Feminism and Feminist Movements in America

Feminism and Feminist Movements in America

An Encyclopedia of Ideals and Activism

Editor
Sarah Kornfield

BLOOMSBURY ACADEMIC
NEW YORK • LONDON • OXFORD • NEW DELHI • SYDNEY

BLOOMSBURY ACADEMIC
Bloomsbury Publishing Inc, 1359 Broadway, New York, NY 10018, USA
Bloomsbury Publishing Plc, 50 Bedford Square, London, WC1B 3DP, UK
Bloomsbury Publishing Ireland, 29 Earlsfort Terrace, Dublin 2, D02 AY28, Ireland

BLOOMSBURY, BLOOMSBURY ACADEMIC and the Diana logo are trademarks of Bloomsbury Publishing Plc

First published in the United States of America 2026

A catalog record for this book is available from the Library of Congress.

ISBN: HB: 979-8-2161-8440-9
ePDF: 979-8-2161-8442-3
eBook: 979-8-2161-8441-6

Typeset by Deanta Global Publishing Services, Chennai, India
Printed and bound in the United States of America

For product safety related questions contact productsafety@bloomsbury.com.

To find out more about our authors and books visit www.bloomsbury.com and sign up for our newsletters.

To a feminist future

Contents

List of Entries

Reading Guide

There are many possible paths through *Feminism and Feminist Movements in America: An Encyclopedia of Ideals and Activism*. The following reading guide offers some potential routes by organizing the entries into topical clusters along with recommended starting points for each topic. Some entries clearly fit in more than one topic, creating necessary overlaps among the clusters.

BODIES

Start with Biopower and follow up with: Beauty; Bioethics; Bodily Autonomy; Body Positivity; Disability; Essentialism; Fat; Gender Performance; Intersex; Mind/Body Split; Nonbinary; Phallocentrism; Right to Privacy; Sexual Objectification; Sexual Pleasure; and Virginity.

CAPITALISM, ECONOMICS, AND EQUAL PAY

Start with Capitalism and follow up with: Domestic Labor; Equal Pay; Feminization of Poverty; Labor Activism; Lilly Ledbetter Fair Pay Act; Neoliberalism; Reproductive Labor; Pink Tax; and Socialism.

COLONIALISM AND DECOLONIALISM

Start with Colonialism and follow up with: Decolonialism; Matriliny; Missing and Murdered Indigenous Women and Girls; National Indigenous Women's Resource Center; Postcolonial Feminism; Settler Colonialism; Transnational Feminism; and Witches.

CONTEMPORARY ACTIVISM AND ORGANIZATIONS

Start with #MeToo and then follow up with: #BlackLivesMatter; #SayHerName; Asian American Feminist Collective; Cyberfeminism; Equal Rights Amendment (ERA); Feministing.com; Guerrilla Girls; Hashtag Activism; MANA: A National Latina Organization; National Indigenous Women's Resource Center; National Organization for Women; Prison Abolition Movement; SisterSong; and the Woman's March on Washington (2017).

CONTEMPORARY FEMINISTS

Start with Crenshaw, Kimberlé, and then follow up with: Burke, Tarana; Butler, Judith; Collins, Patricia Hill; Davis, Angela Y.; Gay, Roxane; Haaland, Deb; and Hill, Anita.

FEMINIST CONCEPTS, THEORIES, AND PRACTICES

Start with Standpoint Theory and follow up with: Anger; Biopower; Bodily Autonomy; Choice; Consciousness Raising; Cyborg Manifesto; Deconstruction; Disciplinary Power; Emotional Labor; Feminist Killjoy; Feminist Methodologies; Feminist Pedagogy; The Lesbian Continuum; Male Gaze; The Personal Is Political; Queer Theory; Strategic Essentialism; Trans Theory; and Tokenism.

FEMINIST IDEOLOGIES

Start with Radical Feminism and follow up with: Anarchy; Environmental Feminism; Liberal Feminism; Marxist Feminism; and Socialism.

GENDER

Start with Gender and follow up with: Gender Discrimination; Gender Performance; Gender-Neutral Language and Pronouns; Intersex; and Nonbinary.

HISTORIC MOMENTS AND MOVEMENTS

Start with Suffrage and follow up with: Black Arts Movement; Civil Rights Movement; Combahee River Collective; Dress Reform Movement; *The Feminist Mystique*; Lacks, Henrietta; Punk Feminism and the Riot Grrrl Manifesto; The Redstockings and the Redstockings Manifesto; Seneca Falls Convention (1848); Stonewall Riots (1969); Sexual Revolution; Temperance; Third World Women's Alliance and Black Woman's Manifesto; the Women's Liberation Movement; and the Vagina Monologues.

INTERSECTIONAL FEMINISM

Start with Intersectionality and follow up with: Anzaldúa, Gloria; Combahee River Collective; Critical Race Theory; Disability; Interlocking Oppression; hooks, bell; Huerta, Dolores; Kochiyama, Yuri; Lorde, Audre; Third World Women's Alliance and Black Woman's Manifesto; and Womanism.

LEGAL LANDMARKS

Start with Nineteenth Amendment and follow up with: Affirmative Action; *Bostock v. Clayton County* (2020); Civil Rights Act (1964); Civil Rights Act: Title VII; Divorce; Family and Medical Leave Act (FMLA, 1993); *Eisenstadt v. Baird* (1972); First Step Act (2018); *Griswold v. Connecticut* (1965); *Lawrence v. Texas* (2003); *Obergefell v. Hodges* (2015); Pregnancy Discrimination Act (1978); *Roe v. Wade* (1973); Survivor's Bill of Rights Act (2016); Title IX (1972); and the Violence Against Women Act (1994).

LGBTQ+

Start with Queer Theory and follow up with: Butch; Drag; Femme; Intersex; *Lesbian Connection*; *Lawrence v. Texas* (2003); The Lesbian Continuum; Kramer, Larry; The May Test; Nonbinary; *Obergefell v. Hodges* (2015); Stonewall Riots; Trans Theory; Trans-exclusionary Radical Feminists (TERFs); and Woman-Identified Woman Manifesto.

PATRIARCHAL OPPRESSION

Start with Patriarchy and follow up with: Backlash; *Dobbs v. Jackson Women's Health Organization* (2022); Eugenics; Essentialism; Gaslighting; Hegemonic Masculinity; Internalized Sexism; Men's Rights Movements; Mind/Body Split; Phallocentrism; Sexual Objectification; and Structural Oppression.

POLITICS AND POLITICIANS

Start with Right to Privacy and follow up with: Anti-Miscegenation Laws; Haaland, Deb; Hyde Amendment; Men's Rights Movements; Neoliberalism; Post-racism; Rankin, Jeannette; Religious Right; and Schlafly, Phyllis.

POPULAR CULTURE

Start with Girl Power and follow up with: Backlash; Beauty; The Bechdel Test; Body Positivity; Cult of True Womanhood; Fat; Intensive Mothering; Male Gaze; The May Test; Online Dating and the Burned Haystack Dating Method; Popular Feminism; and Postfeminism.

RACISM AND WHITE SUPREMACY

Start with Racist Stereotypes and follow up with: Post-racism; Racist Stereotypes of Arab and Muslim People; Racist Stereotypes of Asian People; Racist Stereotypes of Black People; Racist Stereotypes of Indigenous People; Racist Stereotypes of Jewish People; Racist Stereotypes of Latinx People; White Privilege; White Supremacy; and Whiteness as Property.

RELIGION AND SPIRITUALITY

Start with Feminist Theology and follow up with the entries on: Biblical Complementarianism; Black Liberation Theology; Cult of True Womanhood; Deconstruction; Mind/Body Split; Purity Culture; Religious Right; Witches; and Womanism.

ROMANCE, RELATIONSHIPS, AND FAMILY

Start with Enthusiastic Consent and follow up with: Anti-Miscegenation Laws; Biblical Complementarianism; Divorce; Domestic Labor; Emotional Labor; Intensive Mothering; Male Gaze; Matriliny; *Obergefell v. Hodges* (2015); Online Dating and the Burned Haystack Method; The Personal Is Political; Reproductive Labor; and Sexual Pleasure.

SEX AND REPRODUCTIVE HEALTH

Start with Reproductive Justice and follow up with: Abortion; Enthusiastic Consent; Kinsey Institute; Menstruation; Menstruation Activism; Partial Birth Abortion Ban Act (2003); Sex Education; Sexual Pleasure; Vagina Monologues; and Virginity.

WOMEN WHO LED THE WAY

Start with hooks, bell, and follow up with: Anzaldúa, Gloria; Bethune, Mary McLeod; Butler, Octavia E.; Chisholm, Shirley; Dworkin, Andrea; Friedan, Betty; Huerta, Dolores; Kochiyama, Yuri; Lorde, Audre; Morrison, Toni; and Rankin, Jeannette.

VIOLENCE AND VIOLENT STRUCTURES

Start with Rape Culture and follow up with: Gaslighting; Intimate Partner Violence; Military-Industrial Complex; Misogyny; and Missing and Murdered Indigenous Women and Girls.

Preface

The entries in this encyclopedia were selected in a collaborative way. I have been teaching feminist theory for roughly fifteen years, and I started with a list of the concepts, events, people, and activism that students find most pressingly relevant to their lives. Then, in conversation with contributors, I expanded the list to include entries based on their advice and expertise. Occasionally, a topic that I had originally conceived as a single entry became so important that it had to be subdivided into two entries in order to do it justice. For instance, the entry on domestic labor became two entries, domestic labor and reproductive labor.

This encyclopedia is not comprehensive: it does not contain *every* person and event important in the history of feminist activism and theory in the United States. Such a book would be impossibly large. Instead, this encyclopedia focuses on what the contributors and I thought was most relevant, most important, and least likely to be already understood by students today.

The entries are arranged alphabetically, with entries for people listed by their surnames. Entries contain a "see also" list of other entries that readers can also explore in order to learn more about related topics. Additionally, each entry concludes with a "further reading" section where readers will find all of the sources that were cited in that entry and other sources—books and research—they might also like to read in order to deepen their knowledge on the subject.

This encyclopedia was not designed to be read from cover to cover. It is more like a handbook or a field guide. It is designed for readers to pick up and read an entry that is pressingly relevant to their lives and to learn more about the concepts and topics that they care about. For instance, a reader who is curious about the rise of podcasts and online forums that teach young men how to enact chauvinist and selfish versions of masculinity (e.g., Andrew Tate's work) might open this encyclopedia to the entry on Men's Rights Movements to learn the history behind this sexist activism. From there, a reader might follow the "see also" recommendations to read more broadly on patriarchy and hegemonic masculinity. Likewise, this encyclopedia contains feminist entries on the key concepts and events—such as "neoliberalism" and the Stonewall Riots—that are often mentioned in passing ways in contemporary society. Readers can jump straight to the entries on Neoliberalism and the Stonewall Riots, and so on, in order to better understand this world and speak to these important topics with depth and nuance. Additionally, this encyclopedia is designed to be a resource for those teaching about feminism in the United States; each entry can be assigned as a stand-alone reading or topically paired with other course materials.

This encyclopedia was written by so many contributors—a whole community of feminists who worked across time and space to make this encyclopedia real. In the final pages of this encyclopedia, readers will find brief biographical statements for each contributor. When I invited contributors to author the entries in this encyclopedia, I told them that the goal was for each entry to be an expert, scholarly, and enthusiastically feminist introduction to the topic. Their entries have exceeded all my expectations.

Finally then, I would like to thank the contributors. I am extremely grateful for all of your expertise and feminist enthusiasm. I have enjoyed collaborating with you on this project more than I can say. Thank you.

Editor's Introduction

Feminism and Feminist Movements in America: An Encyclopedia of Ideals and Activism is an enthusiastically feminist, scholarly introduction to US feminism's most pressingly relevant concepts, events, people, and activism. Authored by feminist scholars, activists, and practitioners, this encyclopedia presents up-to-date, succinct, and engaging introductions to the topics that matter most.

This book is enthusiastically feminist: each entry provides a scholarly introduction to the topic at hand while foregrounding feminist concerns and principles. This encyclopedia does not offer "both sides" of an issue. There is enough sexism in this world! This encyclopedia should not and does not present sexist perspectives alongside feminist perspectives as if both were equally valid. Likewise, this encyclopedia does not pretend to be objective because "objectivity" is largely a façade. People are not objective. Instead of pretending to be objective, the entries in this encyclopedia are honest about their feminist commitments.

The entries in this book are clear, concise, and easy to read. Each entry deals with complex material and yet is written for a mass audience. Black feminist theorist bell hooks lamented that too much of feminism is written in academic jargon and intended for academic readers. Such an elitist version of feminism is counterproductive; feminism is for everybody but it cannot reach a mass audience if it cannot speak in everyday language. This book answers her call for feminist writing that is clear, concise, and easy to read (hooks 2015, ix). Each of the contributors lovingly tailored their entries for a mass audience, ensuring that this book uses everyday language.

The entries compiled here speak to urgent contemporary concerns and span a breadth of topics. For instance, this book contains feminist discussions of concepts such as capitalism, cyberfeminism, queer theory, beauty, virginity, and misogyny. It provides feminist analyses of laws and policies that shape life in the United States, such as Supreme Court cases, the Family Medical Leave Act of 1993 (which is broadly known as maternity leave), the Lilly Ledbetter Fair Pay Act of 2009, and the Pregnancy Discrimination Act of 1978. It features feminist movements and activism such as #BlackLivesMatter, #MeToo, the Stonewall Riots, and the Women's March on Washington. It showcases foundational texts and documents, such as the 19th Amendment, the Cyborg Manifesto, the Redstockings Manifesto, the Seneca Falls Convention and Declaration of Sentiments, and the Third World Women's Alliance and Black Woman's Manifesto. Additionally, featuring feminists, such as Anita Hill, Roxane Gay, Yuri Kochiyama, Judith Butler, Deb Haaland, and Betty Friedan, and feminist organizations, such as the National Organization for Women, the Asian American Feminist Collective, and SisterSong, this encyclopedia foregrounds the strategies and work that feminists and feminist organizations have championed in the United States.

Each entry was chosen for its ability to speak to the crises caused by contemporary sexism. Yet the entries speak in different ways. Some entries—such as the Feminization of Poverty—analyze the reality of our current crises, explaining how and why oppression targets women and other minoritized people. Other entries—such as the Guerrilla Girls—feature feminist activism, demonstrating how to resist. Still other entries—such as Enthusiastic Consent—introduce feminist concepts, explaining how feminist theory works to end violence and oppression. And finally, some entries—such as the Combahee River Collective—are designed to address the voids in patriarchal histories and surveys of US life. When we don't know what feminists have already accomplished, contemporary feminism is much reduced. We draw the strength needed to meet our present reality from knowing our history, from knowing the rich legacy of activism and organizing that has gone before us.

Ultimately, this book gathers entries that are both scholarly and practical. They feature feminist theories and the work of feminist sociologists, psychologists, historians, philosophers, librarians, political scientists, communication scholars, religion scholars, and the like, with each writing from their own areas of expertise. These entries, then, provide an interdisciplinary perspective across the book, drawing readers' attention to the breadth of feminist scholarship and the importance of being able to think broadly and make connections across different topics. For instance, the matter of "equal pay" is a legal issue since anti-discrimination laws are typically the only recourse for someone who realizes they have received unequal pay. Yet "equal pay" is also a sociological issue since women and migrants are typically funneled into low-paying and temporary work. It is also a psychological issue since employers rely on unconscious bias when hiring, deciding salaries, and issuing promotions in sexist ways. Putting an end to wage discrimination and accomplishing "equal pay" is one of the most practical feminist goals; it is also a thoroughly scholarly endeavor, requiring the insights and resources of at least three scholarly disciplines—political science, sociology, and psychology. Throughout this book, the entries emphasize the practicality of feminist thought and activism, highlighting the importance of understanding how oppression works and how feminists can resist—developing new ways of being and organizing that are grounded in liberation, not oppression.

TELLING FEMINIST HISTORIES AND USING FEMINIST WORDS

Feminist thinkers and activists all generally agree that sexism needs to end, but we come from different backgrounds, focus in different areas, and use different tools and schools of thought in our work to end sexism. We do not always agree on the same priorities, approaches, or premises. For instance, we have historically disagreed about the role of Marxist and anarchist thought in feminist theory and we have often splintered along regional lines in addition to being divided by race, class, and sexuality.

This book is not a history; it does not chronologically walk through time attempting to document and explain the paths and trajectories that feminists have taken over the years. Yet it does feature the work of feminists and feminist organizations throughout US history. In so doing, the contributors and I have faced decisions regarding how to tell these stories.

In mainstream US culture, the story of feminist activism is told as a story of at least "three waves." The first wave is summarized as women's efforts from 1848 to 1920 to get the vote. It is a story of suffrage. The second wave is summarized as women's efforts in the 1960s and 1970s to obtain equal rights. It is a story of protests and consciousness-raising regarding equal pay, equal opportunity, and equal access. The third wave is summarized as women's efforts from the 1990s onward to undo power hierarchies. It is a story about choice and empowerment. Sometimes people add more "waves" for the recent decades. For instance, a fourth wave is sometimes described as focusing on online activism. These stories are simplified accounts—and that makes them easy to tell and therefore quite popular as a broad overview.

The "wave" metaphor, however, imagines feminist activism as ocean waves that occasionally crash upon the shore. This presents feminism as a sort of swelling of thought and activism that occasionally pulses through the United States. This is quite frankly inaccurate: feminist thought and activism is ongoing—a constant across US history. Feminist movement certainly becomes more visible in certain eras. For instance, the so-called "second wave" was a period in which feminist organizing achieved heightened visibility by building coalitions with the protest movements of liberal student activism, Civil Rights activism, anti-Vietnam War activism, and so on. But the "wave" metaphor implies that feminism dies out in between these eras of heightened visibility, and this is simply inaccurate.

The second reason this book avoids the "waves" metaphor is because its simplified stories are likewise inaccurate. The women's rights activists who worked to get women the vote were often also abolitionists and labor rights activists—and sometimes anarchists. To simplify the feminist thought and activism from 1848 to 1920 to "suffrage" is to do a great injustice to the work being done during this time. Such a simplification also deprives contemporary feminists from drawing strength and developing creative solutions based on the riches of our history. Likewise, to simplify the work of women's liberation activists and theorists during the 1960s and 1970s down to "equal rights" is to ignore the (sometimes international) coalitions built by Black women and feminists of color that theorized "triple jeopardy," identifying how racism, sexism, and colonialism interact to uniquely impact women of color—a concept now typically referred to as "intersectionality."

For these reasons, this book avoids the language of the "waves." Instead, the entries situate ideas and activism in time, working in nuanced ways. Rather than discussing the "second wave" in broad and oversimplified terms, this book—for instance—details the nuances of how the Redstockings feminist organization originated in 1969 and championed what was then known as the Women's Liberation Agenda.

This brings us to another consideration: language itself. Languages change. Words that were once used one way—such as the phrase "identity politics," which was coined by the Black feminist organization known as the Combahee River Collective—have taken on new meanings in contemporary discourse. Other words and phrases that were popularly used—such as "third world"—have fallen into disgrace and been removed from mainstream discourse. Even what we call feminists has changed over time. Before 1920, the people we think of as feminists self-described as suffragists or people who supported "Woman Rights." Over time, people stopped using the term "Woman Rights" and started using phrases such as "women's liberation" or "women's rights." Likewise, when colleges and universities started teaching feminism, it was often called "Women's Studies." Now, this academic discipline is often referred to as "Women's, Gender, and Sexuality Studies" or sometimes simply "Gender Studies" or "Feminist Studies." These changes—and many others like them—were not easy or simple. They represent enormous cultural shifts, backlash, and strategic feminist activism.

These changes also represent a significant challenge for contemporary authors who wish to discuss feminism with nuance and clarity. It is hard to be specific without getting tangled up in words. In general, the approach throughout this book has been for contributors to name their language choices—to explain in the entries themselves how words were used and the politics of how they changed. As such, the entries in this book address the politics of terminologies such as "third world," "socialism," "identity politics," "neoliberalism," "consent," "post-feminism," and so on.

Similarly, the standards for capitalization have changed over time—again, as a result of cultural shifts, backlash, and strategic activism. For instance, while it is customary to capitalize "America" as a proper noun, feminist author and theorist Audre Lorde often used lowercase letters when writing about "america" in order to call attention to the way this country belittled, demonized, and oppressed her and her communities.

More broadly, the standard conventions for capitalization when talking about race and ethnicity have shifted in complex ways. This encyclopedia follows the style currently used by the Associated Press, capitalizing Black, Brown, and Indigenous when referring to people and communities with "strong historical and cultural commonalities," including the "shared experience of discrimination due solely to the color of one's skin." The Associated Press does not capitalize "white," largely because white supremacists have a long history of capitalizing "white" and the Associated Press does not want to follow the lead of white supremacists or legitimize their practices (Meir 2020). These are fraught decisions. For instance, the progressive MacArthur Foundation argues that "white" should be capitalized and that the capitalization of Black, Brown, and Indigenous but not "white" subtly reinforces the idea that whiteness is normal—as opposed to other races and ethnicities that are marked through capitalization (Mack and Palfrey 2020). Still others argue that by not capitalizing "white," authors and publishing houses perform a sort of reverse racism against white people. Generally, I find that students are confused about why and how to use capitalization when it comes to race and ethnicity. I acknowledge the problems of capitalizing Black, Brown, and Indigenous but not white when referring to race and ethnicity. Yet I am swayed by the same reasoning that proved persuasive to the Associated Press: I do not want to follow the lead of white supremacists or legitimize their practices. As such, this encyclopedia capitalizes Black, Brown, and Indigenous but not white when referring to race and ethnicity.

A PERSONAL NOTE FROM THE EDITOR

I was raised in fairly white, conservative, Christian communities. Which is to say, I spent my high school years homeschooled in Texas and I attended a Christian college that did not allow dancing (except at school-sponsored dances—a paradox to be sure). It was at this Christian college that I first met feminists. Over the next ten years, during which I obtained an MA and a PhD in rhetoric and a graduate minor in women's and gender studies, it was feminists who taught me how to love my neighbor by caring for the most oppressed and practicing radical solidarity. It was feminists who taught me—as bell hooks would say—*all about love.*

The point of this book—and for me, its only measure of success—is the extent to which it helps readers love themselves, love their neighbors, and transform US and global systems into lovingly feminist futures.

Sarah Kornfield

Further Reading

hooks, bell. 2015. *Feminism Is for Everybody*. New York: Routledge.

hooks, bell. 2000. *All About Love: New Visions*. New York: William Morrow.

Mack, Kristen, and John Palfrey. 2020. "Capitalizing Black and White: Grammatical Justice and Equity." *MacArthur Foundation*, August 26, 2020. Accessed March 11, 2025. https://www.macfound.org/press/perspectives/capitalizing-black-and-white-grammatical-justice-and-equity.

Meir, Nicole. 2020. "Why We Will Lowercase White." *Associated Press*, July 20, 2020. Accessed March 11, 2025. https://www.ap.org/the-definitive-source/announcements/why-we-will-lowercase-white/.

A to Z Entries

A

ABORTION

Abortion is one of the most discussed medical procedures in the United States. This is because abortion is a highly politicized topic—people tend to have strong opinions. But what exactly is it and how long has it been around? When politicians and pundits speak about abortion, they are often discussing it for the social and political implications. In other words, people are concerned with how abortions shape populations and bodily autonomy. While abortion is important to politics, it is important to also discuss abortion for what it is—healthcare.

Abortions are medical procedures, and there are several different types. For instance, there are medication-based abortions where someone takes pills (usually mifepristone and misoprostol) to terminate a pregnancy in its initial weeks. There are also surgical abortions. One common type of surgical abortion is known as dilation and curettage—or D&C for short—in which the lining of one's uterus is cut or scraped away and the uterus is emptied of its tissue. While this type of abortion can be used to terminate a pregnancy, people who have miscarried, who have heavy bleeding, or who have other uterine conditions also have this type of abortion. Again, "abortion" refers to a medical procedure—which may have nothing to do with terminating a pregnancy. Additionally, abortions are used to save lives in the instance of ectopic pregnancies. Roughly 2 percent of all pregnancies in the United States are ectopic pregnancies, meaning that a fertilized egg implants outside the uterus—typically in the fallopian tube ("Ectopic Pregnancy" 2024). If an egg grows there, it will rupture the tube causing life-threatening bleeding in the pregnant person. The pregnancy is not viable, and the pregnant person's life is at risk. In these instances, abortions are clearly life-saving medical procedures.

History of Abortion

Abortion has been a part of medical history for as long as people have been keeping records. In fact, for long stretches of history, ending an unwanted pregnancy was a relatively uncontroversial procedure. Egyptian papyrus, Greek plays, ancient biographers, and more suggested that abortions were fairly common. The first written reference to abortion is contained in an Egyptian medical text, *The Ebers Papuris*, in around 1550 BCE, which suggests that "plant-fibre tampon coated with a compound that included honey and crushed dates" would rid someone of an unwanted pregnancy (Hunt 2023). Even some Catholic, medieval Irish saints celebrated the ending of pregnancy as a miracle (Hunt 2023). A longer historical view of abortion is necessary because it demonstrates that the public opinion of abortion shifts regularly, which has the power to change abortion politics all together.

Within the United States, abortion has been a moral battleground that reflects what the public thinks about population control, bodily autonomy, and identity. Feminist activist and scholar Rickie Solinger notes that "until the 1820s, abortion, according to English common law, was generally not a crime" and that women would often report the procedure as necessary to "restore an absent menstrual period" (2007, 61). The criminalization of abortion aligned with an increase of both advertisements for abortionists and abortions, as well as shifts in who was getting abortions (Solinger 2007, 62). Prior to the nineteenth century, married women and enslaved women were more likely to terminate a pregnancy. Then in the 1800s there was a shift, and more unmarried white women began having abortions; these women were painted as promiscuous and sexually irresponsible. The early American Medical Association began a campaign against abortion in 1859, and "physicians combined political advocacy and public condemnation, echoed by some religious leaders and newspapers, to make abortion a public scandal" (Stormer 2015, 3). In fact, many feminist activists at the time opposed abortion. For example, suffragist Elizabeth Cady Stanton called abortion "the degradation of women" (Solinger 2007, 114). The Comstock Laws of 1873 censored materials that related to fertility control, making it much more difficult for women to end unwanted pregnancies.

Between the mid-1800s and the 1960s, abortion was considered illegal in most circumstances (Gold 2003). During this time, countless illegal abortions took place. "Estimates of the number of illegal abortions in the 1950s and 1960s ranged from 200,000 to 1.2 million per year" (Gold 2003). In the 1960s, states began to revise their strict abortion laws. Even still, ending a pregnancy often involved "securing the approval of a standing hospital committee established specifically to review abortion requests" (Gold 2003). In 1973, the Supreme Court decided state governments and the US federal government could not constitutionally criminalize abortion in the landmark case *Roe v. Wade*. Over the next fifty years, the protection provided by *Roe* was slowly whittled away. Then, in 2022, the Supreme Court's ruling in *Dobbs v. Jackson Women's Health Organization* overturned *Roe*, allowing states to make their own laws criminalizing or legalizing abortion.

Whether legal or illegal, abortion access has always been stratified across race, class, and gender lines. Since the 1970s, even when abortion is legal, it is more difficult for people of color and people living in poverty to receive abortion care—a reality that has intensified for those living in states where abortion is currently illegal.

Abortion Today

The medical practice and the technologies of abortion have evolved rapidly since the 1970s, and legislation is not always accurate, clear, or up-to-date with current medical procedures.

When an abortion is used to terminate a pregnancy, the type of abortion procedure (medication based or surgical) is typically determined by the stage of pregnancy. Those in the first twelve weeks of a pregnancy often have medication-based abortions, taking pills (mifepristone and misoprostol) that stop the pregnancy from developing and trigger the uterus to empty (Satmary 2023). A surgical abortion usually takes place after week twelve through dilation and curettage or another procedure known as vacuum aspiration. Both procedures use suction to empty the uterus. In very few cases, terminating a pregnancy after the twenty-seventh week requires what is known as a labor-induced abortion, which anti-abortion activists often call a "partial-birth abortion." This type of abortion is exceptionally rare and really only used when the pregnant person's life is in danger. Based on the Center for Disease Control Monitoring (2024), we know that about 91 percent of abortions take place before thirteen weeks of pregnancy. Moreover, despite the prevalence of abortion in public conversations, there has been a steady decline in procedures since 1995 (Kortsmit et al. 2022). There are several causes for this decline, including greater access to birth control, restrictive laws, and an overall decline in pregnancy rates.

Following the overturning of *Roe v. Wade* (1973) in the summer of 2022, the availability of abortion care is largely determined on a state-to-state basis. *Dobbs v. Jackson Women's Health Organization* (2022) removed federal protections for abortion and turned determination of these various procedures back to the states. The public's opinion of abortion also depends primarily on location. A Pew Research

Study (2023) found that a majority of people (56 percent) living in states with restricted access say it is difficult to get an abortion, and that a third of adults say it should be easier to access abortions. This is an increase of 9 percent from 2019 (Pew Research Center). As of 2024, over half of US states have some restriction on abortion, ranging from almost complete bans to bans after twenty-four weeks (Guttmacher 2024). These laws are changing rapidly across the country and will continue to shift based on who has the political power to create laws.

Beyond the politicization of the procedure, the inability to terminate an unwanted pregnancy has remarkably adverse outcomes for people's financial, physical, and mental health. The Turnaway Study—a landmark research project that conducted nearly 8,000 interviews with women who sought abortions between 2010 and 2016—found that there were significant mental health and life consequences based on whether or not the women were granted the procedure (2021). First, there were significant financial differences: "Women denied a wanted abortion who have to carry an unwanted pregnancy to term have four times greater odds of living below the Federal Poverty Level" (Foster 2021). The study also found that the mental health impacts of denied abortions were profound. For example, they noted that women who were denied abortions were more likely to have anxiety, and women who were granted an abortion were more likely to have better self-esteem. Overall, 95 percent of the women who had abortions reported that it was the right decision for them over five years after the procedure (Foster 2021). These outcomes are rarely discussed in policy decisions about abortion. Diane Greene Foster (2021), a demographer and the director of research at UCSF's Advancing New Standards in Reproductive Health (ANSIRH) program, stated that the study highlighted that "the debate about abortion rarely focuses on what happens to the pregnant person." Instead, abortion is "framed as an abstract moral question in which everyone else weighs in without considering why someone would be in the circumstances where they want an abortion—and what happens to them and their lives when they can't get one" (Foster 2021). It is important that when we talk about abortion that we center discussions on pregnant people and their right to healthcare.

As was the case throughout US history, abortion access will continue to shift and evolve as technology, politics, and medicine do. One thing we know for certain is that pregnant people who do not want to be pregnant will continue to seek care through legal and illegal channels.

Hannah Taylor

See Also: Biopower; Birth Control; Bodily Autonomy; *Dobbs v. Jackson Women's Health Organization* (2022); Partial Birth Abortion Ban Act (2003); Reproductive Justice; *Roe v. Wade* (1973)

Further Reading

Center for Disease Control. 2024. "Abortion Surveillance Findings and Reports." *CDC Reproductive Health*, May 15, 2024. Accessed August 24, 2024. #https://www.cdc.gov/reproductive-health/data-statistics/abortion-surveillance-findings-reports.html.

Cleveland Clinic. 2024. "Ectopic Pregnancy." Accessed July 16, 2024. https://my.clevelandclinic.org/health/diseases/9687-ectopic-pregnancy.

Diaman, Jeff, Besheee Mohamed, and Rebecca Leppert. 2024. "What the Data Says About Abortion in the US." *Pew Research Center*, March 25, 2024. Accessed August 24, 2024. https://www.pewresearch.org/short-reads/2024/03/25/what-the-data-says-about-abortion-in-the-us/.

Foster, Diana Greene. 2021. *The Turnaway Study: Ten Years, a Thousand Women, and the Consequences of Having—or Being Denied—an Abortion*. New York: Simon and Schuster.

Foster, Diana Greene, and M. Antonia Biggs. 2018. "The Mental Health Impact of Receiving vs. Being Denied a Wanted Abortion." *Bixby Center for Global Reproductive Health*, July 22, 2018. Accessed August 24,

2024. https://www.ansirh.org/research/brief/mental-health-impact-receiving-vs-being-denied-wanted-abortion.
Fost, Dan. 2022. "UCSF Turnaway Study Shows Impact of Abortion Access on Well-Being." *USCF*, June 30, 2022. Accessed August 24, 2024. https://www.ucsf.edu/news/2022/06/423161/ucsf-turnaway-study-shows-impact-abortion-access.
Gold, Rachel Benson. 2003. "Lessons from Before Roe: Will Past be Prologue?" *Guttmacher Policy Review* 6, no. 1. https://www.guttmacher.org/gpr/2003/03/lessons-roe-will-past-be-prologue.
Guttmacher Institute. 2024. "Interactive Map: US Abortion Policies and Access After Roe." *Guttmacher Institute*, June 26, 2024. Accessed August 24, 2024. https://states.guttmacher.org/policies/nevada/abortion-policies.
Hunt, Katie. 2023. "Abortion is Ancient History: Long Before Roe, Women Terminated Pregnancies." *CNN*, June 23, 2023. https://www.cnn.com/2023/06/23/health/abortion-is-ancient-history-and-that-matters-today-scn/index.html.
Kortsmit, Katherine, Antoinette T. Nguyen, Michele G. Mandel, Elizabeth Clark, Lisa M. Hollier, Jessica Rodenhizer, and Maura K. Whiteman. 2022. "Abortion Surveillance — United States, 2020." *CDC: Morbidity and Mortality Weekly Report, Surveillance Summaries*, 71, no. 10 (November 25): 1–27.
Pew Research Center. 2023. "Nearly a Year After Roe's Demise, Americans' Views of Abortion Access Increasingly Vary by Where They Live." *Pew Research Center,* November 25, 2022. Accessed August 24, 2024. https://www.pewresearch.org/politics/2023/04/26/nearly-a-year-after-roes-demise-americans-views-of-abortion-access-increasingly-vary-by-where-they-live/.
Satmary, Wendy A. 2023 "What are the Different Types of Abortion?" *Medical News Today*, May 31, 2023. https://www.medicalnewstoday.com/articles/325582.
Solinger, Rickie. 2007. *Pregnancy and Power: A Short History of Reproductive Politics in America.* New York: New York University Press.
Stormer, Nathan. 2015. *Sign of Pathology: US Medical Rhetoric on Abortion, 1800s–1960s.* Pennsylvania: Penn State Press.

AFFIRMATIVE ACTION

In the United States, affirmative action refers to policies that seek to counteract racism, sexism, and other systems of oppression. These policies typically incentivize corporations and organizations such as colleges and universities that receive federal money to hire or admit a person from oppressed/minoritized groups rather than a person from a dominant group when their credentials are otherwise equal. For example, most large public universities receive federal support through grants and other systems. Affirmative action offered these universities an incentive to admit a Latinx student rather than a white student when their admission materials were otherwise equal. Likewise, for instance, affirmative action incentivized computer science corporations that do contract work for the federal government to hire a woman rather than a man for a software engineer position when their application materials were otherwise equal. The premise is that without such incentives, racist and sexist logic would typically win the day, unfairly advantaging white and male applicants. In that sense, affirmative action is understood as a necessary intervention that attempts to level the playing field within organizations and corporations that receive government money.

In 1961, President John F. Kennedy first used the term "Affirmative Action" in its current sense in an executive order, requiring government contractors to "take *affirmative action* to ensure that applicants are employed, and employees are treated [fairly] during employment without regard to their race, creed, color or national origin" (see MacLaury 2010). President Lyndon B. Johnson added a provision for women in the late 1960s, making white women such as myself beneficiaries of affirmative action policies across the country—although most white women remain unaware that they are or could be beneficiaries of affirmative action. During the 1970s, affirmative action was expanded to include people with disabilities and Vietnam veterans.

Across the United States, affirmative action is often perceived as "reverse-racism" against white people. Americans—especially white Americans—rarely understand that affirmative action only exists within organizations and corporations that receive government money, and even fewer Americans understand that white women not only directly benefit from affirmative action but are also the "greatest beneficiaries of affirmative action" across "college campuses" and "the American workplace" (Crenshaw 2007; Guynn 2023).

Almost since its inception, affirmative action has been under fire as white men and women seek to end these policies, especially through judicial rulings. Famously, Abigail Fisher began a lengthy court battle, which culminated in a 2016 Supreme Court ruling after being denied admission to the University of Texas Austin (UT Austin) in 2008. Abigail Fisher is a white woman and thus a viable beneficiary of affirmative action. Nonetheless, she and her sponsors and lawyers argued in court that she had been denied admission to UT Austin and her rightful place given to a less qualified student of color (Massie 2016). Fisher had a 3.58 high school GPA and a 1180 SAT score; she was neither admitted to UT Austin nor offered conditional admission through a "provisional slot" involving summer requirements prior to fall coursework. "One black student, four Latino students, and 42 white students with lower scores than Fisher were accepted" under these provisional terms while "168 African-American and Latino Students with better scores than Fisher" were rejected (Massie 2016). Regardless, Fisher carried her anti-affirmative action suit to the US Supreme Court, where her suit was rejected by a 4-3 ruling that held UT Austin's affirmative action admission policy procedures as constitutional.

In 2023, however, the US Supreme Court ruled against affirmative action admission policies in higher education in cases regarding the admission policies at Harvard and the University of North Carolina. In so doing, the Supreme Court essentially ended affirmative action within US college and university admissions. This ruling essentially said that it was unconstitutional to consider race when deciding who is a qualified college or university applicant (Totenberg 2023). Dissenting, Supreme Court Justices Sonia Sotomayor and Ketanji Brown Jackson (both women of color) argued that this majority decision smacks of legal "colorblindness" or post-racism that actually benefits white people. As Justice Jackson put it, "deeming race irrelevant in law does not make it so in real life" (quoted in Totenberg 2023).

Moreover, this pair of 2023 rulings (*Students for Fair Admissions, Inc [SFFA] v. President & Fellows of Harvard College* and *SFFA v. University of North Carolina*) left the door open for military academies to continue recruiting students through affirmative action and race-conscious admissions processes (Totenberg 2023). One feminist response to these 2023 rulings and their exception for military academies is to note that the US government has a history of recruiting people of color into an inherently risky and violent national project—the military—and that the United States has difficulty recruiting middle-class and wealthy white people into the military. As such, this Supreme Court ruling can be interpreted as crassly opportunistic: it refuses to recognize racist oppression as relevant to college and university admissions but leaves the door open for purposefully recruiting people of color into the military.

Sarah Kornfield

See Also: Liberal Feminism; Military-Industrial Complex; Post-racism

Further Reading

Crenshaw, Kimberlé W. 2007. "Framing Affirmative Action." *Michigan Law Review First Impressions* 105: 123–33.

Guynn, Jessica. 2023. "White Women Benefit Most from Affirmative Action. So Why do They Oppose It?" *USA Today*, June 30, 2023. https://www.usatoday.com/story/money/2023/06/29/affirmative-action-who-benefits-white-women/70371219007/.

MacLaury, Judson. 2010. "President Kennedy's E.O. 10925: Seedbed of Affirmative Action." *Federal History* 2: 42–57.

Massie, Victoria M. 2016. "White Women Benefit Most from Affirmative Action—And Are Among Its Fiercest Opponents." *Vox.com*, May 25, 2016. https://www.vox.com/2016/5/25/11682950/fisher-supreme-court-white-women-affirmative-action.

Totenberg, Nina. 2023. "Supreme Court Guts Affirmative Action, Effectively Ending Race- Conscious Admissions." *NPR.org*, June 29, 2023. https://www.npr.org/2023/06/29/1181138066/affirmative-action-supreme-court-decision.

ANARCHY

There are several definitions of anarchy, but it generally refers to political movements or ideologies that reject hierarchical institutions, such as the state. Instead, anarchy favors autonomous self-governance that provides freedom from economic and political injustices.

Emma Goldman, one of the founding mothers of anarchism in the United States, described anarchy around 1900 as "a social order based on the free grouping of individuals for the purpose of producing real social wealth, an order that will guarantee to every human being free access to the earth and full enjoyment of the necessities of life" (Antliff 2007, 57).

In order to achieve this freedom, anarchists believe the elimination of any hierarchal domination or social stratification (i.e., classification by wealth, sex, or power) is necessary to lead to a truly democratic and self-managing society. This critique and rejection of hierarchal power has attracted a wide variety of social movements, from feminist to postcolonial movements that seek to dismantle white, heterosexual, patriarchal power within government and social institutions.

Since the 1970s, anarchy and anarchist movements are often known by their most prominent symbol, a circled A.

The concept of anarchy is often represented by this symbol. Anarchist movements favor self-governance in place of hierarchical institutions such as the state (Thinglass/Dreamstime.com).

A Brief US History of Anarchy

Anarchism came to the shores of the United States during the mid-nineteenth century, rising in popularity with workers' organizations and immigrants through the early twentieth century. Influenced by prominent European anarchists, such as French philosopher Pierre-Joseph Proudhon and Russian revolutionaries Mikhail Bakunin and Peter Kropotkin, US anarchists played a contentious role in revolutionary tactics geared toward overthrowing state institutions.

Propaganda of the deed, which refers to bombings and targeted killings in the name of anarchy, lent to the reputation that early US anarchists were inherently violent. However, not all anarchists were associated with violent tactics, and many aligned peacefully with workers' and women's movements during the Industrial Age.

The US government was quick to quell the growing anarchist movement by pointing to violent tactics, such as the bombing of Wall Street in 1920, which was presumed by officials to be a result of anarchist retaliation (FBI.gov n.d.). In a move commonly known as the first Red Scare, the Justice Department deported many immigrants active in the anarchist community, including Emma Goldman—a famous anarchist revolutionary who was deported to Russia (Shepley 2015). This mass hysteria, and the slow downfall of the Socialist party in the United States, a key anarchist ally, further removed anarchy from the main political stage.

Today, the anarchist movement is not as impactful as it was during its heyday in the early 1900s. Yet many of the anti-authoritarian figures and movements in recent US history owe their politics to anarchist influences, including the anarcho-pacifist counterculture of the 1960s, the punk anarchism of the 1980s, and the environmental anarchist collectives of the 2000s. As such, a significant portion of US counterculturalism has been shaped by anarchist ideologies and politics.

Feminism and Anarchy

Feminist anarchism largely arrived in the United States with the immigration wave of the late nineteenth century. By the beginning of the twentieth century, many women who aligned with the anarchist party moved their alliances closer to socialist parties as they sought women's suffrage. While these socialist and liberal feminist movements were more reformist than their radical anarchist allies, many women felt that the then current anarchist movements were ignoring women's rights in favor of the collective.

During the 1970s, feminists organized into "anarcho" or "anarcha-feminist" movements that remain influential today. For example, the popular contemporary blog, *anarcha library*, defines anarcha-feminism as not "just a response to anarchism and feminism" but rather "its own entity: an anti-authoritarian, anti-capitalist, anti-oppression way of addressing gender issues—and addressing other issues with a radical critique of patriarchy" (Sallydarity 2010). Likewise, during the 1990s, anarcha-feminists in the United States were involved in the anarcho-punk scene that inspired the Riot Grrrl subculture and thus much of US punk music (Kaltefleiter 2016).

Feminist versions of anarchism continue to influence US politics. In the past decade, the global justice movement has allied with many self-titled anarcha-feminists (Maiguashca 2014). Ultimately, anarcha-feminists offer important and substantive intersectional critiques of injustice, highlighting the ways in which race, gender, and sexuality are further oppressed by a patriarchal hierarchy that seeks domination over the state and its affiliated institutions.

Kelsey Taylor Alexander

See Also: Labor Activism; Punk Feminism and the Riot Grrrl Manifesto; Radical Feminism; Socialism

Further Reading

Antliff, Allan. 2007. "Anarchy, Power, and Poststructuralism." *SubStance* 36, no. 2: 56–66. http://www.jstor.org/stable/25195125.

FBI.gov. n.d. "Wall Street Bombing 1920." Accessed August 24, 2024. https://www.fbi.gov/history/famous-cases/wall-street-bombing-1920.

Kaltefleiter, C. K. 2016. "Start Your Own Revolution: Agency and Action of the Riot Grrrl Network." *International Journal of Sociology and Social Policy* 36, no. 11/12: 808–23. https://doi.org/10.1108/IJSSP-06-2016-0067.

Maiguashca, Bice. 2014. "'They're Talkin' Bout a Revolution': Feminism, Anarchism and the Politics of Social Change in the Global Justice Movement." *Feminist Review* 106: 78–94. http://www.jstor.org/stable/24571940.

Sallydarity. 2010. "What is Anarcha-Feminism?" *Anarcha Library*. Accessed August 24, 2024. http://anarchalibrary.blogspot.co.uk/2010/09/what-is-anarcha-feminism-2005.html.

Shepley, Nick. 2015. *The Palmer Raids and the Red Scare: 1918–1920: Justice and Liberty for All*. Luton: Andrews UK Limited.

ANGER

Anger is often considered a negative emotion, but anger is important to creating change on large and small scales. According to the Black feminist poet Audre Lorde (1984), the goal of anger is change, which stands in contrast to hatred with its goal of destruction. Many scholars argue that anger is the key to social change, as it can build community and spark community action (Gould 2009; Rand 2012). An example is the AIDS Coalition to Unleash Power, also known as ACT UP. ACT UP was a "diverse, non-partisan group of individuals united in anger and committed to direct action to end the AIDS crisis" (Olson 2011, 288). Anger was so central to their cause that the documentary about the history of ACT UP is titled *United in Anger: A History of ACT UP* (2012), foregrounding the role of anger in uniting and motivating the group. Beyond ACT UP's explicit activism and protests, anger was also central to the media that brought awareness to the AIDS crisis. As Isaac West illustrates, during the 2011 revival of *The Normal Heart*—a play focusing on the beginning of the AIDS epidemic in New York City during the 1980s—the producers "had to take steps to motivate audiences to translate their emotions into action once they left the show" (2012, 100). To ensure the crowd acted on the anger generated by the play, after each show volunteers handed out letters in which the playwright Larry Kramer explained the inspiration for the characters and described how the AIDS crisis had grown worse, not better, in the twenty-six years since the play premiered. The goal of ACT UP and media like *The Normal Heart* was not to destroy or bring harm to others; rather, it was to change legislation and public policies to improve the lives of people with AIDS. This goal was accomplished through the uniting force of anger.

Despite anger being a key emotion in creating change, too often women are discouraged from expressing anger. Rebecca Traister demonstrates that when women express anger it is deemed "ugly, unappealing, dangerous, something to be shut down or jeered" by others—not just men but often by other women as well (2018, 19). This is especially true for Black woman, whose anger may be dismissed due to the racist stereotype known as "the angry Black woman" (Ahmed 2009; Griffin 2012; hooks 2000). Men, on the other hand, are not only permitted but also encouraged to express anger as a part of their masculinity (Connell 1995). In Brett Kavanaugh's Supreme Court Justice nomination hearing, for example, he yelled and cried his way through his testimony, and many observers considered this to be a strong performance of a man in touch with his feelings. If, however, a woman had expressed herself in a similar way, more than likely she would be dismissed as hysterical (Campbell 1994). Christine Blasey Ford, who testified about Kavanaugh sexually assaulting her, was criticized for being too emotional during her hearing, despite being far more restrained than

Kavanaugh. While anger can be motivating, angry women (particularly women of color) have been diminished and dismissed when they become "too emotional."

While anger is a useful tool for creating change and too often denied from women, feminist scholar Sara Ahmed (2010) cautions against assuming because we are angry, we are also right. As she argues, "When anger becomes righteous it can become oppressive; to assume anger makes us right can be a wrong" (4). Indeed, while anger can motivate people to create change, it can also be used to alienate and discriminate against others. Celeste Condit (2018) demonstrates how angry rhetoric can be directed at out-group members in order to rally in-group members to attack them. An in-group is a social grouping with which a person identifies—it can be related to race, gender, nationality, political party, even sports team fandoms. A person in the out-group, then, would be someone or a group of people with whom you do *not* identify. Out-groups are often seen as minorities to the in-group majorities. When anger is directed at the out-group, it can be performed in a way that casts the out-group as the reason for the in-group's supposed harm. This is evident in a controversy known as PuppyGate, where a group of reactionary authors and fans grew upset over how the most prestigious award in science fiction and fantasy (the Hugo Awards) was increasingly won by women and people of color. These reactionaries organized a campaign called the "Sad Puppies" that was driven by anger (Dosser 2023). As is often the case with anger, the aim of the campaign coordinators was to use angry rhetoric "to make an audience angry (or angrier) and to have them direct this anger toward a particular agent, policy, or idea" (Zagacki and Boleyn-Fitzgerald 2006, 295). The Sad Puppies' goal was to fill the ballots with "popular" literature, literature they deemed message-free (and not so coincidentally, largely written by white male authors), and, through doing so, change the Hugo Awards back to what they preferred—when fewer women and people of color won accolades for their writing. Here, the anger may have felt right and justified to the Sad Puppies, but it caused harm for many authors who were targeted due to their identities.

Anger is apolitical. It can be used in progressive and conservative movements, and the presence of anger is not an indication of being right or wrong. Rather, as Ahmed writes, "Feminist emotions are mediated and opaque; they are sites of struggle, and we must persist in struggling with them," and this is especially true for the assumed "negative" emotion of anger (2010, 4). Anger binds people together and motivates them to work toward a common goal, but it is always important to consider who is angry, who is allowed to be angry, and what is the goal of that anger. Anger is a common emotion in ACT UP, the Women's Liberation Movement, and many other intersectional feminist movements that work not to destroy but to create change for a more accepting future.

Max Dosser

See Also: Feminist Killjoy; Hegemonic Masculinity; Women's Liberation Movement

Further Reading

Ahmed, Sara. 2009. "Embodying Diversity: Problems and Paradoxes for Black Feminists." *Race Ethnicity and Education* 12, no. 1: 41–52. https://doi.org/10.1080/13613320802650931.

Ahmed, Sara. 2010. "Feminist Killjoys (And Other Willful Subjects)." *The Scholar & Feminist Online* 8, no. 3: 1–8. https://sfonline.barnard.edu/polyphonic/print_ahmed.htm

Campbell, Sue. 1994. "Being Dismissed: The Politics of Emotional Expression." *Hypatia* 9, no. 3: 46–65. https://www.jstor.org/stable/3810188.

Condit, Celeste Michelle. 2018. *Angry Public Rhetorics: Global Relations and Emotion in the Wake of 9/11.* Ann Arbor: University of Michigan Press.

Connell, Raewyn W. 1995. *Masculinities*. Berkeley: University of California Press.

Dosser, Max. 2023. "When Puppies Start to Hate: The Revanchist Nostalgia of the Hugo Awards' PuppyGate Controversy." *Communication and Critical/Cultural Studies* 20, no. 4: 453–70. https://doi.org/10.1080/14791420.2023.2267656.

Gould, Deborah. 2009. *Moving Politics: Emotion and ACT UP's Fight Against AIDS.* Chicago: University of Chicago Press.

Griffin, Rachel Alicia. 2012. "I AM an Angry Black Woman: Black Feminist Autoethnography, Voice, and Resistance." *Women's Studies in Communication* 35, no. 2: 138–57. https://doi.org/10.1080/07491409.2012.724524.

hooks, bell. 2000. *Feminist Theory: From Margin to Centre*. London: Pluto Press.

Lorde, Audre. 1984. "Uses of Anger: Women Responding to Racism." In *Sister Outsider: Essays & Speeches by Audre Lorde*, edited by Audre Lorde, 124–33. Freedom, CA: Crossing.

Olson, Lester C. 2011. "Anger Among Allies: Audre Lorde's 1981 Keynote Admonishing the National Women's Studies Association." *Quarterly Journal of Speech* 97, no. 3: 283–308. https://doi.org/10.1080/00335630.2011.585169.

Rand, Erin J. 2012. "Gay Pride and Its Queer Discontents: ACT UP and the Political Deployment of Affect." *Quarterly Journal of Speech* 98, no. 1: 75–80. https://doi.org/10.1080/00335630.2011.638665.

Traister, Rebecca. 2018. *Good and Mad.* New York: Simon & Schuster.

Zagacki, Kenneth S., and Patrick A. Boleyn-Fitzgerald. 2006. "Rhetoric and Anger." *Philosophy & Rhetoric* 39, no. 4: 290–309. https://doi.org/10.1353/par.2007.0006.

ANTI-MISCEGENATION LAWS

Miscegenation is defined as "the mixing of two or more races," which means that the term "anti-miscegenation" refers to opposing or being against interracial mixing (Bhusal 2017, 84). Anti-miscegenation laws in the United States, however, primarily prohibited the "mixing" of the "white race" with people of color—especially opposing sexual unions between white women and Black men.

Anti-miscegenation laws date back to colonial America. For instance, in 1660, colonial Maryland created such a law, opposing miscegenation by stipulating that "any white woman who married a black man" would "become a slave" and so would her children (Wallenstein 2014, 23). Maryland set the tone for anti-miscegenation laws and other colonies followed. For example, in 1662 Virginia passed a similar law and then in 1691 Virginia banned interracial marriage and stated that if a white woman conceived a child with a person of color (even out of wedlock), they would have to pay a fine or they would be sold into indentured servitude and their child would likewise become an indentured servant until the age of thirty-one (Wallenstein 2014, 24). These laws not only penalized interracial couples but also punished their children. By 1866, all but sixteen states had anti-miscegenation laws in force (Pascoe 2009, 42).

Anti-miscegenation laws were designed to protect and privilege whiteness in colonial America and in the United States. During these eras, most Western Europeans and American colonists believed that "races" were biologically distinct and that the "white race" was biologically (and thus intellectually and morally) superior to other "races" (Bhusal 2017, 86). This perspective insisted that interracial marriage and procreation were "unnatural" (Pascoe 2009, 2).

In reality, "race" is a "virtually pure construct," meaning that "races" exist because of geographical, social, and legal segregations, not because of nature (Pateman and Mills 2007, 5). Which is to say, unless people who live in the same area are purposefully prevented from procreating together, after a few generations the offspring in that area will be a mixture of all the available genetics. From 1660 until 1967, anti-miscegenation laws maintained the "purity" of the "white race"—preventing white women from procreating with people from other "races"—by criminalizing interracial marriage for white women and by punishing (e.g., lynching) men of color, especially Black men, who were thought or said to have had sex with white women.

Loving v. Virginia (1967)

When Richard Loving (a white man) and Mildred Jeter (a Black woman) met in Virginia, it was illegal for them to marry according to Virginia's Racial Integrity Act of 1924. They fell in love and traveled to Washington, D.C. to wed. The Lovings returned home to Virginia. The police raided their home, finding the married couple sharing a bed and locating their marriage certificate. Virginia charged them with breaking the state's laws, and the Lovings pled guilty and ultimately had to leave Virginia. They moved back to Washington, D.C., but shortly thereafter wanted to move home again—back to Virginia.

When Mildred Loving contacted the ACLU for help in 1964 through Attorney General Robert F. Kennedy, the Lovings joined a movement that was hard at work overturning the nation's anti-miscegenation laws. The ACLU and the Japanese American Citizens League (JACL) had been trying to find the right case to bring before the US Supreme Court and thus overturn all anti-miscegenation laws in a single judicial ruling. As the JACL's Masao Satow stated, "our overall philosophy . . . has been to look for a suitable case for the US Supreme Court review. We feel it would be better to rid all the States of such statues at one time" (Pascoe 2009, 231). Specifically, they were looking for a case where they could "excite public sympathy" for the interracial couple. They imagined that a case involving a white Second World War veteran who was married to "a Japanese or Korean bride" would be ideal (Pascoe 2009, 232). They were looking specifically for cases where white men were married to women of color. The ideal couple, however, proved elusive: some couples had children out of wedlock, others did not have marriage licenses, others were unwilling to endure the "embarrassing publicity" of a national case, and still others had their cases resolved too quickly and did not reach the Supreme Court (Pascoe 2009, 235). When Mildred Loving contacted the ACLU, the ACLU saw an opportunity to expand Civil Rights across the United States. The Supreme Court ultimately ruled in the Loving's favor, making anti-miscegenation laws unconstitutional.

Interracial Couples Today

When anti-miscegenation laws were struck down as unconstitutional by *Loving v. Virginia* in 1967, approximately 3 percent of new marriages in the Unites States were interracial marriages. Today, approximately 17 percent of newlyweds are interracial couples (Livingston and Brown 2017). Historically, anti-miscegenation laws focused on keeping white people (especially women) from marrying and procreating with people of color. Since these laws ended, white people have increasingly married people of color. For instance, in 1980, only 4 percent of newlywed white people were married to people of color compared to 2015 when 11 percent of newlywed white people were married to people of color (Livingston and Brown 2017). Even though racist oppression remains routine in the United States, the increase in interracial marriage provides some optimism.

Isabella M. Rodriguez

See Also: Civil Rights Act (1964); Cult of True Womanhood; Intersectionality; White Privilege; Whiteness as Property

Further Reading

Bhusal, Ashok. 2017. "The Rhetoric of Racism and Anti-Miscegenation Laws in the United States." *IAFOR Journal of Arts & Humanities* 4, no. 2: 83–9.

Livingston, Gretchen and Anna Brown. 2017. "Intermarriage in the US 50 Years After *Loving v. Virginia*." Pew Research Center (blog), May 18, 2017. https://www.pewresearch.org/social-trends/2017/05/18/intermarriage-in-the-u-s-50-year s-after-loving-v-virginia/

Livingston, Gretchen, and Anna Brown. 2017. "Trends and Patters in Intermarriage." *Pew Research Center*, May 18, 2017. https://www.pewresearch.org/social-trends/2017/05/18/1-trends-and-patterns-in-intermarriage/.

Pascoe, Peggy. 2009. *What Comes Naturally: Miscegenation Law and the Making of Race in America.* New York: Oxford University Press.

Pateman, Carole, and Charles W. Mills. 2007. *Contract and Domination.* Cambridge: Polity Press.

Wallenstein, Peter. 2014. *Race, Sex, and the Freedom to Marry.* Lawrence: University Press of Kansas.

ANZALDÚA, GLORIA

Gloria Anzaldúa (1942–2004) was a feminist scholar, cultural theorist, and activist who contributed to many fields, including border studies, feminism and feminist theory, literary studies, and queer theory. Anzaldúa was born in south Texas, and her geographic location near the Mexico-US border shaped much of her thinking and writing. Anzaldúa was a prolific feminist author who expressed herself through a variety of genres, including essays, poetry, short stories, autobiographical narratives, fiction, children's stories, and more.

Contributions to Feminism

Anzaldúa is widely known for her writing on the concept of the borderlands—a space of hybridity, conflict, and creative transformation. To understand the "borderlands," we have to think of borders not as a line in the sand that cleanly divides two things but as a region where one thing overlaps with, mixes with, clashes with, and gives way to another. For instance, people often think there is a clear dividing line between the United States and Mexico. Anzuldúa, however, argued that instead of a clear, binary divide, there is really a "borderland" or region where cultures, languages, and people mix, clash, and intermix. For instance, Spanish is the primary language spoken in Mexico and English is the primary language spoken in the United States, but in the borderlands there is no clear dividing line and lots of people speak both languages or mixtures of Spanish and English—which are commonly known as "Spanglish." For Anzaldúa, the borderlands are real and also a metaphor for all sorts of instances where people imagine a clear binary divide but the reality is more complex.

In her book *Borderlands/La Frontera: The New Mestiza*, Anzaldúa examines the "borderlands" or intersectionality of race, gender, sexuality, and culture. This book blends autobiography, poetry, and theory, serving as a crucial text in feminist, queer, and postcolonial studies. She focuses primarily on Chicana identity while weaving in her own experiences as a queer woman of color. Chicana typically refers to a woman or girl living in the United States who has Mexican or Latino ancestry and some would use the term Mexican Americans in its place. Another notable aspect of Anzaldúa's writing is that she uses a mix of English and Spanish, refusing to conform to mainstream ways of expression. Her use of Spanish, without translations, is an intentional literary choice to represent the merging of cultures and a shift away from binary language. In *Borderlands/La Frontera: The New Mestiza*, Anzaldúa writes, "The US-Mexican border es una herida abierta where the Third World grates against the first and bleeds. And before a scab forms it hemorrhages again, the lifeblood of two worlds merging to form a third country—a border culture" (1987, 6). Anzaldúa's mix of Spanish and English models her own experience in the borderlands. By switching languages within sentences and not translating "es una herida abierta" for English readers, Anzaldúa rejects monolingual hegemony and embraces her bilingual identity. She challenges mainstream feminism by refusing to write solely in the dominant culture's language.

Scholars often cite this work for its groundbreaking articulation of "mestiza consciousness," a concept that encourages fluidity of identity across borders, both literal and metaphorical. Mestiza consciousness, as described by Anzaldúa, challenges the traditional notion of the mestiza, which was historically based on racial purity and hierarchy. The "old mestiza" reinforced colonial ideas of superiority by emphasizing bloodlines and divisions between races. In contrast, Anzaldúa's "new mestiza consciousness" dismantles this hierarchy, embracing the complexity of intersectional identities—racial, cultural, gender, and spiritual. It encourages fluidity and multiplicity, allowing individuals to navigate and merge the many layers of their identities rather than conform to rigid categories. An example of mestiza consciousness can be found in the experience of Afro-Latinx individuals, who navigate both African and Latinx heritages while often confronting racism within both communities. Afro-Latinx people might embrace their Blackness while also celebrating Latinx cultural traditions, such as food, music, and language. Mestiza consciousness, in this context, allows for the blending of these identities and challenges the idea that they must choose one over the other. It dismantles the racial and cultural hierarchies that often marginalize Afro-Latinx identities, instead embracing their intersectionality and complexity.

Anzaldúa also coedited *This Bridge Called My Back: Writings by Radical Women of Color*, which is a landmark collection that gathers writings from women of color on issues of race, class, gender, and sexuality. The collection confronts mainstream feminism's neglect of women of color and provides a space for these voices to articulate their unique struggles and strengths.

Likewise, Anzaldúa challenged mainstream feminism by writing queer theory. Not only does she bring sexuality into her writing, but she also challenges the dominant culture's queer labels, saying, "for me the term lesbian es un problema. As a working-class Chicana, mestiza—a composite being, amalgama de culturas y de lenguas—a woman who loves women, 'lesbian' is a cerebral word, white and middle-class, representing an English-only dominant culture" (1991, 249–50). Overall, Anzaldúa pushes the boundaries of language, identity, and culture, insisting that scholars reimagine the binaries they write within.

Feminist Legacy

Anzaldúa deeply influenced feminist thought through her writing on intersectionality, identity, and inclusion of women of color in academic spaces. Many scholars have highlighted her international impact, arguing that her work transcends borders both geographically and culturally. Norma Cantú (2011) highlights how Anzaldúa's concept of the borderlands and mestiza consciousness resonates with marginalized communities across the globe, making her work relevant in global feminist movements. Melissa Castillo-Garsow (2012) addresses Anzaldúa's legacy in academia, especially her efforts to create space for women of color. Her work is recognized for challenging the exclusionary practices of academia, where women of color often struggle for visibility and acknowledgment. Anzaldúa's impact is seen in the growing inclusion of intersectional frameworks and cultural studies in higher education.

Finally, her feminist legacy is rooted in her development of a "mestiza consciousness," which blends multiple, often conflicting, identities into a fluid, hybrid form. Erika Aigner-Varoz (2000) argues that this mestiza consciousness is central to Anzaldúa's feminist legacy, offering a model for understanding identity beyond binary thinking and rigid categories. Overall, Anzaldúa's feminist legacy lies in her commitment to deconstructing borders, whether cultural, racial, or academic, and her visionary contributions to the inclusion and empowerment of marginalized identities.

Anna Whittle

See Also: Intersectionality; Postcolonial Feminism; Queer Theory; Transnational Feminism

Further Reading

Aigner-Varoz, Erika. 2000. "Metaphors of a Mestiza Consciousness: Anzaldúa's Borderlands/La Frontera." *MELUS* 25, no. 2: 47–62. https://doi.org/10.2307/468218.
Anzaldúa, Gloria. 1987. *Borderlands/La Frontera: The New Mestiza*, 1st ed. San Francisco: Spinsters/Aunt Lute.
Anzaldúa, Gloria. 1991. "To(o) Queer the Writer—Loca, escritora y chicana." In *Versions: Writing by Dykes, Queers & Lesbians*, edited by Betsy Warland, 249–63. Vancouver: Press Gang.
Cantú, Norma E. 2011. "Comparative Perspectives Symposium: Gloria E. Anzaldúa, an International Perspective." *Signs: Journal of Women in Culture & Society* 37, no. 1: 1–5. https://doi.org/10.1086/660168.
Castillo-Garsow, Melissa. 2012. "The Legacy of Gloria Anzaldúa: Finding a Place for Women of Color in Academia." *Bilingual Review / La Revista Bilingüe* 31, no. 1: 3–11. http://www.jstor.org/stable/24705991.
Moraga, Cherríe, and Gloria Anzaldúa, eds. 1981. *This Bridge Called My Back: Writings by Radical Women of Color*, 1st ed. Watertown: Persephone Press.

ASIAN AMERICAN FEMINIST COLLECTIVE

"We make histories." This phrase, printed boldly in the Asian American Feminist Collective's (AAFC) second published zine, reflects the communal, determined, and creative empowerment for which the AAFC stands (Kuo 2019, 1). Launched in 2018, this organization was formed by four Asian women in response to both the 2016 US election and the mainstream erasure of women of color at the 2017 Women's March and Strike ("About" n.d.). Founders Julie Ae Kim, Rachel Kuo, Senti Sojwal, and Tiffany Diane Tso joined together to create a New York City-centered political coalition for people whose backgrounds include "East, Southeast, and South Asian, Pacific Islander, multi-ethnic and diasporic Asian identities" ("Asian American Writers' Workshop" n.d.). Focused on goals of "collective liberation and organizing," the AAFC has become recognized today for its honesty and intersectionality ("About" n.d.). The AAFC operates through a variety of initiatives, including educational workshops, public events, and digital campaigns. These activities amplify feminist perspectives within the Asian-American and Pacific Islander (AAPI) community and mobilize collective action.

Publications, Media, and Events

AAFC leadership emphasizes the importance of championing accessibility and affordability alongside their goal of collective liberation (Dadlani 2019). Their online publications, social media series, and expert-led events are open to the public, demonstrating how integral sharing resources is to their work. From 2018 to 2021, the AAFC published annual zines (small, handmade magazines) with titles such as "Building an Asian American Feminist Movement," "How to Make History," "Care in the Time of Coronavirus," and "To Us & Ours." Together, they cover themes of community building, identity exploration, and political education. Other items featured on their website include Covid-19 mutual aid resources such as domestic violence helplines and funds for people in need ("Resources" n.d.).

The AAFC's social media presence is also significant, with various series like #ThisIsAsianAmerica or #FeministAntibodies creating online "communal site[s] of resistance" that collect firsthand responses to experiences such as racial discrimination or identity-based harassment (Kuo et al. 2020, 2). Examining the impact of digital records such as these, researchers Rachel Kuo, Amy Zhang, Vivian Shaw, and Cynthia Wang emphasize the power of these "collective politics . . . to imagine new systems" (Kuo et al. 2020, 8).

Notably, the collective collaborates with other feminist and social justice organizations to advocate for policy changes impacting Asian American and Pacific Islander (AAPI) communities. Their writer workshops feature authors from across the Asian diaspora, and collaborations with groups such as Q-Wave, which builds community for AAPI queer and trans-identifying people in New York, to demonstrate their commitment to intersectional solidarity (@aafc.nyc n.d.).

Intersectional Solidarity

Much of the AAFC's collaborative work, as well as their own feminist foundation, is grounded in intersectional feminism. Paying respect to Black feminist thought and the "multi-dimensional ways Asian/Asian American people confront systems of power at the intersections of race, gender, class, sexuality, religion, disability, migration history and citizenship and immigration status," the organization utilizes existing methods to fight connected forms of discrimination ("About" n.d.). By bringing lived experiences from AAPI communities and this intersectional solidarity to their work, the AAFC has succeeded in supporting collective responses to pressing topics. For example, a joint discussion with AAFC and the Black feminist advocacy group Black Women Radicals featured conversations about "Black and Asian feminist perspectives on immigration as strategies towards liberation" (@aafc.nyc n.d.).

Carole Yoke-kew Chee

See Also: Combahee River Collective; Intersectionality

Further Reading

"About." n.d. *Asian American Feminist Collective*. Accessed July 5, 2024. https://www.asianamfeminism.org/about.

@aafc.nyc. n.d. *Instagram*. Accessed July 5, 2024. https://instagram.com/aafc.nyc.

"Asian American Feminist Collective." n.d. *Asian American Writers' Workshop*. Accessed July 5, 2024. https://aaww.org/postauthor/asian-american-feminist-collective/.

"Building an Asian American Feminist Movement." 2018. *Asian American Feminist Collective*. Accessed July 5, 2024. https://www.asianamfeminism.org/s/AAFC_Zine1.pdf.

"Care in the Time of Coronavirus." 2020. *Asian American Feminist Collective*. Accessed July 5, 2024. https://www.asianamfeminism.org/s/AAFCZine3_CareintheTimeofCoronavirus.pdf.

Dadlani, Priya. 2019. "SPICY Q&A: AAFC on Interrogating What It Means to be Asian in America." *SPICY*, July 3, 2019. https://spicyzine.wordpress.com/2019/07/03/spicy-qa-with-asian-american-feminist-collective-the-importance-of-sharing-stories-movement-building-and-interrogating-what-it-means-to-be-asian-in-america/.

Kuo, Rachel. 2019. "How to Make History." *Asian American Feminist Collective*. Accessed August 24, 2024. https://www.asianamfeminism.org/s/AAFC_HistoryZine.pdf.

Kuo, Rachel, A. Zhang, V. Shaw, and C. Wang. 2020. "FeministAntibodies: Asian American Media in the Time of Coronavirus." *Social Media + Society* 6, no. 4: 1–11. https://doi.org/10.1177/2056305120978364.

"Resources." n.d. *Asian American Feminist Collective*. Accessed July 5, 2024. https://www.asianamfeminism.org/resources.

"To Us and Ours." 2001. *Asian American Feminist Collective*. Accessed July 5 2024. https://www.asianamfeminism.org/s/ToUsandOurs_FinalZine3.pdf.

B

BACKLASH

"Backlash" is a term used to explain a negative reaction to political and cultural change; it is an attempt to push back against the gains of an oppressed group. Such pushback is a response to perceived advances, such as reproductive rights, greater political representation, or gaining the legal right to marry by LGBT people. The backlash against feminism has been particularly evident throughout the twentieth and twenty-first centuries in response to advancements in women's rights. The term was made popular in the 1990s to explain a rising anti-feminist backlash.

In her 1991 bestselling book *Backlash: The Undeclared War Against American Women*, Susan Faludi applied this concept to her reporting on the anti-feminist backlash in US culture and politics specifically in the 1980s. Faludi's book was a bestseller and is now a feminist classic rereleased in 2020. In the more than three decades since its original publication, the book has continued to frame the conversation about women's advancement and the far right's war on women. Though Faludi examined the 1980s in her work, the trends that she uncovered in her research also applied to the backlash against the gains women made in the early twentieth century, particularly the right to vote.

In her research, Faludi found a pervasive myth across the media—that the fight for women's equality had been won but that women had never been more miserable. Women "had it all" including corporate jobs, access to education, access to credit and wealth, access to politics but as a result had become ugly, aging, depressed alcoholics. And for this, feminism was to blame.

The anti-feminist backlash in the 1980s that Susan Faludi described had two messages. One, that feminism was over, that women had already achieved equality, thus no further equal opportunity policies, including the Equal Rights Amendment, were needed. The second message was that women were more miserable than ever and that equality and feminism were to blame. Faludi found that women were indeed unhappy, but that the unhappiness was caused not by feminism but, rather, by the lack of equality they were still experiencing.

In her work, Faludi examined media and popular culture from the previous decade, the 1980s, such as film, television, media like *Time* and *Newsweek*, and popular psychology that shifted the discourse about women's happiness and success. Faludi's research also delved into demographic shifts, psychology, politics, and more to uncover the myths being perpetuated about women's lives in these various areas. Again and again, her work turned up a pervasive set of myths fueled by anti-feminist sentiments that pitted women's social and political progress against their own well-being and that of their male counterparts, family, and the nation.

The message that women were miserable took the form of news stories focusing on working women experiencing burnout, career women delaying motherhood and then struggling with infertility, single women facing a shortage of men that meant they might never marry. For instance, the June 1986 *Newsweek* cover posed the question, "Too Late for Prince Charming?" and reported that college-educated women over forty had less than a 3 percent chance of getting married; in fact that they were "more likely to be killed by a terrorist than find a mate."

The backlash message was that women would pay the price for their independence with misery, loneliness, and infertility. These stories were countered by the romanticization of traditional wives and stay at home mothers, who were supposedly in danger as a result of feminism's creation of independent and working women. These messages appeared across popular culture, with prominent magazine covers and headlines, and films like *Fatal Attraction* (1987), in which a traditional wife and mother was threatened by a desperate, miserable working woman.

Some scholars see backlash as constant, particularly in terms of racist backlash against women of color, which Faludi did not examine in her work. The fight against oppression is ever present, so while waves of backlash seem sudden, such as when there are public policy changes that roll back rights or protections for an oppressed group, the constant cultural and media messages that undermine progress mean that backlash is also ongoing.

Danielle M. DeMuth

See Also: Beauty; Men's Rights Groups; Misogyny; Patriarchy; Postfeminism

Further Reading

Cohen, Nancy L. 2020. "Toward a Feminist Future: A Political Strategy for Fighting Backlash and Advancing Gender Equity." *Signs: Journal of Women in Culture and Society* 45, no. 2: 328–36.
Faludi, Susan. 1991. *Backlash: The Undeclared War Against American Women*. New York: Random House.
Mansbridge, Jane, and Shauna L. Shames. 2008. "Toward a Theory of Backlash: Dynamic Resistance and the Central Role of Power." *Politics and Gender* 4, no. 2: 623–34.
Piscopo, Jennifer M., and Denise M. Walsh. 2020. "Introduction" *Signs* 45, no. 2: 265–78.
Rowley, Michelle V. 2020. "Anything but Reactionary: Exploring the Mechanics of Backlash." *Signs: Journal of Women in Culture and Society* 45, no. 2: 278–87.
Townsend-Bell, Erica. 2020. "Backlash at the Moment of Revelation." *Signs*: *Journal of Women in Culture and Society* 45, no. 2: 287–94.

BEAUTY

When "beauty" appears in feminist discourse, it evokes images of rigid beauty standards that discipline and confine women's bodies to unattainable ideals. In this context, beauty standards often lead to issues, such as body dissatisfaction, eating disorders, and low self-esteem, and point to beauty practices, such as dieting, makeup, and plastic surgery, that perpetuate a narrow understanding of beauty as a mechanism of control. Naomi Wolf (2002, 28) states in *The Beauty Myth*, "The central rule of the myth: For every feminist action there is an equal and opposite beauty myth reaction." Wolf's understanding of beauty encapsulates the notion that the progress of feminism stands in opposition to beauty, understanding beauty as a mechanism of control that reinforces gender norms and the male gaze, ultimately limiting women's bodies to objectification.

However, bell hooks (2000, 36) in *Feminism Is for Everybody* recognizes the significance of beauty along the trajectory of feminism, stating, "Rigid feminist dismissal of female longings for beauty has undermined feminist politics . . . Until feminists go back to the beauty industry, go back to fashion, and create an ongoing, sustained revolution, we will not be free. We will not know how to love our bodies as ourselves." hooks advocates for a feminist perspective that engages with beauty rather than completely rejecting it, urging feminists to reimagine and reclaim beauty as a site of empowerment and self-expression. Despite the detrimental effects of the beauty industry, beauty is also a tool of empowerment, enabling women to express their creativity, make choices, and practice self-care. In this context, beauty exists at the intersection of agency and oppression, inevitably tying back to beauty's relationship with women's bodies.

Feminist Theories on Beauty and Beauty Practices

Feminist scholars have long debated whether beauty is truly liberating or oppressing women. Focusing on beauty practices, plastic surgery, in particular, the 1990s and early twenty-first century marked a hotbed of feminist discourses surrounding feminism and beauty. Specifically, feminists Susan Bordo and Kathy Davis held differing views on plastic surgery, and their debate reflected the larger tensions, particularly concerning whether women have agency through the process of body modification. Plastic surgery has been at the heart of feminist discourses, debated as a technology "ideally suited to altering the body in accordance with an individual's personal preferences" (Davis 2003, 6) or "the surgically perfected body" that sets the benchmark for what is considered a "normal body," rendering "the ordinary body" as "the defective body" (Bordo 2003, 28).

In *Unbearable Weight*, Susan Bordo criticizes plastic surgery for "effac[ing], not only the inequalities of privilege, money, and time that prohibit most people from indulging in these practices" (2003, 402), emphasizing that a "Western" appearance is the widely acknowledged beauty standard within the history of racism. Bordo further claims that the absence of individuals actively "choosing" to look more African or Jewish demonstrates that plastic surgery is "a burgeoning industry and an increasingly normative cultural practice" (2003, 24). The word "normative" means establishing or reflecting social norms, shaping the perception of what is considered normal—even natural—and Bordo's point is that plastic surgery is contributing to the uniformity of beauty ideals by promoting Western beauty ideals as the norm as individuals use plastic surgery to achieve a more Western appearance around the world.

Kathy Davis, on the other hand, sees plastic surgery as a "strategy for becoming an embodied subject" (2003, 96), reflecting the ongoing processes of negotiating and (re)constructing the relationship between the self and the body. Davis views an individual's decision to undergo plastic surgery as a "moment of triumph" (2003, 22), wherein a person seizes control of their own body. Writing specifically about women and plastic surgery, Davis saw plastic surgery as allowing each woman to determine the degree of suffering she deems appropriate for herself.

This debate highlights the complexity of feminist perspectives on beauty, underscoring the need to consider diverse experiences and viewpoints in discussions about women's autonomy and cultural gender norms. In addition to the feminist debates about whether plastic surgery modifies or mutilates the feminine body, feminist scholars have pointed out that beauty is an effective tool for managing and disciplining bodies. Approaching beauty as less philosophical—such as Kant's notion of the sublime—and more within social and political contexts, Genevieve Clutario notes that beauty reveals "social formations, commerce, consumption, labor, social interactions and control, and policy" (2023, 4).

Beauty is also an index of history as S. Heijin Lee, Christina H. Moon, and Thuy Linh Nguyen Tu suggest, as beauty provides "indexes of the modern formations taking place" (2019, 5). Put more simply, this means that we can study the history of femininity and feminine bodies by studying the history of beauty. In *Fashioning Diaspora*, Vanita Reddy situates beauty as "an assemblage [of] demands attending to the materialities and affectivities of beauty in diaspora" (2016, 24). This means that beauty is material or physical in the sense that it is the literal embodiment of the histories of migration, race, gender, class, and sexuality and it is a physical practice or embodiment that produces material effects.

It is impossible to detach beauty from the body or the material more broadly, as beauty is closely tied to capitalist processes of production, circulation, and consumption that exist in the form of labor, capital, technology, and material objects of desire. In this sense, beauty is not an ideal abstraction (although it materializes promises of personhood and citizenship) but something that builds racial and gendered embodiments and that is shaped by particular historical contexts.

Feminist Activism: Embracing or Rejecting Beauty

Feminist activism surrounding beauty is indeed complex, inviting the question: "Is beauty liberating or oppressive?" Nonetheless, throughout US history, beauty has been intricately linked with feminist activism, often serving as an integral component of it. For instance, the suffrage movement in the United States, which spanned from the late nineteenth century until 1920 when women gained the right to vote, exemplifies the connection between beauty and women's empowerment. During the early twentieth century, women advocating for their voting rights viewed beauty as a significant symbol of their strength. Red lipstick, in particular, emerged as a symbol of their resilience and power, worn proudly as they fought for equality. In 1912, women who marched in New York wore bright red lipstick as a way of visually expressing their rebellion and liberation. Red lipstick, which once had been socially and morally condemned for visualizing women's sexuality and femininity, had now taken on a form of protest against the constraints placed on women, highlighting their defiance and solidarity. By strategically embracing a once-condemned item, suffragists transformed it into a symbol of resistance and empowerment, challenging traditional notions of beauty and reclaiming control over their own bodies and rights.

The "Black is Beautiful" movement is another significant feminist movement in the history of the United States that deeply intersects with beauty. Emerging in the 1960s, Black feminists of the "Black is Beautiful" movement challenged the dominant standards of beauty that favored white, middle-class ideals (such as straight or gently curled hair), instead promoting Black aesthetics (such as afros and braids) and reclaiming Black identity.

As the Civil Rights Movement gained momentum during the 1960s, Black feminists celebrated the beauty of dark skin, textured hair, and distinctive facial features as a means of promoting appreciation for Black heritage and reclamation of cultural identity within the United States. By embracing and celebrating Blackness, Black feminists aimed to redefine beauty standards, ultimately challenging the systemic racism and colorism that pervade beauty standards in US society. The influence of Black feminists who sought to affirm Black beauty not only highlights the complex relationship between beauty, power, and race in the United States but also paves the way for greater inclusivity and representation in the country.

Beauty and feminist movements share a complex and intertwined history. While it is undeniable that unrealistic beauty standards can have detrimental effects on women, labeling beauty as inherently oppressive or objectifying women overlooks the complicated relationship between beauty and feminist activism. Feminist discourses on beauty and US feminist activism reveal that beauty can both perpetuate oppressive myths, subjecting women to unattainable standards, and serve as a tool for resistance against the structural violence that oppresses women.

Soyeon Kim

See Also: Body Positivity; Capitalism; Civil Rights Movement; hooks, bell; Male Gaze; Nineteenth Amendment; Suffrage

Further Reading

Bordo, Susan. 2003. *Unbearable Weight: Feminism, Western Culture, and the Body*, 10th ed. Berkeley: University of California Press.

Clutario, Genevieve Alva. 2023. *Beauty Regimes: A History of Power and Modern Empire in the Philippines, 1898–1941*. Durhan, NC: Duke University Press.
Davis, Kathy. 2003. *Dubious Equalities and Embodied Differences: Cultural Studies on Cosmetic Surgery*. Lanham, MD: Rowman & Littlefield.
hooks, bell. 2000. *Feminism is for Everybody: Passionate Politics*. London: Pluto Press.
Lee, S. Heijin, Christina H. Moon, and Thuy Linh Nguyen Tu, eds. 2019. *Fashion and Beauty in the Time of Asia*. New York: New York University Press.
National Museum of African American History and Culture. 2024. "Black is Beautiful: The Emergence of Black Culture and Identity in the 60s and 70s." Accessed May 31. https://nmaahc.si.edu/explore/stories/black-beautiful-emergence-black-culture-and-identity-60s-and-70s#:~:text=The%20phrase%20%E2%80%9Cblack%20is%20beautiful,pride%20in%20contemporary%20black%20achievements.
Palumbo, Jacqui. 2022. "Empowering, Alluring, Degenerate? The Evolution of Red Lipstick." *CNN Style*. Accessed May 31, 2024. https://www.cnn.com/style/article/red-lipstick-history-beauty/index.html.
Reddy, Vanita. 2016. *Fashioning Diaspora: Beauty, Femininity, and South Asian American Culture*. Philadelphia: Temple University Press.
Wolf, Naomi. 2002. *The Beauty Myth: How Images of Beauty Are Used against Women*. New York: HarperCollins Publishers.

THE BECHDEL TEST

Sexism is so routine that it can be hard to notice but once you see it, it can't be unseen. This is the scenario in which Alison Bechdel, a queer comic artist, found herself. She noticed the ways in which films are absolutely dominated by men: most of the actors are men and most of the dialogue is by men. Often, women exist in films only to be looked at—a phenomenon Laura Mulvey identified as the "male gaze." Drawing awareness to the overwhelming sexism in films, Bechdel developed a "tongue-in-cheek set of criteria" for identifying blatant sexism in cinema (Donald 2015; O'Meara 2016). In 1985, Bechdel published these criteria in her comic strip, "Dykes to Watch Out For." In the comic strip, two queer women walk past a movie theater and one remarks "that she will only see a film if it meets a certain set of requirements" (Neville 2023). These requirements are now known as the "Bechdel Test," and in order to "pass" the test, a film must have at least two women in it, and they have to talk to each other about something other than a man (Bechdel 1985).

The Bechdel Test and Mainstream Entertainment

The Bechdel Test has become quite popular, with mainstream media and websites such as BechdelTest.com routinely using the Bechdel Test to discuss films and other media—such as television series, video games, plays, and literature (Neville 2023).

The Bechdel Test is simplistic. It offers a "bare-minimum" set of criteria, and people typically use it in popular culture to identify overt sexism. Yet many popular films fail this test, including *Breakfast at Tiffany's* (1961), all three films in the *Lord of the Rings* trilogy (2001–3), *The Avengers* (2012), *Arrival* (2016), and *Oppenheimer* (2023). Indeed, a study of the "fifty highest grossing films in 2013" found that only 36 percent of the films passed "with flying colors" and another 7 percent "dubiously" passed. This means that 57 percent failed the Bechdel Test.

It is important to note that even if a film passes the Bechdel Test, it can still be sexist. Imagine, for instance, a scene in a film where two women talk to each other about the weather while wearing bikinis and lounging on a beach while the camera pans over their bodies. Technically, this scene would mean its film passes the Bechdel Test—but such a scene would also sexually objectify these women, presenting their bodies for masculine consumption. Media scholar Jennifer O'Meara cautions that even when films pass the Bechdel Test, audiences ought to ask many more questions as we consider whether a film is sexist. For instance, honing in on the criteria that there must be a conversation between two women, O'Meara (2016, 1121) suggests that we ask questions such as, "What do they discuss? When and where do they discuss it? How do they phrase it? How is it performed? Are their words acknowledged, praised, or dismissed by other characters? Are their words repeated by filmgoers, and immortalized in lists of memorable dialogue?"

Moreover, the mainstream use of the Bechdel Test does not attend to the ways in which interlocking oppression silences women of color, older women, queer women, and women for whom English is not their first language in blockbuster films (O'Meara 2016, 1121). That is, most of the films that pass the Bechdel Test do so by having two young, white, thin, heterosexually attractive women speak to each other in unaccented English. Using the Bechdel Test as a sort of "thumbs up/thumbs down" categorization of a film as sexist or not sexist fails to account for sexism's intersectional nature.

Origins and a More Feminist Use of the Bechdel Test

The Bechdel Test was never designed to assess whether or not a film is sexist. Describing the criteria as "a little lesbian joke in an alternative feminist newspaper," Alison Bechdel explains that the "test" emerged from her conversation with a friend, Liz Wallace—whom she credits in the comic strip. Within the comic strip, the criteria are presented as a way in which lesbians might decide whether to see a film. The Bechdel Test—which Alison Bechdel refers to as the Bechdel-Wallace Test—is a starting point, not an end point.

Moreover, if you haven't seen a film yet, you don't know for sure if there are two women who speak to each other about something other than a man. Instead, you have to use the movie's trailer and posters to get a sense of the film, a point that is reinforced in Bechdel's comic as the lesbian couple walks past movie posters with hypermasculine men posing with weapons for imaginary films with titles such as "The Mercenary," "The Barbarian," and "The Vigilante." Based on these posters, the women decide not to see those films.

As such, the Bechdel Test's criteria were first imagined in a more evocative or holistic sense than the way in which they are currently implemented in popular culture. Essentially, rather than being used to assess a film *after* watching it, the criteria were designed to be used *before* watching a film.

Before watching a film, we might ask ourselves, "Based on this film's poster and trailer, do I have reason to believe there are at least two women in the film, and that they will talk to each other about something other than a man?" If the movie poster is of Hollywood's leading men plus, possibly, a woman in the background (e.g., the posters for *Ocean's Eleven, The Avengers*, the *Fast and the Furious* series, *The Magnificent Seven,* etc.) or if the poster is of a single male actor in a powerful pose (e.g., the posters for *Rambo*, *Rocky*, *Taken, Oppenheimer*, etc.), we might surmise that these films will likely not have feminist portrayals of women.

The Bechdel Test is joined by a wide variety of other "tests" that draw attention to sexism and heterosexism in entertainment. For example, the Mako Mori Test requires that a film include a female character who has her own narrative arc and that her narrative arc does not support a man's story. The "Sexy Lamp Test" simply stipulates that if you can "take out a female character and replace her with a sexy lamp, without the story falling apart, then you fail!" (Kannan 2022). The May Test offers criteria for the portrayal of trans characters. It requires that trans actors portray trans characters, and that trans characters are depicted as "safe, stable, and secure," as "happy" and "in love," and not be a "sex worker, dealer, or thief." Moreover, trans identity "cannot be used to produce humor or generate a plot twist, and gender transition should not be the focus of the story" (May 2019). Like the Bechdel Test, these tests are starting places and offer a bare-minimum threshold that can help people determine whether or not they want to spend their time watching a film.

Sarah Kornfield

See Also: Interlocking Oppression; Intersectionality; Male Gaze; May Test

Further Reading

Bechdel, Alison. 1985. "The Bechdel Test." In *Dykes to Watch Out For*. Accessed August 14, 2024. http://bechdeltestfest.com/about/.

Donald, Alexandra. 2015. "Girls Against the World." *Screen Education* 76 (Summer): 60–7.

Kannan, Lakshmi. 2022. "Measuring the Feminism in Movies: Bechdel and Other Tests." *Medium*, October 12, 2022. https://medium.com/@kplakshmi.97/measuring-the-feminism-in-movies-bechdel-and-other-tests-dba1bbae1e88.

May, Kiley. 2019. "There Wasn't a Bechdel Test for Trans Representation, So I Made One." *Vice*, November 26, 2019. www.vice.com/en/article/7x5nje/there-wasnt-a-bechdel-test-for-trans-representation-so-i-made-one.

Morlan, Kinsee. 2014. "Comic-Con vs. The Bechdel Test." *San Diego City Beat*, July 23, 2014. Accessed August 14, 2024. https://web.archive.org/web/20150316161800/http://www.sdcitybeat.com/sandiego/article-13243-comic-con-vs-the-bechdel-test.html.

Neville, Lois. 2023. "What is the Bechdel Test?" *Backstage Magazine*, May 30, 2023. Accessed August 14, 2024. https://www.backstage.com/magazine/article/what-is-the-bechdel-test-75534/.

O'Meara, Jennifer. 2016. "What 'The Bechdel Test' Doesn't Tell Us: Examining Women's Verbal and Vocal (Dis)empowerment in Cinema." *Feminist Media Studies* 16, no. 6: 1120–3.

BETHUNE, MARY MCLEOD

Mary McLeod Bethune (1875–1955) is best known for founding the National Council of Negro Women (NCNW) in 1935 and her decades of civil rights activism, political leadership, work as an educator, and prolific writing.

Born Mary Jane McLeod in 1875, Bethune was one of seventeen children raised in South Carolina by their formerly enslaved parents—Sam and Patsy McLeod. When she was approximately ten years old, she began attending Trinity Mission School, a one-room Black schoolhouse. Her teacher Emma Jane Wilson helped Bethune receive a scholarship to attend Scotia Seminary, which is now known as Barber-Scotia College from 1888 to 1894. This education not only gave Bethune the tools for her future work but also brought her joy in learning. Indeed, Bethune would later describe her work in educational leadership as the "unfolding of my soul" (McCluskey 1999, 74).

In 1904, Bethune founded a school for Black girls in Daytona, Florida, which is now known as the Bethune-Cookman College. There were no hospitals for Black people in Daytona, so in 1911 Bethune founded McLeod Hospital—named in honor of her parents—next door to her school: the student nurses at her school worked alongside physicians at McLeod Hospital to care for both Black and white community members. Similarly, Bethune opened her school's library to the community, making it the first free library Black people could enter in Florida (Dionne 2020). Bethune soon began working to improve housing for Black people in Daytona, becoming the only Black member of the city's housing board and leading the city to develop affordable housing near her school (Robertson 2015). Bethune's leadership and example provides a gorgeous model of local activism as she worked to right the wrongs of racism, Jim Crow laws, poverty, and sexism in her own community.

Mary McLeod Bethune was dedicated to achieving social, economic, and educational opportunities for African Americans and particularly African American women (Library of Congress).

Beyond her work in Daytona, Florida, Bethune was active in regional and national organizations for Black women. In 1935 she founded the National Council of Negro Women (NCNW), arguing that Black women needed a national organization with international reach through which to lobby for equality and help others. The founding by-laws state that the organization is designed to provide a voice "for the millions of Negro women of this country in their struggle for opportunity and equality" (Preston 2023, 41).

The NCNW worked to unite Black women in the United States with women of color in Cuba, Haiti, as well as in Europe and Africa as they struggled together for access and equality. In 1940, the NCNW launched a magazine, the *Aframerican Woman's Journal*, which was published "in English, French, and Spanish and distributed globally" (Preston 2023, 41). In the magazine's first issue, Bethune wrote that the magazine would "go to many places, perhaps to far away countries where we ourselves may never travel, but even then it will tell our story, and serve to mirror for many people the uneven gradations of the Negro women's progress and the larger progress of the Race achieved through the years." She continues, writing that the magazine would serve an even greater mission by deepening Black women's consciousness of the part they "must play in helping to bring to past America's true Democracy." Bethune concluded that these were the dreams that guided the magazine, and with those goals in mind she and the other editors were sending "our Journal down the years" (1940, 2).

Bethune understood her work as bringing about "America's true Democracy." She worked across the United States and internationally, building schools, redesigning curriculum, arguing for civil rights for people of color—especially women of color—building coalitions and activist organizations, and lobbying business and government agencies. She "leveraged relationships" to bring NCNW council members "to the White House to discuss with government officials the issues faced by

African Americans," and she became the "unofficial leader of the Black Cabinet, a group of Black federal employees who came together to 'channel their individual campaigns against discrimination and transform them into an unofficial lobby for African American concerns'" with the White House (Preston 2023, 40–1; Watts 2020, xii).

Mary McLeod Bethune's work at the local, national, and international levels continues to inspire feminists and civil rights activists—and her work continues through the NCNW. To this day, the NCNW continues Bethune's mission to "lead, empower, and advocate for women of African descent, their families and communities" (NCNW 2025).

Sarah Kornfield

See Also: Civil Rights Movement; Suffrage; Third World Women's Alliance and Black Woman's Manifesto; Womanism

Further Reading

Bethune, Mary McLeod. 1940. "From the President." *Aframerican Woman's Journal* 1, no. 1: 2.

Dionne, Evette. 2020. *Lifting as We Climb: Black Women's Battle for the Ballot Box*. New York: Viking.

McCluskey, Audrey Thomas. 1999. "Introduction: Educational Leadership." In *Mary McLeod Bethune: Building a Better World*, edited by Audrey Thomas McClusky and Elaine M. Smith, 67–74. Bloomington: Indiana University Press.

National Council of Negro Women (NCNW). 2025. "Our Mission." Accessed February 26, 2025. https://ncnw.org/our-mission/.

Preston, Ashley Robertson. 2023. *Mary McLeod Bethune the Pan-Africanist*. Gainesville: University Press of Florida.

Robertson, Ashley N. 2015. *Mary Mcleod Bethune in Florida: Bringing Social Justice to the Sunshine State*. Charleston, SC: The History Press.

Watts, Jill. 2020. *The Black Cabinet: The Untold Story of African Americans and Politics during the Age of Roosevelt*. New York: Grove Atlantic.

BIBLICAL COMPLEMENTARIANISM

Biblical complementarianism is a theological belief that asserts distinct but "equally" important (binary) gender roles for men and women. Men are meant to be providers and protectors, while women are meant to partake in a more passive role, letting men lead them while taking care of the home and children. Women are also forbidden from taking leadership positions in the church, including teaching or preaching to men. The Council for Biblical Manhood and Womanhood developed complementarian doctrine in the 1980s as a response to feminist theology and to feminist activism and the more equitable gender roles developing in the 1960s and 1970s ("The Danvers Statement" 1988). The Council for Biblical Manhood and Womanhood maintains that gender roles are God-given and laid out clearly in scripture. Complementarian doctrine is mainstream in evangelical churches, the Southern Baptist Convention, and many nondenominational churches.

Biblical complementarianism argues that women are meant to submit to men's authority as a representation of the "relationship between Christ and the earthly church," where men represent Christ and women represent the earthly church (Sheldon 2017, 981). Women's submission and passivity is meant to *complement* patriarchal authority and dominance, and thus these gender roles work together to "sustain and protect Christian family values" (Marsden 2018, 82). Indeed, these gender roles are believed to be biologically based. According to biblical complementarianism, there are only two sexes and heterosexual marriage is the only type of romantic relationship that should exist because the two sexes complement each other.

Feminist activists and theologians have critiqued complementarian doctrine as inherently misogynistic and heteronormative with racist undertones. For instance, because complementarianism is patriarchal, churches and organizations that follow complementarian doctrine often become breeding grounds for sexual abuse. Christian feminists have consistently drawn connections between the two. During the #MeToo Movement, hundreds of women came forward using the hashtag #ChurchToo, revealing how church leaders had sexually abused them and detailing the church's abysmal handling of abuse (Shellnutt 2018). Many of these women state that they were told to forgive their abusers, were blamed for the abuse by being called "promiscuous," and were ostracized from their church communities (Du Mez 2020, 290). In cases of domestic abuse, women were encouraged to stay married to their abusers (Marsden 2018, 78; Du Mez 2020, 276, 292–3).

While complementarian leaders like John Piper have argued that patriarchal doctrine will end abuse when men step up as "leaders," Christian feminists such as Rachel Held Evans have criticized such beliefs, stating, "banning women from the pulpit," "misusing Scripture to reinforce gender stereotypes," and telling women to endure abuse at the hands of their husbands "doesn't protect women; it harms them" (Held Evans 2018).

There is a distinct connection between encouraging women's submission and the abuse that takes place in the home and church. Citing one study, Meredith Whitnah states that "men who hold more conservative theological beliefs about scriptural authority than their wives have been found to be more likely to perpetrate violence" (Whitnah 2022, 432). When men are given total authority in the church and home, there is no accountability, justice, or love. Encouraging and sometimes requiring women to be submissive paves the way for an abuse of power in families and churches.

Biblical complementarianism exclusively endorses heterosexual relationships and is inherently homophobic. Those in favor of complementarianism often use anti-LGBTQIA+ rhetoric, stating that anything but celibacy or a heterosexual relationship is unbiblical (Shorter 2023, 135). Believing that sex determines gender, biblical complementarianism works to erase the existence of gay, transgender, and nonbinary people by claiming binary gender roles are natural and God ordained (Sheldon 2017, 978).

In addition to being heteronormative, complementarian doctrine automatically assumes that women have the ability to manage the home and take care of children without having to work. For low-income women and women of color this has never been the case as "becoming an expert in domesticity has generally required the support of a (white) man with a (middle-to upper-class) stable income" (Birch 2018, 237). Complementarianism makes little to no room for women and men of different backgrounds. Rather, it treats middle- and upper-class, white, heterosexual couples as the norm and fails to acknowledge the systemic injustice that plagues our society.

Ultimately, biblical complementarianism reinforces patriarchal beliefs about men and women. Women are seen as strictly made for domesticity and motherhood while men are seen as leaders and providers. By working to deconstruct patriarchy, feminists break the misogynistic binary rooted in complementarianism.

Sage Mikkelsen

See Also: Compulsory Heterosexuality; Deconstruction; Feminist Theology; Purity Culture; Religious Right

Further Reading

Birch, Jessica E. 2018. "Love, Labor, and Lorde." In *Introduction to Women's. Gender and Sexuality Studies: Interdisciplinary and intersectional Approaches*, edited by L. Ayu Saraswati, Barabara L. Shaw, and Heather Rellihan, 234–8. New York: Oxford University Press.

"The Danvers Statement." 1988. *Center for Biblical Manhood and Womanhood.* Accessed April 25, 2024. https://cbmw.org/about/danvers-statement/.

Du Mez, Kristin Kobes. 2020. *Jesus and John Wayne: How White Evangelicals Corrupted a Faith and Fractured a Nation.* New York: Liveright Publishing Corporation.

Held Evans, Rachel. 2018. "Patriarchy Doesn't 'Protect' Women: A Response to John Piper." *Rachel Held Evans*, March 21, 2018. https://rachelheldevans.com/blog/me-too-john-piper.

Marsden, Daphne. 2018. "The Church's Contribution to Domestic Violence: Submission, Headship, and Patriarchy." In *Rape Culture, Gender Violence, and Religion*, edited by Caroline Blyth, Emily Colgan, and Katie B. Edwards, 73–95. Cham: Springer International Publishing.

Sheldon, Myrna Perez. 2017. "Wild at Heart: How Sociobiology and Evolutionary Psychology Helped Influence the Construction of Heterosexual Masculinity in American Evangelicalism." *Signs: Journal of Women in Culture and Society* 42, no. 4: 977–98.

Shellnutt, Kate. 2018. "Hundreds Accuse Independent Baptist Pastors of Abuse." *Christianity Today*, December 12, 2018. https://www.christianitytoday.com/news/2018/december/independent-fundamentalist-baptist-church-abuse-scandal.html.

Shorter, Rosie Clare. 2023. "Complementarianism, Heteronormativity and the Future of the Anglican Church: Tensions in Lived Sydney Anglicanism." *Journal for the Academic Study of Religion* 36, no. 1: 118–44.

Whitnah, Meredith. 2022. "Evangelical Organizations' Responses to Domestic Violence: How the Cultural Production of Religious Beliefs Challenges or Enshrines Patriarchy." *Review of Religious Research* 64, no. 3: 427–50.

BIOETHICS

We can think of bioethics as, roughly, the interdisciplinary study of ethical questions that took shape in the 1960s and 1970s in response to developments in the health-related life sciences, health care, health policy, and their applications. Put more simply, bioethics refers to the ways different branches of research and thought come together to study the ethics of health-related and life-related technology, care, science, and policies. For example, feminist bioethics stresses the importance of social identities on women's health. Feminist approaches to bioethics emerged beginning in the 1980s, challenging gendered norms and assumptions in traditional approaches to bioethics, seeking to take gender and other forms of social inequality seriously as a morally relevant category within the field. For instance, feminist bioethics have directed attention to the importance of the exclusion of women from medical research and how women of color have a significantly higher maternal mortality rate in the United States. The point of this work, however, isn't merely academic. By showing the importance of bioethical investigation on specific issues thought to be neglected by traditional bioethics, feminist bioethics also works toward the political goal of justice for women.

There are two clear avenues through which feminism has furthered bioethics. The first is by expanding the field of bioethics to topics such as reproductive health, the commodification of women's bodies, and ways that medical research ignores or marginalizes women. Second, feminist bioethicists have transformed the entire field of bioethics by challenging patriarchal assumptions and pioneering feminist methodologies—or ways of researching—within the field of bioethics. Feminist methodologies have shaped approaches to ontology, epistemology, and ethics within philosophy. All of these influence feminist bioethics. Ontology is that part of philosophy that deals with what things exist and their natures. Large swaths of Western philosophy have thought about moral agents in individualistic and idealized ways. In contrast, feminist ontologies stress the relational dimension of human existence. This is seen, for instance, in the importance of relational accounts of autonomy. Feminists such as Susan Wendell and Elizabeth Spelman also stress the importance of reflection on embodiment. Reason, or rationality, is traditionally most closely associated with the mind or soul. Reflection on agency often downplays the body while stressing rationality and impartiality. Characteristics more associated with women, such as emotions and partiality, are denigrated. Feminists stress that humans are not only rational but also emotional, relational agents. Bioethics needs to incorporate this broader understanding.

Epistemology deals with how and what we know. Feminist epistemologists stress the importance of power dynamics and social position. In this vein, feminist bioethics pays special attention to power hierarchies and social contexts, recognizing that "what" we know is often dependent on "who" the knower is. Knowledge is socially constructed and influenced by our identities, including though not limited to our genders. Some feminists argue not only that knowledge is situated without our social locations but also that marginalized individuals are often better positioned epistemically:

> when standpoint is taken into account, often the epistemic tables are turned. Those who are economically dispossessed, politically oppressed, socially marginalized and are therefore likely to be discredited as epistemic agents—e.g., as uneducated, uninformed, unreliable—may actually have a capacity, by virtue of their standpoint, to know things that those occupying privileged positions typically do not know, or are invested in not knowing. (Wylie 2003, 31)

For instance, it is especially women of color who have direct awareness of how both the economic precarity of hospice care and the desire for greater profits negatively impact those receiving such care.

Tom Beauchamp and James Childress developed four principles that have been extremely influential in bioethics: autonomy, beneficence, nonmaleficence, and justice. Feminist bioethics stresses that in addition to these principles, issues of care and vulnerability are also crucial for ethical reflection. Care ethics emphasizes the importance of relationships and questions the usual assumed split between reason and emotion. Care ethics, and feminist bioethics more generally, criticizes overly abstract and rule-based approaches. Our responsibilities come not from abstract rules but from the relationships we have with particular people. The moral decisions we make in bioethics thus need to be sensitive to the contexts of those relationships.

Kevin Timpe

See Also: Disability; Feminist Methodologies; Mind/Body Split; Reproductive Justice; Standpoint Theory

Further Reading

Beauchamp, Tom L., and James F. Childress. *Principles of Biomedical Ethics*, 8th ed. Oxford: Oxford University Press.

Fricker, Miranda. 2007. *Epistemic Injustice: Power and the Ethics of Knowing*. Oxford: Oxford University Press.

Noddings, Nel. 2002. *Starting at Home: Caring and Social Policy*. Berkeley, CA: University of California Press.

Scully, Jackie Leach. "Feminist Bioethics." 2023. In *Stanford Encyclopedia of Philosophy*, edited by Edward N. Zalta and Uri Nodelman. https://plato.stanford.edu/archives/fall2023/entries/feminist-bioethics/.

Scully, Jackie Leach, Laurel Baldwin-Ragaven, and Petya Fitzpatrick, eds. 2010. *Feminist Bioethics: At the Center, on the Margins*. Baltimore, MD: Johns Hopkins University Press.

Wylie, Alison. 2003. "Why Standpoint Matters." In *Science and Other Cultures: Issues in Philosophies of Science and Technology*, edited by Robert Figueroa and Sandra G. Harding. New York: Routledge.

BIOPOWER

When activists and scholars discuss biopower, they are discussing two interconnected ideas. The first concerns who has power over bodies and how those bodies can move about in the world. In other words, this aspect of biopower is when institutions—such as governments, religions, medical systems, prisons, and schools—have control over how individuals move and exist in the world. Most often, this type of power is enacted through surveillance. Take a school dress code, for example. A powerful group, usually a school board, votes on what students can wear, removing choice and imposing a set of values. Teachers and administrators take up the role of enforcing the dress code, participating in the system of control and surveilling students as they walk about school. When people dress outside of the code, there are real consequences—missing school, missing tests, or suspension. Many students, then, internalize the dress code so much that it becomes second nature to dress within its boundaries and enforcement is no longer necessary. This is exactly how biopower works.

The second aspect of biopower is institutions' control of life—typically in terms of population control and maintenance. For example, anti-miscegenation laws in the United States prohibited white people from marrying and reproducing with people of color (Washington 2012). These laws were about maintaining a "pure" white population; they were a form of population control and maintenance. Similarly, tax laws that incentivize birthing more children, such as the tax and related benefits for families who have a third child in France, are a way of controlling the population—in this case, attempting to increase the population (Commander n.d.). A different type of example would be mandatory vaccines. Consider, for instance, how in 2008 the state of Texas required immigrant women and girls (age eleven to twenty-six) who were applying to become legal permanent residents in the United States to receive the human papillomavirus (HPV) vaccine as part of their qualifications—while not requiring it of other women in the state. The HPV vaccine protects against a sexually transmitted virus; requiring it for immigrant women and girls fed into stereotypes that portray women of color as dirty, impure, and promiscuous. Moreover, the HPV vaccine is expensive, creating an additional financial burden for immigrant women and girls. This policy was a clear instance of biopower, working to "maintain" the health of Texas' population. It clearly violated immigrant women and girls' bodily autonomy, and a coalition of over hundred immigrant and health and women's advocacy groups challenged the requirement, successfully overturning it in 2009 as reported by the National Latina Institute for Reproductive Justice ("HPV Vaccine" 2009).

The theory of biopower was first developed by Michel Foucault (1977), a philosopher and historian, who worked to define the relationship between power, knowledge, and freedom within society. Foucault initially discussed biopower in the prison system using a concept called the panopticon. Picture it: a prison where the guards are set up in the center, looking at every move that the inmates make. The inmates feel so surveilled in every action that they eventually begin surveilling themselves. Foucault was referencing an actual prison, but the disciplinary power that the guards have is a demonstration of biopower.

Biopower can be used to describe many social issues within the United States. Many feminist issues are concerned with biopower. Most prominently, birth rights and abortion are wrapped up in this. When the choice to have a child, be on birth control, or have sex is controlled by a government, that is a matter of biopolitics. Overall, biopower reduces individuals and their choices to a population that can be controlled. It is a dangerous tool used by systems to enforce a set of beliefs on entire groups of people.

Hannah Taylor

See Also: Abortion; Birth Control; Bodily Autonomy; Disciplinary Power; Eugenics; Patriarchy

Further Reading

Commander, Emily. n.d. "How Tax for Families in France Plays a Big Part in Life." *The Good Life France*. Accessed July 17, 2024. https://thegoodlifefrance.com/how-tax-for-families-in-france-plays-a-big-part-in-life/.

Foucault, Michel. 1977. *Discipline and Punish*. Translated by A. Sheridan. New York: Pantheon.

"HPV Vaccine." 2009. *National Latina Institute for Reproductive Justice*, November 16, 2009. Accessed July 17, 2024. https://www.latinainstitute.org/news/immigrant-seekers-wont-have-to-get-hpv-vaccine/.

Washington, Myra. 2012. "Interracial Intimacy: Hegemonic Construction of Asian American and Black Relationships on TV Medical Dramas." *Howard Journal of Communications* 23, no. 3: 253–71.

BLACK ARTS MOVEMENT

The Black Arts Movement (BAM) was a cultural and artistic revolution that emerged in the mid-1960s and lasted through the 1970s. Often described as the "aesthetic and spiritual sister of the Black Power Movement," BAM used literature, theater, music, and visual arts to advocate for Black liberation, self-determination, and cultural pride (Neal 1968). Rooted in resistance to systemic racism and the legacy of white supremacy, the movement also critiqued Western aesthetic norms as it redefined Black identity and artistry. While the movement is often associated with male-dominated spaces, feminist contributions to BAM have been central to its enduring legacy. Black women artists and activists expanded the movement's scope by addressing the intersections of race, gender, and class oppression.

The Black Arts Movement was founded by poet and playwright Amiri Baraka, who established the Black Arts Repertory Theatre/School (BARTS) in Harlem in 1965. Baraka's vision inspired artists and activists across the United States to develop community-based art spaces, independent publishing houses, and Black theaters. These spaces, such as Chicago's Organization of Black American Culture (OBAC) and Detroit's Broadside Press, became incubators for radical creativity and political expression.

The movement aligned itself with Black nationalism, emphasizing the importance of art as a tool for political change. BAM rejected assimilationist narratives and sought to cultivate an art form rooted in the Black experience. Writers like Sonia Sanchez, Nikki Giovanni, and Audre Lorde emphasized themes of community, resilience, and resistance, often challenging patriarchy and male dominance within the movement.

Feminist and Intersectional Interventions in BAM

While BAM as a whole championed Black liberation, its early iterations often marginalized the voices of Black women and failed to address gender oppression. Black women writers and artists played a crucial role in pushing the movement toward an intersectional understanding of oppression. For instance, Audre Lorde's poetry and essays bridged the personal and political, exploring issues like sexism, homophobia, and racism. Similarly, playwright Adrienne Kennedy interrogated the psychological impacts of systemic oppression in her experimental works.

Feminist thinkers within the movement insisted on including gender equity in the broader struggle for racial justice. Sonia Sanchez, in her poetry and plays, highlighted the complexities of Black womanhood, while Nikki Giovanni's works celebrated Black motherhood and community. These artists not only contributed to the movement's creative output but also challenged its limitations, calling for an inclusive vision of liberation that accounted for the lived experiences of Black women.

The Black Arts Movement demonstrated the interconnectedness of race, gender, and class oppression. For example, Lorraine Hansberry's play *A Raisin in the Sun* (1959) predated BAM and profoundly influenced its aesthetics and activism. The play addresses the double burden of racism and sexism faced by Black women, foreshadowing the intersectional concerns later taken up by BAM. Similarly, Gwendolyn Brooks's poetry, such as "We Real Cool," explores the struggles of working-class Black communities, making visible the class dimensions of Black life.

BAM also intersected with the burgeoning women's liberation movement of the 1960s and 1970s. However, many Black women in BAM distanced themselves from mainstream feminism, critiquing its whiteness and failure to address the unique challenges faced by women of color. Instead, they developed frameworks like womanism, as articulated by Alice Walker, to describe their dual commitment to racial and gender equity.

Legacy and Impact

The Black Arts Movement transformed US culture, laying the groundwork for contemporary Black feminist thought and activism. It inspired future generations of artists, from Toni Morrison to Ava DuVernay, who continue to challenge the intersections of systemic oppression through their work. BAM's emphasis on community-centered art has also influenced feminist organizing practices, emphasizing the role of art in creating social change.

Despite its achievements, the movement faced criticism for its male-dominated leadership and exclusionary practices. The feminist critiques leveled by Black women during BAM remain relevant today, offering valuable lessons for building inclusive movements.

Sage Drisker

See Also: Intersectionality; Lorde, Audre; White Supremacy; Womanism; Women's Liberation Movement

Further Reading

Christian, Barbara. 1985. *Black Feminist Criticism: Perspectives on Black Women Writers.* New York: Teachers College Press.
Collins, Patricia Hill. 2000. *Black Feminist Thought: Knowledge, Consciousness, and the Politics of Empowerment.* New York: Routledge.
Lorde, Audre. 1984. *Sister Outsider: Essays and Speeches.* Berkeley, CA: Crossing Press.
Neal, Larry. 1968. "The Black Arts Movement." *Drama Review* 12, no. 4: 29–39.
Walker, Alice. 1983. *In Search of Our Mothers' Gardens: Womanist Prose.* New York: Harcourt Brace Jovanovich.

BLACK LIBERATION THEOLOGY

Black Liberation Theology was created amid the US Civil Rights Era. The theology's founder, James H. Cone, established Black Liberation Theology in a slate of publications: *Black Theology and Black Power* (1969), *A Black Theology of Liberation* (1970), and *God of the Oppressed* (1975). Black Liberation Theology's most basic tenet is the express belief that God sides with the oppressed and is concerned with the needs of the poor and needy.

Cone defines liberation as "a divine gift of freedom . . . wherein the oppressed realize that their fight for freedom is a divine right of creation" (Cone [1975] 1997, 127). Black Liberation Theology follows in the tradition of Liberation Theology, which was founded in Latin America by Peruvian Catholic priest, Gustavo Gutiérrez. Liberation Theology asserted that the Catholic Church was charged to care for the poor and needy and to address structural oppression instead of ignoring or perpetuating it.

Black Liberation Theology adapted a similar theology for the Black community and the Black Church to the context of a contentious, racially oppressive US society. Due to the extensive history of Black oppression in the United States, from the Transatlantic Slave Trade to Jim Crow segregation, Black Liberation Theology was an attempt to disconnect the ideas that God justified the mistreatment and oppression of people of color, particularly Black people and that Black people were part of a divinely subordinate race. Underlying this racist assumption was the belief that Black Christians were properly practicing their faith and its customs if they accepted their subordinate status in US and global society. Cone's theology of Black liberation was a direct affront against this racist perspective and approach to Christianity, with a special emphasis on the teachings in the Black Church.

Cone went so far as to connect the suffering reality of Black people in the United States to the death of Jesus Christ, Savior of the Christian faith. He described the method of Jesus' death as a form of lynching in his book, *The Cross and Lynching Tree*. He writes that the cross is the universal symbol of the Christian faith and the lynching tree is the "quintessential symbol" of Black oppression in the United States, but both are symbols of death. He concludes that by recognizing the resonances between the cross and the lynching tree, Christians can live into the "hope that we may heal the wounds of racial violence that continue to divide our churches and society" (Cone 2011, xiii).

Other foundational Black Liberation Theologians include Dr. Gayraud S. Wilmore, Dr. Cain Hope Felder, Dr. Vincent Harding, Dr. Albert Cleage, and William A. Jones. There are two additional scholars who lived prior to the era of Black Liberation Theology but their theology would certainly place them squarely in alignment with Black Liberation Theologians: Dr. Howard W. Thurman and Bishop Henry McNeal Turner. Thurman was a Christian mystic and theologian whose philosophy of liberatory theology influenced Dr. Martin Luther King's approaches to the Civil Rights Movement and a host of other global leaders, including Mahatma Gandhi and Pauli Murray. Bishop Turner was one of the first Black preachers in the African Methodist Episcopal Church and was known for his controversial views on Blackness and religion. He is one of the first Black pulpiteers who claimed that God was Black and that the first people on Earth were also Black, encouraging his parishioners to adopt the view of God as Black too.

Criticism of Black Liberation Theology

Black Liberation Theology has centered on Black men, following in the patriarchal norm of US religion and excluding Black women from its pursuit of liberation. As such, many Black women theologians confronted the issue, often directly. Jacqueline Grant, a prominent womanist theologian, insisted that "Black theology cannot continue to treat Black women as if they are invisible creatures." She continued, arguing that since "Black women represent more than 50 percent of the Black community and more than 70 percent of the Black Church," there can be no "authentic theology of liberation" that does not specifically address the liberation of Black women. Finally, Grant confronted the argument that racism and sexism are hard enough to battle on their own and thus their problems should not be confused and conflated by stating, "the elimination of both racism and sexism is so crucial for the liberation of Black persons that we cannot shrink from facing them together" (Grant in Cone and Wilmore 1993, 334).

Stephanie House-Niamke

See Also: Civil Rights Movement; Feminist Theology; Womanism

Further Reading

Cone, James H., and Gayraud S. Wilmore. 1993. *Black Theology: A Documentary History Volume One: 1966–1979*. Maryknoll, NY: Orbis Books.

Cone, James H., and Gayraud S. Wilmore. 1993. *Black Theology: A Documentary History Volume Two: 1980–1992*. Maryknoll, NY: Orbis Books.

Cone, James H. [1975] 1997. *God of the Oppressed*. Maryknoll, NY: Orbis Books.

Cone, James H. 2011. *The Cross and the Lynching Tree*. Maryknoll, NY: Orbis Books.

Jones, William R. 1973. *Is God a White Racist? A Preamble to Black Theology*. Boston: Beacon Press.

Wilmore, Gayraud S. 1998. *Black Religion and Black Radicalism: An Interpretation of the Religious History of African Americans*. Maryknoll, NY: Orbis Books.

#BLACKLIVESMATTER

The #BlackLivesMatter movement emerged in 2013 as a powerful challenge to racism, police brutality, and state-sanctioned violence against Black people in the United States. Founded by three Black queer women, from its inception this movement has been shaped by a Black feminist lens and praxis—a fusion of theory and activism. #BlackLivesMatter has reshaped the landscape of social justice activism, employing decentralized digital organizing tactics to mobilize protests, influence policy, and change public discourse. While focused on anti-Black racism, the movement is fundamentally intersectional, addressing the interlocking systems of oppression that impact all Black lives.

The Origins of #BlackLivesMatter

#BlackLivesMatter began as a hashtag on social media in July 2013, after the acquittal of George Zimmerman for the murder of seventeen-year-old Trayvon Martin. Activists Alicia Garza, Patrisse Cullors, and Opal Tometi created #BlackLivesMatter in an act of resistance and affirmation, sparking a broader conversation about anti-Black racism. The hashtag went viral and quickly became a rallying cry for a new generation of organizers (Edgar and Johnson 2018).

In 2014, #BlackLivesMatter erupted into a national mass movement in the streets after the police killing of Michael Brown in Ferguson, Missouri (Taylor 2016). Protesters faced down militarized police, tear gas, and rubber bullets to demand justice and declare that Black lives matter. Demonstrations spread to cities across the country as activists responded to a devastating succession of police killings of Black people that were caught on camera and shared on social media, from Eric Garner in New York to Walter Scott in South Carolina to Sandra Bland in Texas.

A Movement Grounded in Black Feminist Politics

From the beginning, the founders of #BlackLivesMatter situated the movement in a Black feminist political framework. In "A Herstory of the #BlackLivesMatter Movement," Alicia Garza (2014) writes,

> #BlackLivesMatter is a unique contribution that goes beyond extrajudicial killings of Black people by police and vigilantes. It goes beyond the narrow nationalism that can be prevalent within some Black communities, which merely call on Black people to love Black, live Black and buy Black, keeping straight cis Black men in the front of the movement while our sisters, queer and trans and disabled folk take up roles in the background or not at all. Black Lives Matter affirms the lives of Black queer and trans folks, disabled folks, Black-undocumented folks, folks with records, women, and all Black lives along the gender spectrum.

This expansive view of whose Black lives matter is rooted in the Black feminist politics of intersectionality, which recognizes that race, class, gender, sexuality, and other identity markers do not exist in isolation from each other but are interlocking systems that work together to produce inequality (Crenshaw 1991). Black women experience both racism and sexism, and these cannot be understood separately. Moreover, Black women are not a monolithic group—they have different experiences based on their class position, sexual orientation, immigration status, disability status, and other factors. Black feminism insists on centering the most marginalized and building movements that address the full complexity of Black people's lives.

Queer Black Feminist Praxis

#BlackLivesMatter exemplifies what historian and activist Barbara Ransby (2018) calls "Black feminist queer praxis," a politics and practice based in the leadership of Black queer feminist organizers. Indeed, #BlackLivesMatter founders Alicia Garza, Patrisse Cullors, and Opal Tometi have deep roots in community organizing. Their experiences of intersectional oppression and resistance directly shaped the movement's trajectory.

Other Black queer women like Charlene Carruthers, director of Black Youth Project 100, and Elle Hearns, director of the Marsha P. Johnson Institute, have also been central leaders in the Movement for Black Lives. This is no coincidence but rather a reflection of the pivotal role that Black queer women have long played in Black freedom struggles, from the civil rights and Black Power movements to the fight against AIDS. Black feminist queer praxis is characterized by several key elements (Ransby 2018):

(1) Centering Black women and queer folks in leadership
(2) Employing an intersectional analysis that connects multiple systems of oppression
(3) Engaging in collective care and healing as integral to organizing
(4) Using artistic and cultural expression as a mode of resistance
(5) Embracing decentralized digital organizing tactics to build grassroots power

By putting these principles into practice, #BlackLivesMatter has modeled a new paradigm of social movement building that is deeply rooted in Black feminist and queer politics.

#BlackLivesMatter and Police Violence Against Black Women

While many of the highest-profile cases of police violence have involved Black men, #BlackLivesMatter has insisted on also highlighting the experiences of Black women who have been killed by police. The #SayHerName campaign, launched by the African American Policy Forum and Center for Intersectionality and Social Policy Studies, has drawn attention to Black women like Sandra Bland, Rekia Boyd, Korryn Gaines, and others whose stories have received less public attention.

Police violence against Black women is often rendered invisible in mainstream discourse, but it is a pervasive reality. Black women are disproportionately targeted for sexual assault by police officers, and they experience unique forms of racialized gender violence such as being brutalized while pregnant or with their children (Ritchie 2017). Black women are also frequently criminalized and arrested for acts of self-defense against domestic abusers and sexual assailants.

#BlackLivesMatter activists have challenged the narrow framing of police brutality as primarily an issue facing Black men by centering Black women's experiences and demanding a gender-inclusive approach to justice. This work builds on a long history of Black feminist organizing against state violence, from the campaign to free Joan Little, who killed a white prison guard in self-defense against sexual assault in 1974, to the protests led by Black women after the 1999 police killing of Amadou Diallo in New York City (Ransby 2018).

#BlackLivesMatter and Reproductive Justice

#BlackLivesMatter has also taken up issues of reproductive justice as integral to the fight for Black liberation. Reproductive justice, a framework developed by Black women in the 1990s, refers to the human right to maintain personal bodily autonomy, have children, not have children, and parent children in safe and sustainable communities (Ross et al. 2017). It goes beyond the narrow focus on abortion rights to encompass a wide range of issues affecting Black women's reproductive lives, including environmental racism, inadequate health care, economic insecurity, and state violence.

Police brutality and mass incarceration are reproductive justice issues because they interfere with Black people's ability to parent their children in safety and dignity. Black women have long been targets of forced sterilization and coercive birth control policies. Today, many Black women live in constant fear that their children will be harmed or killed by police, and Black mothers are frequently separated from their families by incarceration or child welfare interventions.

In 2015, activists disrupted a presidential campaign rally for Bernie Sanders in Seattle to demand that he address police violence and reproductive justice. Leaders from the #BlackLivesMatter network issued a statement affirming that "reproductive justice is very much situated within the Black Lives Matter movement . . . We absolutely stand in solidarity with all folks fighting for reproductive justice and bodily autonomy" (Ransby 2018). By articulating and fighting for an expansive vision of reproductive freedom, #BlackLivesMatter has helped to bring the reproductive justice framework to a wider audience and build bridges between movements.

#BlackLivesMatter's Global Impact

While focused on anti-Black racism in the United States, #BlackLivesMatter has had a profound global impact. Activists around the world have taken up the mantle of #BlackLivesMatter to challenge anti-Black racism and state violence in their own contexts, from Brazil to Australia to South Africa. In doing so, they have highlighted the global nature of anti-Blackness and the need for transnational solidarity in the fight against white supremacy (Davis 2016).

At the same time, #BlackLivesMatter has also sparked difficult conversations within Black communities about how to build a truly inclusive and liberatory movement. Some activists have critiqued the movement for neglecting the experiences of Black immigrants, who face both anti-Black racism and xenophobia. Others have pointed out the need to challenge homophobia and transphobia within Black communities and center the leadership of Black queer and transgender people.

Despite these challenges, #BlackLivesMatter has succeeded in changing the terms of public debate and catalyzing a new wave of anti-racist organizing around the world. Its impact can be seen in everything from the toppling of Confederate monuments to the uprising against police brutality in Nigeria to the global outpouring of support for Black Lives Matter protests in 2020 after the police killing of George Floyd.

Ultimately, the #BlackLivesMatter movement is a testament to the power of Black feminist queer praxis to transform society. By centering the most marginalized, employing an intersectional lens, and using creative digital tactics, #BlackLivesMatter has built a mass movement that is fundamentally shifting the political terrain. As Barbara Ransby (2018) argues, "Black queer feminist politics are driving this new moment of Black insurgency in ways we have not seen in a generation. Shaped by their leadership and their radical politics, #BlackLivesMatter has ushered in a new Black freedom movement for the 21st century—one that has the potential to transform not only US society but the world."

Theon E. Hill

See Also: Intersectionality; Prison Abolition Movements; Prison-Industrial Complex; Reproductive Justice; #SayHerName; White Supremacy

Further Reading

African American Policy Forum and Center for Intersectionality and Social Policy Studies. n.d. "#SayHerName." Accessed October 1, 2023. https://www.aapf.org/sayhername.

Carruthers, Charlene. 2018. *Unapologetic: A Black, Queer, and Feminist Mandate for Radical Movements*. Boston: Beacon Press.

Crenshaw, Kimberlé. 1991. "Mapping the Margins: Intersectionality, Identity Politics, and Violence against Women of Color." *Stanford Law Review* 43, no. 6: 1241–99.

Davis, Angela Y. 2016. *Freedom Is a Constant Struggle: Ferguson, Palestine, and the Foundations of a Movement*. Edited by Frank Barat. Chicago, IL: Haymarket Books.

Edgar, Amanda Nell, and Andre E. Johnson. 2018. *The Struggle over Black Lives Matter and All Lives Matter*. Lanham, MD: Lexington Books.

Garza, Alicia. 2014. "A Herstory of the #BlackLivesMatter Movement." *The Feminist Wire*, October 7, 2014. https://thefeministwire.com/2014/10/blacklivesmatter-2/.

Khan-Cullors, Patrisse, and Asha Bandele. 2018. *When They Call You a Terrorist: A Black Lives Matter Memoir*. New York: St Martin's Press.

Ransby, Barbara. 2018. *Making All Black Lives Matter: Reimagining Freedom in the Twenty-First Century*. Berkeley: University of California Press.

Ritchie, Andrea J. 2017. *Invisible No More: Police Violence Against Black Women and Women of Color*. Boston: Beacon Press.

Ross, Loretta, Lynn Roberts, Erika Derkas, Whitney Peoples, and Pamela Bridgewater, eds. 2017. *Radical Reproductive Justice: Foundation, Theory, Practice, Critique*. New York: Feminist Press.

Taylor, Keeanga-Yamahtta. 2016. *From #BlackLivesMatter to Black Liberation*. Chicago, IL: Haymarket Books.

BODILY AUTONOMY

Bodily autonomy is the idea that each person's body is theirs and theirs alone and that only they have the right to determine what happens to and with their own body. If you've ever heard the slogan "my body, my choice," you may think that it only applies to the pro-choice movement and primarily to pregnant people's decision whether to have an abortion. Although that is one important context relevant to bodily autonomy, it is but one of many.

Underpinning the idea of bodily autonomy is the related idea of consent, and not just consent for romance and sex. At least in theory, our bodies belong only to us, and nobody else should be able to tell us what to do with them. Indeed, nothing should happen to us without our consent. From pregnancy and birth to death, we make many choices related to our own bodies and often try to keep those choices to ourselves unless we wish to seek out advice or support from others.

Bodily Autonomy during Pregnancy

Those who are familiar with the abortion debate know that bodily autonomy during pregnancy is a complicated matter depending on whether one defines life as beginning at conception, birth, or somewhere in between. There is a process between an egg's fertilization and its development into a baby. That process is not as straightforward as a tiny, fully formed baby with all of its organs intact at the moment of fertilization that just grows and grows until it is born. Instead, fetuses develop more piecemeal than that, and even the best religious, scientific, and philosophical experts struggle to pinpoint the exact moment at which life begins (Bradshaw et al. 2015; Dias 2022).

For those who see life as beginning at conception or early in pregnancy, the bodily autonomy of the fetus tends to be weighed heavily against the bodily autonomy of the mother. For those who see life beginning later in pregnancy (for instance, at what medical professionals call "fetal viability," or the point at which a fetus could survive outside of the womb if it were born—typically not until the third trimester, or around twenty-seven weeks), the mother's bodily autonomy may weigh more heavily (Taylor 2021). According to the Centers for Disease Control, in 2020, almost 81 percent of abortions were performed at or before the ninth week of gestation, and nearly all abortions (93 percent) were performed at or before the thirteenth week of gestation. Just less than 6 percent of abortions occurred during gestational weeks fourteen to twenty, and less than 1 percent of abortions occurred after the twenty-first gestational week (Kortsmit et al. 2022). As such, over 99 percent of abortions in the United States occur well prior to the threshold of fetal viability.

Further complicating matters of bodily autonomy during pregnancy are factors like the circumstances under which the fetus was conceived (for instance, whether it was a planned or unplanned pregnancy, or whether it was a product of rape or incest) or various medical conditions like ectopic pregnancies or preeclampsia that could threaten the health, future reproductive capabilities, or life of the mother, or chromosomal abnormalities that could threaten the health, well-being, or lifespan of the fetus after birth. Choices around bodily autonomy during pregnancy are not always easy or straightforward; much depends on the unknown and perhaps unknowable question of whether and when a fetus becomes viable as an autonomous living being with a fully functioning body of its own.

Bodily Autonomy at Birth

Several matters related to bodily autonomy also present themselves at birth. Maintaining bodily autonomy for newborn babies can be tricky, as infants have few ways of expressing consent beyond latching onto a breast (or not) or bottle to feed or crying or flailing to express discomfort. However, some newborns are born with various medical conditions that may require or present the opportunity for parents to make bodily decisions on their children's behalf. For instance, a child born with a malfunctioning kidney may require emergency surgery.

Alternatively, parents of intersex children (possessing a combination of male and female parts) sometimes subject those children to unnecessary medical interventions, which many intersex people and others consider controversial or even unethical (Carpenter 2016). Meanwhile, it is also fairly common for cultural, religious, medical, or aesthetic reasons for parents to conduct infant circumcisions. Although male and female circumcisions differ considerably in terms of what doctors, surgeons, or religious figures remove and how it affects those who have them, there is some debate about whether one or both practices should be allowed, particularly without a person's consent (Bodenner 2015). Although some people recommend waiting until children are old enough to consent to surgeries like these, others argue that there are good reasons to perform them during infancy, as it is less likely that infants will remember having them.

Bodily Autonomy in Childhood and Adolescence

As children grow up, they will express more bodily autonomy through various choices about the clothes they wear, how they cut and do their hair, whether they wear makeup, whether they get piercings or tattoos, what hobbies they enjoy, or other aspects of their physical appearance or behavior. They also may set boundaries around who may hug, kiss, or touch them. Some may express themselves in socially constructed gender-conforming ways, and others may not. Some of those who are exploring their gender identity may choose, usually after consultation with parents, doctors, and/or mental health professionals, to go on puberty blockers to delay the onset of puberty and/or consider hormone replacement therapy or other gender-affirming care later in life. Meanwhile, as they approach puberty and adulthood, others will make choices about whether, when, with whom, how, and how often to become sexually active, whether to use birth control (which can have medical benefits beyond contraception), and other ways of exploring and performing their gender identities and sexual orientations.

Bodily Autonomy in Adulthood

In adulthood, people usually will continue to express bodily autonomy in similar ways to how they did during adolescence. In addition to the choices that they make in adolescence, bodily autonomy may extend to a variety of adult decisions like what we put into our bodies, how frequently we exercise, what nutritional and medical advice we follow, whether we will have one or many partners over the course of a lifetime, whether to have children, whether to leave an abusive partner, whether to have surgery, or whether to embrace or try to resist the natural process of aging.

Although adults are the group most likely to enjoy the most bodily autonomy, it is worth noting that even in adulthood, bodily autonomy is not unlimited. Adult bodies still have to navigate the world with other bodies and forces (laws, cultural practices, medical conditions, injuries, and natural processes) that restrain their full bodily autonomy. Some people will have greater bodily autonomy than others, but feminists and other equal rights activists strive to give as many people as much bodily autonomy as possible, as long as their exercises of bodily autonomy do not harm others.

Bodily Autonomy at the End of Life

Meanwhile, later in adulthood, bodily autonomy issues also extend to end-of-life care. Unless people die unexpectedly, many have decisions to make about whether they can take care of themselves or need care workers, whether, when, and how to engage in palliative care, whether to sign a "do not resuscitate" (DNR) order, whether and when to go on hospice, and, under some circumstances, whether they can partake in assisted suicide to end their lives.

One such example was that of Brittany Maynard, a 29-year-old woman who chose death with dignity after being diagnosed with a severe brain tumor that doctors estimated would give her six months to live. Upon hearing her prognosis, Maynard (2014) wrote that she reached a "heartbreaking conclusion" that there was "no treatment that would save [her] life, and [that] the recommended treatments would have destroyed the time [she] had left." Regarding her own bodily autonomy, she explained that she "would not tell anyone else that he or she should choose death with dignity" but also asked, "Who has the right to tell me that I don't deserve this choice? That I deserve to suffer for weeks or months in tremendous amounts of physical and emotional pain? Why should anyone have the right to make that choice for me?" When Maynard made that choice and went public with it, she became a face of the death with dignity movement, which strives to allow people maximal bodily autonomy over how they die.

Bodily Autonomy for Life

In practice, our bodies exist in a world with other people's bodies, some of whom may try to exert authority over our bodies. Throughout the life cycle, we make many choices about our bodies. Although nobody experiences full bodily autonomy, most people seek to maximize control over the choices that they make over their own bodies. As we navigate the world with other people's bodies, there are many things to consider, and some choices can be tough ones. However, maximizing equal access to bodily autonomy helps ensure greater agency and equality for as many people as possible.

Brad Serber

See Also: Abortion; Bioethics; Body Positivity; Enthusiastic Consent; Fat; Gender; Intersex; Nonbinary; Queer Theory; Right to Privacy; Trans Theory

Further Reading

Bodenner, Chris. 2015. "How Similar Is FGM to Male Circumcision? Your Thoughts." *The Atlantic*, May 13, 2015. https://www.theatlantic.com/health/archive/2015/05/male-circumcision-vs-female-circumcision/392732/.

Bradshaw, Gideon, Helen Thomas, Jonathan Renouf, David Barker, and Naomi Austin. 2015. "Countdown to Life: The Extraordinary Making of You." Presented by Michael Mosley. *BBC* in partnership with The Open University, September 28-October 1, 2015. Documentary series, 177 min.

Carpenter, Morgan. 2016. "The Human Rights of Intersex People." *Reproductive Health Matters* 24, no. 47: 74–84. https://doi.org/10.1016/j.rhm.2016.06.003.

Dias, Elizabeth. 2022. "When Does Life Begin?" *New York Times*, December 31, 2022. https://www.nytimes.com/interactive/2022/12/31/us/human-life-begin.html.

Kortsmit, Kathryn, et al. 2022. "Abortion Surveillance — United States, 2020." *Centers for Disease Control and Preventions*, November 25, 2022. https://www.cdc.gov/mmwr/volumes/71/ss/ss7110a1.htm#T10_down.

Maynard, Brittany. 2014. "My Right to Death with Dignity at 29." *CNN*, November 2, 2014. https://www.cnn.com/2014/10/07/opinion/maynard-assisted-suicide-cancer-dignity/index.html.

Taylor, Marygrace. 2021. "What is the Age of Fetal Viability?" *What to Expect*, August 2, 2021. https://www.whattoexpect.com/first-year/preemies/fetal-viability#point.

BODY POSITIVITY

Body positivity challenges white supremacist and patriarchal beauty standards by promoting "an all-encompassing respect and love for one's body" no matter its perceived imperfections (Brathwaite, DeAndrea, and Vendemia 2023, 2). The Body Positivity or the #BoPo Movement is extremely prevalent on social media, where it challenges traditionally idealized standards by encouraging representation and normalization of those with marginalized bodies (Brathwaite and DeAndrea 2021). The movement emphasizes body appreciation, and some scholars consider body positivity to be a form of self-love (Leboeuf 2019).

The Body Positivity movement is needed for many reasons. First, studies show that consistent exposure to extremely thin bodies leads to body dissatisfaction (Moreno-Domínguez et al. 2018). This dissatisfaction leads to an increase in eating disorders and depression (Brathwaite and DeAndrea 2021). Body dissatisfaction is particularly prevalent among those who are considered overweight or obese. Additionally, obesity and weight are the number one reason for childhood bullying (Manne 2022).

The relationship between weight and health is complicated; many fat people are healthy and many thin people are not. However, fat people are often discriminated against in healthcare settings, with doctors pushing understudied and sometimes unnecessary procedures (Manne 2022; Gunter 2018). Body positivity seeks to undo these harmful attitudes, assumptions, and behaviors—and their negative consequences—creating a world that is accepting of all bodies.

Feminist Approaches to Body Positivity

The Body Positivity movement developed out of the 1960s feminist fat-acceptance movement. During the 1960s, feminists responded to widespread anti-fat rhetoric, mobilizing to counteract this harmful and often sexist discourse. Feminists lobbied for anti-discrimination measures for those with larger bodies and promoted a rethinking of the relationship between health and attractiveness. Born from this fat-acceptance feminist activism, the Body Positivity movement promotes body diversity, acceptance, and a positive body image while challenging widely held, restrictive ideals of beauty and body size (Brathwaite, DeAndrea, and Vendemia 2023).

Currently, the Body Positivity movement is quite broad. There are several approaches under the body positivity umbrella, but the main three are known as Mainstream Body Positivity (or just Body Positivity), Radical Body Positivity, and Fat Positivity = Body Positivity.

Mainstream Body Positivity emphasizes women's self-love as a psychological act of resistance in a society that objectifies them (Darwin and Miller 2020). To bring about societal change and recover self-acceptance, mainstream body positive activists often launch internet campaigns, largely relying on social media like Instagram and hashtags including #Loveyourbody and #bodypositivity (Legault and Sago 2022). These hashtags convey a body positive message and attempt to empower everyone to feel beautiful. The focus within this mainstream approach to body positivity emphasizes individuals' self-acceptance as resistance.

In contrast, the Radical Body Positivity movement argues that the focus of the movement should be on "combating systemic rather than individual experiences of oppression" (Darwin and Miller 2020, 883). For instance, rather than telling women to love themselves, the Radical Body Positivity movement focuses on changing policies and laws. The Radical Body Positivity movement celebrates changes such as the CROWN Act. So far, twenty-four states in America have passed the CROWN Act, which "prohibits hair-based discrimination at work and school," creating protections for Black people and other people of color (Payne-Patterson 2023). Notably, the Radical Body Positivity movement has shifted away from a central concern with fat positivity, conceptualizing body positivity in much broader terms.

The Fat Positivity = Body Positivity, meanwhile, focuses on the discrimination against fat people, especially women. Fat activists are most concerned with the systemic prejudice against fat women, highlighting the importance of obese women's marginalization from Western beauty standards (Darwin and Miller 2020). This branch of the movement has sparked a lot of discussion on the varied consequences of fat stigma and how to define fatness. Additionally, fat activists including Marilyn Wann, Sonya Renee Taylor, and Aubrey Gordon promote the idea that "fat bodies can be not only healthy but also athletic, beautiful, and sexy" (Manne 2022).

Feminist Critiques of Body Positivity

In many ways, body positivity has been commodified by corporations—as a way to sell soap and makeup—and watered down by nonfeminist activists, celebrities, and well-meaning people who have turned body positivity into the generalized advice to "just love yourself!" When feminist activism—such as girl power and popular feminism—is commodified, it often becomes something that primarily benefits white girls and women who are middle or upper class. Responding to mainstream body positivity, then, feminist activists argue that the movement, particularly on social media, focuses on the "experiences of the wealthy, white, straight, able-bodied women who already have more than their fair share of social privilege," yet liken their own experiences to the discrimination faced by women of color and disabled women (Hay 2019). Mainstream body positivity has evolved to represent women who are "mostly white and still relatively thin" (Legault and Sago 2022, 226). Again, this is linked to the commodification of body positivity.

Corporate interests undermine the movement's radical activism. One example of this is the 2004 Dove "Real Beauty" campaign. On their website during the campaign, there were sections with titles such as "Let's Dare to Love Our Hair," which was followed by a list of Dove shampoos, conditioners, and styling tools, all of which seamlessly connect to the body positive message while selling traditional beauty products. In another section, the phrase "Let's Make Peace with Our Bodies" appears before a list of Dove lotions and antiperspirants. Dove's corporate representatives explicitly stated that this combination of body positivity and product sales is intentional: Dove's two main objectives are to increase sales of Dove beauty products and to help women feel more beautiful (Johnston and Taylor 2008). Scholars argue that this focus on beauty perpetuates "the demand that we (especially women) should all want to be beautiful" and ultimately reinforces fairly narrow standards of beauty and normalizes the daily expenses, time commitments, and labor that are part of "beauty" routines (Leboeuf 2019, 123).

A second critique of mainstream body positivity has to do with "toxic" positivity. Toxic positivity makes people feel like they have to have a positive outlook or they are a bad person, even when a situation is so dire that there is no reasonable basis for optimism. Toxic positivity can lead to feeling guilty over one's own negative emotions, to ignoring one's own negative emotions and problems, and to minimizing or dismissing others' difficult emotions. Some feminist activists see mainstream body positive advice, such as "love yourself!" and "feel beautiful!," as toxic positivity and argue instead for body neutrality (Legault and Sago 2022).

Body neutrality is a neutral stance. Body neutrality directly opposes the mainstream body positivity emphasis on appearance and self-love (Darwin and Miller 2020), especially since it is challenging if not impossible for many people whose bodies are socially excluded or othered to transition from body hatred to self-love. Rather than investing time, emotional energy, and money into hating or loving one's body, body neutrality recommends a neutral stance—feeling "OK" about one's body and reserving one's time, emotional energy, and money for other matters. Body neutrality attempts to shift society's emphasis away from beauty and appearance and toward appreciating bodily talents and health (Brathwaite, DeAndrea, and Vendemia 2023).

Joanna Thornburg

See Also: Beauty; Fat; Girl Power; Hashtag Activism; Popular Feminism; Radical Feminism

Further Reading

Brathwaite, Kyla N., and David C. DeAndrea. 2021. "Bopopriation: How Self-Promotion and Corporate Commodification Can Undermine the Body Positivity (Bopo) Movement on Instagram." *Communication Monographs* 89, no. 1: 25–46. https://doi.org/10.1080/03637751.2021.1925939.

Brathwaite, Kyla N., David C. DeAndrea, and Megan A. Vendemia. 2023. "Non-Sexualized Images and Body-Neutral Messaging Foster Body Positivity Online." *Social Media + Society* 9, no. 4. https://doi.org/10.1177/20563051231207852.

Darwin, Helana, and Amara Miller. 2020. "Factions, Frames, and Postfeminism(s) in the Body Positive Movement." *Feminist Media Studies* 21, no. 6: 873–90. https://doi.org/10.1080/14680777.2020.1736118.

Gunter, Jen. 2018. "Your Vagina Is Terrific (and Everyone Else's Opinions Still Are Not)." *The New York Times*, December 21, 2018. https://www.nytimes.com/2018/12/21/style/jen-gunter-says-your-vagina-is-terrific.html.

Hay, Carol. 2019. "Who Counts as a Woman?" *The New York Times*, April 1, 2019. https://www.nytimes.com/2019/04/01/opinion/trans-women-feminism.html.

Johnston, Josée, and Judith Taylor. 2008. "Feminist Consumerism and Fat Activists: A Comparative Study of Grassroots Activism and the Dove Real Beauty Campaign." *Signs: Journal of Women in Culture and Society* 33, no. 4: 941–66. https://doi.org/10.1086/528849.

Leboeuf, Celine. 2019. "What Is Body Positivity? The Path from Shame to Pride." *Philosophical Topics* 47, no. 2: 113–27. https://doi.org/10.5840/philtopics201947218.

Legault, Lisa, and Anise Sago. 2022. "When Body Positivity Falls Flat: Divergent Effects of Body Acceptance Messages That Support vs. Undermine Basic Psychological Needs." *Body Image* 41: 225–38. https://doi.org/10.1016/j.bodyim.2022.02.013.

Manne, Kate. 2022. "Diet Culture Is Unhealthy. It's Also Immoral." *The New York Times*, January 3, 2022. https://www.nytimes.com/2022/01/03/opinion/diet-resolution.html.

Moreno-Domínguez, Silvia, Fátima Servián-Franco, Gustavo A. Reyes del Paso, and Antonio Cepeda-Benito. 2018. "Images of Thin and Plus-Size Models Produce Opposite Effects on Women's Body Image, Body Dissatisfaction, and Anxiety." *Sex Roles* 80, no. 9–10: 607–16. https://doi.org/10.1007/s11199-018-0951-3.

Payne-Patterson, Jasmine. 2023. "The CROWN Act: A Jewel for Combating Racial Discrimination in the Workplace and Classroom." *Economic Policy Institute*. Last modified July 26, 2023. https://www.epi.org/publication/crown-act/.

Rupp, Kristie, and Stephanie M. McCoy. 2023. "Understanding Health Behaviors, Weight Perceptions, and Body Appreciation of Young Adult Women Engaged in the Body Positivity Movement." *Women's Health Issues* 33, no. 5: 551–59. https://doi.org/10.1016/j.whi.2023.05.004.

BOSTOCK V. CLAYTON COUNTY (2020)

On June 15, 2020, the Supreme Court released a decision, *Bostock v. Clayton County*, which could have major historical significance and implications, providing civil protections to LGBTQ people.

Until this decision, gay and transgender people have never been protected by civil rights legislation. Indeed, until this decision, in the majority of states a person could be fired for being gay or transgender. The LGBTQ rights movement has been working for decades for civil rights legislation, and this Supreme Court decision is a major step in that direction.

Textualism and Originalism

Much of the decision rests on a constitutional theory known as textualism. Textualism is a theory of legal interpretation championed by the late Supreme Court Justice Antonin Scalia, and the current Supreme Court Justice Neil Gorsuch, who was brought in specifically to fill Scalia's shoes. Textualism is a theory of the law that focuses on what is called the "ordinary" meaning of a text, or the common meaning of a text. Nontextual sources are not considered. For instance, the problem the law was meant to remedy or legislative history is not important for a textualist judge. Sometimes textualism is misconstrued with originalism, which is actually quite different. Originalism argues that the laws must be considered from the viewpoint of the original understanding of the authors who wrote the law. The theory of originalism understands the law as stable and that the law can only be changed through legislative means.

That last part is important. Both theories, textualism and originalism, reject the notion of "legislating from the bench." They believe the job of creating law lies strictly with the legislative branch. The judiciary's job is just to explain or at best help apply the law. Scalia was sometimes hesitant to do even that much. In the decision of *Bostock v. Clayton County* (2020), it becomes clear that this case turned over an argument regarding how to understand the law and what textualism (and to some extent originalism) means.

Discrimination Law

In brief, prior to this case, in many states a person could be fired for being gay or transgender. Now they cannot because this ruling makes work place discrimination against gay and transgender people a violation of Title VII. Title VII of the Civil Rights Acts makes it unlawful "for an employer to fail or refuse to hire or discharge any individual, or otherwise to discriminate against any individual . . . because of such individual's race, color, religion, sex, or national origin." Notably, the phrasing in Title VII does not specify sexual orientation, and—historically—anything not listed is not a protected class, meaning they can be discriminated against. The decision of *Bostock v. Clayton County* (2020) changed this, considering sexual orientation and gender presentation as part of the category of "sex." Basically, Gorsuch posits, an employer who fires an individual for being homosexual or transgender fires that person for traits they would not have questioned in a person of a different sex. As such, sex plays a necessary role in the decision to fire the person, which is forbidden by Title VII. The legislators who created Title VII of the Civil Rights Act may not have anticipated their work would lead to this result, but according to Gorsuch—who is a textualist and not an originalist—the "limits of the drafters' imagination supply no reason to ignore the law's demands" (*Bostock v. Clayton County* 2020).

The only question at hand in this case was "sex."

Arguing for the right to discriminate against gay and transgender people, the employers in this case appealed to contemporaneous dictionaries from 1964, claiming that "sex" referred only to one's "status as either male or female as determined by reproductive biology."

Gorsuch agrees that this was the meaning of "sex" in 1964. But for Gorsuch, that's just a starting point. The question isn't just what "sex" means but what Title VII says about it.

Title VII states that it is illegal to discriminate against a person "because of" their race, color, religion, sex, or national origin. The phrase "because of" includes what is known as a "but for" causation. The idea is that the outcome (the effect) would not have happened "but for" a specific cause.

In this scenario, the question is, "would the person have been fired 'but for' their sex?" Or to put it another way, "if it weren't for their sex, would they have been fired?" It is also important to note that Title VII is meant to be applied to individuals, not groups. A Title VII violation is about whether an *individual* has been discriminated against, not a group of people. So if one woman is discriminated against, even if not all women are discriminated against, it is still a Title VII case. For example, if a woman refuses sexual advances from her boss and then her career stalls, she has been discriminated against, even if other women have not. Title VII protects individuals. The decision in *Bostock v. Clayton County* (2020) is simple and momentous—an individual's homosexuality or transgender status is not relevant to employment decisions because it is impossible to discriminate against a person for being homosexual or transgender without discriminating against that individual based on sex.

To illustrate, consider two hypothetical employees who are both attracted to males. By the employer's reckoning their employment merits are exactly the same, except that one is male and the other female. Their work quality is the same, their output is the same, they have the same level of job experience. If the employer fires the male employee for no other reason than the fact that he is attracted to males, then that employee is being discriminated against for actions that the employer tolerates in the female colleague. In other words, the employers intentionally single out this male employee to fire partially based on the employee's sex. This means that sex is a "but for" cause of his termination.

Similarly, imagine an employer who has a policy that they will fire anyone known to be a homosexual. During an office party, a model employee with a perfect record shows up with their wife, Susan. Will that employee be fired? It totally depends on whether the employee is male or female. Their sex is a "but for" cause. Whether this person gets fired rests on or is "caused" by their sex. The goal might be to discriminate based on sexual orientation, but the practice is discriminating on the basis of sex.

During the *Bostock* (2020) case, the employers offered two main arguments, but both arguments failed to persuade Gorsuch and the other justices. Their first argument relied on appealing to the original purpose or intent behind creating Title VII. But this failed to persuade Gorsuch because it went beyond the text itself. Their second argument focused on warning against what they saw as the dire consequences of preventing employers from discriminating based on sexuality and gender presentation. But again, this argument failed to persuade since it was not about what the law actually says. In response, Gorsuch offered a textualist argument par excellence in the *Bostock v. Clayton County* (2020) decision, laying out what the text of Title VII says and attending closely to the "common meaning" of the law's text.

The *Bostock* (2020) decision is controversial. Most obviously, those who disagree with the decision argue that discrimination on the basis of homosexuality and transgender status are not referred to as sex discrimination in ordinary conversation. In conversation, a person in this situation would not say they were fired for sex-based discrimination; they would typically say they were fired for discrimination against homosexuals or gender expression. But these conversational conventions do not control Title VII's legal, textual analysis, which simply asks whether sex was a "but for" cause.

Ultimately, the case of *Bostock v. Clayton County* (2020) was a stunning victory for the queer community, but as is always the case, the question remains whether the law will be executed.

M. Elizabeth Thorpe

See Also: Civil Rights Act: Title VII; *Lawrence v. Texas* (2003); Queer Theory; Trans Theory

Further Reading

Bostock v. Clayton County, Georgia. 590 U.S. 17. 2020. https://www.google.com/url?sa=t&source=web&rct=j&opi=89978449&url=https://www.supremecourt.gov/opinions/19pdf/17-1618_hfci.pdf&ved=2ahUKEwix4_z3iN2FAxXLlYkEHRvrAL4QFnoECB0QAQ&usg=AOvVaw3OeHHuN8GO6L_AiO24vz1c.

BURKE, TARANA

Tarana J. Burke (1973–) is a US feminist activist who has committed her life to fighting against systems of oppression, including white patriarchy. Burke is best known for founding a movement and related organizations that use the phrase "me too." This entry follows Burke by referring to the *"me too." Movement*. Burke's choice of capitalization and punctuation calls attention to the solemnity of naming oneself as a victim of sexual assault by saying "me too." Burke is best known for founding the "me too." Movement and serving as a leader in the fight against sexual violence, advocating for women's rights, and supporting survivors of sexual assault. Further, she advocates for racial equality and empowerment. Her activism is driven by an investment in addressing intersectional oppression worldwide, beginning with community organizing and advancing toward structural and systematic change.

Tarana Burke, best known for founding the "me too." Movement, is an activist committed to addressing intersectional oppression around the world through community organizing and working toward systemic change (Hutchinsphoto/Dreamstime.com).

The Beginnings

Born in New York City on September 12, 1973, Tarana Burke grew up in a working-class neighborhood and was raised by a single mother (Burke 2021; "Tarana Burke Biography" 2018). Burke struggled as a child. She was sexually assaulted and raped multiple times in her childhood and was subjected to overt acts of discrimination and violence on the basis of her gender, race, and physical appearance (Burke 2021). From a young age, she learned the impact one's appearance can have on how they are treated by others as well as how intersecting identities can exacerbate these shows of force. She writes that her experiences as a child and as a young woman have instilled within her a sense that she is "hardwired to respond to injustice" (Burke 2021, 11). It is this hardwiring that launched her career as an activist.

While Burke is popularly known for her work with the "me too." Movement, she has demonstrated a steadfast commitment to social justice issues more broadly. As a young adult, she joined the 21st Century Youth Leadership Movement, an organization dedicated to empowering youth to identify their strengths as future leaders in their communities ("About Tarana Burke" 2024). Burke advocated for just responses to "issues like police brutality, housing inequality, and economic justice" in New York City ("About Tarana Burke" 2024; Alexander 2020). She continued to advocate for social justice during college while she attended Alabama State University and the University of Auburn at Montgomery, organizing protests for economic equality and racial justice (Alexander 2020; Colville 2018). Tarana Burke advocates for justice by adopting an intersectional lens, bringing awareness to the ways in which race, class, gender, and other factors influence one another to bring privilege to some and marginalizing others (Collins 2009; Collins and Bilge 2020; Crenshaw 1989).

Just Be Inc. and the "me too." Movement

In 2003, Burke founded the first of many organizations aimed at supporting young women, particularly women of color and survivors of sexual assault. The first organization she created is Jendayi Aza, "an African-centered Rites of Passage program for girls" ("Tarana Burke Biography" 2018). In 2006, this organization evolved into Just Be Inc. Today, Just Be Inc. serves as a youth organization dedicated to the "health, well being [*sic*] and wholeness of young women of color," empowering these young women to grow and thrive in a sociocultural environment that is often oppressive, discriminatory, and violent toward women of color ("Purpose" 2013). Burke's commitment to serving marginalized communities, particularly young girls and women of color, is evident in the organizations she has built.

Shortly after developing Just Be Inc., Tarana Burke set out to address one issue that plagues young girls and women of color, in particular—sexual violence. Burke sees sexual violence against young girls and women of color as a systemic issue that requires systemic, community-based, and interpersonal attention, and thus, the "me too." Movement was born ("About Tarana Burke" 2024; Burke 2021). In 2006, Tarana Burke founded the "me too." Movement as a tool for building community and providing resources, support, and healing to survivors of sexual violence ("Tarana Burke Founder" 2024). By sharing two simple words, "me too," Burke believes that some barriers to understanding and healing may be overcome ("Tarana Burke Founder" 2024). Sexual violence is underreported, particularly by members of marginalized communities, and is one of the most stigmatized crimes to report (Boyle 2019; French and Brown 2011; Gilmore 2017). Tarana Burke believes that voicing one's own experiences with sexual violence can challenge common cultural assumptions that sexual violence is rare or shameful and can reduce stigmatization.

Her extensive experience with community organizing informed her choice to make this a movement for and by the people. A fellow survivor of sexual assault and rape, Burke understands how alienating and lonely it can be, leading her to establish a theory of "empowerment through empathy" and an orientation toward healing that she carries through her work today ("Tarana Burke Founder" 2024). In this way, Burke embraces a spirit of sisterhood and solidarity through hardship, a core tenet of Black feminist theory (hooks 2000). The "me too." Movement empowers women through finding community and support in one another first, then advocating for systematic and structural change together as a coalition. Burke's "me too." Movement has been hard at work since 2006.

#MeToo and Beyond

In 2017, however, Tarana Burke's "me too." Movement changed forever. One morning in October, Tarana Burke was awakened with text and Facebook messages informing her of Alyssa Milano's now infamous Tweet reading "If you've been sexually harassed or assaulted write 'me too' as a reply to this tweet" (Milano 2017). As Burke writes in her book, *Unbound: My Story of Liberation and the Birth of the Me Too Movement,* "I grabbed my phone off of its charger in a panic [. . .] I'd been doing the work of bringing empathy into the fight against sexual violence for many years now using this language [. . .] I didn't want to diminish it by creating a simple hashtag" (Burke 2021, 3). She continues to write about how seeing the phrase being used by people outside of the community she had developed was "jarring" at first (Burke 2021, 3). There is a legacy in the United States in which the hard work of Black women is co-opted by other groups, their contributions ignored and covered over, and Burke was concerned that the community she had been so involved with creating would crumble around her.

However, as she began to see how the hashtag was being used by hundreds of thousands of users in the first day of its creation, she realized that "my work was happening right in front of me" (Burke 2021, 11). She notes that as she was reading the tweets using the hashtag, she realized that complete strangers were finding the comfort and belonging they had been desperate to find. Burke released a statement on her social media pages calling for people to join her movement, that "It's beyond a hashtag. It's the start of a larger conversation and a movement for radical community healing" (Burke 2021, 10). Burke's involvement in the "me too." Movement and pivot to adopt the hashtag catapulted her into the spotlight. Named one of "The Silence Breakers" of 2017, Tarana Burke was named Time Person of the Year alongside other activists, survivors, and advocates (Zacharek, Dockterman, and Sweetland Edwards 2017).

Realizing the power of the hashtag and its ability to reach survivors across the globe, Burke founded "me too." International, a global nonprofit organization aimed at furthering the reach and scope of the original "me too." Movement ("About Tarana Burke" 2024). This organization also furthers her dedication to advancing an intersectional approach in her activism, as "me too." International addresses "systems that allow for the proliferation of sexual violence, specifically in Black, queer, trans, disabled, and all communities of color" ("About Tarana Burke" 2024). Her work in this field has been continuously recognized. For instance, Burke has been named one of Time's 100 Most Influential People in 2018, was awarded the 2019 Sydney Peace Prize and 2019 Harvard Gleitsman Citizen Activist Award, was named one of USA Today's Women of the Decade in 2020, and was named one of BBC's 100 Women of 2022, among other acknowledgments (BBC.com Staff 2022; Carroll 2020; Harris 2019; Sydney Peace Foundation 2019; Union 2018).

Tarana Burke's work continues to be recognized and celebrated, but her work is far from complete. She remains dedicated to serving her communities and advocating for justice for survivors of sexual violence, as well as other forms of systematic oppression and discrimination.

Amanda N. Brand

See Also: #MeToo; Intersectionality; Rape Culture; Violence Against Women Act (1994)

Further Reading

"About Tarana Burke." 2024. *Tarana Burke.* 2024. https://www.taranaburke.com/bio.

Alexander, Kerri Lee. 2020. "Tarana Burke." *National Women's History Museum.* https://www.womenshistory.org/education-resources/biographies/tarana-burke.

BBC.com Staff. 2022. "BBC 100 Women 2022: Who Is on the List This Year?" *BBC News*, December 6, 2022. https://www.bbc.co.uk/news/resources/idt-75af095e-21f7-41b0-9c5f-a96a5e0615c1.

Boyle, Karen. 2019. *#MeToo, Weinstein and Feminism.* Cham: Palgrave Macmillan. https://doi.org/10.1007/978-3-030-28243–1.

Burke, Tarana. 2021. *Unbound: My Story of Liberation and the Birth of the Me Too Movement*, 1st ed. New York: Flatiron Books.

Carroll, Nicole. 2020. "Tarana Burke on the Power of Empathy, the Building Block of the Me Too Movement." *USA Today*, August 19, 2020. https://www.usatoday.com/in-depth/life/women-of-the-century/2020/08/19/tarana-burke-me-too-movement-19th-amendment-women-of-century/5535976002/.

Collins, Patricia Hill. 2009. *Black Feminist Thought: Knowledge, Consciousness, and the Politics of Empowerment*, 2nd ed. Routledge Classics. New York: Routledge.

Collins, Patricia Hill, and Sirma Bilge. 2020. *Intersectionality*, 2nd ed. Cambridge; Medford, MA: Polity Press.
Colville, Waverly. 2018. "#MeToo Movement Speaker Founder Speaks to Capacity University of Missouri Crowd." *Columbia Daily Tribune*, February 21, 2018. https://web.archive.org/web/20190828215800/http://www.columbiatribune.com/news/20180221/metoo-movement-founder-speaks-to-capacity-university-of-missouri-crowd.
Crenshaw, Kimberlé. 1989. "Demarginalizing the Intersection of Race and Sex: A Black Feminist Critique of Antidiscrimination Doctrine, Feminist Theory and Antiracist Politics." *University of Chicago Legal Forum* 1989, no. 1: 139–67.
French, Sandra L., and Sonya C. Brown. 2011. "It's All Your Fault: Kenneth Burke, Symbolic Action, and the Assigning of Guilt and Blame to Women." *Southern Communication Journal* 76, no. 1: 1–16. https://doi.org/10.1080/10417940903419235.
Gilmore, Leigh. 2017. *Tainted Witness: Why We Doubt What Women Say About Their Lives*. New York: Columbia University Press.
Harris, Lael. 2019. "#MeToo Founder Tarana Burke to Receive Gleitsman Citizen Activist Award." *The Harvard Gazette*, October 10, 2019. https://news.harvard.edu/gazette/story/newsplus/metoo-founder-tarana-burke-to-receive-2019-gleitsman-citizen-activist-award/.
hooks, bell. 2000. *Feminist Theory: From Margin to Center*, 2nd ed. Cambridge, MA: South End Press.
Milano, Alyssa. 2017. "If You've Been Sexually Harassed or Assaulted Write 'me Too' as a Reply to This Tweet." *Twitter* (blog), October 15, 2017. https://twitter.com/alyssa_milano/status/919659438700670976?lang=en.
"Purpose." 2013. *Just Be Inc*. 2013. https://justbeinc.wixsite.com/justbeinc/purpose-mission-and-vision.
Sydney Peace Foundation. 2019. "2019 The Me Too Movement." *Sydney Peace Foundation*, 2019. https://sydneypeacefoundation.org.au/peace-prize-recipients/2019-me-too/#:~:text=Tarana%20Burke%20and%20Tracey%20Spicer%20win%20Sydney%20Peace%20prize%20for,in%20media%20workplaces%20in%20Australia.
"Tarana Burke Biography." 2018. *Biography.com,* March 2, 2018. https://web.archive.org/web/20180422054552/https://www.biography.com/people/tarana-burke.
"Tarana Burke Founder." 2024. *Me Too*. 2024. https://metoomvmt.org/get-to-know-us/tarana-burke-founder/.
Union, Gabrielle. 2018. "Time 100: The Most Influential People of 2018: Tarana Burke." *Time Magazine*, 2018. https://time.com/collection/most-influential-people-2018/.
Zacharek, Stephanie, Eliana Dockterman, and Haley Sweetland Edwards. 2017. "Time Person of the Year 2017: The Silence Breakers." *Time Magazine*, December 18, 2017. https://time.com/time-person-of-the-year-2017-silence-breakers/.

BUTCH

Butch is a deeply influential lesbian term with a storied history and a significant contribution to the queer liberation movement (López 2024). Butch is a genre, not a strictly defined category. It is a queer way of being that invites complex intersections of gender and sexuality—and invites our communities into greater reflection on sex, gender, and relationality. Butch is both an identity marker and an orientation of values. Whether or not someone is butch is not something an outsider can determine; it is a felt sense of being. Self-identification as butch is the only definitive shared quality of butch representations (Hale 1998, 325).

Historical Context

Historically, butch has been rigidly defined by characteristics (such as short haircuts) and denoted a particular embodiment of lesbian masculinity. Derived from the word "butcher," the term was used to convey toughness. The term grew in popularity among Black and working-class lesbians to describe masculine-presenting queer folks (who typically dated folks of the complementary identifier, femmes) through the 1940s and 1950s (López 2024; Liesch 2024). Indeed, both butch and femme identities functioned as "social roles" that informed "community norms and dating expectations" in the twentieth century, as well as "making sexual-minority women visible to each other in a society that was hostile to their existence" (Herbitter and Levitt 2016).

As the queer liberation movement responded to the Stonewall uprising and its aftermath, butch-femme labels were criticized by some lesbians for imitating heteronormativity, but this critique ignores the ways that butch and femme identities have historically subverted traditional understandings of what it means to be a woman, at both a personal and interpersonal scale (Liesch 2024). For example, butch-femme relationships obtained financial and relationship security outside of heteronormative structures (i.e., without a patriarchal husband). Often, in butch-femme pairings during the mid-1900s, both partners would work outside the home, but butches often worked in factories—doing so-called "men's work" and thus commanding wages that made their butch-femme partnerships more financially stable. This historical context intertwines butch identities with labor movements and especially with women's labor rights ("LGBT Labor History" 2020)

Theorizing Butch

Butch traits are invitations, not prescriptions. Someone who identifies as butch can perform some of the classic butch traits and perform contradictory traits and still be butch. Butch presentations include stereotypical media representations, like Big Boo from *Orange Is the New Black*, but it is important not to get lost in aesthetics. Most butches include some masculine presentations (e.g., more masculine hairstyles, fashions, or hobbies) as part of their gender performance; butches may also engage in medical transitions and/or use gender-neutral pronouns or pronouns that do not match their sex as assigned at birth. There is no one defining criteria that can qualify or disqualify someone from being butch (López 2024; Hale 1998, 322). Butch, transmasculine, and lesbian are not exclusive categories; they are fluid and exist in generative relation, personalized to each individual who self-identifies with any to all of the labels (Crawley 2008, 370).

Leslie Feinberg's novel *Stone Butch Blues* (1993) is one of the most important meditations on butch as a lived experience. In the novel, Feinberg presents butch as a multifaceted and evolving practice that foregrounds tenderness and complex understandings of lived masculinity. The novel's protagonist, Jess, uses a variety of pronouns and undergoes a double mastectomy to affirm their felt sense of gender—which is articulated as butch. Near the end of the novel, Jess describes butch grief, confiding in a fellow butch that they've "got no language" to express their experience; there are no accessible "butch words to talk about butch feelings," which in turn inhibits their ability to communicate the complexity of being butch (Feinberg 1993, 301). In response, Jess's butch friend replies that if butch words did exist, they would sound "like thunder" and "yearning" (Feinberg 1993, 301). Here, Feinberg characterizes butch as strength in tenderness to loved ones, and the sense that something needs to be articulated but cannot be. To be butch is to be powerful, like thunder—to pause for a moment after the flash of lightning has passed. To be butch is an assessment of the strength needed to respond before taking action.

In the novel, Jess has a variety of lovers, including trans and cis women, and many of the novel's butch characters love other butches—perhaps even including men (Feinberg 1993, 300). As such, Feinberg articulates a variety of butch identities and relationships that are not confined to one particular understanding of gender or sexuality; this helps to theorize butch as a complicated intersection of nonnormative genders and sapphic sexualities without being constrictive.

Butch Politics Today

Butches often serve as role models for younger queer folk, providing examples of different ways to ethically approach masculinity (López 2024). This model and rich history is key—especially as TERF feminists and lesbians exclude trans lesbians from queer feminist communities (López 2024). These exclusions often ignore or erase butches, and butches can offer a rich counter to anti-trans rhetoric.

When queer folk and feminists get caught up debating and defining what is and is not butch, it saps our energy—and we need our energy for activism such as labor rights, anti-racist work, harm reduction, affirming health care, and sex worker liberation. Feinberg highlighted how butches blend and merge these different areas of activism, underscoring the importance of cross-movement organizing and the central role butches play in cross-movement organizing (López 2024; Herbitter and Levitt 2016).

Ultimately, butch history and theory insists that it is better to form alliances rather than define and exclude. There can be no definitive characterization of butch. Every butch experience is unique and finds queer kinship in the unique conditions they experience. Butch is a valuable and affirming queer term with ongoing intersectional impact (López 2024).

Terrence Adams

See Also: Femme; Gender Performance; Labor Movement; Nonbinary; Pronouns and Gender-Neutral Language and Pronouns; Queer Theory; Stonewall Uprising; Trans-Exclusionary Radical Feminists (TERFs); Trans Theory

Further Reading

Brindley, Michael. 2018. "The Butch Monologues." *Stage Whispers*. Accessed December 21, 2024. https://www.stagewhispers.com.au/reviews/butch-monologues.

Coyote, Ivan. 2019. *Rebent Sinner*. Vancouver, Canada: Arsenal Pulp Press.

Crawley, Sara L. 2008. "The Clothes make the Trans: Region and Geography in Experiences of the Body." *Journal of Lesbian Studies* 12, no. 4: 365–79.

Feinberg, Leslie. 1993. *Stone Butch Blues*. Firebrand Books.

Hale, C. Jacob. 1998. "Consuming the Living, Dis(Re)Membering the Dead in the Butch/FTM Borderlands." *GLQ: A Journal of Lesbian & Gay Studies* 4, no. 2: 311–48.

Herbitter, Cara and Heidi M. Levitt. 2016. "Butch-Femme." In *The SAGE Encyclopedia of LGBTQ Studies*, edited by Abbie E. Goldberg. Sage Publications, Inc.

"LGBT Labor History is All Our History." 2020. *Autostraddle*, September 7, 2020. Accessed December 21, 2024. https://www.autostraddle.com/lgbt-labor-history-is-all-our-history/.

Liesch, Syaa. 2024. "A Brief History of Butch and Femme: Living Gender Outside the Binary." *One Woman Project*, April 23, 2024. https://www.onewomanproject.org/lgbtqia/2024/4/23/a-brief-history-of-butch-and-femme-living-gender-outside-the-binary.

López, Quispe. 2024. "The Queer History of Butches." *Them*, April 11, 2024. https://www.them.us/story/what-does-butch-mean.

BUTLER, JUDITH

Judith Butler (1956–) is a feminist theorist who is most well known for two key arguments within feminist theory: that gender is a performance and that sex has been gender all along. The first concept, that gender is a performance, is where Butler claims that gender is "an identity instituted through a stylized repetition of acts," pointing out that gender is a set of actions and behaviors rather than an "essence" or something that is an innate behavior (Butler 1988, 519). This means that the gender we embody only exists during action, making gender a verb in this sense. By "doing" gender, we are acting or presenting ourselves in a way that is legible for others in society to recognize based on preconceived notions about what each gender should look and act like. For example, the concept of drag performances by drag queens and kings reveals the performative nature of gender and how clothing, hair, makeup, body shape, and movement are all signifiers for how we interpret someone's gender since the "way in which bodily gestures, movements, and enactments of various kinds" build what we perceive as a "gendered self" (Butler 1988, 519).

The second argument Butler makes, the idea that sex has been gender all along, refers to the way society categorizes bodies into two and only two "sexes," focusing on some physical features while choosing to ignore others. This indicates that society is using concepts derived from social understandings of gender to create what we know as sex. Or to put it another way, sex is a category that reflects heterosexual assumptions about who is able to reproduce with who based on genitalia. The category "sex" tells us that our reproductive organs are the most important things about our multifaceted bodies and that they determine our behavior (gender). So "sex" is a cultural interpretation of the body that prescribes behavior—but that is how gender is usually defined! And this leads to Butler's conclusion that sex was gender all along.

Butler's Feminist Career

Butler is a philosopher and gender theorist. Their work has been studied and used to profoundly influence political philosophy, ethics, and feminist, queer, and literary theory. Their most well-known contributions have been within feminist theory through their landmark book, *Gender Trouble: Feminism and the Subversion of Identity* (1990). Within this book, Butler critiques the idea that gender is a stable identity and argues instead that gender is performative. Butler challenges the binary understanding of gender, suggesting that it is fluid and constructed through social norms and expectations of action and appearance (Butler 1990). Their arguments within this book have roots in Simone de Beauvoir's work, who claims that "to be a woman within the terms of a masculinist culture is to be a source of mystery and unknowability for men" and has other similar claims like "one is not born, but, rather, becomes a woman" (Butler 1990). These ideas are the building blocks of Butler's gender performativity claim. Butler also explores how power structures influence our understanding of gender and how certain performances are privileged over others as well (Butler 1990). Overall, they critique the idea of a fixed identity and call for a more inclusive understanding of gender that recognizes its complexity and diversity when it comes to different people and bodies (Butler 1990).

Butler has also written many other books throughout their life that expand on their claims about bodies, gender, and feminism, such as *Bodies That Matter* (1993), *Undoing Gender* (2004), and *Antigone's Claim: Kinship Between Life and Death* (2000). While their main body of work is in gender studies and they are best known for gender theory, Butler has also produced significant work in political activism and ethics. For example, their book *Frames of War: When Is Life Grievable?* (2009) discusses Western media portrayals of state violence and how this plays into how the West wages modern war in a way that deems people unsavable and/or existential threats. Their other works within the same arena include *Precarious Life: The Powers of Mourning and Violence* (2004) and *The Force of Nonviolence: An Ethico-Political Bind* (2020), among many others.

Butler's more recent works center around progressing their aforementioned claims about gender, sex, and ethical issues. Their most recent book, *Who's Afraid of Gender* (2024), continues their work surrounding gender and sexuality. Within this book Butler tackles ideas surrounding contemporary attacks on gender by right-wing "anti-gender ideology movements" that are currently working to undermine rights pertaining to women, queer, and trans communities and reproductive justice (Butler 2024). This book works to address modern attacks by trans-exclusionary radical feminists (TERFs), religious organizations, and governments on feminine and queer communities (Butler 2024). It has been critiqued for being "tepid" and "uninspiringly careful" due to the book's calm critique of these issues, but arguably, the book is a great way to bring these issues to the forefront of feminist critique and activism (Szalai 2024).

Butler's other most recent work, *What World Is This? A Pandemic Phenomenology* (2022) is based more in their work around ethics and talks about questions of what it means to be human in a "post" Covid-19 world and the consequences we now see from the global pandemic (Butler 2022). Drawing on Max Scheler's and Maurice Merleau-Ponty's work, Butler discusses the ethical and political lessons we can learn from our collective experiences during the Covid-19 pandmeic (Butler 2022).

While Butler's works are very well known, they are not without critique. The main critique Butler faces "is related to [their] style of writing," which has been described as "ponderous and obscure" due to how dense and riddled with jargon it can be at points (Cadwallader 2009, 289). Many others, such as Moya Lloyd, Vicki Kirby, and Martha Nussbaum, have all come forward with similar complaints of how Butler's work may be prolific but is difficult to understand and not accessible to most people (Cadwallader 2009, 289). People have even accused Butler of elitism due to their difficult writing style. Despite these issues of accessibility, Butler still remains a prevalent writer within many different areas of study.

Furthering Feminism with Butler

Overall, feminist ideology and theory has been furthered by Butler's work. Their most well-known arguments that gender is a performance and that sex has been gender all along have built on earlier feminists' work and have provided the grounds for new critical research and feminist theory. While Butler's work is critiqued as inaccessible, they remain a prolific feminist theorist and an important feminist voice in contemporary society. They have helped give form to our current understanding, as feminists, of what sex and gender mean and they continue to shape these meanings as we head into the future.

Cherokee S. Bauer

See Also: Drag; Gender; Gender Performance; Queer Theory; Trans Theory; Trans-Exclusionary Radical Feminists (TERFs)

Further Reading

Butler, Judith. 1988. "Performative Acts and Gender Constitution: An Essay in Phenomenology and Feminist Theory." *Theatre Journal* 40, no. 4: 519–31. https://doi.org/10.2307/3207893.

Butler, Judith. 1990. *Gender Trouble: Feminism and the Subversion of Identity*. New York: Routledge.

Butler, Judith. 2022. *What World Is This? A Pandemic Phenomenology*. New York: Columbia University Press.

Butler, Judith. 2024. *Who's Afraid of Gender?* New York: Farrar, Straus and Giroux.

Cadwallader, Jessica. 2009. "How Judith Butler Matters." *Australian Feminist Studies* 24, no. 60: 289–94. https://doi.org/10.1080/08164640902852506.

Szalai, Jennifer. 2024. "A Gender Theorist Who Just Wants Everyone to Get Along." *The New York Times*, April 3, 2024. www.nytimes.com/2024/04/03/books/review/a-gender-theorist-who-just-wants-everyone-to-get-along.html#:~:text=So%20Butler%20set%20out%20to,that%20biology%20does%20exist%2C%20that.

BUTLER, OCTAVIA E.

Born on June 22, in Pasadena, California, to parents who worked as a shoe-shiner and a maid, Octavia E. Butler (1947–2006) grew up knowing what it meant to be poor, Black, and female. A Hugo and Nebula award-winning science-fiction writer of twelve novels and two short story collections (one published posthumously), Butler is the foundational figure in Black women's speculative fiction. Her work introduced African American women's perspectives into a literary genre almost exclusively dominated by white men. But her contributions extend beyond storytelling and accolades to her insightful commentaries on varied topics from public libraries to environmental sustainability. Whether in fiction or nonfiction, Butler used her science fiction and the platform it afforded her to tell truths by posing questions—What if? If only? If this goes on?—as a way to point to things we can do for ourselves to make a better, more livable present and future.

Work and Activism

In interviews, Butler often reflected on her experiences as a Black girl turned woman, from being taunted for her shyness to misgendered because she was broad-shouldered, deeper voiced, and quite tall—nearly 6 feet as a twelve-year-old. As she lived and reflected on these experiences, Black feminist theorists like bell hooks (1981, 1992) and Audre Lorde (1979) were exploring how Black women are often misgendered or coded as masculine, resulting in them being denied the full expression of their femininity. Recognizing these limiting stereotypes, Butler reimagined the strong, Black, sexual woman in several career-spanning works. *Survivor* (1978), *Kindred* (1979), *Dawn* (1987), and *Parable of the Sower* (1993) feature protagonists who physically resemble the Butler who was teased for her androgynous appearance, and these protagonists enjoy healthy sexual relationships with their male partners. While Butler did create smaller, more delicate women—like Anyanwu in *Wild Seed* (1980)—who also had a healthy sexual appetite, she frequently wrote characters who looked like her enjoying sexual encounters without their femininity, gender identity, or sexuality being under scrutiny like hers was. Ultimately, she was interested in creating worlds for people who were not often written in, and the personal soon became the thread that undergirded her writing career.

Parallel to her sex-positive reimagination of Black women was her critique of racism in the science-fiction community in "The Lost Races of Science Fiction" (2016). Originally published in 1980, Butler's essay challenged anti-Blackness and racism that a prominent science-fiction writer and keynote speaker flaunted at a science-fiction conference. Her words echo Lorde's (1979) sentiments in "The Master's Tools Will Never Dismantle the Master's House," where Lorde criticized a conference for its failure to incorporate perspectives from Black feminists, lesbians, and women of color. Both Butler and Lorde underscore the interconnected struggles against racism and discrimination faced by Black women in various spaces, and they urge for more inclusive approaches by white people in their respective disciplines.

Furthermore, Butler's impassioned plea for the preservation of public libraries (1993a) stressed the humanitarian importance of accessible knowledge and opportunity, aligning with her broader commitment to social justice and equity. Butler's op-ed issued a call to save libraries amid the divestments from public libraries and investments in prison systems. In the op-ed, she combined personal anecdotes, references to current events, and her novel, *Parable of the Sower* (1993b), to reinforce the urgent need to address the challenges facing these vital institutions. She began by recounting the devastating 1986 fire at the Los Angeles Central Library, using vivid imagery to evoke a sense of urgency and impending crisis. She warned of the dangers of allowing libraries to be defunded or neglected, framing it as part of a larger social crisis rooted in capitalism. Butler emphasized the necessity of public libraries, portraying them as accessible havens of knowledge and opportunity, particularly for historically marginalized communities. By drawing on her own experiences as a writer and the daughter of working-poor parents who valued education, she affirmed the personal significance of libraries in her life and called upon readers to recognize their essential role in shaping the future.

Response to Religious Fundamentalism

Similarly, Butler's critical stance toward religious fundamentalism and political corruption highlights her holistic approach to addressing social challenges, rooted in inclusivity, skepticism toward authority, and a commitment to fostering empathy and understanding among diverse communities. As part of recognizing one's role as a participant in shaping their future, Butler hoped that people would be critical thinkers when it came to religion. She was an atheist and quite critical of organized religion. However, she credited her Baptist upbringing and her mother's religion for giving her a moral compass, which influenced her life philosophy and work and, ironically, her critical stance toward religious fundamentalism. She shared in a 1980 interview,

> I was raised a Born Again Baptist and I remember a minister from a different church coming to our church . . . spewing out prejudice against the Jews and Catholics and anyone else who disagreed with him. Just as telling, he didn't get the kind of congregational feedback that you would expect from people who worshiped the Prince of Peace. The kind of religion that I'm seeing now is not the religion of love and it scares me. We need to outgrow it. (Francis 2009, 9)

In recounting her disillusionment with the prejudiced and intolerant rhetoric within her Born Again Baptist upbringing, Butler reflected on the necessity of departing from divisive theological attitudes, advocating for a more inclusive and loving application of religion, a goal she realizes in *Sower* and its sequel *Parable of the Talents.*

Her creative approach to offering a new religion in The Parable duology aligns with Black feminist and womanist theologians Delores S. Williams (2013), Renita J. Weems (1988), Jacquelyn Grant (1989), and Katie G. Cannon (2021) whose works emerged in the 1980s and early 1990s. Rather than rejecting Christianity altogether, Williams, Weems, Grant, and Cannon sought to reclaim and reinterpret scripture in ways that affirmed the dignity and liberation of marginalized communities by prioritizing justice, compassion, and solidarity and challenging fundamentalist readings that perpetuate oppression and exclusion. *Sower* and *Talents* do not seek to reclaim Christian scripture; in fact, the protagonist invents new ones along with a new religion, Earthseed. But, Earthseed does prioritize justice, compassion, and solidarity embraced by Black feminist and womanist theologians, becoming a viable and attractive alternative to the Christian fundamentalist state depicted in the novels. The SolSeed Movement (www.solseed.org) emerged from the novels and exists as one attempt to practice Earthseed as a religion. Butler's approach and the real-world impact of her novels exemplify Afrofuturist Feminism, a theoretical framework that seeks to critique and challenge existing power structures and a critical practice that imagines new possibilities for liberation and empowerment, particularly for Black women, queer, and nonbinary individuals. Through the Parable duology, Butler offered a liberating vision that honored her upbringing and channeled her disdain for Christian fundamentalism.

Response to Political Corruption and Environmental Injustice

Her disillusionment with religious fundamentalism extended to politics, where she highlighted the potential misuse of power: "Yet a politician may become angry and say, 'I'm not going to let this bill go through, even though it will help millions of people, because you didn't respect my authority, my personal power.' Of course, politicians never actually say that, but we know it happens" (Francis 2009, 19). If personal motivations could hinder the passage of bills that would benefit the public, what does it say about those politicians and those leaders? Butler was concerned about the prioritization of personal power over the greater good. So skeptical of those who sought power, she struggled to write *Sower* because she did not believe she could write about a person who actively sought a platform to spread ideas until she realized that power was not the problem but the type of person who would wield it. As part of challenging who was in power and how power should be wielded for the greater good, her works often depict a challenge to gender stereotypes about leadership. In a 1997 interview, Butler shared the following one-liner: "It's not women with their periods who were out there starting shooting wars" (Francis 2009, 109), succinctly challenging the notion that menstruating women are emotionally unstable and therefore prone to irrationality, violence, and aggression. She demonstrated this in her fiction, where she often—but not always—painted men who were invested in heteropatriarchy as violent from Coranesee in *Patternmaster* (1976) to the Silks in *Fledgling* (2005).

Beyond her disillusionment with politicians, Butler was a student of history and a self-proclaimed news junkie; therefore, her concern for environmental wellness emerged as a central theme in her later work, notably *Parable of the Sower*. Her concerns were being amplified and given real consideration partly due to the groundbreaking work of Robert D. Bullard (1993, 1994, 1990/2020), who paved the way in addressing environmental racism. In 2000, Butler emphasized the interconnected nature of global warming and climate change and their far-reaching consequences for agriculture, disease spread, and sea level rise in interviews (Francis 2009). In her commentary, Butler connects the dots between global warming, agriculture, disease spread, and sea level rise, underscoring the urgent need for collective action to address these interconnected challenges and reflecting her concern for the far-reaching impact of these interconnected issues on humanity.

Butler's legacy transcends the boundaries of literature, encompassing a profound commitment to social justice, equity, and environmental sustainability. Through her powerful storytelling and social commentary, Butler leaves a transformative legacy that inspires readers, activists, and scholars alike. As her work emerged alongside feminist research and theory-making, sometimes preceding it, she played a vital role in shaping feminist discourse and challenging conventional narratives, suggesting she was part and parcel of helping develop feminist theory even if her work isn't traditionally considered feminist theory/theoretical. By integrating feminist perspectives into her narratives, Butler expanded the possibilities of speculative fiction and challenged readers to confront the complexities of power and injustice in our world. As we reflect on Butler's contributions, we are reminded that her science fiction was not merely a means of escape but also a tool for envisioning and shaping a more just and equitable future for all.

Kendra R. Parker

See Also: Environmental Feminism; hooks, bell; Lorde, Audre; Womanism

Further Reading

Bullard, Robert D. 1990/2000. *Dumping in Dixie: Race, Class, And Environmental Quality*, 3rd ed. Boulder, CO: Westview Press.

Bullard, Robert D. 1993. *Confronting Environmental Racism: Voices from the Grassroots*. Boston: South End Press.

Bullard, Robert D. 1994. *Unequal Protection: Environmental Justice and Communities of Color*. New York: Random House.

Butler, Octavia E. (1976) 2020. *Patternmaster*. New York: Grand Central Publishing.

Butler, Octavia E. 1978. *Survivor*. New York: Doubleday.

Butler, Octavia E. (1979) 2003. *Kindred*. Boston: Beacon Press.

Butler, Octavia E. (1980) 2020. *Wild Seed*. New York: Grand Central Publishing.

Butler, Octavia E. (1987) 2021. *Dawn*. New York: Grand Central Publishing.

Butler, Octavia E. 1993a. "Free Libraries: Are They Becoming Extinct?" *Omni* 15, no. 10: 4.

Butler, Octavia E. (1993b) 2000. *Parable of the Sower*. New York: Grand Central Publishing.

Butler, Octavia E. (1998) 2000. *Parable of the Talents*. New York: Grand Central Publishing.
Butler, Octavia E. 2002. "Eye Witness." *O, The Oprah Magazine*, May. https://www.oprah.com/spirit/octavia-butlers-aha-moment/all.
Butler, Octavia E. (2005) 2007. *Fledgling*. New York: Grand Central Publishing.
Butler, Octavia E. 2016. "The Lost Races of Science Fiction." In *Octavia E. Butler*, edited by Gerry Canavan, 181–6. University of Illinois Press.
Cannon, Katie Geneva. 2021. *Katie's Canon: Womanism and the Soul of the Black Community,* Rev. and expanded 25th Anniversary ed. Minneapolis, MN: Fortress Press.
Francis, Conseula, ed. 2009. *Conversations with Octavia Butler*. Jackson: University Press of Mississippi.
Grant, Jacquelyn. 1989. *White Women's Christ and Black Women's Jesus: Feminist Christology and Womanist Response*. Atlanta: AAR Academy.
hooks, bell. (1981) 2014. *Ain't I a Woman: Black Women and Feminism*. New York: Routledge.
hooks, bell. (1992) 2014. *Black Looks: Race and Representation*. New York: Routledge.
Lorde, Audre. (1979) 2007. "The Master's Tools Will Never Dismantle the Master's House." In *Sister Outsider: Essays and Speeches*. Berkeley, CA: Crossing Press.
Weems, Renita J. 1988. *Just a Sister Away: A Womanist Vision of Women's Relationships in the Bible*. Silver Spring, MD: Innisfree Press.
Williams, Delores S. 2013. *Sisters in the Wilderness: The Challenge of Womanist God-Talk*. Maryknoll, NY: Orbis Books.

C

CAPITALISM

Capitalism is an economic system developed by human beings that creates what Holly Lewis terms a "system of social relations" (2016, 35). This means that capitalism is a way of managing value, commodities, and money that creates and defines social roles and relationships—between, for example, factory laborers, factory owners, investment financiers, and stock owners but also in terms of gender, race, and even nationality or ethnicity. Capitalism exists through policies and regulations, daily practices, and human assumptions and perspectives.

Capitalism is a relatively new economic system in human history. It was developed and came to dominance during the age of European imperialism and colonization. At the same time as European aristocrats, governments, and wealthy business owners were stripping other lands of their valuable commodities (for instance, gold) and enslaving people (annexing not just people but also their labor as a commodity), they were also changing things at home. Most famously, in Britain the "Enclosure movement" allowed wealthy people to buy the land that serfs lived on—creating a "class of landless people" who "were forced to survive by selling their labor" (Lewis 2016, 37). This ultimately shifted European countries from a feudal economy to a capitalist economy. To understand this change and thus understand what capitalism is, it is useful to explore the feudal economic system.

The Feudal Economic System

In a feudal economic system, aristocrats—the feudal lords—managed "agricultural domains" where people—known as serfs or peasants—lived on and farmed their own land. Serfs had hereditary rights to their homesteads, typically living there generation after generation and they "generally produced material" such as food and shelter "for their own sustenance at their own pace." The feudal lord protected the serfs, meted out "justice" among the serfs, and was (at least tacitly) responsible for the serfs' well-being—providing resources in common (such as seeds for next year's crops, pastures for animals, wood, water, and machinery) in what was known as "the commons." In return, serfs were beholden to their feudal lord and had to "hand over a fixed portion" or percentage "of their yield" (Lewis 2016, 37–8). For instance, a feudal lord might demand one out of every ten sheep or one out of every four bushels of grain. This was a known rate of exploitation, and while it could be crushing if the feudal lord demanded a large portion of goods, it was obvious how much of the serfs' goods the feudal lord took.

If a serf wanted to expand their livelihood, they often could. For example, a shepherd with ten sheep might owe one to their feudal lord; if they grew their flock to twenty sheep, they owed two sheep to their feudal lord. This fixed rate of exploitation meant—for instance—that a shepherd could increase their flock and livelihood through hard labor, going from nine to eighteen sheep after giving their fixed portion to the feudal lord.

Within feudalism, a feudal lord's demand—and thus serfs' exploitation—was limited or capped by the lord's own usage rate. That is, a feudal lord "might demand that a peasant give him a hundred turnips, or a thousand turnips, or even ten thousand turnips" but a feudal lord would not demand more turnips than they (and their court) could eat before the turnips rotted, and the idea of "a billion turnips" would have been simply absurd—no feudal lord would demand a billion turnips (Lewis 2016, 40). Within a feudal economy, then, more exploitation (more turnips) is not always better for the lord. There are actual limits to how much a feudal lord can take from others.

Within feudal economies, serfs traded commodities (food, cloth, etc.) using money for exchange. This exchange is represented through the syllogism C—M—C, which stands for Commodity-Money-Commodity. Essentially, if I am a shepherd with a flock of sheep and you are a farmer with a crop of carrots, I might be able to trade you a sheep for carrots, creating a direct commodity-commodity exchange. But if you do not want a sheep, we cannot make this trade. Here, money functions as a useful "middle" term in our exchange: if I can sell a sheep and receive money for it, then I can give you the money and receive carrots. This exchange starts with a commodity (a sheep) and ends with a commodity (carrots) and money is in the middle, making the C—M—C exchange. Notably, the middle term (the money) in this exchange is "vanishing" (Lewis 2016, 42). The middle term is empty or meaningless. It exists only to disappear and has no real value. In this example, I (the shepherd) never wanted money—I wanted carrots. The two end terms (the commodities) have value. That is, the sheep and the carrots have value and the money is simply there to facilitate the trade of commodities.

The Capitalist Economic System

Policies such as Britain's "Enclosure movement" privatized the land, robbing people (formerly known as serfs) from "their own land" and access "to the commons" where they pastured animals and gathered wood and water and so on. This created a class of "propertyless people" who "did not own the means to reproduce their existence" (Lewis 2016, 38). Karl Marx famously called this class of people "the proletariat." Unable to shepherd their own flock or cultivate their own orchard—working for their own sustenance and at their own pace—the newly created proletariat had to sell their labor to survive. This remains the case in contemporary capitalist economies. For instance, a person might work alongside many other laborers in an extremely large orchard for fourteen hours a day, receiving a wage at the end of the day. The harvest crop, however, belongs to the orchard owner—who performed no labor. Similarly, a computer scientist might work with other software engineers creating programs for a video game company and receive a hefty salary paid every two weeks. The video game program, however, belongs to the video game company's owner who neither wrote the code nor understands it.

In this capitalist economic system, the rate of exploitation is unknown. In a feudal economy, the exploitation rate is clear: one apple out of every ten—or whatever rate the feudal lord demands. But in a capitalist economy, it is nearly impossible to know how much "profit" a company—such as the orchard or video game company in these examples—makes from the laborers' labor. Feminists and Marxists often refer to this type of "profit" as "wage theft" because it is profit garnered from the workers' labor. The "profit" would not exist without the laborers, and yet they do not receive their portion of the "profit." In other words, it has been stolen from them—taken out of their wages. Returning to the orchard example and putting this in simplistic terms, imagine that I own the orchard. In one year, I spend $100,000 on fertilizer and machinery and I spend another $100,000 paying laborers, but when I sell the crop I receive $500,000. This means that I have made a profit of $300,000. Here, many feminists, Marxists, and Marxist feminists would argue that I have stolen that $300,000 from the laborers by keeping their wages low, hence the term "wage theft." Again, in this capitalist system, the rate of exploitation is largely unknown: the laborers know they receive $10/day and that the crop must be worth more than that, but it is typically impossible for laborers to figure out how much "profit" was garnered off of their labor since they don't know the markup rate for each bushel of apples sold to supermarkets and so on.

Within capitalism, the exchange is also different than it is under a feudal economy. Feudal economics operate through a C—M—C exchange, where commodities (e.g., sheep) are exchanged for money, which is exchanged for a different commodity (e.g., carrots). The capitalist exchange inverts this formula: it starts and ends with money and the commodity is the vanishing middle term. The capitalist exchange is written as M^1—C—M^2, representing Money^1-Commodity-Money^2. Consider the orchard example once more. In this scenario, I (the orchard owner) am a capitalist. I use the capitalist exchange. I start by exchanging $200,000 ($M^1$) for seeds, machinery, and labor to produce a crop, which is the commodity (C). Then I exchange the crop (C) for $500,000 ($M^2$). This creates the exchange M^1—C—M^2. The capitalist's exchange starts and ends with money, and the middle term—the commodity—is irrelevant to the capitalist. In this scenario, I (the orchard owner) never wanted the crop; I wanted to receive more money than I put in. Almost all stock investments work as M^1—C—M^2 exchanges; indeed, most of the middle and upper class use investment firms and the like, which means they typically have no idea what commodities their money is invested in. Likewise, homeownership, investing in "kickstarter" projects, and retirement savings all function according to this capitalist exchange.

Moreover, in capitalist economic systems not only is the rate of exploitation (wage theft) unknown, it is also unlimited. That is, while a feudal lord's demand for turnips is generally capped by the number of turnips they can use, there is no such cap for the amount of money a capitalist can accumulate. Likewise, while more turnips are not always better in the feudal system, in the capitalist system more money is always better. And while a "billion turnips" would have been unfathomable to a British feudal lord, billions and trillions of dollars (or any other currency) is a common-sense idea for contemporary capitalists.

Additionally, while a serf could improve their livelihood through hard work (growing their herd or planting and harvesting more crops), the proletariat typically does not benefit or benefits very little from working harder. For instance, if you work for fourteen hours in an orchard and are paid ten dollars at the end of the day, it does not matter if you work hard or very hard, you are still paid ten dollars at the end of the day. Perhaps, if you are the best laborer and work extremely hard, you might receive ten dollars and fifty cents at the end of the day. Indeed, this "bonus pay" might spur most or all of the laborers to work extra hard as they compete to receive the extra pay. All of this hard work creates increased profits for the orchard owner.

Low Wages and Unemployment Pools

Capitalists make their profit by keeping wages as low as laborers can bear. The materials and machinery required to make a commodity have actual value and a capitalist must invest however much they cost. Let us reconsider the orchard example. The orchard owner must buy seeds and buy or maintain machinery and cannot pay less for them than they are worth. Returning to the same figures used previously in this example, imagine the orchard owner buys the seeds and machinery for $100,000 and sells the crop for $500,00 in a given year. This means the potential profit is $400,000—minus whatever the orchard owner pays the laborers in wages. This means that the profit is determined by how low wages can be set. The lower the wages, the more profit "left over" for the orchard owner. If the orchard owner uses slave labor, the profits would be the full $400,000 difference between the initial investment and the crop's value. If the orchard owner has to pay $100,000 to get laborers to work in the orchard, then the profit is only $300,000.

The capitalist exchange, then, depends on low wages. In order to keep wages low workers need to be frightened of losing their wages. That is, imagine I receive $75,000 per year in exchange for teaching three courses per semester at a university. One day, my supervisor tells me that next semester I will be required to teach four classes without a pay increase. Outraged at being asked to work more for the same pay, I could quit. But really, I would only quit if I believed there was another job I could easily move into that would pay enough to live—or in this example, to live at a middle-class standard. Moreover, if I refuse to teach the fourth course without an increase in pay, the university can simply fire me and hire someone else to teach four classes per semester at the rate of $75,000 per year. As such, to keep wages low, there needs to be a pool of unemployed or underemployed people. This pool supplies companies and organizations with a ready supply of new hires to take current laborers' jobs if they refuse to work more for the same pay (or work the same amount for less pay, which is known as "pay cuts"). Moreover, the presence of this pool of unemployed or underemployed people in society scares currently employed laborers who—seeing how miserable life is for the unemployed and underemployed—would do almost anything (including working incredibly long hours for incredibly low wages) to keep their jobs.

Additionally, capitalist economies can keep wages low through unpaid labor. For instance, if a laborer has someone to do the cooking and cleaning for free, then the laborer doesn't have to pay someone out of their own wages for these services, and an employer need not pay laborers enough for them to in turn pay for these services. And here, capitalism and patriarchy clearly intertwine. When societies are organized into heterosexual family units in which women are expected and/or required to cook, clean, nurture, nurse, child-rear, and so on without wages, then (men's) paid labor can be set at much lower wages than if women were monetarily recompensed for their domestic labor.

The Boom-to-Bust Cycle

The capitalist exchange requires that some commodity (a crop of oranges, or yoga mats, or refrigerators, or thermoses, or the next blockbuster movie, etc.) is sold at a profit. The commodity is the vanishing middle term in the capitalist exchange, meaning that it—in and of itself—is irrelevant, but it has to be made and sold or else capitalists cannot receive profit. However, once the market is saturated, once everyone who wants and/or can afford a commodity has bought it, the capitalists have received their max profit from that commodity and it is time to stop investing in that commodity and start investing in a different one. Consider thermoses for example, first Hydro Flasks, then Yeti, and then Owala thermoses were all the rage. Sequentially, each brand of thermoses saturated the market, and then capitalists moved on to the next in order to receive profit. The stage in which a commodity is selling very well (before saturation) is referred to as a "boom," as in the phrase "business is booming."

However, once a commodity has reached saturation, it stops selling (because everyone who was going to buy it has bought it). The capitalist investors have received their max profit from the commodity, and now the only sensible thing for a capitalist to do is stop investing in that commodity and start investing in something else. This causes the production of that commodity to collapse: the laborers are laid off, the manufacturing equipment is sold for parts, and the raw materials are no longer being bought from the suppliers. This is referred to as a "bust." Busts can create a domino effect in economies through gluts of cheap machinery and rises in unemployment—driving wages even lower—and so on. Although capitalists reinvest in other commodities (creating a cycle), busts can decimate whole industries, communities, and geographies.

This is known as the "boom-to-bust" cycle—and Marxist feminists typically maintain that it is an inherent part of capitalism (Lewis 2016; McNamara 2018). Boom-to-bust is not an accident or the result of badly regulated capitalism. Capitalism functions through the boom-to-bust cycle: without "booms" capitalists would make no profits, and "busts" are the necessary result of a market reaching saturation and capitalists moving on and investing in new commodities from which they can profit.

Feminism: A Movement to End Imperialist White Supremacist Capitalist Patriarchy
bell hooks (2000) describes sexism as an imperialist white supremacist capitalist patriarchy. Capitalism developed alongside imperialism—they have long fueled each other. Indeed, as transnational feminists demonstrate, capitalism, imperialism, colonialism/settler colonialism, and white supremacy typically go hand in hand, and white supremacy not only helps push wages lower for racialized people, but it also helps ensure that a pool of racialized people are unemployed and underemployed, which lowers wages for the whole community. Additionally, patriarchy makes women's labor less valuable, pushing women's wages lower and ultimately keeping all wages low through women's unpaid domestic labor.

Compared to disciplines such as sociology, media studies, and psychology, there are relatively few feminist economists. Feminist movement needs more feminist economists who can help develop more equitable and less destructive economic systems for the future. Capitalism is a lynchpin in imperialism, white supremacy, and patriarchy, which are all, likewise, lynchpins in capitalism. Capitalism is not a neutral system for managing money and economies. Capitalism is an oppressive economic system that structures social relations and creates profits from gendered, classed, and racialized social roles.

Sarah Kornfield

See Also: Colonialism; Domestic Labor; Emotional Labor; hooks, bell; Marxist Feminism; Neoliberalism; Patriarchy; Reproductive Labor; Socialism; Transnational Feminism

Further Reading

hooks, bell. 2000. *Feminism is for Everybody: Passionate Politics*. London: Pluto Press.

Lewis, Holly. 2016. *The Politics of Everybody: Feminism, Queer Theory, and Marxism at the Intersection.* London: Zed Books.

Marx, Karl. 2011. *Capital: A Critique of Political Economy*. Translated by Samuel Moore and Edward Aveling. Edited by Friedrich Engels, 3 vols. New York: Dover.

McNamara, Sallie. 2018. *Tatler's Irony: Conspicuous Consumption, Inconspicuous Power and Social Change.* Cham: Palgrave Macmillan.

CHISHOLM, SHIRLEY

Shirley Chisholm (1924–2005) was a trailblazer in US politics. She is known for being the first African American woman elected to the US Congress and for her historic candidacy for the presidency in 1972. Her life and career exemplify the struggles and triumphs of women, particularly women of color, in the pursuit of equality and representation.

Born Shirley Anita St. Hill on November 30, 1924, in Brooklyn, New York, to immigrant parents from Barbados. Her father a factory worker and mother a seamstress sent her and her sisters to live in Barbados with their grandmother from 1928 to 1934. When her parents saved up enough money to support their family, her mother brought Chisholm and her sisters back to New York (Chisholm 1970). Growing up in a predominantly white neighborhood, she faced racial discrimination, which fueled her desire to advocate for social justice and equality (Chisholm 1970).

Chisholm graduated *cum laude* from Brooklyn College in 1946, earning a degree in sociology and minoring in Spanish. During college, she was involved in the Harriet Tubman Society, Political Science Society, Ipothia, NAACP, and the Debate Society. Her experiences during college shaped her political views and sharpened her feelings for how racism was woven through US life (Chisholm

1970). With professional options limited by racial and gender discrimination, Chisholm entered into early childhood education (Gallagher 2007).

Entry into Politics

In 1964, Chisholm ran for a seat in the New York State Assembly. Chisholm encountered sexist resistance to her political ambitions as the leadership of the Unity Democratic Club was hesitant to support a woman (Gallagher 2007). She won the election and quickly gained a reputation as a passionate advocate for marginalized groups (Chisholm 1973).

During her time in the New York State Assembly from 1965 to 1968, Chisholm worked on various legislative initiatives, including efforts to increase funding for public schools and improve access to healthcare. She was known for her willingness to confront political norms and challenge the status quo, often advocating for policies that prioritized the needs of the poor and disenfranchised (Winslow 2013). Chisholm proposed legislation to eliminate racial discrimination in banking, investment, and insurance practices and to require city police to complete training in civil rights issues. She fought for unemployment benefits to be extended to domestic workers and sponsored the Search for Education, Elevation, and Knowledge (SEEK) program (Gallagher 2007). She proposed bills to benefit women, such as legislation to open day care centers for working women and those on public assistance, and protection for public school teachers who took maternity leave. Her experiences in the assembly prepared her for the next significant milestone in her career—her election to US Congress.

Election to Congress

In 1968, Chisholm made history by becoming the first African American woman elected to the US Congress, representing New York's 12th Congressional District. Her election was a monumental achievement, breaking barriers for women of color in politics and serving as an inspiration for future generations (Winslow 2013). Chisholm's campaign slogan, "Fighting Shirley Chisholm—Unbought and Unbossed," encapsulated her commitment to independent thought and resistance to political pressures, particularly those stemming from gender and racial discrimination (Chisholm 1973).

Once in Congress, Chisholm quickly established herself as a formidable advocate for social justice and the women's movement. She purposely hired a staff composed of young women (Chisholm 1970). Within the first few months of entering Congress, in May 1969, she spoke of the need for an Equal Rights Amendment (ERA), in a speech to the House of Representatives (Gallagher 2007), and fought tirelessly to eradicate the discrimination toward women.

She was a founding member of the Congressional Black Caucus (CBC), which aims to address the legislative concerns of African Americans and other marginalized groups. Chisholm's work focused on a range of issues, including civil rights, education, healthcare, child welfare, and economic opportunities for low-income communities (Winslow 2013).

Presidential Campaign

In 1972, Chisholm took a bold step by announcing her candidacy for the Democratic nomination for president of the United States. Her campaign was groundbreaking as she became the first major party Black candidate and the first woman to seek a major party nomination in her campaign for the presidency. Although she faced immense challenges, including limited media coverage and institutional barriers, her candidacy brought national attention to issues such as poverty, education, and women's rights (Winslow 2013).

Congresswoman Shirley Chisholm, the first African American woman elected to Congress, announcing her candidacy for the presidential nomination, January 25, 1972 (Library of Congress).

Chisholm's campaign was marked by her determination to speak out on behalf of marginalized communities and endorsed an activist federal government. She focused on a platform that included quality education, healthcare, elimination of poverty, commitment to environmental issues, new housing programs, social justice, and more (Chisholm 1973). She struggled to be taken seriously as a candidate and was not supported by her Black male colleagues, saying, "When I ran for the Congress, when I ran for president, I met more discrimination as a woman than for being black. Men are men" (Barron 2005). Despite not securing the Democratic nomination, her candidacy laid the groundwork for future generations of women and people of color in politics, inspiring many to pursue public service (Chisholm 1973). Chisholm continued to speak out about women's rights, specifically pointing out that the women's movement needed to extend beyond the white middle class to Black and Mexican American women who suffer double discriminations (Gallagher 2007). She used her position of power to influence white mainstream feminists to transform the women's movement.

Legacy

Shirley Chisholm's legacy is profound and multifaceted. Her groundbreaking achievements opened doors for countless women and minorities in politics, challenging systemic barriers and inspiring future leaders. Chisholm's contributions to civil rights, women's rights, and social justice continue to resonate today. Her story is often cited in discussions about representation and the importance of diverse voices in shaping public policy. The impact of her work is evident in the increasing number of women and people of color who have entered politics since her time, reflecting her enduring influence on American political life.

Arrington Stoll

See Also: Equal Rights Amendment (ERA); Interlocking Oppression

Further Reading

Barron, James. 2005. "Shirley Chisholm, First Black Woman Elected to Congress, Dies." *New York Times*, January 3, 2005. https://www.nytimes.com/2005/01/03/obituaries/shirley-chisholm-unbossedpioneer-in-congress-is-dead-at-80.html.

Chisholm, Shirley. 1970. *Unbought and Unbossed.* Boston: Houghton Mifflin.

Chisholm, Shirley. 1973. *The Good Fight.* New York: Harper Collins.

Congress.gov. n.d. "Representative Shirley Chisholm." Accessed November 28, 2024 https://www.congress.gov/member/shirley-chisholm/C000371

Gallagher, Julie. 2007. "Waging 'The Good Fight': The Political Career of Shirley Chisholm, 1953–1982." *The Journal of African American History* 92, no. 3: 392–416. https://doi.org/10.1086/jaahv92n3p392.

Winslow, Barbara. 2013. *Shirley Chisholm: Catalyst for Change.* Boulder, CO: Westview Press.

CHOICE

The concept of choice is simultaneously fraught and of central importance in US feminist movements. Communication scholar Celeste Condit writes that "choice" evolved out of the US mainstream feminist movement's activism during the 1960s–80s, noting that there was a need for "real and pressing changes in the public vocabulary describing women's biological choices" and occupational choices (1994, 84). Although "choice" might originally have been linked to both "biological choices" and "occupational choices," today "choice" is most often associated with reproductive rights and abortion activism. Even in this context, though, Nancy Hirschmann (2010, 271) believes "choice" is about more than abortion. She argues, choice "was about recognizing that women are full-fledged human beings, not the half humans that they have been conceived as since Aristotle." Feminists, in this way, herald "choice" as a call for self-determination and bodily autonomy. In other words, feminists' use of "choice" means that gender should not dictate the life paths and options available to someone.

Queer women and women of color have criticized mainstream feminists' use of "choice," illustrating the ways that intersecting identities constrain people's ability to make choices (Luthra 1993). For instance, the classic feminist abortion adage "my body, my choice" or even the term "pro-choice" assumes and implies that the choice to have an abortion is equally available to everyone. Women of color have argued that choices mean little if there is not a way to realize them. If someone wants to *choose* abortion but lives in a rural area without a clinic or experiences medical racism, that choice is not actually available. If a Black woman *chooses* to have a baby and that child is killed by police while playing with a toy gun, that choice is taken from her. In the 1990s, women of color activists proposed a "reproductive justice" framework to expand our ability to think about and advocate for reproductive rights *beyond* choice to emphasize that a myriad of factors affect people's choices and their ability to actualize them.

Choice Feminism

In 2006, feminist political scientist Linda Hirshman coined the term "choice feminism" to describe an orientation to feminism organized around the belief that "the US women's movement has liberated women to make whatever choices they want" (Ferguson 2010, 247). Choice feminism has four primary principles: (1) only an individual woman knows their situation well enough to make decisions for their life; (2) the only time a choice can be "bad" is if it harms someone; (3) the success of earlier feminist movements is unchangeable and guaranteed; (4) restricting a feminist's choice is more harmful than a feminist making a mistake (Kirkpatrick 2010).

Some argue that choice feminism is actually dangerous to the larger feminist movement because it assumes a baseline of gender equity that may not exist. These critics position choice feminism as part of a neoliberal postfeminist movement, which believes "that structural factors which once systematically ordered social relations to the detriment of women have now been largely overcome" and that "individuals will make themselves into responsible, self-monitoring subjects" (Budgeon 2015, 304, 310). Ultimately, critics of choice feminism question if every choice a feminist makes is inherently feminist since, as Nancy Hirschmann (2010, 272) notes, "only now, because in theory women have other options, other possibilities for living their lives, women's taking up the same old responsibilities has the *illusion* of choice."

Overall, "choice" is a significant concept in feminist movements and activism. While there is some disagreement among feminists about how choice functions and the role of choice in feminist politics, the ability to decide for oneself what one does and how one does things is crucial to achieve gender equity—the goal of feminist activism. That said, Hirschmann (2010, 272–3) reminds us that it is essential for feminists to consider the "political and ethical" justifications one makes for their choices and to ask, "How do we know that what I want is 'really' what I want, rather than that I have simply adapted my preferences to an unjustly limited set of options?" While there are more choices available to most US women today than in years prior, it is apparent that these options are not set in stone (e.g., the overturning of *Roe v. Wade*). As such, it is important that feminists continue reflecting on their choices and the sociopolitical impact of those choices.

Cassidy D. Ellis

See Also: Abortion; Intersectionality; Neoliberalism; Postfeminism; Reproductive Justice; *Roe v. Wade* (1973)

Further Reading

Budgeon, Shelley. 2015. "Individualized Femininity and Feminist Politics of Choice." *European Journal of Women's Studies* 22, no. 3: 303–18. https://doi.org/10.1177/1350506815576602.

Condit, Celeste M. 1994. *Decoding Abortion Rhetoric: Communicating Social Change*. Urbana: University of Illinois Press.

Ferguson, Michaele L. 2010. "Choice Feminism and the Fear of Politics." *Perspectives on Politics* 8, no. 1: 247–53. https://doi.org/10.1017/S1537592709992830.

Gill, Rosalind C. 2007. "Critical Respect: The Difficulties and Dilemmas of Agency and 'Choice' for Feminism." *European Journal of Women's Studies* 14, no. 1: 69–80. https://doi.org/10.1177/1350506807072318.

Hirshman, Linda R. 2006. *Get to Work: A Manifesto for Women of the World*. New York: Viking Adult.

Hirschmann, Nancy J. 2010. "Choosing Betrayal." *Perspectives on Politics* 8, no. 1: 271–8. https://doi.org/10.1017/S1537592709992866.

Kirkpatrick, Jennet. 2010. "Introduction: Selling Out? Solidarity and Choice in the American Feminist Movement." *Perspectives on Politics* 8, no. 1: 241–5. https://doi.org/10.1017/S1537592709992829.

Luthra, Rashmi. 1993. "Toward a Reconceptualization of 'Choice': Challenges by Women at the Margins." *Feminist Issues* 13, no. 1: 41–54. https://doi.org/ 10.1007/BF02685647.

Snyder-Hall, R. Claire. 2010. "Third-Wave Feminism and the Defense of 'Choice'." *Perspectives on Politics* 8, no. 1: 255–61. https://doi.org/10.1017/S1537592709992842.

Thwaites, Rachel. 2017. "Making a Choice or Taking a Stand? Choice Feminism, Political Engagement and the Contemporary Feminist Movement." *Feminist Theory* 18, no. 1: 55–68. https://doi.org/10.1177/1464700116683657.

CIVIL RIGHTS ACT (1964)

The Civil Rights Act of 1964 is a landmark piece of legislation that affirms the Constitution's prohibition against denying equal protection under the law, especially related to social justice and social benefits (US Department of Labor 2024). Signed into law by President Lyndon B. Johnson, the Civil Rights Act specifically prohibits discrimination in public places, schools, and employment based on race, color, religion, sex, and national origin (Fisher 2022). While the Act's primary purpose was to support racial equality, its inclusion of "sex" in Title VII widened its impact, both changing the law and challenging systems of power that marginalized women and people of color.

The Intersectional Fight against Inequality

The Civil Rights Act was written during an era of immense social division. In the 1960s, numerous minoritized groups increased their demands for recognition and equal rights under the law. African American men and women were fighting against racism, violence, segregation, and voter discrimination (Carson 2024; Solomon, Maxwell, and Castro 2019) while women across the country faced blatant discrimination in schools and the workplace (Burkett 2024). The National Association for the Advancement of Colored People (NAACP) and leaders like Martin Luther King, Jr., John Lewis, Fannie Lou Hamer, Rosa Parks, Diane Nash, Dorothy Height, and Ella Baker led the fight against Jim Crow laws and racial segregation even as organizations like the National Women's Party (Fredrickson 2019) and activists like Dorothy Height (National Museum of African American History and Culture 2018) and Betty Friedan (National Women's History Museum 2020) inspired women to organize for employment opportunities and equal pay.

Although women and Black people entered the US workforce in large numbers during the Second World War, many were pushed back into traditional and segregated roles when the war ended (Burkett 2024). Job listings were segregated by gender and race, promotions and higher education accolades were often reserved for white men, there were no laws protecting the jobs of women who took time off to give birth, and harassment was common but rarely acknowledged (National Parks Service 2022). Feminist groups like the National Organization for Women (NOW) and civil rights organizations like the NAACP advocated for equal treatment and opportunities for women and people of color (Burkett 2024; Carson 2024), making it clear to elected officials and the public that true justice must be intersectional.

The Purpose of the Civil Rights Act

The Civil Rights Act used four key provisions—known as "Titles"—to dismantle systemic discrimination (Civil Rights Act 1964):

- **Title I** prohibits discriminatory interference in the right to vote.
- **Title II** prohibits segregation in public places.
- **Title IV** prohibits segregation in schools.
- **Title VII** prohibits discrimination in employment based on race, color, religion, sex, or national origin.

In addition, the Civil Rights Act created the Equal Employment Opportunity Commission (EEOC) to implement and enforce the law in the workplace (NARA 2022).

What's Next?

The Civil Rights Act of 1964 was a transformative achievement in the fight for equality, with profound implications for women's rights and racial equality. It provides a legal framework that continues to inspire feminist activism toward justice and equity. As the United States continues to evolve, the Act serves as both a milestone in history and a reminder of the ongoing work needed to achieve true, intersectional equality for all.

Devon S. Torchiana

See Also: Civil Rights Act: Title VII; Interlocking Oppression; Intersectionality

Further Reading

Burkett, Elinor, 2024. "Women's Rights Movement." *Britannica*, December 16, 2024. Accessed January 8, 2025. https://www.britannica.com/event/womens-movement.

Carson, Clayborne. 2024. "American Civil Rights Movement." *Britannica*, December 11, 2024. Accessed January 8, 2025. https://www.britannica.com/event/American-civil-rights-movement.

Civil Rights Act, 78 Stat. 241. 1964.

Fisher, Allen. 2022. "Women's Rights and the Civil Rights Act of 1964." *Women's Rights*, June 17, 2022. Accessed January 8, 2025. https://www.archives.gov/women/1964-civil-rights-act.

Fredrickson, Caroline. 2019. "How the Most Important US Civil Rights Law Came to Include Women." *The Harbinger* 43: 122–7.

National Archives and Records Administration. 2022. "Civil Rights Act (1964)" *Milestone Documents*, February 8, 2022. Accessed January 8, 2025. https://www.archives.gov/milestone-documents/civil-rights-act.

National Museum of African American History & Culture. 2018. "Women in the Modern Civil Rights Movement." National History Day: Conflict & Compromise. Accessed January 8, 2025. https://nmaahc.si.edu/sites/default/files/images/black_women_civil_rights_movement_5.pdf.

National Parks Service. 2022. "The Modern Civil Rights Movement, 1954–1964." *Pivotal Moments*, December 6, 2022. Accessed January 8, 2025. https://www.nps.gov/subjects/civilrights/modern-civil-rights-movement.htm.

National Women's History Museum. 2020. "Feminism: The Second Wave." *Exhibits*, June 18, 2020. Accessed January 8, 2025. https://www.womenshistory.org/exhibits/feminism-second-wave.

Solomon, Danyelle, Connor Maxwell, and Abril Castro. 2019. "Systemic Inequality and American Democracy." *Center for American Progress*. Accessed January 8, 2025. https://www.americanprogress.org/article/systematic-inequality-american-democracy/.

US Department of Labor. 2024. "Legal Highlight: The Civil Rights Act of 1964." *Office of the Assistant Secretary for Administration & Management*, December 15, 2024. Accessed January 8, 2025. https://www.dol.gov/agencies/oasam/civil-rights-center/statutes/civil-rights-act-of-1964.

CIVIL RIGHTS ACT: TITLE VII

The Civil Rights Act of 1964 is most famous for making racial segregation and discrimination illegal, but it also played a pivotal role in advancing women's rights—particularly in the workplace. Title VII, a revolutionary section of the Civil Rights Act, explicitly protects employees and job applicants from discrimination based on race, color, religion, sex, or national origin (Fisher 2022).

As originally written, the Civil Rights Act focused on protecting people from discrimination based only on "race, religion, color, or national origin"; it had no protections against sex-based discrimination (Fisher 2022). However, during debate—before Congress voted to pass the legislation—Representative Howard W. Smith of Virginia "offered an amendment that added sex" but only to Title VII of the Civil Rights Act (Fisher 2022). Representative Smith was a well-known segregationist with a history of opposing civil rights legislation. It is unclear why he proposed adding "sex" to Title VII. Many speculate that he added it to derail the bill or as a joke, but women in Congress like Representative Martha Griffiths (MI) embraced the inclusion and fought to keep it (Butler 2024). This provision allowed women throughout the United States to challenge hiring, promotion, and wage disparities based on the protections outlined in Title VII.

Title VII also planted the seeds for understanding the intersections between racial discrimination and gender discrimination at the federal level. This has proved especially important for women of color who are often doubly marginalized due to racism and sexism.

Feminist Successes Stemming from Title VII of the Civil Rights Act of 1964

Title VII has been the foundation of significant wins for women's rights, particularly in the workplace. Namely, Title VII led to the creation of the Equal Employment Opportunity Commission (EEOC), laid the groundwork for important legal precedents, and contributed to feminist momentum.

The US EEOC was created to enforce Title VII. Initially, it was slow to prioritize sex discrimination cases; it also faced challenges related to being a new government entity and lacked legal precedents for sex discrimination cases. Over time, however, persistent feminist advocacy pushed the EEOC to address sex discrimination complaints, making the EEOC a resource for women facing workplace discrimination based on sex (EEOC 2024).

Title VII paved the way for key court cases such as *Phillips v. Martin Marietta Corp.* (1971), which challenged discriminatory hiring practices (especially for mothers as compared to fathers), and *Meritor Savings Bank v. Vinson* (1986), which established that workplace sexual harassment is a form of discrimination. In 1998, *Oncale v. Sundowner* came before the Supreme Court and built upon *Meritor Savings Bank v. Vinson*, establishing that Title VII also applied to same-sex harassment. Title VII is a bulwark protecting people from sex-based discrimination and providing legal recourse for those who are oppressed based on sex at work.

Activist groups like the National Association of Media Women (Fisher 2022), the National Organization for Women, the American Association of University Women, along with legislators like Shirley Chisholm (Rep., D-NY) and Martha Griffiths (Rep., D-MO) and activists like Betty Friedan and Gloria Steinem built on the Act's success (Burkett 2024), pushing for additional reforms, including the Equal Rights Amendment (ERA) and Title IX of the Education Amendments of 1972, which outlawed gender-based discrimination in education (National Women's History Museum 2020).

What's Next?

Title VII of the Civil Rights Act of 1964 continues to shape the fight for equality. By banning sex-based discrimination, it laid the groundwork for continued advocacy. While much progress has been made, activists and legislators continue to leverage Title VII to address the following injustices:

- **Pay equity:** While the gender pay gap persists, Title VII inspired later reforms, including the Lilly Ledbetter Fair Pay Act of 2009, to combat wage discrimination.
- **Workplace harassment protections:** Title VII remains a key tool in addressing sexual harassment, especially in the wake of the #MeToo movement, which highlighted the challenges women face when they report sexual harassment and discrimination (White 2018).
- **Intersectional advocacy:** While the Act did not specifically address intersectional discrimination, its protections based on multiple aspects of identity (race, religion, color, sex, or national origin) allow for a broader understanding of how systems of oppression can overlap, opening up opportunities to address discrimination in deeper, more inclusive ways.

As a framework, intersectionality reminds activists and legislators to advocate for laws and policies under Title VII that consider how groups of people may be impacted by multiple systems of oppression at once, leading to more inclusive language, interpretations, and impact.

As technological innovations continue to transform society and make it easier to conceal oppressive systems and practices, activists and lawmakers must continue to recognize that true equality must be intersectional. Policies and guidance designed to address the evolving challenges of our time should adopt an intersectional approach, ensuring they account for the interconnected nature of social identities and inequalities.

Devon S. Torchiana

See Also: Civil Rights Act (1964); Civil Rights Movement; Equal Pay; Interlocking Oppression; Intersectionality; Lilly Ledbetter Fair Pay Act (2009); Title IX (1972)

Further Reading

Burkett, Elinor. 2024. "Women's Rights Movement." *Britannica*, December 16, 2024. Accessed January 8, 2024. https://www.britannica.com/event/womens-movement.

Butler, Kristin, producer. 2024. "The Surprising Reason Why Women Were Included in the 1964 Civil Rights Act." *American Experience: What the History?!* Written by Chris Young, featuring Samie Jarroush, February 7, 2024. Digital short. Public Broadcasting System. Accessed January 8, 2025. https://www.youtube.com/watch?v=M6zcET1MLq8&t=54s.

Equal Employment Opportunity Commission (EEOC). 2024. "History of the EEOC." December 15, 2024. Accessed January 8, 2025. https://www.eeoc.gov/history.

Fisher, Allen. 2022. "Women's Rights and the Civil Rights Act of 1964." *National Archives*, June 17, 2022. Accessed January 8, 2025. https://www.archives.gov/women/1964-civil-rights-act.

Meritor Savings Bank v. Vinson, 477 U.S. 57. (1986).

National Women's History Museum. 2020. "Feminism: The Second Wave." *Exhibits*, June 18, 2020. https://www.womenshistory.org/exhibits/feminism-second-wave.

Oncale v. Sundowner Offshore Services, Inc., 523 U.S. 75 (1998).

Phillips v. Martin Marietta Corp., 400 U.S. 542 (1971).

White, Rebecca Hanner. 2018. "Title VII and the #MeToo Movement." *Emory Law Journal Online* 68: 1014–33.

CIVIL RIGHTS MOVEMENT

The Civil Rights Movement of the 1960s is considered by many to be one of the most transformative periods in US history. The movement gave us activist leaders like Coretta Scott and Martin Luther King, Jr., John Lewis, Rosa Parks, Malcolm X, Ella Baker, Fannie Lou Hamer, and Thurgood Marshall (National Museum 2018). Feminist activism intersected with the fight for racial justice, seeking to create equal opportunities for all people and a world without racism or sexism. While history often spotlights the male leaders of the Civil Rights Movement, the efforts of women and feminist organizations were critical to achieving success. Despite much of their work going unrecognized, women worked doggedly to coordinate marches, register voters, and gather people to protest ("Women in the African American Civil Rights Movement" 2025).

Feminism and the Civil Rights Movement

During the mid-twentieth century, members of the Civil Rights Movement and feminist activists worked together toward a common goal: dismantling systems of oppression. Feminist activism highlighted how racism and sexism intersected, especially in the lives of Black women (Fredrickson 2019). This awareness laid the groundwork for the later development of intersectional feminism, which posits that identities like race, gender, and class cannot be separated when attempting to understand oppression (Crenshaw 1989).

Women of color faced unique challenges that white feminists and Black male leaders often overlooked. Within the Civil Rights Movement, Black women had to navigate patriarchal norms that tried to sideline them, even as they did much of the heavy lifting (National Museum 2018). Outside the movement, they dealt with systemic racism and sexism in ways that neither white women nor Black men experienced.

Dorothy Height—known as "The Godmother of the Civil Rights Movement"—was especially influential during this period. She had been involved in the fight for civil rights since the 1930s, and she used her experience and reputation as a formidable activist to influence leaders like Martin Luther King, Jr., and John Lewis (National Museum 2018). Primarily focused on women's rights, Dorothy Height was critical in ensuring the inclusion of women in the fight for equality.

Leveraging the work already being done by Dorothy Height (National Museum 2018) and capitalizing on the popularity of books like *The Feminine Mystique* by Betty Friedan (Burkett 2024), feminists used the momentum of the Civil Rights Movement to advocate for broader feminist issues. The landmark legislation, the Civil Rights Act of 1964 includes women as a protected category in Title VII; although it seems likely that women were added to the Civil Rights Act in an attempt to actually sabotage the legislation, its passing means that the efforts of feminist and civil rights activists succeeded together in ensuring this landmark legislation protected both racial and gender minorities.

What's Next?

The Civil Rights Movement of the 1960s resulted in numerous new legal protections for minority groups in the United States, but the fight for equality did not end with the passing of the Civil Rights Act of 1964. The ongoing #MeToo and #BlackLivesMatter movements demonstrate both how far we've come and also how far we still have to go before we realize true equality. As in the 1960s, activists and their allies in US legislatures continue to push for reforms and policies that address the intersectional challenges still faced by minority groups.

Devon S. Torchiana

See Also: #BlackLivesMatter; Civil Rights Act (1964); Civil Rights Act: Title VII; Interlocking Oppression; Intersectionality; #MeToo; *The Feminine Mystique*

Further Reading

Burkett, Elinor. 2024. "Women's Rights Movement." *Britannica*, December 16, 2024. https://www.britannica.com/event/womens-movement.

Butler, Kristin, producer. 2024. "The Surprising Reason Why Women Were Included in the 1964 Civil Rights Act." *American Experience: What the History?!* Written by Chris Young, featuring Samie Jarroush, February 7, 2024. Digital short. Public Broadcasting System. Accessed January 8, 2025. https://www.youtube.com/watch?v=M6zcET1MLq8&t=54s.

Crenshaw, Kimberlé. 1989. "Demarginalizing the Intersection of Race and Sex: A Black Feminist Critique of Antidiscrimination Doctrine, Feminist Theory and Antiracist Politics." *University of Chicago Legal Forum* 1989 1, no. 8: 139–67.

Fredrickson, Caroline. 2019. "How the Most Important US Civil Rights Law Came to Include Women." *The Harbinger* 43: 122–7.

National Museum of African American History & Culture. 2018. "Women in the Modern Civil Rights Movement." https://nmaahc.si.edu/sites/default/files/images/black_women_civil_rights_movement_5.pdf.

Women in the African American Civil Rights Movement: An Historic Context." 2025. *National Park Services*. Accessed January 12, 2025. https://www.nps.gov/articles/women-in-the-african-american-civil-rights-movement-an-historic-context.htm.

COLLINS, PATRICIA HILL

Born to parents Albert and Eunice Hill, Patricia Hill Collins (1948–) is a prominent Black American scholar and writer. She is best known for her pioneering work in the establishment and development of Black feminist thought. Though her academic roots are in the field of sociology, Collins has made a significant impact on intersectional feminism that continues to be seen across disciplines and beyond the academy.

Background, Education, and Career

Contextualizing Collins's upbringing and parentage, Elizabeth Higginbotham (2009) notes that Collins "is part of a cohort of working-class youth who had educational opportunities long denied their parents." Specifically, Collins grew up during the Civil Rights movement of the 1950s and 1960s. Comparing her experiences within her Black working-class community to the desegregated spaces she entered, Collins writes that during her teenage years, she was "increasingly the 'first,' or 'one of the few,' or the 'only' African-American and/or woman and/or working-class person" in her schools, communities, and work settings. Although she saw nothing wrong with who she was, "apparently many others did," so that while her world grew larger, she often felt that she was growing smaller. Collins writes, "I tried to disappear into myself in order to deflect the painful, daily assaults designed to teach me that being an African-American, working-class woman made me lesser than those who were not. And as I felt smaller, I became quieter and eventually was virtually silenced" (2009, vi).

Collins describes her journey in college and beyond as an "ongoing struggle to regain [her] voice" (2009, vi). This began at Brandeis University in Waltham, Massachusetts, where she graduated with a bachelor of arts in sociology in 1969 (Higginbotham 2009). After earning her bachelor's degree, Collins went on to pursue her master of arts in teaching at Harvard University. Eventually, she would return to Brandeis and gain her doctoral degree in sociology in 1984.

Patricia Hill Collins served as the 100th president of the American Sociological Association in 2009 and was the first Black woman to do so. She has taught across various educational institutions and is currently a Distinguished University Professor Emerita in the University of Maryland's Department of Sociology.

Notable Publications

Patricia Hill Collins's 1986 article, "Learning from the Outsider Within: The Sociological Significance of Black Feminist Thought" is one of her earliest publications, yet it contains key themes that are present throughout her body of scholarship. Arguing "that many Black female intellectuals [make] creative use of their marginality—their 'outsider within' status—to produce Black feminist thought that reflects a special standpoint on self, family, and society," Collins explores the following themes: "(1) Black women's self-definition and self-valuation; (2) the interlocking nature of oppression; and (3) the importance of Afro-American women's culture" (14). In her exploration, Collins cites notable figures in academia and literature, such as Adrienne Rich, Zora Neal Hurston, bell hooks, and E. Frances White (14–15).

Another early article that serves as a foundation for Collins's later work is "The Social Construction of Black Feminist Thought" (1989). Once again, Collins draws from a rich tradition of Black women intellectuals and activists to support her theorizing. She notes how the "two prevailing approaches to studying the consciousness of oppressed groups" (746) are insufficient for investigating Black women's experiences, because "African-American women have been neither passive victims of nor willing accomplices to their own domination" (747). This assertion connects Collins's previous work to her future publications by emphasizing the importance of Black women's self-definition and self-valuation in opposition to institutionalized methods and sites of knowledge.

Patricia Hill Collins defines the "Eurocentric masculinist process . . . as the institutions, paradigms, and any elements of the knowledge-validation procedure controlled by white males and whose purpose is to represent a white male standpoint" (1989, 751). Collins explains how this knowledge-validation process "[works] to suppress Black feminist thought. Since the general culture shaping the taken-for-granted knowledge of the community of experts is one permeated by widespread notions of Black and female inferiority, new knowledge claims that seem to violate these fundamental assumptions are likely to be viewed as anomalies" (1989, 752). Collins highlights this aspect of alternative sources knowledge production and other aspects of Black feminism in what is now known as her central work: *Black Feminist Thought: Knowledge, Consciousness, and the Politics of Empowerment.*

First published in 1990, *Black Feminist Thought* is the first of Collins's five solo authored books (Higginbotham 2012, 23). In the second chapter, Collins (2009) outlines six distinguishing features of Black feminist thought:

1. US Black women have a unique understanding and standpoint that is informed by interlocking and intersecting oppressions, which Collins calls "a unique matrix of domination" (23). Collins notes a "connection between experience and consciousness" (24) within the works of Black women activists, thinkers, and writers, stating that "these ties between what one does and what one thinks illustrated by *individual* Black women can also characterize Black women's experiences and ideas as a *group*" (24, emphasis original).
2. Though US Black women as a group hold collective knowledge, Collins clarifies that Black women are not a homogenous monolith and cautions against "an essentialist understanding of a Black woman's standpoint" which "suppresses differences among Black women in search of an elusive group unity" (28).
3. Black feminist thought is a critical social theory that is necessarily meant to impact social activism. Collins writes that "knowledge for knowledge's sake is not enough—Black feminist thought must both be tied to Black women's lived experiences and aim to better those experiences in some fashion" (31).
4. Black women intellectuals are at the heart of Black feminist thought. This includes, but is not limited to, those found in traditional academic spaces. Collins uplifts and validates a "tradition of using everyday actions and experiences" (33) to inform theory. Knowledge can and should come from community, regardless of formal education and credentials.
5. Black feminist thought is dynamic and changing. As Collins says, "Neither Black feminist thought as a critical social theory nor Black feminist practice can be static; as social conditions change, so must the knowledge and practices designed to resist them" (39). We must continually engage with scholarship *and* the world around us. There is no final and definitive form of Black feminist thought. Though specific articulation is necessary for coalition-building, Collins does not claim to be the ultimate and definitive authority on Black feminist thought.
6. Black feminist thought does not exist in a vacuum. It should be concerned with and support "other social justice projects" (41). Collins sums up this point by saying "that Black women's struggles are part of a wider struggle for human dignity, empowerment, and social justice" (41).

Liberation concerns all those who are oppressed—not just one single group. This fits with the concept of interlocking systems of oppression.

Patricia Hill Collins's scholarly career did not end with *Black Feminist Thought*. She has published four other books and countless other essays and articles. Her contributions to critical theory, both within and beyond the field of sociology, cannot be overstated.

Emma Darby

See Also: Consciousness Raising; Critical Race Theory; Interlocking Oppression; Intersectionality; Standpoint Theory; Womanism

Further Reading

Brown, Melissa. 2021. "What Is Black Feminist Thought?" *Blackfeminisms.com*, February 22, 2021. https://blackfeminisms.com/black-feminist-thought/.

Collins, Patricia Hill. 1986. "Learning from the Outsider Within: The Sociological Significance of Black Feminist Thought." *Social Problems* 33 (6): 14–32. https://doi.org/10.2307/800672.

Collins, Patricia Hill. 1989. "The Social Construction of Black Feminist Thought." *Signs: Journal of Women in Culture and Society* 14 (4): 745–73.

Collins, Patricia Hill. 2009. *Black Feminist Thought: Knowledge, Consciousness, and the Politics of Empowerment*, 2nd ed. New York: Routledge.

Gianoulis, Tina. 2008. "Patricia Hill Collins." In *Contemporary Black Biography*, edited by Paula Kepos and Derek Jacques, 24–7. Detroit, MI: Gale.

Higginbotham, Elizabeth. 2009. "Patricia Hill Collins." *American Sociological Association*, 2009. https://www.asanet.org/patricia-hill-collins/.

Higginbotham, Elizabeth. 2012. "Reflections on the Early Contributions of Patricia Hill Collins." *Gender & Society* 26 (1): 23–7. https://doi.org/10.1177/0891243211426723.

"Patricia Hill Collins, Department of Sociology." n.d. University of Maryland. Accessed December 19, 2024. https://socy.umd.edu/facultyprofile/collins/patricia-hill.

COLONIALISM

Colonialism occurs when one people (often an empire or nation-state) occupies the land of another people, usually to extract resources from the land and to perform violence on the Indigenous people (sometimes referred to as Native, American Indian, Native Alaskan, First Nations, and/or Aboriginal peoples) of that land. Colonialism has been a part of Western culture since ancient Greece and became a dominant feature of modernity, especially as European empires colonized the people and lands of Asia, Africa, the Americas, the pacific islands, and the Caribbean. Although governmental and military-based colonization fell out of favor in the mid-twentieth century, subtler forms of colonization continue to shape the contemporary era, which is often described as a neocolonialism, or a world where direct exploitation has changed into indirect exploitation.

Western Colonialism

Part of what drives colonialism is the figure of the "savage." If another people are deemed to be savage, or less than civilized, colonizers can and have justified terrible atrocities in the name of so-called civilization. As Lumbee legal scholar Robert A. Williams argues, the birth of Western civilization in ancient Greece has within it the figure of the savage or barbarian; for example, the literature of Homer and Hesiod frames outsiders as savages—as do the Socratic dialogues and Aristotle's writings (2012, 11, 36, 71, and 78). Williams argues that this assumed savagery is part of what mobilized coloniality in the ancient period and generations later.

One of the periods of intense colonization started in the late 1400s. During this time, Europe's Modernity emerged during its Renaissance (fourteenth to seventeenth centuries) and Enlightenment (seventeenth to eighteenth centuries) periods, and it simultaneously embarked on expanding its colonial holdings. European empires, such as Britain, France, Portugal, Spain, and the Netherlands, exploited Indigenous lands across the globe and committed atrocities against Indigenous peoples. One of the central contradictions of this period is how thinkers, like John Stuart Mill, for example, could plead for Enlightenment-style democracy in so-called "civilized" places such as Britain but support, even in a limited way, the despotism of the empire in so-called "savage" places like India (see Mehta 1999, 111–12; Pitts 2005, 161; and Chiu and Taylor 2011, 1246–8). Such contradictions motivate literary scholar Walter D. Mignolo to argue that modernity and coloniality are two aspects of the same phenomenon. Modernity tells the story of "Western civilization by celebrating its achievements [and] hiding at the same time its darker side, 'coloniality.' Coloniality, in other words, is constitutive of modernity—there is no modernity without coloniality" (2011, 2–3). European empires, for example, often forced Indigenous peoples into labor that extracted "underpriced raw materials" from the land, such as tobacco, sugar, tea, coffee, opium, and chocolate (Howe 2002). In India, for example, the British used local timber to build navy ships and the railway system that spread across India. These efforts grew the British empire but led to deforestation in India, producing negative effects on water and soil erosion (Beinart and Hughes 2007, 111–19). Like Britian, many European countries exploited their colonial holdings well into the twentieth century.

Neocolonialism

After years of resistance on the part of colonized peoples, many of these empires began the process of removing direct rule from their former colonial holdings, producing a so-called independent condition for many countries in the mid-twentieth century. While places in Africa, Asia, and Latin America became independent, literary scholar Robert J. C. Young explains that such independence was a "relatively minor move from direct to indirect rule" such that formerly colonized nations became "in-dependence" (2003, 3). This position of dependence and exploitation is sometimes referred to as neocolonialism, as the examples of Gabon, Côte d'Ivoire and Ghana, and Nigeria demonstrate.

In Africa, neocolonialism took a variety of forms but includes the ways former colonial powers imposed conditions on newly independent countries (as in the case of Gabon) and maintained trade imbalances (as is the case in Côte d'Ivoire and Ghana). France, by way of example, imposed a range of conditions upon Gabon's independence. The former colonial power retained access to Gabon's raw materials, like uranium and oil; controlled the issuance of and circulation of francs, thus controlling their financial markets; and kept a military presence there and in several African counties (Martin 1985, 197, 200, 204). While technically independent, France exploited and controlled Gabon's raw materials and financial markets, respectively. Furthermore, France's neocolonial control continued, more or less unchanged, until a military coup in late 2023 (Finlator 2023).

Additionally, throughout the twentieth and twenty-first centuries, multinational corporations, like chocolate companies, extract raw goods from poor countries at very low prices. They are, thus, able to preserve massive profits for the corporations themselves. One example of trade imbalance occurs in the $130 billion chocolate industry. While "Côte d'Ivoire and Ghana," former colonies of France and Brittan, "are responsible for 70% of global cocoa production," farmers in these counties make $1 or less a day, far below the poverty line ("Cocoa's Bittersweet" 2020). Much of the wealth generated in the industry stays with chocolate retailers and corporations like Mars, Nestlé, and Hershey ("Cocoa's Bittersweet" 2020). Trade imbalances exist not only throughout Africa but also in Latin America and around the world (Mahoney and Rodríguez-Franco 2018).

Finally, Nigeria's relationship to international financial institutions demonstrates how neocolonialism persists through foreign interventions into the national economy, like so-called debt relief or investment. In an effort to create security for Nigeria after its independence in the 1960s, the country turned, in the 1970s, to oil. Oil became Nigeria's main export, comprising "over 95% of its revenue" (Attah 2013, 75). Overreliance on oil, however, sidelined development in other vital sectors, like agriculture. Without development across the economy, Nigeria had to import a wide variety of goods, not the least of which was food. Importation results in exorbitantly high prices. To keep costs reasonable, the government instituted welfare systems and various kinds of subsidies, all in order to protect the Nigerian citizenry (Ekanade 2014, 2–6).

By the early 1980s, the international price on oil declined, which negatively impacted Nigeria's oil revenue and its ability to fund welfare and subsidies. As a result, Nigeria went into unimaginable debt within a few short years. At this time, international institutions, like the International Monetary Fund (IMF) and the World Bank (WB), provided economic debt relief but only under the implementation of austerity measures, like the removal of welfare services and subsidies. In the wake of these measures, businesses closed, workers became unemployed, and prices for items like food soared (Ekanade 2014, 9). Austerity "produced considerable hardship, poverty, and discontentment across the Nigerian society" (Ekanade 2014, 11). Into the 2020s, the conditions attached to debt relief keep Nigeria in a continual state of indebtedness to foreign organizations.

In the 1990s, still under the pressure of debt relief, the IMF and WB required that Nigeria open itself to foreign investment through public-private partnerships. During this time of privatization, the Nigerian government divested from a range of public services the government could no longer fiscally manage. For example, electricity service was privatized through foreign investment. However, the new management failed to improve the delivery of reliable power service. International relations scholar Olumide Victor Ekanade observes that privatization of the energy sector has not improved the lives of Nigerians. Electric power remains inconsistent, and no new infrastructure was built. As a result, "the manufacturing sector and small-scale businesses" remained "uncompetitive with their imported counterparts" (Ekanade 2014, 17). Such was the case for many elements of privatization across Nigeria, in sectors like healthcare and oil. Foreign investment benefited from a monopoly on the privatized service all without helping Nigerian peoples.

In the 2020s, Nigeria's relation to foreign intervention remains largely neocolonial. After a period of economic growth (2000–14), Nigeria's economy has stagnated in the years following (2015–24). The WB and the US government continue to lobby for measures like austerity and international investment, which arguably continue to place Nigeria in a state of indebtedness, thus preserving neocolonial dependence of foreign powers. What has changed is poverty rates. In 2024, inflation rates hit highs unseen for decades and fuel subsidies were removed. These realities produced, in part, one of the highest poverty rates in the world, second only to India. Although Nigeria is one of the largest economies in Africa, over 100 million people live below the poverty line ("The World Bank" 2024; "2024 Investment Climate" 2024).

As these examples demonstrate, colonialism and neocolonialism cause extreme harm while benefiting colonizers and former colonial powers. There are present-day exceptions: South Korea and Taiwan are both formerly colonized regions that have arguably benefited from neocolonial practices like foreign investments. Feminists around the world are working to end imperialism, colonialism, neocolonialism, and the resulting forms of oppression—poverty, violence, climate crisis—that follow in their wake.

Naaman Wood

See Also: Decolonialism; Patriarchy; Postcolonial Feminism; Settler Colonialism; Structural Oppression; Transnational Feminism; White Supremacy

Further Reading

"2024 Investment Climate Statements: Nigeria." 2024. *US Department of State*. Accessed September 26, 2024. https://www.state.gov/reports/2024-investment-climate-statements/nigeria/.

Attah, Noah Echa. 2013. "The Historical Conjuncture of Neo-colonialism and Underdevelopment in Nigeria." *Journal of African Studies and Development* 5, no. 5: 70–9.

Beinart, William, and Lotte Hughes. 2007. *Environment and Empire*. Oxford: Oxford University Press.

Chiu, Yvonne and Robert S. Taylor. 2011. "The Self-Extinguishing Despot: Millian Democratization." *The Journal of Politics* 73, no. 4 (October): 1239–50.

"Cocoa's Bittersweet Supply Chain in One Visualization." 2020. *World Economic Forum*, November 4, 2020. Accessed September 26, 2024. https://www.weforum.org/agenda/2020/11/cocoa-chocolate-supply-chain-business-bar-africa-exports/.

Ekanade, Olumide Victor. 2014. "The Dynamics of Forced Neoliberalism in Nigeria Since the 1980s." *Journal of Retracing Africa* 1, no. 1: 1–24.

Finlator, William. 2023. "How France Lost Control of Gabon." *UnHerd.com*, September 5, 2023. https://unherd.com/2023/09/how-france-lost-control-of-gabon/.

Howe, Stephen. 2002. *Empire: A Very Short Introduction*. Oxford: Oxford University Press. Apple Books.

Mahoney, James, and Diana Rodríguez-Franco. 2018. "Dependency Theory." In *The Oxford Handbook of the Politics of Development*, edited by Carol Lancaster and Nicolas van de Walle, 22–42. Oxford: Oxford University Press.

Martin, Guy. 1985. "The Historical, Economic and Political Bases of France's African Policy." *The Journal of Modern African Studies* 23, no. 2: 189–208.

Mehta, Uday Singh. 1999. *Liberalism and Empire: A Study in Nineteenth-Century British Liberal Thought*. Chicago: University of Chicago Press.

Mignolo, Walter D. 2011. *The Darker Side of Western Modernity: Global Futures, Decolonial Options*. Durham: Duke University Press.

Pitts, Jennifer. 2005. *A Turn to Empire*. Princeton, NJ: Princeton University Press.

"The World Bank in Nigeria." 2024. *The World Bank Group*, March 21, 2024. Accessed September 26, 2024. https://www.worldbank.org/en/country/nigeria/overview.

Williams, Robert A., Jr. 2012. *Savage Anxieties: The Invention of Western Civilization*. New York: St. Martin's Press.

Young, Robert J. C. 2003. *Postcolonialism: A Very Short Introduction*. Oxford: Oxford University Press.

COMBAHEE RIVER COLLECTIVE

The Combahee River Collective was an organization led by a group of Black feminists, lesbians, and socialists, active in the United States between 1974 and 1980. The organization was primarily based in Boston, Massachusetts. This organization was formed in the wake of the Black Civil Rights Movement and feminist activism during the 1960s and 1970s. The Combahee River Collective organized in response to the sexism and homophobia within the civil rights movement and the racism within the mainstream women's movement, which white middle-class women largely led.

Activist and writer Barbara Smith was the founder of the collective. She named the collective after Harriet Tubman's organized raid on the Combahee River on June 2, 1863, that freed around 750 enslaved Black people. The collective primarily wanted to highlight that both the white feminist movement and the Civil Rights Movement were not addressing the particular issues they faced as Black women or more particularly as Black lesbians.

The Combahee River Collective initially started as a smaller breakaway group from the National Black Feminist Organization (NBFO). The founders of the collective had some major disagreements with the organization's incompetence in addressing class struggles faced by Black women. Historian Duchess Harris concluded that the collective's vision for social change was more radical than the NBFO's (2001, 294). The collective was determined to address the intersectional politics and experiences of poor Black women and lesbians, which seemed to be missing in the work of other feminist organizations of their time.

Since its inception in 1974, the collective met weekly at the Women's Center in Cambridge, Massachusetts. Between 1977 and 1979, they also held retreats throughout the Northeast to discuss the state of the Black feminist movement and develop a comprehensive intervention that they intended to make. The biographer of Black lesbian poet Audre Lorde, author Alexis De Veaux, has described the goal of these retreats as formally establishing the assertions of radical Black feminism, as well as probing the limitations of mainstream white feminists' preoccupation with women's gender as the only form of oppression they face (2004, 237).

A few important members of the Combahee River Collective were the twin sisters Barbara Smith and Beverly Smith and poets Audre Lorde, Akasha Gloria Hul, and Cheryl Clarke, among others. The collective's first retreat (July 1977) was held in Jean Grossholtz's house in South Hadley, Massachusetts. Grossholtz was a lesbian-feminist activist and professor of politics and women's studies at Mount Holyoke College. Six more retreats at different places followed this, the final one in Washington, D.C. in February 1980. In these Black feminist retreats and meetings, they discussed the need to publish their ideas and thoughts and develop a collective statement. This led to their seminal 1978 statement, the Combahee River Collective Statement, in which they outlined their politics and beliefs.

Combahee River Collective's 1978 Statement

The Combahee River Collective's 1978 Statement stemmed from these feminist discussions and was collectively drafted by Black authors and activists Barbara Smith, Demita Frazier, and Beverly Smith. The statement was divided into four sections, namely: (1) "the genesis of contemporary Black feminism"; (2) "what we believe, i.e., the specific province of our politics"; (3) "the problems in organizing Black feminists, including a brief herstory of our collective"; and (4) "Black feminist issues and practice" (Combahee River Collective 1978).

In the first section of the statement, "The Genesis of Contemporary Black Feminism," the statement foregrounded the collective's work and politics within a long lineage of Black feminist struggles, such as those by known Black women activists Sojourner Truth, Harriet Tubman, Frances E. W. Harper, Ida B. Wells Barnett, and Mary Church Terrell, and "thousands upon thousands unknown" (1978). They expressed their dissatisfaction with the mainstream white feminist movement that did not account for race or class and the Civil Rights Movement led by Black men that sidelined the experiences of Black lesbians and women. They also highlighted the "personal genesis" of Black feminism, that is, the connection between their political outlook and "the seemingly personal experiences of individual Black women's lives" (1978). The idea that the "personal is political" was very important to them. That is, Black women's everyday experiences greatly informed their politics.

In the second section, "What We Believe," the authors laid down the beliefs that guided their politics. Identity politics, a term coined by the collective, refers to a kind of feminist politics derived from their identity as Black women and lesbians and is one of their fundamental ideas. Rather than working toward someone else's liberation, they wanted to work toward ending the oppression they faced themselves. They also believed that the systems of oppression, such as class, race, gender, or sexuality, were interlocking. That is, these oppressions work together and are interconnected—as these Black women daily experienced. They did not believe in building their politics on any form of biological determinism, that is, solely based on their sex or gender. Hence, they expressed solidarity with the racial struggles of Black men as part of the larger Black community, while also critiquing Black masculine activists for their sexism, stating, "We struggle together with Black men against racism, while we also struggle with Black men about sexism" (1978). Further, they expressed their ideas of socialism, elaborating that the systems of capitalism and patriarchy are linked, and class struggles are also feminist struggles.

In the third section, "Problems in Organizing Black Feminists," the authors outlined some of the problems that they face as activists. Specifically, declaring oneself as a Black feminist was rarely well-received, especially in the context of the dominant white women's movement. Moreover, Black feminists struggle against multiple oppressions, making their work complicated and tiring. A lot of the time, the material conditions of Black women do not allow them to continue doing this radical feminist organizing. At the time, Black men were also not receptive to feminism, as the collective wrote, "accusations that Black feminism divides the Black struggle are powerful deterrents to the growth of an autonomous Black women's movement" (1978). Finally, disagreements based on class, political ideologies, and beliefs also remain while organizing, including splits based on sexual identities such as a split between lesbian-identifying and heterosexual-identifying Black women. Despite such hardships, the collective wrote that they were determined to collectively fight the interlocking systems of oppression that they found themselves in every day.

In the final section of the statement, "Black Feminist Issues and Projects," the authors end by identifying many issues that are still relevant to Black feminist struggles. They highlight the inclusiveness of their political work and their solidarity with Third World women and working-class people. Some of the key issues the collective worked on were "sterilization abuse, abortion rights, battered women, rape, and health care" (1978). They again asserted that the racism that they faced within the white women's movement had caused them a lot of harm. The narrow politics of the white women's movement did not account for the ways white women are racially privileged, continuing to benefit from the racism against Black people that they perpetuate. The collective ended their statement succinctly, writing, "as Black feminists and Lesbians we know that we have a very definite revolutionary task to perform and we are ready for the lifetime of work and struggle before us" (1978).

Legacy

The Combahee River Collective's 1978 statement continues to resonate within today's feminist movements and politics. Their critique of biological determinism significantly influenced the transgender rights movement. Their ideas of interlocking systems of oppression also form the basis for the development of the theoretical framework of intersectionality by Black feminist and legal scholar Kimberlé Crenshaw. And their solidarity with Third World women and working-class people continues to shape transnational feminism. In our present moment, when the Black Lives Matter movement has seen a resurgence in the wake of increasing police brutality and violence against Black people, especially Black women and trans folx, the Combahee River Collective Statement, and the passion and determination with which it was written in the 1970s, remains powerful.

Tapaswinee Mitra

See Also: #BlackLivesMatter; Civil Rights Movement; Interlocking Oppression; Intersectionality; Lorde, Audre; The Personal is Political; Radical Feminism; Socialism; Third World Women's Alliance and Black Woman's Manifesto; Transnational Feminism

Further Reading

Combahee River Collective. 1978. "The Combahee River Collective Statement." Accessed June 1, 2024. https://americanstudies.yale.edu/sites/default/files/files/Keyword%20Coalition_Readings.pdf.

Decherney, Sophia. 2023. "Combahee River Collective." *Encyclopedia Britannica*. Accessed June 1, 2024. https://www.britannica.com/topic/Combahee-River-Collective.

De Veaux, Alexis. 2004. *Warrior Poet: A Biography of Audre Lorde*. New York: W. W. Norton & Company.

Harris, Duchess. 2001. "From the Kennedy Commission to the Combahee Collective." In *Sisters in the Struggle*, edited by Collier-Thomas et al., 280–305. New York: New York University Press.

Hull, Gloria T., Patricia Bell Scott, and Barbara Smith, eds. 1982. *All the Women Are White, All the Blacks Are Men, But Some of Us Are Brave*. New York: The Feminist Press.

Moraga, Cherríe, and Gloria Anzaldúa, eds. 1981. *This Bridge Called My Back: Writings by Radical Women of Color*. New York: Kitchen Table: Women of Color Press.

Taylor, Keeanga-Yamahtta. 2017. *How We Get Free: Black Feminism and the Combahee River Collective*. Chicago: Haymarket Books.

Ware, Celestine. 1970. *Woman Power: The Movement for Women's Liberation*. New York: Tower Publications, Inc.

CONSCIOUSNESS RAISING

Consciousness raising is a form of feminist activism focused on bringing awareness, education, and action against oppression and injustice. Consciousness raising began with feminists who wanted to better educate themselves and others about women's oppression. Specifically, Kathie Sarachild began forming consciousness-raising groups in the late 1960s. Reflecting on these groups, she stated, "Consciousness-raising was seen as both a method for arriving at the truth and a means for action and organizing" (1975, 147).

In other words, consciousness raising was about analyzing the dominating "structures of society," such as patriarchy, and working toward "radical transformation" (McCarthy and Grosser 2023, 1153). In small group discussion—often meeting in community spaces or women's homes—women were encouraged to discuss their own experiences, unleashing "pent up hostility and rage about being victimized" (hooks 2015, 7). Consciousness-raising groups became a place where women could release and analyze their frustrations with sexism in a safe environment, taking the first step toward change and emphasizing the "importance of learning about patriarchy as a system of domination" (hooks 2015, 7).

Today, consciousness raising has "changed, expanded, and adapted to new social contexts" but remains a critical feminist practice (Sowards and Renegar 2004, 547). Social media in particular has paved the way for feminists across the world to connect, educate, and organize. For example, the Instagram account Feminist (@feminist), which describes itself as "the global hub for intersectional feminism today," educates its nearly six million followers about current and historical events. They have posts dedicated to defining terms such as "menopause" as well as posts highlighting feminist activists, such as Beth Moore Campbell (Feminist 2023, 2024a). For instance, they posted about an issue that took place at a Prague hospital where a patient was accidentally given a procedure that caused a miscarriage because she was mistaken for another Asian patient and because, according to the hospital, there was a language barrier. After giving the details of the event, Feminist asks the question "Why is this a feminist issue?" and then explains how "the mix-up highlights the intersection of language barriers and racism within reproductive health care" (Feminist 2024b). By highlighting instances of oppression such as this and directly demonstrating how feminist theory and activism speaks to these oppressions, this Instagram account participates in consciousness raising.

Consciousness raising started with a group of feminists who wanted to educate themselves and others about oppression, while discussing their own experiences with injustice. Consciousness raising remains an integral aspect of feminist theory building and activism (Turk 2023, 92). Consciousness raising is an essential part of change because it not only asks us to pay attention to injustice but also to examine our own beliefs about women and intersecting identities.

Sage Mikkelsen

See Also: Cyberfeminism; Hashtag Activism; Patriarchy; Women's Liberation Movement

Further Reading

Feminist (@feminist). 2023. "Menopause." *Instagram*, October 18, 2023. Accessed August 24, 2024. https://www.instagram.com/p/Cyiu9JmgIUR/.

Feminist (@feminist). 2024a. "Beth Moore Campbell." *Instagram,* July 1, 2024. Accessed August 24, 2024. https://www.instagram.com/p/C85QLkuJ6JC/.

Feminist (@feminist). 2024b. "Language Barrier at Prague Hospital Causes Mix-up Between Asian Patients, Resulting in Unintended Miscarriage." *Instagram,* April 18, 2024. Accessed August 24, 2024. https://www.instagram.com/p/C56LpboLhaf/?igsh=MTdsZTFiaHQ1dWF1dg%3D%3D&img_index=1.

hooks, bell. 2015. *Feminism Is for Everybody: Passionate Politics*, 2nd ed. New York: Routledge.

McCarthy, L., and Kate Grosser. 2023. "Breaking Isolation: Consciousness-raising as a Methodology for Academic Activism." *Organization* 30, no. 5: 1152–67. https://doi.org/10.1177/13505084231166172.

Sarachild, Kathie. 1975. "Consciousness–Raising: A Radical Weapon." In *Feminist Revolution: An Abridged Edition with Additional Writings*, edited by Redstockings of the Women's Liberation Movement, 144–50. New York: Random House.

Sowards, Stacey K., and Valerie R. Renegar. 2004. "The Rhetorical Functions of Consciousness-raising in Third Wave Feminism." *Communication Studies* 55, no. 4: 535–52. https://doi.org/10.1080/10510970409388637.

Turk, Katherine. 2023. *The Women of NOW: How Feminists Built an Organization That Transformed America.* New York: Farrar, Straus and Giroux.

CRENSHAW, KIMBERLÉ

Kimberlé Crenshaw (1959–) is a feminist legal scholar whose work on Critical Race Theory and intersectionality has been foundational for scholars of all fields. Beginning in the 1980s, Crenshaw's work on intersectionality is an important framework for analyzing how power hierarchies and structures affect people in overlapping—or intersecting—ways based on their identities. Likewise, Crenshaw's insights into Critical Race Theory are necessary examinations of how racial biases are upheld in US laws and policies in ways that are detrimental to the lives of people of color.

Crenshaw is a Distinguished Professor of Law and the Promise Institute Chair in Human Rights at the University of California, Los Angeles School of Law. She holds a joint appointment as the Isidor and Seville Sulzbacher Professor of Law at the Columbia Law School. Crenshaw received her bachelor's from Cornell University, her JD from Harvard Law School, and her LLM from the University of Wisconsin (Crenshaw 2022).

Crenshaw's Scholarship

Crenshaw's scholarship has been an important contribution to feminist theory and practice, helping feminists and activists build an understanding of how people's conditions can change their experiences in the world. In other words, Crenshaw's work gives new perspective to human's relationships to each other, their identities, and structures—such as US laws, HR policies, hiring practices, and police practices. Her scholarship, while foundational to many fields, focuses on legal implications. As a result, the most applicable field for Crenshaw's work is that of legal scholarship and practice.

Nevertheless, scholars in all fields can use Crenshaw's frameworks to inform their own work and deepen the understanding of interlocking oppression and marginalized people.

Crenshaw wrote two popular pieces on intersectionality in 1989 and 1991, well before the public commonly considered the impact of intersecting identities on a person's experiences with oppression. Crenshaw's first article was in the University of Chicago Legal Forum and focused on developing a Black feminist criticism that centered and compared the "multidimensionality of Black women's experience with the single-axis analysis that distorts these experiences" (Crenshaw 1989, 139). This article is a foundational piece and its ideas are amplified by feminists who highlight the inequities that Black women and other women of color face in comparison to their white and/or male counterparts.

Crenshaw's second article was published in the Stanford Law Review and focused on broadening the concept of what is now known as "identity politics" with an intersectional frame, asserting that "identity politics" fail to consider that "the violence that many women experience is often shaped by other dimensions of their identities, such as race and class" (Crenshaw 1991, 1242). Further, the article examines three types of intersectionality: structural, political, and representational. Crenshaw uses these frames to explain intersectionality, making it more detailed and applicable in various realms of life.

In 1995, Crenshaw was one of the editors of a book on Critical Race Theory, which collected foundational writings from people who developed this area of scholarship. Coupled with Crenshaw's previous work on intersectionality and her work highlighting Black women's experiences, Crenshaw became a leading figure in Critical Race Theory and its expansion into wider audiences.

Crenshaw Recently

In recent years, Kimberlé Crenshaw has done a wide range of academic and nonacademic outreach regarding intersectionality and Critical Race Theory. In 2016, Crenshaw delivered a TEDTalk titled "The Urgency of Intersectionality," in which she urged people to pay attention to the experiences of people with multiple marginalized identities. Specifically, Crenshaw champions the #SayHerName campaign, drawing attention to the way racism and sexism combine in police practices, resulting in the disproportionate deaths of women of color during police interactions. In 2024, Crenshaw published an article in *The Guardian* addressing racism within "anti-woke," "All Lives Matter," and "Make America Great Again" (MAGA) extremists, connecting said racism to the destruction of US democracy (Crenshaw 2024).

Crenshaw's contributions to feminism and the feminist movement are vital. Thanks to Crenshaw's scholarship, feminists are now more aware of how power operates in intersectional ways and better able to advocate for the equality for all races and sexes.

Ryan Hall

See Also: #BlackLivesMatter; Critical Race Theory; Interlocking Oppression; Intersectionality; Racist Stereotypes; #SayHerName

Further Reading

Crenshaw, Kimberlé. 1989. "Demarginalizing the Intersection of Race and Sex: A Black Feminist Critique of Antidiscrimination Doctrine, Feminist Theory, and Antiracist Politics." *University of Chicago Legal Forum* 1, no. 8: 139–67.

Crenshaw, Kimberlé. 1991. "Mapping the Margins: Intersectionality, Identity Politics, and Violence against Women of Color." *Stanford Law Review* 43, no. 6: 1241–99.

Crenshaw, Kimberlé. 2016. "The Urgency of Intersectionality." *TED*. https://www.youtube.com/watch?v=akOe5-UsQ2o.

Crenshaw, Kimberlé. 2022. *Curriculum Vitae*. Accessed October 30, 2024. https://www.law.columbia.edu/sites/default/files/2024-09/crenshaw_kimberle_cv.pdf

Crenshaw, Kimberlé. 2024. "American Democracy Is in Peril. And Racism Will be the Sledgehammer That Destroys it." *The Guardian*, September 6, 2024. https://www.theguardian.com/commentisfree/article/2024/sep/06/us-racism-maga-fascism-anti-woke-democracy.

Crenshaw, Kimberlé, Neil Gotanda, Gary Peller, and Kendall Thomas. 1995. *Critical Race Theory: The Key Writings that Formed the Movement*. New York: The New Press.

CRITICAL RACE THEORY

Critical Race Theory (CRT) is historically rooted in Kimberlé Crenshaw's legal scholarship examining how racism is embedded in the legal system and in government policy as opposed to thinking of racism as primarily individual prejudice (Sawchuck 2021; Fortin 2021). Although it began in legal scholarship, CRT is now widely used in academic research as a framework that focuses scholars' attention on studying how racism is embedded in systems themselves—like television's economic system of production, which results in extremely few Black women as TV protagonists.

Since CRT is widely used by scholars in fields such as political science, media and communication, sociology, psychology, computer science, economics, and so on, there can be a lot of differences in how people use CRT and what people mean by CRT. But in general, scholars who use CRT reject "colorblindness" or "post-racism," meaning that they recognize how even neutral policies (structures and systems that are not supposed to "see color") can still be oppressive for marginalized groups. Additionally, when scholars use CRT to focus their research, they are typically asking research questions about how racist hierarchies are enforced and how various systems (such as laws) reinforce racist hierarchies—even among people with good intentions (Fortin 2021).

A law professor at both UCLA and Columbia Law School, Kimberlé Crenshaw's work on intersectionality is considered the foundation of CRT (Fortin 2021). She highlighted the ways that systems such as racism and sexism impact people's lives in multiple and overlapping ways, often obscuring the impacts of each specific form of discrimination (Crenshaw 1989). Other early developers of CRT include Mari Matsuda and the late Derrick Bell, also law professors. Black feminist scholars have embraced CRT, challenging readers to consider identity and politics in an intersectional manner, examining how systems of oppression like sexism converge with racism and other systems, reinforcing each other (Smith 2021).

Feminism and CRT

Feminists use CRT to study how racism, sexism, and other systems, such as political power, social organization, and even language, intersect to create multifaceted experiences of oppression (Sawchuck 2021). By adding a gendered lens to CRT, feminists can better understand how race and gender intersect, revealing the complex, overlapping systems of oppression that shape marginalized people's experiences. Feminist theorists and activists who use CRT often stress the importance of coalition building, arguing that the struggle for racial justice is inseparable from the fight for gender equity.

CRT's influence extends beyond theory, shaping contemporary debates on education, public policy, and social justice. Feminist applications of CRT include:

- **Legal advocacy:** Legal scholars have used CRT to challenge laws and policies that marginalize women and other people of color. For example, CRT-informed legal challenges have exposed discriminatory policing practices (DaViera et al. 2023) and advocated for improvements in the workplace (Hernandez 2024).

- **Education and curriculum:** CRT has influenced educational frameworks, advocating for the inclusion of ethnic studies and anti-racist teaching strategies. Feminist scholars support these efforts, arguing that intersectional education fosters greater empathy and critical thinking (Ladson-Billings in Anderson 2022).
- **Public health and medicine:** CRT's focus on structural racism has informed feminist critiques of healthcare disparities. Black women's disproportionate maternal mortality rates, for example, reflect the intersection of racism, sexism, and inadequate healthcare access (Ogunwole et al. 2023).
- **Workplace and labor rights:** CRT and feminism intersect in workplace advocacy, particularly regarding pay equity, discrimination, harassment, and labor organizing. Feminist CRT activists highlight how women of color are often underpaid and underrepresented in leadership roles, despite diversity initiatives, and often push for unionization as an answer to the challenges of intersectional oppression (Gates et al. 2022).

In addition to helping people study how racism operates within seemingly "colorblind" or neutral systems, and thus helping activists resist systems of oppression, CRT has also offered a critique of "white feminism," arguing that white feminists have co-opted struggles for racial justice while failing to address needs specific to women of color. Examples of these failures include how Black women were pushed to the margins of the women's suffrage movement and mainstream feminism's prioritization of workplace equality in the 1970s and 1980s that ignored racial disparities in things like pay rates and job security.

What's Next?

As the feminist movement continues to evolve and grow, CRT is a valuable tool to address contemporary issues such as:

- **Algorithmic bias:** CRT can be applied to technology and artificial intelligence, examining how algorithms reinforce racial and gender biases, exacerbating and extending the reach of existing systems of oppression.
- **Environmental racism:** Feminist CRT scholars are exploring how race, gender, and class intersect in environmental justice movements (Sovacool et al. 2023).
- **Transnational feminist CRT:** Transnational feminists are expanding CRT beyond the United States, analyzing how colonialism, race, and gender intersect in global contexts (Wing 2000).

By centering the voices and experiences of marginalized communities, feminist CRT challenges the erasure of women of color from mainstream legal, political, and feminist discourses. In a time of escalating political backlash, feminists' use of CRT remains an essential tool for advancing social justice and equity and understanding how race, gender, and other social identities intersect to shape experiences of oppression.

Devon S. Torchiana

See Also: #BlackLivesMatter; Interlocking Oppression; Intersectionality; Labor Activism; Post-racism; Transnational Feminism; White Privilege; Whiteness as Property

Further Reading

Anderson, Jill. 2022. "The State of Critical Race Theory in Education." *Harvard EdCast*, February 23, 2022. Accessed March 26, 2025. https://www.gse.harvard.edu/ideas/edcast/22/02/state-critical-race-theory-education.

Coaston, Jane. 2019. "The Intersectionality Wars." *Vox*, May 28, 2019. https://www.vox.com/the-highlight/2019/5/20/18542843/intersectionality-conservatism-law-race-gender-discrimination.

Crenshaw, Kimberlé. 1989. "Demarginalizing the Intersection of Race and Sex: A Black Feminist Critique of Antidiscrimination Doctrine, Feminist Theory and Antiracist Politics." *University of Chicago Legal Forum* 1, no. 8: 139–67.

DaViera, Andrea L., Marbella Uriostegui, Aaron Gottlieb, and Ogechi (Cynthia) Onyeka. 2023. "Risk, Race, and Predictive Policing: A Critical Race Theory Analysis of the Strategic Subject List." *American Journal of Community Psychology* 73, no. 1–2: 91–103.

Fortin, Jacey. 2021. "Critical Race Theory: A Brief History." *The New York Times*, November 8, 2021. https://www.nytimes.com/article/what-is-critical-race-theory.html.

Gates, Stacey Davis, Sheri Davis, Marilyn Sneiderman, and Alisha Volante. 2022. "Critical Race Feminism and Common Good Unionism." *NonProfit Quarterly*, September 28, 2022. Accessed March 14, 2025. https://nonprofitquarterly.org/critical-race-feminism-and-common-good-unionism/.

Hernandez, Tanya Kateri. 2024. "Can CRT Save DEI?: Workplace Diversity, Equity & Inclusion in the Shadow of Anti-Affirmative Action." *UCLA Law Review* 71: 2–39.

Ogunwole, S. Michelle, Habibat A. Oguntade, Kelly M. Bower, Lisa A. Cooper, and Wendy L. Bennett. 2023. "Health Experiences of African American Mothers, Wellness in the Postpartum Period and Beyond (HEAL): A Qualitative Study Applying a Critical Race Feminist Theoretical Framework." *International Journal of Environmental Research and Public Health* 20, no. 13: 1–29.

Sawchuck, Stephen. 2021. "What is Critical Race Theory, and Why is it Under Attack?" *EducationWeek*, May 18, 2021. Accessed March 14, 2025. https://www.edweek.org/leadership/what-is-critical-race-theory-and-why-is-it-under-attack/2021/05.

Smith, Kaitlin. 2021. "Exploring Audre Lorde's Intersectionality." *Facing History & Ourselves*, June 24, 2021. Accessed March 12, 2025. https://www.facinghistory.org/ideas-week/exploring-audre-lordes-intersectionality.

Sovacool, Benjamin K., Shannon Elizabeth Bell, Cara Daggett, Christine Labuski, Myles Lennon, Lindsay Naylor, Julie Klinger, Kelsey Leonard, Jeremy Firestone. 2023. "Pluralizing Energy Justice: Incorporating Feminist, Anti-racist, Indigenous, and Postcolonial Perspectives." *Energy Research & Social Science* 97: 2–8.

Wing, Adrien Katherine. 2000. *Global Critical Race Feminism*. New York: New York University Press.

CULT OF TRUE WOMANHOOD

Feminist historian Barbara Welter (1966) famously studied and coined the "Cult of True Womanhood," a predominant cultural attitude concerning women around the turn of the nineteenth century. "The Cult," short for culture, endorsed four cardinal virtues—piety (religious devotion), purity (chastity outside of marriage), submissiveness (obedience to husbands), and domesticity (homemaking)—as *ideal* womanhood. From magazines to school textbooks, Welter found that literature idealizing these four virtues as an aspirational form of "true" *femininity* (the expression of womanhood) trained American women to be subservient to, and to depend heavily on, men.

The Cult's aesthetics often depicted women as delicate and frail, making their inferiority seem natural—even romantic. Vintage issues of *The Ladies Home Journal*, for instance, show women constantly positioned in relation to nature (i.e., among trees, meadows, and/or naked infants) and regularly addressed in terms of their relation to men (i.e., articles on how to behave in a new marriage). Conveying femininity through soft, delicate symbols—think flowers, butterflies, flowy white fabrics—was a common feature of poetic realism, a predominant style in the Victorian era; however, such literature helped to sentimentalize *gender essentialism* (the idea that there is a true nature, or *essence*, to being male or female). Representing "woman's" frailty as natural rather than a cultural creation, the Cult's romantic aesthetic concealed anti-feminist principles. In reality, the four virtues functioned together to quietly subjugate mostly middle-class white women to a life under patriarchal domination.

The Victorian era was also marked by major structural shifts in Europe and North America that necessarily modified the ideals associated with "womanhood." Economic factors such as rapid industrial progress, the emergence of class-based societies, and drastic increases in poverty/exploitation all converged with Victorian ideals to devalue "women's roles," further materializing the ideals advanced by the Cult into ordinary systems of oppression. We can still locate this influence in modern expectations of women where traditional, often Eurocentric and white supremacist standards of femininity prevail.

In Christian religious rhetoric, for instance, a Culture of True Womanhood suggests to women that their "virtue," in other words their morality, depends on their embodiment of piety, purity, submissiveness, and domesticity (Kornfield 2023). Here, "good wives" trust husbands to protect the family and concentrate their own efforts on moral enrichment and domestic service. Within this way of thinking, rejecting marriage and mothering or seeking a life of influence outside the home is not just unusual, it is considered unnatural and immoral.

Today, women and gender diverse people who break the mold set out by the Cult of True Womanhood face threats of social intolerance, economic struggles, familial conflict, and, in extreme but common cases, gender-based violence.

Cultural Influences, Imperfections, and Implications

Corresponding with the major shift toward capitalism during the nineteenth-century Market Revolution, American men moved in droves into industrial workplaces while women remained home with the expectation of performing the homestead's "softer" duties. These women were convinced to view themselves as too weak—physically and mentally—for physical labor (excluding reproductive and domestic labor) and instead to concern themselves with moral and domestic enrichment. From here, ideas about "women's work" and "women's roles" developed in contrast to men's public and professional locations.

Paradoxically, while the alleged frailty of white women suggested that they were not well suited for "hard" labor, nonwhite women were routinely exploited for theirs. Glenda Dickerson (1988) highlights the contradiction in which the Cult of True Womanhood ensnared many Black women: firstly, "the 'cult' became virtually synonymous with the upper class because only they had the luxury of leisure. Women of color were triply locked out: by class, by race, and by history—they had been made the mule of the world in slavery, how could they now aspire to silk parasols and satin dresses" (179). Then, and despite many Black feminists and abolitionists "abhorring the 'cult,'" they found themselves inescapably "aspiring to its tenants" in their efforts to "lift up the race" (179; 182).

In a now-famous example, abolitionist Sojourner Truth's (1851) Ohio Women's Rights Convention address "Ain't I a Woman?" asked why her experience as a Black woman should look so unlike white "womanhood." She observed how Black women in general were not treated with equal care: "That man over there says that women need to be helped into carriages, and lifted over ditches, and to have the best place everywhere. Nobody ever helps *me* into carriages, or over mud-puddles, or gives *me* any best place! And ain't *I* a woman?" (emphasis added). Truth's famous question highlighted how the category of "true" womanhood excluded Black women, and it helps to trouble the notion of womanhood in general. The Cult reinforced a narrow view of womanhood but ignored that its ideals were not attainable for, afforded to, or even sought after by many women.

Some people believe that the Cult of True Womanhood weakened around the Civil War or phased out with advances in feminism. However, in many cultures, myths about the virtues of womanhood/femininity endure. The Cult's virtues are visible in religious discourse (especially Christian fundamentalist cultures), popular literature and media (i.e., the classic midcentury housewife trope), political rhetoric (i.e., trans/gender panic from conservative demagogues and trans-exclusionary radical feminists, or TERFs), and even in social media lifestyle trends (i.e., the #TradWife movement on TikTok).

Feminist Reckonings with the Virtues of "Womanhood"

Women's rights activists confronted the Cult of True Womanhood in several ways throughout the twentieth century. While some tried moving beyond essentialist ideals of "womanhood," others leaned into them. Those who viewed women's domesticity as beneficial to society fought to bring respect and technological sophistication to housework. Early feminists like Catharine Beecher (1848) and Ellen Richards championed "domestic femininity" to defend girls' education (home economics) and increase professional opportunities. Comparatively, women's liberationists wanted to free women from domesticity ideologically. In 1898, Charlotte Perkins Gilman's famous manifesto *Women and Economics* urged women to liberate themselves from "domestic mythology" holding them in states of dependence with men (2023).

Merging some of the Cult's ideas about womanhood with socialist ideals, "public housekeeping" feminism argued that the moral and domestic skills associated with womanhood, if used for public service, could help to "clean up" society (Addams 1910). The Woman's Peace Party founded by Jane Addams and Carrie Chapman Catt in 1915, for example, worked to support the First World War soldiers, organize suffrage movements, and reduce corruption in immigration law. The public housekeeping approach provoked some philosophical incongruities among feminist causes. Liberal feminists such as Ellen Key (1914) valorized motherhood as a morally superior endeavor to argue for state-supported caregiving. In contrast, anarchist feminists such as Emma Goldman (1969) downplayed any notion of "special" strengths to redirect focus on how women's domestic exploitation restricted their ability to fight for political and economic autonomy.

In 1963, Betty Friedan's *The Feminine Mystique* (2013) famously revealed the Cult of True Womanhood as a pervasive myth, though in different words. Friedan exposed the psychological distress of suburban housewives aspiring to the image of "true" womanhood, coining "the feminine mystique" to describe this false ideal. She found that housewives often felt unfulfilled by the pursuit of ideal femininity and encouraged women to seek self-actualization through work and intellectual pursuits outside marriage, sex, and motherhood. Importantly, and as bell hooks (2000) critiqued, Friedan's work largely privileged the needs of white middle-class women, neglecting the experiences of those barred from the "true" womanhood ideal, such as single mothers, unmarried women, lesbians, and women without the racial or socioeconomic privilege to live as housewives.

Twentieth-century Marxist feminism altogether rejected the notion of domesticity as leisurely and recast the domestic realm as "domestic enclosure" to argue that women and their domestic labor are "enclosed"—or socially and economically trapped and exploited—by capitalism (Federici 2004). From this standpoint, the naturalization of domestic subservience helps to carry out gendered exploitation via "unwaged" reproductive labor.

Unfortunately, anti-feminists have also drawn on the Culture of True Womanhood's ideals to advance their causes. A famous example of this is "moral conservative" Phyllis Schlafly who organized *against* the Equal Rights Amendment (ERA) in the 1970s, arguing that the ERA would rob housewives of essential privileges like "dependent wife" benefits and exemption from military service.

Schlafly's "family values" campaign relied on essential gender roles, cast women's dependency as idyllic, and ultimately obstructed ratification of the ERA across the United States.

Cultures of Contrasting Femininities

Despite significant and sustained feminist resistance, the Cult of True Womanhood has cast a long shadow over culturally specific and essentialist ideals about womanhood in the United States. Within white middle-class communities, and especially in conservative and religious communities, women are still held to expectations of chastity, submissiveness, and domesticity. They are expected to *want* to marry men and stay home with their children, even though this is often economically impossible even for middle-class families. Young women in college are sometimes denigrated, or themselves identify, as pursuing a "MRS" degree—an assumption that (straight, white, middle- to upper-class) women only attend college to find a husband.

Contemporary queer theory and activism challenge gender essentialism by deconstructing gender and sexuality, but fully escaping the built-in contradictions of "true" womanhood remains complex. For instance, self-identified "cottagecore lesbians" embrace a domestic aesthetic through the online #cottagecore trend. While shared pastoral-feminine aesthetics may make it *appear* as though #CottagecoreLesbians have much in common with #TradWives, in reality their goals differ significantly. Femme/queer cottagecore acknowledges—sometimes satirically—that the concept of "women's work" is a sexist and racist construct invested in male-female relationships and racial capital. As Cora Butcher-Spellman (2024) notes, #queercottagecore pushes back against neoliberal capitalism's hustle culture's #girlboss feminism in favor of slowness, self-sufficiency, resource sharing, and community. Contrastingly, #TradWives view a pastoral lifestyle not as a way to achieve independence but as a way to dodge what they see as a liberal push toward professional wage labor, preferring instead to staying home with their children. While both #cottagecores use a romantic pastoral fantasy to escape modern pressures, #queercottagecore *critiques* capitalism and the essentialist exploitation it engenders, whereas #tradwifecottagecore romanticizes it (Butcher-Spellman 2024). Like when Catharine Beecher and Phyllis Schlafly used similar essentialist ideals of womanhood to support both feminist and anti-feminist agendas, respectively, this highlights the need to recognize which movements fight *for* gender liberation and which rally *against* it.

Talia E. Kibsey

See Also: Domestic Labor; *The Feminine Mystique*; Purity Culture; Queer Theory; Trans-Exclusionary Radical Feminists (TERFs)

Further Reading

Addams, Jane. 1910. *Women and Public Housekeeping*. National Woman Suffrage Publishing Company, Incorporated.

Beecher, Catharine E. 1848. *A Treatise on Domestic Economy, For the Use of Young Ladies at Home, and at School*. New York: Harper.

Butcher-Spellman, Cora. 2024. "Selling Financial Feminism: How Personal Finance Education is Commodified as Feminist Praxis." Conference Presentation, Digital Humanities Summer Institute, Victoria, BC, June 6, 2024.

Christou, Miranda. 2020. "#TradWives: Sexism as a Gateway to White Supremacy." *Open Democracy*, March 17, 2020. Accessed 15 August 2024.

Click Americana. 2020. "Antique Ladies' Home Journal Magazine Covers & Subjects from the Victorian Era." Last updated July 1, 2020. Accessed 12 August 2024.

Dickerson, Glenda. 1988. "The Cult of True Womanhood: Toward a Womanist Attitude in African-American Theatre." *Theatre Journal* 40, no. 2: 178–87.
Federici, Silvia. 2004. *Caliban and the Witch*. Brooklyn, NY: Autonomedia.
Friedan, Betty. 2013. *The Feminine Mystique: 50 Years*. New York: WW Norton & Company.
Gilman, Charlotte Perkins. 2023. "Women and Economics." In *Women's Economic Writing in the Nineteenth Century*, edited by Lana L. Dalley, 132–57. London: Routledge.
hooks, bell. 2000. *Feminist Theory: From Margin to Center*. London: Pluto Press.
Kornfield, Sarah. 2023. "Spiritual Mothers: Evangelical Practices of Mothering in the 21st-Century." In *Refiguring Motherhood: Beyond Biology*, edited by Valerie Renegar and Kirsti Cole. New York: Routledge.
Stage, Sarah. 1997. "Ellen Richards and the Social Significance of the Home Economics Movement." In *Rethinking Home Economics: Women and the History of a Profession*, edited by Sarah Stage and Virginia B. Vincenti, 17–33. Ithaca and London: Cornell University Press.
Truth, Sojourner. 1851. "Ain't I a Woman?" In *Ain't I a Woman?*, edited by Patricia C. McKissack and Fredrick L. McKissack, 1–10. New York: Scholastic, 1992.
Welter, Barbara. 1966. "The Cult of True Womanhood: 1820–1860." *American Quarterly* 18, no. 2: 151–74.
White, Ro. 2020. "What is Cottagecore and Why do Young Queer People Love It?" *Autostraddle*, September 30, 2020. Accessed 15 August 2024.

CYBERFEMINISM

In the 1990s, cyberfeminism emerged as a branch of feminist theory and activism, focused on unpacking how power operates at the intersections of gender, sex, and technology. As with many postmodern theories, cyberfeminism has also been hard to define, although many attempts have been made. *Cyberfeminism Index* (Seu 2023) traces the multiple histories, legacies, and iterations of cyberfeminism. Famously, at the First Cyberfeminist International Conference in Germany, in 1997, participants attempted to define cyberfeminism but instead ended up with 100 anti-theses, which are a set of statements outlining what cyberfeminism is not (Old Boys Network 1997). However, VNS Matrix, an Australian art collective, and Sadie Plant, a feminist academic, are often credited with coining the term "cyberfeminism" to describe feminist work about the internet, online spaces, and digital technologies in the 1990s.

The Evolution of Cyberfeminist Theories

Even prior to the emergence of the term cyberfeminism, feminists had been examining the links between gender and technology. For example, Cockburn (1983) showcased how women's contributions are excluded from discussions of technological development. Relatedly, in *Feminism Confronts Technology*, Wajcman (1991) demonstrated how male biases in the development of reproductive and domestic technologies led to these technologies affirming traditional female social roles. This strand of scholarship, in general, showed how technology might limit gender equality. In contrast, others like Sadie Plant (1997) argued for understanding technology and feminism as particularly well-aligned.

In contrast to Plant's (1997) approach, which has been critiqued for retrenching a very narrow definition of woman, Donna Haraway's (1985) essay "A Cyborg Manifesto" embraced a much more open-ended understanding of sex and gender. Her essay continues to animate contemporary feminist theorizing because her argument moves us away from essentialist understandings of sex and/or gender (i.e., moves us away from the idea that being a woman or a man comprises an essential or unchanging set of characteristics, both biological and social). Haraway proposed the cyborg as a framework for understanding the intimate ways in which humans and technology are integrated (or have the potential to be integrated). Indeed, she claimed we are all cyborgs because technology is now so prevalent that by interfacing with it, we have reworked what it means to be human.

For example, although we might not immediately think of reading glasses as a technology, they are, in fact, a technology that allows us to enhance or correct the biological limits of our vision. Similarly, those of us who use fitness trackers might modify our behaviors and our fitness levels (including weight) in response to data provided by these trackers. This integration between technology and humans is now so intimate, Haraway argued, that it has eliminated "the validity of essentialist understandings of human nature," including the specific "social roles reserved for each of the sexes which are based in biological differences between them, in addition to other differences such as age or race" (Ahmad 2019). For feminists this argument has been enormously generative: if the link between technology and gender is socially constructed rather than natural, then it is open to being reconstructed or reimagined. Thus, technology *can* be used to achieve feminist goals such as challenging the links between bodies and social roles, examining the types of female bodies being fashioned through technology, and critiquing the ways in which technology can be used to limit agency.

Doing Cyberfeminism

Chicana feminist Chéla Sandoval's (1994) work clarified how cyberfeminism, with its goals of destabilizing binaries and exposing the shifting, socially constructed nature of identities, can operate in ways that are aligned with intersectional feminist goals and be helpful in coalition building. Sandoval (1995) developed the idea of cyborg consciousness to articulate the similarities between the political potential of Haraway's cyborg and the theorizing of US women of color feminists. Feminists continue to work on making cyberfeminism more robustly intersectional. Kishonna Gray, for example, developed Black cyberfeminism to address the critique that "traditional virtual feminist frameworks do not effectively grasp the reality of all women" and to "help theorize the digital and intersecting lives of women" (Gray 2015, 176). To negotiate the criticism that cyberfeminism is too abstract and disembodied, Daniels (2009, 101) recommends refocusing cyberfeminism in material realities by emphasizing "the lived experience and actual Internet practices of girls and self-identified women" to learn how "they use the Internet to transform their material, corporeal lives in a number of complex ways that both resist and reinforce hierarchies of gender and race." This refocusing aligns with Radhika Gajjala's (2003, 49) rationale for a "subaltern cyberfeminism from below" that is attentive to issues of labor and globalization wherein women from the Global South are often the ones working to build the technologies used by women in the Global North but rarely reap the benefits of these technologies.

While early cyberfeminists were criticized for being overly optimistic about technology's potential for feminist liberation and echoing narrow definitions of womanhood, today, most cyberfeminists forward a more nuanced version of the role technology plays in achieving feminist goals. As Fellows and Smith (2022, 306) explain,

> technology can bring progress but does not do so uniformly. It can give us hope but also leads to dangers. It can bring power, but that power is not evenly distributed across populations. And it can allow knowledge to be gained, but we should be critical of who is gaining that knowledge and to what purposes they are putting that knowledge towards.

Still, it is important to acknowledge that given the erasures of women of color during early cyberfeminist theorizing, not all the scholars who work at the intersections of feminism and technology use the term "cyberfeminism" to describe their work. For example, in *Digital Black Feminism*, Catherine Knight Steele (2021, 15) uses "the term digital instead of cyber to likewise disrupt cyber studies that place Black women on the periphery."

Key Areas of Cyberfeminism

Cyberfeminism is an exciting and challenging branch of feminism. Cyberfeminism affects many areas of our lives, and below are key areas of cyberfeminist theorizing.

1. *Activist art*: This work often echoes the playful, irreverent, and political tendencies that were centered in the activist art endeavors of early cyberfeminist collectives such as VNS Matrix (n.d.) who sought to "hijack the toys from technocowboys and remap cyberculture with a feminist bent." For example, sub-Rosa is a famous cyberfeminist art collective which derives its name from feminist icons such as Rosa Bonheur, Rosa Luxemburg, Rosie the Riveter, Rosa Parks, and Rosie Franklin; sub-Rosa (n.d.) creates artworks that "explore and critique the effects of the intersections of the new information and biotechnologies on women's bodies, lives, and work."
2. *Online activism*: This encompasses examining the use of platforms and social media to further feminist causes. For example, Rachel Loney-Howes et al. (2022) places the #MeToo movement within a larger global archive of feminist activism regarding sexual violence. Other areas of feminist research include gendered online harassment and digital surveillance and privacy.
3. *Technology development and design*: Much cyberfeminist work has involved recovering the contributions of the women and other marginalized groups in histories of technological innovation. Additionally, some feminists have focused on expanding women's access to technology. Still others have critically examined the design and process via which technologies are developed to show how racism, sexism, and other inequities are baked into the process. Alison Adam (1998), for example, has explored how artificial intelligence models are gendered while also explaining what feminist artificial intelligence might entail.
4. *Cyborg identities*: Jennifer Hites-Thomas (2022, 222) analyzed how the medical discourse around gender-affirming surgeries acts as a form of biased gatekeeping, by "framing male enhancement technologies as augmenting the nature of cis men's bodies and transition technologies as harming the nature of gender/sex congruence." This study is an example of how cyberfeminist scholarship has interrogated very literal ways in which the joining of technology with flesh shapes our understanding of what it means to be human or a particular sex.
5. *Digital culture*: A number of scholars have examined how women and marginalized groups engage with technologies to enact agency by creating communities and exploring their identities. Others have explored how women and marginalized groups might use technology to challenge taken-for-granted ideas about technology. Lisa Nakamura (2002) showed how cyberspace does not necessarily mean leaving behind one's offline social identities and that often, marginalizing experiences can extend into cyberspace. Still others, however, have found online spaces helpful for better understanding their own identities and negotiating challenges that these identities might encounter offline. For example, Marcinao (2014, 834) found that "Using cyberspace as an alternative sphere enables transgender users to undergo meaningful experiences that are hard to attain in the offline world. These experiences include maintaining a chosen identity and building a romantic relationship online." Thus, scholars of digital culture have usually been particularly attentive to how ideas or narratives about technology intersect with how people engage with technology, while avoiding oversimplifications that position technology either as the ultimate solution or problem.

Although this list is not comprehensive, and the categories presented above are interconnected rather than mutually exclusive, it outlines the broad contours of this ever-evolving branch of feminist work.

Marissa Joanna Doshi

See Also: Cyborg Manifesto; Essentialism; Hashtag Activism; #MeToo; Transnational Feminism

Further Reading

Adam, Alison. 1998. *Artificial Knowing: Gender and the Thinking Machine*. New York: Routledge.
Ahmad, Nour. 2019. "We are All Cyborgs: How Machines Can Be a Feminist Tool." *International Media Support*. Last modified May 9, 2019. https://www.mediasupport.org/navigating-a-changing-world/we-are-all-cyborgs-how-machines-can-be-a-feminist-tool/.
Cockburn, Cynthia. 1983. *Brothers: Male Dominance and Technological Change*. London: Pluto Press.
Daniels, Jessie. 2009. *Cyber Racism: White Supremacy Online and the New Attack on Civil Rights*. New York: Rowman and Littlefield.
Fellows, Jennifer Jill, and Lisa Smith. 2022. *Gender, Sex, and Tech! An Intersectional Feminist Guide*. Toronto: Women's Press.
Gajjala, Radhika. 2003. "South Asian Digital Diasporas and Cyberfeminist Webs: Negotiating Globalization, Nation, Gender, and Information Technology Design." *Contemporary South Asia* 12, no. 1: 41–56.
Gray, Kishonna. 2015. "Race, Gender, and Virtual Inequality: Exploring the Liberatory Potential of Black Cyberfeminist Theory." In *Produsing Theory in a Digital World 2.0: The Intersection of Audiences and Production in Contemporary Theory* edited by Rebecca Lind, 175–92. New York: Peter Lang.
Haraway, Donna. 1985. "A Manifesto for Cyborgs: Science, Technology, and Socialist Feminism in the 1980s." *Socialist Review* 80: 65–108.
Hites-Thomas, Jennifer. 2022. "Gatekeeping 'Authentic' Gender: The Somatechnics of Transition Surgery and Male Enhancement." In *Gender, Sex, and Tech! An Intersectional Feminist Guide* edited by Jennifer Jill Fellows and Lisa Smith, 207–29. Toronto: Women's Press.
Loney-Howes, Rachel, Kaitlynn Mendes, Diana Fernández Romero, Bianca Fileborn, and Sonia Núñez Puente. 2022. "Digital Footprints of #MeToo." *Feminist Media Studies* 22, no. 6: 1345–62.
Marciano, Avi. 2014. "Living the VirtuReal: Negotiating Transgender Identity in Cyberspace." *Journal of Computer-Mediated Communication* 19, no. 4: 824–38.
Nakamura, Lisa. 2002. *Cybertypes: Race, Ethnicity, and Identity on the Internet*. New York: Routledge.
Old Boys Network. 1997. "100 Anti-Theses of Cyberfeminism." Accessed April 25, 2024. https://obn.org/obn/inhalt_index.html.
Plant, Sadie. 1997. *Zeroes and Ones: Digital Women and the New Technoculture*. London: Fourth Estate.
Sandoval, Chéla. 1994. "Re-entering Cyberspaces: Sciences of Resistance." *Dispositio* 19, no. 46: 75–93. http://www.jstor.org/stable/41491506.
Sandoval, Chéla. 1995. "New Sciences: Cyborg Feminism and the Methodology of the Oppressed," *Cybersexualities* 23: 374–7.
Seu, Mindy. 2023. *Cyberfeminism Index*. Los Angeles: Inventory Press.
Steele, Catherine Knight. 2021. *Digital Black Feminism*. New York: New York University Press.
sub-Rosa. n.d. Manifesto. Accessed April 25, 2024. http://cyberfeminism.net/about/manifesto/.
VNS Matrix. n.d. "The Artists." Accessed April 25, 2024. https://vnsmatrix.net/the-artists.
Wajcman, Judy. 1991. *Feminism Confronts Technology*. University Park, PA : The Pennsylvania State University Press.

CYBORG MANIFESTO

"A Manifesto for Cyborgs" (1985) is a famous essay by feminist theorist Donna Haraway. In the wake of President Ronald Reagan's conservative administration, Haraway penned a call to action for feminist thinkers. Haraway addresses her main audience, socialist feminists, by critiquing the prevailing Marxist ideology and materialism that had influenced feminist politics in the United States and the United Kingdom since the late nineteenth century (Hennessy 2014).

Haraway's cyborg manifesto offers an alternative approach to materialism that is both innovative and controversial (Sofoulis 2015). Within feminist theory, materialism is the study of actual "stuff" (land, resources, things, commodities, etc.), and feminists typically focus on equity, emphasizing materiality as "what humans need to survive" (Hennessy 2014, 308). Haraway argues that this way of thinking about materiality causes divisions among feminist theorists and activists, creating groups that focus on domestic labor, sexual liberation and reproductive rights, temperance, and so on (Hennessy 2014). By rethinking materialism, Haraway charts a path toward equity that works to deconstruct the boundaries and riffs separating these feminist groups.

Using a postmodern perspective of power and knowledge, Haraway emphasizes the important role of science and technology in understanding social relationships and historical conditions. Haraway argues that power moves through a dispersed "grid" or "web," organizing subjects through "control strategies" (2016, 15–32). She calls for a more nuanced perspective explaining how partial identities (class, race, gender, sexuality, etc.) better articulate lived experiences. She draws from Audre Lorde's groundbreaking book, *Sister Outsider* (1984), to illustrate how partial identities and cyborg writing elucidate more nuanced feminist perspectives.

Using cyborgs as a metaphor, Haraway emphasizes the roles of science and technology while calling for feminists to embrace a nuanced and multifaceted understanding of humanity. Through this metaphor, Haraway argues two key points. First, fidelity to political identifications (thinking of yourself first and foremost as a "woman" or a "man" or a white person, etc.) creates totalizing outcomes, alienating other feminist projects and creating division among feminist groups. For example, during the 1960s and 1970s white feminists often identified as "women" while ignoring race and racism. This created awful divisions within feminism by alienating and subjugating feminists of color. Second, Haraway argued that postmodern approaches to power can enrich feminist politics and unify disparate groups by offering more nuanced critiques of capitalism and creating new possibilities for the survival of the oppressed.

Cyborg Feminists Today

The cyborg manifesto contributes to a wide range of scholarly discussions (Sofoulis 2015; Martin and McIntyre 2019). Haraway's reconceptualization of materialism from a postmodern lens significantly influenced the philosophy of gender, sexuality, and subjectivity under late capitalism (Cox 2018). Here, science and technology are crucial to Haraway's contributions because they help her pose a perspective of reality where it is possible to embody multiple partial identities and even contradictory positions. Again, the goal of cyborg feminism is to completely disrupt the notions that each person has only one identity and that there is only one right way of thinking or being in the world. Haraway disavowed the idea of purity or fidelity to one identity or embodiment of norms. For Haraway, the emphasis on "purity" in life and thought reproduces the patriarchal origin myths of human innocence or "purity" and ultimately constrains women as "impure."

To better imagine the survival of women and other marginalized groups, Haraway encouraged feminists to turn toward what she called "cyborg" texts, figures, and writings. For Haraway, these cyborgs feature disrupted modes of language, cultural norms, and perspectives, showing the dispersed way knowledge is created and contested and shaping new boundaries for subjectivity that transcend Western, patriarchal knowledge, language, and social perspectives.

For example, Rachel Ghansah (2014) uses cyborg feminism to problematize the politics of the famous music entertainer Beyoncé. Ghansah writes, "Is Beyoncé a feminist? Is she a womanist? I don't know. To me, she is a cyborg" (2014, 27). Instead of trying to force Beyoncé into just one identity (e.g., feminist or womanist), Ghansah's cyborg approach recognizes Beyoncé's activism in her multiple and varied contributions to Black women in the music industry, her means of survival, and the ways she creates new space for Black women in US culture. Ghansah's notion of Beyoncé as a cyborg is defined by the ways she is "seizing the tools to mark the world that marked [her] as other" (Haraway 2016, 56).

This cyborg approach is in direct contrast with the way white feminist critics (Holloway 2019) often question Beyoncé's position as a feminist because of her hyperfeminized and sexualized public image (Kendall 2013). Putting boundaries around what it means to be feminist, to perform feminism, and to represent feminism alienates figures such as Beyoncé and discredits the feminist work they perform within US culture. Instead, Haraway's work invites us to recognize Beyoncé as a cyborg since she (1) reclaims the tools of domination, (2) uses them to survive the toxic, patriarchal, and white supremacist music industry, and (3) uses them to create new spaces for Black girls and women to become independent from patriarchal values. Beyoncé may not always perform perfect feminism or fight for Marxist feminist values, but Haraway's point is that these should not be the benchmark for feminist resistance. "I recognize the tools seized. This is not to say that these aspects in Beyoncé align neatly—they are indeed confusing" (Ghansah 2014, 27). Confusion, contradiction, and irony are all tools of cyborg feminism. Cyborg politics is the "struggle for language and against perfect communication, against one code that translates all meaning perfectly" (Haraway 2016, 57).

The cyborg manifesto follows Haraway's claim for the struggle for language as it refuses to fit neatly into any one scholarly box, making it timeless and rich with new possibilities even forty years later. In many ways, this work was ahead of its time in predicting technology's role in individualizing politics and social relations, economic upheaval, and redefining sex and gender relationships in the family and labor force (van Doorn 2017). Haraway and cyborg politics remain crucial to feminism today.

Samantha Gillespie-Hoffman

See Also: Lorde, Audre; Marxist Feminism; Socialism; Standpoint Theory; Temperance; Womanism

Further Reading

Cox, Lara. 2018. "Decolonial Queer Feminism in Donna Haraway's 'A Cyborg Manifesto' (1985)." *Paragraph* 41, no. 3: 317–32. https://www.jstor.org/stable/26538230.

Ghansah, Rachel. 2014. "How Sweet It Is to Be Loved by You: The BeyHive." *The Record: NPR*, March 14, 2014. https://www.npr.org/sections/therecord/2014/03/17/258155902/how-sweet-it-is-to-be-loved-by-you-the-beyhive.

Haraway, Donna. 1985. "A Manifesto for Cyborgs: Science, Technology, and Socialist Feminism in the 1980s." *Socialist Review*, 80:65–108.

Haraway, Donna. 2016. *Manifestly Haraway*. Minneapolis: University of Minnesota Press.

Hennessy, Rosemary. 2014. "Thinking Sex Materially: Marxist, Socialist, and Related Feminist Approaches." In *The Sage Handbook of Feminist Theory*, edited by Mary Evans, Claire Hemmings, Marsha Henry, Hazel Johnstone, Sumi Madhok, Ania Plomien, and Sadie Wearing. Thousand Oaks, CA: Sage Reference.

Holloway, Alexia. 2019. "White Feminists' Critiques of Beyoncé Are Unwarranted." *The Commonwealth Times*, February 13, 2019. https://commonwealthtimes.org/2019/02/13/white-feminists-critiques-of-beyonce-are-unwarranted/.

Kendall, Mikki. 2013. "Beyoncé's New Album Should Silence Her Feminist Critics." *The Guardian*, December 13, 2013. https://www.theguardian.com/commentisfree/2013/dec/13/beyonce-album-flawless-feminism.

Martin, Corey, and Joanna McIntyre. 2019. "The Cyborg Re-manifested: Black Mirror, Cyberfeminism, and Genre Hybridity." *Outskirts* 39: 1–18.

Sofoulis, Zoë. 2015. "The Cyborg, Its Manifesto and Their Relevance Today: Some Reflections." *Journal of Media and Communication* 6, no. 2: 8–15. https://doi.org/10.25595/115.

van Doorn, Niels. 2017. "Platform Labor: On the Gendered and Racialized Exploitation of Low-Income Service Work in the 'On-Demand' Economy." *Information, Communication & Society* 20, no. 6: 898–914. https://doi.org/10.1080/1369118X.2017.1294194.

D

DAVIS, ANGELA Y.

Angela Yvonne Davis (1994–) is a prominent Black feminist political activist, scholar, philosopher, and public intellectual. As a renowned author and public speaker, she has influenced contemporary feminist theory and praxis through her analyses of identity and power, particularly the intersections of gender, race, class, and incarceration. Her work spans feminist studies, critical theory, political philosophy, and Black studies. She is known internationally for her dedication to combating all forms of oppression through her scholarship and activism but gained widespread acclaim initially during the 1970s when a controversial case led to her political imprisonment. Through her lifelong commitment to social justice, Davis advocates for feminism as a collective, revolutionary project aimed at achieving global liberation and dismantling interconnected systems of oppression, including patriarchy, racism, and capitalism.

Early Influences and Activism

Born in Birmingham, Alabama, in 1944, Davis was raised by her father Frank, a service station owner, and her mother Sally, a schoolteacher, alongside her three siblings in "Dynamite Hill"—a neighborhood nicknamed for being frequently bombed by white supremacists resisting Civil Rights integration. Departing from the racial violence and poverty of the segregated South, Davis earned a scholarship to attend Elizabeth Irwin High School, a Quaker school in New York City.

In 1961, she attended Brandeis University and majored in French. Studying abroad at the University of Paris during her junior year expanded Davis's worldview and political commitments, as she interacted with people from the French intellectual community and students from Cuba and Algeria (Davis 2021, 104–7, 119–21). She also started studying philosophy with the Frankfurt School thinker Herbert Marcuse. In 1965, she attended the Goethe University Frankfurt in Germany where she studied with Theodore Adorno and Jurgen Habermas. This training in Marxist ideology and critical theory deeply influenced Davis. The growing Black Freedom movement compelled Davis to return to the United States and resume her studies with Marcuse at the University of California, San Diego, in 1967.

In 1969, Davis accepted a teaching position at UCLA, but her time there was short-lived. Upon hearing of her membership with the Communist Party USA, Governor of California Ronald Reagan ordered the Board of Regents to fire Davis. Although she sued the state and won the case, she was soon after let go due to "inflammatory rhetoric" (James 2024, 119). She became more involved with the Black Panther Party, although her relationship was fraught due to gender dynamics and philosophical differences (Davis 2021, 157–60). She also served as cochair for the Soledad Brothers Defense Committee, an advocacy group supporting three incarcerated Black activists accused of murdering a prison guard. Her involvement shifted her life trajectory dramatically when, unbeknownst to her, weapons registered in her name were used in a deadly armed takeover of the courtroom during the Soledad Brothers' trial. She was charged with conspiracy, kidnapping, and murder and placed on the FBI's most wanted fugitive list. After a highly publicized and politicized trial, she was acquitted of all charges in June 1972. In the wake of her imprisonment, an international "Free Angela Davis" movement formed, making Davis a revolutionary icon (Rosenberg 2020). The lasting influence of her experiences with political repression and grassroots mobilization is evident in her work.

A "Free Angela Davis Now!" poster, published by the New York Committee to Free Angela Davis, *c.* 1971. An activist and academic, Davis was imprisoned after a shooting involving weapons registered in her name (Library of Congress).

Feminist Contributions

A primary contribution of Davis's work to feminist scholarship and activism is her early explication of intersectionality. Her landmark book *Women, Race, and Class* (1981) traced the history of the women's liberation movement through an integrated Marxist analytical lens, challenging the idea that gender, race, and class could be understood in isolation. The book critiqued how, at the time, the white mainstream feminist movement disregarded the struggles and resistance of Black and working-class women by foregrounding the experiences of white, middle-class women. Davis remarks on how the book "was about uncovering the contributions of women who were completely marginalized by histories of the women's movement, especially Black women, but also Latino women and working-class women" (George 2020). Her analysis revealed the complexity of social dynamics of power and privilege even within feminist movements and laid the foundation for the later popularized notion of intersectional feminism.

Davis also draws important connections between feminism and incarceration. Her critique of carceral systems and their impact on women, particularly women of color, is central to her work. In her seminal book *Are Prisons Obsolete?* (2003, 61), Davis argues that those committed to feminist efforts "should not consider the structure of state punishment as marginal to their work" but instead should "recognize that the deeply gendered character of punishment both reflects and further entrenches the gendered structure of the larger society." In her analyses of state violence and the prison industrial complex, she persistently reveals the latent power structures of gender, race, and class.

She is also a leading critic of *carceral feminism*, which is a kind of feminism that relies on the criminal legal system to address gendered violence (Bernstein 2007). For example, advocates often call for harsher sentences or increased policing in cases of gender-based crimes like rape or domestic violence. Instead, Davis argues for *abolition feminism*, which is a feminist approach rooted in intersectionality that combats sexual and gender-based violence by challenging rather than reinforcing the prison system. In their coauthored book *Abolition. Feminism. Now.* (2022, 2), Angela Davis, Gina Dent, Erica R. Meiners, and Beth E. Richie explain that a feminist agenda which is also abolitionist is "the most inclusive and persuasive version of feminism for these times." Abolition feminism adopts a holistic perspective, recognizing the relationship between state and individual violence and emphasizing the need for both supporting survivors and holding perpetrators accountable through community-based solutions as opposed to punitive responses. Importantly, this work created a framework for understanding the feminist and prison abolition movements as interconnected historically and conceptually.

Lasting Impact

Angela Davis continues to be a prominent political icon, highly regarded for her contributions as an academic and activist. In 2020, TIME magazine included her among its most influential people, underscoring her significance in the contemporary political sphere (Common 2020). She has founded several social justice organizations. In 1973, she helped form the National Alliance Against Racist and Political Repression, and in 1997, she and Ruth Wilson Gilmore cofounded Critical Resistance, an organization working to abolish the US prison system (Davis 2021, xvi). Throughout her career, she has written several other books and published collections of speeches and essays that expand her Marxist critiques of capitalism, patriarchy, imperialism, and the prison industrial complex. Davis has fundamentally shaped feminist scholarship by advancing a vision of feminism that is both intersectional and global, and that bridges theory and practice. Her work consistently emphasizes themes of collective action and solidarity, calling for unified efforts across social movements. She maintains a hopeful disposition toward social change, drawing inspiration from ongoing liberatory efforts, including global movements such as Black Lives Matter and Free Palestine (George 2020). Currently, she is a professor emeritus of history of consciousness at the University of California, Santa Cruz.

Dominique Nicole Campbell

See Also: Crenshaw, Kimberlé; Intersectionality; Marxist Feminism; Prison Abolition Movements; Prison Industrial Complex

Further Reading

Bernstein, Elizabeth. 2007. "The Sexual Politics of the 'New Abolitionism.'" *Differences* 18, no. 3: 128–51.
Common. 2020. "The 100 Most Influential People of 2020: Angela Davis." *Time Magazine*, September 23, 2020. https://time.com/collection/100-most-influential-people-2020/5888290/angela-davis/.
Davis, Angela Y. (1974) 2021. *Angela Davis: An Autobiography*. New York: Random House. Reprint, Haymarket Books.

Davis, Angela Y. 1981. *Women, Race, and Class*. New York: Random House.
Davis, Angela Y. 2003. *Are Prisons Obsolete?* New York: Seven Stories Press.
Davis, Angela Y., Gina Dent, Erica R. Meiners, and Beth E. Richie. 2022. *Abolition. Feminism. Now.* Haymarket Books.
George, Nelson. 2020. "The Greats: Angela Davis." *The New York Times Style Magazine*, October 19, 2020. https://www.nytimes.com/interactive/2020/10/19/t-magazine/angela-davis.html.
James, Joy. 2024. *Contextualizing Angela Davis: The Agency and Identity of an Icon*. Bloomsbury Publishing.
Rosenberg, Daniel. 2020. "The Free Angela Movement in the United States, 1969–1991." *American Communist History* 19, no. 3–4: 191–261. https://doi.org/10.1080/14743892.2020.1799600.

DECOLONIZATION

The term "decolonization" is sometimes used to describe the historical process in which European empires left or "decolonized" the lands and peoples they had previously colonized (see Betts 2004 and Kennedy 2016). Today, however, "decolonization" mostly refers to the process by which individuals and society might move away from or dismantle the structures of Western imperialism and center the concerns and knowledge of Indigenous peoples (sometimes referred to as Native, American Indian, Native Alaskan, First Nations, and/or Aboriginal peoples). Essentially, instead of referring to nation-craft, "decolonization" now mostly refers to individual and cultural efforts to stop dismissing or exploiting Indigenous peoples and lands and to start centering Indigenous peoples' knowledge, perspectives, and concerns. The activism around the issue of MMIWG2S (Missing and Murdered Women, Girls, and Two-Spirit Peoples) serves as an example of what women-led, decolonial action looks like.

Defining Decolonization

One of the key texts addressing decolonization is *Decolonizing Methodologies: Research and Indigenous Peoples*, by Maori scholar Linda Tuhiwai Smith. Smith draws upon feminist theory for her conceptual understanding of decolonization (Wilson 2001, 215). In the opening chapters, Smith explains how most Western research is built on assumptions for what counts as "knowledge" and what is "knowable"—and those assumptions often exclude Indigenous ways of knowing. For instance, Smith describes how Maori peoples regard afterbirth as sacred and connected to land. In Western societies, the afterbirth is typically known by medicalized terms such as placenta. The Maori words for "land and afterbirth" are, however, identical to one other (Smith 2012, 104). As a result, Maori traditions involve burying the afterbirth. However, until very recently, hospitals in New Zealand, grounded in Western scientific research and practice, refused to acknowledge Maori knowledge. And they refused to allow Maori patients to leave the hospital with the afterbirth to observe the sacred practice according to their knowledge and traditions (Smith 2012, 104).

By explaining the assumptions of what counts as knowledge within Western societies, and how exclusionary those assumptions are, Smith builds upon the work of earlier feminists who similarly argued that patriarchal ways of knowing marginalized and silenced women academics (Smith 2012, 168). Additionally, Smith draws on the tradition of Black feminism and other women of color in dealing with harmful conditions such as postcolonial poverty, landlessness, sexism, or racism, be they in India, Egypt, or southern Texas. For instance, Smith draws on the writing of feminist Patricia Hill Collins, who argued that Black women have a particular and legitimate standpoint by which they make sense of the world—a standpoint white feminists tend to overlook and ignore. Maori women have used such insights to legitimate their own experience and knowledge (Smith 2012, 170; tebrakunna, Lee, and Evans 2022, 5–6).

For Smith, decolonization centers the concerns and worldview of Indigenous peoples to "offer a language of possibility, a way out of colonialism" (2012, 41). Her account intends to help Native communities specifically (Tuck 2013, 366), and in order to achieve that aim, Smith's decolonization holds together two strands of thought. The first strand looks to the "time before colonization" (Smith 2012, 25). This was a period in which Indigenous peoples possessed autonomy over their existence and lived in a world of their own making. The second includes an inquiry into how colonization took place and its significance for Indigenous peoples. Decolonization poses responses to colonization drawing both on an analysis of colonialism and on past Indigenous wisdom.

Other accounts of decolonization bear some important similarities to Smith's, especially in their insistence on critical accounts of colonialism, resourcing or centering Indigenous knowledge, and a constructive account for living better lives. For example, settler colonial studies scholar Lorenzo Veracini's work implies that decolonization possesses at least two parts. First, students and scholars must draw attention to how settler cultures erase or disavow Indigenous peoples and culture from society, particularly through analysis of popular culture, history, laws, and the like. Second, settlers must support political actions for Indigenous self-determination. This includes, in part, attempts at reconciliation between settlers and Indigenous people such that all peoples can live well with and on the land (see Veracini 2010). In a similar way, literary scholar Walter Mignolo argues that decolonization, or decoloniality as he calls it, involves letting go of (or "delinking" from) colonial knowledge and structures in order to reconstitute "ways of thinking, languages, ways of life and being in the world" that are beyond the colonial imagination (Hoffmann 2017, 2), ways informed by Indigenous wisdom.

Naaman Wood

See Also: Colonialism; Missing and Murdered Indigenous Women and Girls; Patriarchy; Settler Colonialism; Structural Oppression

Further Reading

Betts, Raymond. 2004. *Decolonization.* New York: Routledge.

Hoffmann, Alvina. 2017. "Interview – Walter Mignolo/Part 2: Key Concepts." *E-International Relations*, January 21, 2017. https://www.e-ir.info/2017/01/21/interview-walter-mignolopart-2-key-concepts/.

Kennedy, Dane Keith. 2016. *Decolonization: A Very Short Introduction.* New York: Oxford University Press.

Presley, Rachel. 2020. "Embodied Liminality and Gendered State Violence: Artivist Expressions in the MMIW Movement." *Journal of International Women's Studies* 21, no. 7: 91–109. https://vc.bridgew.edu/jiws/vol21/iss7/8.

Smith, Linda Tuhiwai. 2012. *Decolonizing Methodologies: Research and Indigenous Peoples.* London: Zed Books.

Solway, Susan. 2010. "Red Dresses: There, but Just Not There." *Windspeaker Publication* 28, no. 8 (October 29). https://www.ammsa.com/publications/windspeaker/red-dresses-there-just-not-there.

tebrakunna country, Emma Lee, and Jennifer Evans, eds. 2022. *Indigenous Women's Voices: 20 Years on from Linda Tuhiwai Smith's* Decolonizing Methodologies. London: Zed Books.

Tuck, Eve. 2013. "Commentary: *Decolonizing Methodologies* 15 Years Later." *AlterNative: An International Journal of Indigenous Peoples* 9, no. 4: 365–72.

US Department of Justice. 2008. *Violence Against American Indian and Alaska Native Women and the Criminal Justice Response: What is Known.* Accessed April 25, 2024. https://www.ojp.gov/pdffiles1/nij/grants/223691.pdf.

Veracini, Lorenzo. 2010. *Settler Colonialism: A Theoretical Overview.* London: Palgrave Macmillan.

Wilson, Carla. 2001. "Decolonizing Methodologies: Research and Indigenous Peoples." *Social Policy Journal of New Zealand* 17 (December): 214–17.

DECONSTRUCTION

Deconstruction is a philosophical concept that refers to the practice of dissecting and analyzing social, cultural, and religious beliefs that are presented as inherent or natural truths rather than social constructs. Deconstruction seeks to disrupt beliefs that are treated as universal facts and "involves questioning how organizing power structures and discourse came to be" (Coburn et al. 2019, 189). Put simply, deconstruction is a practice of taking a widely accepted belief, such as "men should initiate romantic relationships," and breaking it into its parts and considering the veracity of each of those parts. In this instance, a deconstructionist approach might ask questions such as, "How are men defined and what characteristics does this definition ascribe to men? Is that definition valid and are those characteristics universally true of men? What does it mean to 'initiate' in romantic relationships? Why are romantic relationships considered different from friendships? What beliefs and expectations follow from the assumption that men should initiate in romantic relationships?"

Feminists have famously deconstructed the gender binary, examining why and how gender is considered binary and has historically been determined at birth by sex. Feminists argue that the gender binary is not something inherent or biologically determined but something that is constructed by society and used in ways that support patriarchal beliefs—for instance, assuming men are natural leaders while women are naturally submissive (Evans 1995, 127). Feminists such as Judith Butler have argued that gender is a performance, something we actively practice in everyday life (Elam 1994, 43; Eschenbacher and Weber 2023, 428). By analyzing and critiquing systematic beliefs about gender, feminists participate in deconstruction; by offering new definitions, feminists participate in the reconstruction of knowledge.

Today, some Evangelical Christians and many Exvangelicals (people who have left Evangelicalism) are using deconstruction to analyze and rethink heteronormative, white supremacist, and patriarchal beliefs taught in the environments within which many Evangelical Christians are raised. For example, many LGBTQIA+ people who grew up Christian have had to rethink conservative Christian doctrine that often insists that their identity is sinful, unnatural, and goes against God's law (Coburn et al. 2019, 176; Hollier 2023, 29). Christians who are deconstructing and reexamining this understanding of scripture often argue that verses in scripture have been taken out of their historical context and used to defend homophobic and patriarchal hierarchies (Moder 2019, 86).

Within Evangelical and Exvangelical contexts, deconstruction often leads to a realization that what is taught about women and sexuality within Christian churches is an abuse of scripture that supports oppression rather than the Gospel. Systems of oppression, such as Christian conservatism, weaponize the idea that heterosexuality and gender hierarchies are natural truths (Elam, 1994, 50; Sewell 2014, 299). Feminists use deconstruction to challenge beliefs and assumptions about human nature that support the powerful and reinforce oppression (Saulnier 1996, 132).

For feminists, deconstruction is a way to rethink how the heteronormative, white supremacist patriarchy has weaponized beliefs about gender, race, sexuality, and so on against women and vulnerable populations. Deconstruction remains an essential part of feminist discourse as we continue to challenge oppression and injustice.

Sage Mikkelsen

See Also: Butler, Judith; Feminist Theology; Gender; Religious Right

Further Reading

Coburn, Katelyn O., Ellory K. Bishop, Jennifer Lambert-Shute, Hoa N. Nguyen, Tabitha L. McCoy, and Christi R. McGeorge. 2019. "The Christian Closet: A Phenomenological Study of Queer Christian Women's Navigation of Church Communities." *Journal of Feminist Family Therapy* 31, no. 4: 165–94. https://doi.org/10.1080/08952833.2019.1640569.

Elam, Diane. 1994. *Feminism and Deconstruction: Ms. En Abyme*. London: Routledge.

Eschenbacher, Saskia, and Nils Weber. 2023. "Deconstructing Gender Identity through Transformative Learning." *Studies in the Education of Adults* 55, no. 2: 427–40. https://doi.org/10.1080/02660830.2023.2243660.

Evans, Judith 1995. *Feminist Theory Today: An Introduction to Second-Wave Feminism*. London: Sage Publications.

Hollier, Joel. 2023. *Religious Trauma, Queer Identities: Mapping the Complexities of Being LGBTQA+ in Evangelical Churches*. Cham: Springer International Publishing. https://doi.org/10.1007/978-3-031-27711-5.

Moder, Ally. 2019. "Women, Personhood, and the Male God: A Feminist Critique of Patriarchal Concepts of God in View of Domestic Abuse." *Feminist Theology* 28, no. 1: 85–103. https://doi.org/10.1177/0966735019859471.

Saulnier, Christine Flynn. 1996. *Feminist Theories and Social Work: Approaches and Applications*. New York: Haworth Press.

Sewell, John Ike. 2014. "'Becoming Rather Than Being': Queer's Double-Edged Discourse as Deconstructive Practice." *The Journal of Communication Inquiry* 38, no. 4: 291–307. https://doi.org/10.1177/0022002714553900.

DISABILITY

Feminist approaches to ethics, political philosophy, and epistemology shape disability studies. Much as feminists have understood patriarchy to be a system of values, domination, and disadvantage that harm women and not just about individual attitudes toward women (see, for instance, Kate Manne's *Down Girl: The Logic of Misogyny*), ableism is often understood as a system of interlocking forces that devalue disabled lives, experiences, and insight. Such an understanding of ableism is closely connected with social models of disability. According to such models, people are disabled not by having a body that is impaired but by environments, attitudes, and social systems that devalue and marginalize disabled people. For instance, under the American Disabilities Act (ADA) a person is disabled if they (1) have an impairment that substantially limits one or more life activities (e.g., quadriplegia or autism), (2) have a history of such an impairment (e.g., cancer that is in remission), or (3) are perceived by others to have such an impairment (e.g., facial scaring). The ADA was intended as a civil rights law for disabled people. It was written specifically to reflect the fact that differences in how bodies and their abilities are socially understood plays a defining role in either marginalizing or preventing discrimination against disabled people.

Both feminist and disability activists have advocated against social exclusion and the limiting of options that women and disabled people often face. Shelley Tremain's work, for instance, draws on the work of Michel Foucault and feminist epistemologists and philosophers of science to explore how responses to disability are shaped by enculturation and social power dynamics. The feminist movement and disability studies have shaped and informed each other's theory and activism in the United States, but *how* feminism and disability have interacted has changed significantly over the years.

History of Interaction between Disability and Feminist Movements

Throughout much of history, concerns about disability were used to marginalize women, who were thought to be frail and especially vulnerable to disability. For instance, concerns about disability were used to oppose the women's suffrage movement in the late nineteenth and early twentieth centuries. Commenting on this phenomenon, Douglas Baynton notes that "two types of disability argument were used in opposition to women's suffrage: that women had disabilities that made them incapable of using the franchise [vote] responsibly, and that because of their frailty women would become disabled if exposed to the rigors of political participation" (Baynton 2001, 41–2). Proponents of women's suffrage tended to argue that women would not be at increased risk of disability due to suffrage or the education required to vote well, rather than question the assumption that disabled people didn't deserve suffrage. This shows that feminist movements have not always been sensitive to concerns about the marginalization of disabled people and their experiences.

Despite this history, disability activists in the latter decades of the twentieth century would use progress in women's rights and racial civil rights movements as a model for their own civil rights movement. Early stages of the disability rights movement focused primarily on issues of accessibility, employment, and the need for anti-discrimination protections; this activism resulted in new laws such as Section 504 of the Rehabilitation Act (1973) and the Americans with Disabilities Act (1990). As the movement expanded, it also highlighted the need to address specific experiences and challenges resulting from gendered expressions of disability, such as disproportionately high rates of gender-based violence. Many insights from feminist scholarship have been applied to issues related to disability. For instance, feminist epistemological insights on the importance of social location not only for *what* a person can know but also *how* that knowledge is received by others inform the need to center disabled contributions in thinking about disability. As the leading slogan of the disability rights movement in the United States puts it, "Nothing about us without us." The disability rights movement also looked to feminist emphases on bodily autonomy as it developed.

Contemporary Theory and Politics

One of the most significant contributions of feminism to the disability rights movement and disability studies has been the concept of intersectionality, focusing on ways that various forms of discrimination intersect and compound each other. For example, it is estimated that between 80,000 and 100,000 disabled people were forcibly sterilized in the United States during the twentieth century. Unsurprisingly, forcible sterilization was performed much more frequently on disabled women, especially women of color, than on disabled men, even though the procedure for men is significantly less invasive than it is for women. More recently, Evelyn Nakano Glenn's *Forced to Care: Coercion and Caregiving in America* explores how various social factors result in women, especially immigrants and women of color, performing the majority of professional care work for disabled individuals.

Just as feminist theory helped disability studies expand to think of gendered components of disability, so too disability studies has helped feminism expand to recognize how disability affects gender. Early US feminists largely disregarded disabled women (Wendell 1996), but now, thanks to disability scholars and activists, the diversity of women's experiences, including disability, is more explicitly recognized. Contemporary feminist and disability activists highlight the need for policies and practices to address intersectional identities and experiences. For instance, disabled people are at increased risk for sexual violence, often by family member or caregivers, and in gendered ways: 80 percent of women with developmental disabilities have been sexually assaulted compared with only 30 percent of men with developmental disabilities. Disability and feminist activists have advocated for stronger legal protections, especially to protect against violence and abuse, for increased public awareness of vulnerability, and for the need for better support services.

Parallels between Disability Studies and Feminism

Not only have feminist and disability studies influenced each other, but there are a number of parallels between the two fields. In the same way that feminism involves both academic study and advocacy drawing on the lived experience of women, so too disability studies draws on the lived experience of disabled people to both shape academic discourse and advocacy for better social and political outcomes. Likewise, feminists typically argue that gender is a social construct. Similarly, disability scholars argue that disability is also a social construct (e.g., Barnes and Tremain). Additionally, both feminism and disability studies argue for the naturalization of the range of "acceptable" bodies and the cultural expectations that shape their reception, especially drawing on claims that both gender and disability are social constructions. Feminists, for instance, have challenged cultural normative beauty standards and other aspects of embodied phenomenology (e.g., Iris Marion Young's "Throwing Like a Girl"). Similarly, disability scholars note how disabled bodies are negatively stigmatized and treated as "deviant" forms of embodiment. For instance, Rosemarie Garland-Thomson's (2011) work shows how disabled and other "extraordinary bodies" have been stigmatized and commodified for others' consumption, furthering feminist critiques of the objectification and marginalization of bodies. In *The Rejected Body*, Susan Wendell (1996) explores how much of the Western philosophical tradition, dating back to Plato, has tended to see the body as not only opposed to the mind (or soul) but also as a hindrance to it. Given that women are often seen as emotional, connected more closely with the body, while men are taken to be more rational, centuries of patriarchy have held that differential treatment of the sexes is needed for societal control. Many of the same pressures are explicit in twentieth-century eugenics but also latent in contemporary assumptions that underwrite what Eli Clare (2017) calls "the ideology of cure." Other topics that both groups have explored include identity, the politics of care, and autonomy (both in general and specifically sexual autonomy).

Despite these similarities, some scholars think that disability studies needs to be more explicitly feminist as a field. Kim Q. Hall argues that feminist disability studies should not be reduced to the combination of feminism and disability studies: "Feminist disability studies does not just add disabled women's experiences to scholarship in disability studies and feminist theory. Instead . . . it transforms both fields" (2011, 1). Similarly, Rosemarie Garland-Thomson argues that feminists have too often ignored how issues such as reproductive technologies are entangled with disability. On the other hand, she also thinks "much of current disability studies does a great deal of wheel reinventing . . . because many disability studies scholars simply do not know either feminist theory or the institutional history of women's studies" (2011, 14). Insofar as both feminism and disability studies engage with often marginalized forms of human diversity, materiality, and the cultural importance of the body, integrating the two approaches deepens both fields. Further mutual engagement should be encouraged.

While there is need for continued mutual engagement, the coming together of feminist and disability rights movements in the United States has led to important advocacy and scholarly work on a wide variety of topics. This should continue as a way of helping bring about a more just and equitable society for all.

Kevin Timpe

See Also: Bioethics; Bodily Autonomy; Eugenics; Mind/Body Split; Reproductive Justice; Standpoint Theory

Further Reading

Barnes, Elizabeth. 2016. *The Minority Body: A Theory of Disability*. Oxford: Oxford University Press.

Baynton, Douglas. 2001. "Disability and the Justification of Inequality in American History." In *The New Disability History: American Perspectives*, edited by Paul K. Longmore and Lauir Umanksy, 33–57. New York: New York University Press.
Clare, Eli. 2017. *Brilliant Imperfection: Grappling with Cure*. Durham, NC: Duke University Press.
Garland-Thomson, Rosemarie. 2011. "Integrating Disability, Transforming Feminist Theory." In *Feminist Disability Studies*, edited by Kim Q. Hall, 13–47. Bloomington, IN: Indianna University Press.
Glenn, Evelyn Nakamo. 2012. *Forced to Care: Coercion and Caregiving in America*. Cambridges, MA: Harvard University Press
Hall, Kim Q. 2011. "Reimagining Disability and Gender through Feminist Disability Studies." In *Feminist Disability Studies*, edited by Kim Q. Hall, 1–10. Bloomington, Ind: Indianna University Press.
Scully, Jackie Leach. 2023. "Feminist Bioethics and Disability." In *The Routledge Handbook of Feminist Bioethics*, edited by Wendy A. Rogers, Jackie Leach Scully, Stacy M. Carter, Vikki A. Entwistle, and Catherine Mills, 181–914. New York: Routledge.
Tremain, Shelley L. 2017. *Foucault and Feminist Philosophy of Disability*. Ann Arbor, MI: University of Michigan Press.
Wendell, Susan. 1996. *The Rejected Body: Feminist Philosophical Reflections on Disability*. New York: Routledge.

DISCIPLINARY POWER

Disciplinary power is a concept developed by Michel Foucault to explain one of the ways power works in modern societies. Disciplinary power refers to the power through which people "punish" or otherwise direct each other—and ultimately themselves—into greater conformity with cultural norms.

Consider a young man who decides to major in nursing while in college. Excited, he tells his friends and family about his educational and career path, only to find that others are skeptical of his choice—often encouraging him to become a doctor instead. Similarly, consider a heterosexual couple with a baby having lunch in a restaurant. The father gets up to change the baby's diaper in the restroom, only to discover that there is no changing table in the men's restroom. In both of these examples, the men's choices and behavior have been "disciplined." They were told *not* to do something. Indeed, they received clear communication (and the father encountered a physical barrier) naysaying their caretaking of others—whether in a profession such as nursing or for members of their own family. At the same time, they were disciplined *toward* a different choice and behavior. They were pushed to do something else: the college student was encouraged to be a doctor and the father to hand the baby and diaper-changing duties to the mother (baby changing stations are much more commonly provided in women's bathrooms). These men can resist disciplinary power. The college student can still choose to study nursing and the father could change the baby's diaper using a table or the floor as a changing station.

Importantly, disciplinary power comes from one's peers and even subordinates—not from the state or government. Imagine a bartender who teases or chides a man who orders a fruity drink with an umbrella. Here, the bartender is not in a position of authority over the man ordering a drink, yet the bartender's teasing clearly communicates that the man has made a wrong choice and ought to amend his ways. Likewise, a boy who wears pink to elementary school and experiences sexist and/or homophobic teasing might choose to never wear pink again in public. In these hypothetical examples, people disciplined each other into conformity with common sense or cultural norms rather than the state stepping in and punishing someone for breaking the law.

Self-Governance and the Panopticon

Ultimately, disciplinary power becomes a form of self-governance that exists even without exterior rewards or punishments. That is, we learn our culture's norms and rules from watching others and from the way others treat us; we then internalize these cultural norms, expectations, and ideals—disciplining ourselves before anyone has a chance to tell us that we have done something wrong. Consider, for instance, a young woman who has grown up watching her mother put on makeup first thing in the morning, every morning. Now an adult, the young woman has an errand to run on a Saturday morning. She has a terrible cold and feels awful. After her errand she plans to take a nap and stay at home. Her errand is to the post office and she can reasonably expect not to bump into anyone she knows during the errand. Nonetheless, she applies a full face of makeup before leaving the house. This is an example of how disciplinary power is *internalized* such that we end up disciplining ourselves into conformity with cultural norms even when no one else (or no one with power over us) would have disciplined us.

The analogy and visual imagery Foucault used to explain disciplinary power is the *panopticon*. Panopticon means something like "all-seeing gaze" or refers to an arena in which all is seen. Specifically, Foucault used it to refer to the architecture of some prisons in which a guard tower with one-way windows was positioned in the middle with prisoners' cells positioned in a circle around it—such that guards could look into any and every prisoner's cell from their central position, but prisoners never knew when the guards were looking at them. While the guard tower has to be initially staffed and punishments meted out in order to achieve compliance with the prison's standards for behavior, eventually the guard tower can be radically understaffed because prisoners internalize the rules and police themselves in order to avoid punishment from the guards. The idea is that even absent external rewards or punishment, people internalize disciplinary power, engaging in self-monitoring and self-discipline, thus bringing their attitudes and behaviors in accord with cultural norms and ideals.

Michel Foucault originally theorized disciplinary power in relation to sexual and gender roles. Subsequently, feminist, queer, and anti-racist scholars have long used this concept to understand how gender roles, heteronormativity, and white supremacy are communicated and reinforced in the United States. Additionally, disciplinary power is related to another type of power that Foucault identified in modern societies—biopower—in which populations become governable not so much by force but through cultural norms, incentives, and internalized disciplinary power.

Activism often focuses on legal or policy changes. For instance, feminist activism often targets sexist institutional policies (like dress codes) or works to create new protections for vulnerable populations (like the 1978 Pregnancy Discrimination Act). However, so many of the injustices, daily humiliations, and oppressions that people experience stem not from institutional policies or governmental laws that prohibit their bodies and ways of life but from disciplinary power—from being teased, chided, mocked, passed over for hiring or promotion, socially ostracized, publicly shamed, beaten, raped, or even murdered for their noncompliance with sexist, racist, and heterosexist cultural norms.

Sarah Kornfield

See Also: Biopower; Compulsory Heterosexuality; Gender Performance; Internalized Sexism; Male Gaze

Further Reading

Foucault, Michel. 2012. *Discipline and Punish: The Birth of the Prison*. Translated by Alan Sheridan. New York: Vintage.

Hoffman, Marcelo. 2014. "Disciplinary Power." In *Michel Foucault: Key Concepts*, edited by Diana Taylor, 27–39. New York: Routledge.
Hole, Anne. 2003. "Performing Identity: Dawn French and the Funny Fat Female Body." *Feminist Media Studies* 3, no. 3: 315–28.
Lynch, Richard A. 2014. "Foucault's Theory of Power." In *Michel Foucault: Key Concepts*, edited by Diana Taylor, 27–39. New York: Routledge.

DIVORCE

Divorce is the dissolution of marriage. People often think about marriage as a private, romantic, and sometimes religious or spiritual union, but marriage is a legal contract—differently regulated by each state and the District of Columbia (DC). Likewise, divorce is regulated by the states and DC; there are no federal marriage or divorce laws. Each state (and DC) is left to its own devices to determine what it considers a legal marriage, upon what grounds it will (or won't) grant a divorce, and how any shared property, child custody, and/or restitution for wrongs might be adjudicated during divorce proceedings. Marriage and divorce laws affect people's legal standing in terms of tax law, insurance policies, child custody, property ownership, inheritance policies, health and end-of-life decisions, retirement savings, citizenship standing, and many other everyday life components (Luongo et al. 2024).

Although marriage (and thus divorce) is left to each state's discretion, the Supreme Court ruled in *Obergefell v. Hodges* (2015) that the states may not discriminate against same-sex couples in their marriage laws. If *Obergefell v. Hodges* were to be overturned (as Justice Clarence Thomas indicated was possible in his concurring opinion to the 2022 ruling *Dobbs v. Jackson Women's Health*, which overturned *Roe v. Wade*), then the states would once again be able to discriminate against same-sex couples if they choose to do so.

History of Divorce Laws: Fault-Based and No-Fault Divorces

In colonial America, marriage was primarily understood in connection to reproduction and economics; divorce, then, was primarily granted if a party could prove they were deceived about their spouse's ability to generate progeny or their financial situation. During the 1800s, divorce laws expanded—varying state by state—to allow the dissolution of marriage on grounds such as "adultery, impotence, extreme cruelty, long-term imprisonment, and confirmed drug or alcohol use" (Luongo et al. 2024, 789). These types of divorce laws are known as "fault-based" divorces: in order to acquire a divorce under "fault-based" divorce laws, one party has to prove that the other was guilty of the type of misconduct that their state considers a rational for dissolving a marriage. During this time, women were more likely to request a divorce than men, but when men requested a divorce, they were more likely to be granted one (Hodes 1997, 68–71).

In fault-based divorces, if the wealthier spouse is found guilty of causing the marriage's failure, judges typically require the wealthier spouse "to support the innocent spouse" (Luongo et al. 2024, 789). If the wealthier spouse is not "at fault," or if both parties are found to be "at fault," the financial arrangements can vary widely at the judge's discretion.

Fault-based divorces are unavailable to couples whose marriages have failed but neither party has engaged in "adultery, impotence, extreme cruelty, long-term imprisonment" or "confirmed drug or alcohol use," which remain the standard grounds for fault-based divorces to this day (Luongo et al. 2024, 789). Prior to the 1960s, fault-based divorces were the only option and couples often perjured themselves in an attempt to end their marriages (Luongo et al. 2024, 790). In response, and after considerable activism, states began to move to no-fault divorce statutes.

No-fault divorces dissolve marriages due to "irreconcilable differences or incompatibility of temperament" rather than misconduct (Luongo et al. 2024, 790). Today, all fifty states and DC have no-fault divorce statutes, although states such as Mississippi and South Dakota impose constraints on no-fault divorces such as requiring that both parties agree to the divorce. Thirty-nine states also maintain their fault-based divorce statutes.

When "no-fault" divorces became available, divorce rates rose—spiking in the 1970s—as couples dissolved bad marriages. The spike in divorce rates fueled backlash against feminist activism during this era as anti-feminists argued that feminism was destroying marriage. Even though divorce rates have been steadily declining since 2000, anti-feminists still claim that feminism is a war on marriage.

Divorce Today

Following the advent of no-fault divorces, the United States saw a reduction in "female suicide, domestic violence, and spousal homicide of women" (Luongo et al. 2024, 792). In many ways, no-fault divorce laws are saving women's lives. Feminists argue that people need to be able to leave bad and abusive marriages—and no-fault divorce makes that easier. As the reductions in women's suicide rates, domestic violence, and the spousal homicide of women demonstrate, no-fault divorce significantly helps women leave bad and abusive marriages before it's too late.

While divorce rates are falling overall, since the 1990s they have been rising for people over fifty; today 40 percent of divorces involve someone over fifty (Harris 2024). As people live longer and women are more likely to have careers later in life (making divorce financially feasible for them), more people are choosing to leave bad marriages later in life (Brown and Lin 2022, 1711). This can wreak havoc on women's retirements: after divorce, women over fifty "see a 45 percent decline on average in their standard of living, versus a 21 percent drop for husbands of the same age" (Harris 2024). Divorce, however, is not the cause of older divorced women's financial trouble. Unequal pay, the devaluation of women's domestic labor, and bias against women during divorce proceedings are the causes of their impoverishment.

Moreover, divorce—even no-fault divorces—are usually expensive. This can put women in heterosexual marriages at a significant disadvantage since sexist gender roles dictate that men control heterosexual couples' finances. Indeed, divorce reform advocate Monica Getz argued that "husbands can fight a war of financial attrition against their spouses" by dragging out appeals and other proceedings (Gabriel 2025).

For LGBTQ+ couples with children, divorce proceedings can be very complicated—especially if the children share a biological link or have a legal adoption with one parent but not the other. Moreover, LGBTQ+ married couples who do not conform to a "middle-class, monogamous model" of marriage can face discrimination and limited "access to justice" in their divorce proceedings (Luongo et al. 2024, 795). Long-term, cohabitating couples who are not legally married likewise have limited "access to justice" compared to their married peers: there are limited legal or formal avenues for such couples, especially regarding child custody and shared property. This puts working-class and less financially stable couples at a significant disadvantage since marriage is increasingly a step only wealthier couples take (Brown and Lin 2022, 1711).

Today, no-fault divorce is under attack from right-wing politicians who continue to claim that feminism and no-fault divorce—rather than bad and abusive marriages—are destroying marriage. For example, a legislator in Louisiana, Nicholas James, drafted "a measure stating, 'Louisiana marriage laws have destroyed the institute of marriage over the past thirty to fifty years'" and the Republican Party of Texas added the "unilateral" termination of "no-fault divorce laws" to their party's platform in 2022 (Jong-Fast 2023; Luongo et al. 2024, 792). Feminist activists spent decades working to achieve no-fault divorce laws, and no-fault divorce laws clearly help people—especially women—escape abusive and bad marriages, becoming better able to determine the course of their own lives. Feminists continue to advocate for divorce reform so that women, LGBTQ+ people, and cohabiting couples are not systematically disadvantaged in the dissolution of marriage and cohabitating unions. The threat of returning to a fault-based divorce system jeopardizes decades of feminist activism and endangers countless people.

Sarah Kornfield

See Also: Bodily Autonomy; Domestic Labor; Emotional Labor; Equal Day; Gaslighting; Intimate Partner Violence; Lesbian Continuum

Further Reading

Brown, Susan L., and I-Fen Lin. 2022. "The Graying of Divorce: A Half Century of Change." *Journals of Gerontology: Social Sciences* 77 (9): 1710–20.

Gabriel, Trip. 2025. "Monica Getz, Advocate for Divorce Court Reform, Dies at 90." *New York Times*, February 7, 2025. https://www.nytimes.com/2025/02/07/us/monica-getz-dead.html?smid=url-share.

Harris, Diane. 2024. "How to Stop a Late-in-Life Divorce from Ruining Your Retirement." *New York Times*, November 17, 2024. https://www.nytimes.com/2024/11/17/business/divorce-retirement-savings.html?searchResultPosition=8.

Hodes, Martha. 1997. *White Women, Black Men: Illicit Sex in the 19th-century South*. New Haven, CT: Yale University Press.

Jong-Fast, Molly. "The Right's Assault on Divorce Will Put More Women at Risk." *Vanity Fair*, May 10, 2023. https://www.vanityfair.com/news/2023/05/no-fault-divorce-gop-right-assault?srsltid=AfmBOopBok_HV5Wxa--fVUju2kPqBGyDKqY5xrt-i6fKXybHwVRBiz1i.

Luongo, Olivia, Hema Gharia, Mell Chhoy, Hattie Phelps, and Jessica Flynn. 2024. "Marriage and Divorce." *Georgetown Journal of Gender and the Law* 25, no. 2: 767–827.

DOBBS V. JACKSON WOMEN'S HEALTH ORGANIZATION (2022)

In 2018, Mississippi passed a law called the "Gestational Age Act," which prohibits abortions (with very few exceptions) fifteen weeks after conception. Jackson Women's Health Organization, the only licensed abortion facility in Mississippi, filed a lawsuit in federal district court challenging the law. Specifically, they challenged the new law because the Supreme Court precedent at the time prohibited states from banning abortions prior to fetal viability—this is when a fetus can survive outside the womb and had been generally set at twenty-four weeks after conception. The district court granted the clinic's motion for summary judgment and found that the state had not provided evidence that a fetus would be viable at fifteen weeks. The case made its way to the Supreme Court, where the question was whether Mississippi's law outlawing abortion after fifteen weeks was constitutional.

The result was a stunning blow to the women's movement. Justice Samuel Alito penned an opinion arguing that abortion is not mentioned in the Constitution, therefore nobody has a right to it. This overturned decades of precedent and the federal precedent set by *Roe v. Wade* (1973) and *Griswold v. Connecticut* (1965). Alito hinted, and Clarence Thomas outright argued, that the right to privacy—through which the Supreme Court had previously granted women's right to choose what happened to their own bodies within the privacy of their own lives and doctors' consultations—was also not really in the Constitution. This argument puts the entirety of the queer movement at risk, since people's rights to make choices about with whom they have sex (a private act) were also granted through the right to privacy.

Second, Alito argued that the right to an abortion is not rooted in US history, nor is it a part of America's desire to maintain ordered liberty. These positions, even though they are rooted in a patently discriminatory paradigm, must be taken seriously. They have been used to try and hold back progress for decades. The argument that a group's or individual's civil or human rights are not deeply rooted in our nation's history has been used for decades to try and deny equality to those demanding it. The argument basically boils down to "historically, we haven't given rights to some people before, so we shouldn't now." It is an unaccountably bigoted position but has been adopted as a constitutional theory for years by those whose goal is to maintain the status quo—including its hierarchies and oppressions.

Finally, in the *Dobbs v. Jackson* (2022) decision, Alito rejects the doctrine of *stare decisis.* "Stare decisis" basically means that precedent should guide legal reasoning. In short, if the decision has already been made, then follow those guidelines. But Alito rejects that out of hand. Certainly, there have been times when precedent was overturned and history has judged the decisions positively. When *Brown v. Board* (1954) overturned decades of law about segregation, it was largely judged as a positive move. But the difference in such rulings is that when precedent is overturned in such cases, it is to *give people more rights*. *Brown v. Board* (1954) changed the law to make things more equal—to make progress. The *Dobbs v. Jackson* (2022) decision is the first time since Prohibition (the 1920s) that the law has been changed to take away a fundamental right. The arc of the law has been to move forward, for the most part, even if it is slowly, and in starts and fits.

The *Dobbs* opinion is an attack on women's rights, but it could also have far-reaching effects on LGBTQ+ rights, and possibly even the rights of people of color, because the right to privacy at the heart of *Roe*, which *Dobbs* overturned, carries so much of the movements that led to the expansion of rights for others.

M. Elizabeth Thorpe

See Also: Abortion; Anti-Miscegenation Laws; *Griswold v. Connecticut* (1965); Reproductive Justice; *Roe v. Wade* (1973)

Further Reading

Dobbs v. Jackson Women's Health Organization. 597 U.S. 19. 2022. https://www.google.com/url?sa=t&source=web&rct=j&opi=89978449&url=https://www.supremecourt.gov/opinions/21pdf/19-1392_6j37.pdf&ved=2ahUKEwi-u7r-i92FAxV7vokEHfLPCAkQFnoECCoQAQ&usg=AOvVaw2eN_ZX02uv5jsaXq-Ghf-r.

DOMESTIC LABOR

For feminism, the term "domestic labor" encapsulates much more than household chores, roles, and responsibilities. Feminist perspectives recognize a range of domestic labor—care labor that is statistically more likely to be performed by women, women of color, and immigrants—as significant to society, including paid and unpaid labor, productive and reproductive labor, as well as emotional labor. Feminists also consider how the notions of *labor* (activity done to improve human welfare) and *domesticity* (the feminized home sphere) intersect with gender, race, immigration status, dis/ability, and class.

According to the US Department of Labor Women's Bureau (2024), women constitute 82 percent of personal care aides, 95 percent of maids and housekeepers, and 97 percent of childcare providers in the United States. Domestic workers are also nearly three times more likely to be immigrants. The average salary for year-round, full-time, domestic work in the United States is less than half of professional sector workers' annual income.

These statistics reflect that the United States' structural adjustments over time, such as the reduction of welfare, have forced women and minorities to shoulder extra labor, both productive and reproductive (Mohanty 2003). Meanwhile, oppressions in the workforce (racism, sexism, ableism, etc.) have routinely pushed vulnerable workers into the low-wage and underregulated domestic labor sector.

Despite being essential to the nation's existence and survival, domestic labor remains severely undervalued. Low wages and weak labor law protections worsen existing disparities among the often-marginalized individuals who perform this labor. Together, feminist and labor activism movements organize to improve labor conditions for domestic workers and to emphasize the value of domestic labor in society.

Domestic Labor as an Economy of Exploitation

Feminist scholars, theorists, and labor activists highlight the cultural contexts through which *domesticity* became linked with "immigrant work" and "women's work." The projects of settler colonization, slavery, and indentured servitude through which the United States was founded created a system where "domesticity" became near synonymous with exploitation. "Domesticating" colonized Indigenous women, for instance, was a key strategy in settler capitalism's policy and practice (Federici 2004; Haskins 2019). Moreover, "free labor" (forced enslavement) built much of the nation, historically—and enduringly—rendering Black women in the United States triply exploited by race, gender, and class hierarchies (Davis 1983; Stevenson 2019).

The nineteenth-century Market Revolution—marking the Western world's shift to industrial capitalism—created a gender divide where "men's work" came to mean professional and "women's work," by opposition, meant domestic. Working-class white men, now finding employment in factories, established the norm of "going to work" whereas middle- and upper-class white women were expected to "stay at home" and manage the household, if married. Lacking rights and their own income streams, married women were made to depend wholly on male heads of households. Poor or unmarried women, on the other hand, might work as domestic servants, usually under poor conditions. Throughout, the feminized reproductive and care labor—necessary for both birthing and supporting a growing capitalist workforce—remained "unwaged" (unpaid/given no value) and "unseen" (mostly conducted in private) (Dalla Costa and James 1975).

Feminist Responses to the Policies and Precarities of Domestic Labor under Globalization

Late capitalism and globalization have had a mixed impact on domestic labor. While the growth of the labor market created job opportunities outside the home for women and globalization enabled transnational solidarities, it also heightened and intensified already existing inequalities that earlier gendered divisions and devaluation of care labor set up. This is why sociologist Valentine Moghadam (1999) says that globalization itself was made possible "on the backs of the poor and especially of poor women" (370). Relatedly though, labor law activism proliferated throughout the twentieth century much to the credit of women of color, immigrant women, and poor women. These women are often recognized as the "unsung heroes" of labor activism (Jones 2009; Amladi and Cobb 2024).

The rise of global neoliberalism in the twentieth century pushed certain populations further into precarious situations. For instance, during the Mexican Border Industrialization Program in the 1960s, many Mexican and Mexican American (Chicana) women found work in textile factories located in US border towns. But when workers at Farah Manufacturing Company in El Paso—where 85 percent of the 4,000 workers were Latina women—went on strike, Farah replaced them with workers from Juárez. This forced workers on both sides to compete for basic survival and turned the El Paso/Juárez border into a "laboratory for a new economic model of exploitable labor" (NDWA). Despite this, the struggle spurred woman-led, working-class organizing on both sides of the border, making the borderlands a key locale of Chicana activism and class struggle.

Civil rights victories throughout the 1960s and 1970s enabled many Black women to leave the domestic sector for the professional sector and prompted domestic labor employers to hire more immigrants from the Global South. State-sponsored recruitment programs disguising economic reforms also helped employers appeal to migrant workers, many of whom faced financial instability and lacked political voice. This shift in the workforce is referred to as the "feminization of labor" (Standing 1989). Here, employers prioritize cheap labor, including women, Black, Indigenous, and people of color, and immigrants of all genders, over traditional labor divisions. Standing argued that this underpaid and exploited labor force—in which women are overrepresented—constitutes a vulnerable "precariat" class, lacking protections like fair pay, job security, and safe working conditions (583). Feminists thus highlight that "feminized" sectors, rooted as they are in racism, sexism, and exploitation, perpetuate global inequalities. Rhacel Salazar Perreñas (2017) refers to such situations, where migrant workers lacking labor protections are made dependent on their employers, as "relationships of indenture" (113).

Reform Era policies in the United States, like the 1963 Equal Pay Act and the 1964 Civil Rights Act, advanced labor equity but excluded most domestic workplaces. The original Fair Labor Standards Act (FLSA) of 1938 did not protect wages for workers employed in households. Other policies, like the Immigration Acts of 1965 and 1986, created legal barriers to citizenship that forced migrants into unregulated sectors like the domestic workforce. A 1974 FLSA amendment now protects minimum wage and overtime for domestic workers but still excludes "casual" services like respite and elder care.

Feminist organizing has worked to redefine domestic/reproductive/care labor as part of the economy and advocate for it to be economically recognized, or "waged." Founded in the 1970s in Italy, the International Feminist Collective started the International Wages for Housework Campaign, imagining what labor equity principles—for instance, wages and strikes—would look like if applied to work like cleaning, meal preparation, and caring for elderly or disabled family members. Placing domestic labor in the context of a strike (asking *what would life look like without this labor?*) reveals it to be troublingly invisible but absolutely essential.

Feminist labor activists also organize to address myriad oppressions built into domestic work. The National Domestic Workers Alliance (NDWA) founded in 2007 centers the legacy of slavery at the root of domestic exploitation, combats domestic work's connection to patriarchy, and challenges corrupt immigration laws that entrench the exploitation of women of color, immigrants, mothers, and low-wage workers in the national economy. NDWA supports grassroots campaigns for the rights and dignities of domestic workers in the United States.

Labor protections for domestic workers remain insufficient and are routinely exploited both locally and globally. According to the US Department of Labor's Women's Bureau, domestic workers typically earn below-average wages, lack certain labor protections, have minimal bargaining power, and face high risks of gender-based violence, abuse, and exploitation due to the isolated nature of their work (2024). The Bureau offers sample employment agreements to help formalize safe working conditions for domestic laborers; however, these agreements are voluntary and not legally required, limiting their effectiveness in preventing exploitation.

In/Visible Labor and Covid-19

For decades, feminist scholars have explained that the capitalist economy *depends on* the exploitation of "unwaged" domestic/reproductive/care labor; and the Covid-19 pandemic made their point strikingly more apparent to many in the United States. As the *New York Times* put it, the pandemic's "cascade of economic, social and political breakdowns" revealed just how important care labor is to the capitalist economy (Kinser 2021). Indeed, the lockdown showed middle- and upper-class people the extent to which their own lives relied on such labor—not just through cleaners and babysitters but also underresourced sectors like daycares, schools, after-school programs, and care homes. One of Covid-19's major shockwaves was the large-scale realization that "the requirements of caring for a family match or even exceed the requirements of the full-time jobs needed to support that family" (Kinser 2021).

Scholar-activist Keeanga-Yamahtta Taylor (2020) wrote of the pandemic that "American life has been suddenly and dramatically upended, and when things are turned upside down, the bottom is brought to the surface, and exposed to the light." With laundry piling up and/or a child interrupting a virtual meeting to ask for lunch, Americans were collectively forced to realize what the capitalist economy has long failed to recognize: that the home space has always been someone's workplace. Against this backdrop we must wonder how different life might look if the domestic care work people did—for themselves, for each other, and for the world around them—was valued at a premium. As the story of domestic labor suggests, major economic shifts are important times to pay attention to who benefits most and at whose expense.

Talia E. Kibsey

See Also: Capitalism; Equal Pay; Feminization of Poverty; Labor Activism; Reproductive Labor

Further Reading

Amladi, Divya and Camryn Cobb. 2024. "Unsung Black Women Heroes of the Labor Movement." *Oxfam,* February 16, 2024. https://www.oxfamamerica.org/explore/stories/unsung-black-women-heroes-of-the-labor-movement/.

BBC. 2022. "We Demand Wages for Housework." September 24, 2022. https://www.bbc.com/news/av/stories-62980454.

Benston, Margaret. 1989. "The Political Economy of Women's Liberation." *Monthly Review* 41, no. 7: 31–44. https://link.gale.com/apps/doc/A8257991/AONE?u=anon~32feccaf&sid=googleScholar&xid=2c8b6300.

Bleiweis, Robin, Jocelyn Frye, and Rose Khattar. 2021. "Women of Color and the Wage Gap." *Center for American Progress*, November 17, 2021. Accessed October 9, 2024. https://www.americanprogress.org/article/women-of-color-and-the-wage-gap/.

Dalla Costa, Mariarosa, and Selma James. 1975. *The Power of Women and the Subversion of the Community.* Bristol: Falling Wall Press.

Davis, Angela Y. 1983. *Women, Race & Class*. Vintage.

Federici, Silvia. 2004. *Caliban and the Witch.* Autonomedia.

Haskins, Victoria. 2019. "Domesticating Colonizers: Domesticity, Indigenous Domestic Labor, and the Modern Settler Colonial Nation." *The American Historical Review* 124, no. 4: 1290–301.

Hondagneu Sotelo, Pierrette. 2007. *Doméstica: Immigrant Workers Cleaning and Caring in the Shadows of Affluence.* University of California Press.

Hudson, Larry E., ed. 1994. *Working Toward Freedom: Slave Society and Domestic Economy in the American South.* University Rochester Press.

Jones, Jacqueline. 2009. *Labor of Love, Labor of Sorrow: Black Women, Work, and the Family, From Slavery to the Present.* Basic Books.

Kinser, Jordan, and Silvia Federici. 2021. "The Lockdown Showed How the Economy Exploits Women. She Already Knew." *New York Times Magazine,* February 22, 2021. https://www.nytimes.com/2021/02/17/magazine/waged-housework.html.

Marquez, Benjamin. 1995. "Organizing Mexican-American Women in the Garment Industry: La Mujer Obrera." *Women & Politics* 15, no. 1: 65–87. https://doi.org/10.1300/J014v15n01_04.

Mitchell, Sophia M. 2024. "Domestic Workers in the United States." *US Department of Labor Women's Bureau.* Accessed October 9, 2024. https://www.dol.gov/sites/dolgov/files/WB/DomesticWorkersFactSheet.pdf.

Moghadam, Val. 1999. "Gender and Globalization: Female Labor and Women's Mobilization." *Journal of World-Systems Research* 2: 366–89. https://doi.org/10.5195/jwsr.1999.139.

Mohanty, Chandra Talpade. 2003. "'Under Western Eyes' Revisited: Feminist Solidarity Through Anticapitalist Struggles." *Signs: Journal of Women in Culture and Society* 28, no. 2: 499–535.

National Domestic Workers Alliance. 2021. "A History of Domestic Work and Worker Organizing." Accessed October 9, 2024. https://www.dwherstories.com/.

Parreñas, Rhacel Salazar. 2017. "The Indenture of Migrant Domestic Workers." *Women's Studies Quarterly* 45, no. ½: 113–27.

Ruiz, Vicki L. 1987. "By the Day or the Week: Mexicana Domestic Workers in El Paso." In *Women of the US-Mexico Border*, edited by Vicki L. Ruiz and Susan Tiano. Allen & Unwin.

Solis, Gabriel. 2022. "Farah's 50 Years Later: A History of Class Struggle in the Borderlands." *Spectre Journal,* June 16, 2022. https://spectrejournal.com/farahs-50-years-later/.

Standing, Guy. 1989. "Global Feminization Through Flexible Labor." *World Development* 17, no. 7: 1077–95. https://doi.org/10.1016/0305-750X(89)90170-8.

Stevenson, Ana. 2019. "'Degrading Servitude': Free Labor, Chattel Slavery, and the Politics of Domesticity." In *The Woman as Slave in Nineteenth-Century American Social Movements*, edited by Ana Stevenson, 159–204. Palgrave Macmillan.

Taylor, Keeanga-Yamahtta. 2020. "Reality Has Endorsed Bernie Sanders." *The New Yorker,* March 30, 2020. https://www.newyorker.com/news/our-columnists/reality-has-endorsed-bernie-sanders.

Vogel, Lise. 2000. "Domestic Labor Revisited." *Science & Society* 64, no. 2: 151–70.

DRAG

Drag is a type of entertainment where people dress up and perform in highly stylized ways. Drag is an entertainment style that often involves cross-dressing for the general purpose of performance. Many consider drag to be a vital form of performance art that spans across artistic disciplines and genres (BREC 2023). For example, a man might wear a dress, high heels, and put on exaggerated feminine makeup for a choreographed lip-sync performance at a bar or restaurant.

Historically, drag was a slang term that began in British theater when women were not permitted to perform in plays, so young men dressed as women to perform the female roles (National Center for Transgender Equality 2017). In the United States, drag performances appeared on the vaudeville circuit and during the Harlem Renaissance ("The History of Drag, and How Drag Queens Got Pulled Into Politics" 2022). As early as 1860s, drag balls began. A drag ball is an event where many of the attendees, typically gay men, wear clothing conventionally associated with the other gender (*Queens and Queers: The Rise of Drag Ball Culture in the 1920s* 2016). Often drag balls featured competitive dressing (e.g., a fashion show), catwalk parading, and stylized dancing. As news of drag balls spread within the gay community, balls became a safe place for gay men to congregate. Drag and drag balls were a significant movement for the gay community, and drag performances are a mainstay at many gay bars to this day. More recently, drag hit mainstream media and gained popularity due to reality television shows such as HBO's *We're Here* and *RuPaul's Drag Race*, an award-winning hit on MTV.

Typically, prominent drag artists are individuals who identify as men and present themselves in exaggeratedly feminine ways as part of their performance. These artists are known as "drag queens." For example, Trixie Mattel is a famous drag queen from Milwaukee, Wisconsin, who gained notoriety after winning the third season of *RuPaul's Drag Race All Stars*, is a co-owner of Milwaukee's oldest gay bar and has her own makeup line, Trixie Cosmetics (About—Trixie Mattel n.d.). "Drag kings" are performers who wear men's clothing and perform stylized forms of masculinity; they are less common and are typically performed by women. However, a person of any gender identity can be a drag queen or drag king. Landon Cinder is a well-known drag king based in Los Angeles, California, whose groundbreaking win on the third season of *The Boulet Brothers' Dragula* paved the way for more representation and inclusion of different forms of drag on television (Dreher 2024).

Many drag performers have a drag persona that is separate from their everyday identity. This persona or personality often looks significantly different from their everyday identity, using different clothing and makeup, a unique name, and may be referred to by different gender pronouns. This does not mean that the performer is transgender. Just as actors do not keep being referred to by their characters' names after stepping offstage, drag performers do not necessarily keep the names or pronouns they use while performing. Drag performers are artists and entertainers, so being in drag is not an essential part of their identity in the same way that gender is.

Feminism, Intersectionality, and Drag

Feminist debates surrounding drag have been controversial. When drag queens first emerged as proud symbols of the gay liberation movement, many felt a need to distance themselves from what they saw as a mocking of women (Coles 2007). Feminists have critiqued drag, especially when drag performances emphasize "traditional" femininity, often sexualizing femininity and performing femininity as something that exists to satisfy masculine desires. In other words, some feminists argued that drag performs and sustains forms of femininity which primarily serve patriarchal interests.

The relationship between feminism and drag king performance is also complicated. While many drag kings believe their performances are feminist, feminists who are critical of drag king performance often accuse drag kings of upholding hegemonic masculinity, reinforcing patriarchal norms, or engaging in the subjugation of femininity through performances that use masculine tropes. Essentially, just as feminists critique drag performances of "traditional" femininity, so too, feminists critique drag performances that enact "traditional" masculinity, because they see these performances as reinforcing the gendered hierarchy in which masculinity oppresses femininity. However, many drag kings understand their performances as specifically feminist because they create feminist-centered spaces with their co-performers and have developed a way of talking (a subcultural language) about gender, drag, and art that resists the typical assumptions that masculinity and femininity are opposites (Basiliere 2019).

While some feminists reject drag as reenacting oppressive gender stereotypes, feminist theorist Judith Butler (1990) famously argued that drag is subversive—that drag undermines sexism by revealing gender as a performance. The idea is that gender is often assumed as a natural part one's life. For instance, people assume that women *naturally* want to wear dresses, high heels, and makeup. When a drag queen wears dresses, high heels, and makeup, his drag performance might be an exaggerated form of femininity, but it is also typically a consummate performance of femininity, which is to say, his performance is very good—better than most women's daily enactment of femininity. This, Butler argued, offers the possibility of subversion. When society sees a drag queen's consummate performance of femininity (or a drag king's consummate performance of masculinity) people can become aware that masculinity and femininity are performances—that the trappings (the clothes and accessories), the behavior, and the knowledges that make up masculinity and femininity are learned and performed, not natural. Indeed, masculinity and femininity cannot be natural if men can perform femininity extremely well and vice versa.

Drag also demonstrates intersectionality because drag performances are a product of multiple, intersecting, and conflicting identities. Hobson (2013) argues, "Drag performance is just one site where we see the dynamics of race, class, gender, and sexuality play out in both oppressive and resistant ways" (48). In other words, drag allows performers to express themselves in creative and liberating ways, has created a safe space for members of the LGBTQIA+ community, and while some feminists see the performance of gender stereotypes as a bad thing, others see these performances as a positive because they can unsettle the assumption that gender is natural.

Samantha F. Quinn

See Also: Gender Performance; Hegemonic Masculinity; Trans Theory

Further Reading

About - Trixie Mattel. n.d.. Trixie Mattel. https://trixiemattel.com/about/.

Basiliere, Jae. 2019. "Staging Dissents: Drag Kings, Resistance, and Feminist Masculinities." *Signs* 44, no. 4 (June): 979–1001. https://doi.org/10.1086/702034.

Brec. 2023. "Drag: A Theatrical Tradition." *BREC*, June 7, 2023. https://www.brec.org/news/drag-a-theatrical-tradition.

Butler, Judith. 1990. *Gender Trouble: Feminism and the Subversion of Identity*. New York: Routledge.

CBS News. 2022. "The History of Drag, and How Drag Queens Got Pulled into Politics." *CBS News*, October 29, 2022. https://www.cbsnews.com/minnesota/news/the-history-of-drag-and-how-drag-queens-got-pulled-into-politics/.

Coles, Charlotte. 2007. "The Question of Power and Authority in Gender Performance: Judith Butler's Drag Strategy." *Esharp: Electronic Social Sciences, Humanities, and Arts Review for Postgraduates* 9: 1–18.

Dreher, Russell. 2024. "Who are the Most Famous Drag Kings?" *AMBER LIVE: The Drag Queen Comedy Talk Show*, February 10, 2024. https://www.amberlive.tv/drag-queens/who-are-famous-drag-kings.

Hobson, Kathryn. 2013. "Performative Tensions in Female Drag Performances." *Kaleidoscope: A Graduate Journal of Qualitative Communication Research* 12, no. 1 (December): 4. https://opensiuc.lib.siu.edu/cgi/viewcontent.cgi?article=1167&context=kaleidoscope.

National Center for Transgender Equality. 2017. "Understanding Drag." April 28, 2017. https://transequality.org/issues/resources/understanding-drag.

"Queens and Queers: The Rise of Drag Ball Culture in the 1920s." 2016. *National Museum of American History*. March 30, 2016. https://americanhistory.si.edu/explore/stories/queens-and-queers-rise-drag-ball-culture-1920s.

DRESS REFORM MOVEMENT

The Dress Reform Movement in the late 1800s and early 1900s was a women's movement that attempted to change the standards for middle- and upper-class white women's clothing in the United States. Coinciding with what is now considered early feminist activism—the suffrage movement and broader activism for women's rights—the Dress Reform Movement was at once immensely practical and out of touch with the more pressing oppressions many women were facing.

During the later 1800s, middle- and upper-class white women were expected to wear floor-length dresses, typically with tight waists. Free women of color often dressed similarly, as did women from lower classes when they could afford to. As described by Marlise Schoeny (2000), these dresses achieved "fashionable" silhouettes not by conforming to the shape of the body but through a "range of undergarments" that supported the dress, creating its silhouette, including "chemise, petticoats, hoops, bustles, and corsets." These fashionable dresses were very time-consuming and difficult to put on. Moreover, if the corset was tightly laced, it could squeeze one's "intestines and internal organs" and could restrict one's breathing. Altogether, these dresses, their undergarments, and the women's coats worn overtop could weigh approximately 25 pounds. They constricted women's movement and made exercise impossible—even going up or down stairs was treacherous. Suffragist Elizabeth Cady Stanton saw these dresses as both a literal and figurative expression of (white) women's role in society, stating, "her tight waist and long trailing skirts deprive her of all freedom" (Schoeny 2000).

Dress reformers focused primarily on the skirt portion of the dress and undergarments. Motivated by both practicality and their cultural sense of modesty, dress reformers designed dresses with shortened skirts worn over trousers called "pantalets" or "pantaloons" (Schoeny 2000; Boissoneault 2018). As such, the entirety of women's legs were covered, but they had freedom of movement. Dress reformers developed these outfits by borrowing from European fashions, specifically from the Turkish and Syrian outfits that women had worn on stage, and French fashion, which had adopted similar outfits for young girls. These outfits were often embellished with lace and ribbons.

The Bloomer Costume, lithograph by N. Currier (1851). With this type of outfit, dress reformers aimed to allow for freedom of movement while maintaining their cultural sense of modesty (Library of Congress).

These outfits—and the women wearing them—became known as Bloomers, taking their name from Amelia Bloomer. Bloomer was a white middle-class woman and suffragist; she was the editor of one of the first women's newspapers, *The Lily*, and she announced her decision to wear the dress reform outfit in the April 1851 edition of *The Lily* (Kesselman 1991). Bloomer included an image of herself wearing the dress reform outfit, and her readers were enthralled. As Bloomer recounted, "As soon as it became known that I was wearing the new dress, letters came pouring in upon me by hundreds from women all over the country making inquiries about the dress and asking for patterns—showing how ready and anxious women were to throw off the burden of long, heavy skirts" (Boissoneault 2018). Soon, Bloomer's name was "inextricably tied to the trend" (Boissoneault 2018).

However, the Dress Reform Movement and the many women activists wearing Bloomers experienced intense backlash. Backlash is a negative response to the progress or perceived progress of minoritized groups. Notably, backlash is not a commensurate response; backlash is wildly over-the-top in its reaction. Bloomers experienced "hostility, ridicule, and ostracism" and were met with reactions "far in excess of the modest changes" to women's fashion (Campbell 1998, 3).

In particular, men objected to the Bloomers' pantaloons. The idea that women would wear trousers was "simply unthinkable," and the backlash was "more vitriolic than anything feminists had yet experienced" (Campbell 1998, 3; Banner 1980, 56). Writing in her autobiography, suffragist and abolitionist Jane Grey Cannon Swisshelm noted that this backlash reflected the belief "that masculine supremacy lay in the form of their garments, and that a woman dressed like a man would be as potent as he" (Swisshelm 1880, 140). Here, it becomes apparent that the idea of "trousers" was tied up with ideas of masculinity, power, and authority. Trousers were symbolic of men and therefore symbolized their power. Indeed, "trousers were the symbol of the male and of male domination, and the proposal that women should adopt them (almost entirely concealed by the skirt as they were) was seen as a threat to the whole structure of society" (Campbell 1998, 3; Gattey 1967).

Remarking on this backlash, abolitionist Angelina Grimké pointed out a sense of hypocrisy circulating in the extreme objections, writing that "if the Bloomer costume had come from a Paris milliner [a fancy dress-maker] it would have been welcomed in Boston, New York and Philadelphia." She continued, stating that the Bloomer "shocks the taste" only because it was developed and worn "from *principle*, from a desire in women to fit herself for daily duty" rather than being developed and worn for fashion, respectability, heterosexual attractiveness, and so on (Girmke in Kesselman 1991, 501).

Met with such extreme backlash, the Dress Reform Movement largely petered out. Suffragists—including Elizabeth Cady Stanton and Amelia Bloomer—unhappily returned to wearing the full dresses they so despised. This was a strategic move: they realized that the Bloomer outfit and the backlash against Bloomer outfits were "drawing attention" away from their core activism for the vote and other rights (Boissoneault 2018).

In many ways, the Dress Reform Movement was practical. It addressed a felt problem that many women experienced every day. On the other hand, it was a movement that continued to focus on wealthier white women's problems rather than working to alleviate the oppressions of poverty and racism that were destroying so many women's lives.

Even so, the Dress Reform Movement and its backlash overtly demonstrated the cultural links between trousers, masculinity, and power in ways that remain insightful for contemporary feminist activism. Indeed, while women now wear jeans and shorts without much thought or backlash, the term "pantsuit" reminds us that we are not too far away from these deeply ingrained assumptions about fashion and power. The term "suit" refers to a *man's* outfit with pants. The term "pantsuit" only applies to women's suits, clearly marking the pants in a "pantsuit" as, well, remarkable (Boissoneault 2018). The backlash against Hillary Clinton's pantsuits during her 2016 presidential campaign and her supporters' strategic wearing of pantsuits reminds us that gender and power are symbolized in fashion and that—as historian Gale Fisher explains—the United States is still uncomfortable "with the idea of women having this kind of masculine power" (Fisher in Boissoneault 2018; Clemente 2016).

Sarah Kornfield

See Also: Backlash; Gender; Gender Performance

Further Reading

Banner, Lois W. 1980. *American Beauty*. Chicago: University of Chicago Press.

Boissoneault, Lorraine. 2018. "Amelia Bloomer Didn't Mean to Start a Fashion Revolution, But Her Name Became Synonymous with Trousers." *Smithsonian Magazine*, May 24, 2018, https://www.smithsonianmag.com/history/amelia-bloomer-didnt-mean-start-fashion-revolution-her-name-became-synonymous-trousers-180969164/.

Campbell, Karlyn Kohrs. 1998. "The Discursive Performance of Femininity: Hating Hillary." *Rhetoric & Public Affairs* 1, no. 1: 1–19.

Clemente, Deirdre. 2016. "A President in a Pantsuit?" *TheConversation.com*, November 7, 2016, https://theconversation.com/a-president-in-a-pantsuit-68286.

Gattey, Charles, N. 1967. *The Bloomer Girls*. New York: Coward-McCann.

Kesselman, Amy. 1991. "The 'Freedom Suit': Feminism and Dress Reform in the United States, 1848–1875." *Gender and Society* 5, no. 4: 495–510.

Schoeny, Marlise. 2000. "Reforming Fashion, 1850–1914: Politics, Health, and Art." *Historic Costume & Textiles Collection: Ohio State University*, April 14, 2000, https://costume.osu.edu/2000/04/14/reforming-fashion-1850-1914-politics-health-and-art/#trousers.

Swisshelm, Jane Gray Cannon. 1880. *Half a Century*. Chicago: Jansen, McClurg.

DWORKIN, ANDREA

Controversial lesbian anti-pornography feminist militant Andrea Dworkin (1946–2005) wrote and gave speeches about sexual violence and what has come to be known as "rape culture" decades before the term was coined. Dworkin wrote and spoke about the most difficult subjects for audiences who almost never wanted to hear what she had to say.

Yet Dworkin's place in the intergenerational canon of feminist must-reads was sealed by the 2025 reissue of her 1983 book *Right-Wing Women*, which insists, in a message more timely than ever, that "Every woman's fate is tied to the fate of women whom she politically and morally abhors" (Dworkin 1983, quoted in Szalai 2025). New editions of two more of Dworkin's books, *Women Hating* and *Pornography*, were also published in 2025.

Dworkin's widower, John Stoltenberg, told *The Guardian* newspaper that these reissues "feel like a vindication" because a new generation of feminists is engaging with Dworkin's writing two decades after her death (Cooke 2025).

Born in Camden, New Jersey, to Jewish immigrants whose own parents had fled oppression in Russia and Europe, Dworkin was raised in a household that valued education, social justice, and literature. After she was molested by a stranger in a movie theater when she was nine, Dworkin's parents moved their family from the integrated city into the white suburbs, where Dworkin was subject to anti-Semitism and resented what she experienced as racist monoculture.

Eighteen years old and a first-year student at Bennington College, Dworkin was arrested for participating in a preapproved anti-Vietnam War protest at the US Mission at the United Nations. Unable to pay the $500 bail, Dworkin was remanded to "the notorious bastille in the heart of Greenwich Village known as the Women's House of Detention" and repeatedly brutally sexually assaulted by guards and a prison doctor, resulting in internal injuries and bleeding that lasted for two weeks (Duberman 2020, 2–3).

After being released without being charged with any crime, Dworkin wrote letters to "every newspaper listed in the Yellow Pages" to describe conditions at the Women's House of Detention (Duberman 2020, 2). Widely read *New York Post* columnist James Weschler responded to Dworkin's letter and, after talking with her, "took down her words in the form of a sworn affidavit" (Duberman 2020, 3). Dworkin's letters and sworn legal statement resulted briefly in her "notoriety as *that* girl in the newspapers" but did not result in charges against any staff at the jail, a pattern noted again and again across Dworkin's voluminous writing and collected speeches on sexual violence and misogyny.

Although much of Dworkin's work "stretched the public's imagination to its conceivable limits" (Palmer-Mehta 2016, 288), for women and other people subject to sexual violence—that is, for somewhere between one-third and one-half of humanity in the early twenty-first century—Dworkin's passion for writing and truth-telling can transform her work into something akin to poetry. In an interview about her 2022 documentary film *My Name Is Andrea*, filmmaker Pratibha Parmar asserts that "I think she was a poet, first and foremost. The way she wrote, she was a wordsmith. These different ways of putting words together, the phrases, the juxtapositions, all of that, was just something that was really both pleasurable and powerful to encounter on the page" (Fox 2022).

Across the history of human affairs, a woman writing is a relatively recent phenomenon. A woman being able to publish her writing is even more recent. A woman writing about rape and other forms of sexual violence and finding a commercial publisher who will pay her enough to pay her bills? Only beginning with feminist activism in the 1960s.

The rise of the #MeToo movement and the mind-bogglingly consistent support of white evangelical women for Donald Trump despite a jury finding him liable for sexual assault have helped keep Dworkin's work more relevant than ever, nearly two decades after her death in 2005 at only fifty-eight.

Along with Catherine A. MacKinnon, Harvard Law professor and Dworkin's coauthor, Dworkin testified before the US Attorney General's Commission on Pornography in 1986 that pornography violates women's civil rights and can lead to sexual violence. Dworkin's arguments against pornography not only increased her profile but also made her subject to hateful responses to her ideas—and to her very presence.

MacKinnon observed that Dworkin's appearance was mentioned in almost everything said or written about her. "Where the physical appearance of male writers is regarded as irrelevant or cherished as a charming eccentricity, Andrea's was reviled and mocked and turned into pornography . . . How [Dworkin] was treated [in life] is how women are treated who tell the truth about male power without compromise or apology. It is why few do" (quoted in Palmer-Mehta 2016, 297).

In addition to her published writing and collected speeches, Dworkin's papers are preserved at the Schlesinger Library at Harvard's Radcliffe Institute for Advanced Study (Palmer-Mehta 2022).

Rosa A. Eberly

See Also: Anger; Radical Feminism; Rape Culture; Sexual Objectification; White Supremacy; Women's Liberation Movement

Further Reading

Cooke, Rachel. 2025. "'It Feels Like a Vindication': Andrea Dworkin's Widower on the Radical Feminist's Rediscovery." Interview with John Stoltenberg. *The Guardian*, February 23, 2025. Accessed March 3, 2025. https://www.theguardian.com/books/2025/feb/23/andrea-dworkins-women-hating-pornography-right-wing-john-stolenberg.

Duberman, Martin. 2020. *Andrea Dworkin: The Feminist as Revolutionary.* New York: The New Press.

Dworkin, Andrea. 1987/2007. *Intercourse*. Free Press.

Dworkin, Andrea. 1976/1981. *Our Blood: Prophecies and Discourses on Sexual Politics*. Harper & Row.

Dworkin, Andrea. 1990. "The Montreal Massacre—A Speech by Andrea Dworkin." *Vancouver Rape Relief & Women's Shelter*, December 7, 1990. Accessed March 4, 2025. https://rapereliefshelter.bc.ca/the-montreal-massacre-a-speech-by-andrea-dworkin/.

Dworkin, Andrea. 1991. *Mercy*. Thunder's Mouth Press.

Dworkin, Andrea. 1993. *Letters from a Warzone*. Lawrence Hill Books.

Dworkin, Andrea. 1997/2002. *Life and Death*. Free Press.

Dworkin, Andrea. 2002. *Heartbreak: The Political Memoir of a Feminist Militant*. Basic Books.

Dworkin, Andrea. 1974/2025. *Woman Hating*. Picador.

Dworkin, Andrea. 1983/2025. *Right-Wing Women*. Picador.

Dworkin, Andrea. 1989/2025. *Pornography: Men Possessing Women*. Picador.

Eberly, Rosa A. 2000. *Citizen Critics: Literary Public Spheres*. Urbana: University of Illinois Press.

Fox, Michael. 2022. "New Film 'My Name Is Andrea' Depicts the Many Sides of Feminist Andrea Dworkin." *KQED*, July 19, 2022. Accessed March 3, 2025. https://www.kqed.org/arts/13916300/my-name-is-andrea-dworkin-documentary-pratibha-parmar.

Palmer-Mehta, Valerie. 2016. "A 'Suitably Dead' Woman: Grieving Andrea Dworkin." *Communication and Critical/Cultural Studies* 13, no. 3: 287–304. https://doi.org/10.1080/14791420.2015.1119291.

Palmer-Mehta, Valerie. 2022. "'It's the Truth about Women — That We Get Lost': Andrea Dworkin, Public Memory, and Archival Resilience." *Quarterly Journal of Speech* 108, no. 3: 292–316. https://doi.org/10.1080/00335630.2022.2088839.

Pratibha Parmar. 2022. *My Name Is Andrea*. Documentary film.

Szalai, Jennifer. 2025. "How 'Right-Wing Women' Found Their Place in the Manosphere." Book review. *New York Times*, February 26, 2025. Accessed February 28, 2025. https://www.nytimes.com/2025/02/26/books/review/right-wing-women-andrea-dworkin.html.

E

***EISENSTADT V. BAIRD* (1972)**

Women and feminist activists have been fighting for women's bodily autonomy for a long time; *Eisenstadt v. Baird* (1972) was a major success in our long-standing efforts. In brief, *Eisenstadt v. Baird* made it unconstitutional to prevent unmarried women from obtaining and using contraception. The case began in 1967, when reproductive rights activist William Baird gave a presentation at Boston University where he demonstrated the use of contraceptive foam. Following his lecture, Baird was arrested and charged with distributing contraceptives to an unmarried woman. At the time, Massachusetts law allowed medical professionals to distribute contraceptives to married couples for family planning purposes but barred distribution to unmarried individuals. This distinction became a focal point of Baird's legal challenge, raising important legal questions about privacy and equal protection under the law.

It had only recently become unconstitutional to prohibit contraception for married people. In 1965, the Supreme Court ruling in *Griswold v. Connecticut* gave married women (well, heterosexual couples) the right to control their fertility. The Supreme Court established this constitutional right to marital *privacy*, basing this right on the Fourteenth Amendment. *Griswold* laid the groundwork and *Eisenstadt v. Baird* expanded it, arguing that based on the right to privacy, women have the right to control their own fertility—regardless of whether they are married.

In short, Baird and the lawyers representing him argued that by permitting doctors and pharmacists to distribute contraceptives to married individuals but not to single individuals, Massachusetts violated the Fourteenth Amendment by discriminating against single people. The case also highlighted concerns about restricting contraceptive distribution (e.g., condoms, contraceptive foam, etc.) to licensed professionals, excluding activists and others involved in educational outreach—which posed potential free speech and due process concerns.

Justice William J. Brennan, Jr., authored the majority opinion in the Supreme Court's decision, ruling in Baird's favor by a 6-1 vote. Justice Brennan argued that the Massachusetts law's differential treatment of married and unmarried individuals lacked a rational basis, thus violating the Fourteenth Amendment's Equal Protection Clause. The Court concluded that Massachusetts's justification for promoting "family stability through marriage" did not warrant denying unmarried individuals access to contraception. In doing so, the Court expanded upon the right to privacy recognized in *Griswold* in a way that acknowledged women's right to control their own fertility. This ruling laid the groundwork for *Roe v. Wade* (1973), which made it unconstitutional to entirely ban abortion until the *Dobbs v. Jackson Women's Health Organization* ruling in 2022.

Eisenstadt v. Baird (1972) was a landmark achievement for bodily autonomy and equality, securing women's reproductive rights and privacy while challenging the social constraints that limit women's autonomy. This case contributed to gender equality, reinforcing the feminist ideal that women should have the freedom to make decisions about their bodies and lives without government interference. The decision not only improved women's access to reproductive healthcare but also strengthened the feminist movement's legal and cultural arguments for greater equality, dignity, and independence for women across all spheres of life.

Mariane Camargo

See Also: Bodily Autonomy; *Dobbs v. Jackson Women's Health Organization* (2022); *Griswold v. Connecticut* (1965); Right to Privacy; *Roe v. Wade* (1973)

Further Reading

Eisenstadt v. Baird, 405 U.S. 438. 1972. https://tile.loc.gov/storage- services/service/ll/usrep/usrep405/usrep405438/usrep405438.pdf.

"Eisenstadt v. Baird." n.d. Cornell Law School. Accessed November 3, 2024. https://www.law.cornell.edu/women-and-justice/resource/eisenstadt_v._baird.

"Eisenstadt v. Baird." 2024. *National Family Planning & Reproductive Health Association.* Accessed November 3, 2024. https://www.nationalfamilyplanning.org/pages/issues/eisenstadtvbairdmain.

EMOTIONAL LABOR

Emotional labor is the gendered expectation that some people—typically women and people of color—must care for the emotional well-being of others, even to their own detriment. Smiling and listening sympathetically while others share their feelings of rage, sadness, or frustration are typical examples of emotional labor.

This expectation is gendered in two ways. First, in intimate relationships and families, women are often expected to be good listeners for all of their male partner's and family members' emotions. Many young girls and women are taught to stifle their own feelings of frustration and anger in the service of making the men in their family happier. This expectation often carries over into the workplace, where women in particular face the second and more structural way in which emotional labor is gendered. The idea of emotional labor came from Arlie Russell Hochschild's study of flight attendants, titled *The Managed Heart*. As the title suggests, Hochschild discovered that flight attendants had to manipulate their own feelings in order to excel at their job—making other people happy and comfortable (Hochschild 1983). If a flight attendant is frustrated or upset when a customer screams in her face, her job requires that she *not* display her own emotions. Instead, she is expected to transform the customer's emotions from negative to positive without any sort of authority to change the situation that created the negative emotions in the first place.

Emotional labor is, at its core, *work*—and that work often goes unpaid. Emotional labor is expected in most or all service occupations, but it is particularly prevalent in female-dominated and poorly paid occupations like social work, nonprofit work, teaching, and salon work (Eschenfelder 2012). Social workers, for example, deal with families and children who are often struggling with money and mental health issues; their day-to-day jobs involve addressing the effects of abuse, neglect, and poverty. The emotional toll of witnessing these difficulties intersecting with the empathy required for such work creates higher levels of burnout and stress among a female-dominated workforce. Despite such difficulties (and the master's degree required for the work), social workers have been notoriously underpaid and experienced high turnover rates for decades (Lushin et al. 2023; Wage Equity Study Team 2023). Additionally, increased emotional labor is often asked of people of color in the form of educating their workplaces on diversity and equity issues, often without any extra pay and little recognition (Allen 1998). When they experience microaggressions on the basis of race and gender, such employees are expected to manage their emotions in ways that protect the very people who have harmed them. Like much emotional labor, this work is often expected of people who are "diverse" (e.g., minorities) and female-presenting and optional for everyone else.

Labor rights activists in the *Wages for Housework* movement have pointed out that the gendering of emotional labor in the workplace is a natural outcome of classed sexism. Emotional labor has perhaps always been expected of women doing (unpaid and underpaid) housework (Federici 1975). Because wealthier families can hire people to clean and cook and tend to their mental health, housework and emotional labor tends to fall even more heavily on the shoulders of women of color from lower socioeconomic situations (Duffy 2007). As Silvia Federici (2020) points out, capitalist social relations actually *rely* on women being unpaid for their work. When a male worker comes home at the end of a frustrating day of working for others, women around him are often expected to "service" him "physically, emotionally, and sexually, to raise his children, mend his socks," and "patch up his ego when it is crushed by the work" so that he can go out and do it again the next day (Federici 2020, 17). This gendered labor benefits companies that want healthy and happy workers without paying for vacation time, higher wages, and parental leave.

Ultimately, emotional labor and the gendered, structural inequity it reproduces remain entrenched in the social fabric of capitalism.

Elaine Schnabel

See Also: Capitalism; Divorce; Domestic Labor; Equal Pay; Labor Activism; Mind/Body Split; Reproductive Labor

Further Reading

Allen, Brenda J. 1998. "Black Womanhood and Feminist Standpoints." *Management Communication Quarterly* 11, no. 4: 499–634.

Duffy, Mignon. 2007. "Doing the Dirty Work: Gender, Race, and Reproductive Labor in Historical Perspective." *Gender & Society* 21, no. 3: 313–36. https://doi.org/10.1177/0891243207300764.

Eschenfelder, Beth. 2012. "Exploring the Nature of Nonprofit Work Through Emotional Labor." *Management Communication Quarterly* 26, no. 1: 173–8. https://doi.org/10.1177/0893318911424373.

Federici, Silvia. 1975. *Wages Against Housework*. Power of Women Collective.

Federici, Silvia. 2020. *Revolution at Point Zero: Housework, Reproduction, and Feminist Struggle*. Oakland: PM Press.

Hochschild, Arlie Russell. 1983. *The Managed Heart: Commercialization of Human Feeling*. Berkeley, CA: University of California Press.

Lushin, Victor, Colleen C. Katz, Francie J. Julien-Chinn, and Marina Lalayants. 2023. "A Burdened Workforce: Exploring Burnout, Job Satisfaction and Turnover among Child Welfare Caseworkers in the Era of COVID-19." *Children and Youth Services Review* 148 (May): 106910. https://doi.org/10.1016/j.childyouth.2023.106910.

Wage Equity Study Team. 2023. "Wage Equity for Non-profit Human Services Workers: A Study of Work and Pay in Seattle and King County." Seattle, WA: University of Washington. Accessed September 14, 2025. https://socialwork.uw.edu/wp-content/uploads/WageEquityStudy_Summary_withAppendices_0.pdf.

ENTHUSIASTIC CONSENT

Consent is the general idea of permitting something. In the context of sexual activity, consent is a basic way of differentiating between something being OK or being abusive, coercive, and/or rape. Enthusiastic consent is a newer model for understanding consent that focuses on a positive expression of consent. Simply put, enthusiastic consent means looking for the presence of a "yes" rather than the absence of a "no" (RAINN 2024). For instance, when teaching about consent, the conversation usually focuses around educating individuals to advocate for and possess the awareness to express and identify needs, desires, and boundaries, particularly within sexual relationships. Enthusiastic consent takes this a step further by focusing on clear communication between partners about what is occurring so that everyone involved is confident and *enthusiastic* about what they are doing.

Essentially, when it comes to questions of consent in a sexual context, the question is almost always, did someone say "No?" And, especially in legal contexts, that question is often something like "Did someone say 'No' in a clear and clearly understood way?" The problem is, as feminist communication scholars such as Celia Kitzinger and Hannah Frith have pointed out, English-speaking Westerners rarely say "No" explicitly in any context—and yet the concept of "No" is clearly conveyed and understood (1999, 301). For instance, when asked "Do you want to order pizza for dinner?" a person who agrees would answer immediately without hesitation. In fact, their yes statement would likely start while the question was still being spoken. But someone who disagrees would hesitate, would likely hedge their answer with filler words such as "well" or "um," and might offer a palliative phrase such as "that sounds great, but . . ." and even include an explanation as part of their answer. Such a negative response might sound like, "Oh! Um. That sounds great. But I'm not really sure I'm hungry right now!" In virtually every context such an answer is understood as a negation—as a "no" or nonconsent. But in sexual instances, this clear negation is often discussed as if it is confusing, ambiguous, and easily understood as a "yes."

By working to make "enthusiastic consent" the standard for consensual sexual activity, feminists are hoping to decrease the regularity in which the supposed absence of a "no" is taken as consent. Instead, feminists are working to make the presence of enthusiastic consent the standard for measuring consensual activity and the absence of it the indicator of nonconsent.

Feminist Activism around Consent

Educational campaigns about consent are heavily encouraged in our modern context as survivors of sexual assault find safe spaces to share their unwanted sexual experiences and, concurrently, their experiences are being validated with working definitions of consent. This has not always been the case.

For instance, in Rome, Italy, in 1992, an eighteen-year-old girl was raped by her 45-year-old driving instructor. She reported the attack, and he was convicted of rape and sentenced to jail. In 1999, the perpetrator appealed the sentence claiming that they had consensual sex, pushing the case all the way to the Italian Supreme Court where the conviction was overturned and the perpetrator was released. Explaining their position, the Italian Supreme Court claimed that because the victim was wearing tight jeans, she must have helped take them off—or at least not hindered their removal—therefore "consenting." This verdict sparked international feminist outrage and a Los Angeles-based nonprofit Peace Over Violence began Denim Day (typically held the last Wednesday in April) to advocate for the ways that harmful misconceptions around consent contribute to women's sexual assault and the discrimination against women under the supposedly neutral eyes of the law and society at large. Since then, Denim Day has been internationally recognized and activists work passionately to end sexual violence by wearing jeans as a protest against the ways false understandings of consent lead to survivors' experiences being minimized under a veil of neutrality that excuses acts of sexual abuse (Denim Day 2024).

Feminist Approaches to Consent

Feminists are always finding ways to describe experiences and advocate for people who experience sexual harassment, coercion, and assault. This involves deconstruction and knowledge reconstruction—essentially, breaking concepts down and redefining them in ways that are rooted in feminist theory.

When it comes to talking about consent, specifically, recognizing the ways that consent takes shape both interpersonally and structurally is essential since our daily interactions function within a white supremacist, patriarchal society. For instance, feminist theorist Catherine MacKinnon explores how ideas of consent operate in our current understandings of sex and sexuality and these structures often place women in impossible scenarios where what victims describe as rape is seen as a "consensual" sexual experience for men (and others in positions of power); moreover, in these scenarios the victim is typically blamed for causing a ruckus if they report their experience as abuse since they are disrupting hierarchal structures that ensure (white) masculine rights of access to women's and other minoritized people's bodies (MacKinnon 1989).

Our society is built on and operates through power structures that are designed to distance women from their own bodies and make women's bodies available to masculine desires—often in abusive ways, as the #MeToo movement highlighted. The lack of comprehensive sex education plays a large part in this system as women are kept from the knowledge of their own bodies and pleasure. Feminists are working to change this by supporting survivors through education. Everyone should have the knowledge and tools to understand what sexual abuse is and should be able to recognize consent—and the lack thereof—within sexual contexts.

Enthusiastic consent, then, is part of the bedrock of a feminist sex education. It is also a key feminist goal for all sexual activity: feminists dream of a future where everyone is enthusiastic about the sexual activity they pursue and experience—and nothing should happen if we aren't enthusiastic about it.

Without the knowledge and tools to understand what sexual abuse is, how to recognize various examples of consent and feminist ideology, believing and supporting survivors becomes inaccessible within a society that is built and operated by power structures meant to disembody and abuse women. Enthusiastic consent is essential for a feminist future.

Sutton Steensma

See Also: Bodily Autonomy; Deconstruction; Intimate Partner Violence; #MeToo; Violence Against Women Act (1994)

Further Reading

Kitzinger, Celia, and Hannah Frith. 1999. "Just Say No? The Use of Conversation Analysis in Developing a Feminist Perspective on Sexual Refusal." *Discourse & Society* 10: 293–316.

MacKinnon, Catherine A. 1989. *Toward a Feminist Theory of The State.* Cambridge, MA: Harvard University Press.

Peace Over Violence. 2024. "Denim Day Through The Years." Accessed July 21, 2024. https://denimday.org/history.

RAINN. 2024. "What Consent Looks Like." Accessed July 21, 2024. https://rainn.org/articles/what-is-consent#:~:text=Simply%20put%2C%20enthusiastic%20consent%20means,maintaining%20eye%20contact%2C%20and%20nodding.

ENVIRONMENTAL FEMINISM

The term environmental feminism (or ecofeminism) encompasses the feminist activism "that sees critical connections between the domination of nature and the exploitation of women" (Lorentzen and Eaton 2002, 1). The term was coined in the 1970s and was first used by French feminist Francoise d'Eaubonne (Mann 2011, 1). Feminist Karen Warren notes that ecofeminism is an umbrella term that covers many different perspectives and approaches since one could be a socialist ecofeminist, cultural ecofeminist, radical ecofeminist, spiritual ecofeminist, climate feminist, and so on (Warren 1996). The overarching main point of environmental feminism, though, is to investigate interwoven forms of domination in relation to "the earth's health and future in the context of women's life experiences" and how these two may be similar in a multitude of ways (Dawson 2014, 335).

While there is a broad range of connections between women and the environment within environmental feminism, three connections are central to the movement: "the empirical, the conceptual and/or cultural/symbolic, and the epistemological" (Lorentzen and Eaton 2002, 1). The empirical connection pertains to how most environmental issues that happen "generally disproportionately affect women" due to the increased burdens women face from environmental deterioration, especially for women in the Global South (Lorentzen and Eaton 2002, 1). The second claim is "that women and nature are connected conceptually and/or culturally/symbolically"; here mainstream symbolism like the idea of "Mother Earth" connects women and nature. Moreover, the domination of women through patriarchy mirrors patriarchal domination over the planet (Lorentzen and Eaton 2002, 1). Finally, the epistemological (knowledge-based) claim is a continuation of the previous two claims: since women are more negatively affected by environmental issues, women are more qualified experts on these conditions and therefore operate from "a position of epistemological" strength that others—especially men—might lack (Lorentzen and Eaton 2002, 1).

The term "environmental feminism" or "ecofeminism" and its associated movements stem from the environmentalism of the late nineteenth century, which was created as "a reaction to how urban, industrial areas were becoming overcrowded, smog-choked, and disease-ridden" due to industrialization and urbanization (Mann 2011, 6). While the environmental problems of the time affected the entire population, they mainly affected poor and working-class people who lived in cities, like immigrants, people of color, and women (Mann 2011, 9). Recognizing the intersectional oppressions of industrialization and urbanization sparked the activism that later started the environmental feminist movement. Most notably, the ecofeminist movement grew among women from the anti-nuclear, environmental, and lesbian-feminist movements, which later all coalesced into the "Women and Life on Earth: Ecofeminism in the Eighties" conference held at Amherst, which was the one of the first of many ecofeminist conferences (Lorentzen and Eaton 2002, 1).

Critiques of Ecofeminism

While environmental feminism provides the vocabulary and ideas to connect feminist ideals to environmental degradation, it is not exempt from critique. The concept or idea of a "Mother Earth" is an important image for feminist environmentalism, but portraying the earth as a mother can also strengthen "a patriarchal, capitalist discourse" that actually harms women and the earth, and "mother earth" imagery is problematically stolen and simplified from Native American ideas (Alaimo 1994). Indeed, the idea of attributing feminine attributes to the environment through images such as "Mother Earth" also leans into a broader critique from other feminists that warn against the essentialist ideas that are prevalent in some forms of ecofeminism. In this context, essentialism in environmental feminism means an "irreducible essence, an innate quality in women that connects them to nature, which is not present or available to men," and this idea creates the risk of essentializing women down to one or two innate characteristics in order to relate them to nature (Nesmith 1993, 383).

In some views of ecofeminism, women in general are painted as empathetic and sensitive, nurturing, spiritually connected with nature, and mothers or mother-like in some form. Using these descriptors to encompass all women ignores the different complexities, contexts, and bodies that women around the world have. In modern day though, ecofeminists have been trying to shift into a more "pluralistic and inclusive" form that "respects diversity and differences" and moves away from "process[es] of abstraction" that prevent us from recognizing the complexity and contexts within both human and nonhuman nature (Ottuh 2020, 176).

Environmental Feminist Movements

One of the most well-known and successful environmental feminist grassroots movements is the Green Belt Movement in Kenya. In 1977, the Green Belt Movement (GBM) was founded by Professor Wangari Maathai under the National Council of Women of Kenya (NCWK) in response to the needs of rural Kenyan women who "reported that their streams were drying up, their food supply was less secure, and they had to walk further and further to get firewood for fuel and fencing" (Green Belt Movement). The movement gave women the ability and resources to work together to plant trees, provide firewood, store and transport rainwater, have food, and receive a small monetary reward for their labor. Their mission statement is as follows: "We strive for better environmental management, community empowerment, and livelihood improvement using tree-planting as an entry point," and their main values are based around environmental conservation, empowerment of community and self, volunteerism, and accountability and honesty (Green Belt Movement). The GBM also provides seminars in environmental and civic education called Community Empowerment and Education seminars "to encourage individuals to examine why they lacked agency to change their political, economic, and environmental circumstances," which helped local people understand and place more accountability on national and local leaders (Green Belt Movement). After receiving the Nobel Peace Prize in 2004, Maathai received worldwide recognition for this movement and it continues to be very prevalent and active today as they continue to expand further and help more communities.

Another example of an environmental feminist-based movement would be the Black Mesa Water Coalition (BMWC). In 2001 a small group of college students, mostly women, responded to a report about dangerously low levels of water from the Navajo Aquifer and harmful deals for coal mining on Native land. This group was led by Enei Begate Peter and Wahleah Johns to form the Black Mesa Water Coalition (Parke-Sutherland 2018, 134). The Black Mesa Water Coalition was led by Indigenous women concerned, like their fellow ecofeminists, with forming a sustainable relationship between human persons and nonhuman persons for the support and health of both sides. They were dedicated to "addressing issues of water depletion, natural resource exploitation, and public health" on the Black Mesa, as well as on fellow Navajo and Hopi communities (Parke-Sutherland 2018, 134). The BMWC organized protests of grandmothers, young mothers, and children as well as allying with other groups working on similar problems, both on the local and national levels. The BMWC, in its beginnings, faced opposition from male-dominated tribal councils within the official governments of the Navajo and Hopi communities who have consistently supported and disproportionately benefited from exploitative, outside deals based on Native lands (Parke-Sutherland 2018, 135). Despite the pushback, the coalition established relations with outside environmentalist groups, worked to educate the younger people around them, held demonstrations and protests, hired lawyers of Native descent to help them argue their case in court, took on volunteers to help, and advocated for "new ways of combining traditional land-based values with innovative, contemporary technologies" (Parke-Sutherland 2018, 135). As of today, the BMWC helps to facilitate Navajo and Hopi joint organizations and projects to combat environmental injustice across the Navajo Nations and throughout North America.

Ultimately, ecofeminism creates a space for people to look at the intersection of how the supremacy over women parallels the suppression of nature and how this mutual domination has led to environmental destruction by white supremacist, imperialist, capitalist, patriarchal society. While this version of feminism needs to confront its own essentialist ideas and practices, it still provides ways for feminists to intertwine their goals with land preservation and conservation. In recognizing how nature is as dynamic and alive as we are and by understanding nature as an agent in its own right, we are able to destabilize the binary categories of active and passive, resource and user, oppressor and oppressed. Indeed, environmental feminism recognizes nature as an agent as much as women are in resisting the domination of both nature and women.

Cherokee S. Bauer

Also See: Colonialism; Cyborg Manifesto; Essentialism

Further Reading

Alaimo, Stacy. 1994. "Cyborg and Ecofeminist Interventions: Challenges for an Environmental Feminism." *Feminist Studies* 20, no. 1: 133. https://doi.org/10.2307/3178438.

Dawson, Melanie. 2014. "Constructing an Interdisciplinary Course on Literature and Environmental Feminism." *Feminist Studies* 40, no. 2: 333–52. https://doi.org/10.1353/fem.2014.0001.

Lorentzen, Lois Ann, and Heather Eaton. 2002. "Ecofeminism: An Overview." *The Forum on Religion and Ecology at Yale*. Accessed August 23, 2024. https://skat.ihmc.us/rid=1174588237625_665601541_9501/ecofeminism.pdf.

Mann, Susan A. 2011. "Pioneers of US Ecofeminism and Environmental Justice." *Feminist Formations* 23, no. 2: 1–25. http://www.jstor.org/stable/41301654.

Nesmith, C., and S. A. Radcliffe. 1993. "(Re)Mapping Mother Earth: A Geographical Perspective on Environmental Feminisms." *Environment & Planning D: Society & Space* 11, no. 4: 379–94. https://doi.org/10.1068/d110379.

Ottuh, Peter. 2020. "A Critique of Eco-Feminism: An Attempt Towards Environmental Solution." *International Journal of Environmental Pollution and Environmental Modelling* 3, no. 4: 167–79.

Parke-Sutherland, Tina. 2018. "Ecofeminist Activism and the Greening of Native America." *American Studies in Scandinavia* 50: 123–49.

The Green Belt Movement. 2024. "Our History." Accessed June 2, 2024. https://www.greenbeltmovement.org/who-we-are/our-history.

Warren, Karen.1996. *Ecological Feminist Philosophies*. Bloomington, IN: University of Indiana Press.

EQUAL PAY

Equal pay is the idea that people should receive the same pay for the same work. In the 1940s, Mary Anderson drafted the first version of the Equal Pay Act (EPA), which prohibits gender-based wage discrimination and was passed in 1963. In the following years, Congress passed laws (Title VII of the Civil Rights Act of 1964; the Age Discrimination Act of 1967) that expanded protections on the basis of race, color, national origin, age, marital status, and political affiliation.

The EPA increased the wages for some women during the 1960s; however, this law did not change the way US culture understands "women's work" or the stereotypes and gender roles that dominate women's lives—for instance, funneling women toward "women's work" as secretaries, nurses, manicurists, and dental hygienists. Nor did the EPA change the way society values "women's work" and thus pays for "women's work." This inequality contributes to the feminization of poverty, as women become trapped in low-paying jobs.

Working to end this inequality, feminists are moving toward a framework known as *pay equity*, which "values women's and men's work equally. It is a broader concept than equal pay" (Gring-Pemble and Chen 2018, 96). Specifically, the idea is to restructure laws to address gender biases instead of writing seemingly neutral laws that ignore gender biases in the marketplace (Zeigler 2006).

Understanding the Gender Pay Gap

Today, the gender pay gap is the smallest it has ever been in the United States, but it is still two and a half times larger than the gender pay gap in other industrialized countries (Javaid 2023). On average, women in the United States make approximately eighty-four cents to a white man's dollar (Javaid 2023). The gap is even larger for women of color and minorities. Compared to the white male's dollar, Latinas make around fifty-seven cents, Native women make approximately fifty-nine cents, and Black women make sixty-nine cents (Javaid 2023).

As such, to understand the pay gap, we must think intersectionally, a term coined by Kimberlé Crenshaw to draw attention to the interlocking oppressions of racism and sexism. In a 2013 study of "dirty work," Urvashi Soni-Sinha and Charlotte Yates examined labor-intensive jobs such as janitorial work and the role of gender and race. They state, "An intersectional analysis is helpful in understanding the simultaneity of class, gender and race in constituting the oppression and resistance of the worker" (Soni-Sinha and Yates 2013, 739). This study found that when workers (who were mainly women) received low wages, they felt unable to negotiate. Often, false narratives or justifications about "women's work" keep employers from listening to women and other minoritized people in the workplace.

Alice Cook (1975, 159) explains six assumptions or justifications that perpetuate unequal pay. First, the idea of "natural causes" is a false narrative that assumes women do "lighter" work and therefore deserve less compensation. For example, nursing is stereotyped as "women's work" and is considered "easier" than a doctor's work. Here, the gender pay gap is attributed to "natural causes" as women are assumed to naturally choose lighter work with less compensated pay. However, "natural causes" is a fallacy because people of all genders hold a wide range of careers.

The second justification, "economic factors," attributes the gender pay gap to women's supposed lack of "commitment" to their job. Here, employers justify paying women less by assuming women are less committed workers. This justification centers around maternity leave and the assumption that women will quit their jobs after having children. However, maternity leave (family medical leave) is incredibly complex and—like quitting one's job—often not an option for working-class people.

The third justification, "educational factors," centers around the myth that women have lower levels of education than men and thus are ineligible for more advanced and higher-paying careers. However, women have been outpacing men in higher education since 1979. For instance, in 2021–2, women earned "63.8% of associate degrees, 58.5% of bachelor's degrees, 62.6% of master's degrees, and 57% of doctoral degrees" (Nietzel 2024).

The fourth justification is known as "convention." Here, employers refuse to hire and/or promote women for better-paying work (e.g., careers in engineering, mathematics, computer science, the military, etc.) and justify this discrimination by essentially saying that hiring or promoting women breaks tradition and that their current (male) employees will not work with or for a woman.

The fifth justification for the gender pay gap is known as "overcrowding." Here, women are blamed for their low wages by the false claim that women's labor floods the marketplace and thus drives wages down. In reality, women significantly help the economy: with higher rates of education women bring knowledge and expertise into the workforce creating new jobs.

Finally, the last justification for unequal pay is known as "nonunion." This rationale again blames women for their low wages by arguing that women have not been participating in labor unions—which are known to help raise workers' pay. However, as the history of labor activism in the United States demonstrates, women have been systematically excluded from unions. As such, women's union rates are lower than men's, but this is a symptom—not a cause—of inequality in the workplace.

Employers continue to use these fallacies as justifications for unequal pay. As Morgan Tufarolo states, "Employers' explanations tend to cover up a much uglier truth: women face a seven percent wage disparity immediately after graduating college . . . even between equally qualified and educated men and women, men continue to earn more than their female counterparts in most fields" (Tufarolo 2016, 307). For instance, directly after graduating from the same college with the same degree, a man might secure a job at $50,000 per year while a woman only receives $46,500 in the same field of work.

Discrimination in the Workplace

Throughout their careers, women face discrimination. Specifically, the "glass ceiling" affects "large segments of the female workforce" (Gregory 2003, 1–2). The glass ceiling is the idea that there are roles or certain jobs that are "reserved" for men. For instance, women run only 10 percent of the Fortune 500 companies (Hinchliffe 2023). This means that the vast majority of C-suite roles and executive positions are held by men. When discussing the glass ceiling, David Purcell, Kelly MacArthur, and Sara Samblanet found that there "are limits to how far women can climb on promotion ladders despite having human capital and motivations that are comparable to their male counterparts" (2010, 707). Thus, even if a woman can enter a well-paying career, there are sexist limits to what roles she can hold and how far up the ladder she can move.

In addition to the glass ceiling, women experience workplace sexual harassment and a "motherhood penalty" (where women's roles and wages stagnate after childbearing). These forms of discrimination significantly affect women's ability to earn equitable wages (Alonso-Almeida 2014). Women of color and immigrant women face additional layers of discrimination that further affect their wages, often trapping women of color and immigrant women in the lowest pay sectors of the US workforce. For example, nearly a third of employed Black women work in service jobs while only a fifth of employed white women work in these low-paying roles (Banks 2019). Again, the intersection of anti-racist activism, feminism, and labor activism is critical in the movement towards equal pay for all women.

Current Movements and Pay Equity

Feminist researchers and activists have recently switched focus from "equal pay" to "pay equity." This new approach focuses on gendered roles within the labor market. For example, the term "fireman" actively excludes women and the term "midwife" clearly implies a gender. The push for pay equity includes wage transparency—so people know if and when they are being underpaid (Trotter et al. 2017). Moreover, the pay equity framework focuses on changing the social system in which "women's work" receives low wages simply because it is considered "women's work." For instance, New Zealand recently passed a pay equity bill that seeks to change wages, so people are compensated for the work they do rather than compensated based on whether their work is perceived as "women's work." For example, this bill would end the pay inequity wherein stereotypically masculine jobs such as sanitation work receive an average salary of $41,400 per year while stereotypically feminine jobs such as house cleaning only receive an average wage of $26,810 a year. Both jobs require similar levels of education, effort, and skill and thus—according to the feminist pay equity framework—ought to receive similar wages (Sussman 2020).

Ultimately, feminists understand pay inequity as the result of sexism and racism (and other forms of interlocking oppression). For instance, sexism and white supremacy combine to create deep-seated stereotypes—known as the Cult of True Womanhood—that cast middle-class white women as nurturing and soft-spoken people whose time is best spent in the home. This stereotype undergirds most of the justifications for the gender pay gap and supports workplace discrimination against women, the "glass-ceiling," and the systems that push women of color and immigrant women into low-paying "dirty work" in the labor force's service sectors. This stereotype also results in the "double bind" where women who work outside the home also do the majority of their family's domestic labor.

Society relies on a system of inequality, creating a cycle in which women are treated unfairly and undercompensated for their work—but change is possible. For example, the World Cup-winning US women's soccer team recently settled a lawsuit with US Soccer. They obtained $24 million in "back pay," which is a "tacit admission that the compensation for the men's and women's teams" was unequal, and obtained a pledge from US Soccer to "equalize pay between the men's and women's national teams in all competitions" (Das 2022). This lawsuit increased awareness about the Equal Pay Act, the gender pay gap, and broader wage inequities (English 2021). Feminist organizations such as the Equal Rights Advocates are working to change legislation around pay and advocating for the Paycheck Fairness Act, which is a proposed US law that would add protections for women in terms of pay and pay transparency. Ultimately, equal pay and living wages are essential to a feminist future and feminists are working to make this future a reality.

Elsie Craig

See Also: Capitalism; Cult of True Womanhood; Domestic Labor; Family and Medical Leave Act (FMLA, 1993); Interlocking Oppression; Intersectionality; Labor Activism; Lilly Ledbetter Fair Pay Act (2009); #MeToo

Further Reading

Alonso-Almeida, María del Mar. 2014. "Women (and Mothers) in the Workforce: Worldwide Factors." *Women's Studies International Forum* 44: 164–71. https://doi.org/10.1016/j.wsif.2014.01.010.

Banks, Nina. 2019. "Black Women's Labor Market History Reveals Deep-Seated Race and Gender Discrimination." *Economic Policy Institute,* February 19, 2019. Accessed September 25, 2024. https://www.epi.org/blog/black-womens-labor-market-history-reveals-deep-seated-race-and-gender-discrimination/.

Cook, Alice. 1975. "Equal Pay: Where Is It?" *Industrial Relations* 14, no. 2: 158–77. https://doi.org/10.1111/j.1468-232X.1975.tb00595.x.

Das, Andrew. 2022. "US Soccer and Women's Players Agree to Settle Equal Pay Lawsuit." May 18, 2022. https://www.nytimes.com/2022/02/22/sports/soccer/us-womens-soccer-equal-pay.html.

English, Ashley. 2021. "Is it a Four-Star movement? Policy Transformation and the US Women's National Soccer Team's Campaign for Equal Pay." *Social Science Quarterly* 102, no. 4: 1966–81.

Equal Pay Act of 1963. n.d. *US EEOC.* Accessed September 25, 2024. https://www.eeoc.gov/statutes/equal-pay-act-1963.

Gregory, Raymond F. 2003. *Women and Workplace Discrimination: Overcoming Barriers to Gender Equality.* New Brunswick: Rutgers University Press.

Gring-Pemble, Lisa, and Cher Chen. 2018. "Patriarchy Prevails: A Feminist Rhetorical Analysis of Equal Pay Discourses." *Women & Language* 41, no. 1: 79–103.

Hinchliffe, Emma. 2023. "Women CEOs Run 10.4% of Fortune 500 Companies. A Quarter of the 52 Leaders Became CEO in the Last Year." *Fortune*, June 5, 2023. https://fortune.com/2023/06/05/fortune-500-companies-2023-women-10-percent/.

Javaid, Sarah. 2023. "A Window into the Wage Gap: What's Behind it and How to Close it." *National Women's Law Center,* January 22, 2024. Accessed September 25, 2024. https://nwlc.org/wp-content/uploads/2023/01/2023-Wage-Gap-Factsheet.pdf.

Nietzel, Michael T. 2024. "Women Continue to Outpace Men in College Enrollment and Graduation." *Forbes*, August 8, 2024. https://www.forbes.com/sites/michaeltnietzel/2024/08/07/women-continue-to-outpace-men-in-college-enrollment-and-graduation/.

Purcell, David, Kelly Rhea MacArthur, and Sarah Samblanet. 2010. "Gender and the Glass Ceiling at Work." *Sociology Compass* 4: 705–17. https://doi.org/10.1111/j.1751-9020.2010.00304.x.

Soni-Sinha, Urvashi, and Charlotte A. B. Yates. 2013. "'Dirty Work?' Gender, Race and the Union in Industrial Cleaning." *Gender, Work & Organization* 20, no. 6: 737–51. https://doi.org/10.1111/gwao.12006.

Sussman, Anna Louie. 2020. "'Women's Work' Can No Longer Be Taken For Granted." *The New York Times*, November 13, 2020. https://www.nytimes.com/2020/11/13/opinion/sunday/women-pay-gender-gap.html?smid=url-share.

Trotter, Richard, Susan Rawson Zacur, and Lisa t. Stickney. 2017. "The New Age of Pay Transparency." *Business Horizons* 60, no. 4: 529–39.

Tufarolo, Morgan A. 2016. "You Haven't Come a Long Way, Baby: The Courts' Inability to Eliminate the Gender Wage Gap Fifty-Two Years After the Passage of the Equal Pay Act." *American University Journal of Gender, Social Policy & the Law* 24, no. 2: 305–36.

Zeigler, Sara L. 2006. "Litigating Equality: The Limits of the Equal Pay Act." *Review of Public Personnel Administration* 26, no. 3: 199–215. https://doi.org/10.1177/0734371X05278404.

EQUAL RIGHTS AMENDMENT (ERA)

In July of 1923, the first iteration of the Equal Rights Amendment (ERA) was proposed to Congress by Alice Paul alongside the National Women's Party on the seventy-fifth anniversary of the Seneca Falls Convention—the first women's rights convention in the United States. The goal of the ERA was to guarantee women would have the same rights as men (Michals 2015). The current iteration of the ERA reads: "Equality of rights under the law shall not be denied or abridged by the United States or by any state on account of sex" (Colohan et al. 2018b). The ERA is a proposed constitutional amendment, meaning that it would change the US Constitution. If enacted, the ERA would set a new precedent for equality in the United States.

For a proposed amendment to become part of the US Constitution, it first has to be introduced to a session of Congress. Then both the House and the Senate have to pass the proposed amendment by a two-thirds majority vote. The proposed amendment is then submitted to the state legislatures for ratification. A proposed amendment "becomes part of the Constitution as soon as it is ratified by three-fourths of the States" (Office of the Federal Register 2016). This means that thirty-eight states (out of fifty) have to approve, or ratify, the proposed amendment before it becomes part of the Constitution.

Journey of the ERA

The political campaign to pass the ERA spread across five decades from 1923 to the 1970s and in many ways is ongoing. After the success of the Nineteenth Amendment, which was ratified in 1920 and allowed (white) women to vote, the ERA was introduced by Alice Paul and coauthored by Crystal Eastman. Both women were active leaders in the suffrage movement and held law degrees—Paul held three degrees herself (Cohen and Codrington 2019). Over the decades, the ERA changed name and phrasing but remained the same in purpose. In 1923 the ERA was known as the "Lucretia Mott Amendment." In 1943, the ERA was dubbed the "Alice Paul Amendment" and its phrasing was revised to its current version, reflecting the language of the Fifteenth and Nineteenth Amendments.

From 1923 through 1971, Congress refused to pass the ERA, and women's rights activists had to routinely reintroduce the proposed amendment for Congress' consideration. By the 1940s the ERA was adopted by both the Republican and Democrat parties. Yet it was not until 1972 that the ERA "passed both the House of Representatives and the Senate" by two-thirds majorities and was sent to the states for ratification. However, Congress set a seven-year time limit for ratification, which they later extended by three years.

Within the time limit, the ERA was ratified by thirty-five of the thirty-eight states needed for federal ratification. The ERA did not become part of the US Constitution. This means that the US

Constitution still does not guarantee that "the rights affirmed by the US Constitution are held equally by all without regard to their sex" ("Equal Rights Amendment" n.d.). Or to put it more simply, without the ERA, the Constitution offers very few protections against sex-based discrimination.

For those opposed to the ERA, it symbolized a sort of doomsday clock: they lived in fear of losing supposed protections for women if it was passed by Congress and then ratified. For instance, they imagined that women might be forced to work outside the home or drafted into military service if the ERA was enacted. These fears were outlandish, but as many scholars have noted, the ERA functioned as a sort of a "political and cultural inkblot" onto which "many people project their greatest hopes or deepest fears about the changing status of women" (Alice Paul Institute n.d.). The ERA remains a powerful symbol for the advocacy of women in the United States.

The ERA's Ongoing Politics

In 1921, the National Consumers' League (NCL) leader Florence Kelley argued the ERA would not be comprehensive enough to protect white and Black women given the sexist racism Black women faced. Kelley also argued, however, that the ERA needed clauses to address the "biological differences" between men and women. As such, Kelley's ideas reinforced a conservative view of women as biologically inferior to men while seeking to address how racism affects women's lives. At the time, Black women and women of color had even fewer legal protections than white women, and Jim Crow laws largely barred Black women and women of color from voting until 1965 (California 2024). As such, Kelley's concerns outlined two continuous politics pertaining to the ERA: the need to ensure racial equality as well as sex-based equality for women and the stiff opposition to the ERA based on assumed differences between women and men.

Those who opposed the ERA largely did and continue to do so in order to ensure women can provide domestic and reproductive labor in society. For instance, in the 1920s, labor activists had won protections for women who worked outside the home, such as "shorter working hours, required rest breaks, prohibitions on night work, and limits on heavy lifting" (Novara 2023). Many were afraid these protections would disappear if the ERA was passed. However, these "hard-won protections" largely assumed women's inferiority in the workplace, allowing employers to abuse the work times and wages of women in the workplace.

Although most of the media coverage of the ERA's history and politics focuses on the 1970s, the ERA experienced decades of revision, activism, and opposition from a wide variety of social movements, such as "labor feminists, African American women, and various women's organizations" (Novara 2023). The ERA remains a site of political activism that draws together women's rights, anti-racist activism, and labor activism.

During the 1970s, Phyllis Schlafly prevented the ERA from being ratified by three-quarters of the states through her STOP (Stop Taking Our Privileges) ERA campaign. Schlafly's campaign amounted to a lot of fear mongering, making middle-class and upper-class families worried that the ERA might *require* (white) women to work outside the home rather than simply outlawing sexism within US laws. Throughout her life—and especially in the STOP ERA campaign—Schlafly's activism persuaded many women that feminism is not in their best interest. This remains an ongoing politic for ERA activism and feminism more broadly.

The ERA Today

In 1972, Congress sent the ERA to the states for consideration for ratification with a seven-year deadline, meaning that ratification efforts would conclude by 1979. However, the actual text of the proposed amendment that Congress sent to the states did not include any timeline or deadline. By 1977, only thirty-five states had ratified the ERA.

In 1978, Congress granted the ERA a three-year extension, offering an additional opportunity for three remaining states to ratify the ERA and thus formally amend the US Constitution. However, during these additional three years, no states ratified the ERA. Moreover, during the ten years during which states had the opportunity to ratify the ERA, several states issued legislation to "rescind" their ratification of the ERA. There is no constitutional guidance for this, and it remains unclear whether states are capable of rescinding a constitutional amendment's ratification.

In 2017, Nevada became the first state to ratify the ERA since 1977. Illinois ratified the ERA in 2018 and Virginia became the thirty-eighth state to ratify the ERA in 2020—reaching the three-quarters mark. The Alice Paul Institute (n.d.) asserts that "constitutional scholars agree the ERA is now part of the Constitution." However, because it was not ratified within the original seven years or the three-year extension (even though no deadline was included in the text sent to states for ratification), and since several states have "rescinded" their ratification, the ERA remains in a constitutional limbo and the National Archivist has yet to initiate the final ministerial process that would induct the ERA into the Constitution as the Twenty-Eighth Amendment.

A. J. Delgado

See Also: Domestic Labor; Labor Activism; Nineteenth Amendment; Reproductive Labor; Schlafly, Phyllis; Seneca Falls Convention (1848); Suffrage

Further Reading

Alice Paul Institute. n.d. *Alice Paul Institute*. Accessed August 29, 2024. https://www.alicepaul.org/.

California, State of. 2024. "Women of Color and the Fight for Women's Suffrage." *CCSWG*. Accessed September 4, 2024. https://women.ca.gov/women-of-color-and-the-fight-for-womens-suffrage/.

Cohen, Alex, and Willfred U. Codrington. 2019. "The Equal Rights Amendment Explained." *Brennan Center for Justice*, October 9, 2019. Accessed August 29, 2024. https://www.brennancenter.org/our-work/research-reports/equal-rights-amendment-explained?amp%3Butm_source=PANTHEON_STRIPPED.&utm_medium=PANTHEON_STRIPPED.

Colohan, Kathryn E., Jillian S Williams, and Niles J. Krista. 2018a. "Equal Rights Amendment Frequently Asked Questions." *Congress.gov.* Accessed August 29, 2024. https://www.congress.gov/116/meeting/house/109330/documents/HHRG-116-JU10-20190430-SD013.pdf.

Colohan, Kathryn E., Jillian S Williams, and Krista J. Niles. 2018b. *Equal Rights Amendment*. Accessed August 29, 2024. https://www.equalrightsamendment.org/.

"Equal Rights Amendment." n.d. *Alice Paul Institute*. Accessed August 29, 2024. https://www.alicepaul.org/equal-rights-amendment-2/.

"Equal Rights Amendment and Why It's Important." 2024. *National Organization for Women*. Accessed August 24, 2024. https://now.org/the-equal-rights-amendment-and-why-its-important/.

"Life Story: Phyllis Schlafly." n.d. *Women & The American Story*. Accessed August 19, 2024. https://wams.nyhistory.org/growth-and-turmoil/feminism-and-the-backlash/phyllis-schlafly/.

Martin, Douglas. 2016. "Phyllis Schlafly, 'First Lady' of a Political March to the Right, Dies at 92." *The New York Times*, September 5, 2016. https://www.nytimes.com/2016/09/06/obituaries/phyllis-schlafly-conservative-leader-and-foe-of-era-dies-at-92.html.

Michals, Debra, ed. 2015. "Alice Paul." *National Women's History Museum*. Accessed August 29, 2024. https://www.womenshistory.org/education-resources/biographies/alice-paul.

Miller, Eric C. 2015. "Phyllis Schlafly's 'Positive' Freedom: Liberty, Liberation, and the Equal Rights Amendment." *Rhetoric & Public Affairs* 18, no. 2: 277–300. Muse.jhu.edu/article/584317.

Novara, Elizabeth. 2023. "The Centennial of the Equal Rights Amendment (ERA): Origins and Early Debates: Unfolding History." *The Library of Congress*, July 27, 2023. Accessed August 29, 2024. https://blogs.loc.gov/manuscripts/2023/07/the-centennial-of-the-equal-rights-amendment-era-origins-and-early-debates/.
Office of the Federal Register. 2016. "Constitutional Amendment Process." *National Archives*. August 15, 2016. Accessed September 14, 2025. https://www.archives.gov/federal-register/constitution.

ESSENTIALISM

Essentialism is the assumption that differences between categories (such as women/men; Black/white; American/unamerican) are natural and fixed or permanent, and that those differences are prototypical—meaning the different characteristics have always existed and are of the utmost importance. Put another way, essentialism understands categories (women/men) as having a particular essence. When it comes to gender, essentialism "refers to the attribution of a fixed essence to women" (Grosz 2013, 334). This means that women and men are seen as naturally containing particular attributes—and it is those attributes that define them as women or men. These characteristics can not only be biological or physical (having certain body parts, hormones, etc.) but also psychological and emotional (being nurturing, supportive, etc.).

Essentialism is a way of thinking that assumes all women share the same "essence" and thus naturally all share the same set of "core" characteristics (Grosz 2013, 334). This way of thinking marks clear boundaries or gender roles, making it hard for women and men to act differently or create change. Indeed, essentialist views on femininity and womanhood have long been used to prevent feminist activism. For instance, many found it easy to dismiss and reject the women's suffrage movement by claiming that the suffragists were "unwomanly." In this sense, essentialist perspectives on womanhood follow psychoanalyst Sigmund Freud's assertion that "anatomy is destiny" (Greene 2020, 23). Many feminist movements have fought this claim that any particular characteristics are essential to being a woman or man. As Simone de Beauvoir states in *The Second Sex* (2011), "[o]ne is not born a woman but becomes one" (330). Many feminists understood de Beauvoir's statement as anti-essentialist and suggesting a lack of fixity in what defines a woman. This openness "held the door open to change and provided a platform for feminist activism" (Greene 2020, 23).

For instance, in the late 1960s and 1970s, many feminist scholars asserted that the subordinate position of women in society was greatly shaped by the patriarchal context and gender stereotyping, rather than any fixed characteristics of women. That is, women are not submissive because it is their natural essence to submit but because women have been conditioned to do so. For instance, Betty Friedan's *The Feminist Mystique* (1963) questioned women's roles and duties in the domestic sphere. Her book pushed back against the essentialist suggestion that a woman's sense of fulfillment could only be satisfied as a housewife and mother. In the text, Friedan suggested that there was no one single thing or act that could make all women content, but that the life of a housewife was not the ideal lifestyle for many women who wanted to receive an education, engage with politics, and voice their opinions in the public sphere.

Even while feminists pushed back against essentialist understandings of gender, biological explanations for the differences between women and men have continued to be pursued by many authors and public intellectuals. For instance, the extremely successful book *Men Are from Mars, Women Are from Venus* (1992) used essentialist logic to suggest that women have special qualities innate in their femininity and that this is natural—and how things ought to be. Even when essentialist language and arguments assert a positive viewpoint on femininity, it is still deeply tied to imagining women as one, unchanging thing. Martha Mednick (1989) significantly notes, "arguments for women's intrinsic difference (from men), whether innate or deeply socialized, support conservative policies" and maintain "the status quo vis a vis gender politics" (1122). When we imagine women as one fixed entity, that leaves little room for growth, transformation, or change.

On the other hand, the complete rejection of an essentialist notion of womanhood might then beg the question: If there is no common essence for women, how can we argue for "women's rights?" The scholar Gayatri Spivak argued that a particular "strategic essentialism" was sometimes needed in the political sphere. In this sense, women would, for a moment, set aside differences (of race, ethnicity, class, etc.) and "adopt the shared identity of woman" but only for political purposes (Spivak 1988, 283). Other feminist scholars reject any form of essentialism but call for women to attempt to find unities in their shared oppression and "shared aspects of their current social positioning" (Greene 2020, 24).

Essentialism can be seen in twenty-first-century conversations regarding the discrimination of trans women in cis women's spaces, such as women's sports. Cis women are understood as containing particular essential biological traits and hormones that mark them as "real" women. Yet, sexual categories do not exist in nature as a separated binary; it is humans, through discourse, who draw the line separating men and women. Physiological markers that we take for granted as gendered and sexed (as a binary), such as hormones and chromosomes, "need not—and perhaps should not—be considered markers of biological sex" (Blithe and Hanchey 2015, 488). As geneticist Anne Fausto-Sterling (2000) has long argued, the manner in which we categorize these alleged biological markers are greatly influenced by societal and aesthetic constraints that play a role in our mapping of these characteristics. Therefore, when trans girls and women are legally barred from playing sports with cis women and girls, this divide is deeply entrenched in essentialist logics. This sort of biological essentialism suggests that any woman who falls outside of particular normative bodily functions is not a woman. Yet, this proposition seems preposterous because scientists have proven the diversity and variability of human genetics and biological traits. This essentialist logic also denies any nonnormative female body the right to exist in the world as their true self.

Dafna Kaufman

See Also: Gender; Gender Performance; Intersex; Mind/Body Split; Strategic Essentialism; Trans-Exclusionary Radical Feminists (TERFs)

Further Reading

Beauvoir, Simone de. 2011. *The Second Sex*, First Vintage Books ed. New York: Vintage Books.

Blithe, Sarah, and Jenna Hanchey. 2015. "The Discursive Emergence of Gendered Physiological Discrimination in Sex Verification Testing." *Women's Studies in Communication* 38: 486–506.

Burns, Katelyn. "The Ride of Anti-trans "Radical" Feminists, Explained." *Vox*, September 5 2019. https://www.vox.com/identities/2019/9/5/20840101/terfs-radical-feminists-gender-critical.

Fausto-Sterling, Anne. 2000. "The Five Sexes, Revisited." *Sciences* 40, no. 4: 18–23.

Friedan, Betty. 1963. *The Feminine Mystique*. London: Penguin.

Greene, Sheila. 2020. "Biological Determinism and Essentialism." In *Companion to Feminist Studies*, edited Nancy A. Naples, 15–34. New Jersey: Wiley Blackwell.

Grosz, Elizabeth. 2013. "Conclusion: A Note on Essentialism and Difference." In *Feminist Knowledge: Critique and Construct*, edited Sneja Gunew, 15–34. London: Routledge.

Hall, Stuart. 1996. "What is this 'Black' in Black Popular Culture?" In *Stuart Hall: Critical Dialogues in Cultural Studies*, edited by David Morley and Kuan-Hsing Chen, 465–75. London: Routledge.

Hay, Carol. 2019. "Who Counts as a Women?" *The New York Times*, April 1 2019. https://www.nytimes.com/2019/04/01/opinion/trans-women-feminism.html?searchResultPosition=4.

hooks, bell. 1991. "Essentialism and Experience." *American Literary History* 3, no. 1: 172–83.

Lewis, Lark, and Jordan Reynolds. 2023. "Happy Pride. Don't be a TERF." *The National Women's Law Center*, June 21 2023. https://nwlc.org/happy-pride-dont-be-a-terf/.
Mednick, Martha T. 1989. "On the Politics of Psychological Constructs: Stop the Bandwagon I Want to Get Off." *American Psychologist* 44: 1118–23.
Spivak, Gayatri. 1988. "Can the Subaltern Speak?" In *Marxism and the Interpretation of Culture*, edited by Cary Nelson and Lawrence Grossberg, 271–313. London: Routledge.

EUGENICS

White supremacy has dominated the United States for centuries, pushing a heteronormative, ableist, racist, and patriarchal agenda. Part of the story of white supremacy is the story of eugenics. In 1883, Francis Galton founded eugenics as a scientific study based on completely ill-founded, Social Darwinist assumptions. Put most simply, eugenics combines the beliefs that (1) races are distinct in their biology and thus character, potential, and intellect, (2) the white race is superior biologically to all other races, (3) characteristics such as intelligence and morality are biologically inherited, and (4) society should control reproduction in order to manufacture a future with only by the best (white) people.

Overtly white supremacist, eugenics is also ableist and sexist. Consider, for example, the case of Carrie Buck. Carrie survived rape and became pregnant; her foster parents (whose nephew had raped and impregnated Carrie) committed her into the Virginia Colony for Epileptics and Feeble-Minded, claiming she was feebleminded and promiscuous. Two months later, she gave birth to her baby—a girl who died of measles at age eight. Believing Carrie (and her mother and sister) to be feebleminded and promiscuous, the state of Virginia sought to sterilize her, resulting in the 1927 Supreme Court Case *Buck v. Bell* that rendered forced sterilization constitutional. Both Carrie and her sister Doris Buck were sterilized without their consent, based on the logic—as stated by Supreme Court Justice Oliver Wendell Holmes—that "three generations of imbeciles are enough" (*Buck v. Bell* 1927). Carrie's mother, herself, and her daughter were the "three generations" Justice Holmes believed to be "imbeciles."

As seen in this example, eugenicists in the early 1900s believed that physical, mental, and moral characteristics were hereditary, thus predetermining the destiny of each individual (Pohlová 2022). In turn, eugenicists insisted that the US population could be improved by eliminating "undesirable" groups—such as the "feebleminded," racial minorities, and new immigrants—from the reproductive pool. As eugenics became increasingly popular, hitting its peak between the 1920s and 1930s, the United States implemented a variety of tactics to "purify" the population through pseudo-scientific methods that were built on racist, ableist, sexist, and homophobic teachings.

Negative Eugenics

Negative eugenics refers to the practices and policies that attempt to prevent those deemed "unfit" from reproducing. Some examples of "unfit" individuals are those classified as criminals, sexually deviant, lower class, disabled, mentally ill, and racial and ethnic groups not of Anglo-Saxon descent (i.e., people of color). During the early 1900s, negative eugenics relied on three primary strategies to rid society of such individuals: anti-miscegenation, institutionalization, and sterilization.

First, anti-miscegenation opposes miscegenation, or the sexual relations and intermarriage of individuals from different racial groups. Basically, this approach understood different races as practically different species and considered interracial sex and marriage (and thus procreation) as unnatural and immoral. Feminists, however, note that eugenicists typically allowed and continue to allow the "miscegenation" between nonwhite racial groups (e.g., a Latinx and Asian couple). Anti-miscegenation is typically about protecting the "purity" of the white race by preventing people of color from procreating with white women.

Second, institutionalization is the practice of isolating supposedly "unfit" individuals—such as Carrie Buck—from society, often by placing them in asylums. Institutionalization existed long before the eugenics movement, but eugenics significantly increased institutionalization in the United States. This method failed, however, to prevent the supposedly "unfit" individuals from reproducing as they sometimes reproduced with each other inside the institutions, and the institutions were expensive to maintain. Today, asylums are much less common, but the high rates of US incarceration suggest that institutionalization is still a factor in US population control.

Finally third, eugenicists use sterilization to control the population. Sterilization is a medical procedure that prevents people from reproducing, typically by severing women's fallopian tubes, a medical practice known as tubal litigation. During the early 1900s, eugenicists often sterilized women without their consent—and sometimes without their knowledge during other medical procedures. Sterilization is arguably the most controversial yet influential eugenics practice. In the early 1900s, scientists and politicians supported sterilization: over thirty states legalized forced sterilization for "all sorts of individuals including criminals, the insane, epileptics," and those deemed feebleminded (Pohlová 2022). The Supreme Court agreed, sanctioning forced sterilization in the 1927 *Buck v. Bell* decision where Justice Oliver Wendell Holmes summarized the eugenicist argument, notoriously stating, "It is better for all the world, if instead of waiting to execute degenerate offspring for crime, or to let them starve for their imbecility, society can prevent those who are manifestly unfit from continuing their kind." Forced sterilization was even considered beneficial "for the individual in question": once sterilized, they could be released back into "the normal population" since they could no longer reproduce (Pohlová 2022).

By 1936 over 60,000 people were forcibly sterilized in the United States (Farber 2008). Racial minorities were significantly affected as eugenicists concentrated on "breeding out" Native Americans, African Americans, and Asian populations as well as the "feebleminded" and impoverished (Farber 2008). Today, society tends to frown on forced sterilization, but it can still happen. For instance, between 2006 and 2010, at least 144 tubal ligations were performed on women prisoners in California alone (Whatcott 2018).

Positive Eugenics

While negative eugenics attempts to prevent "unfit" procreation, positive eugenics aims to encourage those deemed "fit" to reproduce—specifically, to have many children—thereby supplying "the human race with superior genes" (Pohlová 2022). Often, nation-states support positive eugenics by financially compensating families with two or more children.

Today, white supremacists and white nationalists bemoan what they see as "race suicide," arguing that white women are having too few babies and thus the "white race" is dying out. For example, the conspiracy theory known as "Replacement Theory" warns against a "white extinction" in which the "white race" is supposedly "replaced" by people of color. Deeply rooted in eugenics, this far-right ideology is currently gaining momentum in the United States. For example, the recent mass shooting in Buffalo, New York, was carried out in the name of "Replacement Theory." Arrested in 2022, Payton Gendron is accused of targeting Black people, shooting thirteen people and killing ten; he published a 180-page Replacement Theory manifesto prior to the attack.

Significant violence is carried out in the name of protecting the "white race." For example, during the 1980s, the white nationalist group, The Order, terrorized and assassinated people, working to spark a "white revolution." They popularized the white supremacist mantra known as the 14-words, which states, "we must secure the existence of our people and a future for white children." Although

The Order does not exist any longer, this slogan has continued to influence other white supremacist groups such as the Active Club, American Freedom Party, and the Patriot Front.

Less violently, contemporary white evangelical communities dabble in positive eugenics. Fixating on gender roles, white evangelicals often encourage (white) women in their communities to have many children as a way to win the "culture wars." For example, Kevin Deyoung (2020) wrote that "the future belongs to the fecund" and encouraged Christian women to "win the culture war" by having more children than their secular neighbors.

Feminist Opposition to Eugenics

Eugenics is a baseless pseudoscience. With time it became increasingly obvious to the scientific community that Galton's eugenicist theories were bogus. And yet, eugenicist thought still circulates today. For example, both historical and present-day Nazis are eugenicists, believing Jewish people to be racially inferior and demanding their extermination. Hitler developed his extermination plans by adopting Francis Galton's theories of eugenics. While Nazism primarily targets people of Jewish descent, it also targets LGBTQIA+ people, disabled people, and Black communities. Most people in the United States agree that Hitler's Nazi regime was wrong, but feminists help peel back the layers to better understand eugenics as a racist, sexist, ableist, and heteronormative ideology that continues to affect people today.

Historically, many white feminists in the United States supported eugenics. Today, however, feminist theory is firmly against eugenics—especially against sterilizing women without their consent. Moreover, feminist theory rejects the idealization of white, able-bodied, nuclear families with heterosexual parents as the "normal" or best type of family in the United States. Feminist theorists and activists typically recognize a wide range of family and living arrangements as beautiful and worthy of respect.

Feminist theorists and activists further note that eugenics claims to be about developing the ideal society, but in practice, eugenics is largely about controlling women's bodies and generally treats women as sexual/procreative objects—often shaming and blaming women. For example, Walter E. Fernald, a board member for the Eugenics Society, once stated, "It is well known that feeble-minded women and girls are very liable to become sources of unspeakable debauchery and licentiousness which pollutes the whole life of young boys and youth of the community" (Lombardo 2024).

Eugenics is a completely flawed and terrible ideology. It dominated scientific and political thought in the early 1900s, and, while soundly debunked today, it still influences US society. Currently, the specter of eugenics is at work not just in white nationalism but also in the industry of for-profit genetic engineering and screening (colloquially known as "designer babies") and in commercial reproductive medicine and technology such as IVF. Feminist groups such as SisterSong actively reject eugenics, working instead for reproductive justice so that all people have the right to have children if they want to, the right not to have children if they don't want to, and the right to nurture their children in safe and healthy environments.

Amber Sodemann

See Also: Anti-Miscegenation Laws; Reproductive Justice; SisterSong; White Supremacy

Further Reading

Buck v. Bell, 274 U.S. 200. 1927.

Cartwright, Ryan L. 2022. "Sissies, Loafers, and the Feebleminded: Disability and Nonheteronormativity in Rural White Eugenic Family Studies." *GLQ: A Journal of Lesbian & Gay Studies* 28, no. 4: 515–40. https://doi.org/10.1215/10642684-9991313.

Clark, Maggie. 2024. "Institutionalized: The Ever-Current Condition of the Formerly Incarcerated." *Fresh Writing (University of Notre Dame)*, January 6, 2024. Accessed November 7, 2024. https://freshwriting.nd.edu/essays/institutionalized-the-ever-current-condition-of-the-formerly-incarcerated/.

Collins, Ben. 2022. "Buffalo Shooting Suspect: Alleged Manifesto Cited "Great Replacement" Theory." *NBCNews.com*, May 15, 2022: https://www.nbcnews.com/news/us-news/buffalo-supermarket-shooting-suspect-posted-apparent-manifesto-repeate-rcna28889.

Deyoung, Kevin. 2020. "It's Time for a New Culture War Strategy." *The Gospel Coalition*, June 17, 2020. Accessed September 26, 2024. https://www.thegospelcoalition.org/blogs/kevin-deyoung/its-time-for-a-new-culture-war-strategy/.

Farber, Steven A. 2008. "US Scientists' Role in the Eugenics Movement (1907–1939): A Contemporary Biologist's Perspective." *Zebrafish* 5, no. 4: 243–45. https://www.ncbi.nlm.nih.gov/pmc/articles/PMC2757926/.

"Hate Map." 2024. *Southern Poverty Law Center*. June 21, 2024. Accessed November 7, 2024. https://www.splcenter.org/hate-map.

Kennedy, Angie C. 2008. "Eugenics, 'Degenerate Girls,' and Social Workers During the Progressive Era." *Affilia: Feminist Inquiry in Social Work* 23, no. 1: 22–37. https://doi.org/10.1177/0886109907310473

Lombardo, Paul A. 2024. "'Ridding the Race of His Defective Blood' — Eugenics in the Journal, 1906–1948." *The New England Journal of Medicine* 390, no. 10: 869–73. https://doi.org/10.1056/NEJMp2307346.

Pohlová, Hedvika. 2022. "Social Impact of the American Eugenics Movement." *American and British Studies Annual* 15: 148–63. https://doi.org/10.46585/absa.2022.15.2437.

Trent, James W. 1993. "To Cut and Control: Institutional Preservation and the Sterilization of Mentally Retarded People in the United States, 1892–1947." *Journal of Historical Sociology* 6, no. 1: 56–73. https://doi.org/10.1111/j.1467-6443.1993.tb00040.x.

Whatcott, Jess. 2018. "No Selves to Consent: Women's Prisons, Sterilization, and the Biopolitics of Informed Consent." *Signs: Journal of Women in Culture & Society* 44, no. 1: 131–53. https://doi.org/10.1086/698280.

Wilson, Jason, and Aaron Flanagan. 2022. May 17. "The Racist 'Great Replacement' Conspiracy Theory Explained." *Southern Poverty Law Center*, May 17, 2022. Accessed November 7, 2024. https://www.splcenter.org/hatewatch/2022/05/17/racist-great-replacement-conspiracy-theory-explained.

F

THE FAMILY AND MEDICAL LEAVE ACT (FMLA, 1993)

The Family and Medical Leave Act, or FMLA, is a federal policy that attempts to provide equal access to caretaking leave to employees of all genders. The policy was intended to minimize inconveniences for employers by offering unpaid leave while offering equal amounts of leave and job protection to employees regardless of gender, thus achieving equality for women and men in the workplace (Grossman 2004).

In practice, the FMLA requires any private employer with more than fifty employees (e.g., Google, the Philadelphia Eagles, your local supermarket) and all public agencies (e.g., the NYPD, the TSA, your local school district) in the United States to provide up to twelve weeks of unpaid leave of absence to their employees every twelve months. Employees qualify for this leave if they experience any of the following circumstances:

- The birth, adoption, or placement of a child
- The need to care for a child, spouse, or parent who is seriously ill
- A serious illness of their own

The FMLA has been amended since it was originally enacted so that it now also provides up to twenty-six weeks of leave for employees with family members in the armed services who need to deal with matters related to their family member's foreign deployment or if they need to care for a service member who has suffered a serious injury or illness (US Department of Labor 2013).

The FMLA offers job protections for employees, requiring that employers allow employees to return to the same job they were performing prior to their leave of absence once their FMLA leave is over. The FMLA makes it illegal to reduce the job duties and responsibilities, rate of pay, job title, access to benefits, or any other terms and conditions of employment simply because a person is on FMLA leave. Specifically, "the law protects employees from interference and retaliation for exercising or attempting to exercising their FMLA rights" (US Department of Labor n.d.). Someone who believes they have been retaliated against for exercising or attempting to exercise their FMLA rights should file a complaint with the US Department of Labor's Wage and Hour Division, as they are responsible for administering and enforcing the FMLA as well as investigating complaints (US Department of Labor n.d.).

Within US policy, there is no such thing as "maternity leave"; there is only the FMLA. When a pregnant person gives birth and goes on what is often colloquially referred to as "maternity leave," they are exercising their right to leave time as granted through the FMLA.

When President Bill Clinton signed the Family and Medical Leave Act into law in 1993, it was thanks to the tireless work of feminist organizations and activists. The FMLA was first introduced to Congress in 1984, but it took seven years before it passed through both the House and the Senate before being sent to the president's desk for signature. Then, President George H. W. Bush vetoed the bill in 1991 and again in 1992, which meant it couldn't become law until President Clinton signed it in 1993 (National Partnership for Women & Families).

FMLA and Intersectionality

In 1989—halfway through the fight to pass the FMLA—Kimberlé Crenshaw launched the concept of intersectional feminism into US politics. She argued that we should approach the law in ways that recognize how "various forms of inequality often operate together and exacerbate each other" (Steinmetz 2020). This is essential because people often have more than one social identity, which can result in simultaneous experiences of discrimination (UN Women 2020).

Even before Crenshaw popularized the term "intersectionality," the National Partnership for Women & Families (NPWF), a feminist organization that was instrumental in writing the first draft of the FMLA, attempted to take an intersectional approach, recognizing that they would need a varied coalition of organizations drumming up support for the law and lobbying political officials in both political parties if they wanted to realize their goal of passing federal leave legislation. The NPWF succeeded in bringing together the League of Women Voters, the Children's Defense Fund, unions including the Service Employees International Union, the National Education Association and United Steel Workers, the American Association for Retired Persons, and even the United States Catholic Conference.

By focusing on the intersectional needs of employees, this coalition rallied public and political support behind the idea that "employees shouldn't have to choose between the jobs they need and the families they love" (National Partnership 2024). They also deftly avoided anti-feminist and conservative-led debates about whether mothers even belonged in the workplace by redirecting focus to the law's equal application for employees of all genders, as well as the law's provisions for leave to cover circumstances beyond becoming a parent, highlighting that the FMLA also protected circumstances where an employee might need time to care for themselves, a spouse, or an elderly parent (National Partnership 2024).

Persisting Problems and Injustices

No discussion of FMLA can be intersectionally feminist without a discussion of its challenges and the injustices that still persist in the United States' medical and family leave process.

The largest obstacle to achieving the original intent of the FMLA—gender equality for medical and family leave—is *gender norms*. Specifically, the behaviors that we consider to be ideal standards of masculinity and femininity routinely subvert our ability to achieve equality for medical and family leave.

When Congress passed the FMLA, they assumed that, if it was available, men would take unpaid leave from their jobs in order to help care for their children or other family members. What they failed to consider was that caregiving is a core component of being a "good woman," and in contrast, masculinity often means being a "breadwinner" and not being a caregiver (because caregiving might make you effeminate!). Under these circumstances, an arrangement that equally offers leave does not, in practice, bring about the equality that is intended (Gerstel and Armenia 2009). To this day, most employees report that they believe women are better caregivers than men, and women—regardless of race and ethnicity—report spending twice as much time as men caring for loved ones (Twomey and Jones 1999; National Partnership 2024).

Studying the patterns of who takes FMLA leave, for how long, and for what reasons, Naomi Gerstel and Amy Armenia (2009) found that women are significantly more likely than men to take leave for any of the covered reasons under the FMLA and for longer periods of time. When men take FMLA leave, they do so for shorter amounts of time and most often for their own health conditions. Leave taken for newborns resulted in the longest leaves for women and the shortest leaves for men.

This disadvantages women in the workplace. Compared to men, women are "missing" from their careers for weeks at a time and losing pay for weeks at a time. Moreover, according to the US Census Bureau (2022), 80 percent of single-parent families are headed by women, making the question of whether to take leave to care for a sick child, family member, or even one's self even more necessary and yet difficult since taking leave means going unpaid for single mothers. This is especially true for Black mothers, 80 percent of whom are either the only, the primary, or the co-breadwinner for their household, which is a significantly greater share than mothers in any other racial or ethnic group (Milli, Frye, and Buchanan 2022).

In addition to gender discrimination, the ability to take FMLA leave and the consequences of that leave time are impacted by a number of additional realities and oppressions.

- **Classism:** Class and gender intersect to impact the ability to take FMLA leave (Gerstel and Armenia 2009). For instance, working-class men are more likely to take FMLA leave than middle-class men—largely because they are more likely to have wives who are employed than middle-class men. Even when middle-class men have wives who work outside the home, the wives of working-class men contribute a larger portion of the overall family income, making it more feasible for working-class men to take unpaid leave (Gerstel and Armenia 2009).
- **Disability:** FMLA leave can be extended beyond twelve weeks if an employee's personal health condition is considered a disability under the Americans with Disabilities Act (ADA). In these cases, employers must grant additional leave as a form of reasonable accommodation under the ADA unless doing so would cause them undue financial hardship or cause a significant disruption in their operations. This provision in the FMLA policy demonstrates how feminism and disability advocates have long been allies in the fight for equal access to civil rights.
- **Race and ethnicity:** African Americans and Latinx individuals are more likely to need healthcare and yet are less likely to have access to healthcare and health insurance (Bulatao and Anderson 2004). The reasons for this are, in and of themselves, intersectional and the result of colonialism and interpersonal, institutional, and structural racism. Additionally, career and wage discrimination mean that people of color are disproportionately likely to be working class—a scenario in which taking unpaid leave is rarely feasible (Gerstel and Armenia 2009).
- **Sexual orientation:** When passed in 1993, FMLA included spouses but not unmarried partners. This meant that until *Obergefell v. Hodges* (2015), same-sex couples could not take FMLA leave to care for their partner if they became unwell or to care for a child if their partner gave birth to the child—unless they were able to successfully petition the court to adopt the child. When the Supreme Court obliviated the right to privacy in the majority decision of *Dobbs v. Jackson Women's Health Organization* (2022) undoing decades of legal precedence, it called the validity of *Obergefell v. Hodges* into question. Feminist and queer rights activists remain uncertain how this ruling will affect a myriad of legal realities, including FMLA.

The Future of FMLA

The United States has perpetually lagged behind its industrialized counterparts on the global stage when it comes to paid family and medical leave. As of 2023, there were 193 countries in the world, and the United States was one of only seven countries that offered no form of national paid maternity leave. Of the 193 countries, 186 of them provide paid leave for new mothers; likewise, 174 of them also provide paid leave for personal health problems such as a heart attack or cancer; and 110 countries offer paid paternity leave (Miller 2023).

The FMLA has set the stage for a national paid leave arrangement that would bring the United States in line with the rest of the world. That said, in order to make such a change we would have to change mainstream attitudes in the United States. Again, it is primarily patriarchal gender roles that are holding us back.

Within US systems, there is a clear path forward: over 80 percent of all adults support expanding disability or unemployment insurance as a vehicle to pay for family leave. Unfortunately, counter-activism has been stiff. The opposition to this measure has been well-organized and well-funded (Lenhoff and Bell 2023). And yet, California and Massachusetts are leading the way with state programs that require insurance policies cover employee wages during employees' FMLA leave time (Employment Development Department 2022; Commonwealth of Massachusetts 2024).

Until we value the domestic and reproductive labor involved in caring for newborns, sick relatives, and elderly parents as much as we value the work that adults provide outside the home and until we are willing to compensate working adults when they provide that care instead of going to their traditional job, the disparities that exist in our family and medical leave structure will remain.

Devon S. Torchiana

See Also: Disability; *Dobbs v. Jackson Women's Health Organization* (2022); Domestic Labor; Feminization of Poverty; *Obergefell v. Hodges* (2015); Pregnancy Discrimination Act (1978); Reproductive Labor

Further Reading

Bulatao, R.A., and N.B. Anderson (eds). 2004. "Understanding Racial and Ethnic Differences in Health in Late Life: A Research Agenda." *National Institute of Health.* Accessed August 24, 2024. https://www.ncbi.nlm.nih.gov/books/NBK24693/.

Commonwealth of Massachusetts. 2024. "An Act Relative to Minimum Wage, Paid Family Medical Leave, and the Sales Tax Holiday." Session Laws: Acts of 2018. April 13, 2024. Accessed August 24, 2024. https://malegislature.gov/Laws/SessionLaws/Acts/2018/Chapter121.

Employment Development Department. 2022. "Fact Sheet: California Paid Family Leave." State of California. June 2022. Accessed August 28, 2024. https://edd.ca.gov/siteassets/files/pdf_pub_ctr/de8714cf.pdf.

Family and Medical Leave Act of 1993, Pub. L. No. 103-3, 107 Stat. 6 (codified as amended at 29 U.S.C. §§ 2601–54).

Gerstel, Naomi, and Amy Armenia. 2009. "Giving and Taking Family Leaves: Right or Privilege." *Yale Journal of Law and Feminism* 21, no. 1: 161–84.

Grossman, Joanna L. 2004. "Job Security without Equality: The Family and Medical Leave Act of 1993." *Washington University Journal of Law & Policy* 15: 17–64.

National Partnership for Women & Families. 2024. "History of the FMLA." *National Partnership for Women & Families.* January 30, 2024. Accessed August 24, 2024. https://nationalpartnership.org/economic-justice/family-medical-leave-act/history-of-the-fmla/.

Lenhoff, Donna R, and Lissa Bell. 2023. "Government Support for Working Families and for Communities: Family and Medical Leave as a Case Study." *National Partnerships for Women and Families.* February 2023. Accessed August 24, 2024. https://nationalpartnership.org/wp-content/uploads/2023/02/fmla-case-study-lenhoff-bell.pdf.

Miller, Claire Cain. 2023. "The United States Is One of the Few Developed Countries Without Paid Leave. Most Americans Need More Than Four Weeks." *The New York Times*, October 25, 2021; updated June 22, 2023. https://www.nytimes.com/2021/10/25/upshot/paid-leave-democrats.html?smid=url-share.

Milli, Jessica, Jocelyn Frye, and Maggie Jo Buchanan. 2022. "Black Women Need Access to Paid Family and Medical Leave." *Center for American Progress.* March 4, 2022. Accessed August 24, 2024. https://www.americanprogress.org/article/black-women-need-access-to-paid-family-and-medical-leave/.

Obergefell v. Hodges, 576 U.S. 644 (2015).

Steinmetz, Katy. 2020. "She Coined the Term 'Intersectionality' Over 30 Years Ago. Here's What it Means to Her Today." *Time*, February 20, 2020. https://time.com/5786710/kimberle-crenshaw-intersectionality/.
Twomey, Rosemarie Feuerbach, and Gwen E. Jones. 1999. "The Family and Medical Leave Act of 1993: A Longitudinal Study of Male and Female Perceptions." *Employee Rights and Employment Policy Journal* 3: 229.
UN Women. 2020. "Intersectional Feminism: What It Means and Why It Matters Right Now." *UN Women*. July 1, 2020. Accessed August 24, 2024. https://www.unwomen.org/en/news/stories/2020/6/explainer-intersectional-feminism-what-it-means-and-why-it-matters.
US Census Bureau. 2022. "Census Bureau Releases New Estimates on America's Families and Living Arrangements." November 17, 2022. Accessed August 24, 2024. https://www.census.gov/newsroom/press-releases/2022/americas-families-and-living-arrangements.html.
US Department of Labor. n.d. "The Employer's Guide to The Family and Medical Leave Act." Accessed April 13, 2024. https://www.dol.gov/sites/dolgov/files/WHD/legacy/files/employerguide.pdf.
US Department of Labor. 2013. "Family and Medical Leave Act Benefits Workers and Their Families, Employers: US Labor Department Releases Key Findings on Act's 20th Anniversary." February 4, 2013. Accessed August 24, 2024. https://www.dol.gov/newsroom/releases/whd/whd20130204-0.
US Equal Employment Opportunity Commission. 2016. "Employer-Provided Leave and the Americans with Disabilities Act." US Equal Employment Opportunity Commission. May 9, 2016. Accessed August 24, 2024. https://www.eeoc.gov/laws/guidance/employer-provided-leave-and-americans-disabilities-act.

FAT

"FAT PEOPLE OF THE WORLD, UNITE! YOU HAVE *NOTHING* TO LOSE." This call to activism is the closing line of the "Fat Liberation Manifesto" (1973), published by the Fat Underground—an organization that was crucial to the fat liberation movement in the 1970s.

"Fat" is a neutral descriptor for primarily plus-size people, used as an objective adjective similar to "tall" or "short." Fat writer and activist Aubrey Gordon writes, "Fat stands in contrast to an endless parade of euphemisms . . . all of which just serve as a reminder of how terrified so many thin people are to see our bodies, name them, have them" (Gordon 2020, 8). While "fat" may be interpreted as "unlovable, unwanted, unattractive, unintelligent, unhealthy," fatness is one small part of who someone is and "deserves to be described as a simple and unimportant fact" (Gordon 2020, 8). Fat activists use a number of terms to describe their work and distinguish it from the body positivity movement (and its "largely interior focus on self-esteem") including body neutrality, fat acceptance, body sovereignty, fat liberation, and fat justice (Gordon 2020, 6).

The work of fat activists is pointedly different from that of the body positivity movement and does not regard body positivity as a force for fat justice and liberation: "While body image is certainly a piece of the puzzle for fat people, it is a relatively small one . . . While the body positivity movement's aims are laudable, they're simply a solution for a very small part of the much larger looming problems faced by fat people—especially fat people at the larger end of the plus-size spectrum" and people in more marginalized bodies, particularly disabled people, transgender and gender-nonconforming people, and people of color (Gordon 2020, 5). There are significant barriers for fat people that cannot and will not be solved by self-esteem or body positivity: access to public spaces and services, freedom from weight discrimination, access to healthcare, and so on. These barriers require "political struggle against economic and social oppressions" (Schoenfielder and Wieser 1983, 33).

Sociologist Sabrina Strings (2019) highlights the role discrimination plays in anti-fatness by tracing its origins to racism and the transatlantic slave trade. During the Renaissance period in Europe, the ideal body type was "full-figured"; then, as Europeans argued for enslaving people from Africa, Europeans justified their so-called "racial superiority" by not just highlighting differences in skin color but also claiming that Europeans were rational and self-controlled while people from Africa were reduced to their bodies. During the 1800s in the United States, white middle- and upper-class women were explicitly cautioned to eat less in order to demonstrate their supposed racial superiority over the women they enslaved (Sofia 2020). From a historic perspective, then, anti-fatness has long participated in overt and overtly racist forms of oppression and discrimination.

Despite what mainstream media and the weight-loss industry may represent, research showing that fatness causes poor health outcomes is questionable at best. For example, government literature frequently cites a statistic that obesity causes 300,000 deaths each year. However, the research supporting this statistic suggests a link, not a cause, and after its publication, the top editors at the *New England Journal of Medicine* called the statistic "by no means well established" and "derived from weak or inconclusive data" (Farrell 2011, 13). In May 2005, the Centers for Disease Control and Prevention (CDC) published a refined study that challenged the 300,000 figure and suggested being moderately overweight was actually linked with increased longevity. The CDC received so much pushback that they pulled the refined study: "In other words, even when the scientific data looked challenging to the earlier statistics, the CDC was going to stick firmly to its war against obesity" (Farrell 2011, 13).

Academic research has consistently found that anti-fat bias is a major problem among medical students, social workers, nurses, doctors, and parents, and even the research that suggests a correlation between size and specific health outcomes is unable to distinguish the effects of fatness from the effects of discrimination (Gordon 2020, 52). The effects of discrimination worsen fat people's health "on all fronts, from the functioning of our brains to the very blood in our veins" (Gordon 2020, 79). Research has debunked a number of myths related to weight loss, including that exercise is a primary driver of weight loss, that diets and "lifestyle changes" result in lasting weight-loss, and that bodies function as calorie-in, calorie-out machines: in reality, body weights are determined by much more complex biological and genetic processes. Regardless of available research and weight-loss methods, the fact remains that "Nearly all available weight-loss interventions are ineffective for most people, most of the time. But each drives towards a proudly exclusionary vision of a world without fat people. And each presumes that fat bodies are broken and must be fixed" (Gordon 2023, 20).

Language around fatness (e.g., "war on obesity") and depictions of fatness in media contribute to how culture "assigns many meanings to fatness beyond the actual physical trait—that a person is gluttonous, or filling a deeply disturbed psychological need, or irresponsible and unable to control primitive urges" (Farrell 2011, 6). As a result, myths about fatness and fat people persist: that fat people are unlovable, or weak-willed, or hate themselves, or are unable to live fulfilling lives. Gordon offers a more resonant vision of fatness:

> We live extraordinary lives, beloved by our families, partners, communities. Fat people fall wildly in love . . . Fat people have phenomenal sex. Fat people are impossibly happy. Those fat people live in defiance of the expectations set forth for them. Their fat lives are glorious and beautiful things, vibrant and beyond the reach of what the rest of us have been trained to imagine. Let's imagine more. (Gordon 2020, 138)

Hannah Jones

See Also: Beauty; Body Positivity; Disability; Intersectionality; Mind/Body Split

Further Reading

Farrell, Amy Erdman. 2011. *Fat Shame: Stigma and the Fat Body in American Culture*. New York University Press.

Freespirit, Judy, and Aldebaran. 1979. "Fat Liberation Manifesto." *Off Our Backs* 9 (4): 18. http://www.jstor.org/stable/25773035.

Gordon, Aubrey. 2020. *What We Don't Talk About When We Talk About Fat*. Beacon Press.

Gordon, Aubrey. 2023. *"You Just Need to Lose Weight": And 19 Other Myths about Fat People*. Beacon Press.

Schoenfielder, Lisa and Barb Wieser. 1983. *Shadow on a Tightrope: Writings by Women on Fat Oppression*. Aunt Lute Book Co.

Sofia, Maddie. 2020. "Fat Phobia and its Racist Past and Present." *NPR.com*, July 21, 2020. https://www.npr.org/transcripts/893006538.

Strings, Sabrina. 2019. *Fearing the Black Body: The Racial Origins of Fat Phobia*. New York University Press.

THE FEMININE MYSTIQUE

Betty Friedan published her groundbreaking book *The Feminine Mystique* in 1963. In this bestseller, she defines "the problem with no name" for US housewives as a dissatisfaction (white) women experienced with the forms of fulfillment to which they were typically limited. In so doing, Friedan describes the institutions and assumptions that kept (white) women in the home in the 1960s and that continue to define femininity today.

Cultural beliefs, such as assuming that housework is "women's work" and that women are innately more nurturing than men, often trap women in household labor. In turn, these beliefs free men to earn paychecks and engage in leisure activities such as sports, working out, reading, watching TV, hobbies, and other forms of leisure. When Friedan used the phrase "the feminine mystique," she referred to the sort of mythical aura around and idealization of patriarchal versions of femininity. For instance, consider how a movie might glamorize a feminine character who is heterosexually attractive and generally passive. Or consider the way "traditional" femininity is glamorized as "grace and elegance," in which the ideal woman is "strong but submissive," "smart but not too smart," and "sexy but also chaste" (Gaddini 2019). This is the "feminine mystique": a patriarchal idealization or myth of femininity that suits heterosexual men and patriarchy more generally and that reinforces the idea that women exist to support and satisfy men.

The Feminine Mystique has helped generations of feminists realize it is okay for women to want more from life than cooking, organizing school carpools, and PTA meetings. As a testament to its impact, *The Feminine Mystique* spent six weeks on *The New York Times* bestseller list and its first paperback printing sold 1.4 million copies. *The Feminine Mystique* has been translated into at least a dozen languages, and over three million copies were sold during Friedan's lifetime (Muñoz 2021).

The Problem with No Name

Writing about middle- and upper-class (white) women's dissatisfaction with their lives, Friedan defined this dissatisfaction as "the problem with no name." For Friedan, it was especially horrible that so many people could be so dissatisfied and yet the problem went unacknowledged and unnamed in patriarchal society. Acknowledging the "problem with no name" helped women realize that they were not alone in their struggles and that there was nothing wrong with them. Reflecting on why she wrote *The Feminine Mystique* ten years after it was published, Betty Friedan stated, "I, like other women, thought there was something wrong with *me* because I didn't have an orgasm waxing the kitchen floor" (Friedan 1963, 511).

Despite the fact that many women struggled with deep depression due to how confined their lives were within patriarchal society during the 1950s and 1960s, their concerns were often dismissed by psychiatrists or treated with heavy medications, including tranquilizers such as oxazepam or laudanum. For instance, one of Friedan's interviewees described her problems as a housewife, stating, "I feel empty somehow . . . incomplete . . . I feel as if I don't exist" (Friedan 1963, 8). Women had been taught their entire lives that being a wife and mother was all they could ask for. What more could they want? Another housewife Friedan interviewed responded, "The problem is always being the children's mommy, or the minister's wife and never being myself" (Friedan 1963, 17). The problem with no name is always being someone's mother, or wife, or daughter—and never being *somebody* in your own right.

MRS Degree

The "feminine mystique" generally affected upper- and middle-class white women who married right out of high school as well as college-educated white women. Indeed, college-educated women were expected to find husbands, not careers during their time at college. This expectation created the stereotype and the running joke of the "MRS Degree," which refers to a woman who is supposedly only in college to find a husband. This hypothetical woman wants to walk out of college with a diamond engagement ring—and thus a marriage commitment to a middle- or upper-class man.

Colleges even marketed themselves to women as *the* place to find a man, rather than the place to get an education (Friedan 1963, 192). In the 1950s, professors at the prestigious women's colleges Vassar, Smith, and Barnard noted, "The girls seemed suddenly incapable of any ambition, any vision, any passion, except the pursuit of a wedding ring. In this pursuit they seemed almost desperate as early as freshman year" (Friedan 1963, 172). Women were taught to view marriage as their life's end goal and their entire purpose—and college was often seen as women's last and best chance of securing a good marriage proposal.

The college environment pushed women toward a "MRS degree." Women who took challenging classes were shunned by their peers and seen as "unfeminine." In order to be seen as "normal," women were encouraged to focus on getting married and having babies (Friedan 1963, 179). Even college professors told women to only take classes where they would learn what they needed to know for marriage. Harder classes such as biology and architecture were seen as "unfeminine," and the women who took them were seen as undesirable.

Reflecting on her own college experience, Friedan told PBS, "Well at Smith we certainly were not geared [toward] having careers. You were going to get married, you were going to have kids and you were going to be a leader, a community leader, a leader of the volunteer effort" (Wattenberg 2000). A college education was not to prepare women for the workforce but to be the perfect housewife and a pillar of the (white) suburban community.

However, as Friedan asked in *The Feminine Mystique*, "What is femininity, if it can be destroyed by an education which makes the mind grow?" (Friedan 1963, 199). And here, Friedan points out how ludicrous the "feminine mystique" is: if women supposedly stop being "true women" or become less feminine by learning interesting and useful things, then far from being natural or biological such "femininity" is a patriarchal design for women's lives.

Response and Criticism

The Feminine Mystique has been criticized for overlooking the struggles of poor women and women of color, who—unlike the middle- and upper-class (white) women Betty Friedan wrote about—have always worked outside the home. Friedan centered her landmark book around the white-collar workplace and thought of this workplace as a skills-based marketplace that was personally rewarding. This perspective did not acknowledge the wage labor poor women and/or women of color were already doing because they had to work outside the home to survive (Turk 2015). Indeed, it is a major failure that *The Feminine Mystique* does not practice intersectionality. It was written almost exclusively for middle- and upper-class white women. Systemic classism, racism, heterosexism, and other oppressions are not addressed in Friedan's landmark publication, leaving many excluded from its feminist contributions.

Friedan's proposed solution to the "problem with no name" is for women to enter the white-collar workplace and thus gain a sense of purpose. This overlooks all of the women who were already working to survive. While *The Feminine Mystique* inspired workplace feminist activism, it did so only for the most privileged women to enter into elite fields. As such, this book's recommended solution made some (mostly white) women's lives more fulfilling, but it largely failed to address the needs of women of color and working-class women. For instance, recommending that housewives pursue white-collar careers does nothing to dismantle the systematic barriers that women face in the workplace, such as lack of accessible childcare and the expectations of the housework still being "women's work."

Despite this criticism, *The Feminine Mystique* changed many women's lives. It helped women realize that they weren't crazy for being unhappy in their suburban "paradise" and that their "gilded chains" were still chains. Friedan received many letters over the years from readers whom she had greatly impacted. For instance, women wrote testimonials such as, "I can't express how freeing it was for me to realize that my predicament was not all my own fault"; "[Your book gave me] the courage to decide that the world wouldn't end if I left my husband"; and "I felt as though Betty Friedan had looked into my heart, mind, and psyche and . . . put the unexplainable distress I was suffering into words" (Coontz 2012). *The Feminine Mystique* gave many women the knowledge that they were not alone and that they were not irrational or ungrateful for wanting more. This caused a feminist spark in the 1960s by transforming public awareness of the struggles women face.

The Feminine Mystique Today

Even though *The Feminine Mystique* was published in 1963, it is still relevant today. Each generation seems to launch a new version of the "feminine mystique" such as the so-called "tradwives" on social media today. Analyzing the tradwife movement, Devin Proctor defines a tradwife as "a woman who believes in traditional gender roles and family dynamics" (2022). There has been a rise of tradwives on online platforms such as YouTube and TikTok, making videos showcasing "mommy hacks" and how to be a better wife for your husband. Famed British tradwife Alena Kate Pettitt has said on her blog *The Darling Academy,* "you may have noticed a new movement of ladies calling themselves 'Traditional Housewives.' Homemakers of our generation who are happy to submit to, keep house, and spoil their husbands" (Pettitt 2022). This new tradwife trend is 1950s domesticity wrapped in a different package and being promoted through social media. The #tradwifelife promotes a rise in domesticity and tells women to return to the household that Friedan describes as trapping so many women in the 1950s and 1960s. Without any awareness of *The Feminine Mystique,* new generations of women may find themselves trapped by the problem with no name that controlled their grandmother's lives.

The Feminine Mystique was a groundbreaking publication in 1963. It helped ignite the feminist movement in the 1960s and 1970s, laying the groundwork for the creation of the National Organization of Women (NOW). By defining the "problem with no name," Friedan gave many white upper- and middle-class housewives the words to realize they were not crazy and they were not alone. Patriarchy's "feminine mystique" is most powerful when women are convinced that this version of femininity is their life's purpose. Friedan's *The Feminine Mystique* exposes the deep depression many women experience under this myth and helps women understand that it is okay to want more out of life.

Riley Gruppen

See Also: Compulsory Heterosexuality; Equal Rights Movement (ERA); Friedan, Betty; Hegemonic Masculinity; Intersectionality; National Organization of Women (NOW)

Further Reading

Coontz, Stephanie. 2012. *A Strange Stirring: The Feminine Mystique and American Women at the Dawn of the 1960s*. New York, New York: Basic Books.

Friedan, Betty. 1963. *The Feminine Mystique*. London: Penguin.

Gaddini, Katie. 2019. "Donald Trump: Why White Evangelical Women Support Him." *TheConversation .com*, February 19, 2019. Accessed July 22, 2024, https://theconversation.com/donald-trump-why-white -evangelical-women-support-him-112041.

Menand, Louis. 2011. "Books as Bombs." *The New Yorker*, January 11, 2016. https://www.newyorker.com/ magazine/2011/01/24/books-as-bombs.

Michals, Debra. 2017. "Biography: Betty Friedan." *National Women's History Museum*. Accessed August 23, 2024. https://www.womenshistory.org/education-resources/biographies/betty-friedan#:~:text=Her%201963 %20best%2Dselling%20book,public%20activism%20for%20gender%20equality

Muñoz, Jacob. 2021. "The Powerful, Complicated Legacy of Betty Friedan's 'The Feminine Mystique.'" *Smithsonian.com*. Accessed August 24, 2024. https://www.smithsonianmag.com/smithsonian-institution/ powerful-complicated-legacy-betty-friedans-feminine-mystique-180976931/.

Pettitt, Alena Kate. 2022. "The Darling Academy: Home of the Traditional Housewife." *The Darling Academy Etiquette Books*. Accessed August 24, 2024. https://www.thedarlingacademy.com.

Proctor, Devin. 2022. "The #Tradwife Persona and the Rise of Radicalized Domesticity." *Persona Studies* 8, no. 2: 7–26. https://doi.org/10.21153/psj2022vol8no2art1645.

Turk, Katherine. 2015. "'To Fulfill an Ambition of [Her] Own': Work, Class, and Identity in The Feminine Mystique." *Frontiers: A Journal of Women Studies* 36, no. 2: 25–32. https://doi.org/10.1353/fro.2015 .a589410.

Wattenberg, Ben. 2000. "Betty Friedan Interview." *PBS*. Accessed August 24, 2024. https://www.pbs.org/fmc/ interviews/friedan.htm.

FEMINIST KILLJOY

Broadly, a killjoy is someone who eradicates the enjoyment or pleasure of a space or environment. In Sara Ahmed's piece (2010), "Feminist Killjoys (and Other Willful Subjects)," she explores the feminist killjoy as a particular brand of joy killer. She examines people's desire for or insistence on happiness and how that shapes our understandings of feminism and activism.

Ahmed (2010, 2) explains that sometimes becoming a feminist can seem like "an alienation from happiness." This feeling of alienation comes from being out of step with society's feelings and approach to happiness. In this sense, the things society claims will make you happy do not necessarily move you to happiness. While this alienation might create frustration or anxiety, Ahmed believes that this gap between how one *actually* feels and how one supposedly *should* feel is where activist possibilities lie. Those who cannot accept the happiness attached to certain objects ("happy" objects) create dissidence and often threaten social norms. Ahmed provides the example of a family joining together for a meal. While this occurrence is considered a happy one, a time where family can come together and enjoy each other's company, the event becomes more complex for the feminist killjoy. While together, appreciating a shared meal among loved ones, someone makes a comment that you feel is problematic or concerning. The normalized reaction is to allow the comment to float by and preserve the feeling of happiness and "good image of the family" (2). But instead, the feminist killjoy speaks up and critiques the comment disrupting and distorting the "happy" world and family occasion—perhaps ruining the dinner. While in this example, the feminist killjoy perhaps alienates their family and meddles with the group's happiness, they do so because they see a better potential world—and are willing to go against the normative social order to move toward that possibility.

Feminist killjoys are prepared to go against particular social and moral orders of happiness and are "willing to cause unhappiness, even if unhappiness is not [their] cause" (Ahmed 2010, 3). Pointing out sexism, the feminist killjoy does "kill joy in a certain sense" by threatening the "very fantasy that happiness can be found in certain places" (Ahmed 2010, 4). Ahmed considers the work of these willful feminist killjoys a way of producing knowledge and "a world-making project" (2010, 5). That is, by resisting and speaking up against sexist assumptions, actions, policies, and practices, feminist killjoys lead the way toward making a new way of living, a world without oppression.

The feminist killjoy disrupts the image of the compliant, docile woman. Her anger and frustration with inequitable systems moves her to speak and unsettle discriminatory norms. While anger, particularly women's anger, is often critiqued as irrational and hysterical, many feminist scholars argue for anger's energizing and clarifying potential. For instance, feminist scholar Audre Lorde (1981) argued that anger is useful for knowledge. In her piece entitled, "The Uses of Anger," Lorde asserts, "Women of Color in America have grown up within a symphony of anguish at being silenced, at being unchosen . . . and I say 'symphony' rather 'cacophony' because we have had to learn to orchestrate those furies so that they do not tear us apart" (1981, 9). Professor and activist Brittany Cooper (2018) takes up Lorde's assertion in her collection, *Eloquent Rage: A Black Feminist Discovers Her Superpowers*. In this text, Cooper maintains "individualized acts of eloquent rage have limited reach. But the collective, orchestrated fury of Black women can move the whole world" (2018, 168). Here, Lorde and Cooper not only contend that anger has powerful political possibilities but that this anger can bring oppressed groups together to enact a sort of refusal needed to combat the status quo. While anger is often depicted as an isolating or volatile emotion, Soraya Chemaly argues, "in fact, it is an emotion that demand(s) communication and conversation . . . finds strength in community . . . [and] creates powerful opportunities" for valuable social action (2018, 276). Not only does anger have the potential to unite oppressed groups—for many, it has been a means of survival.

In the early twenty-first century, we have seen major collectivist feminist movements relying on the feminist killjoy's logic of confrontation and critique of norms. While women's anger in the public sphere has existed historically, we have seen a marked increase in the expression of public anger by women. In particular, the election of Donald Trump as president of the United States in November 2016 left many American women disappointed and disturbed. Trump's overt and unapologetic misogyny inspired a swell in women's activism. Ashwini Tambe, a transnational feminist scholar, notes that running through this activism and political moment was a passionate fury about the election of Donald Trump and his overtly misogyny (2018, 198). Trump's blatantly misogynistic rhetoric motivated women to take to the streets. Soraya Chemaly suggests that women's shared anger is what drove them to march in worldwide protest the day after Trump's inauguration (2018, 535). The Women's March, spanning hundreds of cities, assembled an estimated five million attendees—the protest is thought to be one of the largest protests in American history.

Subsequently, almost exactly one year after Trump's election, in October 2017, actress Alyssa Milano released a tweet using the hashtag #MeToo urging people to speak out in order to demonstrate the extent to which women were the victims of sexual violence on an everyday basis. Milano's tweets employing the #MeToo hashtag focused on sexual assault allegations against Harvey Weinstein, a famous and influential Hollywood producer. Within twenty-four hours of Milano's post, the tweet generated an explosive response: half a million retweets. The #MeToo movement did not focus exclusively on Hollywood celebrities but rather on a multitude of influential cis men. Almost no industry remained untouched, and many men resigned from powerful positions when the allegations of their sexual misconduct came to light. Through the #MeToo hashtag, women enacted killjoy feminism. Speaking about sexual assault and harassment seems to suck all the happiness from a room, yet these feminists were driven by the need to end sexual violence and they were willing to kill the joy in order to make change. In so doing, they helped reveal to many Americans how prevalent sexual coercion is throughout all realms of life.

Many feminists and cultural critics celebrated #MeToo and believed in its ability to stimulate change. For many, #MeToo opened up an international dialogue regarding anger, power, sexual misconduct, and the workplace. Yet, even this feminist movement had its critics. Due to the media focus on white women and the disregard for Tarana Burke's original Me Too movement, many also came to see the #MeToo movement as another historical example of the marginalization of women of color. Instead of centering women of color, media coverage focused and spotlighted white women's rage and suffering. Similar to many other Western feminist movements, #MeToo centered white women's anger and pain—eclipsing the visibility of Black women's struggles, activism, and feminist leadership. The example of #MeToo demonstrates how the feminist killjoy must always work intersectionally—resisting the intertwined oppressions of sexism, racism, classism, and the like—because even the work of the feminist killjoy can be tainted by its own hierarchies and norms. In order to build a new world, the feminist killjoy must face the discomfort of refusing normative "happiness" and confront inequality whole heartedly.

Dafna Kaufman

See Also: Anger; Burke, Tarana; hooks, bell; Intersectionality; Lorde, Audre; #MeToo; The Personal Is Political; Women's March on Washington (2016)

Further Reading

Ahmed, Sara. 2010. *The Promise of Happiness*. Durham: Duke University Press.

Ahmed, Sara. 2010. "Feminist Killjoys (and Other Willful Subjects)." *The Scholar and Feminist Online* 8, no. 3. http://sfonline.barnard.edu/polyphonic/print_ahmed.htm.

Ahmed, Sara. 2017. *Living a Feminist Life*. Durham: Duke University Press.

Chemaly, Soraya. 2018. *Rage Becomes Her: The Power of Women's Anger*. New York: Atria Books.

Cooper, Brittany. 2018. *Eloquent Rage: A Black Feminist Discovers Her Superpowers*. New York: St. Martin's Press.

Gay, Roxane. 2016. "Who Gets to Be Angry?" *The New York Times*, June 10 2016. https://www.nytimes.com/2016/06/12/opinion/sunday/who-gets-to-be-angry.html.

Hill Collins, Patricia. 2009. *Black Feminist Thought: Knowledge, Consciousness, and the Politics of Empowerment*. 2nd ed. New York: Routledge.

hooks, bell. 2014. *Talking Back: Thinking Feminist, Thinking Black*. New York: Routledge.

Jaggar, Alison. 1996. "Love and Knowledge: Emotion in Feminist Epistemology," in *Women, Knowledge and Reality: Explorations in Feminist Philosophy*, edited by Ann Garry and Marilyn Pearsall, 166–90. New York: Routledge.

Boyce Kay, Jilly. 2019. "Introduction: Anger, Media, and Feminism: The Gender Politics of Mediated Rage." *Feminist Media Studies* 19, no. 4: 591–615. HTTPS://DOI.ORG/ 10.1080/14680777.2019.1609197.

Kay, Jilly Boyce. 2020. *Gender, Media and Voice: Communicative Injustice and Public Speech*. Cham, Switzerland: Palgrave Macmillan.

Lorde, Audre. 1981. "The Uses of Anger," *Women's Studies Quarterly* 9, no. 3: 7–10.

Topping, Alexandra. 2021. "Endemic Violence Against Women is Causing a Wave of Anger." *The Guardian*, March 11, 2021. https://www.theguardian.com/world/2021/mar/11/endemic-violence-against-women-is-causing-a-wave-of-anger.

Traister, Rebecca. 2018. *Good and Mad: The Revolutionary Power of Women's Anger*. New York: Simon & Schuster.

FEMINIST METHODOLOGIES

There are many ways of knowing and perceiving the world. For example, five commonly accepted ways of knowing are: intuition, authority, rationalism, empiricism (observation), and science (the scientific method). Regardless of *how* we know what we know, methodologies are chosen perspectives about the ways in which we measure and evaluate that knowledge. Alan Bryman defined methodology as "the study of the methods that are employed" to collect and/or analyze data. Methodology is "concerned with uncovering the practices and assumptions" that research methods are built on (2008, 160). Generally speaking, "methodology" is the premise or principle that connects an "epistemology" to a research "method" (Sprague 2016).

An epistemology is what an individual or a culture thinks counts as knowledge. Typically, this includes ideas about *who* can know things, *what* can be known, and *how* a knower discovers the known. For instance, a researcher might think that only a trained, "objective," "nonbiased" scientist can know things; that only observable behavior (not intent or internal emotions) can be known; and—as such—the way to knowledge is through a trained researcher's observation of people's behaviors. Again, epistemology is the theory or assumptions that shape what "counts" as knowledge for a community.

"Methods," meanwhile, refer to the actual protocols, steps, or guidelines that researchers practice in order to generate knowledge. For instance, a method might provide a step-by-step list of "to-do" items for studying how Gen Z develops romantic relationships. There are hundreds of methods to choose from when conducting research.

A "methodology," then, is the typology or principle that connects an epistemology and a specific research method. There are three general methodologies: quantitative, qualitative, and rhetorical.

Quantitative methodologies generally accept epistemologies that assume empirical data points can be known and that we can understand the world through empirical observations. These methodologies use methods such as surveys, experiments, and content analysis to create numerical data that is used to investigate the relationship between identified variables. For example, using a survey to gather responses about how age can influence information-seeking behaviors.

Qualitative methodologies generally accept epistemologies that assume personal perceptions can be known and that we can understand the world through lived experiences. These methodologies use methods such as interviews, focus groups, and ethnographies to create narrative data that is used to understand the rich, nuanced complexities of the world. For instance, interviewing and then sifting through the responses from first responders, emergency room medical staff, and patients to identify the dynamics of medical communication and patient experiences.

Mixed methodologies generally accept epistemologies from both quantitative and qualitative methodologies. These methodologies will combine quantitative and qualitative methods, so the empirical and experiential data informs each other. Doing so provides a fuller, more in-depth analysis. For example, conducting local focus groups about civic engagement and political communication that will be used to construct and inform a nation-wide survey on the same topic.

Finally, *rhetorical methodologies* generally accept epistemologies that assume worldviews can be known and that we can understand the world through the persuasive elements of artifacts (e.g., news articles, TV shows, clothing, propaganda). These methodologies use methods such as rhetorical criticisms, textual analyses, and discourse analyses to create thematic data that is used to investigate an artifact's message about the world. For instance, analyzing magazine covers to determine what beauty standards are being created and communicated to audiences.

Assumptions of Feminist Methodologies

First, as described above, feminist methodologies assume there is a relationship between knowledge, knowledge production, and power. In contrast, most patriarchal approaches pretend that these items are all the same or are connected intuitively and absolutely by common sense. Feminists, however, demonstrate how elements like language, privilege, and social construction impact what knowledge is valued, whose voices are included, and who gets to control such value attributions (Burns and Walker 2005). One key focus of power in feminist methodologies is the researcher themselves. The researcher's positionality—their identities, biases, experiences, and privileges—dictates knowledge production. Feminist scholar Sandra Harding (1987) argued that this sort of privileged positioning in knowledge construction is a primary reason why traditional "objective" methodologies are so problematic. If meaning and truth are impacted by "who is speaking and who is listening" (Alcoff 1991, 12), then researchers must be mindful of their own positions of power as well as how societal power structures directly influence knowledge production.

Second, feminist methodologies assume that research norms shape knowledge. Because traditional methodologies are androcentric and WEIRD (White, Educated, Industrialized, Rich, and Democratic; Henrich, Heine, and Norenzayan, 2010), feminist scholars advocate for decolonizing research methodologies. According to Vivetha Thambinathan and Elizabeth Kinsella (2021, 2), decolonizing our methodologies means "centering concerns and worldviews of non-Western individuals, and respectfully knowing and understanding theory and research from previously 'Other(ed)' perspectives" (Battiste 2000; Datta 2017; Smith 2012).

For example, in risk and crisis communication, traditional constructs of crises center on a functionalistic perspective where crises are linear, rational, and an objective "real" thing happening "out there" (Zhao, Falkheimer, and Heide 2017; Zhao 2020). One alternative understanding of crises, however, understands them to be nonlinear and engaged in dynamic interactivity (Lee 2005). In this example, feminist methodologies decolonize traditional, Western methodological perspectives on crises to help researchers more fully investigate risk and crisis events.

Feminist scholars have critiqued traditional epistemologies and methods by arguing that they are based on male-centric (androcentric) assumptions about the world, which makes them less likely to be fully valid and more likely to marginalize women, racialized minorities, and poor people (Gray et al. 2007; Wigginton and Lafrance 2019). Thus, while feminist researchers still use quantitative, qualitative, and rhetorical methodologies, they operationalize them differently.

Ultimately, feminist methodologies ask researchers to engage in a fuller understanding of research by using alternative ways of knowing. This requires researchers to reflect on their own positionalities and the power dynamics that might be at work in their study. Such power dynamics heavily impact knowledge production, the value of certain types of knowledge, and who gets to contribute to the process. Thus, feminist methodologies offer a different perspective on methods that decolonize and turn away from androcentrism.

Lakelyn E. Taylor

See Also: Decolonialism; Feminist Pedagogy; Standpoint Theory; Structural Oppression

Further Reading

Alcoff, Linda. 1991. "The Problem of Speaking for Others." *Cultural Critique* 48, no. 20: 5– 32.
Battiste, Marie. 2000. *Reclaiming Indigenous Voice and Vision*. Vancouver: UBC Press.
Bryman, Alan. 2008. "Of Methods and Methodology." *Qualitative Research in Organizations and Management: An International Journal* 3, no. 2: 159–68. https://doi.org/10.1108/17465640810900568.
Burns, Diane, and Melanie Walker. 2005. "Feminist Methodologies." In *Research Methods in the Social Sciences*, edited by Bridget Somekh and Cathy Lewin, 66–73. Thousand Oaks: SAGE.
Datta, Ranjan. 2017. "Decolonizing Both Researcher and Research and Its Effectiveness in Indigenous Research." *Research Ethics* 14, no. 2 (September): 1–24. https://doi.org/10.1177/1747016117733296.
Gray, Paul S., John B. Williamson, David A. Karp, and John R. Dalphin. 2007. "Feminist Methods." In *The Research Imagination: An Introduction to Qualitative and Quantitative Methods*, edited by Paul S. Gray, John B. Williamson, David A. Karp, and John R. Dalphin, 211–40. Cambridge: Cambridge University Press.
Harding, Sandra. 1987. "The Method Question." *Hypatia* 2, no. 3: 19-35. https://doi.org/10.1111/j.1527-2001.1987.tb01339.x.
Henrich, Joe, Steven J. Heine, and Ara Norenzayan. 2010. "The Weirdest People in the World?" *Behavioral and Brain Sciences* 33, no. 2–3 (May): 61–83. https://doi.org/10.1017/S0140525X0999152X.
Lee, Betty Kaman. 2005. "Crisis, Culture, Community." In *Communication Yearbook*, edited by Pamela J. Kalbfleisch, 275–309. London: Routledge.
Smith, Linsa Tuhiwai. 2012. *Decolonizing Methodologies: Research and Indigenous Peoples*. London: Zed Books.
Sprague, Joey. 2016. *Feminist Methodologies for Critical Researchers: Bridging Differences*. 2nd edition. Lanham, NJ: Rowman & Littlefield.
Thambinathan, Vivetha, and Elizabeth Anne Kinsella. 2021. "Decolonizing Methodologies in Qualitative Research: Creating Spaces for Transformative Praxis." *International Journal of Qualitative Methods* 20 (May): 1–9. https://doi.org/10.1177/16094069211101476.
Wigginton, Britta, and Michelle N. Lafrance. 2019. "Learning Critical Feminist Research: A Brief Introduction to Feminist Epistemologies and Methodologies." *Feminism & Psychology* (May): 1–17. https://doi.org/10.1177/0959353519866058.
Zhao, Hui, Jesper Falkheimer, and Mats Heide. 2017. "Revisiting a Social Constructionist Approach to Crisis Communication – Investigating Contemporary Crises in China." *International Journal of Strategic Communication* 11, no. 5 (September): 364–78. https://doi.org/10.1080/1553118X.2017.1363758.
Zhao, Hui. 2020. "Explicating the Social Constructionist Perspective on Crisis Communication and Crisis Management Research: A Review of Communication and Business Journals." *Journal of Public Relations Research* 32, no. 3–4 (August): 98–119. https://doi.org/10.1080/1062726X.2020.1802732.

FEMINIST PEDAGOGY

Feminist pedagogy can take many forms, making it difficult to provide a singular, precise definition. "Pedagogy" refers to the theory and practice of education, commonly referred to as an approach to teaching. Feminist pedagogy, then, is an approach to teaching informed by feminist theory and frameworks. It promotes the idea that education is a site for social change, transformation, and liberation; it strives to bring about that social change by raising consciousness about marginalization. Feminist pedagogy values lived experience and personal testimony as ways of knowing. Although feminist pedagogy is often associated with women's, gender, and sexuality studies courses, feminist teaching strategies can be used in any classroom. This approach is more concerned with the *way* teachers teach, regardless of the subject matter. Teaching techniques are "anti-hierarchical, student-centered, promote community and collaboration, validate experiential knowledge, discourage passivity, and emphasize well-being and self-actualization" (Accardi 2013, 31; see also hooks 1994).

bell hooks observes that teachers "are faced with the way the politics of domination are often reproduced in the educational setting," and feminist pedagogy argues that the classroom is not a neutral setting: "it is inextricably linked to the culture it lives in" (hooks 1994, 39; Accardi 2013,

46). Echoing hooks's definition of feminism as "a movement to end sexism, sexist exploitation, and oppression," feminist pedagogy seeks to "transform sexist and oppressive systems in a way that disrupts replication in the classroom" (hooks 2015, 1; Accardi 2013, 30).

The Origins of Feminist Pedagogy

Feminist pedagogy was formally developed during the women's movement of the 1970s and sought to connect feminist theory with new teaching practices and concepts of learning. The first mention of the term appears in an essay titled "What Is Feminist Pedagogy?," written by Berenice Fisher and published in 1981 in an issue of *Radical Teacher* (Accardi 2013, 29). Fisher writes, "By most accounts, [feminist pedagogy] is a perspective on teaching which is anti-sexist, and anti-hierarchical, and which stresses women's experience, both the suffering our oppression has caused and the strengths we have developed to resist it" (Fisher 1981, 20). Fisher points to consciousness raising as a tool for education, and feminist pedagogy translates consciousness raising into teaching strategies that promote student learning about societal injustice (Accardi 2013, 30).

Feminist pedagogy also has its origins in critical pedagogy, which can be defined as "an educational theory based on the idea that schools typically serve the interests of those who have power in a society by, usually unintentionally, perpetuating unquestioned norms . . . to combat these taken-for-granted biases in schools, teachers and students must constantly question their world, both inside and outside the classroom" (Billings 2019). Paolo Freire's book *Pedagogy of the Oppressed* (2005) is arguably the most influential work on critical pedagogy. It resisted the traditional banking model of education, in which learners were viewed as passive vessels waiting to receive knowledge from an all-knowing instructor. Instead, Freire's approach embraces learners as knowledge creators. Critical pedagogy is concerned with critical consciousness, a concept referring to the process of learning to recognize injustice and take action in response (Freire 2005). Although critical reflection and motivation, two components of critical consciousness, are important, feminist pedagogy emphasizes the third component, action, "because feminist pedagogy is a form of education to effect social change" (Accardi 2013, 36).

Feminist Pedagogy's Central Tenets in the Classroom

Feminist pedagogy can take a variety of forms in the classroom. Generally, it includes engaged pedagogy and active learning, believing in the importance of student agency and interaction between instructors and learners.

One primary technique of feminist pedagogy is focusing on subject matter concerning oppression. This includes, but is not limited to, sexism, homophobia, transphobia, racism, ableism, and classism. According to many scholars, enacting feminism in the classroom should "take as its primary subject matter issues of patriarchal oppression and sexism, and how these things construct what happens in a classroom and what material is taught" (Accardi 2013, 35). For academic librarian Maria Accardi, this means that when teaching a class primarily about information literacy, she finds ways to achieve her learning outcomes using a feminist approach. Accardi regularly works with students researching topics related to career planning and career choice. During those classes, while demonstrating how to search in databases, Accardi often uses example searches such as "women in computer science" or "women in engineering." Not only does this exercise provide opportunities to discuss keyword searching, topic development, and search results evaluation; it also surfaces results about the underrepresentation of women in traditionally male-dominated fields like computer science, about the challenges women face in those fields, and how sexism impacts the career paths of women in STEM (Accardi 2013, 37). Students leave the class with the information literacy skills they need to complete their assignments, but they also encounter articles that address sexism in their respective fields.

A second primary area for feminist pedagogy is the validity of lived experience as a source of knowledge or way of knowing. In the classroom, this means that instructors treat learners as full human beings with expertise and experience worth contributing. The instructor's voice is not viewed as the ultimate authority, and student knowledge is taken seriously. In *Teaching Critical Thinking: Practical Wisdom*, hooks specifies that while feminist pedagogy assumes that "every student has a valuable contribution to make to the learning process . . . it does not assume that all voices should be heard all the time or that all voices should occupy the same amount of time" (hooks 2010, 21). Attention must be paid to how forces of oppression like sexism influence whose voices are prioritized in the classroom. Beyond the experiences and voices in the classroom, feminist pedagogy values other forms of knowledge production: "knowledge produced in the male-dominated culture is traditionally privileged as valid, true, and important, so an emphasis on legitimizing other forms of knowledge, especially the knowledge of oppressed classes, is a feminist act" (Accardi 2013, 38).

Another aspect of feminist pedagogy is that the classroom is designed to be democratic and collaborative. It is a place "where all voices are valued, and is also a site where students and teachers partner to create a respectful learning community" (Accardi 2013, 40). This requires accountability from instructors and learners alike. hooks writes that "When we all take risks, we participate mutually in the work of creating a learning community. We discover together that we can be vulnerable in the space of shared learning" (hooks 2010, 21). This mutual participation is what creates meaningful relationships between everyone in the room. The feminist classroom is less like a lecture hall and more like a cooperative: "where everyone contributes to make sure all resources are being used, to ensure the optimal learning well-being of everyone" (hooks 2010, 22). With the goal of learning as self-actualization and critical consciousness, a collaborative, democratic approach to teaching can foster an environment where all learners and their experiences are valued.

As touched on previously, feminist pedagogy reenvisions the relationship between teacher and learner. The teacher is no longer seen as the ultimate authority bestowing knowledge; knowledge "is collaboratively discussed and created by the students and the teacher together. The students are not passive vessels waiting to be filled by the teacher's wisdom" (Accardi 2013, 25). By transforming this relationship, instructors aim to disrupt traditional ideas of power and authority in the classroom. Instructors engage in ways of teaching that respect student agency and knowledge, which empowers students to learn, develop their critical consciousness, and influence social change. Feminist pedagogy encourages learners to be active in their education and expects them to share in decision-making; instructors in turn share authority with learners and ask more questions than they answer (Accardi 2013, 43). The reenvisioned relationship between teacher and learner also involves an ethics of care, which means that instructors are expected to treat learners as whole persons, with experiences and feelings that shape the way they learn. Listening to learners, relying on them for examples, and encouraging them to listen to one another each demonstrate an ethics of care. In *Teaching to Transgress*, hooks writes, "To teach in a manner that respects and cares for the souls of our students is essential if we are to provide the necessary conditions where learning can most deeply and intimately begin" (hooks 1994, 13).

Limitations and Beyond

Feminist pedagogy is not without its limitations and criticisms. hooks notes that "the urge to experiment with pedagogical practices may not be welcomed by students who often expect us to teach in the manner they are accustomed to" (hooks 1994, 142–3). Student resistance to feminist pedagogy is especially present where instructors hold marginalized identities. Because educational settings replicate societal biases and systems of oppression, the academy as an institution impacts how effective feminist pedagogy (and other critical pedagogies) can be, broadly. Busse, Krausch, and Liao found that race- and gender-neutral messaging from neoliberal educational institutions is the root of both resistance to teaching methods and skepticism of intellectual validity (Busse, Krausch, and Liao 2021). They argue that educational institutions are inherently antithetical to critical pedagogy and emphasize the need to return critical pedagogy to its context of political organizing beyond the academy.

hooks offers a cautiously optimistic view that recognizes the limitations of educational institutions while carving paths for feminist teaching. She writes,

> The academy is not paradise. But learning is a place where paradise can be created. The classroom, with all its limitations, remains a location of possibility. In that field of possibility we have the opportunity to labor for freedom, to demand of ourselves and our comrades, an openness of mind and heart that allows us to face reality even as we collectively imagine ways to move beyond boundaries, to transgress. This is education as the practice of freedom. (hooks 1994, 207)

Hannah Jones

See Also: Consciousness Raising; Feminist Methodologies; hooks, bell

Further Reading

Accardi, Maria T. 2013. *Feminist Pedagogy for Library Instruction.* Series on Gender and Sexuality in Information Studies. Sacramento, California: Library Juice Press. https://search-ebscohost-com.libpdb.d.umn.edu:2443/login.aspx?direct=true&AuthType=ip,cookie,uid&db=e000xna&AN=2145291&site=ehost-live&scope=site.

Billings, Sabrina. 2019. "Critical Pedagogy." *Salem Press Encyclopedia.* Salem Press.

Busse, Erika, Meghan Krausch, and Wenjie Liao. 2021. "How the 'Neutral' University Makes Critical Feminist Pedagogy Impossible: Intersectional Analysis from Marginalized Faculty on Three Campuses." *Sociological Spectrum* 41, no. 1: 29–52. https://doi.org/10.1080/02732173.2020.1850377.

Fisher, Berenice. 1981. "What Is Feminist Pedagogy?" *Radical Teacher (Cambridge)* 18: 20–4.

Freire, Paulo. 2005. *Pedagogy of the Oppressed.* New York: Continuum.

hooks, bell. 1994. *Teaching to Transgress: Education as the Practice of Freedom.* New York: Routledge.

hooks, bell. 2010. *Teaching Critical Thinking: Practical Wisdom.* New York: Routledge.

hooks, bell. 2015. *Feminism is for Everybody: Passionate Politics.* New York: Routledge.

FEMINIST THEOLOGY

"I am a student of theology; I am also a woman." While this statement is true of me, it is not mine—it is the opening words of one of the earliest essays in the field of feminist theology (Saiving 1960, 100). Over seventy years ago, Valerie Goldstein Saiving wrote "The Human Situation: A Feminine View," pointing out how Christianity's prevailing understanding of sin as pride was reflective of (white, upper-class, Western) men's experiences. Viewing sin in this way not only undermines women's experiences, she argued, but is harmful to women who are socialized to be selfless and humble. Feminist theologies following Saiving's work have criticized and challenged how religion has been formed and wielded by (male) power, by patriarchy. At the same time feminist theologies recover and reinterpret religious texts, traditions, and practices to reflect religious values of liberation and justice.

For example, a range of feminist theologies have critically examined and challenged the cultural presumption of the Divine as male. God only imaged as Father has made "the oppression of women appear right and fitting," Mary Daly argued. "If God in 'his' heaven is a father ruling 'his' people, then it is in the 'nature' of things and according to divine plan and the order of the universe that society be male-dominated" (Daly 1973, 13). Feminist theologians have turned to their respective traditions to counter this patriarchal perspective: from the Goddess movement in Neopagan traditions (e.g., Wicca) that has uplifted the worship of the Divine feminine and Hindu feminist turns to the divine feminine energy of Shakti to attention to the feminine language for God used in Jewish and Christian scriptures and prayer books (Christ 1978; Karmarkar 2024; Janowitz and Wenig 1976; Johnson 1992). Challenging the maleness of the Divine, feminist theologians argue, has significant implications for issues like women's ordination/religious leadership and religious perspectives on gender roles. The gender of the Divine is just one of many arenas in which feminist theologians both challenge and draw on their respective religious traditions to affirm women's equality.

Feminist Theology as Liberation Theology: Justice, Freedom, and Flourishing

Feminist theology emerged as a part of liberation theology, a broader movement in the study of Christianity that developed in the late 1960s, as theologians began to reflect at length on how Christianity aligned with the goals of the civil rights, feminist, and economic justice movements. Looking especially to the story of the Exodus (as God liberates the Israelites from their enslavement to the Egyptians), and to the life and teachings of Jesus, liberation theologians argue that God always stands with the oppressed and seeks justice and liberation—not only with the Israelites who were oppressed by Pharoah or King Herod but also African Americans oppressed by enslavement and segregation, Latin Americans who suffered from poverty due to colonialism and unjust economic structures, and women oppressed by patriarchy and gender roles (Gutierrez 1988; Cone 1969; Daly 1968). Those who believe in and follow God, then, are to join in the pursuit of justice and freedom—seeking the flourishing of all. Feminist theologians across various religious traditions also draw on the history of liberation theology and themes of justice and flourishing. For instance, feminist Sikh activist Valarie Kaur calls for a feminist ethic of revolutionary love. In her address to the Parliament of World Religions, Kaur spoke about the parliamentarians being midwives who "labor for justice," who "can begin to deliver the world we dream" (Kaur 2019).

Feminist Theologies as Intersectional Theologies: Dismantling ~~Patriarchy~~ Kyriarchy!

In their pursuit of freedom and flourishing for all, feminist theologies naturally directed their efforts toward "the promotion of the full humanity of women" (Ruether 1983, 18). Yet, like the broader feminist activist movement in the Global North, feminist theologies have historically struggled with inclusion and difference, privileging the voices and experiences of upper- and middle-class, white, cisgender, and heterosexual women (and thus betraying liberation theology's attention to the oppressed). Just as Saiving challenged how an understanding of sin as pride undermined women's experiences, Black feminist theologians like Jacquelyn Grant drew our attention to how feminist understandings of who Jesus is and what his death and resurrection mean (what theologians call Christology) undermined and ignored *Black* women's experiences—as did Black male theologians who ignored Black *women's* experiences (Grant 1989).

Grant and other Black feminist theologians, seeking to "take seriously (as a primary theological source) the faith, thought, and life struggle of African American women," developed womanist theology (Williams 1993, xi; see also Cannon 1988). Following womanism, there was a proliferation of intersectional feminist theologies, including but not limited to mujerista theologies exploring the struggles facing poor Latinas (Isasi-Díaz 1993), Asian women's theologies attending to immigrant experiences and the impacts of colonization (Chung 1990; Kwok 2005), and "indecent theology," addressing the intersections of gender, sexuality, poverty, and race (Althaus-Reid 2004).

With these diverse, intersectional approaches, feminist theologies seek to not only challenge and dismantle the patriarchy, but they recognize, and seek to challenge and dismantle, how patriarchal oppression is entangled with other forms of domination: white supremacy, colonialism, economic exploitation, cisheteronormativity, and so on. Feminist theologian Elisabeth Schüssler Fiorenza gave the name *kyriarchy* (a neologism derived from the Greek words for "lord" or "master," *kyrios*, and "to rule or dominate," *archein*) to this complexified understanding of patriarchal intersectional structures of domination (1992). Condemnation of and challenges to kyriarchy are clear in diverse forms of feminist theology such as womanist and mujerista theologies, as well as, for instance, ecofeminist theologies, which attend to how systems of domination have damaged the environment and have endangered vulnerable ecosystems.

Reform or Revolution? Feminist Theological Approaches

While feminist theologies seek liberation from kyriarchy and promote the humanity and flourishing of wo/men, *how* they pursue those goals differ. As Rita Gross put it, the "most difficult question facing a feminist who discovers her traditional religion to be patriarchal and sexist is what to do next" (1996, 107). Feminist theologies generally fall into one of two key approaches: reform or revolution (McFague 1982, 152).

Revolutionary feminist theologians have argued that the Christian tradition is irredeemably oppressive and kyriarchal and should be utterly transformed, or even abandoned. The feminist suffragist Elizabeth Cady Stanton is a good example of a revolutionary approach. Stanton famously wrote of the Christian Bible that she knew of "no other books that so fully teach the subjection and degradation of women" (2020 [1898]). To progress beyond patriarchy meant revising Christianity, and Stanton convened a committee to reinterpret Scripture's message, publishing *The Woman's Bible* (1895). Going even further than Stanton, feminist "thealogians" like Mary Daly and Carol Christ have argued that revolution means rejecting and moving beyond Christianity in favor of "Goddess religion"—that "the misogynism of Christian theology is deep rooted and that merely removing symptoms will not cure the disease" (Christ 1978; Daly 1985 [1973], 37).

Other feminist theologians, however, believe that religious institutions and beliefs can (and should!) be reformed, and that religion is not necessarily, and need not be, counter to feminism. For example, after Stanton published *The Woman's Bible*, Stanton's friend and fellow suffragist Susan B. Anthony pushed back, arguing that just as there was space for atheism, there was space for religion in the feminist movement (Barry 2020). And feminist theologians have spoken about how their work reflects a commitment "to keeping or trying to support the continuance of progressive perspectives in Catholicism" and other religions—explaining that they "don't like to see religion used to justify injustice and oppression" and thus seek to change it from the inside (Hinton 2002, 30, 29).

Feminist theologians who seek reform argue that, while it developed in patriarchal social contexts, the heart of Christianity (or Judaism or other religious traditions) is liberation, not patriarchy, and that the task then is to recover or uncover that foundation. For instance, Jewish feminist theologians have argued that while Jewish law, halakhah, is limiting—excluding women from particular religious ceremonies (minyan) or prohibiting women from initiating divorce—that the very nature of halakhah calls for its transformation, "a way for communities of Jews to generate and embody their Jewish moral visions" (Adler 1998, 21). Christian feminist theologians and historians have challenged "biblical womanhood" or complementarianism—the idea that Christian scripture supports male leadership and women's "functional subordination"—demonstrating how patriarchal ideas were cultural by-products of history and how biblical texts and early Christian practices reflect a far more egalitarian and liberative vision of women's place in the church and world (Barr 2021; Fiorenza 1983).

Though feminist theologians hold diverse perspectives of how change happens, they share a commitment to seeking equality and liberation for women and for all, for dismantling kyriarchy and building a more just world. Feminist theologies understand their work both as an end, a vision of a more just world, and a means, the pursuit of that goal through challenging, changing, and constructing religious beliefs and practices.

Brandy Daniels

See Also: Biblical Complementarianism; Black Liberation Theology; Colonialism; Purity Culture; Womanism

Further Reading

Adler, Rachel. 1998. *Engendering Judaism: An Inclusive Theology and Ethics*. Philadelphia: The Jewish Publication Society.

Althaus-Reid, Marcella. 2004. *From Feminist Theology to Indecent Theology*. London: SCM Press.

Barr, Beth Allison. 2021. *The Making of Biblical Womanhood: How the Subjugation of Women Became Gospel Truth.* Grand Rapids: Brazos Press.

Barry, Kathleen. 2020. *Susan B. Anthony: A Biography.* New York: New York University.

Carbine, Rosemary P. 2023. *Nevertheless, We Persist: A Feminist Public Theology.* Maryknoll, NY: Orbis Books.

Cannon, Katie Geneva. 1988. *Black Womanist Ethics.* Atlanta: Scholars Press.

Christ, Carol P. 1978. "Why Women Need the Goddess." *Heresies: A Feminist Publication on Arts and Politics* 2, no. 1 (The Great Goddess Issue): 8–13.

Chung, Hyun Kyung. 1990. *Struggle to be the Sun Again: Introducing Asian Women's Theology.* Maryknoll: Orbis Books.

Cone, James. 1969. *Black Theology and Black Power.* New York: Seabury Press.

Daly, Mary. 1968. *The Church and the Second Sex.* Boston: Beacon Press.

Daly, Mary. 1973. *Beyond God the Father: Toward a Philosophy of Women's Liberation.* Boston: Beacon Press.

Daly, Mary. 1985 [1973]. *Beyond God the Father: Toward a Philosophy of Women's Liberation, with the Feminist Postchristian Introduction and New Archaic Afterwords.* Boston:
Beacon Press.

Fiorenza, Elisabeth Schüssler. 1983. *In Memory of Her: A Feminist Theological Reconstruction of Early Christian Beginnings.* New York: Crossroads Publishing.

Fiorenza, Elisabeth Schüssler. 1992. *But She Said: Feminist Practices of Biblical Interpretation.* Boston: Beacon Press.

Grant, Jacquelyn. 1989. *White Women's Christ and Black Women's Jesus: Feminist Christology and Womanist Response.* Atlanta: Scholars Press.

Gross, Rita M. 1996. *Feminism & Religion: An Introduction*. Boston, MA: Beacon Press.

Gutierrez, Gustavo. 1988. *A Theology of Liberation.* Translated and edited by Sister Caridad Inda and John Eagleston. Maryknoll: Orbis Books.

Hinton, Rosalind. 2002. "A Legacy of Inclusion: An Interview with Rosemary Radford Ruether." *CrossCurrents* 52, no. 1: 28–37.

Isasi-Díaz, Ada María. 1993. *En la Lucha/In the Struggle: A Hispanic Women's Liberation Theology.* Minneapolis: Fortress Press.

Janowitz, Naomi, and Maggie Wenig. 1976. *Siddur Nashim: A Sabbath Prayer Book for Women.* Providence, RI.

Johnson, Elizabeth. 1992. *She Who Is: The Mystery of God in Feminist Theological Discourse.* New York: Crossroad Publishing.

Karmarkar, Richa. 2024. "Hindu Women Look to Ancient Goddesses for Guidance on Modern Feminism." *Religion News Service*, March 13, 2024. https://religionnews.com/2024/03/13/shakti-the-divine-feminine-energy-is-having-her-moment-among-hindu-american-women/.

Kaur, Valarie. 2019. Keynote Address. 2018 Parliament of the World's Religions. February 14, 2019. https://youtu.be/jnCf3NL-0dI?si=H_d7vgUfa5MhG7CW.
Kwok, Pui-lan. 2005. *Postcolonial Imagination and Feminist Theology*. Louisville: Westminster John Knox Press.
McFague, Sally. 1982. *Metaphorical Theology: Models of God in Religious Language*. London: SCM Press.
Ruether, Rosemary Radford. 1983. *Sexism and God-Talk: Toward a Feminist Theology*. Boston: Beacon Press.
Saiving, Valerie Goldstein. 1960. "The Human Situation: A Feminine View." *The Journal of Religion* 40, no. 2: 100–12. https://doi.org/10.1086/485231.
Stanton, Elizabeth Cady. 2020 [1898]. *Eighty Years and More: Reminiscences (1815–1897)*. New York: Simon & Schuster.
Stanton, Elizabeth Cady. 1895. *The Woman's Bible*. New York: European Publishing Company.
Trible, Phyllis. 1984. *Texts of Terror: Literary-Feminist Readings of Biblical Narratives*. Minneapolis: Fortress Press.
Williams, Delores S. 1993. *Sisters in the Wilderness: The Challenge of Womanist God-Talk*. Maryknoll, NY: Orbis Books.

FEMINISTING.COM

Feministing.com was founded in 2004 by sisters Jessica Valenti, a feminist writer and activist, and Vanessa Valenti, a blogger, speaker, and online strategist (Feministing 2024). Launched as a blog, the website emerged during a wave of digital activism to offer a space where readers could engage with feminist perspectives on subjects like gender, race, class, and sexuality in an accessible and inclusive way. Feministing.com quickly became a leading digital platform for feminist thought and, until the time the blog was shuttered in 2019, its collective of authors aimed to close gaps between academic feminism and grassroots activism by providing a forum for conversations about reproductive rights, sexual violence, politics and legislation, pop culture and contemporary news, systemic oppressions such as global colonialism, and more (Feministing 2024).

At its peak, Feministing.com drew over a million unique visitors per month to the site, making it one of the most widely read online feminist publications of its era (Goldberg 2019). A key feature of the blog's approach was its commitment to intersectionality. Embracing this framework, the site regularly amplified the voices and concerns of women of color, the LGBTQ+ community, the Global South, and others whose experiences were often sidelined in mainstream feminist discourse. The platform also relied heavily on personal narratives as a means of engaging readers, reflecting feminist traditions of consciousness raising adapted for the digital age (Baumgardner and Richards 2010).

Despite its popularity and intention, Feministing.com certainly faced some criticisms. Beyond the anti-feminist opposition it faced, some feminists argued that its pop culture focus sometimes overshadowed deeper, systemic critiques, while others pointed out that despite its intersectional aspirations, the platform could have done more to elevate the voices of marginalized feminists, particularly from outside the United States (Cochrane 2013).

Though Feministing.com no longer exists in its original digital format, it is credited for paving the way for similar online outlets (Goldberg 2019). Additionally, it is worth noting that the legacy of Feministing.com has continued in new forms as its contributors have taken to other forums (Feministing 2019; Goldberg 2023). Its influence can still be seen today in the proliferation of feminist blogs, podcasts, and social media channels that continue to advance feminist thought and activism.

Dakota J. Sandras

See Also: Consciousness Raising; Cyberfeminism; Intersectionality

Further Reading

Baumgardner, Jennifer, and Amy Richards. 2010. *Manifesta: Young Women, Feminism, and the Future*. Farrar, Straus and Giroux.

Feministing. 2019. "(B)logging Off: Feministing Forever." *Feministing*, December 8, 2019. https://feministing.com/2019/12/08/blogging-off-feministing-forever/.

Feministing. 2024. "About Feministing." Accessed September 7, 2024. https://feministing.com/about/.

Cochrane, Kira. 2013. *All the Rebel Women: The Rise of the Fourth Wave of Feminism*. Guardian Books.

Goldberg, Emma. 2019. "A Farewell to Feministing and the Heyday of Feminist Blogging." *The New York Times*, December 8, 2019. https://www.nytimes.com/2019/12/08/business/media/feminist-blogs-feministing.html.

Goldberg, Emma. 2023. "Goodbye, Feminist Blogs. Hello, Gen Z Content Creators?" *The New York Times*, November 17, 2023. https://www.nytimes.com/2023/11/17/business/feminism-gen-z.html.

FEMINIZATION OF POVERTY

The feminization of poverty refers to the trend of rising rates of poverty among women in the United States and worldwide. Coined by sociologist Diana Pearce in the late 1970s, the term designates the "trend towards more and more of the burden of poverty being borne by women" (Pearce 1989). Since then, it has been a popular way to describe the widening gender gap in poverty rates within the fields of sociology and anthropology. Contemporary research on poverty, however, typically broadens the scope, providing an intersectional analysis of class, gender, and race on a global scale.

It is important to note that "poverty" here refers to the US definition, meaning "not having enough income to cover basic needs," and poverty in the United States is usually measured at the "household level" (Christensen 2019). This means, according to the 2024 US poverty guidelines, that a household and everyone in it is considered impoverished if their total household income is under $20,440 for a family of two or under $31,200 for a family of four ("Poverty Guidelines" n.d.). Likewise, a household and *everyone in it* is considered not to be in poverty if the household's income is over those thresholds. Alaska and Hawaii have slightly higher thresholds. Notably, this standard threshold ignores the differences in cost of living for rural and urban areas. Moreover, because this standard measures poverty using a "household" income, it may "grossly underestimate women's poverty because women may not necessarily have access" to income from patriarchal male partners (Christensen, 370). That is, patriarchal men may refuse to share their income with the household, impoverishing the women and children who live with them. This is especially dangerous for women when a man is the household's primary income member—which is often known as the "head of household."

When measuring the femininization of poverty, researchers usually use three categories. First, family structures, such as whether or not a household has children, allow for researchers to study the gender gap differences between women-led households and/or single mothers and their male counterparts. Second, education and labor markets help researchers to identify how education and participation in the workforce play a foundational role in women's access to the labor force, while also revealing how the gender pay gap may increase women-led households' poverty rates. And third, welfare/governmental assistance programs allow researchers to see not only who relies on such programs but also whether or not these programs are able to assist in pulling women out of poverty.

In 2019, the Institute for Women's Policy Research found that the gender wage gap is just over 18 percent between men and women ("The Gender Wage Gap" 2020). This means that—on a statistical average—for each dollar a man makes, a woman makes just over eighty-one cents. Or to put it another way—again, on a statistical average—if a man earns a salary of $50,000 a year, a woman only earns $40,750 per year. Because women tend to make less money than their male counterparts, a single woman acting as head of household is at greater risk of poverty than a single male. This risk increases if the woman also cares for children (Christensen 2019). This can be further exacerbated by racial inequality both culturally and economically. Social and cultural norms may also affect women's poverty risks, often creating a negative cycle. Cassandra Lauren Melo argues that in

> societies dominated by patriarchal norms, girls and women are often expected to adhere to strict gender related behaviors and practices, and experience restrictions on their choices and opportunities. . . . The low value placed on women and girls perpetuates a variety of harmful yet common attitudes and practices that can negatively impact them for the rest of their lives. (Melo 2019)

Ultimately then, 70 percent of the people living in poverty in the United States are women and children ("Women and Poverty in America" n.d.). Women are consistently and structurally steered toward low-paying job sectors (e.g., retail and hospitality), and women are often paid less than male peers even within those jobs. Additionally, women's ability to earn a living wage is compounded by factors such as a lack of affordable childcare, workplace discrimination, and intimate partner violence in which a woman's partner might prevent her from working outside the home or might garnish her pay. All of this adds up to the feminization of poverty.

Intersectional Analysis of Poverty

Currently, feminists studying poverty highlight the importance of an intersectional analysis. This means thinking along multiple axes of oppression rather than solely focusing on gender. For example, an intersectional analysis would address the systemic racism operating within the feminization of poverty.

To demonstrate an intersectional analysis, it is important to revisit the gender pay gap discussed above. If one looks at the average of men's pay and the average of women's pay, then women are making only just above eighty-one cents per male dollar. But if we think intersectionally, we can see how racism impacts the feminization of poverty. For instance, in 2024, for every dollar that white men earned, Latinas were paid approximately fifty-five cents, Native American women were paid approximately fifty-nine cents, and Black women were paid approximately sixty-four cents (Haan 2024). All of this adds up. For instance, the medium income (as measured in 2019) for Black women was over 10,000 dollars less than white women, with 25 percent of all Black women living below the poverty line in the United States (The Women's Fund of the Greater Cincinnati Foundation 2020).

Feminist Activism Confronting Poverty

Many feminist activists are involved in fighting to end the feminization of poverty and poverty more broadly. The organization UN Women addresses the gender poverty gap through initiatives such as the Generation Equality Action Coalition on Economic Justice and Rights. By promoting gender equality, sustainable economies, and access to the workforce, Generation Equality generated $32 billion toward such initiatives in 2022 (UN Women 2024). The Feminist Majority Foundation (FMF) also organizes projects and programs that work to end the sexism and racism that impoverishes women, along with several other initiatives toward equality. Educational programs, such as Girls Learn International (GLI), are helping to educate students and increasing girls' education.

Overall, by highlighting the gender disparity among poverty rates, feminist scholars focusing on the feminization of poverty aim to reveal the barriers that women face when seeking economic security. Such analysis may also inform and strengthen the initiatives of feminist activists seeking a more equitable future for all.

Kelsey Taylor Alexander

See Also: Domestic Labor; Equal Pay; Gender Discrimination; Intersectionality; Transnational Feminism

Further Reading

Christensen, M.A. 2019. "Feminization of Poverty: Causes and Implications." In *Gender Equality: Encyclopedia of the UN Sustainable Development Goals*, edited by W. Leal Filho, A. Azul, L. Brandli, P. Özuyar, and T. Wall. Springer. https://doi.org/10.1007/978-3-319-70060-1_6-1.

Haan, Katherine. 2024. "Gender Pay Gap Statistics in 2024." *Forbes*, March 1, 2024. Accessed August 1, 2024. https://www.forbes.com/advisor/business/gender-pay-gap-statistics/#sources_section.

Melo, Cassandra Lauren. 2019. "The Feminization of Poverty: A Brief Analysis of Gender Issues and Poverty among Women and Girls." *CJCND* 1, no. 1: 73–81.

"Our Work." n.d. *Feminist Majority Foundation*. Accessed August 24, 2024. https://feminist.org/our-work/.

Pearce, Diana M. 1989. "The Feminization of Poverty: A Second Look." *Institute for Women's Policy Research*. Accessed August 24, 2024. https://www.google.com/url?sa=t&source=web&rct=j&opi=89978449&url=https://iwpr.org/wp-content/uploads/2021/01/D401.pdf&ved=2ahUKEwjc58OL5JWIAxWEGtAFHToaCg4QFnoECBMQAQ&usg=AOvVaw3MpNYoL5y2L4zFHxD0CiFt.

"Poverty Guidelines." n.d. *The US Department of Health and Human Services*. 2024. Accessed August 8, 2024. https://aspe.hhs.gov/topics/poverty-economic-mobility/poverty-guidelines.

"The Gender Wage Gap: 2019 Earnings Differences by Race and Ethnicity." 2020. *Institute for Women's Policy Research*. Accessed August 24, 2024. https://iwpr.org/wp-content/uploads/2020/07/2020-Weekly-Wage-Gap-2020-FINAL.pdf.

UN Women. 2024. "How Can Gender Equality Reduce Poverty?" February 28, 2024. Accessed August 24, 2024. https://www.unwomen.org/en/news-stories/explainer/2024/02/how-can-gender-equality-reduce-poverty.

"Women and Poverty in America." n.d. *The Women's Legal Defense and Education Fund*. Accessed August 1, 2024. https://www.legalmomentum.org/women-and-poverty-america.

Women's Fund of the Greater Cincinnati Foundation. 2020. "Analysis of Black Women's Historical Labor Trends and Systemic Barriers to Economic Mobility." Accessed August 24, 2024. https://www.womensfundingnetwork.org/wp-content/uploads/2020/10/Final_Hist_Black_Women__Report_Design_reduced.pdf.

FEMME

Femme is a descriptor for a queer person who presents themselves and acts in a traditionally feminine manner (e.g., wearing makeup or feminine clothing). For example, celebrities like Kate McKinnon (former Saturday Night Live comedian) and Portia de Rossi (actor and spouse of Ellen DeGeneres) present as femme. Both identify as members of the LGBTQIA+ community and depict a traditionally feminine outward appearance. Historically, the term describes a lesbian woman who exhibits a feminine identity or gender presentation; it now applies more broadly to also include transgender people, gender-nonconforming people, nonbinary people, and others whose performance of femininity is out of step with social norms.

Although femme and femininity are closely related, the terms are not interchangeable. Femininity refers to the socially constructed idea of what is feminine and is not necessarily queer. Femme includes the queering of femininity—not just identifying as queer but the embodiment and embracing of queerness in the full meaning of the word (Jones 2016). Femme is also distinct from femininity in its refusal to accept the patriarchal norms for femininity that only recognize cisgender, female-bodied, white, heterosexual, able-bodied, and heterosexually attractive women as "feminine" (Blair and Hoskin 2014).

Additionally, there is a sense of reclamation in the use of the term "femme." For many, it is about owning the stereotypes and expectations traditionally placed on women and making them one's own. "Intentionality is the key to distinguishing a femme identity from a traditionally feminine one" (Urquhart 2015). Being femme is not about acting feminine or "girly" in the ways mainstream society feels that female-presenting people should act. Instead, being femme is about challenging the expectations that women face purely for being women. Society's promotion of heteronormativity—the socially enforced idea that everyone is male and masculine or female and feminine, and that everyone is heterosexual—is harmful as it erases identities and denies the reality that our identities are unique and complex.

Femmephobia/Anti-Femininity

Since the 1970s, social science researchers have documented the cultural devaluation of femininity and its impact on experiences of discrimination among sexual and gender minorities. The devaluing of femininity is a social problem resulting in or exacerbating the violence against women, men, transgender people, and racial minorities (Hoskin 2020). Femmephobia or anti-femininity refers to the devaluation and regulation of femininity and suggests a separate phenomenon specific to gender (e.g., femininity), rather than gender/sex (e.g., woman/female; Hoskin, 2020). For instance, on the dating application, Grindr, which is typically used by gay men to meet other gay men, a person's dating profile might specifically state "no femmes." This deliberately excludes and devalues femininity as a quality in a romantic partner. That is, a gay man with feminine qualities is less desirable than a stereotypical masculine-presenting man. Many experience femmephobia as a regulatory power within LGBTQ+ communities and society at large as well as a target in their experiences of gender policing and discrimination (Hoskin 2019).

Feminists have long addressed the systematic discrimination against women. In so doing, sometimes feminists have thought of femininity as a patriarchal construction—as a way of being in the world through which women embody patriarchy's desires. This ultimately devalues femininity, seeing it as succumbing to patriarchy, and sometimes even blames women who are feminine for participating in their own oppression (Serano 2007). In response, scholars of femme point out that femininity is not the problem; instead femmephobia—the systematic devaluation and regulation of femininity—is the problem. Currently, there is comparatively little research studying femme, and feminists and feminist theory must continue to explore femme identity and its role in the feminist movement.

Samantha F. Quinn

See Also: Gender; Gender Performance; Patriarchy; Queer Theory

Further Reading

Blair, Karen L., and Rhea Ashley Hoskin. 2014 "Experiences of Femme Identity: Coming Out, Invisibility and Femmephobia." *Psychology and Sexuality* 6, no. 3: 229–244. https://doi.org/10.1080/19419899.2014.921860.

"Gender Diversity Terminology | Penn State Student Affairs," n.d. Accessed April 25, 2024. https://studentaffairs.psu.edu/csgd/explore-lgbtq-resources/identity-based/gender-terms.

Hoskin, Rhea Ashley. 2019. "Femmephobia: The Role of Anti-Femininity and Gender Policing in LGBTQ+ People's Experiences of Discrimination." *Sex Roles* 81, no. 11–12 (February): 686–703. https://doi.org/10.1007/s11199-019-01021-3.

Hoskin, Rhea Ashley. 2020. "'Femininity? It's the Aesthetic of Subordination': Examining Femmephobia, the Gender Binary, and Experiences of Oppression among Sexual and Gender Minorities." *Archives of Sexual Behavior* 49, no. 7 (March): 2319–2339. https://doi.org/10.1007/s10508-020-01641-x.

Jones, Gina. 2016. "What Does Femme Mean? The Difference between Being Femme & Being Feminine." *Bustle*, August 24, 2016. https://www.bustle.com/articles/166081-what-does-femme-mean-the-difference-between-being-femme-being-feminine.

Serano, Julia M. 2007. *Whipping Girl: A Transsexual Woman on Sexism and the Scapegoating of Femininity.* Da Capo Press.

Urquhart, Evan. 2015. "Not Your Great-Aunt's Girly Lesbian. What Does Femme Mean Today?" *Slate Magazine*, March 12, 2015. https://slate.com/human-interest/2015/03/femme-lesbians-shouldnt-be-defined-by-their-butches.html.

FIRST STEP ACT (2018)

On December 21, 2018, President Donald Trump signed the First Step Act into US law. The law, also known as the Formerly Incarcerated Reenter Society Transformed Safely Transitioning Every Person Act, was established as part of a bipartisan effort to improve criminal justice outcomes by bettering prison conditions, promoting rehabilitation, and decreasing excessive prison sentencing. One essential facet of the First Step Act's betterment of prison conditions is its mandate that the Bureau of Prisons make tampons and sanitary napkins "available to prisoners for free, in a quantity that is appropriate to the healthcare needs of each prisoner" (First Step Act 2018).

Prior to the 2018 First Step Act, only twelve states and the District of Columbia mandated free access to menstrual products for those in need. As a result, incarcerated people who menstruate experienced high rates of what is known as "period poverty" (Lee 2023). Period poverty is the lack of access to the necessary menstrual products and knowledge to use them properly.

Menstruation within prisons and jails is expensive. The cost of menstrual products within the commissary—the in-prison store—is often too high for individuals to afford appropriate supplies to care for their menstrual cycles (Haven 2019). Often, period poverty leads to menstruating inmates reusing hygiene products or using old clothes or rags rather than new, sterile sanitary pads or tampons. The lack of access to proper menstrual products, in conjunction with the lack of access to laundry facilities and showers within jails and prisons, leads to complications such as bacterial infections, yeast infections, and toxic shock syndrome (Golding 2024).

The First Step Act provides access to free menstrual care products such as tampons and pads for those within federal prisons, but it only applies at a federal level, meaning that state-level prisons are not required to provide free menstrual products—and the majority of menstruating inmates are housed at state-level prisons, leaving countless imprisoned individuals experiencing period poverty (Golding 2024). For instance, a recent survey by Shilpa Darivemula and her colleagues (2023) found that of a survey of 106 imprisoned respondents, more than half received fewer than five menstrual products upon intake and almost 30 percent had to trade or barter for menstrual hygiene products monthly.

The Robert F. Kennedy Human Rights Institute has named period poverty a human rights issue and an urgent health and hygiene problem. Although the First Step Act has made strides in addressing period poverty within federal prisons, it has its shortcomings even at the federal level. Due to the ambiguity of the wording, there is a large margin for interpretation within each prison, meaning that some menstruating individuals in federal prisons may still not receive what they need even if the supply meets the loose standards of the First Step Act's mandate.

This gap in care and overarching implications of period poverty for incarcerated individuals are being addressed in several ways. Many private institutions and nonprofit organizations donate menstrual products to those within prisons and jails. Unfortunately, this remains an inadequate solution. For instance, journalist Jessica Kane (2015) provided a rough estimate of menstrual product use, offering a conservative calculation that an average menstrual cycle might require twenty tampons and five liners over the course of a five-day flow. Taking those conservative figures and applying them to contemporary incarceration rates reveals that—since three-quarters of incarcerated women are of reproductive age—incarcerated menstruators in the United States would need more than 800,000 liners and three million tampons per month in a given year (Alves and Spears 2022). Donated menstrual products are incredibly important but not an adequate solution given the need.

Proper state and federal legislation is the best way to address period poverty within incarcerated populations (Kindelan 2019). At a state level, this looks like California's 2020 Reproductive Dignity for Incarcerated People Act, which mandates jails and prisons provide free tampons and sanitary pads as well as mandating better access to perinatal medical care and bans the use of tasers and chemical weapons on pregnant inmates in California (Sosa and Blakinger 2024). At a federal level, the First Step Act is a first step toward addressing this problem.

Feminist activism has been a vital component of the changes seen in US legislation regarding period equity. US Congress Representative Grace Meng (D-NY) has made significant strides in ensuring that menstruating individuals in schools, prisons, and homeless shelters have access to proper menstrual hygiene products. Rep. Meng's period equity activism started with a letter from a teenager in her district writing to tell her about gaps in period equity within homeless shelters. This led Rep. Meng to research period equity status at a local and federal level and to find a startling reality: public schools, prisons, and homeless shelters lack even rudimentary provisions for menstrual products. Rep. Meng first wrote the Obama administration in 2015, expressing concerns about the lack of menstrual products in homeless shelters, soon after the Federal Emergency Management System (FEMA) announced that they would allow homeless shelters to use federal grants to buy menstrual products. Next, Rep. Meng began addressing period equity within prisons. Rep. Meng again wrote a letter to the Obama administration, but the request stalled as President Obama's second term came to an end. Shortly after the inauguration of President Trump, the new administration expressed its support for Rep. Meng's concerns. A year later, President Trump signed the First Step Act into law, creating provisions for menstrual products in federal prisons. Rep. Meng's advocacy and its origins in a teenage constituent's letter helped pave the way for the First Step Act to be signed into law (Kindelan 2019). This is only one example of how feminist activism has been crucial to legislative developments for period equality.

Although the First Step Act would benefit from more stringent regulations and firmer language, it is an important step toward seeking period equity for incarcerated populations.

Josephine McClure

See Also: Interlocking Oppression; Intersectionality; Menstruation; Menstruation Activism

Further Reading

ACLU. 2019. "The Unequal Price of Periods: Menstrual Equity in the United States." *American Civil Liberties Union*, November 6, 2019. Accessed August 24, 2024. https://www.aclu.org/publications/unequal-price-periods.

Alves, Thais, and Emily Spears. 2022. "The Period Project: The Fight for Menstrual Equity in Prisons." *Ms.*, February 24, 2022. https://msmagazine.com/2022/02/24/period-project-menstrual-equity-women-prisons/.

Darivemula, Shilpa, Andrea Knittel, Lisa Flowers, Shawana Moore, Bianca Hall, Hebron Kelecha, Xinyang Li, Megha Ramaswamy, and Patricia J. Kelly. 2023. "Menstrual Equality in the Criminal Legal System." *Journal of Women's Health* 32, no. 9: 927–31. https://doi.org/10.1089/jwh.2023.0085

Federal Bureau of Prisons. 2018. "An Overview of The First Step Act." Accessed July 2, 2024 https://www.bop.gov/inmates/fsa/overview.jsp.

First Step Act of 2018, Pub. L. No. 115-391, 132 Stat. 5194 (2018).
Golding, Tanesha. 2024. "Supporting Rights of Incarcerated Women by Providing Free Period Products." *Robert F. Kennedy Human Rights*. Accessed July 2, 2024. https://rfkhumanrights.org/our-voices/supporting-rights-of-incarcerated-women-by-providing-free-period-products/.
Haven, Kimberly. 2019. "Why I'm Fighting for Menstrual Equity in Prison." *ACLU,* November 8, 2019. Accessed August 21, 2024. https://www.aclu.org/news/prisoners-rights/why-im-fighting-for-menstrual-equity-in-prison.
Kane, Jessica. 2015. "Here's How Much a Woman's Period Will Cost Her Over a Lifetime." *Huffington Post,* May 18, 2015. Accessed July 9, 2024. https://www.huffpost.com/entry/period-cost-lifetime_n_7258780.
Kindelan, Katie. 2019. "This Congresswoman Nicknamed 'Period Lady' is on a Mission to Give All Women Access to Period Products." *ABC*, October 18, 2019. https://abcnews.go.com/GMA/Wellness/congresswoman-nicknamed-period-lady-mission-give-women-access/story?id=66232513.
Law, Victoria, and Rachel Kauder Nalebuff. 2023. "How Prisons Use Menstruation as a Form of Punishment." *Time,* March 29, 2023. https://time.com/6265653/prison-menstruation-punishment/.
Lee, Jean. 2023. "5 Pads for 2 Cellmates: Period Inequality Remains an Issue in Prisons." *USA Today*, July 13, 2023. https://www.usatoday.com/story/news/nation/2021/07/13/lack-access-period-products-prisons-widespread-us/7932448002/.
Monazzam, Niki, and Kristen Budd. 2023. "Incarcerated Women and Girls." *The Sentencing Project*, April 3, 2023. Accessed August 24, 2024. www.sentencingproject.org/fact-sheet/incarcerated-women-and-girls/.
Parrish, Danielle E. 2020. "Achieving Justice for Girls in the Juvenile Justice System." *Social Work (New York)*, vol. 65, no. 2: 149–58. https://doi.org/10.1093/sw/swaa005.
Sosa, Anabel, and Keri Blakinger. 2024. "For Some Incarcerated Women, Getting Ahold of Menstrual Products is a Nightmare." *Los Angeles Times*, June 2, 2024. https://www.latimes.com/california/story/2024-06-02/for-some-incarcerated-women-getting-ahold-of-menstrual-products-isnt-easy.
US Department of Justice, Memorandum. 2017. "Provision of Feminine Hygiene Products." August 17, 2017. Accessed August 21, 2024. https://www.bop.gov/policy/om/001_2017.pdf.

FRIEDAN, BETTY

Betty Friedan (1921–2006) was born in Peoria, Illinois, as Bettye Goldstein. In 1942, she graduated from Smith College *summa cum laude* in psychology. She spent a year doing a graduate fellowship in psychology at the University of California Berkeley before she was encouraged by her then boyfriend to drop out, since he did not receive a similar scholarship (Friedan 1963, 68). She followed him to New York where she worked as a reporter for the Federated Press and UE News.

In 1947, Betty Goldstein married Carl Friedan and soon had three children in the suburbs. She found herself living with what she would later call the "problem with no name." This was the problem countless (white) women faced in the suburbs: surrounded by everything they were told should be fulfilling for women, they were not fulfilled. Friedan drove the school carpool, went to PTA meetings, and had dinner on the table every night at six o'clock. But she was not fulfilled. She missed her work, both in writing and psychology, and felt a deep sense of emptiness in her life.

In 1963, Betty Friedan published *The Feminine Mystique*. Although she published six books over the course of her lifetime, *The Feminine Mystique* remains her most famous and most influential. This book originated in a survey Friedan sent out for her fifteen-year Smith class reunion. Friedan realized that many other women were feeling the same dissatisfaction with their lives that she was, and thus she started writing a book that would give name to the "problem with no name" and ultimately influence the course of the twentieth century.

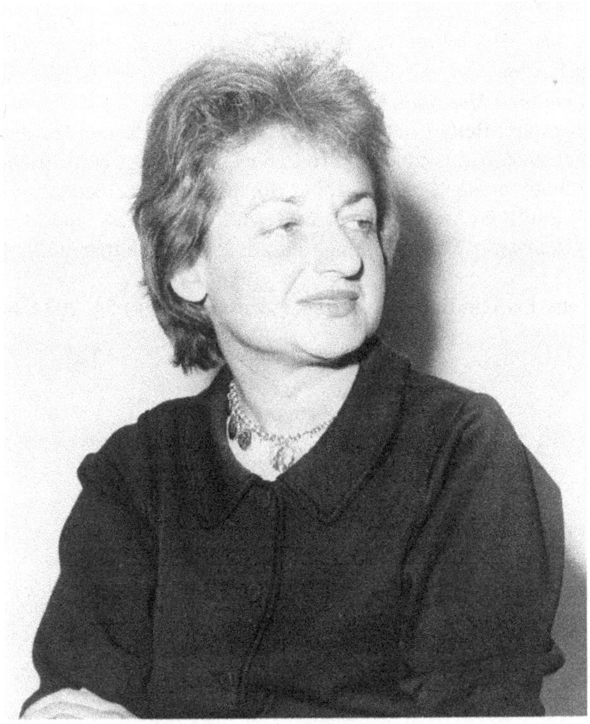

Best known for her 1963 book *The Feminine Mystique*, Betty Friedan cofounded the National Organization of Women and laid the foundation for the mainstream women's movement in the United States (Library of Congress).

Betty Friedan was active in the women's movement until her death in 2006. She cofounded the National Organization for Women (NOW) in 1966 and was elected as its first president. Leading this activist organization, Friedan pushed for equal employment opportunity, ending discrimination in workplace advertising. For instance, Friedan was essential in the push to change "help wanted-male" signs (and hiring realities) into "help-wanted" signs, and she advocated for equal pay and supported the ratification of the Equal Rights Amendment (Michals 2017).

In many ways, Friedan's leadership steered NOW toward liberal feminism instead of radical feminism during the 1960s and 1970s. Specifically, Friedan excluded lesbian priorities from NOW's political agenda, famously referring to lesbians as the "lavender menace," by which she meant that lesbians threatened feminists' respectability in mainstream culture and that if NOW was associated with lesbianism, feminism would be thought of as "man-hating."

Ultimately, Friedan's work laid the foundation for much of the mainstream women's movement in the United States. While excluding many women, her work paved the way for women such as Ruth Bader Ginsburg and Hillary Clinton to continue shattering glass ceilings.

Riley Gruppen

See Also: Equal Rights Amendment (ERA); *The Feminine Mystique*; Liberal Feminism; National Organization for Women (NOW); Radical Feminism; Woman-Identified Woman Manifesto

Further Reading

Coontz, Stephanie. 2012. *A Strange Stirring: The Feminine Mystique and American Women at the Dawn of the 1960s*. New York: Basic Books.

Friedan, Betty. 1963. *The Feminine Mystique*. London: Penguin.

Michals, Debra. 2017. "Biography: Betty Friedan." *National Women's History Museum*. Accessed August 24, 2024. https://www.womenshistory.org/education-resources/biographies/betty-friedan#:~:text=Her%201963%20best%2Dselling%20book,public%20activism%20for%20gender%20equality.

Turk, Katherine. 2015. "'To Fulfill an Ambition of [Her] Own': Work, Class, and Identity in The Feminine Mystique." *Frontiers: A Journal of Women Studies* 36, no. 2: 25–32. https://doi.org/10.1353/fro.2015.a589410.

Wattenberg, Ben. 2000. "Betty Friedan Interview." *PBS*. Accessed August 24, 2024. https://www.pbs.org/fmc/interviews/friedan.htm.

G

GASLIGHTING

Gaslighting is psychological manipulation, usually over an extended period of time, that causes the victim to question the validity of their own thoughts, perception of reality, or memories ("Gaslighting" 2024). Gaslighting can lead to confusion, loss of confidence, uncertainty of one's emotional or mental stability, and a dependency on the perpetrator. In short, gaslighting is psychological abuse aimed at making victims seem or feel "crazy" (Sweet 2019). For example, someone who is gaslighting their romantic partner might use phrases like, "You're overreacting" or "Can't you take a joke?" This abuse can happen in many different relationships including child–parent relationships, romantic partnerships, teacher–student relationships, doctor–patient relationships, among others (Angermann 2022). The term "gaslighting" comes from the 1938 stage play *Gas Light*, in which a husband attempts to drive his wife crazy by dimming the lights (which were powered by gas) in their home, and then he later denies that the light changed when his wife points it out ("What Is Gaslighting?" 2023).

Overall, there are five main categories of gaslighting including lying, trivializing, reality manipulation, coercion, and scapegoating (Angermann 2022).

- *Lying*: Gaslighting may include subtle or blatant lies. When the abuser is confronted with the lie, they will often repeat the lie or make excuses for why the evidence against them is supposedly untrue. According to the National Domestic Violence Hotline (2023), examples of this include statements like "I don't know what you're talking about" and "you're just making stuff up."
- *Trivializing*: Abusive gaslighters may also trivialize their victim's wants and needs by making their feelings seem unimportant. This can be done through statements and questions such as "you're too sensitive" and "you're going to get angry over a little thing like that?" (Angermann 2022).
- *Reality Manipulation*: This type of gaslighting occurs when abusers attempt to make their victim question their own reality. This is done by countering their victim's memory of events and might include statements like "that's not what happened" and "you're wrong, you never remember things correctly" (Angermann 2022).
- *Coercion*: Coercion or coercive control includes humiliation and verbal abuse, making the victim feel guilty for spending time with friends and family and guilting and/or manipulating the victim into doing things they do not want to do (Flannery 2023). The gaslighter may also withdraw affection or act cruel to provoke rage from their victim. Once their victim gets angry, they might say something like "I'm not abusive; you are the one yelling and losing control!"
- *Scapegoating*: This final form of gaslighting blames the victim, so the gaslighter never has to take responsibility for their actions (Angermann 2022). Instead, abusers turn the situation around and blame their victims for their own actions. Gaslighters will often make false accusations and blame those around them. They may also call their victims "crazy" or emotionally unbalanced to distort victims' valid reactions as "oversensitivity" and "overreactions."

Gaslighting, Intimate Partner Abuse, and Feminism

Intimate partner violence refers to violence and abuse between individuals in an intimate relationship and includes not only physical violence but also psychological and emotional abuse (Jewkes 2002; World Health Organization: WHO 2024). Gaslighting is often deployed in intimate relationships with an unequal power balance and is considered a core feature in intimate partner abuse (Sweet 2019). Unlike other forms of intimate partner abuse where there may be overt indicators of abuse, gaslighting may operate on a covert level with the goal of destabilizing the victim (March et al. 2023). By destabilizing the victim, gaslighting prevents them from seeking support and resources that could help them escape the abuse (Sweet 2019).

Gaslighting should be understood as rooted in social inequalities, including gender, and executed in intimate relationships with unequal power. Specifically, gaslighting is gendered due to the association of femininity with irrationality. In other words, the stereotype that women are more emotional and, therefore, less logical than men perpetuates this type of abuse. Furthermore, the effects of gaslighting are more dramatic for women on the margins, those often seen as vulnerable or lacking in credibility (Sweet 2019). These societal vulnerabilities depend on gender, sexual, and racial inequalities, which are built into the way women are viewed and treated in institutional settings. For example, an undocumented, Latina woman might receive threats and made-up stories about the immigration system from their abuser to amplify her insecurity, destabilize her sense of reality, and increase her dependence on her abuser.

In summary, gender stereotypes, intersecting inequalities, and institutional discrimination create unequal conditions in intimate relationships. The association of femininity with irrationality, alongside intersecting inequalities, is built into interpersonal relationships and social institutions, generating gender-based vulnerabilities to abuse (Sweet 2019). Therefore, it is crucial to consider gaslighting as part of a broader system of oppression and abuse mainly experienced by marginalized populations, such as women, people of color, undocumented individuals, individuals with disabilities, and members of the LGBTQIA+ community.

Samantha F. Quinn

See Also: Gender; Intersectionality; Intimate Partner Violence; Mind/Body Split

Further Reading

Angermann, Marlena. 2022. "The 5 Types of Gaslighting With Examples." *Utopia*, December 21, 2022. https://utopia.org/guide/the-5-types-of-gaslighting-with-examples/.

Flannery, Shelley. 2023. "A Guide to Coercive Control." *DomesticShelters.org*, August 11, 2023. https://www.domesticshelters.org/articles/identifying-abuse/a-guide-to-coercive-control.

"Gaslighting." 2024. In *Merriam-Webster Dictionary*. https://www.merriam-webster.com/dictionary/gaslighting.

Jewkes, Rachel. 2002. "Intimate Partner Violence: Causes and Prevention." *The Lancet* 359, no. 9315: 1423–9.

March, Evita, Cameron S. Kay, Bojana M. Dinić, Danielle Wagstaff, Beáta Grabovac, and Peter K. Jonason. 2023. "'It's All in Your Head': Personality Traits and Gaslighting Tactics in Intimate Relationships." *Journal of Family Violence* 40: 259–68. https://doi.org/10.1007/s10896-023-00582-y.

National Domestic Violence Hotline. 2023. "What Is Gaslighting?" July 4, 2023. https://www.thehotline.org/resources/what-is-gaslighting/.

Sweet, Paige L. 2019. "The Sociology of Gaslighting." *American Sociological Review* 84, no. 5: 851–75. https://doi.org/10.1177/0003122419874843.

World Health Organization: WHO. 2024. "Violence Against Women." March 25, 2024. https://www.who.int/news-room/fact-sheets/detail/violence-against-women.

GAY, ROXANE

Roxane Gay is widely known for her book *Bad Feminist* (2014a), a key work in contemporary Black feminism. Her writing challenges stereotypes around race, sexuality, body image, and feminism. Gay is a pivotal voice in fat studies, LGBTQ+ advocacy, and sexual assault, offering nuanced perspectives on body politics and rape culture. Gay's career spans academia, multiple bestselling books, and writing for *The New York Times* as a contributing opinion writer. Her work bridges academic theory with accessible cultural critique.

Bad Feminist

In her own words, Gay says, "I would rather be a bad feminist than no feminist at all," which explains her embrace of contradictions and imperfections with feminist identities (2014a, 318).

According to feminist author Naomi Wolf, *Bad Feminist* stands out for offering sharp cultural criticism with an accessible, humorous voice, making feminist theory widely relatable while delving into the complexities of race, class, and gender. Wolf highlights Gay's achievement in bridging personal narrative and political analysis, positioning *Bad Feminist* as an essential volume for both feminist theory and popular culture, without sacrificing critical depth or engagement.

Black feminist Brittney Cooper also praises how Gay's writing frees young people, particularly women of color, from the rigid expectations of feminist identity, acknowledging that contradictions exist in feminist practice. Gay's unapologetic embrace of these complexities, Cooper argues, allows for a more livable and breathable feminist politic—one that makes room for imperfection, growth, and a liberation that aligns with being one's "very best, badass self" (2016, 705).

Feminist Contributions and Legacy

Gay's influence is broad, resonating with feminist scholars like Sara Ahmed, who coined the term feminist killjoy. She's also gained recognition for advocating for social justice, such as supporting WNBA star Brittney Griner during her imprisonment in Russia. Other notable books include *Hunger* (2017), *Difficult Women* (2017), and *Not That Bad: Dispatches from Rape Culture* (2018). Overall, Gay's role as a public intellectual and prolific writer has given her household name status in contemporary feminism.

Gay's work continues to inspire and push for more inclusive feminism. Her feminist legacy lies in her unapologetic embrace of complexity and contradictions within feminist identity. Through her groundbreaking book *Bad Feminist*, she redefined feminism by acknowledging that one can hold feminist ideals while being imperfect in practice. Her work offers space for those who resist rigid definitions, encouraging authenticity and inclusivity. Gay critiques privilege, pop culture, and social norms, all while advocating for a feminism that is livable and adaptable, particularly for marginalized communities. Her legacy challenges the perfectionism often expected within feminist movements.

Anna Whittle

See Also: Anger; Feminist Killjoy; Rape Culture; Womanism

Further Reading

Cooper, Brittney. 2016. "Feminism for Badasses." *Signs: Journal of Women in Culture & Society* 41, no. 3: 704–5. https://doi.org/10.1086/684255.

Gay, Roxane. 2014a. *Bad Feminist: Essays*, 1st ed. New York: Harper Perennial.

Gay, Roxane. 2014b. "Roxane Gay: The Bad Feminist Manifesto." *The Guardian*, August 2, 2014. www.theguardian.com/world/2014/aug/02/bad-feminist-roxane-gay-extract.

Gay, Roxane. 2017. *Hunger: A Memoir of (My) Body*, 1st ed. New York: Harper Collins Publishers.
Wolf, Naomi. 2016. "'Bad Feminist,' Great Rhetorician." *Signs: Journal of Women in Culture & Society* 41, no. 3: 709–12. https://doi.org/10.1086/684258.

GENDER

Gender refers to the social and cultural differences between masculinity and femininity, where sex refers to the biological distinctions between men and women. Gender describes the expectations regarding how men and women are expected to look, behave, communicate, and live (Alberts, Nakayama, and Martin 2021). For example, in the United States and in many similar cultures, women are expected to express femininity through behaviors such as being a caregiver or homemaker, being polite, not speaking in a loud or aggressive manner, and wearing dresses or makeup. On the other hand, men are expected to be strong and assertive, act as the provider, and wear clothing such as pants or suits.

Gender identity refers to what extent a person identifies with the social construction of masculinity or femininity. In other words, someone's gender identity is their innermost concept of self as man, woman, a blend of both or neither, and it can be the same or different from their sex assigned at birth (Human Rights Campaign 2024). For example, an individual born as a biological male might feel that they are a boy/man and accept the traditional notions of what it means to be a man. However, gender roles and expectations have evolved over time and different cultures have differing gender expectations. Essentially, what it means to "be a man" has changed across time and varies across cultures. Individuals learn about gender and come to understand their own gender identity through communication. That is, we learn about gender through listening to how people talk about gender, observing the images portrayed in media, and by observing how people communicate to men and women. For example, films and television shows like *The Stepford Wives* and *Mad Men* portray men as leaders, authority figures, and the head of the household, and the male characters treat women with disrespect, expecting them to be stay-at-home mothers and to obey the demands of their male spouse or boss.

An individual's gender identity is not biological but based on performance or self-presentation. Self-presentation refers to how an individual attempts to present themselves to control or shape how others view them. Many people express their gender identity based on how they have seen masculinity or femininity performed by family, peers, authority figures, and media representations. Because traditional expressions of masculinity and femininity are heavily repeated in a culture and because society typically downplays changes in gender performances—especially changes to masculinity—many see the behaviors of masculinity and femininity as normal or natural. Other people show their gender identity in nontraditional ways such as wearing clothing that does not match what society deems is normal for a man or a woman. For example, a woman with a more masculine gender identity attending a wedding might wear a tuxedo. Indeed, at the 2024 Grammy Awards, members of the band Boygenius (well known for their androgynous style) wore matching white suits and ties.

Although many gender identities exist and a person's gender identity is dynamic and can change, sometimes people distinguish between cisgender, transgender, or nonbinary to understand gender. Cisgender means that a person's gender identity is what society expects from someone born with their type of body. In other words, a cisgender woman identifies with their biological body and presents themselves in ways that align with societal or cultural norms of being a woman. Pew Research Center defines a transgender person as someone who identifies with a gender that is different than their biological body. A transgender woman is someone who identifies as a woman but was born into a male body. Nonbinary refers to a person who does not identify as a man or a woman or who does not strictly identify as one or the other. Just over 5 percent of adults younger than thirty identify as transgender or nonbinary, including 2 percent who are a transgender man or transgender woman and 3 percent who identify as nonbinary (Pew Research Center 2022). These rates are lower in older age groups in the United States.

Finally, according to the Human Rights Campaign, some individuals experience gender dysphoria, which is the significant distress caused when an individual's assigned gender at birth is not the same gender with which they identify.

Feminist View of Gender and Intersectionality

Feminist theory examines the reinforcement of gender roles and inequalities, highlighting the role of the patriarchy in maintaining the oppression of women (hooks 2000). In patriarchal societies, the perspectives and contributions of men are considered more valuable, resulting in the silencing and marginalization of women and other minority groups. For example, the United States values male leadership as seen in the fact that the country has yet to see a female president and of the 500 CEOs of "Fortune 500 Companies" only 53 are women (Forbes 2023).

Additionally, more recent scholarship on the feminist perspective of gender inequality considers intersectionality suggesting that various biological, social, and cultural categories, including gender, race, class, sexuality, and ethnicity, contribute to systematic social inequality (Lewis 2009). Therefore, different forms of oppression do not act independently of one another; instead, they form a system of oppression that reflects the intersection of multiple types of discrimination. In other words, the marginalization of women is not only shaped by gender but also by other factors such as race and class.

Samantha F. Quinn

See Also: Crenshaw, Kimberlé; Gender Discrimination; hooks, bell; Intersectionality; Gender Performance; Hegemonic Masculinity; Trans Theory

Further Reading

Alberts, Jess, Thomas Nakayama, and Judith Martin. 2021. *Human Communication in Society*. Upper Saddle River: Pearson.

Elting, Liz. 2023. "New Year, New Glass Heights: Women Now Comprise 10% of Top US Corporation CEOs." *Forbes*, January 27, 2023. https://www.forbes.com/sites/lizelting/2023/01/27/new-year-new-glass-heights-for-the-first-time-in-history-over-10-of-fortune-500-ceos-are-women/?sh=38f2b6abe77f.

hooks, bell. 2020. *Feminist Theory: From Margin to Center*. London: Pluto Press. http://ci.nii.ac.jp/ncid/BA49808302.

Human Rights Campaign. n.d. "Sexual Orientation and Gender Identity Definitions." Accessed April 25, 2024. https://www.hrc.org/resources/sexual-orientation-and-gender-identity-terminology-and-definitions.

"Intersectionality – the Feminist Perspective." 2020. *Pressbooks*, October 31, 2020. https://viva.pressbooks.pub/hum210/chapter/the-feminist-perspective/.

Lewis, Gail. 2009. "Celebrating Intersectionality? Debates on a Multi-Faceted Concept in Gender Studies: Themes from a Conference." *European Journal of Women's Studies* 16, no. 3 (July): 203–10. https://doi.org/10.1177/1350506809105310.

Pew Research Center. 2022. "About 5% of Young Adults in US Are Transgender or Nonbinary." June 7, 2022. https://www.pewresearch.org/short-reads/2022/06/07/about-5-of-young-adults-in-the-u-s-say-their-gender-is-different-from-their-sex-assigned-at-birth/.

GENDER DISCRIMINATION

Gender discrimination refers to a wide variety of acts, behaviors, and processes that treat people differently because of their gender identity. Generally, gender discrimination refers to the unfair treatment of women and other gender minorities, although there is increased interest among some sociopolitical circles—especially Men's Rights Movements—in the experiences men have with gender discrimination. Regardless of the victim, gender discrimination occurs on interpersonal and structural levels, ranging from passive prejudice to active bigotry, and it is often related to other forms of discrimination, such as racism, homophobia, and ableism. Thus, gender discrimination is best understood as one component in what Patricia Hill Collins calls the "matrix of domination" (Collins 2009, 26).

Many forms of gender discrimination often go overlooked, as they represent the status quo in patriarchal societies (Wade and Ferree 2019). In patriarchal societies, men or masculine-presenting people possess a disproportionate share of the power, interpersonally, socially, culturally, and legally. As a result, behaviors such as spousal rape or inequitable hiring practices were historically not questioned, despite their discriminatory qualities. Feminist projects in fighting gender discrimination, then, focus on identifying forms of discrimination, raising awareness about their prevalence, and advocating for change at myriad levels.

Identifying and Addressing Discrimination

Gender discrimination occurs within personal relationships, social circles, schools, workplaces, places of worship, and healthcare facilities, among other spaces, and feminist theorists often categorize discrimination as a mixture of intersecting interpersonal/individual and structural forces (Wade and Ferree 2019). Interpersonal or individual discrimination refers to the unfair treatment women or members of other gender minorities (such as trans people and nonbinary folks) experience in their daily lives while interacting with family, friends, or members of their communities. On the other hand, structural discrimination refers to the unequal distribution of power between genders in larger arenas, such as workplaces, legal systems, and cultural environments. Women and other gender minority groups regularly experience discrimination on both interpersonal and structural levels and are often blamed for their own victimization (Gilmore 2017; Wade and Ferree 2019).

Feminist activists have worked for decades to define and identify interpersonal gender discrimination, calling attention to day-to-day issues like catcalling, workplace sexual harassment, and domestic violence (Wade and Ferree 2019). Interpersonal gender discrimination derives from an understanding of women as objects who exist to serve male/masculine desire or as people who need male/masculine assistance. Historically, women have been expected to perceive catcalls and unsolicited sexual advances in the workplace as compliments that need not be questioned and abuse at home as something that must not be disclosed. Feminist activists have worked to challenge this narrative, instead asserting that a woman's body is her own and does not exist purely for the enjoyment of men. Much of this work takes place in online spaces, as hashtags like #MeToo and #TimesUp empower survivors of sexual harassment and abuse to disclose their trauma, seek support, and find solidarity with other victim-survivors (Boyle 2018).

Other forms of interpersonal discrimination stem from what feminists call benevolent sexism, a term that is regularly conflated with chivalry. Benevolent sexism may be understood as sexism with (possibly) good intentions or with the intentions of potentially helping women by offering a strong, knowing, and capable (often masculine) hand (Wade and Ferree 2019). At the root of benevolent sexism is a belief that women lack the strength, knowledge, and capability to manage life on their own, necessitating masculine intervention or help. Thus, built into many contemporary societies is a chivalrous code or religious doctrine in which men are expected to honor, serve, and support women by, for instance, opening doors for them, mansplaining concepts, and financially providing for their families. While these practices may appear to serve women on the surface, they often cultivate a relationship of dependence and male authority. This culture of dependence regularly results in spousal abuse, sexual objectification, and other forms of gendered violence. Across the globe, these practices take on different tones. Feminist activists labor to identify and name these forms of discrimination, holding that identifying and raising awareness is crucial in fighting against them.

Feminist activists also endeavor to demonstrate that many of these individual behaviors are enabled, allowed, and/or excused by structural affordances because they are encoded into law and other guiding doctrines. While identifying and raising awareness about these forms of structural discrimination are crucial processes, structural problems require structural solutions. For instance, in the US Constitution, only white men were granted the rights to vote, hold political office, and own property. Feminists advocated for decades for women's suffrage, challenging the existing legal structures that prevented them from enjoying equal rights. In 1920, these efforts proved successful as women were granted the right to vote (US Congress 1920). Feminist activists were also instrumental in passing the Civil Rights Acts of 1964 and 1991, legislation that prohibits workplace discrimination on the basis of race, color, religion, sex, and national origin (US Congress 1991). Constitutional amendments and legislation like the Civil Rights Act provide systemic solutions to structural discrimination.

While early feminist movements achieved suffrage and other steps toward gender equality, women are still subject to structural barriers, including a lack of access to fair pay and reproductive rights. Women continue to be paid less money than men, even when they have the same education, experience, and job titles. Though the wage gap has improved over time, as of 2022, women were paid 82 cents for every dollar that men were paid (Aragão 2023). The persistence of the wage gap suggests the limited success of legislation such as the Civil Rights Acts of 1964 and 1991. Similarly, although *Roe v. Wade* protected women's access to safe and legal abortions in 1973, this precedent was overturned when the US Supreme Court heard the *Dobbs v. Jackson Women's Health Organization* case in 2022 *(Dobbs v. Jackson Women's Health Organization* 2022; *Roe v. Wade* 1973). The Dobbs ruling has implications for other women's health issues, such as in vitro fertilization and miscarriage. These examples demonstrate that the feminist project of fighting against discrimination is far from complete.

Future Directions

Current feminist interventions in gender discrimination necessitate and prioritize an intersectional approach, attending to the ways in which race, class, geographic location, and other factors coincide and influence the types of discrimination members of gender minority groups experience. Thus, feminist efforts to combat discrimination have extended to include trans people, gender-nonconforming folks, and nonbinary individuals to advocate for increased protections for them in the workplace and other public spaces, advocating for their right to work and use public restrooms that align with their gender identity. Other efforts are focused on bringing the right to education to girls across the globe, which would also enable girls to become more financially independent and able to provide for themselves. Further, as women of color are disproportionately likely to experience violence and lower pay, intersectional feminists are advocating for increased structural attention to these inequalities.

The fight against gender discrimination is a storied one. Due to sustained feminist activism, women's rights across the globe have progressed significantly in the past century, largely beginning with women's suffrage. Since then, cultural and structural shifts have contributed to a safer and more empowering environment for women. Nonetheless, interpersonal and structural gender discrimination persists across the globe as women and other gender minorities continue to live within inequitable systems, which illustrates the need for feminist activism to endure.

Amanda N. Brand

See also: Civil Rights Act (1964); *Dobbs v. Jackson Women's Health Organization* (2022); Equal Pay; Feminization of Poverty; Internalized Sexism; #MeToo; Men's Rights Movements; Nineteenth Amendment; Reproductive Justice; Suffrage; Violence Against Women Act (1994)

Further Reading

Aragão, Carolina. 2023. "Gender Pay Gap in US Hasn't Changed Much in Two Decades." *Pew Research Center*, March 1, 2023. https://www.pewresearch.org/short-reads/2023/03/01/gender-pay-gap-facts/.
Boyle, Karen. 2018. "What's in a Name?" Theorising the Inter-Relationships of Gender and Violence." *Feminist Theory* 20, no. 1: 19-36.
Collins, Patricia Hill. 2009. *Black Feminist Thought: Knowledge, Consciousness, and the Politics of Empowerment*, 2nd ed. Routledge Classics. New York: Routledge.
Dobbs v. Jackson Women's Health Organization. 597 U.S. 19. 2022.
Gilmore, Leigh. 2017. *Tainted Witness: Why We Doubt What Women Say About Their Lives.* New York: Columbia University Press.
Roe v. Wade. 410 U.S. 113. 1973.
US Congress. 1920. *19th Amendment to the US Constitution.* https://www.archives.gov/milestone-documents/19th-amendment#page-header.
US Congress. 1991. *Civil Rights Act of 1991.* https://www.eeoc.gov/civil-rights-act-1991-original-text.
Wade, Lisa, and Myra Marx Ferree. 2019. *Gender: Ideas, Interactions, Institutions*, 2nd ed. New York: W. W. Norton & Company.

GENDER PERFORMANCE

Gender performance is the idea that gender is something we *do* in our day-to-day lives rather than something we *are*. Much of this "doing" or performance is unconscious. Although we may purposefully accentuate our gender in certain contexts (e.g., putting on mascara and a form-fitting dress for a date), most gender performance occurs outside of our conscious awareness and is the product of years of gendered socialization. From birth, children are taught to dress, act, and even feel in ways considered socially acceptable for their assigned gender. Through repetition, these behaviors and "ways of being" come to feel "natural" and the constructed nature of gender is obscured.

Popularized by the feminist theorist Judith Butler (1990), the theory of gender performativity asserts that gender is created by its own performance. The term "performativity" refers to speech or behaviors that create the thing they describe (Austin 1962). For example, saying "I pronounce you husband and wife" is not simply descriptive—it also creates the marriage. Butler argues that gender works in a similar way: when we label babies who are born with a penis, "boys," and babies who are born with a vagina, "girls," we participate in *creating them* as boys and girls. Consider, for example, the cascade of social scripts set off by a stereotypical gender-reveal party (Gieseler 2017; Toles-Patkin 2021). After detecting the presence or absence of a penis on an ultrasound, soon-to-be parents announce the "gender" of their unborn child to friends and family through gender-coded (pink vs. blue) cupcakes, balloons, or other party favors. Taking the cue, friends and family begin to refer to the baby in gender stereotyped ways ("He has such a strong kick!"), buy them gendered clothes and toys, and even imagine their future personality and interests through a gendered lens. Following birth, this gendered training intensifies and children become well-versed in how to "act like" boys and girls (Bem 1983; Fine 2011). Their convincing performance, in turn, reinforces the idea that gender exists as a binary (that there are only two options, masculine and feminine) and that gender must be an essential part of human nature.

Through this process, gender performance becomes an unquestioned part of our social lives—shaping the way we understand both ourselves and others. For most people, gender is like the air we breathe. It is so pervasive that we generally don't notice it at all. It is only when someone's gender performance violates our expectations—that is, when someone fails to do gender "correctly"—that we pay attention to its production (Lorber 1994). This is particularly true when gender cues are missing or ambiguous. The discomfort and social disorientation people experience when they cannot clearly classify someone as male or female is parodied in a classic *Saturday Night Live* sequence featuring Pat, an androgynous individual, carrying out routine activities like requesting a haircut or striking up a conversation at a party. In each sketch, Pat's interaction partners desperately (and unsuccessfully) seek cues that will allow them to classify Pat as a man or a woman in order to figure out how to treat him or her. The audience's nervous laughter reveals the central role gender plays in organizing social interactions: when someone "fails" to perform gender in the expected manner, people feel unmoored and struggle to navigate even basic social encounters (Ridgeway 2011). Although nonbinary individuals are more visible and accepted today than in the early 1990s when the Pat series ran, the expectation that individuals will clearly signal their membership in one of two gender categories—and the marginalization of those who violate this norm—remains intact (Kaufman, Taniguchi, and Compton 2024; Rosati et al. 2024).

According to Judith Butler (1990), masculine and feminine identities do not exist outside of the ways we express them. There is no essential masculine or feminine nature. Instead, masculinity and femininity simply reflect a society's shared beliefs about who men and women are and ought to be; they are the ideal prototypes of manness or womanness in a particular culture. In US society, the assumptions or expectations for gender that inform our stereotypes tend to be based on the traits and experiences of white, straight, middle-class individuals (Ridgeway 2011). These stereotypes become the default rules or scripts for "doing gender" in public settings. For those who are closer to the "center" of society (e.g., straight, white women or men), femininity and masculinity often *feel* natural because the scripts are likely to resemble their own cultural upbringing. But this "effortlessness" is actually the result of years of lessons (both subtle and blatant) on how to groom, arrange, and present one's body in ways that are "properly" feminine or masculine. And even with extensive early training, most people fall short of the gender ideals prescribed by their culture. Consider the popular storyline of a (typically straight) man losing his "man card" for engaging in any number of "unmanly" behaviors like crying in public or buying almond milk. If gender was an essential quality following from biological sex, manhood could not be earned or lost—it would just *be*. Anxieties and jokes about losing or turning in one's man card reveal gender for what it is: an achieved status that must be actively maintained through the performance of masculinity and femininity (Bosson, Vandello, and Caswell 2013).

Importantly, the notion that gender is a performance does not imply that gender is optional—that we can simply choose which gender (if any) we would like to display on a given day and be seen accordingly. Although people may choose to bend or ignore gender expectations (often at their own social peril), they generally do not have the option of being seen by others as man or woman, masculine or feminine. Sociologists Candace West and Don Zimmerman (1987) contend that, whether we want to or not, we "do gender" every day, all the time, and that "virtually any activity can be assessed as to its womanly or manly nature" (136). This does not mean that everything we do will conform to society's ideal standards for femininity or masculinity, but that any behavior we perform runs "the risk of gender assessment." Even activities with no apparent relevance to gender, like brushing your teeth, can be evaluated with respect to their gender appropriateness. A high school boy may receive shade for using a pink toothbrush; a woman brushing her teeth in a public bathroom might be judged for spitting too loudly. From this perspective, gender is compulsory—you can embrace the gender scripts you are given or you can resist and rebel against them, but you cannot opt out of performing altogether.

Ultimately, gender performance is about *creating* difference and is closely tied to the maintenance of power dynamics in society (Lorber 1994). Although feminist scholars debate the extent to which gender has a biological basis, there is widespread consensus that any small differences that may exist have been exaggerated and distorted beyond recognition by compulsory gender performance. Once gender differences have been constructed, their continual production and reproduction justifies the use of gender as one of the most fundamental divisions in society. If people were not, *on average*, seen as fitting neatly into one of two distinguishable genders, the legitimacy of linking people's social status, rights, and roles to these categories would be called into question. By making gender differences appear natural and essential, gender performance plays a critical role in maintaining the status quo of women's subordination.

Carrie A. Bredow

See Also: Butler, Judith; Essentialism; Gender; Hegemonic Masculinity; Nonbinary

Further Reading

Austin, John L. 1962. *How to Do Things with Words*. Cambridge: Harvard University Press.

Bem, Sandra. 1983. "Gender Schema Theory and its Implications for Child Development: Raising Gender Aschematic Children in a Gender-Schematic Society." *Signs: Journal of Women in Culture and Society* 8 (4): 598–616. https://doi.org/10.1086/493998.

Bosson, Jennifer K., Joseph A. Vandello, and T. Andrew Caswell. 2013. "Precarious Manhood." In *The Sage Handbook of Gender and Psychology*, edited by Michelle K. Ryan and Nyla R. Branscombe. SAGE Publications.

Butler, Judith. 1990. *Gender Trouble: Feminism and the Subversion of Identity*. New York: Routledge.

Fine, Cordelia. 2011. *Delusions of Gender: How Our Minds, Society, and Neurosexism Create Difference*. New York: W. W. Norton.

Gieseler, Carly. 2017. "Gender-Reveal Parties: Performing Community Identity in Pink and Blue." *Journal of Gender Studies* 27, no. 6: 661–71. https://doi.org/10.1080/09589236.2017.1287066.

Kaufman, Gayle, Hiromi Taniguchi, and D'Lane Compton. 2024. "Life Satisfaction and Negative Affect Among Trans Men, Trans Women, and Nonbinary Individuals in a US National Sample." *LGBT Health* 11, no. 1: 57–65. https://doi.org/10.1089/lgbt.2022.0350.

Lorber, Judith. 1994. *Paradoxes of Gender*. New Haven: Yale University Press.

Ridgeway, Cecilia L. 2011. *Framed By Gender: How Gender Inequality Persists in the Modern World*. New York: Oxford University Press.

Rosati, Fau, Maric Martin Lorusso, Jessica Pistella, et al. 2024. "Nonbinary People Living in a Binary World: Minority Stress in Public and Gendered Places." *International Journal of Transgender Health* 26, no. 2: 360–77. https://doi.org/10/1080/26895269.2024.2338152.

Toles-Patkin, Terri. 2021. "Gender Reveal Parties and the Construction of the Prenatal Gendered Environment." *Explorations in Media Ecology* 20 (2): 175–93. https://doi.org/10.1386/eme_00083_1.

West, Candace, and Don H. Zimmerman. 1987. "Doing Gender." *Gender & Society* 1, no. 2: 125–51. https://doi.org/10.1177/0891243287001002002.

GENDER-NEUTRAL LANGUAGE AND PRONOUNS

In recent years, feminists have increasingly advocated for gender-neutral language and the correct use of pronouns, such as "she/her," "they/them," "he/him," "xe/xem," and other exciting possibilities. For example, many feminists refer to their significant other as their "partner" rather than their "wife" or "husband," thus using a gender-neutral option. Gender-neutral language can call attention to the patriarchal structures within language that support a male-dominated society even while sidestepping such patriarchy (Kabba 2011, 429). Developing a gender-neutral vocabulary and grammar is a vital step toward creating a more inclusive space for women, nonbinary, and trans people—and using people's preferred pronouns moves society in a more accepting direction for people of all genders.

Gendered and Gender-Neutral Language

Gendered language is found in everyday phrases that are often not considered gendered. For example, consider how you might address a crowd of people as "you guys," whether or not the group was comprised of just men. This is an example of gendered language and its naturalized role in society. Nobody would question a mixed-gendered group being referred to as "you guys," because that phrase has been taught as a *normal* mode of address—but referring to a mixed-gendered group as "you gals" would likely make people uncomfortable. Patriarchal, masculine language is often framed as gender neutral, as if "he," "guys," and "men" encompass "she," "gals," and "women," despite their explicit exclusions. As communication scholar Helen Sterk (1989, 24–5) noted, truly generic language shocks because "it removes maleness as the definitional criterion for being 'generic.'"

In contrast to gendered language, gender-neutral language avoids implying gender. As words like "sibling" and "spouse" demonstrate, English gender-neutral words have always been around—and they are becoming more common through feminist activism. Rather than using gendered language (typically masculine) as our default vocabulary, feminists often recommend gender-neutral language—such as "folks" or "you all" instead of "you guys." The result is a more inclusive society that does not frame the masculine as the default, does not assume gender, and can help destigmatize gender transitions.

Pronouns

Pronouns are words such as "I," "she," "he," "they," "you," "it," and "we," which are "used as substitutes for nouns or noun phrases" and which clearly refer to someone or something within a context (Merriam-Webster n.d.). Pronouns are routinely used in everyday writing and conversation—and a lot of English pronouns are gender specific. Just as people want others to remember and pronounce their names correctly, people also want to be referred to by the pronouns that match their gender. It is often insulting when someone purposefully uses pronouns that misgender others.

In recent years, feminist and LGBTQ+ activism has worked to loosen patriarchal language's grip on US society by normalizing sharing one's pronouns. You may see pronouns listed next to names in places like email signatures and social media profiles or on name badges. The fact that social media platforms added the option to choose and include one's pronouns is a direct result of feminist and LGBTQ+ activism. When everyone chooses and shares their pronouns, it creates a more comfortable society—especially for nonbinary and trans people.

Feminists and queer communities have fought for gender-neutral pronoun options, especially "they/them" in official spaces and in colloquial language. Sometimes people push back against using "they/them" pronouns for a singular person, insisting that "they/them" grammatically refers to multiple people. This objection, however, is largely bogus. We routinely use "they/them" pronouns to refer to a singular person when that person's gender is unknown. For example, when asking expecting parents about the gender of their baby, it's common to ask, "what gender are they?" or "are they a boy or a girl?" Additionally, using "they/them" as a singular pronoun is routine throughout history. Feminists and LGBTQ+ activists aren't exactly doing something new: "they has been used as a singular pronoun since at least the late 14th century," with famous literary examples. For instance, Jane Austen used "they" in this way in *Pride and Prejudice* (Meagley 2021).

We are taught language from a very young age. It can be difficult to use truly gender-neutral language (e.g., "folks" instead of "guys") and to use "they/them" as singular pronouns if you haven't practiced. So practice!

Ryan Hall

See Also: Gender; Gender Performance; Internalized Sexism; Nonbinary; Trans Theory

Further Reading

Kabba, Kadija. 2011. "Gender-Neutral Language: An Essential Language Tool to Serve Precision, Clarity and Unambiguity." *Commonwealth Law Bulletin* 37, no. 3: 427–34. https://doi.org/10.1080/03050718.2011.595141.

Meagley, Desmond. 2021. "They/Them Pronouns: All Your Questions About Gender Neutral Pronouns Answered." *Teen Vogue*, December 15, 2021. https://www.teenvogue.com/story/they-them-questions-answered.

Merriam-Webster. n.d. Pronoun. *In Merriam-Webster.com dictionary*. Retrieved October 31, 2024, from https://www.merriam-webster.com/dictionary/pronoun.

Sterk, Helen M. 1989. "How Rhetorical Becomes Real: Religious Sources of Gender Identity." *Journal of Communication & Religion* 12, no. 2: 24–5.

GIRL POWER

"Girl power" refers to a trend in popular culture that celebrates girls and women feeling empowered in their femininity. Or, as Zaslow (2009, 3) puts it, girl power media "encourages girls and women to identify both as traditionally feminine objects *and* as powerful feminist agents." Under the banner of "girl power," women are encouraged to pursue careers, view themselves as men's equals, be resilient both physically and mentally, and achieve financial independence. They are also encouraged to pursue romance and marriage, have children, and embrace their sexuality. Thus, "girl power" is closely linked with the 1990s–2010s cultural sensibility of postfeminism and the more contemporary cultural sense of popular feminism, since they all highlight individual choice as central to female empowerment. This means that women are encouraged to decide when to express themselves as sexy, professional, or nurturing and to embrace all of these identities as part of their femininity.

"Girl power" first emerged as a cultural force in the 1990s. One of the most well-known early instances of "girl power" is the 1990s British girl group, The Spice Girls, whose music highlighted themes of female empowerment, female friendship, and sexual freedom. The Spice Girls even offered female fans five distinct models of femininity to admire and emulate: athletic, cute, sexy, posh, and fierce. Since then, "girl power" has been adopted as one of the key marketing strategies for media and products aimed at girls and women. Some examples of "girl power" media include TV shows such as *The Gilmore Girls* and *Buffy the Vampire Slayer* and musical artists such as Taylor Swift, Beyoncé, and Olivia Rodrigo.

Feminist scholars often see the "girl power" promoted by mainstream media to be "almost exclusively about consumer power"; that is, mainstream media uses "girl power" to sell things, rather than actually challenging gendered hierarchies and power relations (Banet-Weiser, Gill, and Rottenberg 2020, 8). In other words, mainstream culture suggests that girls and women show their power through their purchasing decisions: buying items with feminist slogans, supporting female musicians by purchasing their albums, and so on. Because of "girl power's" inherent connection to consumerist products, it cannot ever truly challenge preexisting power structures or gender inequalities. Instead, it uses appeals to the least political or radical aspects of feminism to sell products that benefit large-scale corporations (Durham 1998). When girls and women buy into "girl power" media and products, they often think they're taking a stand for feminism. However, the larger systems of gender inequality typically remain unchallenged and unchanged.

And yet, despite being a marketing tactic, "girl power" can still offer empowerment and inspiration—sometimes even provoking protest and resistance. In her study of how women and girls respond to "girl power" culture, Zaslow (2009, 9) found that even though "girl power *is* a watered-down feminist position," it is "also a meaningful and widespread embodiment of some feminist positions that girls draw upon as they create their gender identities." Moreover, women of color and LGBTQIA+ individuals have created alternative media to challenge the stereotypes found in mainstream "girl power" representations, which typically depict white, heterosexual, middle-class women (Gonick et al. 2009).

One example of "girl power" media is the 2023 film *Barbie*, directed by Greta Gerwig and based on Mattel's toy line. Notably, Gerwig's film uses Barbie as a lens to make a feminist argument about the persistence of gender inequality. When Barbie departs from the matriarchal society of Barbieland to enter the Real World, she encounters the consequences of gender inequality and the patriarchy for the first time, drawing viewers' attention to the larger cultural and political structures that still exist in contemporary society. However, the ideals of "girl power" are still very much front and center throughout the film. The various types of Barbies living in Barbieland continue to emphasize the idea that feminism is rooted, at least in part, in the ability to individually choose your own preferred form of femininity. Moreover, the film's marketing campaigns encouraged fans to show their support by purchasing a wide array of Barbie-branded merchandise, including Xboxes, hoodies, and Barbie dolls. There was a Barbie Dreamhouse-themed Airbnb that fans could rent to get the true Barbie experience. And fans showed up to the theaters dressed in full Barbie-themed costumes. The hyperfeminity of Barbie as a consumerist product, then, became an expression of "feminist" girl power (Rosenblatt and Tolentino 2023). In this way, support for the film and any feminist messages it contains was couched in terms of consumption. To support the "girl power" messages of *Barbie*, fans were encouraged to both buy Barbie and become Barbie, thus continuing the "girl power" trend of turning feminist activism into acts of personal expression.

Ultimately, while "girl power" may serve as an enjoyable motivational tool for inspiring girls and women, it has its limitations in terms of its ability to bring about gender equality and societal change. Additionally, its tendency to push consumerism as a form of feminist expression means that it is firmly rooted in capitalistic systems that view women and girls primarily as a demographic to be targeted and marketed to. That does not, however, mean that women and girls are unable to derive a sense of empowerment from "girl power" or utilize it as a starting point for engaging in feminist activism and effecting genuine societal change.

Courtlyn Pippert

See Also: Capitalism; Popular Feminism; Postfeminism

Further Reading

Banet-Weiser, Sarah, Rosalind Gill, and Catherine Rottenberg. 2020. "Postfeminism, Popular Feminism and Neoliberal Feminism? Sarah Banet-Weiser, Rosalind Gill and Catherine Rottenberg in Conversation." *Feminist Theory* 21, no. 1: 3–24.

Barksdale, Sheryl Sandberg, and Latricia Barksdale. 2023. "Girls Make Great Leaders. So Why Do We Often Tell Them Not to Lead?" *USA Today*, July 27, 2023. https://www.usatoday.com/story/opinion/voices/2023/07/27/sheryl-sandberg-lean-in-girls-women-leadership-inequality/70468645007/.

Currie, Dawn, Deirdre M. Kelly, and Shauna Pomerantz. 2009. *"Girl Power": Girls Reinventing Girlhood.* New York: Peter Lang.

Durham, Meenakshi Gigi. 1998. "Dilemmas of Desire: Representations of Adolescent Sexuality in Two Teen Magazines." *Youth and Society* 29, no. 3: 369–89.

Friedman, Vanessa. 2024. "What Girl Power Looks Like Now." *The New York Times*, February 16, 2024. https://www.nytimes.com/2024/02/16/style/new-york-fashion-week-trends.html.

Gonick, Marnina, Emma Renold, Jessica Ringrose, and Lisa Weems. 2009. "Rethinking Agency and Resistance: What Comes After Girl Power?" *Girlhood Studies* 2, no. 2: 1–9.

Rosenblatt, Kalhan, and Daysia Tolentino. 2023. "The 'Barbie' Movie Ushers Bimbo Feminism and Hyperfemininity into the Mainstream." *NBC News*, July 20, 2023. https://www.nbcnews.com/pop-culture/barbie-movie-ushers-bimbo-feminism-hyperfemininity-mainstream-rcna94892.

Rubin, Rebecca. 2023. "Inside 'Barbie's' Pink Publicity Machine: How Warner Bros. Pulled Off the Marketing Campaign of the Year." *Variety* (blog), July 23, 2023. https://variety.com/2023/film/box-office/barbie-marketing-campaign-explainedwarner-bros-1235677922/.

Woodcock, Adara. 2022. "What Does 'Girl Power' Really Mean?" *Smithsonian Magazine*, October 11, 2022. http://www.smithsonianmag.com/blogs/national-museum-american-history/2022/10/11/girl-power/.

Zaslow, Emilie. 2009. *Feminism, Inc.: Coming of Age in Girl Power Media Culture.* New York: Palgrave Macmillan US.

GRISWOLD V. CONNECTICUT (1965)

Griswold v. Connecticut was a landmark case in 1965, which finally struck down crucial elements of the Comstock Act, which Congress passed in 1873 and has haunted women ever since. The Comstock Act—among many other problematic things—made birth control illegal. The Comstock Act defined birth control as obscene and illicit, making it a federal offense to dispense birth control through the mail or across state lines. Soon after the federal law was passed, several states passed even more restrictive laws to restrict birth control on the state level.

This was the state of things for almost 100 years. Then, in 1965, birth control came before the Supreme Court. Estelle Griswold and C. Lee Buxton, a gynecologist, opened a birth control clinic in New Haven, Connecticut. They were subsequently arrested, and their convictions were affirmed by higher courts. But Buxton and Griswold were prepared. All along they had planned to use their case to challenge the constitutionality of the Comstock Act.

The *Griswold* decision set up a framework that would be essential to understanding the relationship between sex, gender, and the law for decades to come.

The Court decided that the right to privacy, which could be extrapolated from the First, Third, Fourth, and Ninth Amendments, is sacrosanct in marital relationships. This is an important element to understand about the women's and LGBTQ movements—the right to privacy is at the heart of much of their progress, but it is technically not guaranteed in the Constitution. And yet, we believe we have it. That is because for over 100 years the judicial branch has interpreted the law and Constitution to protect this right, which they have argued is implicit in the law, even though it is not directly stated. This slippage between what is stated and what is extracted because of interpretation is important in understanding the full narrative of the fight for gender equality. And this protection, this right to make decisions privately between a married couple and their doctor, protects the intimate decision of whether to take birth control.

In any Supreme Court case, the decision is defined by the majority opinion and the dissenters. The majority opinion, or the "winning" opinion, is the side that has the most justices that agree with that argument. They write an "opinion," which becomes the guiding principle by which we interpret the Constitution. But, the dissenters, or the justices who disagree with the decision, also write an "opinion." They detail why they disagree with the decision and what they think the prevailing argument should be. This is done not just for posterity's sake, but in some cases, history will eventually come to favor the dissenter's opinion and it may become the more heavily cited one, as society and contexts change. The justices who "dissented" in *Griswold* acknowledged that the Comstock Act is "uncommonly silly" but not unconstitutional. This may seem odd, but it speaks to the unique role of the Court. The Supreme Court's job is not to decide whether a law is "good" or "bad." And they don't decide if somebody is "guilty" or "innocent." If a case comes before the Supreme Court a person is almost always "guilty." But the question is, is the law that person broke unconstitutional? And that question just means the justices have to decide does the law in question match up with the Constitution? Simply put, does the law break the law of the Constitution? Guided by this logic, dissenters in *Griswold* acknowledged that the Comstock Act was a ridiculous law but noted that it didn't contradict the Constitution. As such, they argued they were just doing their jobs.

However, the majority of the justices decided that the best interpretation of the Constitution granted a right to privacy, and that right to privacy included the decisions married couples (in consultation with their doctors) made about their sex lives and families—and thus birth control.

The *Griswold* case set into motion what would become the next sixty years of women's and LGBTQ+ rights. The right to privacy is at the heart of much of the progress made by the queer community in the past half century, and the progress made in women's reproductive health, though that has been stymied since 2022.

On the one hand, one cannot understand social movements in the twentieth and twenty-first centuries without understanding protest activism and social media. For example, Black Lives Matter (BLM) has engaged in demonstrations that one might call "extra-rhetorical," which just means outside of the normal modes of discourse. BLM has protested, and this has ranged from silent sit-ins to marches in the street. And, they have made great use of social media and online activism. Similarly, one of the most galvanizing moments in the women's movement was the #MeToo movement of the twenty-first century. But on the other, the women's movement and the LGBTQ movement have used some very institutional means to address their concerns. Both movements have made great use of the legal system and the Courts—using the establishment's own tools against them. And much of this work has been built upon the legacy of *Griswold.* So, this understanding of the importance of the right to privacy is quintessential to understanding how the movement for equality had progressed since the 1960s. It undergirds much of the work activists and lawyers have laid for future leaders.

M. Elizabeth Thorpe

See Also: Choice; *Lawrence v. Texas* (2003); *Roe v. Wade* (1973)

Further Reading

Griswold v. Connecticut. 381 U.S. 479 (1965).

GUERRILLA GIRLS

Formed in 1985 by a group of women in New York City, the Guerrilla Girls are an anonymous collective of art activists who use media such as posters to express their "anger and frustration at the art world's exclusionary practices" (Leng 2020, 111). Their inciting incident was a 1984 exhibition at the Museum of Modern Art in New York. Out of the 169 artists featured in this exhibition's "International Survey of Painting and Sculpture," only thirteen were women. This gross inequality prompted a women's protest outside the museum. However, the protest made little impression on passersby, and irritated by not being taken seriously, the Guerrilla Girls were born (The Guerrilla Girls 1995). As their renown grew beyond the art world, they began tackling sexism in Hollywood and the military and addressing issues such as reproductive rights and racial inequality (Leng 2020; Raizada 2007). The Guerrilla Girls produced about eighty posters between 1985 and 2000. They also produce stickers, billboards, bus ads, magazine spreads, newsletters, and exhibits. In addition, they frequently appear in public at museums, colleges, and protests. They have also released three volumes examining Western art history and stereotypes about women (Leng 2020).

The name Guerrilla Girls refers to the Spanish term referring to "a group of radical, unconventional fighters" (Uribe 2022). The group said in an interview, "We wanted to play with the fear of guerrilla warfare, to make people afraid of who we might be and where we would strike next" (The Guerrilla Girls 1995). Additionally, like Riot Grrrl, the Guerrilla Girls wanted to reclaim the word "girl" so that it could not be used against them (The Guerrilla Girls 1995).

The Guerrilla Girls remain anonymous. This is achieved in two main ways: gorilla masks and code names (Martorana 2017). The gorilla mask itself is said to come from a founding member misspelling guerrilla as "gorilla." This "enlightened mistake" gave the group their "mask-ulinity" (The Guerrilla Girls 1995). The group wears these masks during public speaking engagements and appearances. The tactic focuses attention on the issues central to their activism, not the members' looks or personalities (Martorana 2017). Originally, the Guerrilla Girls wore masks to protect their lives and their work, but the practice has evolved into a way for the group to represent all women, not just their members (Raizada 2007). The second factor of their anonymity is the code names assigned to each member. Each member (except for one who prefers to be called GG1) is assigned the codename of a deceased woman artist. Members include "Frida Kahlo," "Alma Thomas," "Rosalba Carriera," and more (The Guerrilla Girls 1995). This practice is the group's attempt to "avenge the omission of women artists from art history textbooks and museum exhibitions by [. . .] reintroducing women artists (past and present) into the public view and exposing the legacy of art world discrimination" (Demo 2000, 144).

One scholar states that the hallmark of Guerrilla Girl activism is "the humorous and sarcastic tone" that permeates throughout their posters and other works (Martorana 2017, 12). When asked to describe their work, one Guerrilla Girl said that they usually "start with an outrageous statement that introduces a subject and makes you laugh. Then we back it up with some information that makes you think about things a little differently" (Raizada 2007, 52).

THE ADVANTAGES OF BEING A WOMAN ARTIST:

Working without the pressure of success
Not having to be in shows with men
Having an escape from the art world in your 4 free-lance jobs
Knowing your career might pick up after you're eighty
Being reassured that whatever kind of art you make it will be labeled feminine
Not being stuck in a tenured teaching position
Seeing your ideas live on in the work of others
Having the opportunity to choose between career and motherhood
Not having to choke on those big cigars or paint in Italian suits
Having more time to work when your mate dumps you for someone younger
Being included in revised versions of art history
Not having to undergo the embarrassment of being called a genius
Getting your picture in the art magazines wearing a gorilla suit

A PUBLIC SERVICE MESSAGE FROM **GUERRILLA GIRLS** CONSCIENCE OF THE ART WORLD

"Advantages of Being a Woman Artist" poster, 1988. The Guerrilla Girls use humor and sarcasm in their artwork to grab people's attention, express their frustration at exclusionary practices in the art world, and affect change (Copyright © Guerrilla Girls, courtesy guerrillagirls.com).

For example, their 1988 poster "The Advantages of Being a Woman Artist" satirically lists "advantages," such as "Not having to be in shows with men," because women artists are often excluded from shows featuring men's work, and "Being reassured that whatever kind of art you make it will be labeled feminine." This poster was one of Guerrilla Girl's first works. While developing this poster, the group discovered that humor creates "an IV" into viewers' brains and makes it easier to create change (Raizada 2007, 49).

Their work illustrates how "feminists can subvert a static definition of femininity through mimicry" and that Guerrilla Girls place "femininity within the lens of a fun-house mirror" (Demo 2000, 141). This fun-house mirror approach leads the group to make both clever and damning critiques of the treatment of women in the art world and beyond.

Joanna Thornburg

See Also: Black Arts Movement; Intersectionality; Punk Feminism and the Riot Grrrl Manifesto; Tokenism

Further Reading

Demo, Anne Teresa. 2000. "The Guerrilla Girls' Comic Politics of Subversion." *Women's Studies in Communication* 23, no. 2: 133–56. https://doi.org/10.1080/07491409.2000.10162566.

Leng, Kirsten. 2020. "Art, Humor, and Activism: The Sardonic, Sustaining Feminism of the Guerrilla Girls, 1985–2000." *Journal of Women's History* 32, no. 4: 110–34. https://doi.org/10.1353/jowh.2020.0042.

Martorana, Christine. 2017. "Enacting Feminist Agency: Responsible Anonymity Visual Parodox, and the Guerrilla Girls." *Women & Language* 39, no. 2: 7–30. https://search-ebscohost-com.ezproxy.hope.edu/login.aspx?direct=true&db=hus&AN=124204810&site=ehost-live.

The Guerrilla Girls. 1995. "Confessions of the Guerrilla Girls." *Guerrilla Girls*. Accessed April 25, 2024. https://www.guerrillagirls.com/confessions_interview.

Uribe, Serena. 2022. "Guerrillas in Gorilla: The Feminist Art Activists." *Medium*, March 14, 2022. https://themedium.ca/guerillas-in-gorilla-the-feminist-art-activists/.

Raizada, Kristen. 2007. "An Interview with the Guerrilla Girls, Dyke Action Machine (DAM!), and the Toxic Titties." *NWSA Journal* 19, no. 1 (Spring): 39–58. https://doi.org/10.2979/NWS.2007.19.1.39.

H

HAALAND, DEB

Deb Haaland's (1960–) political career has cemented her place in US history. In 2021, Deb Haaland became the first Indigenous person to serve in the US Presidential Cabinet when the Senate confirmed her as Secretary of the Interior. In this role, Haaland became "the second-highest-ranking person of Native American ancestry in the history of American government" (Kamisar 2025). In 2018, Haaland also "made history," along with Sharice Davids, in becoming the first Indigenous women members of the House of Representatives (Reilly 2018). During the process of writing this entry, Haaland announced she would be running for governor of New Mexico (Kamisar 2025).

Haaland's and Davids's election victories prompted the question why it took so long for Indigenous women representatives to become elected. Commentators discussed contemporary and historical barriers to political participation faced by Indigenous people (Reilly 2018). For example, Indigenous people face disproportionate challenges when attempting to vote, including long travel times to voting locations and laws preventing them from using their Tribal Identification as proof of residency (Jones and Grange 2024).

Representation of and for Indigenous people is necessary but not sufficient. Scholars like Taylor N. Johnson (2021, 2) have even argued that working toward inclusion within US institutions can undermine political sovereignty of Indigenous communities: "the pursuit of decolonization and the pursuit of inclusion within a public sphere that centers the improvement and continuance of a settler state run counter to one another."

Fortunately, Haaland used her position to advocate for and ensure progress on an array of critical issues, including the conservation of public lands, strengthening Indigenous communities and expanding their decision-making authority, and she created a unit dedicated to addressing the ongoing tragedy of missing and murdered Indigenous women and children (Villagomez, Zeno, and Moffett 2024). Haaland also spotlighted the issue of Indigenous boarding school abuses, advocating for an official apology to Indigenous people for the deaths that occurred at boarding schools (Denetclaw 2025).

Deb Haaland's mark on history rests not only in being the first Indigenous person to serve in the Presidential Cabinet but also in her landmark efforts to bring Indigenous and environmental policy matters to the forefront.

Joshua H. Miller

See Also: Chisholm, Shirley; Missing and Murdered Indigenous Women and Girls; National Indigenous Women's Resource Center; Rankin, Jeannette

Further Reading

Denetclaw, Pauly. 2025. "Deb Haaland's Enduring Legacy Lives on at Interior Department." *ICT News*, January 15, 2025. https://ictnews.org/news/deb-haalands-enduring-legacy-lives-at-interior-department.

Johnson, Taylor N. 2021. "Indigenous Publicity in American Public Lands Controversies: Environmental Participation in the Fight for Bears Ears National Monument." *Frontiers in Communication* 6: 1–16. https://doi.org/10.3389/fcomm.2021.673115

Jones, Chelsea, and Coryn Grange. 2024. "Study Finds Extensive Barriers Restrict Native Americans from Voting." *Brennan Center*, November 19, 2024. https://www.brennancenter.org/our-work/analysis-opinion/study-finds-extensive-barriers-restrict-native-americans-voting. Accessed March 4, 2025.

Kamisar, Ben. 2025. "Former Interior Secretary Deb Haaland Launches New Mexico governor campaign." *NBC News*, February 11, 2025. https://www.nbcnews.com/politics/elections/former-interior-secretary-deb-haaland-launches-new-mexico-governor-cam-rcna191581.

Reilly, Katie. 2018. "Democrats in Kansas, New Mexico Become First Native American Women Elected to Congress." *Time*, November 6, 2018. https://time.com/5446593/sharice-davids-deb-haaland-first-native-american-woman-congress/.

Villagomez, Angelo, Sam Zeno, and Joel Moffett. 2024. "Secretary Deb Halland Has Hade Historic Progress at the Department of the Interior." *Center for American Progress*, June 3, 2024, https://www.americanprogress.org/article/secretary-deb-haaland-has-made-historic-progress-at-the-department-of-the-interior/. Accessed March 4, 2025.

HASHTAG ACTIVISM

Hashtag activism is the use of social media to promote cultural and political movements. More specifically, hashtag activism refers to the phenomenon wherein individuals and organizations mobilize support, raise awareness, and foster community around various issues on platforms like Twitter/X, Instagram, Facebook, and TikTok. Originating on Twitter, hashtags function to link posts together through keywords marked with a pound sign, thus allowing users to follow and contribute to shared conversations on social media. Hashtags can be used for cause-based movements (e.g., #MeToo) and for all sorts of other possibilities, such as expanding meaning by using hashtags within photo captions (e.g., #Blessed) (Bailey, Jackson, and Foucault Welles 2020).

The term "hashtag activism" became popular during movements such as #BlackLivesMatter, #MeToo, and #LoveWins. For example, the #BlackLivesMatter movement, which began in response to George Zimmerman's acquittal in the murder of Trayvon Martin in 2013, quickly became a recognizable global call for justice against systemic racism and police brutality (Bonilla and Rosa 2015). Similarly, although MeToo was founded by Tarana Burke to highlight the prevalence of sexual harassment and assault, the #MeToo movement did not gain national prominence until 2017 when it was amplified on social media in connection to Harvey Weinstein. As a result, this movement has been credited with shifting and even popularizing the cultural conversation around consent and accountability (Stubbs-Richardson et al. 2023).

In *#HashtagActivism: Networks of Race and Gender Justice*, authors Angela Bailey, Sarah Jackson, and Brooke Foucault Welles describe the ways hashtags can serve as tools for activism and can facilitate communities that challenge oppressive power structures and social norms. These digital spaces can enable nuanced discussions around issues of race, gender, and justice, helping activists build solidarity across diverse identities (2020). Toward that end, one significant advantage of hashtag activism is its ability to democratize participation in social movements. Traditional forms of activism often require substantial resources, such as funding or physical presence at protests. In contrast, hashtag activism allows individuals to engage from the convenience of their personal devices, breaking down barriers to participation (Atuk and Cole 2024). This accessibility has led to increased visibility for marginalized voices, particularly among younger generations adept at navigating digital platforms.

At the same time, hashtag activism has drawn both social and academic criticism. Most commonly, people argue it can foster "slacktivism," where individuals engage in minimal actions or virtue signaling—such as liking or sharing posts—without committing to deeper involvement (Zohouri, Darvishi, and Sarfi 2020). In this way, critics argue hashtag activism can create an illusion of engagement with feminist and other social causes without producing meaningful change. Additionally, the rapid nature of social media can lead to hashtag or "favoriting fatigue," where the constant onslaught of trending topics can desensitize audiences, diminishing the impact of the important messages to which they are connected (Carr 2012). The capitalistic and algorithmic nature of social media further complicates this. Corporations often co-opt social justice hashtags for marketing, diluting the original message and commodifying social movements (Bennett and Segerberg 2012). This extends the significance of critical questions about authenticity when it comes to engaging in activism on digital platforms, both in terms of what is shared and what is consumed.

Despite its ongoing challenges, hashtag activism remains a powerful tool for social change, capable of fostering community, building solidarity, and amplifying marginalized voices. The immediacy and reach of social media can mobilize people quickly and can connect them to more tangible work, as seen in movements like the Women's March (Einwohner and Rochford 2019). While hashtag activism is vital in the digital age and can extend the reach of important feminist movements and causes, it is always most effective when it leads to real-world action.

Dakota J. Sandras

See Also: #BlackLivesMatter; Cyberfeminism; #MeToo; #SayHerName

Further Reading

Atuk, Sumru, and Alyson Cole. 2024. "Bodies on the Line vs. Bodies Online: A Feminist Phenomenology of Digitally Mediated Political Action." *Women's Studies in Communication* 47, no. 1: 63–86. https://doi.org/10.1080/07491409.2023.2297288.

Bailey, Angela, Sarah Jackson, and Brooke Foucault Welles. 2020. *#HashtagActivism: Networks of Race and Gender Justice*. Cambridge: MIT Press.

Bennett, W. Lance, and Alexandra Segerberg. 2012. "The Logic of Connective Action: Digital Media and the Personalization of Contentious Politics." *Information, Communication & Society* 15, no. 5: 739–68. https://doi.org/10.1080/1369118X.2012.670661.

Bonilla, Yarimar, and Jonathan Rosa. 2015. "#Ferguson: Digital Protest, Hashtag Ethnography, and the Racial Politics of Social Media in the United States." *American Ethnologist* 42, no. 1: 4–17. https://doi.org/10.1111/amet.12112.

Carr, David. 2012. "Hashtag Activism, and Its Limits." *The New York Times*, March 25, 2012. https://www.nytimes.com/2012/03/26/business/media/hashtag-activism-and-its-limits.html.

Einwohner, Rachel L., and E. Burke Rochford. 2019. "After the March: Using Instagram to Perform and Sustain the Women's March." *Sociological Forum* 34, no. 1: 1090–111. https://doi.org/10.1111/socf.12542.

Stubbs-Richardson, Megan, Shelby Gilbreath, MacKenzie Paul, and Audrey Reid. 2023. "It's a Global #MeToo: A Cross-National Comparison of Social Change Associated with the Movement." *Feminist Media Studies* 24, no. 6: 1330–49. https://doi.org/10.1080/14680777.2023.2231654.

Zohouri, Mostafa, Morteza Darvishi, and Majid Sarfi. 2020. "Slacktivism: A Critical Evaluation." *Journal of Cyberspace Studies* 4, no. 2: 173–88. https://doi.org/10.22059/JCSS.2020.93911.

HEGEMONIC MASCULINITY

Hegemonic masculinity is a set of practices that lead to the societal structuring of men as dominant and women as subordinate to men. In other words, it is the set of practices men are meant to engage in to appear "masculine" and therefore dominant over those who are nonmale and/or considered "feminine." Often associated with white, heterosexual men, Sue Curry Jansen and Don Sabo describe the values of hegemonic masculinity as "aggression, competition, dominance, territoriality, [and] instrumental violence" (1994, 10). In some ways, this appears to be a very narrow description of masculinity. Can men not also be passive, noncompetitive, gentle, sharing, and peaceful? Or perhaps some combination of the two lists? While men embody a wide variety of character traits, hegemonic masculinity endorses a *particular kind* of masculinity as dominant and uses this dominance to legitimize the whole system of patriarchy (Connell 1995). Victoria Pruin DeFrancisco and Catherine Helen Palczewski demonstrate that within patriarchy, men who do not engage in these overtly hegemonic practices are encouraged "to remain silent to protect their own masculinity" and status "when others commit such practices" (2007, 147). This means that not all men will exert the values of hegemonic masculinity, though their actions (and silences) as well as media depictions often reinforce these ideals as correct and desirable.

Importantly, hegemonic masculinity is not stable because, as James W. Messerschmidt argues, it is "open to historical change" (2018, 29). Its instability means that the dominant masculine values can shift as time progresses. An example of this comes from Brent Malin (2005), who describes how the shift from a hypermasculinity in the 1980s into a more conflicted masculinity in the 1990s and 2000s can be seen through Bill Clinton's simultaneous performance of *hyper* and *hypo*masculinity while running for US president and during the scandal surrounding his affair with Monica Lewinsky. His so-called "*hyper*masculinity" aligns with a depiction of an insensitive, nonemotional, philandering lady's man, while "*hypo*masculinity" is used to describe Clinton as hypersensitive and overly emotional, especially when describing his experience with anxiety—two forms of masculinity that should conflict with each other but are ascribed to Clinton simultaneously by a variety of parties. Even though Clinton was engaging in a different form of masculinity by being more emotional, it still served to reinforce a "correct" masculinity, one that privileges a white, heterosexual male expression, as opposed to masculinities more aligned with nonwhite, queer men (Schippers 2007). This reinforcing of a so-called correct masculinity is the goal of hegemonic masculinity, as it privileges one performance of masculinity over others.

While there has been a rise in so-called "alpha males" providing instructions on how to be "truly masculine" (Russell 2021), we mostly learn what is "masculine" and what is "feminine" through interactions with our family, our friends, the schools we attend, and the media we consume. As Joshua Atkinson and Bernadette Calafell (2009) illustrate, film narratives can educate audiences about hegemonic masculinity, entrenched femininity, and other gender expressions. This is true for media aimed at adults as well as media more explicitly intended for children. Much has been written about how Walt Disney Animation Studio has depicted masculinity and femininity in their films and how these depictions shift as the cultural opinion on what is "properly" masculine changes (Davis 2015). For example, Susan Jeffords (1995) demonstrates how in *Beauty and the Beast* (1991), the Beast is presented as a "new '90s man," one who, like Bill Clinton, is a conflicted masculine presence—his appearance and initial demeanor present the older form of hegemonic masculinity (territorial, violent, deep voiced, a towering physical presence, etc.) but as the film progresses he is revealed as also sensitive and emotional—not only angry, which is the main emotion hegemonic masculinity permits and encourages (Connell 1995). By combining traits, the Beast embodies the newer form of hegemonic masculinity popular in the 1990s.

Unfortunately, even films that seem to explicitly set out to critique and challenge hegemonic masculinity can often end up reinforcing it. An example is *Ralph Breaks the Internet* (2018), which attempts to tackle "toxic masculinity" in a way that appeals to children (Dosser 2022). Its protagonist, Wreck-It Ralph, acts possessive of the woman in his life, dismisses any ideas that come from women, and frequently engages in physical violence, but in the end he ultimately lets his female best friend do what she wants. While the film attempts to have Ralph grow from the experience, it depicts all the characters completely forgiving him for his actions and acting like this behavior was an aberration to his usually "nontoxic" ways, despite Ralph never apologizing or accepting the blame for his actions. In this way, the film, while having good meaning in its demonstration of ways to overcome "toxic" behaviors, reinforces the idea that men can and should be excused for any misogynistic, racist, homophobic actions they may show. This is an example of what Kate Manne refers to as "himpathy," or the "the excessive sympathy sometimes shown toward male perpetrators of sexual violence," especially extended to "white, nondisabled, and otherwise privileged 'golden boys'" (2018, 197). As described by Max Dosser, "while Ralph does not perpetuate sexual violence, the film does suggest that Ralph's wrongs should be forgiven largely due to the simple fact that he has been sweet, caring, and likable in the past" (2022, 341). *Ralph Breaks the Internet* is an example of the more insidious way that hegemonic masculinity reestablishes itself, as it is not always about being misogynistic, violent, or territorial. It can often be as simple as receiving unjust rewards, thanks, and forgiveness due to the dominant position men hold over women and femininity in society (see Hoskin 2019).

Hegemonic masculinity is rooted in maintaining not only the dominance of men but also the subordination of women. While hegemonic masculinity shifts over time, it is clear with the rise and fall and reemergence of "alpha male" masculinity in the 1980s and again in the 2020s that even as the specific values associated with hegemonic masculinity may change, its goal remains the same. These values are reproduced in our media, school lessons, sermons, and other discourses and can greatly impact how women, nonbinary people, and nonwhite, nonheterosexual men are treated in society.

Max Dosser

See Also: Anger; Gender; Misogyny; Patriarchy

Further Reading

Atkinson, Joshua, and Bernadette Calafell. 2009. "Darth Vader Made Me Do It! Anakin Skywalker's Avoidance of Responsibility and the Gray Areas of Hegemonic Masculinity in the *Star Wars* Universe." *Communication, Culture & Critique* 2, no. 1: 1–20. https://doi.org/10.1111/j.1753-9137.2008.01026.x.

Connell, R. W. *Masculinities*. Berkeley: University of California Press, 1995.

Davis, Amy M. 2015. *Handsome Heroes and Vile Villains: Men in Disney's Feature Animation*. Bloomington: Indiana University Press.

DeFrancisco, Victoria Pruin, and Catherine Helen Palczewski. 2007. *Communication Gender Diversity: A Critical Approach*. Thousand Oaks: Sage.

Dosser, Max. 2022. "I'm Gonna Wreck It, Again: The False Dichotomy of 'Healthy' and 'Toxic' Masculinity in *Ralph Breaks the Internet*." *Critical Studies in Media Communication* 39, no. 4: 333–46. https://doi.org/10.1080/15295036.2022.2067347.

Hoskin, Rhea Ashley. 2019. "Femmephobia: The Role of Anti-Femininity and Gender Policing in LGBTQ+ People's Experiences of Discrimination." *Sex Roles* 81: 686–703. https://doi.org/10.1007/s11199-019-01021-3.

Jansen, Sue Curry, and Don Sabo. 1994. "The Sport/War Metaphor: Hegemonic Masculinity, the Persian Gulf War, and the New World Order." *Sociology of Sport Journal* 11, no. 1: 1–17. https://doi.org/10.1123/ssj.11.1.1.

Jeffords, Susan. 1995. "The Curse of Masculinity in Disney's *Beauty and the Beast*." In *From Mouse to Mermaid: The Politics of Film, Gender, and Culture*, edited by Elizabeth Bell, Lynda Haas, and Laura Sells, 161–72. Bloomington: Indiana University Press.

Malin, Brenton J. 2005. *American Masculinity Under Clinton: Popular Media and the Nineties "Crises of Masculinity."* New York: Peter Lang.

Manne, Kate. 2018. *Down Girl: The Logic of Misogyny*. New York: Oxford University Press.

Messerschmidt, James W. 2018. *Hegemonic Masculinity: Formulation, Reformulation, and Amplification*. Lanham: Rowman & Littlefield.

Russell, Eric Louis. 2021. *Alpha Masculinity: Hegemony in Language and Discourse*. London: Palgrave Macmillan.
Schippers, Mimi. 2007. "Recovering the Feminine Other: Masculinity, Femininity, and Gender Hegemony." *Theory and Society* 36: 85–102. https://doi.org/10.1007/s11186-007-9022-4.

HILL, ANITA

Anita Hill (1956–) is a US lawyer, professor, author, and advocate. A lifelong legal scholar and civil rights advocate, Hill has effectively changed the social and political landscape, bringing awareness to social issues like sexual harassment in the workplace and influencing legislation to protect women from violence.

Early Life and Career

Born on July 20, 1956, Anita Hill was raised by her parents in Lone Tree, Oklahoma, on a family farm, alongside her twelve siblings (Hill 1998; Tikkanen 2024). She excelled at school, describing herself as "very bookish" and always looking for the next academic challenge (Hill 1998, 45). Often finishing her work early, she would spend spare time reading at the library and completing extra work that was assigned to students at higher grade levels. Hill graduated from high school as valedictorian before attending Oklahoma State University, where she majored in psychology (Hill 1998). Ultimately, Hill earned her Juris Doctor from Yale Law School, was admitted to the District of Columbia Bar, and began practicing law (Hill 1998; Tikkanen 2024).

Hill's early career would set the stage for her becoming a public figure. In 1980, Hill joined the Washington, D.C. law firm, Wald, Harkrader and Ross, but, while she did not experience direct discrimination at the firm, it quickly became clear that she needed to explore other options (Hill 1998). Thus, in 1981, she left the firm to work at the US Department of Education's Office for Civil Rights as a legal adviser to Clarence Thomas, citing a perceived shared commitment to civil rights as a deciding factor to join his team (Hill 1998; Tikkanen 2024). Thomas accepted a new position as chair of the Equal Employment Opportunity Commission in 1982, and Hill followed him as his assistant until she left in July of 1983 (Hill 1998; Tikkanen 2024). As would later become clear, Clarence Thomas had been sexually harassing Anita Hill during the time they worked together, a pattern of behavior that catalyzed her decision to leave D.C. and begin her career as a professor at Oral Roberts University (Hill 1998; Tikkanen 2024). She would later teach at the University of Oklahoma and Brandeis University (Hill 1998; Tikkanen 2024). Unfortunately, while Hill had physically and professionally distanced herself from Thomas, she never escaped the fallout of the harassment she experienced while working for him.

Clarence Thomas Nomination and Confirmation Hearings

In July of 1991, George H. W. Bush nominated Clarence Thomas to the Supreme Court, a nomination that would compel Anita Hill's testimony to the US Senate Judiciary Committee. Thomas, a judge for the US Court of Appeals in Washington, D.C., was already a controversial selection, particularly given his Conservative politics regarding issues like abortion and racial equality (Congressional Black Caucus Foundation 1991; Tribe 1991). Hill writes that the FBI contacted her in July regarding her experiences working with Thomas, and that reporters from the *New York Times* and *Washington Post* had reached out to her for comment, but she was reluctant to disclose any of the harassment she had experienced (Hill 1998). However, during Thomas's confirmation hearings in the fall of 1991, she broke her silence and agreed to testify before the Senate Judiciary Committee, the body of the US Congress responsible for confirming justices to the US Supreme Court (Hill 1998; Tikkanen 2024).

The confirmation hearings began on September 10, 1991. The initial hearings unfolded with the committee questioning Thomas about his judicial record and positions on issues of popular concern (Totenberg 2018). Following the initial hearings, the FBI continued investigating the allegations against Thomas and the Judiciary Committee met for a preliminary vote on the nomination. However, Hill's allegations were absent from the public view. News of Hill's allegations did not reach the public until October 6, 1991, when Nina Totenberg published a story detailing Hill's allegations (Totenberg 2018). Hill held a press conference the following day agreeing to testify, prompting a reopening of the hearings to confirm Clarence Thomas (Totenberg 2018).

On October 11, 1991, the Senate Judiciary Committee reopened the confirmation hearings for Clarence Thomas, as both Thomas and Hill testified to the Senate Judiciary Committee to address the allegations against Thomas ("Nomination of Judge Clarence Thomas to Be Associate Justice of the Supreme Court of the United States" 1991). Clarence Thomas testified first, characterizing the allegations against him as a "high-tech lynching," asserting that Hill's claims were politically motivated and untrue (Hill 1998; "Nomination of Judge Clarence Thomas to Be Associate Justice of the Supreme Court of the United States" 1991). Later that day, Hill testified to the committee, detailing the sexual harassment she suffered while working for Clarence Thomas (Hill 1998; Tikkanen 2024; Totenberg 2018). Hill testified that Thomas routinely asked her to go on dates (while he was married), "graphically described pornographic films" to her during the workday, and made other inappropriate sexual comments in the workplace ("Nomination of Judge Clarence Thomas to Be Associate Justice of the Supreme Court of the United States" 1991; Tikkanen 2024). Members of the committee questioned her about the abuse she suffered; however, they were often critical of her testimony and questioned her motives.

Detailing sexual harassment she suffered while working for Clarence Thomas, Anita Hill testifies to the Senate Judiciary Committee during Thomas's Supreme Court confirmation hearing, October 11, 1991 (Library of Congress).

Although Anita Hill is widely known to be one of the most credible witnesses in a high-profile sexual harassment case, Clarence Thomas was confirmed to the Supreme Court. Feminist scholars note that women (and Black women, in particular) are often disbelieved or blamed for their own victimization (Collins and Bilge 2020; Gilmore 2017). Hill's identity as a young, Black woman intersected with her lack of political power during the confirmation hearings, rendering her unintelligible to the predominately white and male members of the Judiciary Committee. In fact, some members of the Black community challenged Hill's testimony, accusing her of being a race traitor or of betraying her race by coming forward (Okeowo 2016). Despite these obstacles and accusations, her testimony in these hearings and her work following them have brought about meaningful social and political change.

Moving beyond Clarence Thomas

Following Thomas's confirmation, Anita Hill returned to her teaching position in Oklahoma. She received thousands of letters from people who had been following the hearings, some of them offering enthusiastic support and some of them containing death threats (Hill 1998; Okeowo 2016). Both types of letters signify the overwhelming public attention Anita Hill and Clarence Thomas received, and they also signify a shift in public perception of sexual harassment in the workplace.

Prior to this case, there were no strong legal protections in place to address sexual harassment in the workplace, and violence against women was often overlooked. But, after Thomas's confirmation, cultural shifts catalyzed political change. In 1991, Congress passed the Civil Rights Act of 1991, an amendment of sorts to the Civil Rights Act of 1964 that extended protections and rights for victims of workplace discrimination (US Congress 1991). Additionally, in 1994, Congress passed the Violence Against Women Act, which revolutionized the ways in which violent crimes against women were addressed (US Congress 1994). For instance, it authorized funding for investigations and gave victims the right to pursue civil trials against their abusers if state prosecutors dropped any charges (US Congress 1994). These acts are crucial pieces of legislation in advocating for women's rights.

Anita Hill continues to advocate for social change and the improved rights and living conditions of women. She empowers her students to identify and combat injustices they might encounter, and she inspires those outside of her classrooms by sharing her experiences in her books. While Hill first entered the public eye because of the abuse against her, Hill's legacy far surpasses her testimony against Clarence Thomas. Anita Hill continues to serve as a role model for speaking truth to power.

Amanda N. Brand

See Also: Civil Rights Act (1964); Gender Discrimination; Intersectionality; Violence Against Women Act (1994)

Further Reading

Collins, Patricia Hill, and Sirma Bilge. 2020. *Intersectionality*. Second edition. Cambridge; Medford, MA: Polity Press.

Congressional Black Caucus Foundation. 1991. "In Opposition to Clarence Thomas: Where We Must Stand and Why." *The Black Scholar* 22, no. 1–2: 126–37. https://doi.org/10.1080/00064246.1992.11413029.

Gilmore, Leigh. 2017. *Tainted Witness: Why We Doubt What Women Say About Their Lives*. New York: Columbia University Press.

Hill, Anita. 1998. *Speaking Truth to Power*. New York: Anchor Books.

"Nomination of Judge Clarence Thomas to Be Associate Justice of the Supreme Court of the United States." 1991. Washington, D.C. https://www.govinfo.gov/content/pkg/GPO-CHRG-THOMAS/pdf/GPO-CHRG-THOMAS-4.pdf.

Okeowo, Alexis. 2016. "Still Thinking About Anita Hill." *The New Yorker*, May 23, 2016. https://www.newyorker.com/culture/cultural-comment/still-thinking-about-anita-hill#:~:text=Hill%20faced%20the%20opposite%20sentiment,of%20a%20target%20for%20criticism.

Tikkanen, Amy. 2024. "Anita Hill." In *Encyclopedia Britannica*. https://www.britannica.com/biography/Anita-Hill.

Totenberg, Nina. 2018. "A Timeline of Clarence Thomas-Anita Hill Controversy as Kavanaugh to Face Accuser." *NPR.org*, September 23, 2018. https://www.npr.org/2018/09/23/650138049/a-timeline-of-clarence-thomas-anita-hill-controversy-as-kavanaugh-to-face-accuse.

Tribe, Lawrence H. 1991. "Clarence Thomas and 'Natural Law.'" *The New York Times*, July 15, 1991, sec. A.
US Congress. 1991. *Civil Rights Act of 1991*. https://www.congress.gov/bill/102nd-congress/senate-bill/1745.
US Congress. 1994. *Violence Against Women Act of 1994*. https://www.congress.gov/bill/103rd-congress/senate-bill/11.

HOOKS, BELL

bell hooks (1952–2021) was an American author, activist, and feminist best known for her writings on race, feminism, and class. hooks defined feminism as "a movement to end sexism, sexist exploitation, and oppression," and her definition has been widely adopted by feminists in the United States (hooks 2015, 1). This definition makes the aims of feminism clear: though misconceptions persist (e.g., the idea that feminists hate men), the movement is focused on combating sexist thought and action regardless of who perpetrates it or where it takes place. As hooks notes, "that clarity helps us remember that all of us, female and male, have been socialized from birth on to accept sexist thought and action" (hooks 2015, xii).

hooks is known for several key contributions to the feminist movement, including her book *Feminist Theory: From Margin to Center*; the phrase or idea of moving "from margin to center" is now used widely within activist groups and academia. In hooks's original use of the phrase, she is referring to the ways in which Black women's lived experiences, perspectives, and contributions exist on the margins of society, as well as within the margins of the feminist movement. *Feminist Theory: From Margin to Center* advocates for a feminist movement that centers, or prioritizes, the needs, experiences, and contributions of those existing in marginalized communities (e.g., Black women, disabled people, those living in poverty, etc.). hooks demonstrates how the feminist movement has historically privileged the needs and issues of white, educated, middle- and upper-class women at the expense of Black women specifically and those existing in the margins more generally.

hooks frequently discussed what she called the "politics of dominance," a way of articulating the interlocking systems of oppression (e.g., patriarchy, capitalism, racism, imperialism, etc.) and referring to the common ideological ground that these systems share (hooks 2023, 20). In clear contrast to the "politics of dominance," hooks described visionary feminism as "a wise and loving politic." Likewise, she emphasized mutuality and interdependency, writing, "Feminist politics aims to end domination to free us to be who we are—to live lives where we love justice, where we can live in peace. Feminism is for everybody" (hooks 2015, 118).

Feminism Is for Everybody: Passionate Politics, a feminist primer published by hooks in 2000, illustrates another important focus of her career: that the feminist movement and feminist theory should be accessible to everyone, regardless of their educational background and ability to understand academic prose. hooks explained that feminist theory "became and remains a privileged discourse available to those among us who are highly literate, well-educated, and usually materially privileged," but she advocated for feminist literature "written in a range of styles and formats," ultimately stating, "we need feminist studies that is community-based" (hooks 2015, 5, 22–3). Since there is no one path to feminism, there must be a diverse range of theory that speaks directly to people's lives. While some feminists have argued that the focus of the movement should be on activism, not on theory, hooks argued that theory itself can be liberating: "in its production lies the hope of our liberation, in its production lies the possibility of naming all our pain—of making all our hurt go away . . . we will have no difficulty building a mass-based feminist resistance struggle. There will be no gap between feminist theory and feminist practice" (hooks 1991, 12).

Other notable contributions by hooks include her books *Ain't I a Woman?: Black Women and Feminism* (1981), *Teaching to Transgress: Education as the Practice of Freedom* (1994), *Killing*

Rage: Ending Racism (1995), *Bone Black: Memories of Girlhood* (1996), *All About Love: New Visions* (2000), *The Will to Change: Men, Masculinity, and Love* (2004), and *Teaching Critical Thinking: Practical Wisdom* (2010). hooks published roughly forty books, including essays, poetry, and children's literature. She authored numerous scholarly articles, appeared in documentaries, and gave public addresses. hooks received her bachelors in English literature from Stanford University in 1973, her masters from the University of Wisconsin in 1976, and her PhD from the University of California, Santa Cruz, in 1983 (Britannica 2025). She taught at several academic institutions throughout her career. The name "bell hooks" is a pseudonym that hooks adopted during her career. It contains a reference to her maternal great-grandmother and is spelled all lowercase in an effort to focus attention on her work and ideas, rather than on herself as a person (hooks 2023, 94). Her birth name is fairly easy to discover for those who are curious, but in making her pseudonym, hooks asked people to call her "bell hooks" when talking about her work, theory, and career—and honoring her wishes is the right thing to do.

bell hooks was born in 1952 and she died in 2021 at her home in Kentucky. In a 1991 interview, when asked how she would describe herself, she responded,

> If I were really asked to define myself, I wouldn't start with race; I wouldn't start with gender; I wouldn't start with feminism. I would start with stripping down to what fundamentally informs my life, which is that I'm a seeker on the path. I think of feminism, and I think of anti-racist struggles as part of it. But where I stand spiritually is, steadfastly, on a path about love. (hooks 2023, 27)

Hannah Jones

See Also: Capitalism; Feminist Pedagogy; Intersectionality; Patriarchy; Reproductive Justice; Structural Oppression; Woman-Identified Woman Manifesto

Further Reading

Britannica. 2025. "bell hooks." Last updated February 8, 2025. Accessed February 12, 2025. https://www.britannica.com/biography/bell-hooks.

hooks, bell. 1984. *Feminist Theory: From Margin to Center*. Cambridge, MA: South End Press.

hooks, bell. 1991. "Theory as Liberatory Practice." *Yale Journal of Law and Feminism* 4, no. 1: 1–12.

hooks, bell. 2010. *Teaching Critical Thinking: Practical Wisdom*. New York: Routledge.

hooks, bell. 2000/2015. *Feminism Is for Everybody: Passionate Politics*. New York: Routledge.

hooks, bell. 2023. *bell hooks: The Last Interview and Other Conversations*. Brooklyn: Melville House.

HUERTA, DOLORES

"¡Sí, se puede!" Yes, we can! Whenever someone chants these words, Dolores Huerta's (1930–) legacy as a critical figure in labor rights, immigrant rights, and women's rights activism is further solidified. Credited with creating this familiar chant, Huerta was the cofounder of the National Farm Workers association, which later became the United Farm Workers of America (UFW) (Godoy 2017). She helped organize and lead many demonstrations, strikes, and boycotts for better living conditions and wages for farm workers, including the 1965 grape workers' strike. Later, in 1973, Huerta launched another boycott of grapes, which contributed to the successful passage of the California Agricultural Labor Relations Act of 1975. The legislation established collective bargaining rights for farm workers and was the first of its kind (Quinnell 2019). Her efforts secured UFW's first negotiation of a union contract for farm workers. A community activist for sixty years, she earned several awards for her labor, including the Presidential Medal of Freedom in 2012.

Her success came with significant challenges. As a female activist of color, Huerta navigated multiple forms of bias and discrimination both from those outside the movement and those within it. She often had to work to highlight her accomplishments and negotiate her place in the movement (Sowards 2012). In addition, many of her accomplishments remain relatively unknown to many members of the public; to correct this, several scholars and filmmakers have worked to spotlight her and her advocacy. For example, the 2017 documentary, *Dolores*, both demonstrated and extended Huerta's legacy as a critical activist in US history (Guadalupe 2017).

Today, one part of Huerta's legacy is her foundation: the Dolores Huerta Foundation. In addition to promoting equitable economic development and education, the foundation also prepares people to run for elected office and promotes "get out the vote" efforts. Such efforts extend Huerta's long-standing commitment to and effort to enfranchise marginalized people, especially working people, women, and Mexican Americans (Sowards 2020).

That's why commentators have called her "one of the most influential labor activists in the 20th century" (Conde 2023).

Joshua H. Miller

See Also: Anzaldúa, Gloria; Davis, Angela; Interlocking Oppression; Intersectionality; Labor Activism

Further Reading

Conde, Arturo. 2023. "Civil Rights Icon Dolores Huerta Discusses Music's Key Role in the Latino Farmworker Movement." *NBC News*, October 13, 2023. https://www.nbcnews.com/news/latino/dolores-huerta-song-cesar-music-sparked-farmworker-movement-rcna120262.

Doss, Erin F., and Robin E. Jensen. 2013. "Balancing Mystery and Identification: Dolores Huerta's Shifting Transcendent Persona." *Quarterly Journal of Speech* 99: 481–506. https://doi.org/10.1080/00335630.2013.833667.

Godoy, Maria. 2017. "Dolores Huerta: The Civil Rights Icon Who Showed Farmworkers 'Sí Se Puede." *National Public Radio*, September 17, 2017. https://www.npr.org/sections/thesalt/2017/09/17/551490281/dolores-huerta-the-civil-rights-icon-who-showed-farmworkers-si-se-puede.

Guadalupe, Patricia. 2017. "Documentary Gives Labor Activist Dolores Huerta Her Place in US History." *NBC News*, August 30, 2017. https://www.nbcnews.com/news/latino/documentary-gives-labor-activist-dolores-huerta-her-place-u-s-n797361.

Murphy, Mollie K. 2022. "Granting Standpoint as a Strategy for Promoting Social Justice Activism: An Analysis of Dolores Huerta's Rhetoric." *Southern Communication Journal* 87: 476–87. https://doi.org/10.1080/1041794X.2022.2117403.

Quinnell, Kenneth. 2019. "Women's History Month Profiles: Dolores Huerta." *AFL-CIO*, March 21, 2019. Accessed March 26, 2024. https://aflcio.org/2019/3/21/womens-history-month-profiles-dolores-huerta.

Sowards, Stacey K. 2012. "Rhetorical Functions of Letter Writing: Dialogic Collaboration, Affirmation, and Catharsis in Dolores Huerta's Letters." *Communication Quarterly* 60: 295–315. https://doi.org/10.1080/01463373.2012.669341.

Sowards, Stacey K. 2019. *Sí, Ella Puede!: The Rhetorical Legacy of Dolores Huerta and the United Farm Workers.* Austin, TX: University of Texas Press.

Sowards, Stacey K. 2020. "Dolores Huerta, the United Farm Workers, and People Power: Rhetorical Participation in Latina/o/x Suffrage and Social movements." *Quarterly Journal of Speech* 106: 285–90. https://doi.org/10.1080/00335630.2020.1785635.

HYDE AMENDMENT

During legislative debates in the US Congress about funding for abortion access and reproductive healthcare, usually someone will point out Congress has already banned federal funding for abortions, expect in cases involving rape, incest, or danger to life of the pregnant person. Such an argument is possible because of the Hyde Amendment, which prohibited such use of federal funds. As a "rider" amendment, the provision is attached to other legislation. Since 1980, Congress has included this amendment in its annual appropriations bills, including legislation funding the Department of Health and Human Services. Thus, the Hyde Amendment is actively reauthorized by Congress every year (Rappazzo 2024).

The restriction broadly applies to many federal programs, including Medicare, Medicaid, and the Indian Health Services, which helps support healthcare access for Indigenous Americans (Arnold 2014). For example, because Medicaid is funded through the annual appropriations budget, those who rely on Medicaid, such as poor and/or disabled individuals, cannot access abortion care (Lin and Shen 2022). The Hyde Amendment therefore creates an additional barrier to reproductive healthcare for anyone who relies on such programs. The Hyde Amendment disproportionally affects Black, Brown, and Indigenous people and poor people (Rappazzo 2024).

As such, many reproductive rights organizations and activists have criticized the law as discriminatory. For example, Jessica Arons and Lindsay Rosenthal of the Center for American Progress argued, "The Hyde Amendment therefore does not only undermine gender equity, but it also violates principles of racial and economic justice" (2013). Natasha Rappazzo of Physicians for Reproductive Health frames the problem succinctly: "Each year Congress chooses to push abortion care out of reach for Black, Brown, and Indigenous people, young people, those living in rural areas, and people with low incomes—all of whom are more likely to rely on government-sponsored insurance because of systemic barriers and inequities" (2024). Such advocates have called for the repeal of the Hyde Amendment to ensure equitable access to reproductive care, which the amendment continues to prevent.

Joshua H. Miller

See Also: Abortion; *Dobbs v. Jackson Women's Health Organization* (2022); Interlocking Oppression; Reproductive Justice; *Roe v. Wade* (1973)

Further Reading

Arnold, Shaye Beverly. 2014. "Reproductive Rights Denied: The Hyde Amendment and Access to Abortion for Native American Women Using Indian Health Services Facilities." *American Journal of Public Health* 104: 1892–3. https://pmc.ncbi.nlm.nih.gov/articles/PMC4167108/.

Arons, Jessica, and Lindsay Rosenthal. 2013. "How the Hyde Amendment Discriminates Against Poor Women and Women of Color." *Center for American Progress*, May 10, 2013. Accessed March 26, 2025. https://www.americanprogress.org/article/how-the-hyde-amendment-discriminates-against-poor-women-and-women-of-color/.

Liu, Edward C., and Wen W. Shen. 2022. "The Hyde Amendment: An Overview." *Congressional Research Service Reports*, July 20, 2022. Accessed March 26, 2025. https://www.congress.gov/crs-product/IF12167#:~:text=Covered%20Abortions,these%20two%20exceptions%20since%20FY1994.

Rappazzo, Natasha. 2024. "The Hyde Amendment Turns 48." *Physicians for Reproductive Health*, September 30, 2014. Accessed March 25, 2025. https://prh.org/updates/hyde-amendment-48/#:~:text=The%20Hyde%20Amendment%20restricts%20access,the%20military%2C%20among%20many%20others.

Williamson, Heidi, and Jamila Taylor. 2016. "The Hyde Amendment Has Perpetuated Inequality in Abortion Access for 40 Years." *Center for American Progress*, September 29, 2016. Accessed March 26, 2025. https://www.americanprogress.org/article/the-hyde-amendment-has-perpetuated-inequality-in-abortion-access-for-40-years/.

I

INTENSIVE MOTHERING

Motherhood is a socially constructed identity that places women in a defined role in society (Phoenix and Woollett 1991). This means that the role of "mother" is socially determined; motherhood is different from and more than giving birth to a child. For instance, Sharon Hays (1996) explained that motherhood is not a natural or essentialist identity but a socially constructed identity with socially constructed demands. Motherhood is perceived as the emotional, psychological, and sociological relationship between a mother and her children. Mothers are expected to take on the full responsibility in taking care of children and do most if not all of the housework. This idea or ideology of motherhood as a social identity that demands women be emotionally and physically present for their children and the sole houseworker is known as intensive mothering (Izhak and Aharoni 2023).

Coined by Sharon Hays in 1996, intensive mothering is a cultural ideology and model that encourages mothers to altruistically make a "tremendous investment in their child" even while sacrificing any and all of their own goals (Verniers, Bonnot, and Assilamehou-Kunz 2022, 1). Lynn O'Brien Hallstein (2006) explained that Hays's intensive mothering contains three key tenets: first, it demands that women "be the primary [and] central caregivers of children" (97); second, it requires mothers spend substantial amounts of their time and energy focusing on their children; and third, intensive mothering separates mothers' unpaid domestic labor from professional paid work under the assumption that domestic work is a private sphere matter, which should be separate from the outside labor market. Intensive mothering discourses, such as magazine and blog posts, tradwife Instagram influencers, and political speeches, set "high demands on maternal performances" by demanding that women place their energy on their caregiving responsibilities and disregard anything in their lives that may interfere with parenting (D'Enbeau and Buzzanell 2016, 15).

Intensive mothering expects women to be "intensely devoted and constantly attuned to their child's emotional, physical, and educational needs" (Barnes 2015, 352). This expectation is premised on the belief that motherhood is instinctive, natural, and driven by a biological need within women to have children (Verniers, Bonnot, and Assilamehou-Kunz 2022). This logic posits that all women have an innate drive to give birth and raise children, which is considered the most rewarding task a woman could ever do. Intensive mothering deems women who choose to become mothers (and then stay at home, work from home, or work part-time) as good moms and thus good women, while women who work full-time outside of the home or are childless are considered immoral and selfish.

Intensive Mothering in Television and Social Media

According to D'Enbeau and Buzzanell (2016, 15) "contemporary discourses and media representations of gender and mothering . . . often are informed by assumptions of intensive mothering, depicting mothers who either do or do not conform to these ideals." These media depictions mirror social expectations for women to not only become mothers but also how mothers should behave.

For example, historically, in popular television series such as *Leave It to Beaver* (1957–63), June Cleaver is depicted as a good mom who engages in intensive mothering. She dedicates her life to her home and family, prioritizing their well-being over her own. June is depicted as always being in the kitchen preparing dinner when her sons arrive home from school and when her husband comes home from work. Her children are happy and healthy while her house is organized and clean. June's social life revolves around her children as she spends her time at school events where she attends meetings or plays. June's entire character upholds traditional gender roles and mothering expectations set by intensive mothering as she is centered on attending to her sons' and husband's needs. Performing intensive mothering, June Cleaver has gone down in television history as a selfless, good mother.

In contemporary media, intensive mothering has found a place in online social networks known as mommy blogs. Even in online spaces, mothering influencers behave in ways that represent intensive mothering. These mommy blogs teach other women, sometimes unconsciously, the social expectations of good mothering even as these influencers present themselves as alpha moms or the ideal mother who sets the standards for others to emulate (Izhak and Aharoni 2023, 2). Mommy bloggers present themselves as happy mothers who are organized and are always emotionally and physically present for their children (Orton-Johnson 2017).

Although these online spaces allow mothers to receive and provide support, they also pressure mothers to present a good mother personality and identity, even online (Izhak and Aharoni 2023). Mothers online are expected to present themselves as fulfilled in their roles as mothers while providing support to other mothers. For example, the homepage of the mommy blog titled *FreshMommyblog* features a photo of the mommy blogger on a beach, dressed up and put together as she smiles while holding her child. The photo features a short bio: "A Life Coach, Speaker, Author, Mom of 6 & Professional Encourager who created this space to support, equip and inspire you on your journey to creating a life you love" (Blue n.d.). Links within the blog include Life Coaching; Recipes; Style & Beauty; Home & DIY; Motherhood; Travel; and many others. These links and photos throughout the blog portray the happy and fulfilled mother who is a creation of intensive mothering.

In conclusion, intensive mothering creates strong social pressures on mothers to be selfless and available to their children at all times. It leads society to think that motherhood is natural and essentialist, which places a demand on women to become mothers. Television and social media routinely feature images, narratives, and messages that encourage women to embody intensive mothering; these messages lead everyday women, men, and families to expect women to sacrifice everything in the name of "motherhood."

Jessica Marinho

See Also: Domestic Labor; Essentialism; Gender; Gender Performance; Reproductive Labor

Further Reading

Barnes, Medora W. 2015. "Gender Differentiation in Paid and Unpaid Work During the Transition to Parenthood." *Sociology Compass* 9, no. 5: 348–64. https://doi.org/10.1111/soc4.12263.

Blue, Tabitha. n.d. Fresh Mommy Blog. Accessed November 15, 2024. https://freshmommyblog.com/.

D'Enbeau, Suzy, and Patrice Buzzanell. 2016. "Counter-Intensive Mothering: Exploring Transgressive Portrayals and Transcendence on Mad Men. "In *Mediated Moms Contemporary Challenges to the Motherhood Myth*, edited by Heather L. Hundley and Sara E. Hayden. New York: Peter Lang.

Hallstein, D. Lynn O'Brien. 2006. "Conceiving Intensive Mothering." *Journal of the Motherhood Initiative for Research and Community Involvement* 8, no. 1–2: 96–108.

Hays, Sharon. 1996. *The Cultural Contradictions of Motherhood.* New Haven: Yale University Press.

Izhak, Inbal, and Matan Aharoni. 2023. "Beyond Intensive Motherhood: Performing Online Cross-border Motherhood on Social Media." *Women's Studies International Forum* 100: 1–8. https://doi.org/10.1016/j.wsif.2023.102820.
Phoenix, Ann, and Anne Woollett. 1991. "Motherhood: Social Construction, Politics and Psychology." In *Motherhood: Meanings, Practices, and Ideologies*, edited by Ann Phoenix, Anne Woollett, and Eva Lloyd, 13–27. London: Sage Publications, Inc.
Orton-Johnson, Kate. 2017. "Mummy Blogs and Representations of Motherhood: 'Bad Mummies' and Their Readers." *Social Media+ Society* 3, no. 2: 1–10. https://doi.org/10.1177/2056305117707.
Verniers, Catherine, Virginie Bonnot, and Yvette Assilaméhou-Kunz. 2022. "Intensive Mothering and The Perpetuation of Gender Inequality: Evidence from a Mixed Methods Research." *Acta Psychologica* 227: 1–14. https://doi.org/10.1016/j.actpsy.2022.103614.

INTERLOCKING OPPRESSION

Interlocking oppression refers to the ways in which different types of oppression (e.g., racism, sexism, ageism, ableism, heterosexism) "interlock" with each other to become more oppressive and affect people in different ways. Interlocking oppression can be pictured through the metaphor of weaving threads together. When a cloth is woven, some of the threads go horizontally and others go vertically, and the threads are woven over and under each other until the cloth is whole. Many of us wove together pot holders and friendship bracelets through this "over-under" intertwining—or interlocking—of threads when we were younger. Interlocking oppression is the weaving together of different threads or strands of oppression. By interlocking these "threads," oppression becomes stronger, harder to resist, and affects people in different ways.

For example, sexism, heterosexism, and racism are woven together so that Black lesbian women face a tapestry of oppression meant to demean, dismiss, and punish their existence into annihilation. As Audre Lorde wrote, "As a Black, lesbian, feminist, socialist, poet, mother of two including one boy and a member of an interracial couple, I usually find myself part of some group in which the majority defines me as deviant, difficult, inferior or just plain 'wrong'" (Lorde 1983, 76). Lorde continues, describing her existence as a death she is expected to live and writing that Black women, especially Black lesbians, were never "meant to survive" in the "mouth of this dragon we call america" (1984, 38, 42).

In many ways, intersectionality is the analysis of interlocking oppressions—and both concepts were theorized by Black feminist scholars and activists, most famously by the Combahee River Collective (CRC) as they worked on identity politics.

Theorizing Interlocking Oppression

Now a buzzword, "intersectionality" was popularized in 1989 by Kimberlé Crenshaw's work. Before then, however, Black and women of color feminists had long been studying interlocking oppression and using what we now refer to as "intersectional" analyses. Most famously, the CRC formed in 1974 as a radical alternative to the National Black Feminist Organization (NBFO), which was created in response to white feminist organizations whose work inadequately addressed racism in the United States. However, the NBFO centered racism alone in the lives of Black women, and its theory and activism were politically insufficient to fully address Black women's experiences of oppression (Taylor 2017, 4).

In response, the CRC focused on what it called "identity politics." In its 1977 mission statement, the CRC wrote that "the most profound and potentially most radical politics come directly out of our own identity, as opposed to working to end somebody else's oppression" (2017, 19). Here, the CRC drew on their experiences with other political organizations (e.g., white feminist groups and the NBFO), realizing those other organizations had focused on the oppression of women (but really *white* women) or the oppression of Black people (but really Black *men*) and left Black women in the political lurch.

For the CRC, the key to achieving revolutionary, systemic transformation was to center Black women's political realities and experiences in order to address the interlocking oppressions that have sedimented Black women's oppression. By highlighting the interlocking oppressions that exclude Black women from mainstream activism and progressive political movements, the CRC highlighted Black women as the most minoritized national subjects and argued that liberating Black women will liberate everyone minoritized in the United States. That is, to liberate Black women, feminists and other activist groups in the United States have to unweave the interlocking oppressions of sexism, racism, classism, heterosexism, ableism, and so on that have historically—and continuously—oppressed Black women. By unweaving that tapestry, we would dismantle all the "isms" that oppress every minoritized group.

Classism as an Interlocking Oppression

When analyzing or organizing against interlocking oppression, it is essential that feminists understand classism as one of those interlocking oppressions. Here again, the CRC led the way. Classism was central to the CRC's understanding of Black women's lives, and their focus on classism distinguished radical Black feminist politics from the emerging middle-class orientation of Black politics in the 1970s (Taylor 2017, 9). Drawing attention to the close connection between the theory of interlocking oppression and intersectionality, Carolyn Pedwell explains, "Intersectionality was initiated through Black feminists' potent critiques of middle-class bias within mainstream feminist theory and practice" in the 1970s and 1980s (2007, 46).

Many women—especially white women—during the 1960s–1980s focused on the notion of common or shared experiences of oppression and expressions of sisterhood that supposedly united all women. The idea was to unify women into a strong political collective. But this "unity" ignored the differences created by interlocking oppressions. It ignored how racism and classism are interwoven with sexism so that working-class women's experiences of sexism are different from middle- and upper-class women's experiences of sexism, and so on. This meant that a lot of the mainstream feminist activism in the 1960s–1980s did not sufficiently address the interests of working-class women of color. This was especially true because many middle- and upper-class white women were not interested in challenging the structures of racial capitalism that dominated the women working under them (hooks 2014, 44–5).

Identity politics helped the CRC identify how oppressions interlock, wholistically oppressing minoritized people through different aspects of their identity—gender, race, class, sexuality, and so on. By identifying interlocking oppressions, radical Black feminists in the CRC confronted the racist, classist structures within patriarchy and within mainstream feminism that uphold elite (white) women's interests while largely dismissing the oppressions women of color and working-class women face.

For the CRC, identity politics was a source of political radicalization emphasizing not just who you were but also how you could become politically active to confront the interlocking oppressions you faced. Today, feminists are still learning from the CRC. When feminists describe themselves as "intersectional feminists" or describe their theory or activism as "intersectional," they often mean that they are trying to learn from past mistakes in the mainstream (white) feminist movement and trying to address interlocking oppressions.

Today, the theory of intersectionality emphasizes how oppressions interlock and the need to transform systems and structures—and our own political activism—to build solidarity across difference (hooks 2014, 55). Instead of a shallow political bond of "sisterhood" that ignores interlocking oppression and pretends differences don't exist, Black feminists and feminists of color—such as the CRC—have led the way by theorizing interlocking oppressions and forming political coalitions across difference (Taylor 2017, 11).

Sergio Peña

See Also: #BlackLivesMatter; Capitalism; Combahee River Collective; Crenshaw, Kimberlé; Intersectionality; Lorde, Audre; Third World Women's Alliance and Black Woman's Manifesto

Further Reading

Combahee River Collective. 1977 (2017). "Combahee River Collective Statement." In *How We Get Free: Black Feminism and the Combahee River Collective*, edited by Yeeanga-Yamahtta Taylor, 15–27. Chicago: Haymarket Books.

Crenshaw, Kimberlé. 1989. "Demarginalizing the Intersection of Race and Sex: A Black Feminist Critique of Antidiscrimination Doctrine, Feminist Theory and Antiracist Politics." *University of Chicago Legal Forum* 1, no. 8: 139–67.

hooks, bell. 2014. *Ain't I a Woman: Black Women and Feminism*, 2nd ed. New York: Routledge.

Lorde, Audre. 1983 (2018). "There Is No Hierarchy of Oppressions." In *Introduction to Women's, Gender & Sexuality Studies: Interdisciplinary and Intersectional Approaches*, edited by L. Ayu Saraswati, Barbara L. Shaw, and Heather Rellihan, 76. New York: Oxford University Press.

Lorde, Audre, 1984. *Sister Outsider: Essays and Speeches by Audre Lorde*. Berkeley, CA: Crossing Press.

Pedwell, Carolyn. 2007. "Gender, Embodiment and Cultural Practice: Towards a Relational Feminist Approach." PhD diss., London School of Economics and Political Science.

Taylor, Keeanga-Yamahtta, ed. 2017. *How We Get Free: Black Feminism and the Combahee River Collective*. Chicago: Haymarket Books.

INTERNALIZED SEXISM

Internalized sexism refers to the way women and queer folk often internalize sexist attitudes, thoughts, and ideas, coming to believe what their oppressors say about them is true. E. J. R. David explains this, saying, "the oppression that permeates the environment is able to seep into oppressed individuals who, in turn, begin to think, feel, and behave in biased ways toward themselves and their own group" (David 2013; David and Derthick 2017, 86). Or, as communication scholar Karlyn Kohrs Campbell put it, women aren't just fighting sexism out there, we "fight an enemy who has outposts" in our own heads (1973, 86). Internalized sexism, like all forms of internalized oppression, is a social problem rooted in cultural norms, not an individual, personal flaw.

Different Forms of Internalized Sexism

In 1997, social psychologists Peter Glick and Susan Fiske pioneered the scholarly discussion of internalized sexism by theorizing "hostile" and "benevolent" sexism as two conflicting but coexisting and mutually reinforcing ways of thinking. Both "hostile" and "benevolent" sexism seek "to justify male power, traditional gender roles, and men's exploitation of women as sexual objects" (Glick and Fiske 1997, 121). Hostile sexism, however, does so "through derogatory characterizations of women," while benevolent sexism "relies on kinder and gentler justifications of male dominance and prescribed gender roles; it recognizes men's dependence on women (i.e., women's dyadic power) and embraces a romanticized view of sexual relationships with women . . .[encompassing] feelings of protectiveness and affection toward women" (Glick and Fiske 1997, 121). Both hostile and benevolent sexism can be internalized.

Consider this example of internalized *hostile* sexism from YouTube influencer Pearl Davis (2023). On November 7, 2023, Davis tweeted that "Women are so exhausting to talk to" because "women make everything about them," "women change the subject constantly," "women go on long tangents and never get to the point," "women are much more passive aggressive than men," because women are "so flakey and always late," and because women "make no sense 99% of the time" (Davis 2023). Davis's tweet is explicitly hostile or negative toward women, despite the author being a woman herself.

In contrast, *benevolent* sexism is more subtle, appearing to be positive toward women while maintaining and justifying traditional gender roles and patriarchal power structures. Women can internalize "benevolent" forms of sexism, which often sound nice but reinforce oppression.

For example, white women who identify as "traditional" wives, or tradwives, draw on "the antebellum US South's Cult of True Womanhood, which stressed a vision of women as innocent, domestic and childlike, placed on a pedestal and too pure for the masculine world" (Tebaldi 2023, 18; Coontz 1992). For example, on Instagram, tradwife Ekaterina Andersen (2022) posted about her "escape from feminism," defining "the idea of womanhood as something thoroughly good, something sacred." This sounds lovely, but tradwives' resurrection of the Cult of True Womanhood enforces essentialist ideas about gender and is inseparably tied up in notions of whiteness and purity, contributing to and compounding misogynoir.

The Cult of True Womanhood and tradwives are often linked to white US Christian fundamentalism, but internalized sexism also affects those outside white US femininity. For example, within Latin American gender studies, the term *marianismo*—connected to the Roman Catholic figure of the Virgin Mary—is used as the counterpart to *machismo*. Originally coined by Evelyn Stevens, *marianismo* is defined as "the cult of female spiritual superiority, which teaches that women are semidivine, morally superior to and spiritually stronger than men" (1973, 315). For example, a woman influenced by *marianismo* may believe that it is her religious responsibility to prevent masculine sexual advances by dressing more modestly, excusing men's sexual harassment by reasoning that men are spiritually inferior and "can't control themselves." Like most benevolent sexism, *marianismo* places women on a pedestal rather than being hostile toward women. Yet *marianismo* ultimately reinforces patriarchal power structures by limiting women to roles focused on chastity, submission, and increased emotional and domestic labor.

Internalized Sexism's Intersection with Trans Identities

Internalized sexism—whether hostile or benevolent—ultimately works to control and define "correct" femininity. Strictly controlling gender expression based on patriarchal social norms and expectations has negative consequences across the spectrums of gender and sexual identity. For example, the belief that women are inherently weaker than men is one of the primary driving forces behind trans exclusion in sports.

Communication scholar Jennifer McClearen (2023) argues that the portrayal of "girl power" in sports advertisements often serves cisgender white women at the expense of trans women and women of color. Analyzing "girl power" advertisements alongside anti-trans legislation, McClearen demonstrates how trans people and cisgender women of color are aligned with "biological men" who are positioned as threats to (white) women, supposedly stealing their confidence and their ability to win (2023, 1361). Many "girl power" advertisements and sports policies reinforce the belief that people assigned female at birth are all physically inferior to people assigned male at birth; this negatively affects trans athletes and women of color since racism often positions women of color as outside traditional (white) femininity.

For example, boxer Imane Khelif faced extreme scrutiny and hate during the 2024 Summer Olympics after her first opponent—Italian boxer Angela Carini—cried and quit after only forty-six seconds in the ring (Beacham 2024). Due to her physical prowess and athletic ability, Khelif (like many other cisgender female athletes—especially athletes of color) was asked to "prove" her femininity (Nasir 2024). As you can imagine, this scrutiny, hate, and gender questioning is even more intense for trans athletes, such as swimmer Lia Thomas, who was banned from competing in the 2024 Summer Olympics (Lavietes 2024). Here, it becomes clear that benevolent sexism—including internalized benevolent sexism from other female athletes—is one of the "central weapons used against trans women" and women of color (McClearen 2023, 1370).

Internalized Sexism's Intersection with Lesbianism

Internalized sexism affects lesbian individuals in several ways. Lesbians are infinitely creative in their gender expression; historically, however, lesbian expression has been categorized on a Butch-Femme continuum, where "butch" indicates a more masculinized gender expression and "femme" indicates a more feminine expression. Lesbians and straight people have used this continuum to layer patriarchal misogyny onto lesbians and lesbian relationships. For instance, writing about her experiences as a butch, Kate (2013) observes that when she is surrounded by men and butch lesbians, the way people talk treats women like "objects rather than humans." Continuing, Kate writes that the objectification of women "seems to be a bonding mechanism for the butches and men," concluding that "patriarchy barters and trades with women as currency, and in those moments, we [butch lesbians] are doing the same thing" (2013).

Clearly, internalized sexism can lead some lesbian women to objectify femmes and femininity. Maya (2016), a self-identified femme, explains this misogynistic treatment, recalling instances of catcalling and other treatment that reflects the overall belief that she and other femmes are sexually passive and submissive. Yet, butch women can also be on the receiving end of misogynistic beliefs and behaviors from other women who have internalized sexism: femme lesbians might expect them to take the lead—forcing them to occupy a dominant role—and straight women often disavow butch women as *women*.

Internalized sexism can also lead to questioning queer identities. Anika Stafford notes that "Queer femmes in 1950s bar cultures were often not viewed as 'real lesbians'; radical feminism condemned femmes as trying to please patriarchy" (2010, 81). Sadly, this pattern of criticizing women's gender expressions in the name of "feminism" continues to this day.

"Pick-Me Girls" and Hegemonic Femininity

When women internalize sexism, they often perform hegemonic femininity, meaning they train themselves to live out—or try to live out—a version of femininity that makes patriarchal men the happiest. In the contemporary era, when a lot of patriarchal men claim to believe in women's empowerment, this can be really complicated: for instance, women walk the line of being attractive to patriarchal men but somehow not appearing to wear much makeup and attempt to have fulfilling careers while still dropping everything for a man or their families.

The stereotype of the "Pick-Me Girl" is a prime example of what internalized sexism and thus hegemonic femininity can look like. Originating on Twitter/X, the term skyrocketed in popularity in 2021 via TikTok (Banet-Weiser and Maddocks 2023). As the name suggests, Pick-Me Girls are women who support and, at times, embody internalized sexism in pursuit of masculine attention and validation, distancing "themselves from other women to be more attractive" and thus "'picked' by men" (Rosenbluth 2021). Pick-Me Girls are frequently associated with the phrase "I'm not like other girls."

Internalized sexism can take many forms and affects women and queer people in many ways. Ultimately, feminist theorists and activists hope that society will view masculinity and femininity not as places within a hierarchy but as equal and valid aesthetic and behavioral expressions.

Emma Darby

See Also: Biblical Complementarianism; Butch; Compulsory Heterosexuality; Cult of True Womanhood; Domestic Labor; Emotional Labor; Essentialism; Femme; Gender; Misogyny; Patriarchy; Trans-Exclusionary Radical Feminists (TERFs)

Further Reading

Andersen, Ekaterina. 2022. "Traditional Femininity. My Collected Thoughts about It and about My Escape from Feminism." *Instagram*, June 22, 2022. https://www.instagram.com/p/CfHTikQI9mp/.

Banet-Weiser, Sarah, and Sophie Maddocks. 2023. "Networked Misogyny on TikTok: A Critical Conjuncture." In *The Routledge Companion to Gender, Media and Violence*, edited by Karen Boyle and Susan Berridge. London: Routledge.

Beacham, Greg. 2024. "Algeria Boxer Imane Khelif Wins First Olympic Fight When Opponent Angela Carini Quits." *AP News*, August 1, 2024, sec. Sports. https://apnews.com/article/olympics-2024-boxing-gender-4b6eb881cce9c34484d30c68ad979127.

Campbell, Karlyn Kohrs. 1973. "The Rhetoric of Women's Liberation: An Oxymoron." *The Quarterly Journal of Speech* 59, no. 1: 74–86.

Coontz, Stephanie. 1992. *The Way We Never Were: American Families and the Nostalgia Trap*. New York: Basic Books.

David, E. J. R. 2013. *Brown Skin, White Minds: Filipino -/ American Postcolonial Psychology*. Charlotte, NC: IAP.

David, E. J. R., and Annie O. Derthick. 2017. *The Psychology of Oppression*. New York: Springer Publishing Company, Incorporated. http://ebookcentral.proquest.com/lib/unt/detail.action?docID=5106035.

Davis, Pearl [@pearlythingz]. 2023. "After 2 Years of Shows – There Is a Reason I Do Pearl Daily and the Panel Shows Only Once a Week Now. Women Are so Exhausting to Talk to – Women Make Everything about Them - Women Change the Subject Constantly - Women Go on Long Tangents and Never Get to the Point - Women." Tweet. *Twitter*. https://x.com/pearlythingz/status/1722066591313961033.

Glick, Peter, and Susan T. Fiske. 1997. "Hostile and Benevolent Sexism: Measuring Ambivalent Sexist Attitudes Toward Women." *Psychology of Women Quarterly* 21, no. 1: 119–35. https://doi.org/10.1111/j.1471-6402.1997.tb00104.x.

Junn, Jane. 2017. "The Trump Majority: White Womanhood and the Making of Female Voters in the US" *Politics, Groups, and Identities* 5, no. 2: 343–52. https://doi.org/10.1080/21565503.2017.1304224.

Kate. 2013. "Butch Please: Butch With A Side of Misogyny." *Autostraddle* (blog), April 26, 2013. https://www.autostraddle.com/butch-please-butch-with-a-side-of-misogyny-174442/.

Lavietes, Matt. 2024. "Trans Swimmer Lia Thomas' Olympic Hopes Are Dashed after a Losing Legal Battle." *NBC News*, June 12, 2024. https://www.nbcnews.com/nbc-out/out-news/lia-thomas-loses-legal-battle-2024-olympics-hopes-dashed-rcna156808.

Maya, M. 2016. "Can Lesbians Be Misogynistic? The Answer Is Yes & Here's Why It Happens." *Bustle*, March 14, 2016. https://www.bustle.com/articles/147623-can-lesbians-be-misogynistic-the-answer-is-yes-heres-why-it-happens.

McClearen, Jennifer. 2023. "'If You Let Me Play': Girls' Empowerment and Transgender Exclusion in Sports." *Feminist Media Studies* 23, no. 4: 1361–75. https://doi.org/10.1080/14680777.2022.2041697.

Nasir, Noreen. 2024. "For Female Athletes of Color, Scrutiny around Gender Rules and Identity Is Part of a Long Trend." *AP News*, August 4, 2024, sec. Sports. https://apnews.com/article/olympics-2024-gender-racism-female-athletes-49b79a6b7ae76afaebb00319732d6486.

Rosenbluth, Amy. 2021. "The Toxic Trajectory of the #PickMeGirl Trend." *The McGill International Review*, April 29, 2021. https://www.mironline.ca/the-toxic-trajectory-of-the-pickmegirl-trend/.
Stafford, Anika. 2010. "Uncompromising Positions: Reiterations of Misogyny Embedded in Lesbian and Feminist Communities' Framing of Lesbian Femme Identities." *Atlantis: Critical Studies in Gender, Culture & Social Justice* 35, no. 1: 81–91.
Stevens, Evelyn P. 1973. "The Prospects for a Women's Liberation Movement in Latin America." *Journal of Marriage and Family* 35, no. 2: 313–21. https://doi.org/10.2307/350661.
Tebaldi, Catherine. 2023. "Tradwives and Truth Warriors: Gender and Nationalism in US White Nationalist Women's Blogs." *Gender & Language* 17, no. 1: 14–38. https://doi.org/10.1558/genl.18551.

INTERSECTIONALITY

Intersectionality is an analytical perspective that identifies how systems of oppression, such as racism, sexism, and classism, converge and reinforce each other to produce different forms of violence and shape lived experiences across shared aspects of identity. For example, an intersectional analysis helps parse how racism and sexism intertwine to make Black women's experiences with oppression both similar to and different from white women's and Black men's experiences with oppression. Intersectionality rejects essentialist frameworks; this means that intersectionality refuses to focus on a "single axis" of oppression, such as only sexism or racism, as the primary cause of a group's oppression. Because essentialist frameworks focus on one aspect of identity—a single axis—they tend to ignore intragroup differences, such as how Black women experience forms of sexism uniquely shaped by racism, and thus the sexism Black women face is different from the sexism other women experience.

For example, feminists have long been working to end the pay gap between men and women. During 2002–22, women in the United States typically earned between 80 and 82 cents for every dollar earned by white men. This is a huge improvement. In 1982, US women earned just 65 cents for every dollar white men earned (Kochhar 2023). However, while the pay gap narrowed for all groups of women from 1982 to 2022, white women experienced the most economic advancement. That is, as measured in 2024, for every dollar that white men earn, white European American women earn approximately 81 cents, but Latinas are paid approximately 55 cents, Native American women are paid approximately 59 cents, and Black women are paid approximately 64 cents (Haan 2024). When accounting for differences in education, experience, and occupation, racial hiring discrimination emerges as a significant systemic mechanism that impacts pay equity across gender. That is, both sexism *and* racism have to be accounted for in order to understand wage gaps. Feminists need intersectional analyses and activism to address the interlocking oppressions that shape pay discrimination and inequity more broadly.

Theorizing Intersectionality

In 1989, Kimberlé Crenshaw published one of the foundational articles formally theorizing intersectionality, writing that a "focus on the most privileged group members [e.g., white women] marginalizes those who are multiply-burdened [e.g., women of color, lesbians, disabled women, etc.] and obscures claims that cannot be understood as resulting from discrete sources of discrimination" (Crenshaw 1989, 140). Crenshaw frames the concept of intersectionality as a metaphor, using the image of a four-way traffic intersection. In the traffic metaphor, roads (or systems, such as racism and sexism) converge and can move in more than one way, illustrating the complexity of how these systems interact with each other.

Intersectionality is built on an understanding of interlocking oppression—the idea that different forms of oppression interact, connect, shape, and strengthen each other. The Black feminist group known as the Combahee River Collective (CRC) theorized this, focusing on what they called "identity politics" in their 1977 mission statement. Coining the phrase, "identity politics," the CRC used it to refer to the different and interlocking ways in which oppression targets minoritized people based on aspects of their identity within society—based on their race, sex, sexuality, and so on (Taylor 2017, 8).

Identity politics originally referred to what we now typically call intersectional analyses and activism, foregrounding the study of how power works to oppress along multiple axes. As Sumi Cho, Kimberlé Crenshaw, and Leslie McCall explain, intersectionality "primarily concerns the way things work rather than who people are" (2013, 797). That is, intersectionality and identity politics are concerned with how and why identity categories (such as race and gender) exist—studying how and why identity categories are made, reinforced, and used to oppress or privilege people in society. The phrase "identity politics" has been appropriated and exploited in patriarchal and white supremacist backlashes against the CRC and intersectional feminism more broadly. Today, "identity politics" is often used to demean an activist group or political organization by suggesting they are "playing the gender card" or "playing the race card." This fundamentally misunderstands the ways in which our identities are always more than one thing—always intersectional—and entirely misses the point that identity politics and intersectionality are about how oppression works.

Intersectionality and Critical Race Theory

Crenshaw's work on intersectionality emerges from critical race studies, "a scholarly movement born in the legal academy committed to problematizing law's purported colour-blindness, neutrality and objectivity" (Nash 2008, 2). This context is significant because Crenshaw demonstrates how the oppression of Black women is implicitly written into US law through their exclusion in legal cases about gender and race discrimination.

Additionally, Crenshaw observes a similar privileging of white women's and Black men's experiences in the feminist and Black liberation movements, respectively. Instead of adopting a top-down approach to activism, she suggests beginning "with the needs and problems of those who are most disadvantaged and with restructuring and remaking the world where necessary" (Crenshaw 1989, 167). This call-to-action manifests in the activist, intellectual, and political work of Black feminists like the Combahee River Collective in the 1970s and ongoing activism today.

Black Feminist Activism and Intersectionality in the Twenty-First Century

Movements such as #SayHerName and #BlackLivesMatter (BLM) exemplify how intersectionality has shaped the work of Black feminist activism and organizing in the twenty-first century. For instance, founded by three radical Black feminist organizers—Alicia Garza, Patrisse Cullors, and Opal Tometi—#BlackLivesMatter is organized around resisting the cultural and systemic criminalization and murder of Black people in the United States (Black Lives Matter 2017). As an organization, BLM intervenes in Black cisheterosexual men's domination of Black liberation politics to center how Black women and Black queer, trans, and disabled people experience criminalization and oppression. The movement affirms its political commitment to *all* Black people's humanity and resilience by centering intersectionality as a framework to analyze and organize against anti-Black oppression.

BLM has been especially successful at raising awareness of and resistance to anti-Black police and state violence. Yet here again, interlocking oppressions come into play to make the deaths of Black *men* more newsworthy in mainstream news coverage. In response, Black feminists in the African American Policy Forum (AAPF) launched the intersectional social media campaign #SayHerName to raise awareness of and organize around police killings of Black women and Black women's unique experiences with police violence (Crenshaw et al. 2015, 3).

Without an intersectional framework in social movements or politics related to anti-Black police violence, we could not account for the extent of systemic anti-Black oppression nor could we attempt to dismantle this unjust system. As a framework, intersectionality first reminds feminist theorists and activists to analyze the concealed forms of interlocking oppression, working to understand how oppression targets the least powerful and least visible people within a system. Second, an intersectional framework urges feminists to center the most minoritized and oppressed people within our activism, organizing around their liberation as a catalyst for the liberation of everyone. As systems of oppression become more sophisticated in concealing their appearance, particularly in the digital age, intersectionality remains a necessary analytical tool to understand how systems of oppression interlock with each other and to dismantle these interlocking oppressions.

Sergio Peña

See Also: #BlackLivesMatter; Combahee River Collective; Crenshaw, Kimberlé; Equal Pay; Essentialism; Interlocking Oppression; #SayHerName

Further Reading

Black Lives Matter. 2017. "Herstory." *Black Lives Matter*, July 7, 2017. Accessed August 24, 2024. https://blacklivesmatter.com/herstory/.

Cassidy, Megan. 2015. "Phoenix Police: 2014 Fatal Shooting of Michelle Cusseaux was 'Outside' Policy." *The Arizona Republic*, September 17, 2015. https://www.azcentral.com/story/news/local/phoenix/breaking/2015/09/17/phoenix-police-michelle-cusseaux-shooting-outside-policy/72370792/.

Cho, Sumi, Kimberlé Williams Crenshaw, and Leslie McCall. 2013. "Toward a Field of Intersectionality Studies: Theory, Applications, and Praxis." *Signs* 38, no. 4: 785–810.

Combahee River Collective. 1977 (2017). "Combahee River Collective Statement." In *How We Get Free: Black Feminism and the Combahee River Collective*, edited by Yeeanga-Yamahtta Taylor, 15–27. Chicago: Haymarket Books.

Crenshaw, Kimberlé. 1989. "Demarginalizing the Intersection of Race and Sex: A Black Feminist Critique of Antidiscrimination Doctrine, Feminist Theory and Antiracist Politics." *University of Chicago Legal Forum* 1989 1, no. 8: 139–67.

Crenshaw, Kimberlé W., Ritchie, Andrea J., Anspach, Rachel, Gilmer, Rachel and Luke Harris. 2015. "Say Her Name: Resisting Police Brutality Against Black Women." *African American Policy Forum*, July 2015. Accessed August 8, 2024. https://www.aapf.org/_files/ugd/62e126_9223ee35c2694ac3bd3f2171504ca3f7.pdf.

Haan, Katherine. 2024. "Gender Pay Gap Statistics in 2024." *Forbes*, March 1, 2024. Accessed August 1, 2024. https://www.forbes.com/advisor/business/gender-pay-gap-statistics/#sources_section.

hooks, bell. 2014. *Ain't I a Woman: Black Women and Feminism*, 2nd ed. Routledge: New York.

Kochhar, Rakesh. 2023. "The Enduring Grip of the Gender Pay Gap." *Pew Research Center*, March 1, 2023. https://www.pewresearch.org/social-trends/2023/03/01/the-enduring-grip-of-the-gender-pay-gap/.

Lowery, Wesley. 2017. "Black Lives Matter: Birth of a Movement." *The Guardian*, January 17, 2017. https://www.theguardian.com/us-news/2017/jan/17/black-lives-matter-birth-of-a-movement.

Nash, Jennifer C. 2008. "Re-thinking Intersectionality." *Feminist Review* 89, no. 1: 1–15.

Pedwell, Carolyn. 2007. "Gender, Embodiment and Cultural Practice: Towards a Relational Feminist Approach." PhD diss., London School of Economics and Political Science.

Taylor, Keeanga-Yamahtta, ed. 2017. *How We Get Free: Black Feminism and the Combahee River Collective*. Chicago: Haymarket Books.

Thebault, Reis. 2022. "Trayvon Martin's Death Set off a Movement that Shaped a Decade's Defining Moments." *The Washington Post*, February 25, 2022. https://www.washingtonpost.com/nation/2022/02/25/trayvon-martins-death-set-off-movement-that-shaped-decades-defining-moments/.

INTERSEX

"Intersex" is a term used to describe human bodies that exist outside the binary of male and female. While there are many ways that someone can be intersex, this term generally refers to individuals whose reproductive or sexual anatomy does not neatly fall into the categories of male or female. Intersex traits are naturally occurring and not inherently a medical problem, yet often when babies demonstrate intersex traits at birth, doctors and family members decide on one of the binary sex options, male or female—routinely altering the infant's body through surgery—and raise the child as that sex.

In the twenty-first century, activists have pushed back against these medically unnecessary infant surgeries and the choices being made for these infants. For instance, the documentary *Every Body* (2023) tells the stories of three intersex people whose childhoods and teenage years were marked by indignity, concealment, and nonconsensual surgeries (Cohen 2023). In the film, these three people discuss their upbringings and demonstrate how they are exploring their bodies and sexualities as adults and as part of a growing international movement promoting greater understanding and acceptance of the intersex community (Cohen 2023).

Anne Fausto-Sterling, a leader in feminist scientific research of genetics, sex, and sexuality, argues that the treatment of intersex individuals speaks to a particular Western political project interested in the control of particular bodies. Fausto-Sterling contends that in order "to maintain gender divisions, we must control those bodies that are so unruly as to blur the borders" (Fausto-Sterling 2020, 8). Bodies that exist outside the binary categories of biologically male and female, such as many intersex individuals, weaken mainstream culture's "common-sense" declarations regarding sexual difference and therefore challenge the assumptions, laws, and policies that maintain patriarchal gender roles.

Scholars like Fausto-Sterling and Judith Butler question the stability and objectivity of the "biological" categories of "man" and "woman"—both in terms of gender and biological sex. Fausto-Sterling notes that "our beliefs about gender affect what kinds of knowledge scientists produce about sex in the first place" (Fausto-Sterling 2020, 3). Therefore, until we accept and acknowledge intersexed people and their right to remain outside of the sex binary, the scientific community and larger culture will continue to force such people to take on identities that do not truly fit their experiences in the world.

In the landscape of sports, the twenty-first century has seen a reckoning with intersex athletes, particularly those who are performing in the female athletic category. The most infamous case has been the global media controversy surrounding South African runner, Caster Semenya. After her dramatic success at the 2009 World Championships in track and field, institutions, fellow athletes, and the Western media questioned and challenged Semenya's femaleness. Semenya's body was subjected to public scrutiny, and some observers suggested that she was not 100 percent female. According to information leaked through news media sources, Semenya's natural testosterone level is much higher than the "normal" testosterone level for a woman. Commentators concluded that even while Semenya was not intentionally doping or cheating, she had an unfair advantage due to her natural biology. In current terminology, Semenya is best understood as intersex, carrying both male and female sexual traits (supposedly diverging from the feminine norm in terms of hormone levels), yet Semenya has always considered herself a woman—having been born and raised as one. Semenya's body has been pushed out of athletic competition for its natural biological traits. Her experiences have raised many questions regarding the use of the sex binary as the organizing structure of athletics.

Dafna Kaufman

See Also: Bodily Autonomy; Butler, Judith; Essentialism; Gender

Further Reading

Beck, Max. 2001. "My Life as an Intersexual." *PBS*, October 30, 2001. https://www.pbs.org/wgbh/nova/article/intersexual-life/.

Cohen, Julie. 2023. *Every Body*. Focus Features.

Dreger, Alice D., and April M. Herndon. 2009. "Progress and Politics in the Intersex Rights Movement: Feminist Theory in Action." *GLQ: A Journal of Lesbian and Gay Studies* 15, no. 2: 199–224.

Fausto-Sterling, Anne. 2000. "The Five Sexes, Revisited." *Sciences*, 40, no. 4: 18–23.

Fausto-Sterling, Anne. 2020. *Sexing the Body: Gender Politics and the Construction of Sexuality*. New York: Basic Books.

Lindahl, Hans. 2019. "9 Young People on How They Found Out They Are Intersex." *Teen Vogue*, October 25, 2019. https://www.teenvogue.com/gallery/young-people-on-how-they-found-out-they-are-intersex.

Ryzik, Melena. 2023. "For a Documentary on Intersex Lives, a Director Champions the Power of Activism." *The New York Times*, June 30, 2023. https://www.nytimes.com/2023/06/30/movies/intersex-documentary.html.

Semenya, Caster. 2023. *The Race to Be Myself: A Memoir*. New York: W.W. Norton & Company.

INTIMATE PARTNER VIOLENCE

"Intimate partner violence" (IPV) is an all-encompassing term that describes any type of violence between those who are or previously have been involved in some sort of intimate relationship. This violence may be verbal, physical, or sexual in nature and can include a wide variety of violent or abusive acts. Under the umbrella of intimate partner violence are terms you have probably heard before: domestic abuse, dating violence, sexual abuse, coercion, gaslighting, and stalking. There is no conclusive list of examples of IPV, but they all share a common denominator: intimate partner violence is the use of power to harm and control those in a close relationship with their perpetrator.

It is important to note that more than half of rape victims in the United States report being raped by an intimate partner (National Sexual Violence Resource Center n.d.). As a result, sexual violence is often discussed in combination with IPV. However, not all sexual assaults are considered intimate partner violence.

It is also worth noting that intimate partner violence has historically been discussed in very limited, heteronormative terms. IPV is not specific to heterosexual relationships, and it is not exclusively perpetrated by men against women (Penone and Guarnaccia 2018). While some people are statistically more at risk for experiencing IPV than others, intimate partner violence can target, or be carried out by, individuals of any gender identity, race, age, or sexual orientation.

Feminist Theory and Intimate Partner Violence

Due to mainstream conversations about intimate partner violence, many of us have very specific ideas of what this violence may look like and why it occurs. Books, movies, and social media often depict abusive relationships with a gendered power dynamic. While these relationships do exist, feminist scholars have expanded our understandings of IPV by creating two categories (Johnson 2008; Johnson and Ferraro 2000).

First, "situational couple violence" describes violent acts that stem from short-term stressors and conflicts within a relationship (think financial struggles or household responsibilities). These acts are committed more equally across different gender identities, as they are more about escalating conflict than grabs for power and control (2008). For example, if one partner is found to be cheating, the other might react with an outburst of yelling, name-calling, and belittling. While this behavior is violent, it occurs as a reaction to conflict in the relationship rather than a premeditated action taken to gain control.

Second, "intimate terrorism" describes the power-based violence used repeatedly to gain control in an intimate relationship (2008). This form of violence has historically been tied to hegemonic masculinity and tends to be used against intimate partners who show feminine qualities. This form of IPV is directly linked to patriarchal values because "under patriarchy, masculinity is equated with dominance, independence, rationality, and strength; by contrast femininity is associated with dependence, emotiveness, passivity, and weakness" (De Coster and Heimer 2021, 288).

Another term often used in discussions about IPV is "coercive control." Unlike overt forms of physical violence that are widely recognized as abuse, coercive control is not always so easy to spot. This tactic includes a variety of behaviors that when combined, create an imbalance of power in the relationship, robbing a victim of their right to freely make decisions and exercise autonomy (Mitchell and Raghavan 2019). A perpetrator may use threats or coercion to gain sexual or financial control, or they may monitor their partner's whereabouts to keep them isolated from others. Due to the power dynamic formed under coercive control, it is considered a form of intimate terrorism; this is a form of abuse often rooted in hegemonic masculinity to maintain patriarchal dominance.

After decades of research focused on IPV survivors, activists and feminists adopted the Cycle Theory of Violence (Walker 1979), which we refer to today as the cycle of abuse. The original theory described three phases of abuse: tension building, the acute battering incident, then kindness and contrite loving behavior. In the cycle of abuse, the tension builds via smaller acts of violence, escalates to a major incident of abuse, then immediately calms as the batterer reconciles with their victim to produce a "calm after the storm." Eventually, the shower of affection and gifts ends and the escalation of tension and conflict begins again. Over the years, different disciplines have adapted the cycle and its phases, but the pattern of intensification and de-escalation remain the same.

The cyclical nature of abuse leads to a great deal of victim blaming and misunderstandings regarding intimate partner violence, but let's be clear: violence is never the fault of the survivor. Many victims endure the cycle over and over out of self-preservation and/or the effects of manipulation by their perpetrator. The brain's reaction to trauma is complex and may cause a survivor to suppress memories, form a bond to their abuser, or doubt if they are even experiencing violence in the first place (Arabi 2016). Common discourse that instructs victims to "just leave" the relationship is rarely helpful. As a result, feminist activists and advocates have begun to adopt a more trauma-informed approach to their conversations with survivors.

Feminist Movements to End Intimate Partner Violence

The history of feminist movements in the United States surrounding IPV is long and complex. The Women's Christian Temperance Union was an early advocate against domestic abuse, citing alcohol abuse by men as a factor of violence against women in the 1870s (Connection for Abused Women and their Children 2023). In 1871, Alabama and Massachusetts outlawed the use of physical violence by husbands against their wives. At the turn of the century, "wife beating [became] a relevant topic of discussion in America as it related to the temperance movement, the social purity movement and the women's suffragist movement" (Trieu n.d.).

Over the course of the next several decades, rape crisis lines were established to support survivors, crisis centers and domestic violence shelters opened their doors, and feminist activists and advocates pushed for legal protections against intimate partner violence. In the 1970s, feminist activism gave rise to the Battered Women's Movement (Coene, Vergaert, and Withaeckx 2021). These activists achieved increased resources for survivors, won court cases in all fifty states to outlaw marital rape as a crime, and successfully advocated for the authorization of the Violence Against Women Act

(Trieu n.d.). The foundation built by early feminists has carried us well into the twenty-first century, even as the policies revolving IPV constantly change and evolve.

With activist efforts, education and resources surrounding intimate partner violence have increased greatly over the years. Currently, all fifty states have domestic violence shelters and advocacy centers. Colleges and universities across the country offer bystander intervention programs to teach students about preventing and responding to IPV. National hotlines and networks connect survivors with advocates who can help them seek counseling or make a safety plan. Even with these improvements, feminist activists continue to push for legislative change in pursuit of a world free of intimate partner violence.

Camryn E. O'Riley

See Also: Gaslighting; Hegemonic Masculinity; Patriarchy; Temperance; Violence Against Women Act (1994)

Further Reading

Arabi, Shahida. 2016. *Becoming the Narcissist's Nightmare: How to Devalue and Discard the Narcissist While Supplying Yourself.* New York, NY: SCW Archer Publishing.

Coene, Gily, Eva Vergaert, and Sophie Withaeckx. 2021. "Researching Intimate Partner Violence. Gender, Intersectionality, and Policymaking." *Tijdschrift Voor Genderstudies,* 24, no. 2: 83–8. https://doi.org/10.5117/TVGN2021.2.001.COEN.

Connection for Abused Women and their Children. 2023. "Things to Know About the History of Domestic Violence." *Connection for Abused Women and their Children,* September 7, 2023. Accessed September 16, 2024. https://www.cawc.org/news/things-to-know-about-the-history-of-the-domestic-violence-movement/#:~:text=Early%201970s%3A%20Galvanized%20in%20part,by%20feminist%20activists%20and%20survivors.

De Coster, Stacy, and Karen Heimer. 2021. "Unifying Theory and Research on Intimate Partner Violence: A Feminist Perspective." *Feminist Criminology* 16, no. 3: 286–303. https://doi.org/10.1177/1557085120987615.

Johnson, Michael. 2008. *A Typology of Domestic Violence: Intimate Terrorism, Violent Resistance, and Situational Couple Violence*. Lebanon, NH: Northeastern University Press.

Johnson, Michael, and Kathleen Ferraro. 2000. "Research on Domestic Violence in the 1990s: Making Distinctions." *Journal of Marriage and the Family* 62, no. 4: 948–63. https://search.ebscohost.com/login.aspx?direct=true&db=edsjsr&AN=edsjsr.1566718&authtype=shib&site=eds-live&scope=site&authtype=shib&custid=s8516548.

Mitchell, Jenny, and Chitra Raghavan. 2019. "The Impact of Coercive Control on Use of Specific Sexual Coercion Tactics." *Violence Against Women* 27, no. 2: 187–206. https://doi.org/10.1177/1077801219884127.

National Sexual Violence Resource Center. n.d. "Statistics In-Depth." *National Sexual Violence Resource Center*. Accessed August 24, 2024. https://www.nsvrc.org/statistics/statistics-depth.

Penone, Giulia and Cinzia Guarnaccia. 2018. "Intimate Partner Violence Within Same Sex Couples: A Qualitative Review of The Literature From A Psychodynamic Perspective." *International Journal of Psychoanalysis and Education* 10, no. 1: 32–46. https://search.ebscohost.com/login.aspx?direct=true&db=sxi&AN=130348215&authtype=shib&site=eds-live&scope=site&authtype=shib&custid=s8516548.

Trieu, Sarah. n.d. "History of Intimate Partner Violence Reform." *Freedom and Citizenship.* Accessed August 23, 2024. https://freedomandcitizenship.columbia.edu/ipv-history.

Walker, Lenore. 1979. *The Battered Woman.* Harper Perennial.

K

KINSEY INSTITUTE

The Kinsey Institute is a research center housed at Indiana University with a two-prong mission of continuing Alfred Kinsey's initial team research on human sexuality and to administer the research findings held by the institute. The Kinsey Institute was incorporated as the Institute of Sex Research on April 8, 1947 ("Learn Our History" 2024). However, the origins of what became the Kinsey Institute date back to the petitioning of Indiana University by the Association of Women Students in 1938 for a course for students who were already married or considering the prospect of marriage ("Learn Our History" 2024). Alfred Kinsey was designated to coordinate this new course. Kinsey was a Harvard-trained zoologist who had a passion for research and a burgeoning interest in human sexual behavior—which he thought was severely understudied. By 1940, the administration at Indiana University asked Kinsey to choose between teaching the course on marriage and researching human sexual behavior. Kinsey jumped at the chance to research human sexuality full-time.

Within a year, Kinsey and his team of research associates and assistants had collected over 2,000 sex histories, funded by a newly founded National Council for Research on the Problems of Sex, which was bankrolled by the Rockefeller Foundation. By 1947, Kinsey had secured the Institute of Sex Research as a clearinghouse to hold and preserve his sex research in all its cutting-edge glory. Through a partnership with Indiana University, Kinsey transferred the ownership of all of his research materials to the institute for $1.00, with initial trustees of the institute being listed as Alfred Kinsey, Paul Gebhard, Clyde Martin, and Wardell Pomeroy (Allen et al. 2017). Kinsey's landmark texts *Sexual Behavior in the Human Male* and *Sexual Behavior in the Human Female*, published in 1948 and 1953, respectively, were comprised from studies carried out by Kinsey and colleagues while at the helm of the institute. Kinsey remained in charge of the institute until his death in 1956 (Jones 2013).

In 1981, the Institute of Sex Research was renamed in its founder's honor as the Kinsey Institute for Sex Research. Colloquially known as the Kinsey Institute since the 1980s, the facility is now home to interdisciplinary research spanning areas such as sex, gender, reproduction, and public health, to name a few. Functioning as equal parts archives, sexual histories repository, and research collective, the Kinsey Institute is currently engaged in novel and timely research spanning topics including, but not limited to, gender equity in business, a research initiative devoted to sexual assault, disability, and sexual health, as well as intersectional research regarding sexual health and the Covid-19 pandemic ("Highlights of Research" 2024). Additionally, the Kinsey Institute is currently home to two academic scholarships: the Gina Ogden Curatorial Scholarship for Integrative Approaches to Sex Research and Therapy and the Scholars of Sexology Fellowship. The Kinsey Institute provides distinguished awards for innovative and key contributions to the field of sexology and sexual research, continuing the legacy of its founder, Alfred Kinsey, and cementing the institute's place as an incubator of research and knowledge on all things sexual.

Jeffrey "JJ" Jones

See Also: Sexual Pleasure

Further Reading

Allen, Judith A., Hallimeda E. Allinson, Andrew Clark-Huckstep, Brandon J. Hill, Stephanie A. Sanders, and Liana H. Zhou. 2017. *The Kinsey Institute: The First Seventy Years.* Bloomington, IN: Indiana University Press.

Highlights of Kinsey Institute Research. 2024. *Kinsey Institute.* Accessed February 7, 2025. https://kinseyinstitute.org/research/index.php.

Jones, James H. 2013. *Alfred C. Kinsey: A Life.* New York: W.W. Norton & Co.

Kinsey, Alfred C. 1947. *Sexual Behavior in the Human Male.* Bloomington, IN: Indiana University Press.

Kinsey, Alfred C. 1953. *Sexual Behavior in the Human Female.* Bloomington, IN: Indiana University Press.

Kinsey Archives. 2024. *The Kinsey Institute.* Accessed February 7, 2025. https://archives.iu.edu/repositories/kinsey.

Learn Our History. 2024. *Kinsey Institute.* Accessed February 7, 2025. https://kinseyinstitute.org/about/history/index.php.

Reinisch, June M., and Ruth Beasley. 1991. *The Kinsey Institute New Report on Sex.* New York: Macmillan.

KOCHIYAMA, YURI

Yuri Kochiyama (1921–2014) was a pioneering figure in US Civil Rights and social justice movements. Her life's work is a testament to resilience, transformation, and a deep commitment to justice, making her story essential for understanding intersectional activism.

Born Mary Yuriko Nakahara on May 19, 1921, in San Pedro, California, to Japanese immigrant parents Seiichi Nakahara and Tsuyako "Tsuma" Sawaguchi Nakahara, Kochiyama's early life was marked by a strong sense of community and cultural pride within a Japanese American enclave. Growing up, she experienced race-based discrimination and class-based privilege "as a middle-class *Nisei*, or second-generation Japanese American" (Kao 2019, 61).

The trajectory of her life, however, changed dramatically after the attack on Pearl Harbor in 1941. In the wake of this event, President Franklin D. Roosevelt issued Executive Order 9066, which led to the forced relocation and incarceration of approximately 120,000 Japanese Americans, including the Nakahara family. The anti-Japanese sentiment that followed was intense, with people yelling to "get the 'Japs' out of California" (Kochiyama 1992, 11). Kochiyama's father was detained just hours after the attack, which led to his health decline and death at fifty-four (Kao 2019, 62–3). Kochiyama, alongside her mother and brother, was interned at the Jerome War Relocation Center in Arkansas.

Postwar Activism

Recounting the impact of the war and internment on her identity formation, Kochiyama wrote, "I was one of these real American patriots then. I've changed now" (1992, 15). After the war, Kochiyama moved to New York City and married Bill Kochiyama, a Japanese American Second World War veteran. They had six children together: Billy, Audee, Aichi, Eddie, Jimmy, and Tommy (Fujino 2005). Living in Harlem, a predominantly African American neighborhood, transformed Kochiyama's perspective. She became deeply involved in local activism and began to see the connections between different struggles against oppression.

One significant contribution was her involvement in the Asian American Movement during the 1960s and 1970s. She helped organize and participate in protests and educational campaigns highlighting the contributions and challenges of Asian Americans. Her advocacy for reparations was particularly notable. She was a key member of the National Coalition for Redress/Reparations (NCRR), which successfully campaigned for the Civil Liberties Act of 1988 (Fujino 2005, 270). This act granted an official apology and financial compensation to Japanese Americans interned during the Second World War.

A turning point in her activism came when she met Malcolm X in 1963. Their friendship profoundly influenced her political views. When Kochiyama was introduced to Malcolm, she expressed disagreement about his political attitude toward integration but soon learned more about the nuance of the Civil Rights Movement (Kochiyama 136). His ideas about self-determination and systemic racism deeply resonated with Kochiyama, and she supported his efforts by attending his Organization of Afro-American Unity (OAAU) meetings. They kept connected by writing to each other, and their families became very close. Kochiyama was present at the Audubon Ballroom on February 21, 1965, the day Malcolm X was assassinated. In a now-iconic photograph, Kochiyama is seen cradling Malcolm X's head as he lay dying (Cosgrove 2014). Later, she wrote, "Malcolm is that North Star . . . triumphantly illuminating today's stark atmosphere, giving light and direction, invincible and inextinguishable" (Fujino 2005, 161).

Kochiyama led and participated in a number of activist movements. For instance, she led a letter-writing campaign to support the 442nd Infantry Regiment—an all-Japanese American unit during the Second World War (Kao 2019, 68). She also founded the Concerned Japanese Americans organization (CJA) with her husband Bill "in response to the surge in anti-Iranian sentiment following the November 1979 seizure of the US embassy in Tehran" (Kao 2019, 70). Likewise, she worked with the Commission on Wartime Internment and Relocation of Civilians (CWIRC), pressing for a review of the internment camps' circumstances and impacts (Kao 2019, 71).

Kochiyama's primary passion, however, was fighting "unjust imprisonment" (Kao 2019, 65). Her dedication to prisoners' rights extended to high-profile cases like that of David Wong, whose exoneration she supported, and Mumia Abu-Jamal, a former Black Panther on death row.

Kochiyama's activism addressed issues of race, class, and gender and demonstrated international solidarity. She was involved in numerous movements, including the fight for reparations for Japanese American internees, Puerto Rican independence, and the anti-Vietnam War movement. Her work demonstrated the interconnectedness of different struggles for justice and the importance of solidarity across communities.

Legacy

Yuri Kochiyama's legacy is one of tireless dedication to justice and human rights. Her life exemplifies the importance of recognizing interconnected struggles, as she believed that "historically, Americans have always been putting people behind walls" and emphasized the need to speak out against such injustices (Kochiyama 1992, 18).

Kochiyama died at her home in Berkeley, California, on June 1, 2014, at the age of ninety-three. Her countless speeches, publications, nominations, awards, and recognitions demonstrate the incredible impact Kochiyama had worldwide. In 2005, she was nominated for the Nobel Peace Prize as part of the "1,000 Women for the Nobel Peace Prize 2005" initiative, which highlighted her significant contributions to global peace and justice (PeaceWomen n.d.). Her activism earned her the 1993 Martin Luther King Jr. Humanitarian Award from Hunter College, acknowledging her unwavering dedication to civil rights (Fujino 2005). Additionally, she was honored with the 2010 Community Activist Award from the Asian American Legal Defense and Education Fund, reflecting her lifelong commitment to fighting for marginalized communities.

Kochiyama's legacy has been extensively documented in biographies and autobiographies that celebrate her life's work. Diane C. Fujino's *Heartbeat of Struggle: The Revolutionary Life of Yuri Kochiyama* (2005) provides a comprehensive look at her activism and influence, while Kochiyama's

(2004) own collection of interviews and writings, *Passing It On: A Memoir*, offers personal insights into her experiences and enduring legacy. These works, alongside her numerous speeches and publications, continue to inspire and educate future generations about the importance of intersectional activism. Yuri Kochiyama's life is a powerful reminder of the enduring impact one individual can have on the fight for justice and equality, and her contributions will continue to resonate for years to come.

Carole Yoke-kew Chee

See Also: Civil Rights Movement; Intersectionality; Prison Abolition Movements

Further Reading

"1000 PeaceWomen." n.d. *PeaceWomen Across the Globe.* Accessed July 13, 2024. https://1000peacewomen.org/en/network/1000-peacewomen.

Cosgrove, Ben. 2014. "Yuri Kochiyama, at Malcolm X's Side When He Died, Is Dead at 93." *Time*, June 2, 2014. https://time.com/3880035/yuri-kochiyama-at-malcolm-xs-side-when-he-died-is-dead-at-93/.

Fujino, Diane C. 2005. *Heartbeat of Struggle: The Revolutionary Life of Yuri Kochiyama.* Minneapolis: University of Minnesota Press.

Kao, Grace Y. 2019. "Setting the Captives Free: Yuri Kochiyama and Her Lifelong Fight against Unjust Imprisonment." In *Can I Get a Witness? Thirteen Peacemakers, Community Builders, and Agitators for Faith and Justice*, edited by Charles Marsh, Shea Tuttle, and Daniel P. Rhodes. Grand Rapids: Eerdmans Publishing Co.

Kochiyama, Yuri. 1992. "Then Came the War." In *Asian Americans: Oral Histories of First to Fourth Generation Americans from China, the Philippines, Japan, India, the Pacific Islands, Vietnam, and Cambodia,* edited by Joann Faung Jean Lee. New York: The New Press.

Kochiyama, Yuri. 2004. *Passing It On: A Memoir.* Los Angeles: UCLA Asian American Studies Center Press.

KRAMER, LARRY

Silence=Death. When the HIV/AIDS crisis started in the early 1980s, Larry Kramer's (1935–2020) voice became one of the first to proclaim inaction and silence would kill more queer people. Known for his blunt and crude language, Kramer's advocacy worked to shock people, especially other gay men, into action (Ulaby 2020). Upon his death in 2020, commentators cited Kramer's essay "1,112 and Counting" as a critical turning point in the nation's response to HIV/AIDS. In this essay, Kramer (2020) declared, "If this article doesn't scare the shit out of you, we're in real trouble. If this article doesn't rouse you to anger, fury, rage, and action, gay men may have no future on this earth." According to Bonnie Dow (1994), his provocative language provided gay men with another way to understand themselves, which included a newfound dedication to the survival of their community.

Among one of Kramer's first accomplishments as an advocate was the founding of Gay Men's Health Crisis—an organization dedicated to providing services to people with HIV/AIDS. Because many in government and the medical industry were slow to respond to HIV/AIDS, Gay Men's Health Crisis's services were crucial (Ulaby 2020). Yet, Kramer disagreed with members of the organization over their messaging and tactics. Writing about his struggle with Gay Men's Health Crisis, Kramer wrote his semi-autobiographical play, *The Normal Heart*, and made his mark on popular culture (Miller 2022).

Larry Kramer's advocacy work helped to bring awareness to the HIV/AIDS crisis, in part by shocking people, especially other gay men, into action (Laurence Agron/Dreamstime.com).

Later, Kramer helped form the AIDS Coalitional to Unleash Power, better known by its acronym, ACT UP. ACT UP used visible, direct action tactics to ensure media attention. Such tactics included protesting at church services and "die ins" to dramatize the death toll of HIV/AIDS and inaction surrounding the issue (Montalvo 2021). If silence is death, Kramer's loud and fierce advocacy helped ensure many would survive the HIV/AIDS crisis.

Joshua H. Miller

See Also: Anger; Feminist Killjoy; *Lawrence v. Texas* (2003); *Obergefell v. Hodges* (2015); Stonewall Riots (1969)

Further Reading

Dow, Bonnie J. 1994. "AIDS, Perspective by Incongruity, and Gay Identity in Larry Kramer's '1,112 and Counting.'" *Communication Studies* 41: 225–40. https://doi.org/10.1080/10510979409368426.

Kramer, Larry. 2020. "March 27, 1983: 1,112 and Counting." *Los Angeles Blade*, May 27, 2020. https://www.losangelesblade.com/2020/05/27/march-27-1983-1112-and-counting/. Accessed March 9, 2025. Original published March 27, 1983.

Miller, Joshua H. 2022. "*The Normal Heart* and 'Sickly' Body: The Case of Matthew Bomer's Extreme Weight Loss." *Communication Quarterly* 70: 365–81. https://doi.org/10.1080/01463373.2022.2073827.

Montalvo, David. 2021. "How AIDS Activists Used 'Die-Ins' to Demand Attention to the Growing Epidemic." *History*, June 2, 2021. https://www.history.com/news/aids-activism-protests-act-up-die-ins. Accessed Mary 9, 2025.

Rand, Erin J. 2008. "An Inflammatory Fag and a Queer Form: Larry Kramer, Polemics, and Rhetorical Agency." *Quarterly Journal of Speech* 94: 297–319. https://doi.org/10.1080/00335630802210377

Ulaby, Neda. 2020. "Larry Kramer, Pioneering AIDS Activist and Write, Dies at 84." *NPR*, May 27, 2020. https://www.npr.org/2020/05/27/512714500/larry-kramer-pioneering-aids-activist-and-writer-dies-at-84. Accessed March 9, 2025.

L

LABOR ACTIVISM

Labor activism refers to efforts by workers to change their working conditions and/or compensation. You may have felt the impact of labor activism when the Writers Guild of America and actors in SAG-AFTRA went on strike in the summer of 2023. Popular television shows and movies stopped production, and viewers were left with reruns. That same summer and fall, UPS drivers and United Auto Workers went on strike to leverage their power while negotiating new contracts. Amazon and Starbucks employees at several shops and warehouses as well as nurses and healthcare workers across the United States took steps to organize unions and gain recognition by their companies. Metro bus drivers in Los Angeles staged a sick-out in May of 2024 to call for added protections after bus drivers were stabbed and assaulted. All of these activities leveraged the collective power of workers to raise awareness and support from the public to put pressure on employers to meet worker demands.

Workers have organized for the eight-hour day, sick days, paid time off, the right to have meal and bathroom breaks as well as for contracts setting wages and benefits like health and life insurance. In the United States, workers have historically formed labor unions and allied with other groups to advocate for their needs. Labor activism consists of efforts ranging from picketing and strikes, to slow downs, to sick-outs, to collective bargaining, and organizing to pass laws. While some labor activism is focused on working conditions and compensation at individual shops or businesses, labor activism has also been used to pass laws such as the Fair Labor Standards Act (FLSA), the Lilly Ledbetter Act, and the Family and Medical Leave Act (FMLA). Organized labor, another term for labor unions, has had a tumultuous relationship with the feminist movement—sometimes working in concert when their objectives aligned and sometimes at odds when interests diverged. However, since the mid-1800s when labor unions began to form, women have been working and organizing to improve their working conditions. This entry explores the intersection of women, labor activism, and feminism.

When industry was in its infant stages in the mid-1800s, early trade unions sought to protect middle-class lifestyles for their members. They called for a family wage so that a man could provide for a family. Labor scholar Martha May explained that the assumption was that such a wage would preserve the distinction between the public and domestic spheres, help maintain social order, and keep tradesmen in the middle class as opposed to sliding into the poorer working class (2013). The wage was a class issue that capitalists (business owners) opposed. Because women were also typically discounted in the public sphere (business, politics, etc.), the men who were organizing labor unions typically excluded women in the unionizing efforts rather than fight for union rights and fight for women's rights.

This, however, changed with the Knights of Labor. The preamble of the Constitution of the Knights of Labor in 1878 pledged, "To secure for both sexes equal pay for equal work." By 1886 there were approximately 50,000 women in the union (Illinois Labor History Society). Through most of the twenty-first century, women's participation in unions lagged behind men's participation. Some scholars posit that one contributing factor to women's lagging participation is that household responsibilities end up taking time and attention from women that is subsequently unavailable for labor activism (Cornfield, Filho, and Chun 1990; Hyman 2013). That said, many women have played important roles in labor activism. Housewives supported striking workers because household life has always been impacted by how workers are treated and paid. During this era, Mary G. Harris Jones—known as Mother Jones—was one of the most prominent labor rights and union organizers; she famously advocated for miners' safety, and she remains a well-known labor rights activist. Moreover, women were members of skilled trades like the cigar makers and autoworkers. Women such as Frances Perkins were appointed to the New York State Industrial Commission. She later became Secretary of Labor in President Franklin Delano Roosevelt's administration (Frances Perkins Center). Women's auxiliaries were organizations of the wives of male union members. They played important roles providing food, first aid, and administrative work for unions during strikes (Lasky 2013).

Class and Diversity in Women's Labor Activism

The Industrial Workers of the World (IWW) organized factory workers regardless of gender, race, or ethnicity. Indeed, African Americans, immigrants, and Americans forced off land into industry formed the bulk of the membership of the IWW, making it the most representative union (Dubofsky 2000, 13). Suffragist and labor rights activist Elizabeth Gurley Flynn, a member of the IWW, helped organize strikes of textile workers and raised money and support for miners on strike. She went on to cofound the American Civil Liberties Union (ACLU).

The Women Trade Union League (WTUL), founded in 1903, saw middle-class women helping working-class women organize through the first part of the twentieth century. The WTUL was a diverse organization in terms of both class and culture. Members leveraged existing networks of women and reached out in immigrants' native languages to help working-class women overcome obstacles to organizing. English-speaking members taught English, helping women immigrants advocate for themselves. They met in homes and neighborhoods where women were comfortable, instead of distant union halls. The WTUL grew out of principles from social feminism (Hyman 2013).

On March 25, 1911, the Triangle Shirtwaist Fire killed hundreds of women seamstresses working inside a building that the owner had locked to ensure no worker could leave early. This horrific event called attention to the dangers women workers faced. Feminists argued that the right to vote would help women workers bring about changes to their working conditions. They marched alongside women factory workers. At that time, the leaders in the feminist movement tended to be middle-class or wealthy women who did not have paid jobs. Nonetheless, they picketed, marched in parades, and advocated for worker rights alongside poorer and lower-class working women. This tragic event galvanized both women and workers and connected issues of labor and feminism.

Women's Concerns and Organized Labor

In the first half of the twentieth century, though there were some women's union chapters, many union chapters set up women's committees that, while giving women a space to articulate their concerns and needs, did not provide a mechanism for enacting change with the backing of the union. In the early 1900s, company owners justified paying women less than men on the grounds that women's needs would be paid for out of the wages of their husband or father. Women's wages were to supplement those basic needs, which meant that unmarried, widowed, and independent women did not earn enough to pay for their basic needs or those of any children they might care for. Martha May argues that this was a consequence of the earlier family wage arguments that unions promoted (2013). Women and their allies called for seamstresses and other women workers to be paid enough to care for themselves and their children. However, the American Federation of Labor (AFL) worked against a living wage for women workers, thinking that raising women's wages would restrict men's ability to negotiate higher pay for men's wages.

The labor market changed during the First World War when young men left vacant positions in factories that women subsequently filled. The AFL's priorities included protecting men's jobs, which conflicted with women's priorities. This is when the family wage arguments became a tool of gender division rather than class distinction. Men argued that to be men, men needed to be able to work, and if women were taking those jobs, men could not have a job to provide for their family (May 2013). The 1919 Spanish flu pandemic further strained the workforce. Due to illnesses and the high death toll, more women needed to earn enough to provide for their families. With the ratification of the Nineteenth Amendment granting women the right to vote, women had more political power than ever before to advocate for their needs once men began returning from war. Though the public narrative was that women would return home to care for their families, those in government knew that women's presence in the workforce would not subside to prewar levels (Hendrickson 2008). A similar pattern was seen with the Second World War a few decades later.

President Wilson established the Women's Bureau to investigate working conditions women faced (Boris and Orleck 2011; Hendrickson 2008). Through its research, this agency showed that women's concerns were not always or even often represented by unions. When women separated into their own union chapter or caucus, they were able to bargain with employers to protect gender-specific work concerns such as minimum wages and maximum hours (Cobble 1990, 534).

Entangled Interests of Feminism and Women Workers

During the 1960s and 1970s feminist activism especially sought to create equal opportunities for women and men, but some of the arguments to advance this cause did not align with the interests of women—particularly in women-dominated working professions such as nursing. While feminists called for women to become doctors, many nurses felt their professional accomplishments were brushed aside by feminists (Lingel, Clark-Parsons, and Branciforte 2022). Through the 1970s and beyond, many women in predominantly female professions sought to be recognized as competent, valuable, and professional with needs and concerns that deserved increased pay and safety standards. They argued that even caring fields—such as teaching and nursing—need to be paid well; loving one's job will not keep a roof over your head.

Even as interests of predominantly female trade unions sometimes clashed with goals promoted by mainstream feminists (who were predominantly white and middle or upper class) during the 1960s and 1970s, more women than ever before became union members. Part of this was due to increased public sector unionizing and the increased number of public jobs from 1965 to 1975 (Bell 2013). Teachers, some nurses, clerical staff for government offices, and other such jobs became more powerful particularly as they gained the legal protection for collective bargaining after 1975. As some of these professions like nursing and teaching were predominantly female, women began not just participating in union activities but also leading them. Deborah Bell argues that "an ongoing impact of the Women's movement has been to legitimate the economic and political activism of women on their own behalf, part of which is a more positive attitude toward unions" (2013).

In recent years, feminists have faced economic pressure to commodify their activism. Though many feminists are white middle-class women, the economic and social pressures from the Covid-19 pandemic have made their class status more precarious than ever. Many have found ways to earn money from their skills learned through public feminist activism. Kaitlynn Mendes dubs these activists "fempreneurs," noting how they write blogs advancing women's concerns, sell branded merchandise, or become paid journalists to provide financial compensation for their efforts (2022).

The story of women, work, feminism, and labor intersects in activism, or when individuals join together in action on their behalf. Women, even when not unionized or paid for their labor, have played an important role advocating for protections for workers. Through contributions to unions and by leveraging their own social networks, women have advanced their concerns to public notice. While there have been times when class and cultural differences have set women workers and the women's movement at odds, feminist labor scholars note that solidarity and progress is possible the more people come together. In recent years the bulk of union growth has come from women and people of color (Torre 2023).

Kristin Summer-Mathe Coletta

See Also: Capitalism; Equal Pay; Family and Medical Leave Act (1993, FMLA); Liberal Feminism; Lilly Ledbetter Fair Pay Act (2009)

Further Reading

Bell, Deborah E. 2013. "Unionized Women in State and Local Government." In *Women, Work and Protest: A Century of US Women's Labor History*, edited by Ruth Milkman, 280–99. New York: Routledge. https://doi.org/10.4324/9780203104026-13.

Boris, Eileen, and Annelise Orleck. 2011. "Feminism and the Labor Movement: A Century of Collaboration and Conflict." *New Labor Forum* 20, no. 1: 33–41. http://www.jstor.org/stable/27920539.

Cobble, Dorothy Sue. 1990. "Rethinking Troubled Relations Between Women and Unions: Craft Unionism and Female Activism." *Feminist Studies* 16, no. 3: 519–48. https://doi.org/10.2307/3178018.

Cornfield, Daniel B., Hilquias B. Cavalcanti Filho, and Bang Jee Chun. 1990. "Household, Work, and Labor Activism: Gender Differences in the Determinants of Union Membership Participation." *Work and Occupations* 17, no. 2: 131–51. https://doi.org/10.1177/0730888490017002001.

Dubofsky, Melvyn. 2000. *We Shall be All: A History of the Industrial Workers of the World.* Edited by Joseph A. McCartin. Urbana: University of Illinois Press.

Frances Perkins Center. 2023. "Her Life." Accessed May 14, 2024. https://francesperkinscenter.org/learn/her-life/.

Hendrickson, Mark. 2008. "Gender Research as Labor Activism: The Women's Bureau in the New Era." *Journal of Policy History* 20, no. 4: 482–515. https://doi.org/10.1353/jph.0.0025.

Hyman, Colette A. 2013. "Labor Organizing and Female Institution-Building: The Chicago Women's Trade Union League 1904–24." In *Women, Work and Protest: A Century of US Women's Labor History*, edited by Ruth Milkman, 22–41. New York: Routledge. https://doi.org/10.4324/9780203104026-2.

Illinois Labor History Society. 2024. "When Women Were Knights." Accessed May 14, 2024. https://www.illinoislaborhistory.org/labor-history-articles/when-women-were-knights.

Lasky, Marjorie Penn. 2013. "'Where I was a Person': The Ladies' Auxiliary in the 1934 Minneapolis Teamsters' Strikes." In *Women, Work and Protest: A Century of US Women's Labor History*, edited by Ruth Milkman, 181–205. New York: Routledge. https://doi.org/10.4324/9780203104026-9.

Lingel, Jessa, Rosemary Clark-Parsons, and Kim Branciforte. 2022. "More than Handmaids: Nursing, Labor Activism and Feminism." *Gender, Work & Organization* 29, no. 4: 1149–63. https://doi.org/10.1111/gwao.12816.

May, Martha. 2013. "Bread Before Roses: American Workingmen, Labor Unions and the Family Wage." In *Women, Work and Protest: A Century of US Women's Labor History*, edited by Ruth Milkman, 1–21. New York: Routledge. https://doi.org/10.4324/9780203104026-1.

Mendes, Kaitlynn. 2022. "Digital Feminist Labor: The Immaterial, Aspirational, and Affective Labor of Feminist Activists and Fempreneurs." *Women's History Review* 31, no. 4: 693–712. https://doi.org/10.1080/09612025.2021.1944353.

Milkman, Ruth. 2013. "Women Workers, Feminism and the Labor Movement Since the 1960's." In *Women, Work and Protest: A Century of US Women's Labor History*, edited by Ruth Milkman, 300–22. New York: Routledge. https://doi.org/10.4324/9780203104026-14.

Torre, Margarita. 2023. "Women and the New Labor Activism: Gender Trends and Attitudes Toward Unions." *Work and Occupations* 50, no. 3: 412–19. https://doi.org/10.1177/07308884231162950.

LACKS, HENRIETTA

Henrietta Lacks (1920–51) was an African American woman who became a pivotal figure in medical research and ethical discussions surrounding informed consent and racial disparities in healthcare. Her legacy is intimately tied to the HeLa cells, which were derived from her cervical cancer tumor without her knowledge or consent and which are named after her.

Early Life

Lacks was born on August 1, 1920, in Roanoke, Virginia, in a family of farmers. She was the granddaughter of enslaved individuals and grew up in a segregated society that limited opportunities for people of color. In 1935, her family moved to Clover, Virginia, where they continued to work on tobacco farms (Skloot 2010).

At the age of fourteen, she married David Lacks, and the couple eventually moved to Baltimore, Maryland. They had five children together, and she worked various jobs to support her family (Skloot 2010). Despite her limited education, Lacks was a devoted mother and provided for her children in a society that often marginalized their existence.

Diagnosis and Treatment

In January 1951, Lacks sought medical attention at Johns Hopkins Hospital and was diagnosed with cervical cancer. During her treatment, physicians took a biopsy of her tumor without informing her or her family of their intention to culture the cells (Skloot 2010). The biopsy of Lacks's tumor was sent to George Gey, the director of the Tissue Culture laboratory at John Hopkins University (Lucey 2009). Lacks's tumor cells were the first human cells successfully cultured and maintained outside the human body, leading to what became known as HeLa cells (Lyapun 2019). Lacks passed away shortly after the medical breakthrough on October 4, 1951, and the discovery was not communicated to her family until decades later in 1975 (Skloot 2010).

The Rise of HeLa Cells and Ethical Implications

The HeLa cells were named after Henrietta Lacks in a way that concealed her identity by using only the first two letters of her first and last name. Lacks's cells revolutionized medical research. They were the first immortal human cell line, meaning they could divide indefinitely in laboratory conditions (Lyapun 2019). Scientists quickly recognized their potential for research and cloned the cells in 1955 (Piccotti 2024). HeLa cells were instrumental in developing the polio vaccine, studying cancer, gene mapping, AIDS, the effects of radiation and toxic substances, in vitro fertilization, and more (Skloot 2010). HeLa cells also enabled the development of Covid-19 vaccines (Piccotti 2024).

The widespread use of HeLa cells in research raises ethical questions regarding consent. Lacks never gave permission for her cells to be harvested, cloned, or sold without her knowledge or any compensation for her family. In the 1950s, the medical community largely ignored the rights of patients, particularly those from marginalized communities (Skloot 2010). The requests for HeLa cells were extensive during the 1950s and supplied to scientists in the United States and internationally (Lucey 2009). They continue to be widely used today.

The story of Henrietta Lacks and the HeLa cells brought to light significant ethical issues in medical research, particularly concerning informed consent and the exploitation of vulnerable populations. Informed consent is a fundamental principle in medical ethics, requiring that patients are adequately educated about the nature of medical procedures and research before agreeing to participate, enabling them to make autonomous decisions about their care (Shah 2024). Lacks's case exemplifies the historical exploitation of African Americans in medical research. Lacks's experience, alongside other historical abuses, highlighted the need for reform in how medical research is conducted, particularly concerning marginalized groups (Skloot 2010). In 1974, the National Research Act was passed in the United States, establishing the National Commission for the Protection of Human Subjects of Biomedical and Behavioral Research. This act emphasizes the importance of informed consent and the ethical treatment of research subjects, making Lacks's legacy a catalyst for change in research ethics and practices (Skloot 2010).

The medical community's historical exploitation of Black bodies is rooted in a legacy of racism and sexism that continues to affect healthcare access and treatment today. The lack of informed consent in Lacks's case exemplifies the broader systemic injustices faced by women of color in medical settings, where their voices and rights are often overlooked.

The cells of Henrietta Lacks have led to some of the most remarkable innovations in science. Her HeLa cells are still alive today and with approximately 55 million or more used in at least 75,000 studies to date; it can be assumed that her HeLa cells are in almost every biological laboratory in the world (Starkman 2022). Lacks has saved countless lives and sparked the creation of the entire field of virology.

Arrington Stoll

See Also: Bioethics; Bodily Autonomy

Further Reading

Lucey, Brendan P., Walter A. Nelson-Rees, and Grover M. Hutchins. 2009. "Henrietta Lacks, HeLa Cells, and Cell Culture Contamination." *Archives of Pathology and Laboratory Medicine* 133, no. 9: 1463–7. https://doi.org/10.5858/133.9.1463.

Lyapun, I. N., B. G. Andryukov, and M. P. Bynina. 2019. "HeLa Cell Culture: Immortal Heritage of Henrietta Lacks." *Molecular Genetics, Microbiology and Virology* 34, no. 4: 195–200. https://doi.org/10.3103/s0891416819040050.

Piccotti, Tyler. 2024 "Henrietta Lacks: Biography, Cervical Cancer Patient, HeLa Cells." *Biography*, January 24, 2024. https://www.biography.com/history-culture/henrietta-lacks.

Shah, Parth. 2024. "Informed Consent." *StatPearls* [Internet], October 15, 2024. https://www.ncbi.nlm.nih.gov/books/NBK430827/.

Skloot, Rebecca. 2010. *The Immortal Life of Henrietta Lacks*. New York: Crown Publishing Group.

Starkman, Evan. 2022. "*What Are HeLa Cells?" WebMD*, January 22, 2022. https://www.webmd.com/cancer/cervical-cancer/hela-cells-cervical-cancer.

LAWRENCE V. TEXAS (2003)

Lawrence v. Texas (2003) was a pivotal case in the fight for LGBTQ+ rights, which built on the legacies of *Griswold* (1965) and *Roe* (1973), overturning previous decisions that outlawed homosexual sex. But a complete understanding of this case requires some contextualization from past cases.

Loving v. Virginia was a 1967 case about interracial marriage. At that point in much of America, it was illegal for white people be in interracial relationships. The Supreme Court struck down those laws in 1967 and in the process established that marriage—to the partner of an individual's choice—is a constitutional right. A person, the Court opined, has a constitutional right to decide with whom they are going to spend their life. Decades later, this would become an integral piece of the puzzle as the argument for LGBTQ+ equality went forward.

In 1986 a very different decision was handed down in the *Bowers v. Hardwick* (1986) case. Here, the Court decided that a Georgia law outlawing homosexual sex was constitutional. In other words, it was perfectly fine to criminalize homosexuality. One of the opinions went so far as to quote a famous

British politician who said homosexual sex was an "infamous crime against nature," worse than rape, and "a crime not fit to be named" (*Bowers v. Hardwick 1986*).

Notably, the Court reasoned, "the fact that homosexual conduct occurs in the privacy of the home does not affect the result." The majority opinion argued that since the majority of people believed homosexuality was immoral, it was perfectly fine to legislate morality. The dissenters, however, saw this as a completely different issue. They stated,

> I believe we must analyze respondent Hardwick's claim in the light of the values that underlie the constitutional right to privacy. If that right means anything, it means that, before Georgia can prosecute its citizens for making choices about the most intimate aspects of their lives, it must do more than assert that the choice they have made is an "*abominable crime not fit to be named among Christians*." (*Bowers v. Hardwick* 1986)

Here we must observe that the dissent was couched in the right to privacy. As noted in the entry for *Griswold* (1965), sometimes the dissent comes to carry the day. Ultimately, privacy came to be the heart of this movement. The impact of this dissent for *Bowers* (1986) is clear in *Lawrence* (2003).

The reason it is important to understand the nature of *Bowers* (1986) is because *Lawrence* (2003) overturned *Bowers* (1986). The Court had already decided a person could marry who they want to marry in *Loving v. Virginia* (1967). One would think that could mean a person could be in a relationship with whom they wanted to be in a relationship. But for many this was a thornier issue than what appeared on the surface. To some it seemed so simple—a person has the right to a relationship, and that's it. But for others, it led to hard questions about "what IS a marriage?" or "what IS a relationship?" *Lawrence* (2003) cut through some of that by establishing that laws that criminalized homosexual sex were unconstitutional, thereby overturning *Bowers* (1986).

The specifics in the *Lawrence* (2003) case are instructive. In 1986, Houston police entered John Lawrence's apartment because of a weapons complaint and saw him and another adult man, Tyron Garner, engaging in a private, consensual sexual act. Lawrence and Garner were arrested and convicted of deviant sexual intercourse in violation of a Texas statute forbidding two persons of the same sex to engage in intimate sexual conduct. But this time the Court veered sharply from their *Bowers* opinion. They argued that just because some see something as immoral doesn't mean we should criminalize it. And building on the legacy of *Griswold* (1965), the Court argued that this act did not involve coercion or anything public—it was private and consensual—so there was no compelling interest for government intrusion. Here again we see the importance of privacy to equality.

Ultimately, *Lawrence* (2003) proved to be a turning point in the fight for equality. It led the way for future cases that would ultimately legalize gay marriage and even leave a path open for transgender rights.

M. Elizabeth Thorpe

See Also: Anti-Miscegenation Laws; *Griswold v. Connecticut* (1965); Queer Theory; Right to Privacy; Stonewall Riots (1969)

Further Reading

Bowers v. Hardwick, 478 U.S. 186. 1986.
Lawrence v. Texas, 539 U.S. 558. 2003.

LESBIAN CONNECTION

Lesbian Connection (*LC*) is a magazine "for, by, and about lesbians," first published in 1974 (Elsie Publishing Institute n.d.). *LC* is a grassroots forum, written and majority funded by readers, and each cover states "Free to lesbians worldwide: but the suggestion donation is $7/issue (more if you can, less if you can't)." Magazine content includes information for lesbians on places to live and travel, websites, lesbian cultural events, conferences, lesbian land and retirement communities, items like books and CDs, lesbian lawyers and other professionals, and a range of additional topics relevant to its readership. *LC* also includes reviews, articles, and letters "dealing with whatever issues *LC*'s readers are thinking about, from gay marriage to health issues, relationships and politics" (Elsie Publishing Institute n.d.).

Women in the lesbian collective Ambitious Amazons began *Lesbian Connection* in an effort to communicate with a broader audience of lesbians who would otherwise be unable to learn about the events, communities, and information within its pages. The group decided that the content of the magazine should be created by readers, with editors acting as "'caretakers of [the] forum' and not as writers" (Whitt 2008, 163). They gathered in East Lansing, Michigan, to mimeograph and mail 400 copies of the first issue in October 1974, then 1,200 copies by the third issue. In an unpublished history of *Lesbian Connection*, editor Margy Lesher shared that the women "envisioned it as a place to be able to announce what was going on for lesbians, which would encourage more things to happen for lesbians . . . We wanted to try to encourage the growth of the lesbian movement" (Whitt 2008, 164).

One unique feature of *Lesbian Connection* is the section "Contact Dykes," which includes names and contact information for lesbians worldwide who are willing to provide information on lodging, food, and activities to other women traveling near their area. It also includes the weekly comic strip *Dykes to Watch Out For*, which ran from 1983 to 2008 and was created by cartoonist Alison Bechdel (author of graphic memoir *Fun Home*). A 1985 strip titled "The Rule" inspired what would become known as the Bechdel Test, a measure for the representation of women in film and television.

Throughout its history, there have been occasions in which issues of *Lesbian Connection* have been rejected by women's prisons, often due to the existence of an image or drawing that features nudity, such as a bare-chested woman at a festival (Amazons 2024). The fifty-year anniversary issue of *LC* notes recent challenges in the state of Texas: between 2019 and 2021, eight issues were rejected, one for including an ad with a small drawing of a woman, one for a review of the book *Headcase: LGBTQ Writers and Artists on Mental Health and Wellness*, and the rest for *Dykes to Watch Out For* comic strips. Two of the rejected strips are about the birth of a lesbian couple's son—as the Ambitious Amazons put it, "you tell us if these are 'sexually explicit images.' By the way, according to the Prison Policy Initiative, more than half (58%) of women in US prisons are mothers, as are 80% of the women in jails" (Amazons 2024). Since it began publication, *Lesbian Connection* has been mailed to readers in a plain envelope, without the word "lesbian" appearing anywhere on the outside (Elsie Publishing Institute n.d.).

Scholar Jan Whitt writes that *LC* is among the alternative publications that "helped lesbians build communities, and they gave readers ways to combat feelings of marginalization" (Whitt 2008, 166). These publications "gave voice to a nearly silent minority and disseminated news about events that spawned profound social change . . . it is impossible to gauge the importance of lesbian newsletters, magazines, journals, and newspapers in terms of circulation figures, income, or even the longevity" (Whitt 2008, 166).

Hannah Jones

See Also: Bechdel Test; Consciousness Raising; Queer Theory; Women's Liberation Movement

Further Reading

Ambitious Amazons. 2024. "Lesbian Connection Banned in Texas." *Lesbian Connection* 51, no. 3: 6. Seattle, WA: Elsie Publishing Institute.

Elsie Publishing Institute. n.d. "Welcome to Lesbian Connection." Accessed December 7, 2024. https://www.lconline.org/about/welcome/.

Evans, Robert C. 2017. *Great Events from History: LGBTQ Events*, Vol. 1, 2nd ed. Detroit, MI: Salem Press.

Whitt, Jan. 2008. *Women in American Journalism: A New History*. Urbana: University of Illinois Press. http://www.jstor.org/stable/10.5406/jj.11249270.10.

LESBIAN CONTINUUM

Writer, poet, and radical feminist Adrienne Rich introduced the concept of the lesbian continuum in her article "Compulsory Heterosexuality and Lesbian Existence," published in 1980. She defines the lesbian continuum as "a range—through each woman's life and throughout history—of woman-identified experience; not simply the fact that a woman has had or consciously desired genital sexual experience with another woman" (Rich 1980, 648). Or to put it another way, the lesbian continuum encompasses the variety of ways (including sex) that women support one another, working together to survive and thrive, and draw their life's joy and sustenance from relationship with each other. In the essay, Rich sets out to critique compulsory heterosexuality—more specifically, the "virtual or total neglect of lesbian existence" in writing, including feminist scholarship, and how and why women's relationships with one another have been invalidated throughout history (Rich 1980, 632).

Compulsory Heterosexuality and Lesbian Existence

Rich argues that across time and cultures, women have cultivated "independent, nonheterosexual, woman-connected existence" within their contexts, and that many have believed they are alone in doing so (Rich 1980, 635). She outlines the "pervasive cluster of forces, ranging from physical brutality to control of consciousness," that enforce patriarchy and describes how some of these forces are easier to recognize than others (Rich 1980, 640). This range of patriarchal forces teaches women that marriage and attraction toward men are inevitable, regardless of how unsatisfying or harmful that may be.

Essentially, from birth, girls are raised to idealize heterosexual marriage and family as the only expression of true love and their life's ultimate goal and fulfillment. Practically every movie made for girls involves a heterosexual romance. The children's toys made for girls (e.g., babydolls) often encourage them to play by imagining themselves as already married with children. Women and girls are encouraged to spend enormous energies planning their weddings even before they are old enough to date. Historically, women have been forced into heterosexual marriages, and today, sexist pay gaps and wage inequities can make it difficult for women to live without a man's salary contributing to the household income. These are all factors that make heterosexuality "compulsory" for women—and historically, a lot more brutal means were employed to force women into heterosexual couplings and keep them there.

Compulsory heterosexuality just assumes that women are naturally heterosexual. This is a significant barrier: lesbian existence has been historically erased or considered deviant. Acknowledging that heterosexuality for women may not be a natural preference (or a preference at all), but rather something that is managed, propagandized, and maintained by force, can be difficult when one considers themself freely and "innately" heterosexual (Rich 1980, 648). Ultimately, Rich writes that questioning compulsory heterosexuality will result in "a freeing-up of thinking, the exploring of new paths, the shattering of another great silence, new clarity in personal relationships" (Rich 1980, 648).

Rich explores the term "lesbian continuum," defined as a range "through each woman's life and throughout history" of "woman-identified experience; not simply the fact that a woman has had or consciously desired genital sexual experience with another woman" (Rich 1980, 648). This understanding of woman-identified experience allows for a wider understanding of women's resistance. In a particularly poignant section of the essay, Rich states, "If we consider the possibility that all women—from the infant suckling her mother's breast . . . to the woman dying at ninety, touched and handled by women—exist on a lesbian continuum, we can see ourselves as moving in and out of this continuum, whether we identify ourselves as lesbian or not" (Rich 1980, 650–1). The lesbian continuum demonstrates that women's struggle against patriarchy throughout history includes acts of resistance not perceived as such by men, such as women choosing not to have children and refusing to do unacknowledged, unpaid domestic labor for men as well the acts of care, love, and gentleness women freely offer other women.

The lesbian continuum, as the term suggests, is especially relevant for lesbians. Compulsory heterosexuality distorts women's passion for women and disregards women's choice of women as life partners and community, which restricts the power of women to liberate one another. In response, Rich calls for an expansion "into conscious woman-identification—into lesbian/feminism" (Rich 1980, 659). This call to define the lesbian continuum "is potentially liberating for all women."

Kate Chopin's *The Awakening* and the Lesbian Continuum

In response to Rich's essay, Kathryn Pyne Addelson maps Edna Pontellier, the protagonist of Kate Chopin's novel *The Awakening* (1899), onto the lesbian continuum. Addelson identifies two criteria from Rich's definition to use for placing women along the continuum: "The first involves resistance to male dominance, which she associates paradigmatically with lesbian existence . . . The second criterion involves women bonding with women" (Addelson 1981, 195). Addelson describes Edna as having resisted male dominance all her life, leading up to her first obvious act of resistance: learning to swim. That night, when Edna's husband compels her to reenter the house, Edna refuses until she "cannot hold out against the weight of her surroundings—at a family resort, on the porch of a cottage within which her children are sleeping" and acquiesces. From that point forward, however, Edna no longer participates in her marriage but must "avoid being labeled deviant, for then the retributive machinery of her society would forcibly return her to the normal," another way of articulating the forces of compulsory heterosexuality (Addelson 1981, 196–7).

Despite her husband's efforts, including attempts to get a doctor to label her hysterical, Edna finds a lover. After their first night together, Edna describes a sensation similar to mist being lifted from her eyes and begins to think more critically about her situation. Eventually, Edna dies by suicide after reckoning with the contradiction of motherhood, concluding that despite extramarital attempts at independence, as long as she is a mother, she remains the property of others. Noting that Edna is not a "successful revolutionary fighting for large-scale social change," Addelson writes, "But . . . she broke serious taboos (though not the homosexual one); she rejected a compulsory way of life; she attacked 'legitimate' male right of access to women. Her experience was a woman's experience, and her rebellion came directly out of the fact that she understood the oppressiveness of male dominance" (Addelson 1981, 197).

Despite the ways in which Edna's actions and increased consciousness can be mapped onto Rich's continuum, Addelson believes that the continuum is inadequate for capturing the experiences of women who, like Edna, are not shaped by bonding with other women or being significantly woman-identified and thus do not satisfy the second criterion of Rich's definition. Addelson questions the usefulness of the concept: "Does that mean she does not belong on the lesbian continuum? Or does it mean that we must come to a new understanding of what women's resistance amounts to?" (Addelson 1981, 197).

Scholarly Critique and Conversation

Kathryn Pyne Addelson's essay applying the lesbian continuum to *The Awakening* is one of three responses to Adrienne Rich's 1980 article published in the autumn 1981 publication of *Signs*. *Signs* is a scholarly feminist journal, and it featured three essays that "describe the political, social, and historical significance of the term 'lesbian'" in response to Rich ("Editorial" 1981, 3). Rich's concept of the lesbian continuum received a wide range of reactions from feminists and lesbians—many of whom were uncomfortable with how Rich broadly imagined lesbianism—and Addelson's article "Words and Lives," Ann Ferguson's article "Patriarchy, Sexual Identity, and the Sexual Revolution," and Jacquelyn N. Zita's article "Historical Amnesia and the Lesbian Continuum" illustrate common threads.

Ferguson critiques the continuum model as too linear and ahistorical, arguing that the continuum fails to account for the social and collective aspects of lesbian identity in relation to individual lesbian practices and behaviors (Ferguson 1981, 160). Ferguson offers up a new definition of "lesbian," which, unlike Rich's concepts of lesbian existence and the lesbian continuum, must include self-identifying as a lesbian (Ferguson 1981, 166). She takes issue with the term itself: "One's sexual preference may indeed be a political act, but it is not necessarily the best, nor the paradigmatic, feminist political act. Naming the continuum of resistance to patriarchy the lesbian continuum has the political implication that it is" (Ferguson 1981, 171). Ferguson's critique of Rich's essay centers around Rich's assumptions that compulsory heterosexuality is the central force driving male dominance and that all heterosexual relations are compulsory.

In "Historical Amnesia and the Lesbian Continuum," Zita defends the continuum model, defining it as "the continuity of resistance that women have always undertaken in independent, nonheterosexual, and woman-centered ways" (Zita 1981, 176). Throughout her article, Zita outlines reasons to embrace the continuum model. First, she argues, it promotes *continuity* by demonstrating how the "constant illusion of unique discovery" of lesbian existence results in a lost legacy of women's resistance (Zita 1981, 179). Next, she describes *quality of resistance*, noting that in order to respond to Rich's call for "lesbian/feminism," "we are the ones who must make the connection between the erotic choice and a deeply expanded consciousness of woman identification" (Zita 1981, 180). The third reason is *false inclusion*: the continuum model rids the term "lesbian" from its clinical associations by defining it in political terms. This false inclusion also differentiates lesbian existence from largely male-defined gay rights struggle (Zita 1981, 181). Finally, Zita names *false polarity* as a reason to use the continuum model. The continuum "releases our imagination from the either/or clinical categories of patriarchal sexual orientation," resulting in the ability to appreciate heterosexual women's experiences without losing sight of the material differences between the struggles by and for heterosexual and lesbian women (Zita 1981, 182). The continuum model does not address the success or failure of acts of resistance. While Ferguson considers that a potential flaw, Zita sees an opportunity: "it leaves open to discussion the question of what counts as successful or failed resistance in particular historical circumstances. This omission, however, does not invalidate the usefulness of such a concept" (Zita 1981, 178).

In addition to providing the example of Edna Pontellier in *The Awakening*, Addelson offers a different understanding of the lesbian continuum in her article "Words and Lives." She disagrees with Ferguson's critique that the continuum is ahistorical: "such a notion may let us examine the past (and present) not in terms of hierarchical institutions but in terms of women's own understandings within the historical contexts of life patterns they were creating" (Addelson 1981, 195). Addelson advocates for a definition that appropriately includes and describes resistance to male dominance. This definition "must also allow us to show the immorality of the normal way of doing things while revealing the fact that women in the deviant subcultures and dominant superculture have resisted and have created positive, self-affirming ways of doing things . . . I believe that Adrienne Rich's lesbian continuum may begin to do this work" (Addelson 1981, 191).

Reflecting on and Expanding the Lesbian Continuum

In 2004, Rich published "Reflections on 'Compulsory Heterosexuality,'" in which she looks back on her concept of the lesbian continuum with the context of the "more grounded scholarship, more critical thinking, and, simply, more witnesses than were available" to her in 1980 (Rich 2004, 9). The initial essay was published in 1980 following an explosion of lesbian and feminist consciousness in 1970s United States. This explosion was radical and revolutionary but still wrangling its "historical, intellectual, and analytical tools." Writing in 2004, Rich states that she feels the 1980 essay is "flawed, outdated, and in certain important ways no longer representative of my thinking and the thinking I respected" (Rich 2004, 9).

In "Reflections on 'Compulsory Heterosexuality,'" Rich explains that her initial essay was an exploratory piece intended to view compulsory heterosexuality from new angles, not intended as a manifesto or doctrine. Responses from some separatist lesbians and feminists indicated that it was being used as an argument against heterosexual sex, and Rich felt the tension between "speculative intellectual searching and the need for absolutes in the politics of lesbian feminism" (Rich 2004, 9). Her intention was to address the "disconnect" between heterosexual and lesbian women and overturn the inherent assumption of women's heterosexuality. The fact that generations of women have continued to return to these ideas "only indicates how deeply the presumption [compulsory heterosexuality] still prevails" (Rich 2004, 10).

Rich offers up a wider envisioning of her original exploration. She celebrates gains in the number of young feminists of color, scholars, and activists in queer and academic communities and the increase in Asian and African American studies programs. She addresses the need for an intersectional approach, decrying issues that have arisen or worsened since her original essay in 1980: the lack of universal healthcare and glorification of fitness, the Reagan administration's trickle-down economics, fundamentalist religious ideology and its deep ties to government, increasing rates of incarceration, criminal corporate practice, and the "increasing bondage of both political parties to the protection of private wealth" that has produced an "ever-growing and deadly economic abyss" (Rich 2004, 11). Rich concludes her piece by writing, "The feminist search for justice and freedom is inseparable from the concept of a truly integrated world society. Its horizons have been and must go on being expanded to a degree I did not yet envision when I wrote 'Compulsory Heterosexuality'" (Rich 2004, 11).

Hannah Jones

See Also: Compulsory Heterosexuality; Equal Pay; Feminization of Poverty; Patriarchy; Radical Feminism; Woman-Identified Woman Manifesto

Further Reading

Addelson, Kathryn Pyne. 1981. "Words and Lives." *Signs* 7, no. 1: 187–99. http://www.jstor.org/stable/3173517.

"Editorial." 1981. *Signs* 7, no. 1: 1–3. http://www.jstor.org/stable/3173500.

Ferguson, Ann. 1981. "Patriarchy, Sexual Identity, and the Sexual Revolution." *Signs* 7, no. 1: 158–72. http://www.jstor.org/stable/3173515.

Rich, Adrienne. 1980. "Compulsory Heterosexuality and Lesbian Existence." *Signs* 5, no. 4: 631–60. http://www.jstor.org/stable/3173834.

Rich, Adrienne. 2004. "Reflections on 'Compulsory Heterosexuality.'" *Journal of Women's History* 16, no. 1: 9–11. https://doi.org/10.1353/jowh.2004.0033.
Zita, Jacquelyn N. 1981. "Historical Amnesia and the Lesbian Continuum." *Signs* 7, no. 1: 172–87. http://www.jstor.org/stable/3173516.

LIBERAL FEMINISM

Liberal feminism is a feminist ideology that focuses on women's equality with men, especially focusing on equal pay, reproductive rights, voting rights, freedom from domestic violence, and freedom from sexual abuse. While its roots reach back at least into the 1800s in the United States, liberal feminism had its heyday during the 1960s and 1970s and its activists brought about significant legal reforms. Making it possible, for example, for women to access birth control and have their own credit cards. During the 1960s and 1970s, mainstream media focused on liberal feminist theorists and activists, such as Gloria Steinem and Betty Friedan—who wrote *The Feminist Mystique* and became the first president of the National Organization of Women in 1966—and liberal feminism became the mainstream face of feminism in the United States.

However, both during its heyday and now, liberal feminism faced and still faces criticism by other types of feminism for not supporting LGBTQ+ rights, for not resisting white supremacy, and for focusing too much on individuals. Indeed, feminists of color have especially critiqued liberal feminism as a white version of feminism that is self-centered and lacks a nuanced, intersectional understanding of patriarchy. Additionally, liberal feminism is known for working within existing structures (such as the legal system and capitalism) while other feminist ideologies and activist strategies see these structures as oppressive and work to create new systems.

In order to understand "liberal feminism," one needs to first understand "liberalism," as the two ideologies and their activism during the 1960s and 1970s are connected. In the United States, liberalism is a philosophy that advocates for freedom as pivotal to the life of all individuals. To this, liberal feminists clarify that freedom is pivotal to women's lives as well. The definition of "freedom," however, is not concrete and disagreements about what freedom means and looks like in practice between liberal groups and liberal feminist groups (and the ongoing patriarchy in liberal activist groups) ultimately divided the two movements. Moreover, liberal feminism itself is divided into two main philosophical camps known as egalitarian feminism and classical liberal feminism.

Egalitarian Feminism

Egalitarian feminism is a type of liberal feminism that focuses on personal and political autonomy. One of the main goals for egalitarian feminism is abolishing gender roles; egalitarian feminists argue that gender roles are wrong because they restrict personal and political autonomy. For instance, women should not be responsible for cooking and other household chores just because they are women. Similarly, men should not have a monopoly on office jobs and important positions in the government just because they are men. Some of the noted egalitarian liberal feminists include S. A. Lloyd, Linda McClain, Martha Nussbaum, Gina Schouten, Christie Hartley, Lori Watson, and Amy Baehr.

A good example of egalitarian feminism is in the critiques of how the US presidency remains closed to women. As C. Akça Ataç explains, Hillary Clinton's loss in the 2016 presidential election—especially to a candidate who was underqualified, misogynistic, and racist—underscored how the US presidency is closed to women. Ataç (2019, 1) writes that Clinton's 2016 campaign was inspiring "for the future of feminist politics" and the potential for women to achieve greater political equality and that her loss clearly signals that women do not have equal opportunity for political power or to hold office in US governance.

Classical Liberal Feminism

While egalitarian feminism conceptualizes freedom as ending gender roles so that people have personal and political autonomy, classical liberal feminism's understanding of freedom is more philosophically oriented around setting up legal protections so that everyone—but especially women—can make free choices. Essentially, classical liberal feminism advocates for legal reforms that would protect women's right to choose in every aspect of their daily lives. One prominent example of classical liberal feminism is the Equal Rights Amendment (ERA), which was first introduced to Congress in 1923 and was passed by Congress in 1972 but was not ratified by enough states to become part of the Constitution. The ERA would have enshrined equal rights—ending legal discriminations between men and women, for example, on the basis of divorce, property, employment, and government positions. During the 1960s and 1970s, classical liberal feminists advocated for the ERA, but their efforts fell short at the state level.

Other prominent examples of classical liberal feminism include activism working to end the laws prohibiting unmarried women's access to birth control and the workplace policies prohibiting women from holding managerial roles. Both of these legal discriminations limited women from making free choices about their lives—preventing women from avoiding pregnancies, regulating their menstrual cycles, and from advancing their careers. Liberal feminists were instrumental in the legal reforms that ended such laws and policies and created new laws that now protect women's freedom to choose. Namely, the 1972 Supreme Court decision *Eisenstadt v. Baird* decriminalized birth control for unmarried women; Title VII of the 1964 Civil Rights Act prohibits discrimination against employees on the basis of sex, race, color, and national origin; and the 1972 amendment of Title IV of the Civil Rights Act prohibits public schools and universities from discriminating based on sex in addition to prohibiting discrimination based on race, color, religion, or national origin. Some of the noted classical liberal feminists include Mary Wollstonecraft, Harriet Taylor Mill, John Stuart Mill, Elizabeth Cady Stanton, Sarah Grimke, and Voltairine de Cleyre.

However, the focus on individual choice in classical liberal feminism ends up obscuring structural oppression and marginalizes women of color. Liberal feminism is largely a white supremacist and capitalist take on feminism that endows rights and choices primarily based on white middle-class women's goals in the United States. For instance, consider the 2024 forced resignation of Harvard president, Claudine Gay, whose career was put under intense scrutiny by white conservative forces that accused her of getting her prestigious position "because she is a Black woman" and not on merit (Binkley and Balingit 2024). Racist bias denied Gay the right to hold a prestigious academic position by accusing her of not having earned her position. Any amount of individual choice/effort on Gay's part is not only inconsequential here but it is dismissed as impossible. The idea is that a Black woman could never have earned the position of a Harvard president because she is inherently incapable of holding that kind of merit because of her race. This kind of biased and exclusionary thinking strengthens white supremacy and its capitalist allies because prestigious job positions and the wealth and respect it brings are localized in white hands, irrespective of their gender, and Black people (and particularly, Black women because of the double bind of racism and sexism) remain impoverished, pushed down, and in Gay's case, publicly humiliated.

In the contemporary world, a good example of classical liberal feminism is the "girlboss" culture where "hustling" and "leaning in" (in other words, individual hard work and labor), rather than political change in social and state policies, is perceived as the path to women's empowerment. The term "girlboss" originated in Sophia Amaruso's memoir #Girlboss (2014) and is defined in the Pop Culture Dictionary as "a woman who was financially successful and who held a high-ranking position at a company, often their own company" (2023). A so-called "girlboss" is successful because she works hard despite the sexist conditions of her workplace and rises to the top because of her own efforts in a male-dominated setting. This power of the individual (white) woman, harnessed to bring her own liberation and elevate her to positions of power despite sexism, is the essence of classical liberal feminism.

This kind of liberal feminism is also linked to "popular feminism" and is tied to the harmful ideas that neoliberalism brings to social movements like feminism. As Sarah Banet-Weiser succinctly puts it: "Popular feminism exists along a continuum, where spectacular, media-friendly expressions such as celebrity feminism and corporate feminism achieve more visibility, and expressions that critique patriarchal structures and systems of racism and violence are more obscured" (Banet-Weiser 2018, 4). Popular feminism is therefore the kind of feminism that sells in the neoliberal market economy, the kind of feminism that can be advertised on T-shirts, stickers, and Instagram; it is an air-brushed version of feminism that is the least disagreed upon feminist politics. In this sense, it automatically resists any kind of nuance based on race, religion, and immigration status, to name a few.

Criticisms of Liberal Feminism

Some of the noted critics of liberal feminism are Sarah Banet-Weiser, Brittney Cooper, Kimberlé Crenshaw, Martha Minow, Eva Kittay, and Susan Okin—and many others around the world. They have argued that the focus on individual liberty often becomes apolitical so that any and every choice is seen as inherently good because it is a mark of "liberty." Moreover, the critiques of liberal feminism clearly point out that liberal feminism simply fails to understand how sexism intersects with racism, ableism, anti-immigrant sentiments, and so on and thereby fails to understand the nature of oppression and thus how to end oppression.

For example, the "girlboss" culture has been critiqued by countless feminists as being focused on upper-class wealth accumulation, in which a certain class of women (usually from privileged economic backgrounds) are able to rise up the corporate ladder and do well in business or office jobs because of their individual efforts. Black feminists and queer feminists have also critiqued it as extremely heterocentric and white, where their racial background and a certain way of embodying femininity in the office space are what makes these women rise upward.

Another criticism of liberal feminism is its refusal to focus on the care-deficit phenomenon, which means that these "girlboss" women are able to be successful outside home without any reform in men's willingness to take up care duties at home because, in many cases, Black women and undocumented women (working as house helps and nannies) taking up care duties for minimal wages. The care deficit or a gap in care work left at home is filled up by other more marginalized women, making the classical liberal feminist a white-only and privileged-only activism.

Ultimately, liberal feminism made many significant legal reforms during the 1960s and 1970s and its philosophy infuses much of mainstream feminism to this day. However, by largely failing to reckon with white supremacy, heterosexism, and capitalism, liberal feminism has largely failed to bring about liberation.

Pujarinee Mitra

See Also: Capitalism; Civil Rights Movement; Crenshaw, Kimberlé; *Eisenstadt v. Baird* (1972); Equal Rights Amendment; Interlocking Oppression; Intersectionality; Neoliberalism; The Personal Is Political; Popular Feminism

Further Reading

Ataç, C. Akça. 2019. "Truth, Truth-telling and Gender in Politics: The "Hillary" Experience." *European Journal of American Studies* 14, no. 2: 1–22. https://doi.org/10.4000/ejas.14695.

Baehr, Amy. 2017. "A Capacious Account of Liberal Feminism." *Feminist Philosophy Quarterly* 3, no. 1. https://doi.org/10.5206/fpq/2016.3.4.

Banet-Weiser, Sarah. 2018. *Empowered: Popular Feminism and Popular Misogyny*. Durham, NC: Duke University Press.

Binkley, Collin, and Moriah Balingit. 2024. "Plagiarism Charges Downed Harvard's President. A Conservative Attack Helped to Fan the Outrage." *AP News*, January 3, 2024. https://apnews.com/article/harvard-president-plagiarism-claudine-gay-3b048da1f2ee17b5edec3680b5828e8f.

Clark, Elizabeth B. 1989. "Self-Ownership and the Political Theory of Elizabeth Cady Stanton." *Connecticut Law Review* 21: 905–41.

Cooper, Brittney. 2018. *Eloquent Rage: A Black Feminist Discovers Her Superpower*. New York: St. Martin's Press.

Crenshaw, Kimberle. 1991. "Mapping the Margins: Intersectionality, Identity Politics, and Violence against Women of Color." *Stanford Law Review* 43, no. 6: 1241–99.

Deutscher, Penelope. 2006. "When Feminism Is "High" and Ignorance Is "Low": Harriet Taylor Mill on the Progress of the Species." *Hypatia* 21, no. 3: 136–50.

Hartley, Christie and Lori Watson. 2010. "Is a Feminist Political Liberalism Possible?" *Journal of Ethics and Social Philosophy* 5, no. 1: 1–22. https://doi.org/10.26556/jesp.v5i1.48.

Kittay, Eva Feder. 1995. "Taking Dependency Seriously: The Family and Medical Leave Act Considered in Light of the Social Organization of Dependency Work and Gender Equality." *Hypatia* 10, no. 1: 8–29, https://doi.org/10.1111/j.1527-2001.1995.tb01351.x.

Kittay, Eva Feder. 1999. *Love's Labor: Essays on Women, Equality and Dependency*. New York: Routledge.

Kotef, Hagar. 2009. "On Abstractness: First Wave Liberal Feminism and the Construction of the Abstract Woman." *Feminist Studies* 35, no. 3: 495–522.

Lloyd, S. A. 1995. "Situating a Feminist Critique of John Rawls' Political Liberalism." *Loyola Law Review* 28, no. 4: 1319–44.

Lloyd, S. A. 1998. "Toward a Liberal Theory of Sexual Equality." *Journal of Contemporary Legal Issues* 9: 203–24.

McClain, Linda. 2006. *The Place of Families: Fostering Capacity, Equality and Responsibility*. Cambridge, MA: Harvard University Press.

Mill, John Stuart. (1869) 1989. *The Subjection of Women*. Cambridge: Cambridge University Press.

Minow, Martha. 1990. *Making All the Difference: Inclusion, Exclusion, and American Law*. Cambridge, MA: Harvard University Press.

Nussbaum, Martha C. 1999. *Sex and Social Justice*. New York: Oxford University Press.

Nussbaum, Martha C. 2000. "The Future of Feminist Liberalism." *Proceedings and Addresses of the American Philosophical Association* 74, no. 2: 47–79. https://doi:10.2307/3219683.

Okin, Susan. 1994. "Political Liberalism, Justice, and Gender." *Ethics* 105, no. 1: 23–43, https://doi:10.1086/293677.

Pop Culture Dictionary. 2023. "Girlboss." Online ed. Rockholdings Inc., September 14, 2023. Accessed August 26, 2024.https://www.dictionary.com/e/pop-culture/girlboss/.

Schouten, Gina. 2019. *Liberalism, Neutrality, and the Gendered Division of Labor*. New York: Oxford University Press.

Watson, Lori. 2007. "Constituting Politics: Power, Reciprocity, and Identity." *Hypatia* 22, no. 4: 96–112. https://doi:10.1111/j.1527-2001.2007.tb01322.x.

Wills, Matthew. 2019. "Voltairine de Cleyre: American Radical." *Jstor Daily*, March 27, 2019. Accessed August 24, 2024. https://daily.jstor.org/voltairine-de-cleyre-american-radical/.

Wollstonecraft, Mary. (1792) 1998. *A Vindication of the Rights of Woman*. New York: Norton.

LILLY LEDBETTER FAIR PAY ACT (2009)

In an attempt to address wage inequity in 2009, the US Congress passed and President Barack Obama signed the Lilly Ledbetter Fair Pay Act into law (National Women's Law Center 2013). The law reinforces protections against pay discrimination on the basis of sex, race, national origin, age, religion, and disability. Moreover, as the Equal Employment Opportunity Commission (n.d.) notes, the law clarifies that pay discrimination occurs any time one of the following things takes place: an employer adopts discriminatory compensation decisions or practices, an employee becomes subject to discriminatory compensation decisions or practices, or an individual's compensation is affected by discriminatory decisions and practices, including each time they receive compensation affected by discrimination (e.g., each pay period).

Who Is Lilly Ledbetter?

Lilly Ledbetter was born in Alabama in 1938 and, in 1979, had the unique experience of being hired as one of the first female managers at the Goodyear Tire and Rubber Company in Gadsen, Alabama (Association for American University Women 2024). Upon being hired, Ledbetter was paid the same as her male colleagues, but by the end of her career, Ledbetter learned via an anonymous note left in her locker that she was earning less than any of her male colleagues who worked in the same position as she (National Women's Hall of Fame 2024).

Ledbetter had signed an agreement promising her employer that she would not discuss wages with other employees, so the anonymous note was the only wage information she had. Initially, she considered accepting the information she had received and ignoring the injustice of the inequality in pay she was facing. However, she found that she could not ignore the discrimination she had learned about. Ledbetter chose to file a claim with the US Equal Employment Opportunity Commission (EEOC) and sued her employer for discrimination under Title VII of the Civil Rights Act of 1964 (Ledbetter 2008).

Ledbetter's lawsuit was initially successful. A jury agreed with her, found that her employer had violated the law, and awarded her monetary damages to compensate her for the pay inequity she had experienced. Ledbetter had hoped that her employer would learn a valuable lesson and never treat other women the way they had treated her. However, her employer appealed—all the way to the Supreme Court (Ledbetter 2008).

Ledbetter v. Goodyear Tire & Rubber Co. (2007)

Ledbetter had sued Goodyear Tire & Rubber Co. under Title VII of the Civil Rights Act of 1964, alleging that the difference between her wages and those paid to her male counterparts was because of her gender, a practice prohibited by federal law under the Civil Rights Act. Goodyear Tire & Rubber appealed the initial jury verdict, citing a provision in Title VII that requires complaints be filed within 180 days of the discriminatory conduct. While the case had focused on facts and feedback from Ledbetter's entire career, Goodyear argued that the jury should have considered only the annual review that occurred within the 180-day period prior to the date that Ledbetter had filed her complaint (*Ledbetter v. Goodyear Tire & Rubber Co.* 2007).

In this case, the key question for the Court was whether Ledbetter had grounds to bring a salary discrimination suit under Title VII of the Civil Rights Act of 1964 when the discriminatory pay decision that led to her receipt of disparate pay occurred more than 180 days before she filed her claim, even though she was still receiving an unequal amount of pay compared to her male colleagues within 180 days of filing her claim (*Ledbetter v. Goodyear Tire & Rubber Co.* 2007).

By a 5-4 vote, with Justice Samuel Alito writing for the majority, the Court ruled against Ledbetter, arguing that she needed to have filed her claim within 180 days of the initial decision to pay her less than her male counterparts in order to have proper standing. In the Court's opinion, the 180-day statute of limitations was intended to guarantee quick resolution of pay disputes, which can be difficult to defend against as more time passes. As a result, they sided with Goodyear Tire & Rubber, overturning the prior jury verdict and denying Ledbetter her victory.

In many ways, this ruling feels preposterous since Ledbetter had no way to know when Goodyear Tire & Rubber decided to discriminate against her, and thus she had no way to know a 180-day timeline had started. Justice Ruth Bader Ginsberg recognized how preposterous this situation was, and dissented, stating that the majority failed to understand the realities of wage discrimination.

Ginsberg, and the concurring minority justices, argued that the majority failed to recognize that employers are rarely transparent about comparative pay information (Ginsberg 2007) and often deliberately conceal pay data from their employees, making it difficult for employees to bring claims and resolve challenges within 180 days of discriminatory decisions or the implementation of discriminatory practices, especially as the impacts of those practices on future wages and total earnings may only become obvious over time. According to Ginsberg (2007), "The Court's approbation of these consequences is totally at odds with the robust protection against workplace discrimination Congress intended Title VII to secure."

What's Next?

The good news is, Congress and President Barack Obama agreed with Justice Ginsberg and the minority dissent. Within two years of the Supreme Court's decision in *Ledbetter*, Congress had drafted and passed the Lilly Ledbetter Fair Pay Act, making it exceedingly clear that the 180-day statute of limitations applies to the decision to offer discriminatory compensation or implement discriminatory compensation practices and also to each time compensation is paid out to employees as a result of a discriminatory offer or discriminatory practice (US EEOC n.d.). This means that employees have many more opportunities to seek redress when discrimination occurs.

Despite this legislative win, the work for fair and equal pay is not over.

At the White House on January 29, 2009, President Barack Obama signs the Lilly Ledbetter Fair Pay Act, aimed at addressing discriminatory compensation and wage inequity (The White House).

Women in the United States who work full-time make approximately 84 cents for every dollar made by their male counterparts, which equates to about $9,990 less per year (Javaid 2024). Compared to every dollar made by white, non-Hispanic men who work full-time, white women make approximately 83 cents (Kochhar 2023), and the comparison gets worse for most women of color. Latinas who work full-time make 57 cents, Native women who work full-time make approximately 59 cents, and Black women who work full-time make approximately 69 cents (Javaid, 2024). Asian American, Native Hawaiian, and Pacific Islander women who work full-time do slightly better than all other women but still not as well as white men, making approximately 93 cents for every dollar made by white, non-Hispanic men (Javaid 2024).

Over a forty-year career, these wage disparities can result in an average lifetime earning difference of over $330,000 and a difference of over $1 million for Native women and Latinas. Given that women are outliving their male partners by an average of ten years, it is critical that we solve this challenge for the future well-being of women (AAUW 2024).

The good news is, there are several things that we can do to help solve this challenge:

As individuals:

- Negotiate and do your research. Know what the industry is paying for the role you're applying for and ask for the compensation you know your labor is worth (AAUW 2024).
- Get a mentor to help you with those conversations. Talking to someone who has done this before can help set expectations for what you should say and how you should handle any feedback you receive.

As employers:

- Implement better hiring practices, designed to eliminate bias as much as possible—studies have shown that, when presented with identical resumes, hiring managers will offer male candidates more money than female candidates while also considering them more desirable as candidates. One experiment revealed that hiring managers for a lab manager position offered the candidate named John $4,000 more than the candidate named Jennifer, while also rating John significantly more competent and hirable (Javaid 2024).
- Implementing pay transparency initiatives can help narrow wage gaps (Javaid 2024). Transparency can be improved both internally, with current employees, and externally, with candidates and job applicants.
  - Internally: Develop and publish job grades and pay bands so that employees have a general idea of what compensation to expect in their current role and what compensation to expect when promoted. Develop compensation guidelines to ensure equity in raises and promotion processes across the organization.
  - Externally: Post compensation ranges for roles on job postings to show candidates what you are willing to pay, removing the guesswork for job seekers and limiting the time your recruiters spend talking to candidates who expect more compensation than you are able to offer. Likewise, avoid asking applicants for their salary history. Not only is this practice prohibited by law in many jurisdictions, but solid compensation philosophies allow you to skip these questions. Instead, conduct market research so that you know what wages are competitive in your market. Partner with a firm that is an expert in collecting compensation data and base your compensation budgets and philosophy on their data. Use their data to develop wage ranges

for the roles you're recruiting for, and then be confident in those ranges, knowing that the data you used is high quality. This will enable you to have fully informed conversations with your applicants about the wage range and budget for the role when they negotiate.

- Recognize and pay women for the work that they do. Women's work is often devalued (Javaid 2024), so if you have roles in your organization that women dominate, ensure those roles are compensated for the value they bring to your organization. In addition, recognize the unseen, unpaid labor often performed by female team members. If you have team members who are accomplishing all of their own work and also contributing to the team by checking in on others, planning team events, sending care packages to team members who are out sick, making lunch arrangements, encouraging people to come to happy hour, and doing other work that isn't part of their job description but makes for a great place to work, remember that those tasks frequently fall to women because they are considered "women's work" and it is often assumed that a woman in the office will take on those tasks out of the goodness of her heart. Consider recognizing that person's efforts with more than just a "thank you."

At the macro level:

- We can continue to strengthen our fair pay laws so that it is even easier to fight back against pay discrimination as well as implement additional laws to prohibit asking about salary history and to increase pay transparency (Javaid 2024).
- Increase the opportunities for women to enter male-dominated fields and break down barriers to success, ensuring that women are free from harassment and other forms of discrimination that may force them out of those fields (Javaid 2024).
- Increase the availability and affordability of high-quality childcare, limiting the impact of motherhood on wages and career growth for women (Javaid 2024).

Ultimately, the Lilly Ledbetter Fair Pay Act of 2009 enables employees whose compensation has been negatively impacted due to discrimination on the basis of sex, race, national origin, age, religion, and disability to better seek justice. This is an important step forward in the fight for wage equality, and Ledbetter's courageous pursuit of justice ultimately helped create a major shift in US law that enables women and minoritized people to seek wage justice across the country. In spite of these improvements, in many ways, the onus is still on women and minoritized people to become aware that they are being discriminated against and then to file a complaint with the EEOC and seek reparations in order to achieve wage equality. Which is to say, when it comes to wage discrimination, there is work to be done.

Devon S. Torchiana

See Also: Civil Rights Act: Title VII; Equal Pay; Labor Activism

Further Reading

Association for American University Women. 2024. "Q&A with Lilly Ledbetter." January 29, 2024. Accessed September 9, 2024. https://www.aauw.org/resources/faces-of-aauw/qa-lilly-ledbetter/.

Ginsberg, Justice Ruth Bader, dissenting. 2007. *Ledbetter v. Goodyear Tire & Rubber Company, Inc.* (Supreme Court of the United States). Accessed September 9, 2024. https://supreme.justia.com/cases/federal/us/550/618/.

Javaid, Sarah. 2024. "A Window into the Wage Gap: What's Behind It and How to Close It." *National Women's Law Center*. Accessed September 10, 2024. https://nwlc.org/wp-content/uploads/2023/01/2023-Wage-Gap-Factsheet.pdf.

Kochhar, Rakesh. 2023. "The Enduring Grip of the Gender Pay Gap." *Pew Research Center*, March 1, 2023. Accessed September 9, 2024. https://www.pewresearch.org/social-trends/2023/03/01/the-enduring-grip-of-the-gender-pay-gap/.

Ledbetter, Lilly. 2008. Speech at the Democratic National Convention, August 26, 2008. Transcript and recording. *PBS Newshour Online Archives*. Accessed September 9, 2024. https://web.archive.org/web/20080915163402/http://www.pbs.org/newshour/bb/politics/july-dec08/ledbetter_08-26.html.

Ledbetter v. Goodyear Tire and Rubber Company Inc., 2007. 550 U.S. 853.

National Women's Hall of Fame. 2024. "Lilly Ledbetter." Accessed on September 8, 2024. https://www.womenofthehall.org/inductee/lilly-ledbetter/.

National Women's Law Center. 2024. *Wage Gap Factsheet,* January 2024. Accessed September 9, 2024. https://nwlc.org/wp- content/uploads/2023/01/2023-Wage-Gap-Factsheet.pdf.

National Women's Law Center. 2013. "Lilly Ledbetter Fair Pay Act." January 29, 2013. Accessed September 9, 2024. https://nwlc.org/resource/lilly-ledbetter-fair-pay-act/.

US Equal Employment Opportunity Commission. n.d. "Notice Concerning the Lilly Ledbetter Fair Pay Act of 2009." Accessed September 8, 2024. https://www.eeoc.gov/statutes/notice-concerning-lilly-ledbetter-fair-pay-act-2009.

LORDE, AUDRE

Audre Lorde (1934–92) was a compelling Black feminist author and activist who wrote on and addressed racism, homophobia, classism, ageism, ableism, and more that were evident not only in the larger world but also within the women's rights movement of the mid- and late twentieth century. Lorde artfully, passionately, and profoundly spoke on her experiences as a Black woman, a lesbian, a mother, and other identities in order to illustrate the multifaceted nature of personhood that translates for some to levels of privilege and access and for others to barriers for equity.

Lorde was born on February 18, 1934, in New York City to parents Linda Gertrude Belmar Lorde and Frederick Byron Lorde. Audre Lorde's parents were immigrants from the Caribbean nations of Grenada and Barbados who settled in NYC's Harlem neighborhood. She was also the youngest of three sisters (Brandman 2021).

While growing up, Lorde gravitated toward poetry as a favored form of expression to best articulate her feelings surrounding her personhood and life experiences. For example, in an interview with feminist and poet Adrienne Rich, Lorde recounted, "I saw the way other people thought, and it was an amazement to me—step by step, not in bubbles up from chaos that you had to anchor with words" (Lorde 1984, 72).

Lorde published her first poem, "Spring," in *Seventeen* magazine after it was rejected for a high school class assignment. After high school, she went on to spend a year at the National University of Mexico before returning to NYC. She earned a bachelor's degree from Hunter College and a master's degree in library science from Columbia University. Lorde then began working in the 1960s as a librarian for New York City public schools, while also beginning to publish her poetry and prose in periodicals and books and joining other activists in civil rights, women's liberation, and anti-war social movements. From the 1960s through the 1980s, Lorde published numerous works, such as *From a Land Where Other People Live; Coal; The Black Unicorn; Zami: A New Spelling of My Name; Sister Outsider;* and *The Cancer Journals*.

"Poetry Is Not a Luxury"

For Lorde, poetry exemplified a feminist rhetorical practice of writing the body, which diverges from traditional (male-theorized) rhetorical elements and uses the body and its associated feelings and emotions as a site of discourse (Ritchie and Ronald 2001). Alluding to this notion, as well as her intersecting identities, Lorde wrote in an essay titled "Poetry Is Not a Luxury" that "the white fathers told us, I think therefore I am; and the black mothers in each of us—the poet whispers in our dreams, I feel therefore I can be free" (Lorde 1984, 26).

Poetry and prose served as necessary tools for Lorde to communicate her feminist rhetoric, including her famous essay, "Uses of the Erotic," and even recording her eventual breast cancer diagnosis. According to Lorde, poetry is a "vital necessity of our (women's) existence" and an act of translating powerful feelings into language and action (Lorde 1984, 25).

Furthermore, Lorde considered speaking as an act of survival. In "The Transformation of Silence into Language and Action," Lorde said, "I was going to die, if not sooner then later, whether or not I had ever spoken myself. My silences had not protected me. Your silence will not protect you" (Lorde 1984, 29). Even more, silence was the antithesis of genuine coalition building, a theme that would typify Lorde's life. She said, "for it is not difference which immobilizes us, but silence. And there are so many silences to be broken" (Lorde 1984, 32).

Activism through an Intersectional Lens

Audre Lorde was acutely aware of the different identities and facets of her life that constructed her personhood and experiences. In the same piece as above, "The Transformation of Silence into Language and Action," Lorde said, "Because I am woman, because I am Black, because I am lesbian, because I am myself—a Black woman warrior poet doing my work—come to ask you, are you doing yours?" (Lorde 1984, 29–30). Lorde's life was impacted by overt discrimination and microaggressions concerning her personhood as a woman who was Black and lesbian, the daughter of Caribbean immigrant parents, raised in a working-class family and setting in Harlem, and who was, herself, a parent. She understood and spent much of her writing and activism communicating how these different identities were not mutually exclusive. In her piece, "Learning from the 60s," Lorde said, "There is no such thing as a single-issue struggle because we do not live single-issue lives" (Lorde 1984, 130).

Lorde's praxis reflects several key scholarly concepts that are important to contemporary feminist practice. Years prior to the term "intersectionality" being coined, Lorde and other contemporaries understood how differing identities resulted in interlocking or compounding forms of oppression (Tong and Botts 2018). For instance, Lorde was impacted by discrimination that devalued her Black personhood and experiences in a predominantly white, male, capitalist schema and within a mainly white woman-led, mid-twentieth-century, mainstream feminist movement. She was also a member of a larger US Black community affected by sexism and homophobia. In "There Is No Hierarchy of Oppressions," Lorde said,

> Within the lesbian community I am Black, and within the Black community I am a lesbian. Any attack against Black people is a lesbian and gay issue, because I and thousands of other Black women are part of the lesbian community. Any attack against lesbians and gays is a Black issue, because thousands of lesbians and gay men are Black. (Lorde 1983, 9)

In a similar vein, Lorde and others illustrated the tenets of Black feminism. This line of feminist thought developed in response to the specific structural racism, sexism, and classism before and during the suffragist movement. Black feminism not only critiques these structural oppressions but also mainstream feminist acquiescence to white male privilege, labor and political economies that disadvantage Black women, and the controlling images of Black femininity (Collins 2000).

Moreover, Lorde's perspective involves critiques of the assumptions that all or most women's experiences of struggle are inherently similar. She critiqued mid- to late-twentieth-century white feminist organizers by pointing to the gaps in their practice that largely ignored the compounding oppressions of race, class, gender, and sexuality of marginalized figures who were excluded, or at best tokenized, as potential allies to the mainstream feminist movement. In perhaps one of her most highly regarded essays, Lorde said,

> What does it mean when the tools of a racist patriarchy are used to examine the fruits of that same patriarchy? . . . Those of us who stand outside the circle of this society's definition of acceptable women . . . know that survival is not an academic skill. It is learning how to take our differences and make them strengths. For the master's tools will never dismantle the master's house. (Lorde 1984, 100–2)

Like the "silences" between women that Lorde advocated we break, Lorde implored feminist organizers to keenly observe the differences in the lived experiences of marginalized women. Inclusive, even revolutionary, feminist practice requires the application of this intersectional lens to reflexively bolster the movement in the pursuit of equitable outcomes for multiple identities.

In 1978, Lorde was diagnosed with breast cancer. Her medical diagnosis and experience as the cancer impacted her abilities became an additional lens for Lorde to apply to her intersectional compositions, which she shared in her work, *The Cancer Journals*. The book became a profound narrative that critiqued stigma surrounding other Black and lesbian women afflicted by breast cancer and allowed Lorde to candidly reflect on her mortality. For example, after her diagnosis, Lorde elected for a mastectomy and declined to wear a prosthesis. Lorde wrote, "Prosthesis offers the empty comfort of 'Nobody will know the difference.' But it is that very difference which I wish to affirm, because I have lived it, and survived it, and wish to share that strength with other women" (Lorde 1980, 61). Lorde died from cancer in 1992.

Legacy

The impacts of Audre Lorde's writing, scholarship, teaching, and activism are vast. Lorde's overarching contribution to feminism was her staunch commitment to applying intersectional lenses to not only understand herself but also to understand the oppressed identities around her. She pushed other women to recognize the structural and interlocking oppressions that inhibit effective coalition building. Lorde wrote in "Who Said It Was Simple" that "There are so many roots to the tree of anger" (Lorde 1983), just one of the numerous articulations she made noting that oppression and discrimination run along lines of race, class, gender, sex, sexuality, ability, and more. These characteristics impact the achievement of equitable outcomes for all. Lorde's writing and activism contributed to the power of the Combahee River Collective and subsequent Black feminist writers, such as bell hooks and Kimberlé Crenshaw. Furthermore, Lorde's praxis serves as a grounding and foundational voice for the intersectional practices necessary for just and effective modern-day feminism.

Lorde earned numerous recognitions for her writing, activism, and advocacy for people of color and queer identities. The following are only a few of her recognitions: Lorde was named the Poet Laureate of New York State from 1991 until her passing in 1992; she cofounded Kitchen Table: Women of Color Press to support and publish women of color feminist voices; she earned several university teaching appointments, such as the writer-in-residence at Tougaloo College and a visiting professorship at the Free University of Berlin; and she is recognized on the National LGBTQ Wall of Honor in the Stonewall National Monument in NYC and the Legacy Walk in Chicago.

Kale Wilk

See Also: Combahee River Collective; Consciousness Raising; Crenshaw, Kimberlé; hooks, bell; Interlocking Oppression; Intersectionality

Further Reading

Brandman, Mariana. 2021. "Audre Lorde." *National Women's History Museum*. Accessed December 12, 2024. https://www.womenshistory.org/education-resources/biographies/audre-lorde.

Collins, Patricia Hill. 2000. *Black Feminist Thought: Knowledge, Consciousness, and the Politics of Empowerment*. New York: Routledge.

Lorde, Audre. 1980. *The Cancer Journals*. San Francisco: Aunt Lute Books.

Lorde, Audre. 1983. "There is No Hierarchy of Oppressions." *Interracial Books for Children Bulletin: Homophobia and Education* 14 (3–4): 9.

Lorde, Audre. 1983. "Who Said It Was Simple." *Poetry Foundation*. Accessed December 12, 2024. https://www.poetryfoundation.org/poems/42587/who-said-it-was-simple.

Lorde, Audre. 1984. *Sister Outsider: Essays and Speeches*. New York: Penguin Random House.

Ritchie, Joy, and Kate Ronald, eds. 2001. *Available Means: An Anthology of Women's Rhetoric(s)*. Pittsburgh, PA: University of Pittsburgh Press.

Tong, Rosemarie, and Tina Fernandes Botts. 2018. *Feminist Thought: A More Comprehensive Introduction*. New York: Routledge.

M

MALE GAZE

In 1975, film theorist and filmmaker Laura Mulvey published "Visual Pleasure and Narrative Cinema," changing the way feminists think about camera- and screen-based media by explaining what she called the "male gaze." Put most simply, the male gaze refers to the way in which films (and other entertainment) often portray women on-screen as sexualized spectacles so that the audience looks at a woman's body as a cisgender, heterosexual man might leer at a woman in real life.

In her work, Mulvey was building on John Berger's idea that there are "ways of seeing." Consider, for example, that after a person has learned to read, they usually cannot prevent themselves from reading when they see words. A classic experiment known as the Stroop effect makes this plain (Monahan 2001). The experiment presents respondents with the words for colors (green, blue, red, pink, yellow, purple, etc.), but the words are printed in a font color that does not match the word's meaning. For example, the word "yellow" might be written in red. If you ask a literate person to read the words and then repeat the exercise but ask them to name the colors (rather than reading the words), a literate person will almost always be faster at reading the words than saying the color of the font. This is because our vision is not neutral or objective. We are trained in different "ways of seeing" and these "ways of seeing" dominate our sight. Mulvey identified the male gaze as a way of seeing, explaining how cinematic camerawork from the 1940s through the 1970s trained people to see through the male gaze and theorizing what happens to society—especially women—when the male gaze becomes our way of seeing.

To begin, Mulvey noted that cinema reinforces "pre-existing patterns" and "social formations" (1975, 833). Most basically, this means that a culture's entertainment reflects or reproduces that culture's patterns, assumptions, social hierarchies, and so on. And here, Mulvey noted that during the 1940s–1970s, patriarchy was embedded in US culture. Even anatomy textbooks for medical students used "pinup photographs" so that female anatomy models—even the children—always had "pointed toes and arched backs," implying that they were "carefree" and sexually playful (Friz and Fernholtz 2020). Alongside these pornographic images were "tongue-in-cheek commentary that sexualizes and objectifies women," clearly inscribing a patriarchal hierarchy into "scientific" and "medical" understandings of anatomy (Friz and Fernholtz 2020).

Mulvey understood that what happens in movies is derived from "the unconscious of patriarchal society," explaining that this unconscious patriarchy becomes part of cinema's visual structures—becomes part of the plot sequences, camera angles, editing, and so on (1975, 833). For instance, a camera might pan up and down a woman's body as she enters a scene, or a film might establish that the characters are in Miami, Florida (or any other beach town), by quickly cutting from one bikini-clad woman to another before settling on the main characters as they sit at a beachside café or walk along the shore.

Discussing the male gaze, Mulvey explains that within this way of seeing, women's bodies become spectacles (Kornfield 2025). Essentially, in the cinema Mulvey studied, men act and women exist to be looked at. Men's actions move the plot forward; men are the protagonists. Women, meanwhile, might serve as the love interest, a sassy sidekick, the victim, the mother, or—most classically—the damsel in distress. In all of these roles, women characters exist *to be looked at*; their behavior almost never moves the plot forward. At this narrative level—the plot—Mulvey argues that audiences are expected and encouraged to identify with the masculine protagonist, and that he serves as a "screen surrogate" for the audience (1975, 838).

By "screen surrogate," Mulvey means that audience members imagine themselves in the role of the male protagonist. Essentially, we look as he looks and we imagine his actions as our own. All of this involves technology. Consider the classic "shot-reverse shot" sequence. The camera looks at a character (who looks directly into the camera), then the camera cuts to a shot of a thing or person, and then cuts back to look directly at the actor. This shot sequence not only implies that the actor is looking at the thing or person but also causes the audience to look *with* the camera, seemingly *through* the actor's eyes. But all of this is the magic of technology: the actor might not have even been in the same room with the thing or person they are supposedly looking at. They only stared at the camera. Indeed, the "camera movements" and "invisible editing" create a visual fantasy, allowing audiences to "see" through the male protagonists' eyes and imagine his actions as their own (1975, 839).

The Two Pleasures of the Male Gaze: Scopophilia and Ego Libido

Mulvey describes two different pleasures associated with the male gaze. After all, watching movies is usually quite pleasurable—people do it for fun and relaxation. The first pleasure is *scopophilia*. This is the pleasure of looking at a person as an erotic object. The second pleasure is *ego libido*. This is the pleasure of identifying with an on-screen protagonist. Mulvey argued that these two pleasures exist simultaneously in the male gaze. According to Mulvey, these two pleasures train or seduce people, even women, into accepting and adopting the male gaze as a primary way of seeing.

A lot of leisure industries, such as playhouse theaters, restaurants with sexualized dress codes for waitresses, and strip clubs, display women's bodies for visual consumption—offering the first pleasure, scopophilia. But cinema not only displays women's bodies for visual consumption but also controls how the audience looks at that visual display. For instance, a strip club can control what people see by controlling what happens on stage. The cinema, however, controls not only what people see but also *how* they see it. For instance, in a strip club, a person might choose to look at the stage decorations or backstage performers. And at a strip club, one cannot look through the lead performer's eyes; the audience can only look at the performers.

In the cinema (and a lot of other screen- and camera-based media), however, the editing and camerawork make it nearly impossible to look anywhere except at the shot's central focus. For instance, cinematic camerawork is often so tightly focused that the background is a blur, making it nearly impossible for audiences to look at the background of a shot the way one might study the background set design at a theatrical performance or watch the supporting performers at a strip club. Similarly, cinematic camerawork and editing control how long an audience can look at something, panning from object to object and cutting from scene to scene. Finally, and most importantly for Mulvey, movies often require that the audiences look through a masculine protagonist's eyes. The editing and camerawork so often show audiences what a masculine protagonist is looking at—and here, Mulvey argues that cinema produces "an illusion cut to the measure of [patriarchal] society" (1975, 843). That is, the visual fantasy that movies create for audiences is a patriarchal fantasy.

Throughout a cinematic experience, the pleasures of scopophilia and ego libido combine and collide. The pleasure of ego libido is found in aligning oneself or identifying with the on-screen protagonist, and this pleasure is so often offered through camerawork and editing that present a masculine protagonist's gaze at a woman—whose body is displayed for maximum erotic excitement, which is the pleasure of scopophilia. Again, the pleasures of scopophilia and ego libido are intertwined in the male gaze.

As a medium, cinema often contains a "conscious aim" to "eliminate the intrusive camera presence and prevent a distancing awareness in the audience" (Mulvey 1975, 843). This means that a movie theater's atmosphere (e.g., the dark space, quiet environment, and separated seating) combined with the camerawork, editing, and other cinematic technologies actively help audiences lose themselves in the cinematic action. Instead of noticing how they look at a two-dimensional screen, moviegoers are often subsumed into the camera's way of seeing, merging their "gaze" with the protagonist's and thus embodying the male gaze.

The Male Gaze Today

In 2015, forty years after publishing "Visual Pleasure and Narrative Cinema," Mulvey noted that the male gaze is still rampant in visual entertainment and that "exploitative images" of women and girls are pervasive across a wide variety of screens (Mulvey 2015, 485; Kornfield 2025). Indeed, media such as television and photographic journalism (especially photojournalism of female politicians and athletes) is often rife with versions of the male gaze. There are many important differences among how television, photographic journalism, cinema, and other camera-based media are produced and experienced, and media scholars carefully attend to those nuances. For instance, television lacks a movie theater's quiet and dark environment and this can significantly lessen the likelihood of an audience member losing themself in the on-screen protagonist and experiencing ego libido. And yet, a lot of contemporary screen media portrays women's bodies as erotic spectacles and invites audiences to identify themselves with a patriarchal and masculine vantage point, gazing at and passing judgment on women. As such, although Mulvey's original article focused on Hollywood cinema from the 1940s to 1970s, feminist scholars continue to use the concept of the male gaze to analyze contemporary screen media.

One of the most important and enduring parts of Mulvey's analysis of the male gaze is the way it affects women. Building on John Berger's writing, Mulvey argued that women who are exposed to the male gaze—so basically all of us—often internalize a "way of seeing" so that we "watch" ourselves and other women from a patriarchal viewpoint. Essentially, we are trained to look at other women, and to look at ourselves in mirrors and within our own inner minds, in a way that first and foremost assesses our level of attractiveness to heterosexual men. Just as literate people read first and "see" other aspects later, so too, we "see" women's level of heterosexual attractiveness before becoming cognizant of practically anything else.

We judge our own bodies—and other women's bodies—not by their strength, comfort, effectiveness, capacity, or health but by what our culture dictates as "sexy" and "beautiful" in the eyes of patriarchal, heterosexual men. This effect can be so strong that many women feel disembodied. Rather than living their bodies, many women feel as if they were watching their bodies perform and are conscious of a sense of performance even when they are alone.

I cannot imagine a world in which I don't see women, especially myself, through the male gaze. But I was born only a decade or so after Mulvey published on the male gaze. It is my hope that as media technologies and platforms proliferate, the male gaze might recede in popularity, ultimately becoming an archaic cinematic technique of the past. Afterall, as Mulvey's filmmaking itself demonstrates, there are many ways to visualize a narrative; we need not succumb to patriarchy in order to have beautiful and intriguing screen-based media entertainment.

Sarah Kornfield

See Also: Bechdel Test; Disciplinary Power; Patriarchy

Further Reading
Berger, John. 1972. *Ways of Seeing*. London: Penguin.
Friz, Amanda M., and Marissa L. Fernholtz. 2020. "The Male Gaze in the Medical Classroom: Proximity, Objectivity, and Objectification in 'The Pornographic Anatomy Book.'" *Women's Studies in Communication* 43, no. 3: 292–316.
Kornfield, Sarah. 2025. *Watching Women: Femininity on TV*. Berlin: De Gruyter.
Monahan, John. 2001. "Coloring Single Stroop Elements: Reducing Automaticity or Slowing Color Processing." *Journal of General Psychology* 128, no. 1: 98–112.
Mulvey, Laura. (1975) 1999. "Visual Pleasure and Narrative Cinema." In *Film Theory and Criticism: Introductory Readings*, edited by Leo Braudy and Marshall Cohen, 833–44. New York: Oxford University Press.
Mulvey, Laura. 2015. "Visual Pleasure at 40." *Screen* 56, no. 4: 481–5.

MANA: A NATIONAL LATINA ORGANIZATION

Founded in 1974 by Gloria Hernandez, Bettie Baca, Sharleen Maldonado Cross, and Blandina Cardenas, MANA began as a feminist organization designed to give voice to Mexican American women who were being excluded from important conversations in their communities (Márquez 2003, 91; History 2024). Originally known as the Mexican-American Women's National Association, this organization provided a "platform for leadership in the national discourse." Over time, MANA developed local chapters across the United States and—recognizing the broader need for representation among all women of Hispanic/Latin descent—MANA grew into its current self with a new name, MANA: A National Latina Organization (History 2024).

MANA is organized around the goals of "Leadership, Service, Education, and Advocacy for Latinas nationwide," and their members volunteer in local programs, such as teaching adult financial literacy classes and youth mentoring (History 2024). MANA is especially active in Washington, D.C., where it has maintained an office longer than any other political Mexican American organization (Márquez 2003, 91). In the nation's capital, MANA's members contribute "the leading Latina voice" by advocating in Congress and the White House (Advocacy 2024). For instance, MANA members have testified before Congress regarding topics such as pay equity, adolescent pregnancy, school dropout experiences, and bilingual education (Márquez 2003, 94–5). MANA also advocates on behalf of Latinas through amicus briefs filed with the Supreme Court (Advocacy 2024). The term "amicus" refers to a "friend of the court," and amicus briefs are filed by organizations that are not directly involved in a case but whose members will be affected by the outcome or who have a perspective or expertise that is pertinent to the case but is not being voiced in the case itself.

Historically, male-centered Hispanic/Latino organizations ignored or undervalued both Latinas' leadership and the unique oppressions affecting Latinas. Likewise, mainstream feminist organizations during the 1960s and 1970s were often led by white women and focused on issues affecting white women. As an organization, MANA steps into these gaps, raising up generations of Latina leaders and advocating for reproductive rights, the Equal Rights Amendment (ERA), and the end of intimate partner and sexual violence, knowing that these issues have "a profound impact on the well-being" of Latinx communities (Márquez 2003, 95–6).

Throughout its history and still to this day, MANA partners with a variety of organizations, building coalitions in order to better advocate for Latinas. For instance, they partner with organizations such as the National Hispanic Leadership Agenda (NHLA) and the ERA Coalition.

Knowing that Latinas' accomplishments are routinely overlooked and tired of being asked, "Where are your Latina Leaders?" MANA developed the MANA Las Primeras awards in 1990. These awards recognize Latinas who "demonstrate important 'firsts' in their fields with a national impact," and they celebrate the "important contributions Latinas make to this country" (Las Primeras 2024). Additionally, these awards help make Latina leaders more visible.

Currently, MANA has eighteen regional chapters and a variety of affiliates across the United States. They welcome new members and are actively working with young people through the Hermanitas program and the Hermana Initiative. "Hermanitas" means little sister, and the Hermanitas program partners Latinas aged eleven to eighteen with trained mentors from their local communities. "Hermana" means sister, but the Hermana Initiative is gender-inclusive, inviting community members to pledge to be an "Hermana/Hermano/Hermanx" by being a role model and by serving, educating, and advocating for Latinas in their communities. MANA is an important and influential feminist organization, and their leadership and activism is making the United States a better nation.

Sarah Kornfield

See Also: Equal Rights Amendment (ERA); Intimate Partner Violence; Reproductive Rights

Further Reading

Advocacy. 2024. *MANA: A National Latina Organization.* Accessed March 25, 2025. https://www.hermana.org/advocacy.

History. 2024. *MANA: A National Latina Organization.* Accessed March 25, 2025. https://www.hermana.org/history.

Las Primeras. 2024. *MANA: A National Latina Organization.* Accessed March 25, 2025. https://www.hermana.org/las-primeras.

Márquez, Benjamin. 2003. *Constructing Identities in Mexican-American Political Organizations: Choosing Issues, Taking Sides.* Austin: University of Texas Press.

MARXIST FEMINISM

Marxist feminism is a strand of feminist theory and activism that especially attends to class struggle, financial equity, labor, resources, and the means of production. Marxist feminism expanded across Europe and the United States during the 1900s, becoming more prominent in the United States during the 1960s and 1970s (Anish and Vishnupriya 2019, 25).

Marxist feminists aim for total gender equality—which they see as dependent on reforming "the economic relations of capitalism" (Pietilä 2005, 274). Essentially, Marxist feminists see sexism and oppression more broadly as reliant on and often caused by the inequalities of capitalism. For Marxist feminists, then, any progress toward ending sexism and its interlocking oppressions will be intertwined with economic reforms and, likewise, moving toward economic justice also moves society closer to other forms of equality.

Private Property and Material Inequity

Marxist feminists highlight the role that *material* plays in inequality. They tend to focus on actual stuff—like raw resources, factories, and commodities. More mainstream strands of feminism typically focus on concepts such as "power," "prejudice," "structures," and "oppression," which are real but often intangible and thus can be hard to explain. Marxist feminists, however, tend to focus on more tangible things. For instance, they argue that the privatization of land allows an owner class to monopolize the resources (e.g., wood, aluminum, ore, water) that a community needs by owning the land where those resources are found. Then, the owner class sells the resources—perhaps at exorbitant prices—to other community members, creating a cycle in which the land owners profit and the other community members become impoverished as they buy the resources they need to survive.

Marxist feminists argue that the privatization of property and capitalist economic systems specifically disadvantage women and feminized people by not compensating their labor. Most domestic and reproductive labor (cooking, cleaning, childcare, eldercare, etc.) is done by women and most of it is uncompensated. As such, women typically do the work that is essential to family and community health without any compensation. We live in a capitalist economic system that values waged labor and profit. This means that not only is women's labor exploited (women work without wages) but women themselves become disvalued in society since they work without compensation—doing what has colloquially become known as "women's work."

Feminist Marxist Policies

For more than a hundred years, feminists in the United States have been advocating for economic policies in order to end the intertwined systems of economic, sexist, and racist oppression. For instance, in the late 1800s, Charlotte Perkins Gilman (1898) argued that women should be compensated for their reproductive labor. In the 1940s, Mary Inman helped labor activists organize for women's rights within the labor force (Gabin 2004). In the 1970s, Margaret Benston and Peggy Morton argued that homemakers should receive wages from the state (Vogel 2013). In the 1980s, Angela Davis argued that domestic labor is not just gendered but also raced as she critiqued capitalism's "profit-motive" (1983).

Today, Marxist feminists in the United States often advocate for more socialist policies and reforms such as universal basic income—where every citizen receives a guaranteed stipend from the government. For instance, in his 2020 political campaign, Andrew Yang proposed what he called the "Freedom Dividend," which would have provided "every American adult over the age of 18" with "$1000/month," resulting in $12,000 per year, regardless of their "work status or any other factor" (Yang 2020). A universal basic income would serve as a safety net for people who lose their jobs and it would value—and compensate—the domestic and reproductive labor that currently goes unpaid. Ultimately, Marxist feminism insists that feminists pay attention to the tangible, material, economic ways that injustices take place and advocates for reforms and revolutions that would radically change economic structures . . . thus depriving the imperialist white supremacist patriarchy of its resources and profit.

Sarah Kornfield

See Also: Capitalism; Davis, Angela; Domestic Labor; Equal Pay; Labor Activism; Reproductive Labor; Socialism

Further Reading

Anish, K., and N. S. Vishnupriya. 2019. "Marxist Feminist Approach to R. Chudamani's 'We Don't Know.'" *Language in India* 19, no. 7: 24–8.

Davis, Angela. 1983. *Women, Race and Class*. New York: Vintage.

Gabin, Nancy. 2004. "Review: *Red Feminism: American Communism and the Making of Women's Liberation*." *Labor* 1, no. 2: 142–5.

Gilman, Charlotte Perkins. 1898. *Women and Economics: A Study of the Economic Relation Between Men and Women as a Factor in Social Evolution*. Boston: Small, Maynard, & Co.

Pietilä, Veikko. 2005. *On the Highway of Mass Communication Studies*. Cresskill, NJ: Hampton Pr.

Vogel, Lise. 2013. *Marxism and the Oppression of Women: Toward a Unitary Theory*. Leiden: Brill.

Yang, Andrew. 2020. "The Freedom Dividend." *Yang2020.com*. Accessed December 30, 2024. https://2020.yang2020.com/policies/the-freedom-dividend/.

MATRILINY

A matrilineal society is one in which "descent is traced through the female rather than the male line and property is often inherited in the same way" (Nelson 2023). Or to put it more simply, the family line is passed through the mother. Essentially, matriliny means that when it comes to where you live, who you live with, and what you can inherit, it matters who your mother and grandmother are—not who your father is. In matrilineal societies, both women and men belong to their mother's kin group (Nelson 2023). In matrilineal societies, women invest resources into raising their own children (who are part of their kin group) and men often invest resources into raising their sisters' children (who are part of their kin group). There are over 160 matrilineal populations throughout the world—including Africa, Asia, Australia, and the Americas (Surowiec, Snyder, and Creanza 2019, 3).

Organizing Social and Family Life

There are many ways to arrange social and family life—and anthropologists have a variety of technical terms that help make sense of these arrangements. In addition to patriarchy (which typically includes patriliny—where descent and inheritance follow the father's line) and matriliny, there are arrangements such as matrilocal societies, where women stay with or near their own families after marriage and their husbands move to be with them, and matrifocal societies, in which women are the heads of the family but not necessarily the heads of government or community leaders. And then, of course, there is matriarchy.

To understand matriarchy and how it interacts with matriliny, we need to understand patriarchy. In its simplest form, patriarchal societies are ones in which men have the right to rule: men rule over the distribution of resources, over the family, over the community, and over the government—because they are men. Patriarchal societies are almost always also patrilineal, patrifocal (with men as the heads of households), and patrilocal (women move to their husband's family homes and/or towns).

People are often unaware that real matriarchal societies exist and simply assume that matriarchy would be like patriarchy except flipped so that women rule. However, matriarchy is real, and the study of real matriarchal societies shows that this is not the case. Matriarchy is not the reversal of patriarchy: it does not result in oppressive decision-making structures.

Matriarchal societies often include matrilineal arrangements but have complex governing systems. For example, as Camilla Nelson (2023) explains, the Minangkabau people in West Sumatra are the "world's largest continuing matrilineal society with a population of over 5 million." They pass ancestry and family name through the female line, along with "house, land, and livestock." The Minangkabau are also a matrilocal society, with men "moving into their wives' homes on marriage." This is a matriarchal society, and family and social governance clearly revolves around women, but "all decision-making requires consensus based on principles of mutual responsibility." Which is to say, this matriarchal society governs not by a top-down hierarchy or a "might-makes-right" mentality but through deliberation, mutual care, and compromise.

Sex, Childbearing, and Inheritance

Women in matrilineal societies often have much greater autonomy in deciding whether or not to have sex, in choosing their sexual partners, and in dissolving those partnerships than women who live in patriarchal societies. This is largely due to the way matrilineal societies organize inheritance and family descent.

Consider how (except in the case of surrogacy) when a person gives birth, that person knows for certain that the child who came out of their body is their offspring—and so does everyone else. In matrilineal societies, then, children can inherit property and resources from their birth parent and the family knows for certain that the family's resources are staying within the family line. However, there is no like-type guarantee that a woman's child is any given man's offspring. This means that when property and resources are inherited from father to son in patriarchal-patrilineal societies, there is no way to ensure that children are actually part of the father's kin group—except to exert excruciating control over women's sexuality, and even then there can be doubts.

As such, most patriarchal-patrilineal societies place an emphasis on controlling women's sexuality. This often looks like an obsession with women's virginity and might include cloistering women away from nonfamily men; chastity belts; honor killings; public shaming (and imprisonment or execution) of "loose" women; the murder or abandonment of "illegitimate" children; and so on. Patriarchal-patrilineal societies control women's sexuality in order to ensure the patrilineal line. This comes at an extreme cost to women's autonomy and well-being—and results in the abandonment if not murder of "suspect" offspring.

All of this is different in matrilineal societies. Within a matrilineal system—as Carol P. Christ explains—there is no such thing as "illegitimate children because all children have mothers." Likewise, there are no "loose" women (and here Christ encourages us to think about the meaning of the term "loose" women!) because "women are free to have sex with whomever they choose." There are no "whores" because "there is no shortage of sexual partners" caused by virginity standards and there is "no exchange of sex for money." Additionally, there is no "Virgin-Whore dichotomy" because women are free to have sex or not—there is no shame or praise in either direction (Christ 2016, 218).

The Bantu-Speaking Diaspora

Many of today's matrilineal societies are distant decedents of Bantu-speaking people who lived in a region of Africa where Nigeria and Cameroon are today. Spreading into an ancient diaspora that covered most of Central and Southern Africa, Bantu-speaking people (who are not an ethnic group) carried their matrilineal—and often matrilocal, matrifocal, and matriarchal—systems with them. The geographical regions Bantu-speaking Africans spread throughout are now known by anthropologists as the Bantu Matrilineal Zone or BMZ.

As Christine Saidi (2023) explains, early Bantu-speaking Africans did not have binary understandings of gender and their pronouns (in English, words such as "she," "he," and "them") and possessive pronouns (in English, words such as "hers," "his," and "theirs") were gender neutral. Age and birth order were and are extremely important within the BMZ but gender not so much.

Indeed, as Ifi Amadiume (1987) and Oyeronke Oyewùmí (1997) demonstrated, binary thinking does not "work well in African contexts" where "a more flexible concept of gender is needed in order to capture situations where certain social *positions* may be gendered, but where these positions may be taken up by a man or a woman as the case may be" (Arnfred 2007, 144).

For instance, within many of the BMZ's people groups, maternal uncles (your mother's brother) were referred to as a "mother without breasts" (Saidi 2023, 363–5). Similarly, patrilineal communities within the BMZ were clearly influenced by their matrilineal neighbors, creating the position of "social fathers" for women who had the means and desire to create their own family branches. These were typically older mothers who were often divorced. They married a woman from their community and fathered children with her through "the use of a male surrogate." The children were then part of the social father's line (Saidi 2023, 365).

Around 1500 CE, some men who were traders in the BMZ became increasingly wealthy due to expanded trade routes. Within their matrilineal communities, these men were unable to "create their own branch of the family" and were still "under the authority of sororal groups," a term that refers to the collection of "related mothers and grandmothers" who are the "center of power within the family."

These men were able to become "social mothers," creating positions "of authority for successful traders" and enabling them to start their own families "without seriously disrupting matrilineal social institutions" (Saidi 2023, 365–6).

As these examples demonstrate, gendered identities were far more flexible within the BMZ than in Western patriarchal societies. Moreover, within the BMZ parenthood and family arrangements were approached creatively, with the possibility that all people could potentially become social parents "as either a father or mother" depending on their community (Saidi 2023, 366). European colonialism "attempted to degrade or destroy African" cultures, deeming them barbaric. European colonial invasions of the BMZ instituted patriarchy across this region. The European colonizers, missionaries, and anthropologists who visited the region described "Bantu-speaking people in Western-centric binary and deterministic gendered terms," imposing patriarchal gender hierarchies onto families and communities within the BMZ (Saidi 2023, 366). Despite several hundred years of violent colonization and Western intervention, many Bantu-speaking communities still follow "matrilineal traditions of descent and inheritance of land" within the BMZ today (Nelson 2023).

Benefits of Matriliny

It comes as no surprise to feminists that matriliny is beneficial to women: the ability to provide for one's self and one's family, the stability provided by inheritance, the support provided by close familial ties, and the ability to make one's own sexual and childbearing choices all amount to better outcomes in terms of health, happiness, and longevity. Moreover, as already discussed, when matrilineal societies are also matriarchal (meaning women not only form the line of descent but also occupy the positions of community leadership and governance), decision-making typically "requires consensus based on principles of mutual responsibility" (Nelson 2023). This means that matriliny is also good for men. Again, matrilineal-matriarchal societies are *not* a reversal of patriarchy with its dominating oppressions and hierarchies.

For example, studying the matrilineal-matriarchal Mosuo people in China's Yunnan and Sichuan regions, scholars have noted that women in these communities are "highly autonomous and have a long history of personal freedom beyond that which is known to women in many other cultures" (Hendricks 2021). These women's blood pressure and inflammation rates (chronic and deadly problems for women around the globe) are significantly lower than the norm, even when compared to the rates within neighboring patriarchal communities in the region (Reynolds et al. 2020). The Mosuo men, however, have very similar rates of hypertension and inflammation as the men in the neighboring patriarchal communities—meaning that there is no "adverse health effect" for men "living in a matriarchal society" (Hendricks 2021). Indeed, a team of scholars led by Siobhán Mary Mattison concluded their analysis of health within the Mosuo people, writing that patriarchy and patriliny reduces "autonomy and resource access for women" and "these inequalities can have tangible biological effects that contribute to gender disparities in health" (Reynolds et al. 2020, 30326). Or to put it plainly, oppression is bad for our health (Hendricks 2021).

Matriliny offers a clear and realistic alternative to patriarchy. Human societies are not doomed to oppressive organizational structures. Across the globe, communities have historically chosen and continue to choose matrilineal ways to organize family and social life—with considerable benefits in terms of health, happiness, and longevity for women.

Sarah Kornfield

See Also: Colonialism; Patriarchy; Virginity

Further Reading

Amadiume, Ifi. 1987. *Male Daughters, Female Husbands: Gender and Sex in an African Society*. London: Zed Books.

Arnfred, Signe. 2007. "Sex, Food, and Female Power: Discussion of Data Material from Northern Mozambique." *Sexualities* 10, no. 2: 141–58.

Christ, Carol P. 2016. "A New Definition of Patriarchy: Control of Women's Sexuality, Private Property, and War." *Feminist Theology* 24, no. 3: 214–25.

Hendricks, Scotty. 2021. "Why Living in a Matriarchal Society is Better for Women's Health." *World Economic Forum*, February 11, 2021. Accessed August 15, 2024. https://www.weforum.org/agenda/2021/02/women-matriarchal-society-improved-health-patriarchy/.

Nelson, Camilla. 2023. "Matrilineal Societies Exist Around the World—It's Time to Look Beyond the Patriarchy." *The Conversation*, March 23, 2023. Accessed August 14, 2024. https://theconversation.com/friday-essay-matrilineal-societies-exist-around-the-world-its-time-to-look-beyond-the-patriarchy-200825.

Oyewùmí, Oyeronke. 1997. *The Invention of Women: Making an African Sense of Western Gender Discourses*. Minneapolis: University of Minnesota Press.

Reynolds, Adam Z. et al. 2020. "Matriliny Reverses Gender Disparities in Inflammation and Hypertension among the Mosuo of China." *Proceedings of the National Academy of Sciences (PNAS)* 177, no. 48: 30324–7.

Saidi, Christine. 2023. "My Husband is also My Daughter: The Social History of the Bantu Matrilineal Zone, 1450–1800." *Early Modern Women* 17, no. 2: 362–6.

Saini, Angela. 2024. *The Patriarchs: The Origins of Inequality*. Boston: Beacon Press.

Surowiec, Alexandra, Kate T. Snyder, and Nicole Creanza. 2019. "A Worldwide View of Matriliny: Using Cross-cultural Analyses to Shed Light on Human Kinship Systems." *Philosophical Transactions B* 372. https://doi.org/10.1098/rstb.2018.0077.

THE MAY TEST

The May Test lays out principles or stipulations that entertainment must "pass" in to be considered relatively decent (or at least not terrible) when representing trans people (Kornfield 2025). Drawing inspiration from the Bechdel Test, Kiley May developed the May Test largely because film and television have been portraying trans people in such terrible ways for such a long time.

The May Test is designed to inspire "more original, authentic, and positive representations of transgender people" (May 2019). As written by Kiley May, the May Test has seven stipulations: (1) trans characters should be portrayed by trans actors; (2) trans characters should be "safe, stable, and secure (not homeless, assaulted, or victimized—no more bloody noses!)"; (3) trans characters should be "thriving, healthy, and happy"; (4) trans characters should be "in love, loveable, and dating (not a lonely romantic pariah)"; (5) trans identities should not be "used as a joke" or revealed as a "surprise" or a "gag"; (6) trans characters should not have occupations as sex workers, drug dealers, or thieves; and (7) gender transition "should not be the focus of the story" nor should the storyline focus on a trans character's "struggle" with their identity (May 2019). May adds that films and television series can earn "bonus points" on this "test" if "the trans character is in a lead role or has a gender queer, non-conforming or neutral gender identity" (2019).

Kiley May is a "trans woman working as an actor, screenwriter, and filmmaker," and she developed the May Test precisely because she is "frustrated and offended" by the way films and TV series have been portraying trans characters (2019).

History of Trans Media Representation

Historically, movies and TV series have portrayed trans characters, especially transwomen, as dangerous, as "prostitutes or people who intentionally deceive others in their gender presentations" (Thomas 2020, 530; Bettcher 2007; Booth 2011; McLaren, Bryant, and Brown 2021, 172). For instance, in a 1974 episode of TV series *The Streets of San Francisco*, a "professional female impersonator" psychotically kills people "while in his female persona but doesn't remember doing it when he's a man" (Anderson 2015). Alternatively, television and films have openly mocked trans characters or killed off any briefly sympathetic portrayals of trans characters, as was the case in *All in the Family*, another early TV portrayal of a trans woman (Anderson 2015).

After decades of these types of representation, films and television series began to shift toward less overtly transphobic portrayals. In response, *Time Magazine* declared 2014 the transgender "tipping point" and the *Los Angeles Times* similarly announced 2015 as a "landmark year for transgender people." Both news outlets focused on Laverne Cox's activism and her character, Sophia Burset, on the Netflix series *Orange Is the New Black* (Steinmetz 2014; Anderson 2015).

In general, representations of trans characters have improved in US films and television series. Rather than reinforcing negative stereotypes and horrible myths about trans people, using trans characters as "fodder for sensational storytelling," more recent representation—especially representation that adheres to the May Test—is likely to represent trans characters in positive and relatable ways (Anderson 2015).

Even with more positive portrayals of transgender characters, US society has seen a rise in hostility toward transgender people. Persecution and hostility have actually increased as the "wider public becomes more familiar" with transgender identities (Keegan 2022, 26). In the United States, anti-trans legislation has limited—for instance—the healthcare trans people receive, their ability to use public bathrooms, their ability to play sports, and LGBTQ+ communities' ability to perform drag in public (ACLU 2023).

Gender Queer, Nonconforming, and Gender-Neutral Representations

Cultural theorist Cáel M. Keegan (2022) notes that contemporary mainstream representations of trans characters—the "good" portrayals that pass the May Test—still objectify trans characters. Specifically, the portrayals that are heralded as "good" by mainstream media tend to be the portrayals in which trans characters are fully assimilated into the gender binary. Or to put it more simply, in contemporary films and television, transgender characters are typically the most masculine men or the most feminine women on screen (Kornfield 2025). These characters have almost always already medically transitioned and they follow very stereotypical gender roles. For instance, on *Orange Is the New Black*, Laverne Cox's character, Sophia Burset, works as a hairstylist.

These representations tend to uphold the patriarchal binary that aligns male bodies with masculinity and female bodies with femininity. As such, these representations double down on the idea that bodies, including surgically modified bodies, map onto and predetermine gender expressions (Steinbock 2020). This reinforces the cultural assumption that "someone who looks like a man or woman will have the corresponding sexual organs," an assumption that Kristen Schilt cheekily refers to as "cultural genitalia" (2010, 50). Or to put it another way, these contemporary portrayals of trans characters tend to reinforce essentialist logic by assuming that gender is caused by one's genitals.

And here, Kiley May's tongue-in-cheek recommendation that a film or TV series can earn "bonus points" if a trans character has a "gender queer, non-conforming or neutral gender identity" becomes more salient (2019). Indeed, Cáel M. Keegan likewise recommends that in order to disrupt the patriarchal gender binary, essentialist logic, and the cultural fixation on genitals, we need more representations that are gender queer, gender nonconforming, and gender neutral.

Sarah Kornfield

See Also: The Bechdel Test; Essentialism; Male Gaze; Trans Theory

Further Reading

American Civil Liberties Union (ACLU). 2023. "Mapping Attacks on LGBTQ Rights in US State Legislatures." Accessed August 14, 2024. https://www.aclu.org/legislative-attacks-on-lgbtq-rights?state=.

Anderson, Tre'vell. 2015. "Visibility Matters: Transgender Characters on Film and Television Through the Years." *Los Angeles Times*, December 18, 2015. https://timelines.latimes.com/transgender-characters-film-tv-timeline/.

Bettcher, Talia Mae. 2007. "Evil Deceivers and Make-Believers: On Transphobic Violence and the Politics of Illusion." *Hypatia* 22, no. 3: 43–65.

Booth, Ewan Tristan. 2011. "Queering Queer Eye: The Stability of Gay Identity Confronts the Liminality of Trans Embodiment." *Western Journal of Communication* 75, no. 2: 185–204.

Keegan, Cáel M. 2022. "On the Necessity of Bad Trans Objects." *Film Quarterly* 75, no. 3: 26–37.

Kornfield, Sarah. 2025. *Watching Women: Femininity on TV*. Berlin: De Gruyter Press.

May, Kiley. 2019. "There Wasn't a Bechdel Test for Trans Representation, So I Made One." *Vice*, November 26, 2019. www.vice.com/en/article/7x5nje/there-wasnt-a-bechdel-test-for-trans-representation-so-i-made-one.

McLaren, Jackson Taylor, Susan Bryant, and Brian Brown. 2021. "'See Me! Recognize Me!' An Analysis of Transgender Media Representation." *Communication Quarterly* 69, no. 2: 172–91.

Thomas, Victoria E. 2020. "Gazing at 'It': An Intersectional Analysis of Transnormativity and Black Womanhood in *Orange is the New Black*." *Communication, Culture & Critique* 13, no. 4: 519–35.

Schilt, Kristen. 2010. *Just One of the Guys? Transgender Men and the Persistence of Gender Inequality*. Chicago: University of Chicago Press.

Steinbock, Eliza. 2020. "The Wavering Line of Foreground and Background: A Proposal for the Schematic Analysis of Trans Visual Culture." *Journal of Visual Culture* 19, no. 2: 171–83.

Steinmetz, Katy. 2014. "The Transgender Tipping Point." *Time Magazine*, May 29, 2014. https://time.com/135480/transgender-tipping-point/.

MEN'S RIGHTS MOVEMENTS

The history of men's movements is diverse, with both feminist and anti-feminist groups. Men, at different times, have advocated as men for men regarding family law, conscription, mental health support, circumcision reform, domestic violence against men, and (supposedly) false rape accusations. However, men's rights activists typically focus on finding a "lost masculinity" and blame "the family court system, affirmative action programs, man-hating feminists, gold-digging ex-wives, political correctness, job-taking immigrants, and queer visibility" for "emasculating" men (Kelly 2018, 163).

Men's rights activists are known for portraying men as victims, despite the fact that men (particularly those who are middle and upper class, straight, and white) continue to hold significant positions of privilege in many US and global hierarchies. For instance, less than 20 percent of the world's landholders are women; women make up more than two-thirds of the world's 796 million illiterate people; and women receive lower wages for the same work (Inter-Agency Task Force on Rural Women 2012). Moreover, one in six women in the United States have been the victims of attempted or completed rape (The US Dept. of Justice 2020). As such, while feminists are fighting to end oppression, men's rights movements typically rally to maintain men's power at all costs.

History of Men's Rights Movements in the United States

The roots of the modern men's rights movements can be traced to the pro-feminist Men's Liberation Movement that grew in response to feminist organizing in the 1970s. As feminists began to challenge gender roles, men rightfully asked, "What does that have to do with me?" Educated men began to host men's liberation groups—much like feminists' consciousness-raising groups—where men could talk about their suffering due to gender roles.

Sex role theory (the idea that there are strict sex-segregated gender roles) informed these conversations surrounding men's liberation. While men acknowledged the importance of feminism and the need for gender equality, they stressed "the high costs of the male sex role to men's health, emotional lives, and relationships" as being of equal importance with women's rights (Messner 1998, 256). Men were encouraged to share their emotions by breaking down internalized norms like "boys don't cry." Ultimately, men focused on personal transformation rather than social change. By the mid-1970s, these men's groups had split between those who wanted to do away with men's institutional privilege and those who "angrily disputed feminist claims that patriarchy benefited men at women's expense" (Messner 1998, 256). The Men's Liberation Movement slipped into obscurity by the end of the decade and the (anti-feminist) men's rights movement rose to prominence.

Men's rights turned toward family law as men personally felt and continue to feel a loss of power in the family. Ronald Reagan signed the country's first no-fault divorce bill in 1969, and the first Child Custody Act was passed in 1970; these new family laws chipped away at men's patriarchal control over the family. At the same time, the economy changed: stagnating wages meant that family households needed two incomes—and this chipped away at the power men derived from being the family "breadwinner." The men's rights movement tended to scapegoat women for these changes, stereotyping divorced women as greedy, evil ex-wives and blaming women in the workforce for the economic stagnation.

The men's rights movement rallied around divorced fathers. In many ways, divorced fathers are the perfect symbol for the men's rights movement since their power is challenged by ex-wives in both economic and family terms through custody policies and child support. Men's rights leader Richard Doyle explained men's anger by opining that "Men are regarded as mere guests in their own homes, evictable any time at the whims of wives and judges" (Messner 1998, 267). This perspective is an inversion of reality: for so many years, wives and daughters have been legally beholden to their husbands' and fathers' whims, and women often remain financially dependent on masculine partners in ways that render them powerless in their own homes.

Father's rights activists, who are predominately white and middle- or working-class, argue that courts are biased against men. They bemoan the lack of equal childcare time shared between parents, the supposed unfairness of legal child support obligations, and a general financial "greediness" by mothers (Collier and Sheldon 2006, 15–16). Father's rights activists rarely acknowledge how work and family dynamics benefit fathers, both before and after divorces (Coltrane and Hickman 1992). Additionally, married fathers are statistically unlikely to contribute 50 percent of the household's childcare, which means that fifty-fifty splits in custody time are rarely in children's best interests. The father's rights movement has been successful because "the rhetoric of fathers' rights gives the illusion of equality, but, in essence, the demands are to continue the practice of inequality in postdivorce but now with legal sanction" (Bretoria and Drakik 1995, 252).

Mythopoeticism and Masculinity

During the 1960s–1990s, the men's rights movement worked on legal reforms to increase men's power while also championing a spiritual rediscovery of a supposedly "lost masculinity." Poet and author Robert Bly prescribed wilderness retreats, self-actualization, and homosocial (same-sex) bonding to combat the supposed "sissy-fying" of masculinity—which he blamed on the liberal social policies often championed by the Democratic Party (Gremillion 2011, 44).

This version of the men's rights movement is known as the mythopoetic movement. It calls men to return to their (imagined) natural state. The main themes of most mythopoetic men's screeds are "essentialist assumptions about gender distinctions," a diagnosis of contemporary manhood as too effeminate, "the search for lost fathers (and father figures)," and "a retrieval of heroic archetypes as models for men" (Gremillion 2011, 47). The "lost masculinity" men are encouraged to rediscover in themselves is typically conveyed through Jungian archetypes and the appropriation of Indigenous imagery in order to imagine masculinity as "deep and ancient": both strong and wild (Gremillion 2011, 47).

Presenting masculinity in this way allows men to deal with the suffering they feel because of strict gender roles, but it fails to question the gender binary or systems of power that enforce these roles. Some of these mythopoetic goals align with feminism as they question and refigure gender norms, emphasize men's responsibility to transform masculinity, and value nature (Gremillion 2011, 43). However, this version of the men's rights movement fails to address the realities that privilege men through hegemonic masculinity and that reproduce structural gender inequalities. Essentially, mythopoeticism fails to address the root of the problem: patriarchy. Today, the mythopoetic ideology continues to infuse the men's rights movement. For instance, men's rights activists often assert that men have a natural right to be wild and virile. This claim is dangerous: it often lays the groundwork for violence against women and other men.

The Men's Rights Movement Today

Men's rights efforts today are largely organized online. Collectively known as the "manosphere," this online organizing includes a variety of groups, "including MRAs [men's rights activists], pickup artists, MGOW (men going their own way), incels (involuntary celibates), [and] father's rights activists" (Marwick and Caplan 2018, 546). All these groups share a central belief that feminism and liberalism are corrupting society at large, and that men "must fight back against an overreaching, misandrist culture to protect their very existence" (Marwick and Caplan 2018, 546). Popular figureheads of the movement such as Jordan Peterson and Joe Rogan help men "fight back" against the "crisis of masculinity." Online communities like r/TheRedPill on Reddit give men a place to talk about how to become an "alpha," often focusing on sexual strategies. Others rally community members to harass prominent feminist speakers and thinkers, usually through online methods like "doxing (publishing personal information online), revenge porn (spreading intimate photos beyond their origins), social shaming, and intimidation" (Marwick and Caplan 2018, 544).

Patriarchy is always hierarchical, always obsessed with power and pecking orders. There is a hierarchy within the "manosphere," with alphas on top and incels (or betas) on bottom. Feminist men are also considered betas because they have supposedly fallen victim to women's domination. In theory, alphas have sex easily, with many different women. Following the norms for hegemonic masculinity, this community assumes that when men have sex they gain and assert their power. Tying sex to power typically has poor results for women in patriarchal societies. When men think of sex as "taking" and believe they have a right to "take" women's bodies for their own pleasure, violence often ensues. And here, incels (who are not successful in "taking" women) can use violence to express their resentment at being denied their supposed right to sex with women. For example, 22-year-old Elliot Rodger's manifesto explained that he wanted to "punish women"; he murdered six people and injured fourteen others in 2018 (Center on Extremism 2024). Other incels answered Rodger's manifesto with their own acts of violence, promising to continue the revolution Rodger started.

When facets of the men's rights movement focus on sexual violence, they tend to overestimate the number of men who are sexually victimized by women while also claiming that women falsely report experiencing rape. For instance, the intimate partner violence page of the Wiki 4 Men website features decontextualized reports that make it look like women perpetrate violence against men more often than the other way around (Intimate Partner Violence 2024). Using misleading, decontextualized, and cherry-picked evidence, the men's rights movement attempts to discredit feminism and other social justice movements that work to reduce violence against women and marginalized groups. The US National Crime Survey data shows that 91 percent of people who seek medical care for injuries received during spousal assault are women, and only 9 percent are men. More importantly, 91 percent of perpetrators are men (US Dept. of Justice 2020). Sexual violence against men is an important issue that deserves to be rectified, but to present sexual violence in the United States as if it were gender-neutral is unethical and blatantly false.

Moreover, the men's rights movement often accuses women of making false rape accusations against men. The rate of false accusations of rape is well-documented: of the cases brought to the police, over 90 percent are credible. Moreover, since most instances of rape and sexual assault go unreported, some estimates put the number of false reports at .005 percent (Flood 2022). As such, when men's rights activists claim that women falsely report rape, it capitalizes upon and reinforces rape myths and negative stereotypes of women as malicious liars and further discourages victims from coming forward.

Patriarchy, Men, and Feminism

Patriarchal gender roles urge men to dominate others and to close themselves off from their own emotional well-being. Feminist theorists such as bell hooks argue that while patriarchy offers many men power, it also damages them. bell hooks described patriarchy as a political and social system that "insists that males are inherently dominating" and "superior to women and everyone and everything else deemed weak." Within patriarchy, men's right to rule is maintained through dominance and "through various forms of psychological terrorism and violence" (hooks 2015, 75). Feminists are working to end all forms of domination, but the contemporary men's rights movement reasserts men's right to dominate others.

Feminism is "for everybody" and men are welcome partners within feminism's goal to dismantle patriarchy and end sexist oppression (hooks 2015). Genuinely feminist men recognize their own privilege, confront their own internalized beliefs about gender and power, and work to dismantle patriarchal systems of domination. Together, all feminists can create an inclusive, compassionate society where no one is bound by the limitations of patriarchal expectations, no one is oppressed by masculine domination, and no one is exploited.

Leah Miller

See Also: Consciousness Raising; Essentialism; Gender; Hegemonic Masculinity; hooks, bell; Patriarchy; Rape Myths

Further Reading

Bertoia, Carol E., and Janice Drakich. 1995. "The Fathers' Rights Movement: Contradictions in Rhetoric and Practice." In *Fatherhood: Contemporary Theory, Research and Social Policy*, edited by William Marsiglio. Thousand Oaks, CA: Sage.

Center on Extremism. 2024. "Incels (Involuntary Celibates)." *Anti-Defamation League*. Accessed October 11, 2024. https://www.adl.org/resources/backgrounder/incels-involuntary-celibates.

Collier, Richard, and Sally Sheldon, eds. 2006. *Fathers' Rights Activism and Law Reform in Comparative Perspective*. Oxford and Portland: Hart Publishing.

Coltrane, Scott, and Neal Hickman. 1992. "The Rhetoric of Rights and Needs: Moral Discourse in the Reform of Child Custody and Child Support Laws." *Social Problems* 39, no. 4: 400–20.

Flood, Michael. 2022. "False Allegations of Sexual and Domestic Violence: The Facts." *Men, Masculinities, and Gender Politics*, April 15, 2022. Accessed October 11, 2024. https://xyonline.net/content/false-allegations-sexual-and-domestic-violence-facts.
Gremillion, Helen. 2011. "Feminism and the Mythopoetic Men's Movement: Some Shared Concepts of Gender." *Women's Studies Journal* 25, no. 2: 43–55.
hooks, b. 2015. *Feminist Theory: From Margin to Center*. New York: Routledge.
Inter-Agency Task Force on Rural Women. 2012. "Rural Women and the Millennium Development Goals." United Nations Womenwatch. Accessed October 11, 2024. https://www.un.org/womenwatch/feature/ruralwomen/facts-figures.html.
Intimate Partner Violence. 2024. Wiki 4 Men. Accessed October 11, 2024. https://wiki4men.com/wiki/Intimate_partner_violence.
Kelly, Casey Ryan. 2018. "The Wounded Man: Foxcatcher and the Incoherence of White Masculine Victimhood." *Communication and Critical/Cultural Studies* 15, no. 2: 161–78.
Marwick, Alice E., and Robyn Caplan. 2018. "Drinking Male Tears: Language, the Manosphere, and Networked Harassment." *Feminist Media Studies* 18, no. 4: 543–59.
Messner, Michael. 1998. "The Limits of 'The Male Sex Role': An Analysis of the Men's Liberation and Men's Rights Movements' Discourse." *Gender & Society* 12, no. 3: 255–76. https://doi.org/10.1177/089124329801200300 2.
Straton, Jack. 1994. "The Myth of the 'Battered Husband Syndrome.'" *Masculinities* 2: 79–82.
The US Department of Justice. 2020. *National Archive of Criminal Justice Data*. Bureau of Justice Statistics. Accessed October 11, 2024. https://bjs.ojp.gov/data/national-archive-criminal-justice-data.

MENSTRUATION

Menstruation (also known as a period) is the phase within one's menstrual cycle that encompasses all of the mainstream buzz around this bodily phenomena. This includes three to five days of the uterine lining shedding (bleeding) resulting in cramping, hormonal dips, shifts in daily bodily care and attention, and so on. Periods provide useful information about one's reproductive system, informing the body about health and pregnancy. Every menstruator's experience is different as there are varying biological, social, cultural, political, and personal implications that impact one's ability to feel supported, comfortable, and celebrated; this can create barriers to accessing proper resources, comprehensive sex education, and bodily autonomy, making this a prominent issue within US feminism.

Menstruators are typically subjected to shame-based dialogue, policies, and ideologies surrounding menstruation. The patriarchy intentionally curates this shame-based reality. For instance, insisting that menstruation is unclean and thus people who menstruate are unclean. This ensures that women and girls feel isolated from one another and often causes menstruators to feel disembodied, embarrassed, unequipped, and gaslit about menstruation. Ultimately, the patriarchy has weaponized the very real, very sacred experience of menstruation and used it as a tool to control and abuse women's bodies. This stigmatization has become so integrated into our society that we are still timid while talking about periods, asking for a pad or tampon, and sharing experiences. Indeed, when menstruators discuss our periods, we are often afraid of rejection, embarrassed, and uncomfortable (Okamoto 2018).

The reality of living with a period is a holistic endeavor: the capacity for pregnancy can be anxiety provoking; living/working/parenting/hosting/connecting while actively bleeding is inconvenient; cramping can debilitate body functionality; and worrying that one might bleed through clothing in public is often quite intense.

Feminist Activism around Menstruation

Conversations around periods are becoming more normalized as many women work to dismantle the misogyny around periods. Gloria Steinem's famous essay "If Men Could Menstruate" has long inspired feminist activism around menstruation. In this essay, Steinem imagined a world in which men were the ones who had periods. Writing satirically, Steinem imagines how men would use their periods to reinforce their male privilege and how excellent healthcare for menstruation would be if men were the ones menstruating. For example, she describes how, if men could menstruate, they would brag about the heaviness of their flow or severity of their cramps as some sort of proof of masculinity. Period products would be free and accessible, and period blood would be discussed openly (Steinem 2019).

In 2015, author Rupi Kahr used Instagram to post a photo of herself lying in bed with a period blood stain on her pants; the image was quickly censored and removed by Instagram, which claimed that it was offensive and explicit content, therefore violating Instagram's community guidelines. Kahr took this opportunity to call out such misogyny and argued that Instagram does not do enough to censor actually "explicit" content: the exploitation and objectification of minors that is unmonitored. This is a clear example of how the sexualization of women and girls is excused in patriarchal structures while a menstruator's autonomous choice to use her period as activism was technologically policed.

Activist and August cofounder Nadya Okamoto has a fierce approach to normalizing and celebrating periods through social media and her lifestyle period brand. Okamoto famously embodies the brand's "mascot" known as the Period Fairy where she attends public events in a fairy costume that showcases herself wearing an August pad. She confidently dances and enjoys herself, handing out period products while having a visible pad with no shame. Videos of this activism and brand promotion went viral on Instagram and TikTok, clearly featuring how Okamoto—as the Period Fairy—combats patriarchal social norms and destigmatizes periods and period products. Despite the fact that over half of the population menstruates, menstruators have long lived within a zone of silence surrounding menstruation, and many of us don't even notice how we maintain this period secrecy by our silence, through our code words for periods, and by hiding our liners, pads, tampons, and menstrual cups. Okamoto is tired of such secrecy.

A lot of everyday activism stems from grassroots organizations that are invested in gender equality efforts by equipping public restrooms with period products. These products are accumulated through drives, donations, or fundraisers to amplify the importance of viewing period products as essential items. In many US states, period products are taxed as luxury goods (e.g., alcohol) rather than essential items (e.g., toilet paper); this is informally known as part of the "pink tax." This economic structure is another example of how misogyny is baked into our current social context; it communicates to consumers that period products are specialty items and not a necessity for someone (again, half the population!) who actively bleeds while trying to get a high school degree, give a career presentation, or simply walk to the food bank comfortably. Additionally, period products are also labeled as "feminine hygiene products," which communicates that, first, these products are feminine and, second, that they are hygienic products, which identifies periods as something that is dirty or unclean.

Feminist Approaches to Menstruation

Period poverty is a significant concern for feminists. Poverty is increasingly feminized (meaning that poverty increasingly and disproportionately affects women), and now one in nine women who are eighteen and older live in poverty in the United States. This means that period care—which can be quite expensive and thus inaccessible—is also impacted by poverty (Shengwei 2023). For menstruators who struggle to find or maintain food and shelter, money is typically spent on basic necessities—and period products (and women's health) are typically considered inessential as the luxury tax on period products so clearly indicates.

Period poverty creates health concerns as menstruators use scraps of cardboard, clothing, rags, or even trash to meet menstrual needs (Okamoto 2018). Period poverty is especially prominent in state prisons and jails. Not only are period products usually unavailable in sufficient quantities, but they are often only available through purchase at the commissary (Okamoto 2018).

Being informed about menstruation and the ways in which patriarchy and misogyny have oppressed menstruators and stigmatized periods is important to ending period shame and discrimination. But this information is also an important first step in helping impoverished and imprisoned menstruators who are deeply impacted by such patriarchy within our current justice system, economy, and healthcare.

It is important to center the lived experiences of women and girls when discussing menstruation, but it is also essential that feminist activism around menstruation be inclusive of all menstruators regardless of their sex or gender identities. Lots of people with different types of bodies and gender performances menstruate—including trans men, nonbinary folx, and many others. As such, feminists are working to remove exclusive language. Menstruation is experienced by anyone with a uterus; it is not synonymous with women.

Knowledge is power. The autonomy to ask questions about menstruation and have them answered honestly with accurate information, the ability to nurture your body, and care for your body's capacities are very powerful experiences. Feminists hope that every menstruator has this type of bodily autonomy.

Sutton Steensma

See Also: Birth Control; Bodily Autonomy; Feminization of Poverty; Menstruation Activism; Misogyny; Patriarchy; Pink Tax; Sex Education

Further Reading

Okamoto, Nadya. 2018. *Period Power: A Manifesto for The Menstrual Movement*. New York: Simon & Schuster.
Steinem, Gloria. 2019. "If Men Could Menstruate." *Women's Reproductive Health* 6, no. 3: 151–2. https://doi:10.1080/23293691.2019.1619050.
Sun, Shengwei. 2023. "National Snapshot: Poverty Among Women and Families." *National Women's Law Center*. Accessed July 21, 2024. https://nwlc.org/wp-content/uploads/2023/02/2023_nwlc_PovertySnapshot-converted.pdf.

MENSTRUATION ACTIVISM

Menstruation activism is a global feminist movement working toward menstrual equity. The concept of "menstrual equity," a term coined by menstrual movement activist Jennifer Weiss-Wolf (2017), concerns "the affordability, accessibility and safety of menstrual products for all people—including laws and policies—that acknowledge and consider menstruation." Beyond the availability of products, menstrual activism also works to address other aspects of periods, including the harmful emotions caused by ongoing stigma and shame. Though discussing menstruation has become less taboo in the past decade, menstrual activism really began in the 1970s with books like *Our Bodies Ourselves* and feminist activists like Judy Blume and Gloria Steinem bringing the topic to the forefront of popular discussions (Bobel 2008).

Menstruation activism has looked like a lot of things—protesting, writing, free bleeding, lobbying, and more! There are approximately 1.9 billion girls, women, nonbinary, and trans individuals throughout the world who menstruate, and they all deserve to receive comprehensive information about their menstrual cycle and should be able to participate in daily activities free from shame or discrimination.

Period Poverty, or, Why We Need Menstrual Activism

Period poverty is not a new phenomenon by any stretch but has become a much more publicly discussed issue due to the work of menstrual activists. Period poverty can be broadly defined as the inability to afford or have consistent access to period products without help. I pause to describe the phenomenon of period poverty so that readers can understand what exactly these menstrual activists are up against. It is not necessarily that government and legislative bodies are actively discriminating against menstruators, it's that they are apathetic. Organization leaders have historically mentioned that when talking with lawmakers, they admitted that they simply did not think about periods when drafting tax exemptions (Rovin 2022). In addition to trying to make people with power care about menstruation, menstrual activists must tend to the regular and persistent presence of menstruation. In other words, while activists are waiting for legislators to change or for school systems to provide products, affected populations continue to have periods.

Though period poverty can affect anyone, and is a global issue, research and activism within the United States primarily addresses three groups: students, imprisoned populations, and homeless people. As younger and younger people are beginning to menstruate the need for products in schools increases. According to a 2021 study completed by Thinx and Period, 23 percent of middle- and high school-aged students have struggled to find period products when they need them. This statistic increased from one in five in 2019 (Thinx and Period 2021, 1). A national survey of college students in the same year found that 10 percent of college-aged students were unable to afford menstrual products every month "leading to skipped classes and greater self-reported rates of moderate or severe depression" (Crawford and Gold 2022). These statistics are even more shocking in low-income and diverse communities, where that statistic nearly doubles (Thinx and Period 2021).

Lack of access to products is not just an issue of comfort but one of safety. The Thinx study found that 51 percent of students have worn period products longer than recommended, which can lead to health issues like toxic shock syndrome and, in some rare cases, sepsis (2021, 3). Beyond physical health, lack of attention to menstruation can harm student's emotional health. The study found that "negative associations with menstruation are powerful and contribute to 'self-objectification, body shame, and lack of agency in sexual decision-making' for young people" (2021, 2). This illustrates that to truly solve the issue of period poverty, activists need to address the material and emotional needs of students.

The need for attention to the material and affective toll of menstruation is equally present in homeless populations. The average menstruator spends between 13 and 20 dollars per cycle, totaling hundreds of dollars a year, depending on the regularity of the cycle, and thousands of dollars over a lifetime (Kim 2021). A study by the National Organization for Women (NOW) found that of the more than 210,000 women experiencing homelessness, 75 percent reported trouble obtaining safe and clean menstrual products (Kim 2021).

Perhaps the least discussed and therefore the least researched population likely to experience period poverty is incarcerated menstruators. In general, prisons are not a place that encourage holistic health, but this is particularly true of menstrual and reproductive health. Although the 2018 First Step Act attempts to help menstruators in federal prisons, most menstruators are held in state prisons where they typically must purchase menstrual products or go without. A 2021 study found that prison commissaries charged 2.63 dollars on average for a pack of pads (Lee 2021). Prison jobs pay as low as 30 cents per hour, meaning a menstruator would have to work up to nine hours to afford a single pack of pads. Only twelve states in the United States and Washington, D.C. enforce laws that make menstrual products free in state correctional facilities (Lee 2021). As a result, menstruators who can't afford this increased cost turn to unsafe and unsanitary measures in order to avoid the shame and stigma attached to menstrual blood. Chandra Bozelko, a formerly incarcerated activist, writes that "prisons control their wards by keeping sanitation just out of reach." For instance, stained clothing chips away at one's self esteem and serves "as an indelible reminder of one's powerlessness in prison." Moreover, having to ask "for something you need crystallizes the power differential" between inmates and correctional officers, since the officer can help you or refuse you and there is "little you can do to influence" their choice (Bozelko 2020, 50). Restricting access to menstrual products is not just about a material shortage, then, it is about control and maintaining power inequities through stigma and shame.

Beyond the United States, period poverty affects menstruators throughout the world. According to the UN, 1.5 billion people still lack access to basic sanitation practices, like private bathrooms and clean water. This makes menstruating with dignity even more difficult. Stigma and lack of education also impact people's understanding of their own bodies. When all is said and done, menstrual activists have remarkable social and material barriers to contend with.

What Menstrual Activism Has Accomplished and Where It Wants to Go

Menstrual activism has made incredible strides toward equity in the past decade. Organizations like Period and the Alliance for Period Supplies lobby state governments to eliminate sales tax on menstrual products like pads and tampons. Activist efforts have led to an increased awareness of period poverty, which takes to task the fact that periods and menstrual products are often forgotten in legislation. In 2021, Louisiana, Maine, and Vermont joined twenty other states that have ended sales tax for menstrual products, according to a Pew Research study (Wright 2021). Nebraska, Colorado, Iowa, and Virginia ended their taxes on period products in 2022, followed by Texas in 2023 and South Carolina in 2024 (Alliance for Period Supplies 2024). However, tax issues are only one barrier to access for low-income, imprisoned, and student populations. The social stigma of menstruation and lack of education impact access to menstrual products, as well.

In addition to legislative efforts, menstrual activists have worked toward greater awareness with the observation of Menstrual Hygiene Day. This day is designated to bring attention to the international humanitarian crisis that is period poverty (UNFPA 2024). People around the world gather to raise consciousness and discuss menstruation candidly, hoping to reduce the stigma of having a period.

Though this success has bolstered activists, there is still a long way to go to reach menstrual equity. As of 2024, twenty states still sell period products as luxury items (Alliance for Period Supplies). Aside from access needs, menstruation remains a taboo topic. Until we can talk about periods for what they are—a natural part of life—there will be a need for menstrual activism.

Hannah Taylor

See Also: First Step Act (2018); Menstruation; Pink Tax; Sexual Education

Further Reading

"About the Collective." 2024. *Global Menstrual Health Collective*. Accessed July 19, 2024. https://www.globalmenstrualcollective.org/who-we-are/.

Alliance for Period Supplies. 2024a. "Menstrual Equity Legislation." Accessed July 19, 2024. https://allianceforperiodsupplies.org/period-legislation/.

Alliance for Period Supplies. 2024b. "Tampon Tax." Accessed July 19, 2024. https://allianceforperiodsupplies.org/tampon-tax/.
Bobel, Chris. 2008. "From Convenience to Hazard: A Short History of the Emergence of the Menstrual Activism Movement, 1971–1992." *Health Care for Women International* 29, no. 7: 738–54.
Bozelko, Chandra. 2020. "Opinion: Prisons that Withhold Menstrual Pads Humiliate Women and Violate Basic Rights." In *Palgrave Handbook of Critical Menstruation Studies*, edited by Chris Bobel, 49–52. Cham: Palgrave.
Crawford, Bridget J., and Emily Gold. 2022. "Period Poverty in the United States: What the Law Should Do." *The Gender Policy Report*. University of Minnesota, May, 25 2022. https://genderpolicyreport.umn.edu/period-poverty-in-the-united-states-what-thelaw-should-do/.
Kim. 2021. "Female Homelessness and Period Poverty." *National Organization for Women*, January 22, 2021. Accessed July 19, 2024. https://now.org/blog/female-homelessness-and-period-poverty/.
Lee, Jean. 2021. "5 Pads for 2 Cellmates: Period Inequity Remains a Problem in Prisons." *USA TODAY*, July 18 2021. https://www.usatoday.com/story/news/nation/2021/07/13/lack-access-period-products-prisons-widespread-us/7932448002/.
Rovin, Laurie. 2022. Personal Interview, July 16, 2022.
Thinx and PERIOD. 2021. *State of the Period 2021: The Widespread Impact of Period Poverty on US Students, 2020*. Accessed July 19, 2024. https://period.org/uploads/State-of-the-Period-2021.pdf.
United Nations Population Fund (UNPF). 2024. "Menstrual Hygiene Day." Accessed July 19, 2024. https://www.unfpa.org/events/menstrual-hygiene-day#:~:text=The%20day%20is%20observed%20on,fifth%20month%20of%20the%20year.
Weiss-Wolf, Jennifer. 2017. *Periods Gone Public: Taking a Stand for Menstrual Equity*. New York: Simon and Schuster.
Wright, Aallyah. 2021. "Lawmakers Tackle 'Period Poverty' With Tax Cuts, School Supplies." *PEW*, July 12, 2021. https://www.pewtrusts.org/en/research-andanalysis/ blogs/stateline/2021/07/12/lawmakers-tackle-period-poverty-with-taxcuts-school-supplies.

#METOO

The #MeToo movement was a surge of digital feminist activism that took place on social media platforms in the fall of 2017. Me Too activism was originally started by Tarana Burke, but the #MeToo hashtag took on a life of its own after multiple women accused Hollywood producer Harvey Weinstein of sexual abuse.

In early October 2017, the *New York Times* broke multiple stories detailing accounts of sexual assault and harassment at the hands of Harvey Weinstein. Dozens of women described crude comments, groping, coercion, and rape they experienced while working for Weinstein at Miramax studios (Kantor and Twohey 2017; Chokshi 2017; Barnes 2017; Fortin 2017). The stories drew international attention and had a snowball effect that encouraged other survivors to come forward; eventually, more than 100 women made accusations against Weinstein.

In response to the news, Alyssa Milano took to Twitter (now known as X) and encouraged everyone who had been sexually harassed or assaulted to reply to her tweet with the hashtag #MeToo. Her goal was to "give people a sense of the magnitude of the problem," and it worked: there were half a million "Me Too" tweets just in the first twenty-four hours and thousands more on other platforms like Facebook and Instagram (Milano 2017). While Milano is often associated with the hashtag, the Me Too movement itself began more than a decade before.

In 2006, activist Tarana Burke started the Me Too movement as a way to support girls and women of color who had experienced sexual abuse. Burke described the movement as "a part of a collective vision to see a world free of sexual violence" (2018, 9:58). She explains that this movement is based on empathy between survivors and promoting their healing process. While the hashtag supports Burke's movement, there is so much more to the mission of Me Too.

Me Too as a Movement

As survivors shared their stories on social media, more and more perpetrators were exposed. Many of them were celebrities, professional athletes, politicians, or business executives. However, hundreds of thousands of survivors called out abusers in their everyday lives: coworkers, family members, acquaintances; and many did not name a perpetrator at all, only writing "me too." It is important to note that not all survivors who came forward in the movement were women: for instance, actor and former professional football player, Terry Crews, was one of the many men who shared his story (Zacharek, Dockterman, and Edwards n.d.). Furthermore, while a vast majority of the accused were men, this was not always the case.

#MeToo and the following news coverage drew attention to sexual harassment as an abuse of power, a concept established by feminists decades earlier. By exposing individuals in positions of power and institutions such as media, sports, and politics, the movement brought public awareness to the relationship between structures of power and sexual violence (Rister and McClure 2019).

A #MeToo sign raised high at a Women's March in San Francisco, January 20, 2018. The digital activism of the #MeToo movement brought attention to sexual harassment as an abuse of power (Andreistanescu/Dreamstime.com).

The 2017 Time Person of the Year feature recognized the "silence breakers," like the women who spoke out against Weinstein. This story called on intersectional feminism, pointing out how additional factors like class, race, ability, sexual orientation, and immigration status influence the power dynamics that perpetuate sexual assault and harassment (Zacharek, Dockterman, and Edwards n.d.). Many of the accused perpetrators targeted women who could not afford to lose or quit their job, using the victim's socioeconomic status to ensure silence.

While Me Too and the hashtag itself were feminist movements, they had similarities with and gave way to other digital feminist movements. Just a year before #MeToo took over Twitter, there was #NotOkay, which expressed outrage and disappointment toward the recording of vulgar and predatory comments about women made by Donald Trump. Prior to that #YesAllWomen responded to Elliot Rodger's mass murder in Santa Barbara, California, resisting the misogynist hate and violence he enacted and raising awareness that women everywhere have experienced threatening and/or violent misogyny.

After #MeToo highlighted a history of abuse in Hollywood, a group of over 300 celebrities came together to found the Time's Up movement (also referred to as #TimesUp). Time's Up is described as an actionable step of the #MeToo movement that focuses on safety and equity in the workplace. This movement is based on the belief that "everyone, every human being, deserves a right to earn a living, to take care of themselves, to take care of their families, free of the impediments of harassment and sexual assault and discrimination" (Langone 2018).

#MeToo and US Courts

The attention that #MeToo brought to patterns of sexual abuse in institutions of power was also a catalyst for the 2018 #StopKavanaugh movement. During the Senate confirmation hearings for Brett Kavanaugh's appointment to the Supreme Court, Dr. Christine Blasey Ford testified that she was sexually assaulted by Kavanaugh when they were teenagers (Gross 2019). Survivors across the country watched the hearings in outrage as a new movement took shape. Dozens of activist groups (including Time's Up) partnered to form Women United to Stop Kavanaugh. In addition to hashtag activism, they put out articles, called senators, and organized protests (National Women's Law Center n.d.). Without the moment of reckoning created by #MeToo, feminist digital activism and sexual violence advocacy would look very different than they do today. Yet despite this activism, Kavanaugh was confirmed to the US Supreme Court, where he presides at this time of writing.

In 2020, Weinstein was convicted of rape and sentenced in New York to a twenty-three-year prison sentence. In April of 2024, however, that conviction was overturned by a New York appeals court due to the fact that so many allegations against Weinstein were discussed in trial, especially those that "weren't part of the case." Weinstein's lawyers successfully argued that this prejudiced the trial against Weinstein. Feminists, however, have long understood that victims often cannot win sexual assault trials unless they can show a pattern of assault—which means bringing in multiple allegations. Although New York overturned its ruling, Weinstein remains imprisoned by a sixteen-year conviction and sentencing from a separate California trial (Burke, Dasrath, and Smith 2024).

The Me Too movement and Burke herself say that they are disappointed by the overturning of the New York ruling but not deterred. In a press release by the movement, they write that "the viral moment was a clarion call. This is another. And our steadfast commitment is that the movement to end sexual violence is active, ready, and going nowhere" (Me Too 2024).

Camryn E. O'Riley

See Also: Burke, Tarana; Cyberfeminism; Hashtag Activism; Misogyny; Rape Culture; Violence Against Women Act (1994)

Further Reading

Barnes, Brooks. 2017. "Harvey Weinstein is the (Whispered) Talk of Hollywood." *The New York Times*, October 8, 2017. https://www.nytimes.com/2017/10/08/business/media/harvey-weinstein-harassment-hollywood.html.

Burke, Minnyvonne, Diana Dasrath, and Morgan Smith. 2024. "Harvey Weinstein's 2020 Rape Conviction Overturned by New York Appeals Court." *NBC News*, April 25, 2024. https://www.nbcnews.com/news/us-news/harvey-weinsteins-rape-conviction-overturned-rcna149328.

Burke, Tarana. 2018. "MeToo is a Movement, Not a Moment." Filmed November, 2018, at TED Video. Video. https://www.ted.com/talks/tarana_burke_me_too_is_a_movement_not_a_moment.

Chokshi, Niraj. 2017. "Actresses Respond to Harvey Weinstein's Accusers: 'I Believe You.'" *The New York Times*, October 5, 2017. https://www.nytimes.com/2017/10/05/us/harvey-weinstein-harassment-reaction.html.

Fortin, Jacey. 2017. "The Women Who Have Accused Harvey Weinstein." *The New York Times*, October 10, 2017. https://www.nytimes.com/2017/10/10/us/harvey-weinstein-accusations.html.

Gross, Terry. 2019. "Reporters Dig Into Justice Kavanaugh's Past, Allegations of Misconduct Against Him." *NPR*, September 16, 2019. https://www.npr.org/2019/09/16/761191576/reporters-dig-into-justice-kavanaughs-past-allegations-of-misconduct-against-him.

Kantor, Jodi, and Megan Twohey. 2017. "Harvey Weinstein Paid Off Sexual Harassment Accusers for Decades." *The New York Times*, October 5, 2017. https://www.nytimes.com/2017/10/05/us/harvey-weinstein-harassment-allegations.html.

Langone, Alix. 2018. "#MeToo and Time's Up Founders Explain the Difference Between the 2 Movements–And How They're Alike." *TIME,* March 22, 2018. https://time.com/5189945/whats-the-difference-between-the-metoo-and-times-up-movements/.

me too. 2024. "me too. International's Statement on Weinstein Decision." *me too,* April 26, 2024. https://metoomvmt.org/stay-informed/press/6088/?utm_campaign=later-linkinbio-metoomvmt&utm_content=later-42645807&utm_medium=social&utm_source=linkin.bio.

Milano, Alyssa (@Alyssa_Milano). "If You've Been Sexually Harassed or Assaulted Write 'Me Too' as a Reply to this Tweet." *Twitter*, October 15, 2017. https://x.com/Alyssa_Milano/status/919659438700670976?lang=en.

National Women's Law Center. n.d. "Justice Rising: Women United to #StopKavanaugh." *National Women's Law Center.* Accessed June 1, 2024. https://nwlc.org/justice-rising-women-united-to-stopkavanaugh/.

Rister, Alex and McClure, Christine I. 2019. "The Me Too Movement: A Qualitative Content Analysis of News Featuring #MeToo." *Northwest Journal of Communication* 47, no. 1 (Spring): 153–85.

Zacharek, Stephanie, Eliana Dockterman, and Haley Sweetland Edwards. n.d. "TIME Person of the Year 2017: The Silence Breakers." *TIME.* Accessed June 1, 2024. https://time.com/time-person-of-the-year-2017-silence-breakers/.

MILITARY-INDUSTRIAL COMPLEX

The term "military-industrial complex" (MIC) describes the collaboration between the US military and the industries that sustain it. This collaboration between the military and private corporations has resulted in an interconnected set of interests that motivate public policy and economic activity. Because the MIC has had such a profound influence upon US political and economic policies, feminists have engaged with it in numerous ways.

The Origins of the Military-Industrial Complex

For most of US history, the research, development, and production of military goods was done "in-house," meaning the military branches had their own production facilities, factories, and research labs staffed with enlisted service members. In the years leading up to the Second World War, however, the military began contracting with civilian companies for the production of equipment and for research into new technologies. The anxieties of the Cold War, and then the wars in Korea and Vietnam, meant that by the 1960s the demand for military products and innovations had grown tremendously. This created a system with mutual benefit for the military (which profited from industry knowledge and labor) and for industry (which profited from large government contracts).

In his 1961 Farewell Address, President Dwight Eisenhower dubbed this relationship "the military-industrial complex." He warned of the "unwarranted influence" by the MIC, concerned that the potential profits from military contracts would motivate US leaders to pursue more aggressive foreign policy strategies. And as a former general, he recognized the danger of having taxpayer funds dedicated to classified efforts: military projects are rarely subject to the democratic systems of transparency or accountability meant to protect public money (Ledbetter 2011, 7–11).

Whether "warranted" or not, the MIC had a profound influence on the United States between 1945 and 1990. MIC contracts bolstered university budgets, providing funding for new programs of study in computer science and engineering (Leslie 1993). The MIC-funded "space race" inspired popular culture from *Star Trek* and *Superman* to *The Jetsons* and *2001: A Space Odyssey*. Domestic technologies from home appliances to nylon stockings and cosmetics were developed downstream from military-industrial grants and advertised as proof of the United States' superior political-economic system (Castillo 2010; Colomina 2007). In a Cold War billed as the battle between two competing "ways of life," nearly every aspect of American culture was part of the war effort.

Resisting the MIC

Public critiques of the MIC arose in the late 1960s, mostly in response to the Vietnam War (Roland 2007, 345). Critics used the concept to explain the profit motive behind US foreign policy decisions, recognizing that those in the MIC benefited from the war's continued escalation. As such, anti-war activists targeted the defense industry directly. If the military and industry shared the profits of war, activists argued, then they would also share the blame.

Anti-war protests at universities confronted the MIC by protesting defense contractors who were recruiting on campus and by protesting the faculty and labs whose research was funded by joint military-industrial grants. In 1967, students at UW-Madison interrupted Dow Chemical recruiters and blocked students from attending their job interviews. In March 1969, students and faculty at the Massachusetts Institute of Technology (MIT) held a single-day walkout to protest the complicity of their school in the MIC (Allen 2019). Calling their schools part of the "military-industrial-academic complex," these scholars and students sought to resist the "unwarranted influence" Eisenhower cautioned against.

Feminists linked together numerous critiques of the MIC. The first fights against nuclear weapons proliferation were led by women's peace groups, who called attention to the impact of nuclear testing by using irradiated breastmilk and baby teeth as evidence of radioactive fallout (Swerdlow 1997). White women recognized that their (white) womanhood was being used in the ideological project of the Cold War, and they rejected such objectification. In their 1968 protest at the Miss America pageant, feminists called the annual winner a "Military Death Mascot," since Miss America would visit military bases as part of her reign. "We refuse," the protesters wrote, "to be used as Mascots for Murder" (Dow 2014).

Feminists also called attention to the fact that every dollar spent on military contracts was a dollar not spent on social programs like building schools, repairing roads, or providing food for the hungry. As such, many feminists calling for labor rights, welfare, and public goods found themselves at odds with the military-industrial priorities of US policy (Horowitz 1996; Twarog 2017; Keohane 2018). Anti-colonial feminists in the Civil Rights movement confronted the Department of Defense in 1951 and declared that racial equity could not be achieved while the United States waged war abroad

(Castledine 2008). While the conservative backlash of the Red Scare limited some of these efforts, early intersectional feminists recognized gender liberation and global peace as interconnected aims.

Contemporary Critiques of the MIC

Military and defense budgets receded in scale at the end of the Cold War, but the US economy and military continue to have a vested interest in each other. As such, the concept of the MIC continues to be relevant for those seeking to confront and resist the status quo.

Gender scholars in the late twentieth century identified the military as a key site for the dissemination of patriarchal stereotypes in US culture. Gender roles such as the masculine "protector" and the "damsel in distress," as well as the portrayal of heteronormative family values as patriotic, are all perpetuated by pro-military media. These films are often produced with military locations, equipment, and permission. The mutual benefit of Hollywood and the MIC has even been called the "military-entertainment complex" (Lenoir and Caldwell 2018). Studies have shown, for example, that the rates of military enlistment rose after the success of the film *Top Gun*, so much so that the army publicly prepared for a similar wave of new recruits just after the release of the film's sequel in 2022 (Baldor 2022). Feminist scholars have identified the influence of these films as both popular culture and military propaganda.

Women have attained leadership positions in MIC organizations such as the FBI, CIA, and defense contractors (Brown 2019). However, many feminists have found fault with these advances, since having women making militarist decisions does not lessen their violent impact (Spade and Lazare 2019; Enloe 2007). Since the 1990s, many feminists have taken interest in dismantling rather than leading the MIC, since the intersectional forms of oppression experienced by women globally are often connected to US military policy. Anti-colonial and anti-imperialist feminists recognize that the exploitation of women abroad is often used as justification for US military intervention, and they have sought to resist this rhetoric (Russo 2006; Amos and Parmar 1984).

For feminists resisting the US prison system, the MIC has provided important conceptual frames. Often called the "prison-industrial complex," scholars and critics have noted that carceral and policing policies are deeply indebted to military strategy, and that an interconnected network of industries and organizations profit off the United States' vast prison system (Alexander 2010). Feminist scholar Angela Davis asserted in 1999 that, "short of major wars, mass incarceration has been the most thoroughly implemented government social programme of our time," mirroring the Cold War-era critiques of the MIC and its relationship to government spending (Gordon 1999).

The vested interests between the military and industry have led some contemporary anti-war activists to use economic and industrial forms of agitation—via consumer boycotts, divestment of financial support, and economic sanctions of political parties. For example, the Boycott, Divest, and Sanction (BDS) movement, modeled after the struggle against apartheid South Africa, has recognized that military policy can be pressured through industry and investments (Barghouti 2011). This strategy is now focused on using nonviolent economic pressure to end US military support for Israel (Pessin and Ben-Atar 2018). Campus protests in 2023, like the Vietnam protests of the 1960s, sought to pressure the interconnected military-academic-industrial complex as one united struggle against war.

Finally, the "-industrial complex" suffix continues to be used by feminists drawing attention to the commodification and commercialization of vast aspects of US life. For example, "the wedding industrial complex" describes how an entire industry has arisen to provide products and services for marriage ceremonies, which has caused them to grow in scale, cost, and complexity. By focusing on weddings as an industrial complex, feminists raise questions about how social institutions such as marriage are reinforced by the industries that profit from them. Likewise, examining the "educational-," "beauty-," and "environmental-" industrial complexes (among others), feminists and other activists draw attention to the ways that commercial profit motives influence our ideas about public education, beauty standards, and climate change. As such, the idea of an "industrial complex" is a useful concept for those invested in how ideologies are created and sustained.

The aligning of military and industrial interests has motivated foreign policy strategies, dominated US economic horizons, and curtailed investment in other social programs. It has also embedded militarism in vast sectors of US life, such as leisure activities, popular culture, domesticity, and family rituals. The MIC has provided a useful conceptual lens for feminist critique, demonstrating how challenging militarism and patriarchy necessarily involves confronting their vested economic interests.

Katie P. Bruner

See Also: Capitalism; Colonialism; Intersectionality; Marxist Feminism; Prison-Industrial Complex

Further Reading

Alexander, Michelle. 2010. *The New Jim Crow: Mass Incarceration in the Age of Colorblindness.* New York: The New Press.

Allen, Jonathan, ed. 2019. *March 4th: Scientists, Students, and Society*, Anniversary ed. Cambridge, MA: MIT Press.

Amos, Valerie, and Pratibha Parmar. 1984. "Challenging Imperial Feminism." *Feminist Review* 17, no. 1: 3–19. https://doi.org/10.1057/fr.1984.18.

Baldor, Lolita C. 2022. "As Recruiters Struggle, Air Force Seeks Lift from 'Top Gun.'" *The Associate Press*, July 20, 2022. https://apnews.com/article/navy-air-force-government-and-politics-e742d6563b8c2ec5a3e3d1e70353b108.

Barghouti, Omar. 2011. *BDS: Boycott, Divestment, Sanctions: The Global Struggle for Palestinian Rights.* Chicago: Haymarket Books.

Brown, David. 2019. "How Women Took Over the Military-Industrial Complex." *Politico*, January 2, 2019. https://www.politico.com/story/2019/01/02/how-women-took-over-the-military-industrial-complex-1049860.

Castillo, Greg. 2010. *Cold War on the Home Front: The Soft Power of Midcentury Design.* Minneapolis: University of Minnesota Press.

Castledine, Jacqueline. 2008. "'In a Solid Bond of Unity': Anticolonial Feminism in the Cold War Era." *Journal of Women's History* 20, no. 4: 57–81. https://doi.org/10.1353/jowh.0.0053.

Colomina, Beatriz. 2007. *Domesticity at War.* Cambridge: MIT Press.

Dow, Bonnie J. 2014. *Watching Women's Liberation: Feminism's Pivotal Year on the Network News.* Urbana: University of Illinois Press.

Enloe, Cynthia H. 2007. *Globalization and Militarism: Feminists Make the Link.* Lanham, MD: Rowman & Littlefield.

Gordon, Avery F. 1999. "Globalism and the Prison Industrial Complex: An Interview with Angela Davis." *Race Class* 40, no. 2/3: 145–57. https://doi.org/10.1177/030639689904000210.

Horowitz, Daniel. 1996. "Rethinking Betty Friedan and the Feminine Mystique: Labor Union Radicalism and Feminism in Cold War America." *American Quarterly* 48, no. 1: 1–42. https://www.jstor.org/stable/30041520.

Keohane, Jennifer. 2018. *Communist Rhetoric and Feminist Voices in Cold War America.* Lanham, MD: Rowman & Littlefield.

Ledbetter, James. 2011. *Unwarranted Influence: Dwight D. Eisenhower and the Military-Industrial Complex.* New Haven, CT: Yale University Press.

Lenoir, Timothy, and Luke Caldwell. 2018. *The Military-Entertainment Complex.* Cambridge, MA: Harvard University Press.

Leslie, Stuart. 1993. *The Cold War and American Science: The Military-Industrial-Academic Complex at MIT and Stanford.* New York: Columbia University Press.

Pessin, Andrew, and Doron S. Ben-Atar. 2018. *Anti-Zionism on Campus: The University, Free Speech, and BDS*. Bloomington: Indiana University Press.

Roland, Alex. 2007. "The Military-Industrial Complex: Lobby and Trope." In *The Long War: A New History of US National Security Policy Since WWII*, edited by Andrew J. Bacevich. New York: Columbia University Press.

Russo, Ann. 2006. "The Feminist Majority Foundation's Campaign to Stop Gender Apartheid." *International Feminist Journal of Politics* 8, no. 4: 557–80. https://doi.org/10.1080/14616740600945149.

Spade, Dean, and Sarah Lazare. 2019. "Women Now Run the Military-Industrial Complex. That's Nothing to Celebrate." *In These Times*, January 12, 2019. https://inthesetimes.com/article/women-military-industrial-complex-gina-haspel-trump-feminism-lockheed-marti.

Swerdlow, Amy. 1997. *Women Strike for Peace: Traditional Motherhood and Radical Politics in the 1960s*. Chicago: University of Chicago Press.

Twarog, Emily E. LB. 2017. *Politics of the Pantry: Housewives, Food, and Consumer Protest in Twentieth-Century America*. New York: Oxford University Press.

MIND/BODY SPLIT

Human beings are typically thought of as having a mind that handles nonphysical components like judgments and decision-making and a body that is physical and enacts physical processes. However, there is some debate over how the mind and body operate. One prevailing notion is that the mind and body are separate from each other. This perspective is known as dualism. Within dualism, the mind is usually seen as more important or better than the body. The mind—rationality and logic—is also typically associated with men and masculinity while the body—physicality and emotions—is often associated with women. Feminist scholar Eve Browning Cole points out that mind–body dualism creates a masculine-feminine relationship of dominance and servitude. She argues, "The body's relationship to the mind" is one of "servitude"; the "mind" (and thus masculine gender identity) "properly dominates its body" (feminine gender identity) and "directs its actions while body properly obeys" (1993, 67). As such, mind–body dualism is usually bad for women and feminist scholars typically advocate for different approaches to understanding humanity.

The History of Mind–Body Dualism

Before and during the early years of the Renaissance, people were typically understood to have a mind, body, and soul. The common thought was that people are unexplainably tied to some form of higher power (such as God) and that such a link could help explain the world. For instance, people living during the Renaissance may have attributed an earthquake to the divine's predetermined will rather than the movement of tectonic plates. These ways of thinking about humans and the world could not keep up with emerging scientific developments of the time, which led to major shifts in reasoning during the rise of the Enlightenment in the seventeenth century.

Enlightenment thinkers tended to turn away from divine explanations and often rejected the idea that people have souls. Instead, Enlightenment thinkers like René Descartes gravitated toward a reason-based duality of the mind and body otherwise known as Cartesian Reductionism (Bauman 1997; Haynes 2009; Seaward 2000). The science of humanity replaced biblical and scriptural teachings, arguing that humans—or men at that point in time—did not need any higher power to make sense of the world. Logic and science began to dominate Enlightenment and post-Enlightenment thinkers. The Industrial Revolution emerged from post-Enlightenment thinking and focused on the mechanistic society further cementing mind–body dualism. This era of thinking capitalizes on the mechanistic, organismic, and contextual perspective of human nature.

And yet, the mind–body split cannot capture the full nature of human beings, which is why there has been yet another shift back toward the Renaissance era's way of thinking. For example, feminist scholar Nadia Hashish (2020, 165) revealed, "Whereas in medicine the scientific development in biology is remarkable, in medical practice, biological developments alone fail to address certain human illnesses that physicians encounter in their everyday clinical work. This leads to the rise of a new major critical debate between reductionism and holism in medical theory." Hashish later argues that a holistic approach highlights the limitations of a reductionist approach to medicine. Similarly, feminist scholars have advocated for more holistic approaches in other fields such as in law (Gilligan 1982), education (Hendrix 2010; Miller 1991), and natural science (Scarano 2024).

Holism as a Feminist Alternative

Holism is not an entirely new concept. Philosophically, the idea of holism began with the ancient Greeks with notable people like Aristotle, Plato, and Socrates. Medically, holistic health traces its origins back 5,000 years to India, China, and Indigenous cultures where it was understood that the most effective healing occurs when the whole person is considered (Jackson 2003). As a term, "holistic education" was coined in the late 1800s when Jan Christiaan Smuts proposed a new philosophy of learning and instruction drawn from the ancient Greek notion of holistic education (Smuts 1926).

Holism shifts away from the mind–body split. Holism is defined as "an inclusive, meaning-centered, experience-focused paradigm that emphasizes the intrinsic connectedness in life" (Haynes 2009, 55). Holism considers the entirety of a person as relevant and necessary and advocates that we should honor all four aspects of a person: mind, body, spirit, and emotions (Hendrix 2010). Each element can be defined in the following ways: the mind is a mental or cognitive process, the body is a physical state, the spirit is a transcendent experience, and the emotion is an affective episode (Taylor, Cook, and Strawser 2021).

Holism is not necessarily "spiritual" or "religious" in nature; instead, holism "seeks to reconnect the personal and transpersonal, the egoic self with the true self" (Miller 1991, 55). This process is focused on making whole body connections without the necessity of a higher power. In fact, some scholars in holism are intentional in making the distinction between "religiosity" and "spirituality" even though the terms are not mutually exclusive and can be interrelated. The key philosophical thought behind holism, despite the "religiosity/spirituality" debate, is that the whole is more than the sum of its parts (Haynes 2009).

Mind–body dualism understands human beings as only being comprised of a mind (nonphysical, mental activities) and body (physical, material activities). Feminist scholars have demonstrated how such a reductionistic approach is limited and does not fully consider the complexities of people or the many ways they exist in the world. They have instead advanced holism as a better alternative that honors a person's mind, body, spirit, and emotions—and that avoids the binary juxtapositions of mind/body, men/women, rational/emotional, good/bad that get stereotyped together and negatively affect women.

Lakelyn E. Taylor

See Also: Beauty; Bodily Autonomy; Body Positivity; Gender

Further Reading

Bauman, Zygmunt. 1997. *Postmodernity and Its Discontents.* Cambridge: Polity Press.
Cole, Eve Browning. 1993. *Philosophy and Feminist Criticism: An Introduction.* New York: Paragon House.
Gilligan, Carol. 1982. *In a Different Voice: Psychological Theory and Women's Development.* Cambridge: Harvard University Press.

Haynes, Carter J. 2009. "Holistic Human Development." *Journal of Adult Development* 16 (January): 53–60. https://doi.org/10.1007/s10804-009-9052-4.

Hashish, Nadia. 2020. "Towards Holistic Medical Humanities - نحو شمولية الإنسانيات الطبية." *Alif: Journal of Comparative Poetics*, no. 40: 164–85. https://www.jstor.org/stable/26924870.

Hendrix, Katherine G. 2010. "Communication and the Preparation of Future Faculty: Learning to Manage Incoherencies." In *The SAGE Handbook of Communication and Instruction,* edited by Deanna L. Fassett and John T. Warren, 81–106. Los Angeles: SAGE Publications.

Jackson, Michael C. 2003. *Systems Thinking: Creative Holism for Managers*. Chichester: John Wiley & Sons.

Miller, Ron. 1991. "Educating the True Self: Spiritual Roots of the Holistic Worldview." *Journal of Humanistic Psychology* 31, no. 4 (Fall): 53–67. https://doi.org/10.1177/0022167891314004.

Scarano, Fabio Rubio. 2024. "The Modern Divorce between Nature and Culture." In *Regenerative Dialogues for Sustainable Futures*, edited by Fabio Rubio Scarano, 35–43. New York City: Springer.

Seaward, Brian Luke. 2000. "Stress and Human Spirituality 2000: At the Cross Roads of Physics and Metaphysics." *Applied Psychophysiology and Biofeedback* 25, no. 4 (December): 241–6. https://doi.org/10.1023/A:1026458905835.

Smuts, Jan Christiaan. 1926. *Holism and Evolution.* London: The Macmillan Company.

Taylor, Lakelyn E., Julie A. Cook, and Michael G. Strawser. 2021. "COVID and Congregations: An Analysis of Religious Messages on Facebook during the Coronavirus Crisis." *Howard Journal of Communications* 32, no. 5 (July): 456–73. https://doi.org/10.1080/10646175.2021.191521.

MISOGYNY

Misogyny typically refers to the hatred of women. The term itself is a combination of Greek stems, "*miso-*" (hate) and "*gynaeco-*" (woman), but feminist theories of misogyny are more complex. The term "misogyny" became popular in the 1970s, when the women's liberation movement used it to refer to sexist violence, such as "sexual assault or murder" (Kendall 2024). Sexism, meanwhile, referred to more subtle forms of gender discrimination (Kendall 2024). Today, feminists often use the terms "misogyny" and "sexism" in fairly interchangeable ways (Kendall 2024).

Philosopher Kate Manne, however, offers a more nuanced definition of misogyny, describing it as the "'law enforcement' branch of a patriarchal order" (2017, 78–9). Here, Manne describes sexism as an ideology or a "body of ideas that exists" to justify patriarchal "social relations" (Illing, 2017). Misogyny, then, refers to the practices that police and enforce sexism, often by forcing women and feminized folks to adhere to sexism's "governing norms and expectations" or face "brutal violence for resisting" (Manne 2017, 78–9).

In response, Samantha Pinson Wrisley (2023) argues that Manne's narrow definition of misogyny focuses too much on action and thus downplays the emotional and affective aspects of misogyny—which, for Wrisley, are essential to our understanding of the term. Ultimately, the term "misogyny" shares much in common with sexism, and its meanings are contested and fluid. The following examples of misogyny, then, are designed to demonstrate the broad uses of the term while featuring the nuanced interpretations of misogyny within feminist scholarship.

Examples of Misogyny

David Gilmore begins his book *Misogyny: The Male Malady* with "a brief preview of misogyny around the world," moving from early stone age groups in New Guinea, to the Amazon Basin, to Renaissance France, to ancient Greece, across various religions, and beyond (2010, 2–8). Gilmore describes a range of misogynistic activities during his preview, including acts of gender-based violence, such as gang rape, mockery of women via jokes and costuming, religious and/or medical persecution, and negative artistic representations. Gilmore's history demonstrates that misogyny is not restricted to one specific culture, location, religion, or time period.

In her foundational work *Woman Hating*, Andrea Dworkin (1974) explores specific historical examples of what she calls "gynocide," that is, the mass killing of women. The witch hunts that occurred throughout Europe and colonial America are some of the most well-known examples of misogyny in history. At least 100,000 women were accused and at least 60,000 died during the witch hunts of the Middle Ages (Carradice 2024, xi).

Many famous religious and philosophical texts from antiquity into modernity refer to women as being inferior and/or inherently wicked—and these texts have been and continue to be used to justify witch hunts and other persecutions of women and feminized folks. Philippa Carter (2023), however, relates the violence of witch hunts to a less obvious form of misogyny: the concept of "women's work." During the seventeenth century—much like today—women were often responsible for their families' and communities' housework, food service, healthcare, and childcare. Carter points out that each of these types of work were high risk and high stakes and characterized by "unpredictability, inexplicability, suddenness, [and] strangeness" (2023, 10–11). For instance, even with modern medicine, it can be unpredictable when children will become ill and whether the illness will prove fatal. As such, the division of labor based on perceived gendered traits has held women accountable, for instance, for sudden ailments—and their seemingly supernatural recoveries. This fueled accusations of witchcraft and guilty verdicts, which, in turn, reinforced misogynistic perceptions of women's weakness, corruptibility, and immorality.

Contemporary Misogyny and Intersectional Oppression

There are many instances of misogyny in everyday life. Catcalling, which typically "involves a [stranger] intruding on a woman's attention [in a public place,] using [sexual] words, whistles, sounds, or gestures" (Walton and Pedersen 2022, 689), is a form of misogyny that serves to enforce the idea of women as passive sexual objects meant for other people's pleasure. Adrienne Rich further noted that catcalling raises the specter of violence, reminding women and feminized folks that they are vulnerable in public spaces, punishing them for "behaving as though they were free" (2007, 8). Likewise, many women politicians experience various forms of misogyny, such as constant questions about their romantic relationships, children, and home life and comments on their physical appearance.

An intersectional feminist approach brings related terms, such as misogynoir and trans misogyny, to the forefront. Moya Bailey describes misogynoir as "the uniquely co-constitutive racialized and sexist violence that befalls Black women as a result of their simultaneous and interlocking oppression at the intersection of racial and gender marginalization" (2021, 1). Examples of misogynoir can be found throughout media, including stereotypes and controlling figures such as the "mammy" and the "Jezebel." Misogynoir portrays Black women as "animalistic, strong, and insatiable" (Bailey 2021, 2) and both justifies and causes discrimination and violence against Black women.

Jules Gill-Peterson writes that trans misogyny "refers to the targeted devaluation of both trans femininity and people perceived to be trans feminine, regardless of how they understand themselves" (2024, 7). Trans misogyny persecutes trans feminine people, often predetermining who "qualifies" as a "real" woman based on visual and behavioral assumptions. People assumed to be trans feminine are then viewed as "inherently threatening," and the "threat label" then justifies aggression toward trans feminine people—which is viewed by the perpetrator as a justified response to the trans person's supposed "threat" (Gill-Peterson 2024, 7) Here, the perpetrator routinely identifies as the "victim" of a trans person's supposedly inherent threat.

Gill-Peterson concludes that the people enacting trans misogyny enjoy "the rare privilege of being at once the victim and the judge, jury, and executioner" (2024, 7). Examples of trans misogyny can range from barring trans women from participating in sports and strictly enforcing gendered bathrooms to horrific violence and widespread murder.

Ultimately, as Rhea Ashley Hoskin writes, misogyny, anti-trans discrimination, sexism, rape culture, and homophobia all share the same "underlying component": anti-femininity (2019, 686). Indeed, femininity is often scapegoated—devalued and blamed for the violence enacted against femininity, feminine persons, and those deemed feminine.

Emma Darby

See Also: Biblical Complementarianism; Cult of True Womanhood; Dworkin, Andrea; Essentialism; Gender; Internalized Sexism; Patriarchy; Racist Stereotypes of Black People; Trans-Exclusionary Radical Feminists (TERFs); Witches

Further Reading

ABC News (Australia). 2012. "Julia Gillard's 'Misogyny Speech' in Full (2012)." *YouTube.com*, October 9, 2012. https://www.youtube.com/watch?v=ihd7ofrwQX0.

Bailey, Moya. 2021. *Misogynoir Transformed: Black Women's Digital Resistance*. New York: New York University Press. http://ebookcentral.proquest.com/lib/unt/detail.action?docID=6562312.

Carradice, Phil. 2024. *Witches and Witch Hunts Through the Ages*. Yorkshire: Pen and Sword History.

Carter, Philippa. 2023. "Work, Gender and Witchcraft in Early Modern England." *Gender & History* 37, no. 1: 91–108. https://doi.org/10.1111/1468-0424.12717.

Dworkin, Andrea. 1974. *Woman Hating*. New York: Dutton. http://archive.org/details/womanhating00dwor.

Gill-Peterson, Jules. 2024. *A Short History of Trans Misogyny*. London: Verso.

Gilmore, David D. 2010. *Misogyny: The Male Malady*. Philadelphia: University of Pennsylvania Press.

Holland, Jack. 2007. *Misogyny: The World's Oldest Prejudice*. Philadelphia, PA: Running Press.

Hoskin, Rhea Ashley. 2019. "Femmephobia: The Role of Anti-Femininity and Gender Policing in LGBTQ+ People's Experiences of Discrimination." *Sex Roles* 81: 686–703.

Illing, Sean. 2017. "What We Get Wrong about Misogyny." *Vox*, December 5, 2017. https://www.vox.com/identities/2017/12/5/16705284/elizabeth-warren-loss-2020-sexism-misogyny-kate-manne.

Kendall, Emily. 2024. "Misogyny." In *Encyclopaedia Britannica*. Accessed December 29, 2024. https://www.britannica.com/topic/misogyny.

Manne, Kate. 2017. *Down Girl: The Logic of Misogyny*. Oxford: Oxford University Press.

Rich, Adrienne. 2007. "Introduction from Of Woman Born." In *Maternal Theory: Essential Readings*, edited by Andrea O' Reilly. Bradford, 6–10. Bradford, Canada: Demeter Press.

Walker, Rachel Loewen. 2024. "Call It Misogyny." *Feminist Theory* 25, no. 1: 64–82. https://doi.org/10.1177/14647001221119995.

Walton, Kari A., and Cory L. Pedersen. 2022. "Motivations behind Catcalling: Exploring Men's Engagement in Street Harassment Behaviour." *Psychology & Sexuality* 13, no. 3: 689–703. https://doi.org/10.1080/19419899.2021.1909648.

Wrisley, Samantha Pinson. 2023. "Feminist Theory and the Problem of Misogyny." *Feminist Theory* 24, no. 2: 188–207. https://doi.org/10.1177/14647001211039365.

MISSING AND MURDERED INDIGENOUS WOMEN AND GIRLS

Missing and Murdered Indigenous Women and Girls is a decolonial, women-led movement to end the violence that targets Indigenous women and girls (sometimes referred to as Native, American Indian, Native Alaskan, First Nations, and/or Aboriginal peoples) in the land currently called North America. Known by various names, Missing and Murdered Indigenous Women, or #MMIW (expanded to include girls and Two-Spirit peoples, #MMIWG2S), was coined in 2012 by Cree journalist Sheila North Wilson (The Current 2016). It describes the reality that Indigenous women live lives vulnerable to a range of violent forces in places like Canada and the United States.

In 2016, for example, the US government reported that Indigenous women experience high rates of violence (84 percent) and sexual violence (56 percent) (National Institute of Justice 2016). More specifically, the rates for the murder of Native women are ten times the national average (US Department of the Interior n.d.). They also comprise a significant portion of missing people, making up the second highest rates of homicide in the nation and are often subjected to human trafficking. Actual rates of missing, murdered, and trafficked women are likely much higher, but due to inadequate data and lack of reporting, precise statistics are not available (US Department of Justice 2008).

In Canada, the situation is similar. Reports show that between 1980 and 2012, First Nations women made up only 4 percent of the population, but they comprised around 20 percent of all homicides of women. In the province of Saskatchewan, a 2007 study showed that "Indigenous women made up 6 percent of the population yet accounted for more than 60 percent of all missing persons reports" (Presley 2020, 91).

Activism and the National Inquiry in Canada

Canadian grassroots activism around MMIW2S gained public attention in the late 2000s and early 2010s, and one important moment in that movement was created by artist Jamie Black (Anishinaabe and Finnish). Rooted in Native practice that "creates space and time to connect with and enter into a relationship with the land," Black developed the idea for the REDress Project some time in 2009 (Black 2020, "Artist"). In her installations, the artist hung red dresses in public places to commemorate and raise awareness for missing or murdered women (Canadian Museum of History 2021; Black 2020, "The REDress"). Reflecting on the installations, she says that the empty dresses "call in the energy of the women who are lost," perhaps in part because of the cultural significance of red to Native communities (Bolen 2019). "[R]ed is very sacred and powerful. It relates to our lifeblood and that connection between all of us" (Bolen 2019).

Even though she would not receive an invitation to perform a major installation until March of 2011, her smaller installations garnered enough public attention that the first Red Dress Day was held May 5, 2010, a day that is still observed in Canada, along with October 1, the National Day of Action for Missing and Murdered Indigenous Women and Girls (Solway 2010; CTV News 2010; CBC News 2010; George 2023). Today, people hang red dresses on these days or whenever a community focuses on issue related to MMIWG2S.

In the wake of pressures like the REDress Project and Red Dress Day, the government of Canada commissioned the National Inquiry into Missing and Murdered Indigenous Women and Girls, which ran from 2016 to 2019. A significant portion of the inquiry was spent in a "Truth Gathering Process," which centered the narratives of survivors and their families as "the heart and soul" of the inquiry (National Inquiry n.d.). Commissioners heard 1,484 of these stories. They also held hearings with eighty-three "Knowledge Keepers and experts such as government officials, academics, legal experts and community leaders" (National Inquiry n.d.).

The commissioners submitted their final report in June 2019. The report argued that the status of MMIW2S "amounts to a race-based genocide of Indigenous Peoples" (National Inquiry 2019, 1) and centered "the importance of relationship to ending violence" (National Inquiry 2019, 7). The report concluded with 231 Calls to Justice, addressing eighteen areas of Canadian society, such as governments, institutions, citizenry, and education. In 2023, "only two of the 231 calls have been completed—and more than half haven't even been started" (CBC News 2023).

While there is much work to do and while there are many more activists that have worked and are working in this area, Black's work illustrates how decolonial action can make a difference in the lives of Indigenous peoples. Her work holds together Maori scholar Linda Tuhiwai Smith's strands of past Indigenous teachings (relationality to land, Native cultural significance of red) and an analysis of coloniality (Indigenous women's vulnerability to violence) in order to offer the response of the REDress Project. Black's work not only came to symbolize MMIWG2S, but it also galvanized widespread cultural awareness. Joining with many other grassroots activists, these collective decolonial actions led to the National Inquiry, an important beginning of help to many First Nations peoples and families across Canada.

Naaman Wood

See Also: Colonialism; Decolonialism; Patriarchy; Settler Colonialism; Structural Oppression

Further Reading

Betts, Raymond. 2004. *Decolonization.* New York: Routledge.

Black, Jamie. 2020a. "Artist Statement." Last modified 2020. https://www.jaimeblackartist.com/exhibitions/.

Black, Jamie. 2020b. "The REDress Project." Last modified 2020. https://www.jaimeblackartist.com/exhibitions/.

Bolen, Anne, 2019. "A Place for the Taken: The REDress Project Gives a Voice to Missing Indigenous Women." *American Indian* 20, no. 1 (Spring): https://www.americanindianmagazine.org/story/redress-project.

Canadian Museum of History. 2021. "An Evening with Jaime Black." Last modified October 18, 2021. https://www.youtube.com/watch?v=HHCLIsvu9uE&t=1305s.

CBC News. 2010. "Empty Dresses Honour Missing, Slain Women." October 5, 2010, https://www.cbc.ca/news/canada/manitoba/empty-dresses-honour-missing-slain-women-1.879097.

CBC News. 2023. "A Report Card on the MMIWG Inquiry's Calls for Justice." June 5, 2023, https://www.cbc.ca/newsinteractives/features/cfj-report-cards.

CTV News. 2010. "Artist Aims to Raise Awareness Regarding Missing, Murdered Women." October 5, 2010. https://winnipeg.ctvnews.ca/artist-aims-to-raise-awareness-regarding-missing-murdered-women-1.559505.

George, Robin. 2023. "What is Red Dress Day? How Missing and Murdered Indigenous Women, Girls, and Two-Spirit People are Honoured on May 5." *The Globe and Mail*, May 4, 2023. https://www.theglobeandmail.com/canada/article-red-dress-day-2023-mmiwg2s/#:~:text=Red%20Dress%20Day%2C%20the%20National,%2C%20windows%2C%20fences%20and%20balconies.

National Inquiry into Missing and Murdered Indigenous Women and Girls. 2019. *Reclaiming Power and Place: The Final Report of the National Inquiry into Missing and Murdered Indigenous Women and Girls, Executive Summary of the Final Report.* https://www.mmiwg-ffada.ca/wp-content/uploads/2019/06/Executive_Summary.pdf.

National Inquiry into Missing and Murdered Indigenous Women and Girls. n.d. "Truth Gathering Process." Accessed February 2, 2024. https://www.mmiwg-ffada.ca/how-to-participate/.

National Institute of Justice. 2016. "Violence Against American Indian and Alaska Native Women and Men." June 1, 2016. https://nij.ojp.gov/topics/articles/violence-against-american-indian-and-alaska-native-women-and-men.

Ouellette, Robert-Falcon. 2012. "Artist Jamie Black and the REDress Project." *At the Edge of Canada: Indigenous Research* (January). https://attheedgeofcanada.blogspot.com/2012/01/artist-jamie-black-and-red-dress.html.

Presley, Rachel. 2020. "Embodied Liminality and Gendered State Violence: Artivist Expressions in the MMIW Movement." *Journal of International Women's Studies* 21, no. 7 (2020): 91–109. https://vc.bridgew.edu/jiws/vol21/iss7/8.

Smith, Linda Tuhiwai. 2012. *Decolonizing Methodologies: Research and Indigenous Peoples.* London: Zed Books.

Solway, Susan. 2010. "Red Dresses: There, but Just Not There." *Windspeaker Publication* 28, no. 8 (October 29). https://www.ammsa.com/publications/windspeaker/red-dresses-there-just-not-there.

tebrakunna country and Emma Lee, and Jennifer Evans, eds. 2022. *Indigenous Women's Voices: 20 Years on from Linda Tuhiwai Smith's Decolonizing Methodologies.* London: Zed Books.

The Current. 2016. "'I Understood . . . because I was One of Them.' Sheila North Wilson on Creating #MMIW." Last modified December 8, 2016. https://www.cbc.ca/radio/thecurrent/the-current-for-december-7-2016

-mmiw-winnipeg-public-forum-1.3883544/i-understood-because-i-was-one-of-them-sheila-north-wilson-on-creating-mmiw-1.3883730.
US Department of Justice. 2008. *Violence Against American Indian and Alaska Native Women and the Criminal Justice Response: What is Known* (August). https://www.ojp.gov/pdffiles1/nij/grants/223691.pdf.
US Department of the Interior: Indian Affairs. n.d. "Missing and Murdered Indigenous People Crisis: Violence Against Native Americans and Alaska Natives far Exceed National Averages." Accessed January 31, 2024, https://www.bia.gov/service/mmu/missing-and-murdered-indigenous-people-crisis.

MORRISON, TONI

Born in Lorain, Ohio, to parents George and Ella Ramah Wofford, Chloe Anthony (or Ardelia) Wofford—better known as Toni Morrison (1931–2019)—was an American novelist, book editor, scholar, teacher, and public intellectual (Li 2009, xi and xv; Duvall 2000, 38). During her distinguished career, Morrison wrote a total of eleven novels, two short stories, three theatrical pieces, eleven children's books, and two book-length literary discussions; additionally, she published four edited volumes and multiple speeches, essays, and lectures (Furman 2020). Morrison's work revolves around the complex and intersecting experiences of class, race, gender, and sexuality in the United States. Though she passed away on August 5, 2019, Toni Morrison's life and literary influence left an undeniable impact on contemporary US feminism and activism (Parke 2022).

Morrison's Education and Career

Morrison graduated from Howard University with her bachelor of arts in English in 1953 before continuing her education at Cornell University, where she earned her MA in American literature in 1955 (Wagner-Martin 2015, 6). After graduating with her MA, Toni Morrison began her teaching career; she first spent a couple years teaching at Texas Southern University before returning to teach at Howard in 1957. Though she was not politically active during the 1960s and 1970s due to the age of her children, in an interview Morrison remarked: "I think I knew there was something an art form could do in that milieu that journalism and television could not. It could identify, it could interpret, it could clarify, it could pose all the right questions" (Bigsby 1992, 271). This perspective serves as a fitting backdrop to explain Morrison's intentionality within her written works of fiction.

Rather than writing explanations of Black life directed toward the "white gaze," Toni Morrison's fictional work was primarily focused on portraying the experiences and viewpoints of Black American women *for* Black American women (Morrison 2008, 252). This commitment to her community remained throughout her life, but Morrison's work reached widespread critical acclaim. Most notably, Morrison was awarded the Nobel Prize in Literature in 1993, making her the first African American and the first Black woman to receive the honor (Ducille 2017, 375). Toni Morrison's career can be seen in parallel to the themes addressed in her books and nonfiction essays, as both grapple with the intersecting oppressions experienced by Black women. Writing about the press coverage of Morrison's Nobel Prize win, Ann Ducille (2017) notes that Morrison's victory was undermined by critics on the basis of both race and gender. Ducille (2017) cites Black writer Charles Johnson's comments to the *Washington Post*, in which he claimed that Morrison only won because, in her writing, "Whites are portrayed badly . . . Men are. Black men are," before eventually calling the award "a triumph of political correctness" (qtd. in Streitfeld 1993). However, Toni Morrison's work reaches a depth and sensitivity that cannot and should not be relegated to the simplified themes of "racism" and "sexism."

Morrison as Author

Morrison stated that she accepts and celebrates the identity labels of "Black" and "female" that are often attached to her work as an author, "because being a black woman writer is not a shallow place but a rich place to write from. It doesn't limit my imagination; it expands it" (qtd. in Als 2003). Inspired by her own personal identity, life, and community, Morrison's works clearly and unapologetically center characters who are Black, feminine, and engaged in work both inside and outside the home.

Toni Morrison's most well-known titles include *The Bluest Eye* (1970), *Sula* (1973), *Song of Solomon* (1977), the Pulitzer Prize-winning *Beloved* (1987), and *God Help the Child* (2015). Reviewing the scholarship written about Morrison's most famous works reveals several common themes that are present throughout her bibliography. For instance, Evelyn Jaffe Schreiber (2011) connects Morrison's exploration of racial identity and the search for home and community to the "legacy of slavery" as identified by Berry and Blassingame (1982). Self-subjectivity and home both serve as safety from generational racial trauma, yet, within these units, trauma can still make itself known. The dehumanization of slavery and the following cultural exclusion and discrimination of Jim Crow and segregation led to a pattern of "internalized racism" characterized by "self-destructive rage, hatred, and paralyzing despair" (hooks 2015, 1, 4). Many of Toni Morrison's characters exhibit signs of and are influenced by internalized racism, from Pecola Breedlove's desire to conform to white beauty standards in *The Bluest Eye* to Sethe's poor self-image in *Beloved.*

Morrison's work also displays how internalized racism affects one's treatment of other people. J. Brooks Bouson (2000, 3) writes that Toni Morrison "is intent on portraying the trauma of defective or abusive parenting or relationships and also the black-on-black violence that exists within the African-American community." Morrison viscerally represents the horrors of domestic violence often experienced by Black women while maintaining white supremacy as the ultimate cause. Both *The Bluest Eye* and *Beloved* connect slavery and racism to domestic violence, while other books within her bibliography address the psychological turmoil of violence and the use of violence as a tool of control both socially and within a romantic partnership.

Toni Morrison had far-reaching influence on the literary and political landscape of the United States, bringing attention to the unique experiences and struggles of Black women (Library of Congress).

This serves as merely a glimpse into the themes addressed in Morrison's fiction, but Toni Morrison's involvement and impact in the literary community stretched beyond her own authorship. Indeed, Morrison's own writing was shaped by and shaped the Black women writer's group known as "The Sisterhood," which in addition to Morrison involved other notable figures such as Alice Walker.

Morrison as Editor

Toni Morrison worked as an editor for Random House publishing from 1971 to 1983 (Brier 2022, 651). In this time, she worked with such notable Black writers as Angela Davis and Huey P. Newton and contributed greatly to "the institutionalization of African American writing . . . making it impossible to talk about American literature without talking about African American literature and . . . legitimizing African American literature as a body of study unto itself" (Brier 2022, 652).

One of Toni Morrison's most notable contributions during this time was the editing and publication of *The Black Book*, a "scrapbook-history" that claims to document "the collective 'memory' of African American existence" ("Editorial Fact Sheet" 1973). Evan Brier (2022, 653) aptly notes that *The Black Book* was distinctly radical in that it was "conceived in opposition . . . to a long-standing idea of Western literature that had emerged alongside, and was partially produced by, the publishing business." Unlike other, more conventional works of literature, *The Black Book* contains "an array of verbal and visual texts: posters, newspaper articles, letters, speeches, bills of sale, spirituals and blues, work songs and folk tales, children's rhymes, drawings, advertisements, photographs (both family pictures and documentary photographs of quilts, tools, furniture, and other artifacts), recipes, patent applications, sheet music, playbills and movie stills, formulas for conjure, and dream interpretations" (Wall 2012, 106). Aside from content and authorship, *The Black Book* also employs a nonlinear form of storytelling that, while absent from the majority of Western literature and thinking, is commonly found in African religions and cultures. *The Black Book* prioritizes the language, voice, and life of those who are not usually considered worthy of literary merit, whether due to societal marginalization or lack of formal education. Regardless of financial or commercial success, Morrison's work as editor is notable in the ways in which it broke through and challenged conventional publishing and centered Black people as authors and as an audience.

Discussing her work as an editor, Morrison explained, "I was very busy . . . trying to find writers that agents did not have . . . which meant I was particularly interested in unpublished, or minimally published, black female writers" (Boyd 2008, 89). Toni Morrison's time as an editor for Random House serves as a powerful example of working within an institution to elicit long-lasting progressive change.

Morrison as Social Critic

Although Morrison was not particularly politically active during the tumultuous 1960s and 1970s, she was still engaged in political conversations. In 1971, Morrison published the essay "What the Black Woman Thinks About Women's Lib" in the *New York Times*, discussing the distrust many Black women felt (and still feel) toward white feminists. Throughout her life, she continued writing political essays. Discussing Morrison's social criticism work, Sämi Ludwig observes, "As in her [fiction] work, it contains a strong cognitive element . . . she is primarily occupied with the way in which language is used by human beings and how it shapes what she calls the 'construction of social reality'" (Ludwig 2007, 125). Even in her nonfiction essays, Toni Morrison employs a lens that is very much focused on the ways in which people speak and read.

One of her edited volumes, titled *Race-ing Justice, En-gendering Power. Essays on Anita Hill, Clarence Thomas, and the Construction of Social Reality* (1992), addresses "the dehumanizing nature of racial stereotypes" as present in the Senate's treatment of Anita Hill during the Clarence Thomas hearings (Ludwig 2007, 126). Morrison also edited a volume exploring the O. J. Simpson trial, titled *Birth of a Nation'hood: Gaze, Script, and Spectacle in the O.J. Simpson Case* (1997). In *Birth of a Nation'hood,* Morrison similarly explores Black subjectivity and the racist tropes that control the portrayal of Blackness in America, revealing that, in lieu of a fully realized human being, O. J. Simpson was portrayed as "a disembodied voice, a phantom. A social cadaver and a minor irritant in the official gaze, which cracks occasionally to expose him golfing. A 'dead' man arrogantly alive" (Morrison 1997, xxv, qtd. by Ludwig 2007, 130). In these and other nonfiction works by Toni Morrison, her main concerns were representation and language. This is consistent with the themes present in her works of fiction.

Toni Morrison's influence on the literary community and on the US political landscape is far-reaching. Her time spent as professor, author, editor, and social critic comes together to paint a picture focused on justice and the unique experiences and struggles of Black women. Even after her passing, Toni Morrison's work continues to teach and inspire and will continue to do so into the future.

Emma Darby

See Also: Critical Race Theory; Hill, Anita; hooks, bell; Intersectionality; Standpoint Theory; Womanism

Further Reading

Als, Hilton. 2003. "Toni Morrison and the Ghosts in the House." *The New Yorker*, October 19, 2003. https://www.newyorker.com/magazine/2003/10/27/ghosts-in-the-house.

Berry, Mary Frances, and John W. Blassingame. 1982. *Long Memory: The Black Experience in America*. New York: Oxford University Press.

Bigsby, Christopher. 1992. "Jazz Queen (interview with Toni Morrison)." *The Independent* (London), April 26, 1992. Print.

Bouson, J. Brooks. 2000. *Quiet as It's Kept: Shame, Trauma, and Race in the Novels of Toni Morrison*. SUNY Series in Psychoanalysis and Culture. Albany: State University of New York Press.

Boyd, Valerie. 2008. "'She Was Just Outrageously Brilliant': Toni Morrison Remembers Toni Cade Bambara." In *Savoring the Salt: The Legacy of Toni Cade Bambara*, edited by Linda Janet Holdmes and Cheryl A. Wall, 88–99. Philadelphia: Temple University Press.

Brier, Evan. 2022. "Unliterary History: Toni Morrison, *The Black Book*, and 'Real Black Publishing.'" *American Literature* 94, no. 4: 651–76. https://doi.org/10.1215/00029831-10341720.

Ducille, Ann. 2017. "Of Race, Gender, and the Novel; or, Where in the World Is Toni Morrison?" *NOVEL: A Forum on Fiction* 50, no. 3: 375–87.

Duvall, John N. 2000. *The Identifying Fictions of Toni Morrison: Modernist Authenticity and Postmodern Blackness*. New York, NY: Palgrave Macmillan.

"Editorial Fact Sheet for *The Black Book*." 1973. Box 1265. Random House Papers, Rare Book and Manuscript Library, Columbia University in the City of New York.

Furman, Jan. 2020. "Toni Morrison." In *Oxford Bibliographies*. https://www.oxfordbibliographies.com/view/document/obo-9780190280024/obo-9780190280024-0086.xml.

hooks, bell. 2015. *Black Looks: Race and Representation*. New York, London: Routledge.

Li, Stephanie. 2009. *Toni Morrison: A Biography*. New York: Bloomsbury Publishing USA. http://ebookcentral.proquest.com/lib/unt/detail.action?docID=497247.

Ludwig, Sämi. 2007. "Toni Morrison's Social Criticism." In *The Cambridge Companion to Toni Morrison*, edited by Justine Tally, 1st ed., 125–37. New York: Cambridge University Press. https://doi.org/10.1017/CCOL052186111X.

Morrison, Toni. 1970. *The Bluest Eye: A Novel*. New York: Holt, Rinehart and Winston.

Morrison, Toni. 1971. "What the Black Woman Thinks About Women's Lib." *The New York Times*, August 22, 1971, sec. Archives. https://www.nytimes.com/1971/08/22/archives/what-the-black-woman-thinks-about-womens-lib-the-black-woman-and.html.

Morrison, Toni. 1973. *Sula.* New York, NY: Plume.
Morrison, Toni. 1977. *Song of Solomon.* New York: Knopf.
Morrison, Toni. 1987. *Beloved.* New York: Knopf.
Morrison, Toni, ed. 1992. *Race-Ing Justice, En-Gendering Power: Essays on Anita Hill, Clarence Thomas, and the Construction of Social Reality*, 1st ed. New York: Pantheon Books.
Morrison, Toni. 1998. *Paradise.* New York: A.A. Knopf.
Morrison, Toni. 2008. *Toni Morrison: Conversations*. Edited by Carolyn C. Denard, 1st ed. Literary Conversations Series. Jackson, Miss: University Press of Mississippi.
Morrison, Toni. 2015. *God Help the Child.* New York: Alfred A. Knopf.
Morrison, Toni, and Claudia Brodsky Lacour, eds. 1997. *Birth of a Nation'hood: Gaze, Script, and Spectacle in the O.J. Simpson Case*. New York: Pantheon Books.
Parke, Phoebe. 2022. "Toni Morrison Fast Facts." *CNN*, February 2, 2022. https://www.cnn.com/2013/04/14/us/toni-morrison-fast-facts/index.html.
Schreiber, Evelyn Jaffe. 2011. *Race, Trauma, and Home in the Novels of Toni Morrison.* Southern Literary Studies. Baton Rouge: Louisiana State University Press.
Streitfeld, David. 1993. "AUTHOR TONI MORRISON WINS NOBEL PRIZE." *Washington Post*, October 8, 1993. https://www.washingtonpost.com/archive/politics/1993/10/08/author-toni-morrison-wins-nobel-prize/6077f17d-d7b7-49a3-ad90-8111cf8478d1/.
Wagner-Martin, L. 2015. *Toni Morrison: A Literary Life*. London: Palgrave Macmillan UK. http://ebookcentral.proquest.com/lib/unt/detail.action?docID=2057823.
Wall, Cheryl A. 2012. "Reading The Black Book: Between the Lines of History." *Arizona Quarterly: A Journal of American Literature, Culture, and Theory* 68, no. 4: 105–30.

N

NATIONAL INDIGENOUS WOMEN'S RESOURCE CENTER

The National Indigenous Women's Resource Center (NIWRC) is "dedicated to restoring sovereignty and safeguarding Native women and children" (NIWRC 2025). Their main offices reside on the "ancestral lands of the Tsétsêhéstâhese and So'taeo'o (Cheyenne) People," and they note that the "Cheyenne people and traditional lifeways are beautiful and thriving" in their land (NIWRC 2025).

The NIWRC operates through grassroots advocacy and supports Native women and communities. They host community conversations and conferences, and they develop and distribute informational and activist resources. For instance, they have webinars for how to work with victims of stalking and how to access and use the Tribal Access Project (TAP), which helps Native communities better access data from the US Department of Justice and report crimes committed against tribal members.

Operating through a human rights framework, the NIWRC asserts that "Native women, their children, and Tribal Nations are entitled to": "safety from violence within their homes and in their community"; "justice both on and off Tribal lands"; "access to advocacy designed by and for Native women"; "safe, affordable housing, legal services, childcare, economic security, and other basic resources provided in respectful ways"; "community-driven, trauma and resiliency-informed services"; and "access to Indigenous healing ways" (NIWRC 2025).

The NIWRC plays a key role in the expansion and reauthorization of the Violence Against Women Act (VAWA), working to ensure that Native women are not excluded from VAWA's protections and resources and that VAWA's policies affirm tribal jurisdiction ("Violence Against Women Act" 2025). This work is critical given the ways in which perpetrators of sexual and intimate partner violence target Native women and children. The NIWRC has a dedicated resource library for addressing the ongoing crisis of Missing and Murdered Indigenous Women and Girls.

In collaboration with the National Resource Center on Domestic Violence, the NIWRC developed and published a 2020 report on "Safe Housing for American Indian and Alaska Native Survivors of Gender-Based Violence" (LaPorte 2020). The NIWRC also supports and collaborates with STTARS Indigenous Safe Housing Center, which offers culturally rooted assistance, training, policy development, and "Indigenous-centered resource materials to address the intersection of domestic violence and housing instability" (STTARS 2025).

To put it simply, the NIWRC is a vital nonprofit organization working to end gendered, racist, and colonial violence by promoting the safety, leadership, and sovereignty of Native women and their communities.

Sarah Kornfield

See Also: Decolonialism; Haaland, Deb; Missing and Murdered Indigenous Women and Girls; Postcolonial Feminism; Violence Against Women Act (1994)

Further Reading

LaPorte, Caroline. 2020. "National Workgroup on Safe Housing for American Indian and Alaska Native Survivors of Gender-Based Violence: Lessons Learned." *National Indigenous Women's Resource Center*. https://www.niwrc.org/resources/report/national-workgroup-safe-housing-american-indian-and-alaska-native-survivors-gender. Accessed March 6, 2025.

National Indigenous Women's Resource Center (NIWRC). 2025. "STTARS." https://www.niwrc.org/housing. Accessed March 6, 2025.

National Indigenous Women's Resource Center (NIWRC). 2025. "Who We Are." https://www.niwrc.org/about. Accessed March 6, 2025.

"Violence Against Women Act (VAWA)." 2025. National Indigenous Women's Resource Center (NIWRC). https://www.niwrc.org/policy-center/vawa?utm_term=vawa&utm_campaign=*Awareness+-+Policy+-+MXC&utm_source=adwords&utm_medium=ppc&hsa_acc=8095999829&hsa_cam=17881908641&hsa_grp=138123656063&hsa_ad=613172906563&hsa_src=g&hsa_tgt=kwd-152783025&hsa_kw=vawa&hsa_mt=b&hsa_net=adwords&hsa_ver=3&gad_source=1&gad_campaignid=17881908641&gbraid=0AAAAADKUiyQqOnksXj-G42w3sgBXK3hbD&gclid=EAIaIQobChMIs6mZkvLdjwMVvTYIBR03Ihv8EAAYASAAEgKICvD_BwE.

NATIONAL ORGANIZATION FOR WOMEN (NOW)

The National Organization for Women—known by its acronym, NOW—was founded in 1966 to advocate for women's rights, both politically and socially. The founders decided on using *for* in the title instead of using *of* because they wanted to include masculine allies who believe in women's rights. NOW was created by forty-nine founders at the Third National conference on the Status of Women in DC. Some notable founding members include: Betty Friedan, author of *The Feminine Mystique* and first president of NOW; Pauli Murray, famed civil rights activist; Shirley Anita Chisholm, who became the first Black woman elected to Congress in 1968; Aileeen Hernandez, the second president of NOW; and Bessie Margolin, the US Department of Labor attorney from 1939 to 1972 (Love 2006). These are just a few of the incredibly intelligent, capable, and passionate women who founded NOW.

One of NOW's most famous demonstrations was the Strike for Equality on August 26, 1970. It celebrated the fiftieth anniversary of the passing of the Nineteenth Amendment, which ensured women's right to vote. Tens of thousands of women marched down Fifth Avenue in New York City, blocking traffic during rush hour. The march was led by then president of NOW, Betty Friedan (Cohen 2015). Women held signs saying, "Don't Iron while the Strike is Hot" and "Don't Cook Dinner—Starve a Rat Today" (Cohen 2015). Activists also ate at men's-only restaurants and bars. Coordinated by NOW, the Strike for Equality was a major act of solidarity and activism.

NOW is classified as a 501 social welfare organization by the IRS. This means that it can't be organized for profit and must be operated only to promote social welfare in order to receive tax exemption (IRS 2024). As of 2024, NOW has over 500,000 members and more than 500 local/campus affiliates in all fifty states as well as the District of Columbia, where their headquarters are located (NOW 2014). The founders of NOW envisioned a "NAACP for women" that would mobilize women politically and give women's rights advocates the power to put pressure on the government (Fox 2006). NOW continues to act as a major feminist lobbying group.

NOW and Lesbian Activism

Historically, NOW has had a complex relationship with the lesbian community. In 1969, out lesbian Ivy Bottini designed the NOW logo, which is still used today. Bottini also held a speech in her New York chapter titled "Is Lesbianism a Feminist Issue?" However, the then president of NOW, Betty Friedan, was against overt lesbian participation in the feminist movement. She famously called lesbians "the lavender menace" (Love 2006). Friedan orchestrated a purge of lesbians from the New York chapter of NOW, including Bottini.

At the 1970 Congress to Unite Women, twenty women wore shirts saying "Lavender Menace." They also read "The Woman-Identified Woman," which was one of the first major lesbian-feminist statements. In 1971, NOW passed a resolution saying "that a woman's right to her own person includes the right to define and express her own sexuality and to choose her own lifestyle" ("NOW: Leading the Fight" 2015). In 1973, the NOW Task Force on Sexuality and Lesbianism was established. This task force focuses on introducing legislation that protects lesbian rights. Human rights activist Del Martin and her partner Phyllis Lyon became the first out lesbians to join NOW (Love 2006). Since the early 1970s, NOW has made lesbian rights a priority and welcomes all sexualities to participate in their feminist mission.

NOW and the ERA

NOW has advocated for the Equal Rights Amendment (ERA) since it was reintroduced in the House of Representatives in 1970 (the ERA was originally introduced to Congress in 1923). The ERA passed Congress in 1972 and was then sent to the states for the required three-fourths ratification. By 1977, the ratification had stalled, needing three more states to ratify it in order to meet the three-fourths benchmark and become a constitutional amendment. While the ERA has been stalled for the past five decades, NOW has held protests and marches, endorsed pro-ERA PACs, and sent "feminist missionaries" to states such as Utah—which is heavily influenced by the Mormon church and one of the remaining holdouts (NOW 2025). The ERA, which has still not been passed, continues to be a priority for NOW.

NOW Today

The National Organization for Women was founded by many brilliant women who were passionate about the fight for women's rights. NOW has always been a racially integrated feminist organization with women of color in high-ranking positions and has expanded to be inclusive of the LGBTQ+ community.

NOW believes that we do not live single-issue lives, and that oppressions women of color and lesbians face are feminist issues. NOW continues to fight for the ratification of the ERA among many other significant feminist policies. NOW has been lobbying for feminist goals for generations and remains a strong influence in Washington.

Riley Gruppen

See Also: Equal Rights Amendment (ERA); *The Feminine Mystique*; Friedan, Betty; Woman-Identified Woman Manifesto

Further Reading

Cohen, Sascha. 2015. "Women's Equality Day: The History of When Women Went on Strike." *Time*, August 26, 2015. https://time.com/4008060/women-strike-equality-1970/.

Fox, Margalit. 2006. "Betty Friedan, Who Ignited a Movement with *The Feminine Mystique*, Dies at 85." *The New York Times*, February 6, 2006. https://www.nytimes.com/2006/02/06/obituaries/us/betty-friedan-who-ignited-a-movement-with-the-feminine.html.

Internal Revenue Service. 2024. "Social Welfare Organizations." March 2024. Accessed August 24, 2024. https://www.irs.gov/charities-non-profits/other-non-profits/social-welfare-organizations#:~:text=To%20be%20tax%2Dexempt%20as,exclusively%20to%20promote%20social%20welfare.

Love, Barbara J. 2006. *Feminists Who Changed America, 1963–1975*. Urbana, IL: University of Illinois Press.
National Organization for Women. 2014. "How Many Members Does NOW Currently Have?" February 10, 2014. Accessed September 16, 2025. https://now.org/faq/how-many-members-does-now-currently-have/.
National Organization for Women. 2025. "The Intertwining History of NOW and the ERA." Accessed July 21, 2024. https://now.org/the-intertwining-history-of-now-and-the-era/.
"NOW: Leading the Fight." 2015. *National Organization for Women*, April 9, 2015. Accessed August 24, 2024. https://now.org/resource/now-leading-the-fight/#:~:text=The%20NOW%20Task%20Force%20on,discrimination%20based%20on%20sexual%20orientation.&text=NOW%20members%20resolve%20to%20designate,one%20of%20NOW's%20top%20priorities.
Wattenberg, Ben. 2000. "First Measured Century: Interview: Betty Friedan." *PBS*. Accessed August 24, 2024. https://www.pbs.org/fmc/interviews/friedan.htm.

NEOLIBERALISM

Neoliberalism is an ideology or way of thinking about the economy and government that has dominated policy, politics, and culture in the United States and many other parts of the world since the 1970s (Dardot and Laval 2017; Harvey 2007). At its core, neoliberalism advocates for free markets, deregulation, privatization, individualism, and limited government intervention in the economy. While presented as gender-neutral, neoliberalism has had complex and often detrimental impacts on women and intersects in important ways with feminism and feminist activism.

Neoliberalism's Core Tenets

Neoliberal economic theory, derived from the ideas of economists like Friedrich Hayek and Milton Friedman, asserts that free markets (unregulated markets) are the most efficient way to allocate resources and that government intervention in the economy should be minimal. Key neoliberal policies include lowering taxes (especially on corporations and the wealthy), austerity measures that cut public spending (such as eliminating welfare), deregulating industries (such as removing safety or environmental rules, so corporations and factories can operate however they would like), privatizing public services (such as letting companies own and operate prisons), and promoting free trade (which means eliminating the special taxes and other rules governing imports and exports).

Crucially, neoliberalism is more than just a set of economic policies. It is a governing rationality—a set of beliefs and assumptions that guide policymaking and politics—and it applies market logic to all spheres of life. Within neoliberalism, the ideal citizen is entrepreneurial, self-reliant, and takes personal responsibility for their own well-being through savvy choices in the marketplace (Brown 2015). Public goods like education, healthcare and social services are redefined as private commodities for individual consumption. Inequality is seen as a natural and even desirable outcome of competitive market processes.

Neoliberalism's Ascent and Consequences

The roots of neoliberalism lie in the economic crises of the 1970s, when stagflation threw the post-Second World War Keynesian economic consensus into disarray. Neoliberal ideas gained traction with the elections of Margaret Thatcher in the United Kingdom in 1979 and Ronald Reagan in the United States in 1980. Putting theory into practice, they cut taxes on high incomes, slashed social spending, busted unions, and deregulated sectors like finance and energy.

In the 1980s and 1990s, neoliberalism went global through "structural adjustment programs" imposed on indebted countries by the International Monetary Fund (IMF) and World Bank. Developing countries were pushed to adopt neoliberal policies like trade liberalization, privatization of state-owned enterprises, and deep cuts to subsidies and social programs. After the fall of the Soviet

Union, much of Eastern Europe underwent "shock therapy"—a rapid transition to capitalism under neoliberal prescriptions.

By the 1990s, neoliberalism had become hegemonic—the taken-for-granted "common sense" of how economies should be structured and governed. Center-left parties like Bill Clinton's New Democrats and Tony Blair's New Labour essentially accepted its core premises. Declaring the "End of History," Francis Fukuyama (1989) proclaimed that humanity had reached the endpoint of its ideological evolution in a world in which neoliberal democracy and global capitalism reigned supreme.

Proponents credit neoliberalism with boosting economic growth, lifting millions out of poverty, expanding consumer choice, and ushering in an age of globalization. Critics argue that its benefits have accrued disproportionately to corporations and the rich while its costs have fallen on the working class and the poor. Neoliberalism's consequences have been stark: dramatic increases in inequality, the decline of organized labor, the erosion of social protections, environmental destruction, repeated financial crises, diminished democracy, and the rise of far-right authoritarian populism in its wake.

Neoliberalism's Complex Relationship with Feminism

Neoliberalism has had an ambivalent and often contentious relationship with feminism. In some ways, the neoliberal emphasis on individual freedom, choice, and opportunity aligns with feminist goals of empowering women as autonomous agents. However, the reliance on unregulated markets and the rolling back of state provisions have undermined women's economic position and increased their burden of unpaid care work.

Feminists note that key neoliberal policies and trends have disproportionately impacted women, especially poor women and women of color:

- Austerity measures and social spending cuts have slashed budgets for public services that many women rely on, from childcare to domestic violence shelters. When care is privatized, the burden falls largely on women to fill the gaps with unpaid labor.
- The decline of unions and rise of precarious work arrangements like temp jobs, contract work, and the gig economy have hit women hard, as they are overrepresented in low-wage, nonunionized service sector jobs.
- Globalization has drawn millions of women in the Global South into exploitative jobs in export processing zones and global supply chains where they face low pay, long hours, and poor working conditions.
- The hollowing out of democracy by market forces has limited the scope for feminist interventions in public policy and made institutions less responsive to women's interests.

Critiquing Neoliberal "Choice Feminism"

Under neoliberalism, feminist goals like empowerment and equality are increasingly expressed through an individualistic rhetoric of choice. Within this framework, women are often assumed to be free agents (unaffected or almost entirely unaffected by sexism) in the work marketplace and encouraged to be "empowered" by making good choices as consumers within this marketplace. For example, Sheryl Sandberg's (2013) exhortation for women to "lean in" at work epitomizes the neoliberal view that women's career success is the result of individual drive, ambition, and confidence—and by contrast, women's career stagnation or failure is the result of their lack of ambition and lack of confidence.

Political philosopher Nancy Fraser (2013) argues that feminism's critique of the family wage, especially during the 1970s–1980s, unwittingly converged with neoliberalism's labor market demands. Feminists' critique of the family wage challenged the post-Second World War model of a male breadwinner and female homemaker, often advocating for women's freedom to join the workforce as a way in which women empower themselves. This coincides with neoliberalism's labor market demands, which always needs a flexible, low-wage workforce and is happy to slot women into these underpaid roles.

Critics argue that neoliberal "choice" rhetoric obscures the structural barriers and unequal power relations that constrain women's options. The "choice" to opt out of the workforce when faced with the impossibility of securing affordable childcare is no real choice at all. And entrepreneurial ventures like selling beauty products to friends and neighbors or renting a spare room on Airbnb are recast as empowering choices rather than survival strategies in a precarious economy.

The idea that women can shop their way to empowerment through commodity consumption and savvy personal branding aligns neatly with neoliberal imperatives, but it reduces the collective vision of women's liberation to individual self-improvement pursuits (Hoerl 2021). In this context, feminist slogans like "Girl Power" can become shallow marketing campaigns that corporations exploit to sell everything from deodorant to cigarettes.

Feminist Resistance to Neoliberalism

Feminists have long challenged the neoliberal narrative, calling attention to its gendered impacts and arguing for a more expansive vision of justice. In the 1970s and 1980s, women were on the front lines of anti-austerity protests and mobilizations against structural adjustment in the Global South.

Activist-scholar Chandra Talpade Mohanty (2002) identifies three waves of a transnational feminist challenge to neoliberal globalization: first, the struggle against unrestricted "free" trade that drew millions of women into free trade zones under unsafe, unprotected working conditions; second, a rapid reorientation and more visible anti-corporatist anti-capitalist stance coinciding with the 1999 Seattle World Trade Organization conference; and third, a wave of engagement with various anti-globalization, anti-capitalism mobilizations in which feminist groups are a crucial component.

Today, feminist scholars and activists call for decentering markets and growth as the primary policy objectives and recentering provisioning, care work, ecological sustainability, and human well-being (Kabeer, Razavi, and van der Meulen Rodgers 2021). They demand reinvestment in public goods, universal social protection systems, decent work agendas, minimum living wages, collective bargaining rights, and progressive taxation of corporations and elites to fund social programs.

Feminists envision a world in which both women and men are unburdened from gender oppression, enabled to form equitable families and households, and empowered to participate fully in political and economic life. Getting there will require challenging neoliberalism's dominance and building a new feminist economy.

Theon E. Hill

See Also: Capitalism; Choice; Feminization of Poverty; Girl Power; Labor Activism

Further Reading

Brown, Wendy. 2015. *Undoing the Demos: Neoliberalism's Stealth Revolution*, 1st ed. New York: Zone Books.

Dardot, Pierre, and Christian Laval. 2017. *The New Way of the World: On Neoliberal Society*. Translated by Gregory Elliott. London: Verso.

Fraser, Nancy. 2013. "How Feminism Became Capitalism's Handmaiden—And How to Reclaim It." *The Guardian*, October 14, 2013. https://www.theguardian.com/commentisfree/2013/oct/14/feminism-capitalist-handmaiden-neoliberal

Fukuyama, Francis. 1989. "The End of History?" *The National Interest*, 16 (Summer): 3–18.

Harvey, David. 2007. *A Brief History of Neoliberalism*. Oxford: Oxford University Press.

Hoerl, Kristen. 2021. "The Impossible Woman and Sexist Realism on NBC's Parks and Recreation." *Quarterly Journal of Speech* 107, no. 4: 373–97. https://doi.org/10.1080/00335630.2021.1984552.

Kabeer, Naila, Shahra Razavi, and Yana van der Meulen Rodgers. 2021. "Feminist Economic Perspectives on the COVID-19 Pandemic." *Feminist Economics* 27, no. 1–2: 1–29. https://doi.org/10.1080/13545701.2021.1876906.

Mohanty, Chandra Talpade. 2002. "'Under Western Eyes' Revisited: Feminist Solidarity through Anticapitalist Struggles." *Signs: Journal of Women in Culture and Society* 28, no. 2: 499–535.

Sandberg, Sheryl. 2013. *Lean In: Women, Work, and the Will to Lead*. New York: Alfred A. Knopf.

NINETEENTH AMENDMENT (1920)

The Nineteenth Amendment to the United States Constitution, ratified in 1920, allows women to vote in the United States. It states, "The right of citizens of the United States to vote shall not be denied or abridged by the United States or by any State on account of sex." The right to vote is known as "suffrage" and early women's rights activists—known as suffragists—organized for decades working to change the US Constitution in order to grant women the right to vote. The entry on "suffrage" in this encyclopedia chronicles that activism; this entry focuses on the Nineteenth Amendment itself.

The US Constitution is a living document. This means that it can be changed—or amended. Each constitutional amendment is sequentially numbered, and there are currently twenty-seven amendments. The Constitution and its amendments, however, are each preserved as written. That is, the original Articles of the Constitution as signed in 1787 are preserved and the amendments are added to it rather than rewriting the original language. For instance, the Eighteenth Amendment was ratified in 1919 and prohibited the "manufacture, sale, or transportation of intoxicating liquors." This amendment was born out of anti-alcohol activism, often known as Temperance. In 1933, the Twenty-First Amendment repealed the Eighteenth Amendment, making it legal again to manufacture, sell, and transport liquor. Both of these changes to the US Constitution are preserved, documented in the amendments. This amendment system makes it clear what has been changed and when, leaving a record of the way things were and how they are now.

Ultimately, this means that the US Constitution is divided into three parts. First, the brief Preamble. This is the famous original passage, beginning with "We the People of the United States." The second part is the Constitution's original seven Articles. Together, the Articles describe how the US government works. Famously, Article I describes the legislative branch (Congress); Article II describes the executive branch (the presidency); and Article III describes the judicial branch (the federal court system). For the purposes of understanding the Nineteenth Amendment, however, it is important to note that Article IV discusses citizenship and Article V describes the process of amending the Constitution. The third part of the Constitution is its amendments—the additions, changes, and updates that amend its original articles. The first ten amendments are collectively known as the Bill of Rights; they were ratified in 1791, a mere four years after the Constitution was signed.

Constitutional Amendments: The Process

Article V of the US Constitution outlines two ways in which the Constitution can be amended (Rappaport and Strauss 2024). All twenty-seven amendments—including the Nineteenth Amendment—have followed the first route, which itself has two options: An amendment is proposed to Congress, and both the House and the Senate pass it by at least a two-thirds majority. The proposed amendment is then sent to the states for consideration. This typically means that the proposed amendment is sent to the states' legislatures. If three-quarters of the state legislatures approve the proposed amendment, it is considered "ratified" and becomes part of the US Constitution. Twenty-six of the twenty-seven amendments have followed this first route. Alternatively, Congress can send a proposed amendment not to the state legislatures but to "state ratifying conventions," which are typically composed of average citizens. This enables Congress to bypass state politicians—a method that has only been used once, in the ratification of the Twenty-First Amendment, which repealed the Eighteenth Amendment's prohibition of alcohol (George and Richards 2024).

The second way to amend the Constitution has never been used, but Article V spells out a way in which state legislatures can bypass Congress. If two-thirds of the state legislatures (thirty-four out of fifty states) call a convention, they can develop a proposed amendment at that convention. They would then send the proposed amendment to each state for consideration. If three-quarters of the states (thirty-eight out of fifty) approve the proposed amendment, it would be ratified and become part of the Constitution.

Historically, amendments were proposed without any timeline or due date for state ratification. This is how the Twenty-Seventh Amendment came into being: it affects congressional pay and was originally proposed in 1789 alongside the first ten amendments, which are collectively known as the Bill of Rights. But it was not ratified by three-quarters of the states until 1992, when it became part of the US Constitution (Calabresi and Teachout 2024). In recent years, Congress has specified that a proposed amendment "must be ratified within seven years or it would lapse," which is the situation for the proposed Equal Rights Amendment (ERA) (Rappaport and Strauss 2024). The proposed ERA was sent to the states in 1972 for consideration for ratification with a seven-year clock—and although granted a three-year extension on that clock, the proposed ERA was not approved by thirty-eight states until 2020, leaving its status in a strange sort of constitutional purgatory.

Ultimately then, the process of amending the US Constitution is quite complicated. And it can be stymied by small minorities. For instance, Article I stipulates that each state gets two senators regardless of how many people live in that state—which is to say, regardless of how small a minority those senators represent. Proposed constitutional amendments, however, have to be passed by at least two-thirds or sixty-six senators (out of 100) in order to be sent to the states for ratification. Which means that if thirty-five senators reject the proposed amendment—again, regardless of how few people they represent—the proposed amendment fails. Likewise, the states themselves have very different populations. To be ratified, however, a proposed amendment needs three-quarters or thirty-eight states (out of fifty) to approve of it. Which means that if thirteen states reject it—again, regardless of how few people live in those states—the proposed amendment fails.

The Nineteenth Amendment in Context

Given how difficult it is to amend the US Constitution and how easily this process can be torpedoed by just a few people in Congress, the Nineteenth Amendment is truly shocking.

When the United States was founded, every state except New Jersey "adopted state constitutions that denied women the right to vote" ("US Census Bureau History" 2020). New Jersey followed suit, rescinding women's right to vote in 1807. Women were not universally considered citizens of the United States until the Fourteenth Amendment was ratified in 1868.

In 1919, the year Congress passed the proposed Nineteenth Amendment, every congressperson was a man. Moreover, in 1920, the year the Nineteenth Amendment was ratified, only twenty states out of the then forty-eight states allowed women to vote: Wyoming, Utah, Colorado, Idaho, Washington,

California, Oregon, Montana, Arizona, Kansas, Alaska, Illinois, North Dakota, Indiana, Nebraska, Michigan, Arkansas, New York, South Dakota, and Oklahoma ("19th Amendment by State" 2020). (Alaska and Hawai'i did not become states until 1959.) As such, the Nineteenth Amendment had to be ratified by thirty-six states in order to become a constitutional amendment at a time when only twenty states allowed women to vote.

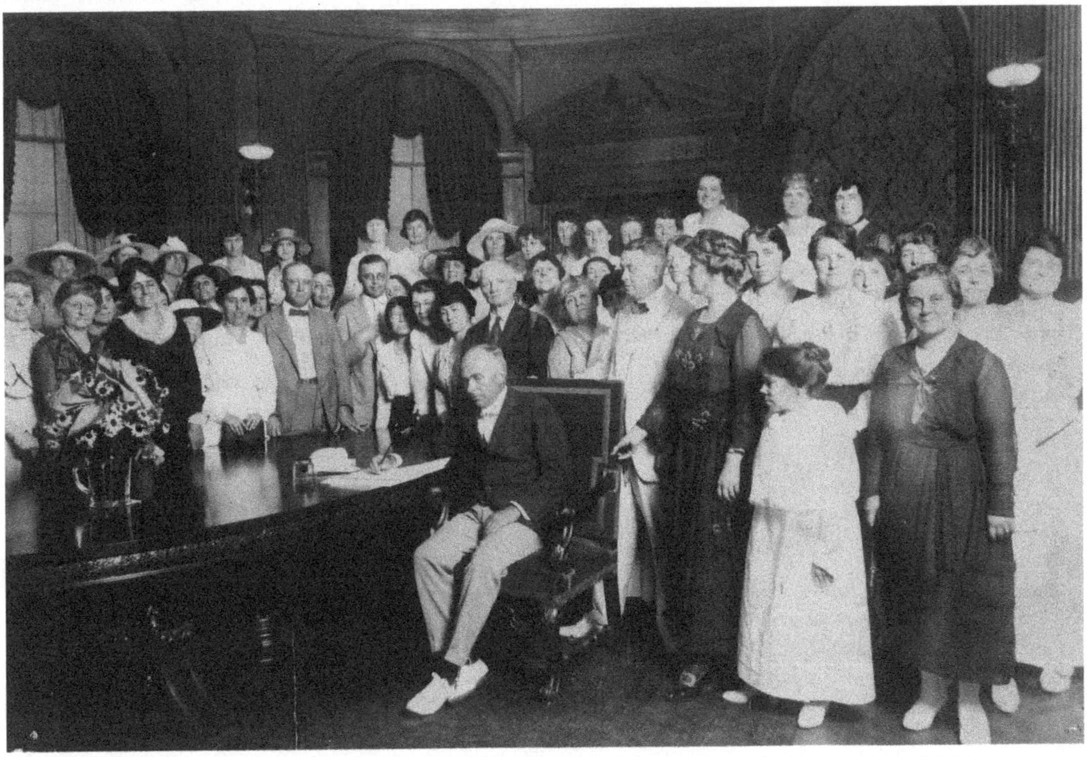

Missouri governor Frederick Gardner signing the resolution ratifying the nineteenth constitutional amendment, allowing women to vote (Library of Congress).

It is a testament to the incredible activism of suffragists across the United States that they successfully petitioned for women's suffrage in an era in which very few of the men who voted on the proposed amendment in Congress and in the state legislatures were beholden in any way to women as constituents. Essentially, since women could not vote in twenty-eight of the forty-eight states, the men who held office representing these twenty-eight states never had to answer to women. They never faced the threat of recall or a failed reelection due to women's votes, and if thirteen of those twenty-eight states had rejected the proposed amendment it would have failed. And yet, it passed.

Women's Citizenship and Suffrage

The Articles of the Constitution do not stipulate who can be a citizen. Rather, Article IV leaves the question of citizenship to each state. Likewise, the rights of citizenship are fairly opaque in the US Constitution's original Articles (Amar and Harrison 2024). Whether or not women were citizens and whether citizenship granted women any rights (such as the right to own property, to receive a wage, to testify in court, or to vote) varied by state. This changed in 1868 when the Fourteenth Amendment was ratified.

The Fourteenth Amendment was part of a slate of three amendments known as the "Reconstruction Amendments" that were ratified after the Civil War and that theoretically outlawed the worst practices of slavery. The opening line of the Fourteenth Amendment states, "All persons born or naturalized in the United States, and subject to the jurisdiction thereof, are citizens of the United States and the State wherein they reside." Although this amendment was designed to make Black men citizens, it also made white and Black women citizens—as well as other people of color who are born within the United States. Notably, the Fourteenth Amendment's phrase "subject to the jurisdiction thereof" excluded many Indigenous people from US citizenship. Essentially, because of the way US governance constrained and excluded Indigenous tribal governance, the Fourteenth Amendment didn't apply to many Indigenous populations. It wasn't until the Snyder Act of 1923 that all Indigenous people in the United States became US citizens (Kornfield 2024).

As such, except for many Indigenous populations, men of color and women born in the United States became US citizens in 1868. However, citizenship does not guarantee rights. As such, the Nineteenth Amendment—ratified in 1920—marked the beginning of women's suffrage across the United States, although Jim Crow laws largely prevented people of color from voting until the Civil Rights Act of 1964. This means that in practice the Nineteenth Amendment only granted white women the right to vote in the United States.

Sarah Kornfield

See Also: Civil Rights Movement; Equal Rights Amendment (ERA); Suffrage

Further Reading

Amar, Akhil Reed, and John C. Harrison. 2024. "The Citizenship Clause: Interpretation and Debate." *National Constitution Center*. Accessed August 31, 2024. https://constitutioncenter.org/the-constitution/amendments/amendment-xiv/clauses/700.

Calabresi, Steven G., and Zephyr Teachout. 2024. "The Twenty-Seventh Amendment: Interpretation and Debate." *National Constitution Center*. Accessed August 31, 2024. https://constitutioncenter.org/the-constitution/amendments/amendment-xxvii/interpretations/165.

George, Robert P., and David A. J. Richards. 2024. "The Twenty-First Amendment: Interpretation and Debate." *National Constitution Center*. Accessed August 31, 2024. https://constitutioncenter.org/the-constitution/amendments/amendment-xxi/interpretations/151.

Kornfield, Sarah. 2024. *Invoking the Fathers: Dangerous Metaphors and Founding Myths in Congressional Politics*. Baltimore: Johns Hopkins University Press.

"19th Amendment by State." 2020. *National Park Service: Women's History*, July 22, 2020. Accessed August 31, 2024. https://www.nps.gov/subjects/womenshistory/19th-amendment-by-state.htm.

Rappaport, Michael B., and David A. Strauss. 2024. "Article V: Interpretation and Debate." *National Constitution Center*. Accessed August 31, 2024. https://constitutioncenter.org/the-constitution/articles/article-v/interpretations/277.

"US Census Bureau History: Ratification of the 19th Amendment." 2020. *United States Census Bureau*. August 2020. Accessed August 31, 2020. https://www.census.gov/history/www/homepage_archive/2020/august_2020.html.

NONBINARY

Nonbinary identities refer to individuals whose gender identity does not conform strictly to the traditional categories of male/masculine or female/feminine (Cordoba 2020). The term "nonbinary" can be an umbrella term encompassing various labels, including genderqueer, agender, bigender, and pangender—and sometimes trans individuals. Often, nonbinary people use gender-neutral pronouns such as they/them. Nonbinary people might feel like a mix of genders or have no gender at all. The term "cisgender" is used for individuals whose gender identity aligns with the sex they were assigned at birth (Cordoba 2020).

Gender is a role we perform in our daily lives (Wilcox 2017). According to West and Zimmerman (1987) in their article "Doing Gender," gender is something we actively "do" through our actions and behaviors—such as choosing our clothes or choosing activities we enjoy. West and Zimmerman explain that our biology does not set gender roles; instead gender roles are learned from society. From a young age, we are taught what behaviors are considered proper for boys and girls, which pressures us to fit these roles. Even small things, like the way we talk or walk, can show these gender norms (West and Zimmerman 1987). These social expectations shape how we act and interact with others, reinforcing the idea that there are strict rules about what is "appropriate" for each gender. West and Zimmerman (1987) argue that these behaviors are not natural but learned. We perform them because we have been taught what is expected based on our gender.

Challenges and Discrimination Faced by Nonbinary Individuals

Many nonbinary individuals face the daily challenge of trying to fit into a binary system that was never designed for them. According to a 2019 Pew Research Center study, about one in five people in the United States know someone who uses gender-neutral pronouns, highlighting the increasing visibility of nonbinary individuals. Despite this, nonbinary people still encounter significant discrimination and misunderstanding.

The US Transgender Survey, one of the most extensive studies of its kind, found that around one-third of transgender and gender-nonconforming respondents identify as nonbinary or genderqueer (James et al. 2016). Nevertheless, nonbinary people continue to face severe stigma and marginalization. Society clings to a binary gender system that assumes everyone must fit into the categories of (cisgender) "men" or "women," or, in some cases, "trans men" and "trans women." While the increased recognition of trans identities is itself a marker of social progress, many nonbinary individuals do not identify as trans. When nonbinary people are labeled as trans, it undermines the very essence of "non" in nonbinary. This exclusion stems from cisnormativity, which assumes a person's gender should align with the sex assigned at birth, further marginalizing nonbinary people.

Heteronormative views perpetuate discrimination against nonbinary individuals, with many dismissing nonbinary identities as temporary or experimental. For instance, nearly two-thirds (63 percent) of nonbinary respondents in the US Transgender Discrimination Survey reported that their identity was frequently dismissed as illegitimate or just a passing phase (James et al. 2016). This skepticism is often rooted in stereotypes that view nonbinary identities as fleeting trends rather than valid, permanent experiences.

Beyond the dismissal of their identities, nonbinary individuals face a wide range of discriminatory experiences. According to the same US Transgender Survey, nonbinary people experience higher rates of harassment, unemployment, and poverty compared to their cisgender counterparts. For example, 30 percent of nonbinary people reported being fired, denied a promotion, or not hired due to their gender identity, and 42 percent experienced some form of housing discrimination (James et al. 2016). Additionally, nonbinary individuals are at a higher risk of physical and sexual violence, with 43 percent reporting that they have been sexually assaulted (James et al. 2016). Cisgender individuals often hold biases against nonbinary individuals, viewing them as "disrupting the binary system in uncomfortable ways" (Fiani and Han 2018). This internalized skepticism, alongside social discrimination, dismissal, and exclusion, exacerbates the challenges nonbinary people face in gaining acceptance and recognition.

Nonbinary Identities in Popular Culture

In the past ten years, the representation of nonbinary identities has increased in popular culture. In television shows, movies, the music industry, social media, and fashion, nonbinary representation is becoming more prominent, reflecting a social shift toward recognizing, validating, and appreciating diverse gender experiences. "Seeing ourselves represented on screen or in literature provides a sense of affirmation and belonging, helping us to feel seen and heard and reducing feelings of isolation" (Hunt 2023).

Seeing oneself represented in the media can positively impact mental health and self-esteem (Impact of Media Representation 2024); good representation can promote a more positive view of one's identity. This was clear in the videos of girls of color seeing their favorite Disney Princess, Ariel, having the same color skin as them in the live action adaptation of *The Little Mermaid* (2023). Seeing people who look and act like you in media can be inspiring. It can also help others be more understanding. As Robin Hunt (2023) explained:

> For everyone else, seeing [non-binary people] in media helps them to understand and relate to them. . . . when realistic narratives and stories are told, others are able to support their community based on facts rather than discriminate against them based on myths and misconceptions. The more realistic stories that are told, the more allies we gain and the louder our collective voice becomes as we fight for equality.

One of the most prominent nonbinary characters in contemporary media is television's Dr. Kai Bartley, a neuroscientist on *Grey's Anatomy*, played by E. R. Fightmaster. Fightmaster praises the show's creators for not reducing Dr. Bartley's identity to a single trait, while also having the rare opportunity to collaborate with writers on how to address gender identity (Hunt 2023). Another standout is Cal Bowman, played by Dua Saleh in *Sex Education*, who quickly became a fan favorite for sparking conversations about gendered dress codes and nonbinary dating (Hunt 2023).

While TV is making progress, the film industry lags behind in nonbinary representation. Yet even here there is some representation, such as Indya Moore's role in *Ma Rainey's Black Bottom* and films such as *Tangerine* and *The Miseducation of Cameron Post*. Books, however, have seen significant growth in nonbinary narratives, thanks in part to platforms like Amazon, Kindle, and Audible, which enable nonbinary authors to self-publish, taking charge of their stories (Hunt 2023). Some notable books include *Loveless* by Alice Oseman, *Chlorine* by Jade Song, *Phoenix Extravagant* by Yoon Ha Lee, *An Unkindness of Ghosts* by Rivers Solomon, and *I Wish You All the Best* by Mason Deaver. Nonbinary representation in the media holds significant potential to challenge the stigma against nonbinary people, validate all identities, and foster understanding. While progress has been made, much work remains to be done (Hunt 2023).

Activism and Advocacy

Nonbinary celebrities such as Indya Moore and Alok Vaid-Menon are also activists and advocates, challenging the rigid boundaries of gender. Their presence in mainstream media brings much-needed representation, and they use their platforms to lead necessary conversations about nonbinary rights and inclusion. These celebrities advocate for and normalize gender fluidity, striving for a world where everyone can express themselves without fear of judgment or discrimination.

For example, Indya Moore (she/they), a 29-year-old actor, writer, model, and social activist, is a trans and nonbinary individual from the Bronx (New York). In 2019, they made history as the first trans person on the cover of *ELLE Magazine* and were named one of *TIME Magazine's* 100 Most Influential People. Reflecting on Moore's role in *Pose,* Janet Mock—a trans author and advocate—

wrote, "In Indya, I see elements of our foremothers: the beauty of Sir Lady Java and Tracey Africa Norman, the brazenness of Miss Major and Sylvia Rivera, and the indelible warmth and spirit of Marsha P. Johnson. She is the living embodiment of our wildest dreams finally coming true" (Mock 2019). Similarly, Alok Vaid-Menon, a globally recognized poet, comedian, and actor, has captivated audiences in over forty countries with their works *Beyond the Gender Binary*, *Femme in Public*, and *Your Wound, My Garden*. Vaid-Menon also appears in activist comedian Hannah Gadsby's *Gender Agenda* on Netflix, where their performance is described as "provocative and powerful" and a "jaw-dropping celestial event" (ALOK 2024).

Several organizations have been pivotal in advancing nonbinary rights and inclusion through various projects. The Transgender Law Center, the largest national trans-led organization, advocates for everyone's bodily autonomy and self-determination. Since its founding in 2002, the Transgender Law Center has been "organizing, assisting, informing, and empowering thousands of individual community members towards a long-term, national, trans-led movement for liberation" (Transgender Law Center 2023). Similarly, the National Center for Transgender Equality (NCTE), a nonprofit organization, works at all levels of government to ensure that trans and nonbinary voices are "not only heard, but embraced in rooms where they have long been ignored" (Advocates for Trans Equality 2024). The Sylvia Rivera Law Project (2024), based in New York City, is likewise dedicated to guaranteeing that all people, regardless of income or race, can freely self-determine their gender identity and expression without facing harassment, discrimination, or violence.

The contributions of nonbinary celebrities like Indya Moore and Alok Vaid-Menon, along with the dedicated efforts of advocacy organizations, have been monumental in advancing nonbinary visibility and rights. By standing in the spotlight, these figures not only inspire nonbinary individuals but also educate broader society, paving the way for a world where gender fluidity is accepted and celebrated. As the movement continues to grow, it is clear that these activists' advocacy is not just about representation; it is about building a future where everyone, regardless of gender, can live authentically and without fear.

Alex Mahan

See Also: Bodily Autonomy; Queer Theory; Trans Theory

Further Reading

Advocates for Trans Equality. 2024. "About Us." Accessed September 19, 2024. https://transequality.org/.

ALOK. n.d. "About." Accessed September 19, 2024. https://www.alokvmenon.com/about.

Cordoba, Sebastian. 2020. "Exploring Non-bianry Genders: Language and Identity." PhD diss., De Montfort University.

Fiani, Chassitty N., and Heather J. Han. 2018. "Navigating Identity: Experiences of Binary and Non-binary Transgender and Gender Non-conforming (TGNC) Adults." *International Journal of Transgenderism* 20, no. 2–3: 181–94.

Hunt, R. [@RobinHunt]. 2023. "Non-binary Representation in Media: Progress and Challenges [LinkedIn post]." *LinkedIn*, July 13, 2023. https://www.linkedin.com/in/robinhunt.

"Indya Moore." 2023. *Unleashed LGBTQ+*. Accessed November 7, 2024. https://www.unleashedlgbtq.com/indya-moore.

James, S. E., J. L. Herman, S. Rankin, M. Keisling, L. Mottet, and M. Anafi. 2016. "The Report of the 2015 US Transgender Survey." Washington, DC: National Center for Transgender Equality. Accessed December 2, 2024. https://transequality.org/sites/default/files/docs/usts/USTS-Full-Report-Dec17.pdf.

Mock, Janet. 2019. "Indya Moore." *Time*. Accessed September 24, 2024. https://time.com/collection/100-most-influential-people-2019/5567698/indya-moore/.

Sylvia Rivera Law Project. 2024. Accessed September 19, 2024. https://srlp.org/.

Transgender Law Center. 2023. "Home." Accessed October 16, 2023. https://transgenderlawcenter.org/.
TransPonder. n.d. "Indya Moore." Accessed September 19, 2024. https://transponder.community/empowering-trans-voices-38-2/.
"The Impact of Media Representation on Mental Health: Why It Matters." 2024. *Trust Mental Health.* July 7, 2024. Accessed November 7, 2024. https://trustmentalhealth.com/blog/the-impact-of-media-representation-on-mental-health-why-it-matters#:~:text=For%20example%2C%20someone%20who%20sees,as%20they%20build%20new%20friendships.&text=Seeing%20oneself%20in%20media%20can%20validate%20one%27s%20identity%20and%20experiences.&text=To%20recap%2C%20meaningful%20representation%20can,and%20improving%20overall%20social%20awareness.
West, Candace, and Don H. Zimmerman. 1987. "Doing Gender." *Gender and Society* 1, no. 2: 125–51. http://www.jstor.org/stable/189945.
Wilcox, Lauren. 2017. "Practicing Gender, Queering Theory." *Review of International Studies* 43, no. 5: 789–808. https://doi.org/10.1017/S0260210517000183.
Youth Radio. 2021. "Will Reality TV Ever Represent My Reality as a Nonbinary Person?" *YR Media*, June 28, 2021. https://yr.media/identity/will-reality-tv-ever-represent-me-as-a-nonbinary-person/.

O

OBERGEFELL V. HODGES (2015)

Obergefell v. Hodges (2015) was the landmark case that legalized gay marriage after a long, fraught battle that lasted over sixty years.

The overall decision was that the Constitution requires a state to license a marriage between two people of the same sex and to recognize a marriage between two people of the same sex when their marriage was lawfully licensed and performed out-of-state. This was a surprising decision in a few ways. One, nobody knew how the Court would decide. People on all sides of the political spectrum were waiting with bated breath for the decision to come out. Second, nobody knew how far the decision would go. If the Court decided gay marriage was legal, that didn't mean they would require that marriages in one state would be recognized in another state. But the Court's decision went as far as it could conceivably go.

The Court argued that petitioners were not seeking to devalue marriage—they were there because they respect marriage. And, the Court observed, the history of marriage is one of change. This was an important point because one of the arguments against gay marriage was that it was outside the bounds of traditional marriage. And tradition carries a lot of weight with some Americans. But, the Court argued, Americans don't pay dowries anymore. Women aren't seen as property anymore. Most Americans don't have arranged marriages anymore. Marriage has changed. It has evolved. That is its nature. And most people would say that is a good thing.

They also argued that the fundamental liberties of the Constitution include intimate choices that define personal identity and beliefs. The Constitution protects our right to make choices about who we are and what we believe—and there is nothing more personal or sacrosanct than the choice about with whom we are going to share our lives. And, as the Court has decided in other cases, such as *Loving v. Virginia* (1967), *Turner v. Safley* (1987), and *Zablocki v. Redhail* (1978), the right to marry is a fundamental liberty. It is a private choice.

As for the argument from previous cases that the right of same-sex couples to marry wasn't protected because it wasn't deeply rooted in our nation's past and traditions, the Court wrote, "If rights were defined by who exercised them in the past, then received practices could serve as their own continued justification and new groups could not invoke rights once denied" (*Obergefell v. Hodges* 2015). In other words, if the only people who had rights were the people who already had rights, then not a lot of people would have rights.

Detractors argued that in a case like this, the Court was "legislating from the bench." That means the Court is making laws instead of the legislative branch making the laws. But the Court specifically addressed that concern. The Court said in the majority decision that they aren't legislating; they are righting a wrong. And that is what the court system exists to do. If a person is wronged, they go to the judicial branch to address their grievances. That is literally what the judicial branch exists to do. And this is a case in which people were wronged, and they went to court to address their grievances. Nothing more.

The Court insisted this would not harm marriage but strengthen it. They stated,

> No union is more profound than marriage, for it embodies the highest ideals of love, fidelity, devotion, sacrifice, and family. In forming a marital union, two people become something greater than once they were. . . . Their plea is that they do respect it, respect it so deeply that they seek to find its fulfillment for themselves. Their hope is not to be condemned to live in loneliness, excluded from one of civilization's oldest institutions. They ask for equal dignity in the eyes of the law. The Constitution gives them that right. (*Obergefell v. Hodges* 2015)

One of the interesting things about *Obergefell* that is different from other decisions and opinions is actually the nature of the decision's prose. Justice Anthony Kennedy penned the *Obergefell* opinion for the majority, and it seems he wrote it with an eye toward the public. Supreme Court opinions are not generally riveting reading. They are somewhat dry, boring, and clearly legalistic. Not many people read them for fun. But the *Obergefell* opinion is written in a very different style. It is actually quite lovely. It is lyrical. Some have described it as poetic. It is definitely romantic. In the years following the decision some even used excerpts from the opinion in their wedding ceremonies because the prose fit so nicely with the event.

It is not far-fetched to say the *Obergefell* changed the course of history. It is imperative we keep an eye on the arguments that both supported and detracted from it, as attacks on the LGBTQ+ community become more and more vitriolic in the twenty-first century.

M. Elizabeth Thorpe

See Also: Anti-Miscegenation Laws; *Lawrence v. Texas* (2003); Queer Theory

Further Reading

Obergefell v. Hodges, 576 U.S. 644. 2015.

ONLINE DATING AND THE BURNED HAYSTACK DATING METHOD

The toxicity of dating apps is well-known, widely discussed in the media, and increasingly studied through an academic lens. The dating app experience is especially toxic for women and exacerbated by identity factors in a variety of ways. Nancy Jo Sales, author of *American Girls: Social Media and the Secret Life of Teenagers*, writes in *Wired Magazine* that "it is women and girls who suffer most often from the abuses of online dating, as well as people of color and those in the LGBTQ community" (2021). In an article about Tinder, feminist media studies scholar Rosalie Gillett (2021) refers to what she calls "intimate intrusions," which are behaviors on the apps that "make women feel uneasy, uncomfortable, or unsafe." Young women absorb an inordinate amount of sexual aggression; women of color are accosted with racial slurs; women of all body types are presented with men's opinions about their particular bodies. Certain demographics—women of color, women with disabilities, women over forty—experience disproportionate degrees of being ignored *and* being fetishized. *All* women encounter exploitation, aggression, objectification, and manipulation.

There are plenty of dating coaches doling out advice, therapists working with individual clients, and articles in mainstream publications addressing these problems on an almost daily basis. But among all the think-piece journalism and the "self-help" advice of varying quality on the free internet, we've been missing an academically informed, rhetorical approach to navigating the dating apps.

Rhetoric and Online Dating

Burned Haystack Dating Method serves as a "feminist correction" to the toxicity and manipulation so salient in the contemporary dating market. The Method is concrete, teachable, and grounded in feminism. I am a professor of rhetoric and women/gender studies, and I developed the Burned Haystack Dating Method based on a practice called "Critical Discourse Analysis," or CDA, which is a method within the broader field of applied rhetoric.

The name of the Method is inspired by the metaphor of "trying to find a needle in a haystack," the needle being that rare good thing that is buried beneath thousands of pieces of hay. The most efficient way to find a needle in a haystack is not to pick through every piece of hay looking for it; it's to burn the entire haystack to the ground so that you can simply pick up the needle left behind, since metal doesn't burn. The "burned haystack" approach to dating focuses on ruling matches OUT rather than in; the goal is to clear away all the people whom you do NOT want to date and, in the process, naturally uncover the ones you might. The most effective way to rule matches out is to become sharply attuned to the red flags of misogyny, aggression, manipulation, and weaponized incompetence. An understanding of rhetoric is the key that unlocks the ability to do this.

The conventional definition of rhetoric is "the art of persuasion," but rhetoricians are just as concerned with *receptive* rhetoric as they are with *productive* rhetoric. Productive rhetoric is what we produce—a speech, a commercial, an argument; receptive rhetoric is what we encounter in the world, and more specifically, what we can analyze. Burned Haystack dwells in this domain: analyzing receptive rhetoric, the rhetoric presented *to* us. Adding the word "applied" in front of rhetoric—"applied rhetoric"—simply means we are applying rhetorical methods to aspects of real life, such as dating and intimate relationships. So when we use Burned Haystack Dating Method, we are using academic methodology to "read between the lines" of people's words on dating apps, in messaging conversations, and in real-life interactions. We are particularly interested in using these methods to figure out what people are revealing about themselves without intending to because this is frequently the most important information to glean. For example, a person who tends toward misogyny or even violence certainly does not want to reveal that in their dating app profile but anyone who encounters that profile needs to be able to read for these "red flag" revelations.

Critical Discourse Analysis, the branch of applied rhetoric we use the most in Burned Haystack, has two primary goals: the first is the one just discussed above—reading language in a way that reveals meaningful information; the second is to use the knowledge gained to make the world better and/or improve the conditions of people who exist in relevant spaces (Fairclough 2010; Gee 2011). In the case of Burned Haystack, the method aims to improve the lives of women in dating spaces by equipping them with analytical tools and the ability to quickly identify problematic patterns that indicate the potential for more bad things—frustration, dishonesty, manipulation, abuse, violence.

Another branch of rhetorical analysis we use in Burned Haystack is "semiotics," which is the branch of analysis concerned with "reading" images for important information. For example, a man who chooses a profile pic that depicts a close-up of his face sneering down at you from above is communicating something specific (and aggressive, in this case); a man who chooses a profile pic of himself climbing a mountain is communicating something else (which could be positive or negative, depending upon how you feel about mountain climbing!). The important thing is that, just like words, images also reveal important underlying truths that should be considered while selecting dating partners.

Using the Burned Haystack Dating Method

Burned Haystack Dating Method articulates ten clear rules that should govern women's use of dating apps; if employed correctly, these guidelines are protective of time, mental health, and physical safety. For example, the Method advises using the dating apps like a practical tool you use a couple times a day for a few minutes (like a toothbrush!) rather than like a video game that is ongoing, attention sucking, addictive, and distracting from real-world interactions with the people in your life. Another rule—the one labeled "Block to Burn"—advises immediately blocking (not just swiping left on but actually blocking) men who remark upon women's appearances or who introduce sexual content in the early phases of dating app interaction; these patterns of communication are boundary violations because they occur without consent and could be indicative of future potential for aggression or abuse.

Two other key components of Burned Haystack Method are a set of thought experiments called "Translate it to Real Life" and "Rhetorical Patterns to Burn." In the first, we take things that happen on the dating apps all the time—for example, men who are strangers demanding that we smile or interact with them sexually—and reimagine that in a different scenario. For example, if an unknown man approached you on the street and demanded that you show him nude pictures of yourself, you would immediately recognize that as inappropriate and threatening. It is no less inappropriate or threatening on a dating app. If it's not okay in real life, it's not okay on a dating app. "Rhetorical Patterns to Burn" are a set of commonly encountered ways of speaking/writing that constitute red flags about a person and indicate that you should avoid or cease interacting with them. For example, the "test and apologize" pattern is when a man begins a conversation by intentionally pushing a boundary—usually by saying something sexual—and then immediately apologizing for it before the woman he's addressing has even responded. This allows him to determine how much he can get away with while preemptively building in the "apology" (which is not sincere) to make himself look like a "good guy." The "disciplinary/directive" rhetorical pattern includes sets of "rules" and expectations of women right in a man's profile. The "designing my AI girlfriend" pattern includes a list of exactly how a man expects a woman to look and behave. The "rescue pup" rhetorical pattern leads off by sharing all of a man's problems, asking for various forms of support, and so on. Once women have learned and internalized these rhetorical patterns, they are immediately identifiable and can be used to quickly "burn the haystack" without further wasted time or uncomfortable interactions.

Holistically speaking, Burned Haystack Dating Method is both an overarching feminist philosophy and a concrete set of guidelines that is intended to empower and protect women in the dating market. Its coverage in major media outlets and its reach on social media have marked it as a distinctive movement in contemporary feminism.

Jennie Young

See Also: Cyberfeminism; Emotional Labor; Feminist Killjoy; Feminist Methodologies; Gaslighting; Rape Culture

Further Reading

Fairclough, Norman. 2010. *Critical Discourse Analysis: The Critical Study of Language*. London: Longman.

Gee, James Paul. 2011. *An Introduction to Discourse Analysis: Theory and Method*. London: Routledge.

Gillett, Rosalie. 2021. "'This is Not a Nice Safe Space': Investigating Women's Safety Work on Tinder." *Feminist Media Studies* 23, no. 1: 199–215. https://doi.org/10.1080/14680777.2021.1948884.

Sales, Nancy Jo. 2021. "Online Dating Apps Are Actually Kind of a Disaster." *Wired*, May 18, 2021. https://www.wired.com/story/online-dating-apps-are-a-disaster/.

P

PARTIAL BIRTH ABORTION BAN ACT (2003)

On November 5, 2003, then president George W. Bush signed the Partial Birth Abortion Ban Act (PBABA) of 2003 into law. The PBABA bans a certain type of abortion procedure that is typically used later in pregnancy (between thirteen and twenty-four weeks' gestation) known as dilation and extraction (also called D&X or intact D&E). This abortion procedure was invented as an alternative to a similar procedure called dilatation and evacuation (also called D&E or nonintact D&E). D&X abortions have a lower risk of complications than D&E abortions because they are "less likely to puncture the uterine wall or cause infection by repeated instrument passes" (Kushnir 2004, 1140). Congress passed earlier iterations of the PBABA bill under President Bill Clinton's administrations, but Clinton vetoed them. Anti-abortion advocates celebrated the 2003 Act being passed into law, while feminists argued the PBABA was a chip in the armor provided by *Roe v. Wade*, which had protected abortion as a constitutional right in the United States since 1973. The PBABA faced many legal challenges and, eventually, was tested in the 2007 Supreme Court case *Gonzales v. Carhart*, which held that the ban was constitutional.

How the PBABA Came to Pass

In 1992 an anti-abortion activist infiltrated a medical conference at which Dr. Martin Haskell, inventor of the D&X procedure, described his new approach for performing abortions after twenty weeks. Anti-abortion activists began calling this procedure a "partial-birth abortion," but this term has no basis in medical fact and is, still, not a term used by medical practitioners or supported by science (Furgerson 2023). The invention of the term "partial-birth abortion" is an example of "strategic ambiguity," a rhetorical strategy used by anti-abortion activists that hides an "independent moral status" of a fetus within a seemingly descriptive and normal term (Furgerson 2023; McCullough and Chervenak 2008). In other words, the PBABA uses strategic ambiguity to create a term that "secured people's abhorrence" of abortion "even before they knew the details of the procedure" (Armitage 2010, 23). The adoption of nonmedical, unscientific, and strategically ambiguous terms like "partial-birth abortion" stirs the public through overly sensationalized descriptions of abortion, in this case implying that the procedure takes place during "birth" (Donley and Lens 2021).

As anti-abortion advocates attempted to pass this federal ban, they learned from other attempts, especially the Supreme Court's decision in *Stenberg v. Carhart* (2000). Here, the Supreme Court ruled that a state-level ban on D&X procedures in Nebraska was unconstitutional because there was no exception for the health of the pregnant person. Anti-abortion actors used this feedback and their earlier failed congressional attempts to refine their approach, including a provision in the 2003 iteration of the PBABA that allows the D&X procedure only to save the pregnant person's life. It is important to note that this is not an exception to preserve the *health* or well-being of the pregnant person but *only* to save their life if in immediate danger as a result of the pregnancy and if no other abortion options are possible.

Implications of the 2003 PBABA for Feminist Activism

There are many ways the 2003 PBABA affected and continues to affect feminist activism around abortion rights. First, the PBAPA is an early example of anti-abortion "guerrilla legislation," which "refers to both a collectivity of pro-life laws, and the litigious and legislative processes by which pro-lifers can propose, pass, and enforce those laws" (Mason 2000, 12). This turn toward legislative attempts to outlaw abortion is known as "guerrilla" legislation because it depends "on independent operators and independent cases of litigation and legislation to sabotage and harass people seeking or providing abortions on an irregular, arbitrary basis" (Mason 2000, 12). Early guerrilla legislation like the PBABA paved the way for TRAP (Target Regulation of Abortion Provider) laws and fetal personhood and protection policies (Coker 2018), and other "trigger laws" (Jiménez 2022). Together, this "guerrilla" strategy contributed to *Roe v. Wade*'s eventual demise.

Anti-abortion activists began using the guerrilla legislation strategy in the 1990s as a move away from the more violent tactics that were endemic to the late 1980s and early 1990s. During this time, feminist abortion activism took a dual focus on protecting *Roe v. Wade* and protecting abortion patients and providers, with most of the focus being on the latter. Feminist activists who focused on abortion rights often served as volunteer clinic escorts or clinic defenders. These volunteers helped people enter clinics and, in some cases, physically defended those seeking or providing care. According to the National Abortion Federation (NAF), by 2003 seven abortion providers (including volunteers) had been murdered by anti-abortion activists, seventeen providers faced attempted murder, and there were hundreds of other instances of anti-abortion clinic violence (like bombings, arson, chemical attacks, death threats, kidnappings, etc.). In addition to individuals' roles as clinic escorts and defenders, a significant role that organizations like NAF and the Feminist Majority Foundation played during this time was keeping track of such statistics and documenting anti-abortion clinic violence. This tracking was necessary because many feminists believed (and still believe) that anti-abortion violence is not taken seriously by law enforcement.

Throughout their guerrilla legislation strategy, anti-abortion activists gained ground in shaping the way abortion is discussed in popular discourse. As Furgerson (2023) notes, the anti-abortion movement has created a lexicon of unscientific and medically inaccurate terms that are used to describe abortion, fetuses, reproductive health, and what we collectively understand as fetal "life." As mentioned earlier, the term "partial-birth abortion" was specifically invented in response to D&E procedures as a means to manipulate public opinion on abortion. Beyond this term, the PBABA advances the anti-abortion movement's goal of reconceptualizing "life" by attaching personhood rights to fetuses. The PBABA further establishes the state's "moral, medical, and ethical" investment in "saving unborn children" through intervening in people's medical decisions and needs. President Bush reflected this investment at the bill's signing ceremony, stating that "Our nation owes its children a different and better welcome" (President Bush Signs 2003) As a specific example of the guerrilla legislation strategy, this stated investment established a precedent that many state-level abortion bans would later follow. Indeed, attorney R. Alta Charo (2007, 2128) writes that the PBABA and subsequent *Gonzales v. Carhart* decision reflect a shift in a social balance of interests in which "women's health [is] no longer paramount but rather societal morality and the state's interest in life even before the point of viability outside the womb" gained precedence.

In addition to legislative implications, the invention of the anti-abortion lexicon also has implications for abortion providers both in terms of how they administer care and how they talk about their work. One, writing in the wake of the 2007 *Carhart* decision, says the ban created an "intimidating environment" for abortion providers working with people at later gestational periods

(Greene 2007, 2128). Greene further expresses how providers were concerned that they would not be treated fairly in the judicial system if they were to be prosecuted under the PBABA. Similarly, a study conducted ten years later found that abortion providers do not openly discuss their work with others and that this self-censoring has implications for the abortion rights movement at large. The authors argue that the dearth of abortion providers' narratives creates "a vacuum in which stereotypical caricatures may dominate the public discourse" (Martin et al. 2017, 76). This study finds that there are many types of stories abortion providers do not share because their lived experience does not reflect the dominant pro-choice narratives (Ellis 2023).

While the dominant feminist narratives emphasize stories about "worthy" abortions that celebrate providers as heroes and the act of abortion as being indicative of women's agency, providers' lived experiences contain more gray areas—things like moral uncertainties, emotional reactions to fetal remains, and experiences with anti-abortion violence, among others (Martin et al. 2017). Lisa Martin and her colleagues identify these narratives as "dangertalk," or what Ludlow (2008) calls the "things we cannot say." An example of "dangertalk" negatively affecting the abortion rights movement can be found here in this entry. When Dr. Martin Haskell described his procedure using nonemotional, medically accurate language for fetal parts and the abortion procedure itself, anti-abortion activists turned this against providers to create their term "partial-birth abortion" and its descriptors like "gruesome." More recently, however, legal scholars have argued that when feminist activists avoid "dangertalk," it only serves the anti-abortion movement by giving narrative and rhetorical power to anti-abortion activists. These scholars argue that "the uncomfortable truths about second-trimester abortion should be met head on and discussed openly by the broader abortion rights movement" in order to push abortion rights forward (Donley and Lens 2021, 2150). This shows that feminist movements around abortion rights are still working to (re)claim the anti-abortion cultural narrative that the PBABA helped solidify.

The Partial Birth Abortion Ban Act of 2003 is a significant piece of legislation in the history of abortion rights in the United States. An exemplar of the anti-abortion "guerrilla legislation" strategy, the PBABA established precedence for the anti-abortion laws that eventually contributed to the overturning of *Roe v. Wade* in 2022. It also firmly cemented ideas of "fetal personhood" into the public's consciousness and significantly contributed to the anti-abortion movement's linguistic rearticulation of abortion as a murderous medical procedure that does more harm (to both women and "unborn children") than good. In 2003, feminist movements concerning abortion were focusing on getting patients into clinics and resisting anti-abortion violence that plagued clinics across the country. As this entry demonstrates there were—and remain—feminist legal scholars, practicing attorneys, researchers, and others who work in tandem with grassroots organizers to help understand and resist anti-abortion legislation like the PBABA of 2003.

Cassidy D. Ellis

See Also: Abortion; Choice; *Dobbs v. Jackson Women's Health Organization* (2022); Reproductive Justice

Further Reading

Armitage, Hannah. 2010. "Political Language, Uses and Abuses: How the Term 'Partial Birth' Changed the Abortion Debate in the United States." *Australasian Journal of American Studies* 29, no. 1: 15–35.

Charo, R. Alta. 2007. "The Partial Death of Abortion Rights." *New England Journal of Medicine* 356, no. 21: 2125–8.

Coker, Calvin R. 2018. "Fetal Protection Policies." In *Women in the American Political System: An Encyclopedia of Women as Voters, Candidates, and Office Holders*, edited by Dianne G. Bystrom and Barbara Burrell, 155–7. ABC-CLIO.
Donley, Greer, and Jill Wieber Lens. 2021. "Second-Trimester Abortion Dangertalk." *Boston College Law Review* 62, no. 2145: 2146–208.
Ellis, Cassidy D. 2023. "Embracing Jane's Uncivil Tongue: Pro-Choice Failures and Post-Roe Futures." *Women's Studies in Communication* 46, no. 4: 375–81. https://doi.org/10.1080/07491409.2023.2264152.
Furgerson, Jessica L. 2023. "A Working Glossary of Key Terms in the Abortion Discourse." *Women & Language* 46, no. 1: 259–65. https://doi.org/10.34036/WL.2023.011.
Greene, Michael F. 2007. "The Intimidation of American Physicians—Banning Partial-Birth Abortion." *New England Journal of Medicine* 256, no. 21: 2128–9.
Jiménez, Jesus. 2022. "What Is a Trigger Law? And Which States Have Them?" *The New York Times*, May 4, 2022. https://www.nytimes.com/2022/05/04/us/abortion-trigger-laws.html.
Kushnir, Tamara F. 2004. "It's My Body, It's My Choice: The Partial-Birth Abortion Ban Act of 2003." *Loyola University Chicago Law Journal* 35, no. 4: 1117–88.
Ludlow, Jeannie. 2008. "The Things We Cannot Say: Witnessing the Trauma-tization of Abortion in the United States." *Women's Studies Quarterly* 36, no. 1/2: 28–41.
Martin, Lisa A., Jane A. Hassinger, Michelle Debbink, and Lisa H. Harris. 2017. "Dangertalk: Voices of Abortion Providers." *Social Science and Medicine* 184: 75–83. https://doi.org/10.1016/j.socscimed.2017.05.001.
Mason, Carol. 2000. "From Protest to Retribution: The Guerrilla Politics of Pro-life Violence." *New Political Science* 22 (1): 11–29. https://doi.org/10.1080/713687891.
McCullough, Laurence B., and Frank A. Chervenak. 2008. "A Critical Analysis of the Concept and Discourse of 'Unborn Child.'" *The American Journal of Bioethics* 8, no. 7: 35–9. https://doi.org/10.1080/15265160802248161.
President Bush. 2003. "President Bush Signs Partial Birth Abortion Ban Act of 2003." *The White House* (blog), November 5, 2003. https://georgewbush-whitehouse.archives.gov/news/releases/2003/11/20031105-1.html.
United States Congress. 2003. *Partial-Birth Abortion Ban Act of 2003*. Public Law 108–5, 117 Stat. 1201. November 5, 2003. https://www.congress.gov/bill/108th-congress/senate-bill/3/text.
Weitz, Tracy A., and Susan Yanow. 2008. "Implications of the Federal Abortion Ban for Women's Health in the United States." *Reproductive Health Matters* 16, no. 31: 99–107.

PATRIARCHY

At its most basic, patriarchy refers to a familial, governmental, or societal structure that is dominated by men. As this definition implies, patriarchy can exist on a variety of levels. One common patriarchal power structure is the perception that the man is the "head" of the family. On a broader scale, the notion of male authority is evident in the fact that to date, all US presidents have been men. Ultimately, patriarchy can be understood as "the organization of society in a way that grants power to men and systematically disadvantages women as women" (Garcia 2021, 13). In patriarchal societies, this power hierarchy is frequently portrayed as the natural order or the most efficient system for maintaining societal stability. While modern society has provided more opportunities for women to attain economic independence and political influence, patriarchy remains a powerful force in shaping contemporary power structures.

Patriarchy's need for a hierarchical family structure is largely tied to economic interests (Lerner 1986). From the earliest periods of human history, women have largely been treated as commodities who were "exchanged or bought in marriages for the benefit of their families" (Lerner 1986, 212–13). As commodities, women held value for their ability to carry on family lineages and contribute to labor on family farms. After the Industrial Revolution, which diminished the significance of farming, patriarchal power shifted to men assuming the role of providers or "breadwinners" for their families (Ruggles 2015, 1800). This is the origin of the "separate spheres" ideology, which argued that men and women were inherently suited to distinct forms of labor. In agricultural societies, all family members, including women and children, worked on family farms (Ruggles 2015, 1799).

As labor increasingly shifted beyond the confines of the home to offices and factories, the idea of "separate spheres" asserted that men were suited to these outside jobs while women should serve as homemakers and mothers. Women belonged in the domestic "sphere" while men belonged in the economic and political one (Davidson and Hatcher 2002). Notably, the separate spheres philosophy largely applied to middle-class families that could survive on a single income. While this "separate spheres" system was never absolute (Vickery 1993), the idea that men and women were inherently predisposed to fulfill distinct societal roles held (and can still hold) considerable influence. This belief was disrupted in the mid-twentieth century when many families found themselves needing two incomes to sustain their livelihoods, leading to married women joining the workforce. Prior to this shift, women who were employed often left their jobs upon marriage. Additionally, the growing availability of jobs for women resulted in an increasing number of women choosing not to marry (Ruggles 2015, 1800, 1804). This increased economic independence coincided with mass-scale feminist activism—known as the Women's Liberation Movement—during the 1960s and 1970s, empowering women to challenge the patriarchal structure of the family unit.

Patriarchal power extends beyond the family to larger social and political arenas. In societies where men are perceived as the leaders of their respective households, they are often regarded as representing the interests of their families within the broader community as both voters and officeholders. Because male heads of household were viewed as the thinking body and voice for their entire family, nonmale family members were seen as simply extensions of their opinions. For example, one common argument against granting women the right to vote was that, because men would dictate the political beliefs for the entire household, giving women the right to vote would just grant additional voting power to fathers and husbands (Lange 2015). Additionally, the ideals and values of patriarchy continue to underpin many institutional powers in the United States. For example, Dubber (2005) has argued that the logics that govern police power are rooted in the same "age-old power of the householder over his household" that underpins all patriarchal power. In this way, patriarchal hierarchies serve as the foundation for much of our modern political and cultural institutions, even as those institutions increasingly, if still disproportionately, allow women to hold positions of power.

Contemporary Examples of Patriarchy

To understand patriarchy's enduring legacy, it is useful to examine the backlashes to feminist movements and increased gender equality. For example, in recent years, an online community of self-described "incels" has emerged around the globe. The term "incel" is short for "involuntary celibate." According to the Anti-Defamation League (2020), incels are "heterosexual men who blame women and society for their lack of romantic success." Incels believe that women's ability to decline relationships or sexual encounters with them indicates that women have too much freedom in selecting romantic partners. Many of their proposed solutions to this problem "involve some form of coercion, rape, or a complete return to enforced monogamy under strict patriarchal rule" (Sparks, Zidenberg, and Olver 2022). As one incel posted in an online forum in 2020, "So why not just help us get laid? Why not have government sponsored girlfriend programs or government sponsored hookers? Seems to be the easiest thing to do" (qtd. in DiBranco 2020).

Incels perceive women's growing capacity to opt out of traditional heterosexual relationships and marriages as a direct denial of something they are entitled to. The denial of this perceived entitlement has driven certain incels to violence, as evidenced by the 2018 mass shooting in Toronto and the 2021 shooting in Oxford, Michigan. As one incel proclaimed, "I will punish all females for the crime of depriving me of sex" (qtd. in Vink et al. 2023).

Patriarchy and Other Power Hierarchies

While patriarchal power in the United States is explicitly about male power, it often implicitly assumes that those men in power are both white and heterosexual. Much as white supremacy sets up a racial hierarchy in which the superiority of whiteness is treated as the natural order of things, patriarchy reinforces similar hierarchies based on gender, race, and class. US imperialism and various wars were justified using the argument that white men had a fatherly responsibility to "protect" nonwhite populations from their perceived political incompetence (Brantlinger 2007). Additionally, patriarchy impacts women of color differently from white women. As Walby (1990) has pointed out, white feminists tend to see the family as "a major, if not the major, site of women's oppression by men," while Black feminist scholars have argued that this is not case for Black women (14). Therefore, it is important to acknowledge that many of the aspects of patriarchy outlined here are not necessarily generalizable across the experiences of all women.

Crucially, Walby (1990) argues that patriarchy is a "system of social structures and practices" used to dominate women (20). Her use of "social structures" is important because, as she argues, it points to the ways that patriarchy is not the result of biological traits that make male domination universal. As Walby (1990) states, not "every individual man is in the dominant position and [not] every woman in a subordinate one" (20). Rather, patriarchy is an overarching system that is encouraged by the norms and structures of society even if it can be resisted at an individual level. That resistance, however, is difficult to achieve. Feminist scholar Manon Garcia argues that women continue to submit to patriarchal systems because "femininity is presented as a desirable norm, submission is depicted as a source of pleasure and power, and the dangers of women's freedom are constantly emphasized" (2021, 132, 204). Postfeminist and popular feminist messages in media and popular culture promote ideas of feminist choice and empowerment that still largely maintain preexisting patriarchal power structures. The omnipresence and perceived normality of these structures means that "submission appears as a destiny to which it is easier to consent than to resist" (Garcia 2021, 204). In this way, patriarchal systems can continue to perpetuate themselves even when their underlying tenets fall out of favor.

Patriarchy remains a powerful force in contemporary society, although it has become more difficult to identify. Earlier forms of patriarchy made male power explicit. For example, for much of US history, men were the only ones who could vote and own property. When a man and a woman married, everything she owned became her husband's property. Before 1970, marital rape was legal in every state, and it was not until 1993 that it became illegal nationwide (Bierschbach 2019). This meant that, prior to the 1970s, no married woman had the right to refuse sexual advances from her husband. Today, these explicit forms of patriarchal power no longer exist. Yet, patriarchy has not gone away completely. One of the best illustrations of this is the continued inability to enshrine gender equality in the US Constitution. While the Equal Rights Amendment was passed in 1972, it failed to garner ratification by the required thirty-eight states within the specified time frame to become official (Cohen and Codrington 2020). Even today, equal legal rights for all Americans regardless of their gender are not guaranteed.

Courtlyn Pippert

See Also: Backlash; Colonialism; Popular Feminism; Postfeminism; White Supremacy

Further Reading

Anti-Defamation League, The. 2020. "Incels (Involuntary Celibates)." July 29, 2020. Accessed March 27, 2024. https://www.adl.org/resources/backgrounder/incels-involuntary-celibates.

Bierschbach, Briana. 2019. "This Woman Fought To End Minnesota's 'Marital Rape' Exception, and Won." *NPR*, May 4, 2019. https://www.npr.org/2019/05/04/719635969/this-woman-fought-to-end-minnesotas-marital-rape-exception-and-won.

Brantlinger, Patrick. 2007. "Kipling's 'The White Man's Burden' and Its Afterlives." *English Literature in Transition, 1880–1920* 50, no. 2: 172–91. https://doi.org/10.1353/elt.2007.0017.

Cohen, Alex, and Wildred U. Codrington III. 2020. "The Equal Rights Amendment Explained." *Brenna Center for Justice*, January 23, 2020. Accessed March 27, 2024. https://www.brennancenter.org/our-work/research-reports/equal-rights-amendment-explained.

Davidson, Cathy N., and Jessamyn Hatcher, eds. 2002. *No More Separate Spheres!: A Next Wave American Studies Reader*. Durham, NC: Duke University Press.

DiBranco, Alex (@alexdibranco). 2020. "Today's Quote From an Incel Forum: 'So Why Not Just Help Us Get Laid? Why Not Have Government Sponsored Girlfriend Programs or Government Sponsored Hookers? Seems to be the Easiest Thing to Do.' BECAUSE WOMEN ARE NOT OBJECTS TO BE DOLED OUT AS SEX OBJECTS BY THE GOVERNMENT." *Tweet*, May 9, 2020. https://twitter.com/alexdibranco/status/1259197900460109827.

Dubber, Markus Dirk. 2005. *The Police Power: Patriarchy and the Foundations of American Government*. New York: Columbia University Press.

Garcia, Manon. 2021. *We Are Not Born Submissive: How Patriarchy Shapes Women's Lives*. Princeton, NJ: Princeton University Press.

Lange, Allison. 2015. "National Association Opposed to Woman Suffrage." *National Women's History Museum* (blog). Accessed March 27, 2024. https://www.crusadeforthevote.org/naows-opposition.

Lerner, Gerda. 1986. *The Creation of Patriarchy*. Oxford: Oxford University Press.

Ruggles, Steven. 2015. "Patriarchy, Power, and Pay: The Transformation of American Families, 1800–2015." *Demography* 52, no. 6: 1797–823. https://doi.org/10.1007/s13524-015-0440-z.

Sparks, Brandon, Alexandra M. Zidenberg, and Mark E. Olver. 2022. "Involuntary Celibacy: A Review of Incel Ideology and Experiences with Dating, Rejection, and Associated Mental Health and Emotional Sequelae." *Current Psychiatry Reports* 24, no. 12: 731–40. https://doi.org/10.1007/s11920-022-01382-9.

Vickery, Amanda. 1993. "Golden Age to Separate Spheres? A Review of the Categories and Chronology of English Women's History." *The Historical Journal* 36, no. 2: 383–414. https://www.jstor.org/stable/2639654.

Vink, Dominique, Tahir Abbas, Yannick Veilleux-Lepage, and Richard McNeil-Willson. 2023. "'Because They Are Women in a Man's World': A Critical Discourse Analysis of Incel Violent Extremists and the Stories They Tell." *Terrorism and Political Violence* 36, no. 6 (March): 723–39. https://doi.org/10.1080/09546553.2023.2189970.

Walby, Sylvia. 1991. *Theorizing Patriarchy*. Hoboken, NJ: Wiley-Blackwell.

THE PERSONAL IS POLITICAL

The phrase "the personal is political" is a feminist mantra associated with Carol Hanisch. Hanisch was a civil rights activist and a community organizer for the Southern Conference Educational Fund (SCEF). Her colleague at SCEF, Dottie Zelner, issued a "scathing" statement describing women's "consciousness-raising" groups as "therapy," not politics. Zelner's vitriolic dismissal of women's liberation groups was fairly standard. As Maureen Freely (2010, 211) writes, activists in "the civil rights movement, the anti-war movement, and the New Left" typically "did not view the fledgling women's liberation movement as truly political." In response, Hanisch wrote a memo titled "Some Thoughts in Response to Dottie's Thoughts on a Women's Liberation Movement"; a year later, a gently revised version of the memo was published under the title, "The Personal Is Political," in *Notes from the Second Year: Women's Liberation, Major Writings of the Radical Feminists*. Hanisch (2006) attributes the now-famous title, "The Personal Is Political," to the book's editors, Shulamith Firestone and Anne Koedt (1970).

During the 1960s and 1970s, the feminist movement in America typically referred to itself as the Women's Liberation Movement—or Women's Lib—and they often met in community groups known as "consciousness-raising groups." These groups were largely nonhierarchical and would share their struggles, educating each other. They took their name "consciousness-raising" groups from the shared goal to raise one another's consciousness—making each other aware of sexism and helping each other devise liberating solutions. Hanisch was a member of the New York Radical Women, a consciousness-raising group that met in the SCEF's New York office, where Hanisch worked. As Hanisch describes, her colleagues at the SCEF were fairly typical in their dismissive attitude toward women's liberation and consciousness raising. She writes, "They belittled us no end for trying to bring our so-called 'personal problems' into the public arena—especially 'all those body issues' like sex, appearance, and abortion. Our demands that men share the housework and childcare were likewise deemed a personal problem between a woman and her individual man" (Hanisch 2006).

In her now-famously titled essay, Hanisch (1970, 76–8) explains that she is writing because Women's Liberation groups are often described as personal therapy, implying that women are "sick" and "messed up." Here, she counters that women are "messed over, not messed up!" Describing personal therapy as "adjusting to your bad personal" situation, she counters, writing that "we need to change the objective conditions, not adjust to them." Continuing, Hanisch writes that by analyzing their daily experiences, the women in consciousness-raising groups engage in "a form of political action." Together, they discover that "personal problems are political problems." Alone, each woman thought they were the only one dealing with a particular problem, but together they realized that the problem is communal—that many if not most women are facing the same problem.

By political, Hanisch meant more than the government and voting—she meant "having to do with power relationships" (2006). In her essay, Hanisch (1970) explains how consciousness-raising groups were developing theory to guide their activism: together, women were working out how power structured their lives and how to best respond. Rather cheekily, Hanisch called this "political therapy."

In many ways, the problems Hanisch was writing about are still problems for women—and they are still political. For instance, if a mother cannot find affordable, quality childcare, she is much less likely to work outside the home, to attend protests, and even to go vote. Similarly, if a woman is routinely denigrated, passed over, belittled, and sexually harassed in the workplace, she is much less likely to rise in the ranks, become a supervisor, or earn a higher salary. The personal is political.

Ultimately then, the title of Hanisch's essay became something of a rallying cry for feminists in the United States. More than that, it serves as a guide for theory building and for activism. In order to understand women's lives and the oppressions women face, feminist theories must understand how power structures our "personal" experiences, and in order to achieve feminist change—change that makes things more equitable—feminist activism has to support women's "personal" lives.

Sarah Kornfield

See Also: Consciousness Raising; Liberal Feminism; Radical Feminism

Further Reading

Firestone, Shulamith, and Anne Koedt, eds. 1970. *Notes from the Second Year: Women's Liberation, Major Writings of the Radical Feminists*. New York: Radical Feminism.

Freely, Maureen. 2010. "When the Personal Became Political: A Reappraisal of the Women's Liberation Movement's Radical Idea." In *Sixties Radicalism and Social Movement Activism: Retreat or Resurgence?* edited by Bryn Jones and Mike O'Donnell, 211–23. London: Anthem Press.

Hanisch, Carol. 1970. "The Personal is Political." In *Notes from the Second Year: Women's Liberation, Major Writings of the Radical Feminists*, edited by Shulamith Firestone and Anne Koedt, 76–8. New York: Radical Feminism.

Hanisch, Carol. 2006. "Introduction." *Index of Carol Hanisch Writings*. Accessed April 1, 2024. http://www.carolhanisch.org/CHwritings/PersonalIsPol.pdf.

PHALLOCENTRISM

Phallocentrism is a way of thinking, talking, and writing that privileges masculine domination. The word "phallus" refers to the symbolism of the penis-as-domination. For instance, if someone scrawled a drawing of an erect penis on the outside of a school locker, it would be a "phallus": it would be a symbolic penis and its presence in public would assert dominance—as if it (and therefore men) has the right to be there, to assert itself in public, and thus the right to control or dominate public space.

In this way, phallocentrism refers to the type of discourse (thinking, talking, and writing) that reinforces patriarchy, that privileges masculinity, and that attempts to control others (e.g., the interlocuter, the reader, or the audience) through "narrative linearity" and the "tendency toward stasis and systematization through opposition and hierarchy" (Worsham 1991, 83; Stroud 2010, 97). For example, imagine you are talking with a peer about high school fashion trends and they proclaim that public schools should have dress codes and then launch into an argument attempting to persuade you toward this idea. They offer three main claims and back each one up with evidence or reasoning. They move through their claims, one right after another, talking over you when you try to get a word in. They talk about clothing as if it could easily be classified as right or wrong according to a dress code, talking about measuring the length of shorts and skirts and the width of shoulder straps, and so on. Finally, they keep contrasting girls and boys, public and private, good and bad, as they talk about school dress codes. This would be an example of phallocentric discourse: they marshaled a linear argument, they saw clothing and bodies as classifiable (or able to be systematized), and they used opposition (contrasts) and hierarchy to defend and explain their argument. Along the way, they worked to control your thinking, your ability to interact with their argument, and ultimately worked to control the way reality (bodies, clothing, school policies) is understood.

Simply—if rather crudely—stated, just as men's lust-based decisions are often described as "thinking with their dicks," phallocentrism is a fancy word that attempts to explain a masculine practice that might be colloquially described as "writing with their dicks." Anyone, however, can be phallocentric. Anyone can think, talk, or write linearly and can insist on linearity as the best or only way to think and communicate correctly. Likewise, anyone can try to classify reality in a systematized framework—essentially compartmentalizing knowledge. Anyone can rely on binary oppositions (up-down, right-wrong, etc.) in their thinking and communication. Which is to say, although the phallus is the symbol of penis-as-domination, anyone can use phallocentric discourse—anyone can think, talk, and write in ways that privilege masculine ways of knowing and being in the world.

Phallocentrism and Western Philosophy

In her witty essay "The Laugh of the Medusa," French feminist Hélène Cixous (1976) describes Western philosophy (such as the work of Descartes, Nietzsche, and Freud) as phallocentric. She imagines Western philosophy as both a statue of a "man-with-rock, standing erect" and as a "self-admiring, self-stimulating, self-congratulatory" way of thinking, talking, and especially writing (1976, 879, 884). Indeed, in many ways, Cixous points out that the history of Western rhetoric and philosophy is phallus worship—meaning that it is a history of people (mostly men) who are admiring, stimulating, and congratulating themselves and their understandings of the world in ways that exclude and dominate everyone else—where everyone else is mostly women and other minoritized people. Cixous is not alone in this critique of Western philosophy. Indeed, philosophers such as Derrida derided much of Western philosophy as phallocentric. Although, ironically, Derrida created his own term for phallocentric discourse, which he called *phallogocentric* discourse, an adjective which is perhaps best, if bluntly, described as "like an arrogant man-mind who is obsessed his own existence and the feeling of empowerment that he derives form hearing himself talk" (Lewis 2016, 74).

If this sounds a little harsh, consider the experience of trying to learn Western philosophical theories. For instance, for someone to understand Nietzsche's work, they need a strong grasp on the ideas of the early Greek rhetoricians known as the Sophists as well as the philosophies of Plato, Aristotle, and Descartes. Even then, Nietzsche's ideas are rather hard to understand—like looking at a library where all the books are clearly organized but one can't make out the system of organization or as if hearing a language where one can pick out the occasional vocabulary term but can't quite grasp the grammatical structure. Clearly, with a good teacher one could learn the library's system of organization or the language's grammar—and so too one can learn to see the world through Nietzsche's way of understanding the world and even recognize a sort of beauty and cleverness in Nietzsche's framework.

What Cixous, however, is trying to point out is that Western philosophical theories, like Freud's and Nietzsche's, are phallocentric. They fawn around prior philosophical works in Western culture in a "self-admiring, self-stimulating," and "self-congratulatory" way. They use their own abstract systems to classify the world, often imposing a rigid moral order onto reality. And they so often are expressed in linear argumentation that has a sort of dogmatic or insistent quality. Or to put it another way, they attempt to dominate, imposing their way of thinking and their way of understanding the world on others. In a word, then, Western philosophical discourse is phallocentric.

Women Write Yourself! Cixous Responds to Phallocentrism

In response, Cixous invites women and other minoritized people to write themselves through the body rather than adopting phallocentrism's way of thinking and writing. Poignantly, Cixous encouraged women, writing, "Woman must write her self: must write about women and bring women to writing, from which they have been driven away as violently as from their bodies—for the same reasons, by the same law, with the same fatal goal." Cixous continues, encouraging her writers to write by saying, "Writing is for you, you are for you; your body is yours, take it" (1976, 875–6).

Cixous's encouragement to write out of feminine embodiment is complex, but one of the clearest ways I understand her challenge is when I think of the body knowledge born from nursing my children. The formal record of my children as infants is all about their height and weight and when they started sleeping through the night. It is about their bodies but it has no body knowledge of them. It is clinical and abstract. It is an imposed order upon a lived experience. In contrast to this sterile, abstract rendering of their earliest months, I have a feminine body knowledge born out of reality and experience. Which is to say, I alone know how their bodies felt while they nursed in my arms. This is an embodied way of knowing and a type of knowledge that phallocentrism can never know. Unless I write myself as Cixous asks me to—unless I write and speak from my feminine body—the truths I experienced and the reality of my children's infancy can never be known.

Ultimately, then, Cixous and feminists more broadly encourage women and other minoritized people to reject phallocentric thinking, talking, and writing and instead to embrace what Cixous called *l'écriture feminine* (feminine writing) as a way of loving and freeing our bodies and thus as a way of knowing and a way of writing.

Sarah Kornfield

See Also: Hegemonic Masculinity; Mind/Body Split; Patriarchy

Further Reading

Cixous, Hélène. 1976. "The Laugh of the Medusa." Translated by Keith Cohen and Paula Cohen. *Signs* 1, no. 4: 875–93.

Lewis, Holly. (2016). *The Politics of Everybody: Feminism, Queer Theory, and Marxism at the Intersection.* London: Zed Books.

Stroud, Mary. 2010. "Eco-Composition Pedagogy: The Environmental Imperative for *L'écriture Féminine*." In *Managing Environmental Justice*, edited by Dennis Pavlich, 93–107. Brill. https://doi.org/10.1163/9789042029385_007.

Worsham, Lynn. 1991. "Writing Against Writing: The Predicament of *Ecriture Féminine* in Composition Studies." In *Contending with Words: Composition and Rhetoric in a Postmodern Age*, edited by Patricia Harkin and John Schlib. New York: Modern Language Association.

PINK TAX

The Pink Tax is a phenomenon where products cost more for women than they do for men. It is called the Pink Tax because many of these products are marketed with pink designs so that consumers know they are intended for women. If you were to go to the store today and buy a razor, it is very likely that a man would pay less for the same razor than a woman would. As one example, an 8-pack of Gillette Men's Disposable Razors would cost $11.00 and a 2-pack of Gillette Women's Disposable Razors disposable (branded Venus) costs $10.00. Essentially, men are paying $1.38 per razor, and women are paying $5.00 (Gillespie 2023). This discrepancy is also present in bigger purchases, like cars. According to feminist scholar Janine Rogan, research has shown that white women were often quoted $200.00 more than their white male counterparts, and Black women were quoted $400.00 more (2023, 3). The Pink Tax can also refer to the tax menstruators pay on products like tampons and pads—a cost most men do not have to consider. Essentially, the Pink Tax describes the fundamental gender discrimination that is present when buying many goods and services.

Though it may seem small, these little price differentials can add up. For example, the California Senate Committee on Judiciary and the Senate Select Committee on Women, Work & Families stated in 2020 that Californian women pay an average of about $2,381 more for the same types of goods and services than men do per year. Over the course of sixty years, the Pink Tax can cost a woman up to $82,000 (Rogan 2023, 3). These little discrepancies add up to a whole lot of money over a lifetime.

Beyond the things we buy on a day-to-day basis, the Pink Tax can also refer to the broader financial disparities between genders in the United States. Women's purchasing power is even further restricted when we consider the fact women are often paid less than men, limiting their ability to fully participate in the economy. As of 2024, white women make approximately 84 cents per dollar of their white male counterparts, and women of color are even more impacted by this difference—Latina women are paid just 55 percent of what their white male counterparts are (Haan 2024). Again, these differences add up. According to the National Women's Law Center, a twenty-year-old woman in a full-time, year-round position stands to lose $407,760 over a forty-year career compared to a similarly employed man (Haan 2024). The Pink Tax reflects a system that prioritizes men's needs over women's and often limits women's ability to be financially stable and free. It is a serious problem that exists on every shelf in every grocery store in the United States.

Activism against the Pink Tax

Because the Pink Tax is developed socially and not created by the government, it has been difficult to stop or change. However, some states, like California, have enacted a retail law that prohibits gender-based price discrimination (Washington 2024). Similarly, New York and Ohio have eliminated the Pink Tax on certain goods and services. In some cases—such as with menstrual products—states have begun to eliminate taxes on certain items. Virginia, Colorado, Iowa, Nebraska, and Texas have eliminated sales tax on menstrual products, marking a step toward financial equality (Taylor 2024). The Pink Tax Repeal Act has been introduced to Congress a number of times but has failed to pass the House of Representatives and the Senate. This leaves it up to individual consumers and activists to demand more of the brands we buy from and up to the government to continue to regulate against this discrimination.

Hannah Taylor

See Also: Capitalism; Equal Pay; Gender; Menstruation; Menstruation Activism

Further Reading

Gillespie, Lane. 2023. "The Pink Tax: Latest Updates and Statistics." *Bankrate,* February 27, 2023. Accessed August 24, 2024. https://www.bankrate.com/personal-finance/pink-tax-how-women-pay-more/#what-is.

Haan, Katherine. 2024. "Gender Pay Gap Statistics in 2024." *Forbes Advisor*, March1, 2024. https://www.forbes.com/advisor/business/gender-pay-gap-statistics/#:~:text=A%2020%2Dyear%2Dold%20woman%20starting%20full%2Dtime%20work,close%20the%20lifetime%20wage%20gap.

Rogan, Janine. 2023. *The Pink Tax: Dismantling a Financial System Designed to Keep Women Broke.* Page Two Press.

Senate Committee on Judiciary and The Senate Select Committee on Women, Work and Families. 2020. *The "Pink Tax": How Gender-Based Pricing and Discrimination Undermines Women's Economic Opportunity and What to Do About It.* February 18, 2020. https://www.google.com/url?sa=t&source=web&rct=j&opi=89978449&url=https://sjud.senate.ca.gov/sites/sjud.senate.ca.gov/files/2.18.2020_sjud_gender_pricing_info_hearing_background_paper.pdf&ved=2ahUKEwiY_ImB7JSIAxU_hIkEHRYPH4oQFnoECBMQAQ&usg=AOvVaw10PRor4iP2IhFbgSuPfj8G.

Taylor, Kelley. 2024. "Pink Tax: What Does Price Discrimination Cost Women?" *Kiplinger*, February 13, 2024. https://www.kiplinger.com/taxes/pink-tax-womens-products-price-discrimination.

Washington, Katelyn. 2024. "California State Tax 2024: Overview." *Kiplinger*, May 3, 2024. Accessed August 24, 2024. https://www.kiplinger.com/state-by-state-guide-taxes/california.

POPULAR FEMINISM

At its most basic, popular feminism is the regular circulation of feminist messages via popular media. This increased visibility can allow feminist ideas to spread to a broad audience. However, it can also undermine the larger political goals of the feminism movement by reducing feminism to a small set of performative, consumerist practices. That is, popular feminism may equate wearing a T-shirt with a feminist message or sharing a feminist post on social media with taking meaningful political action. In the process, the underlying cultural and political systems that enable gender inequality largely remain unchanged and unprotested.

Since the early 2010s, popular feminism has increasingly become a part of popular culture. Celebrities such as John Legend, Lizzo, Emma Watson, Meghan Markle, and Lin Manuel-Miranda have publicly declared themselves feminists. Advertising campaigns like Dove's "Real Beauty" and Always's "LikeAGirl" offer seemingly feminist takes on traditional beauty products. In the latter, Always reclaims the phrase "like a girl," typically used to belittle actions as weak or inferior (e.g., "run like a girl," "hit like a girl," and "cry like a girl"), by inviting real girls to demonstrate what "doing it like a girl" truly means. This marketing campaign challenges the negative stereotypes typically associated with the phrase.

Similarly, social media hashtags like "#girlboss," "#everydaysexism," and "#girlpower" allow users to express both empowerment and their struggles with gender inequality. Girlboss culture in particular spreads the idea that women can attain empowerment by achieving success within a capitalist system, such as running businesses and holding leadership positions. Notably, popular feminism is not limited to the United States, although it can take different forms in different cultures around the world. Take, for example, the increasing popularity of "strong female characters" in Indian cinema who "glare at all men except their (usually misogynistic) love interest, have their hair tied up or cut short, wear a shirt tucked into their pants and stand around with one hand always on their waist" (Verma 2021).

When referring to "popular" feminism, the term "popular" can take on three distinct meanings: (1) widely distributed or mainstream, (2) well-liked, and (3) a site of struggle. This last understanding of popular is the least straightforward. Stemming from cultural studies scholar Stuart Hall's understanding of popular culture as "a space where competing demands for power battle it out" (see Banet-Weiser and Portwood-Stacer 2017, 884), this definition of popular takes seriously the idea that people get much of their understandings about the world from what they see in popular media. Therefore, the competing popular depictions of feminism that circulate throughout popular culture have the power to shape or reshape what feminism means for those who encounter them.

While popular feminism is sometimes seen as a resurgence of feminism after the postfeminist backlash of the 1990s and 2000s, Sarah Banet-Weiser (2018, 19) argues that popular feminism emerged from within the logic of postfeminism. While popular feminism appears to address some of the issues downplayed or dismissed by postfeminism—namely, that gender inequality still exists as a problem in contemporary society—it continues to offer the same solutions as postfeminism: consumerism and individual empowerment. As Banet-Weiser (2018, 21) puts it, while "a feminist standpoint . . . is a political commitment, a struggle over power. . . . There is no postfeminist or popular feminist standpoint; on the contrary, it is more a kind of attitude." And this attitude centers consumption and visibility as the most important components of popular feminism.

Crucially, because popular feminism is predominantly promoted by corporations and media institutions and platforms, much of popular feminism promotes consumption as a key aspect of feminist action. The consumerist nature of popular feminism replaces political and social action with the purchasing of "feminist" products. Magazines like *Cosmopolitan* and websites like Buzzfeed publish articles about feminist-branded merchandise. You can go on a shopping site like Etsy and buy a button that proclaims, "Smash the Patriarchy!" to place on your backpack. This is not a meaningless act. But taken alone, it does not do much to further a feminist cause. As Banet-Weiser (2018, 4) puts it, the problem with the consumerist nature of popular feminism is that "it often stops there, as if *seeing* or purchasing feminism is the same thing as changing patriarchal structures."

Scholars such as Angela McRobbie (2009), Rosalind Gill (2011), Catherine Rottenberg (2014), and Sarah Banet-Weiser (2018) have all pointed to the ways that popular feminism emphasizes visibility over structural changes. That is, popular feminism pushes the idea that simply having women in more visible positions of power—as CEOs, politicians, and celebrity role models—will contribute to gender equality. While representation is important, it does not fix the larger patriarchal and white supremacist power structures that underly much of America's corporate, political, and media landscape. Instead, it allows those structures to go uncritiqued (Banet-Weiser 2018, 4).

Another major critique of popular feminism is the way it limits the visibility of other forms of feminism, namely those that center the voices of marginalized groups traditionally excluded from mainstream feminism, including feminists of color and LGBTQIA+ feminists. While a variety of forms of popular feminism exist, including subsegments dedicated to feminists of color and queer feminists (Banet-Weiser and Portwood-Stacer 2017), mainstream popular feminism is predominantly a white, heterosexual, middle-class form of feminism. For instance, Banet-Weiser (2018) and Anita Harris (2004) contend that mainstream popular feminism often juxtaposes "Can-Do girls" and "At-Risk girls." The typically white, middle-class "Can-Do girls" are depicted as ambitious, confident, and business-oriented, whereas the typically nonwhite, working-class "At-Risk girls" are portrayed as more prone to lack ambition, engage in substance abuse or early pregnancy, and remain impoverished. In this way, "Visibility thus yields different gazes, or forms of surveillance, based on race and class" (Banet-Weiser 2018, 28). Thus, the significant focus on representation can hinder equality when it reinforces racial and class-based stereotypes, perpetuating a version of popular feminism that is primarily centered around whiteness, heterosexuality, and middle-class status.

Ultimately, popular feminism is a complicated phenomenon; its pros and cons must be taken into consideration. While increased visibility and the general acceptance of feminism in mainstream culture is important for the fight against gender inequality, popular feminism should not be seen as the solution. Rather, we need to be aware of the ways that popular feminism can obscure the need for larger structural changes with messages about representation and consumption.

Courtlyn Pippert

See Also: Capitalism; Girl Power; Postfeminism; White Supremacy

Further Reading

Austin, Ainsley G. 2021. "Contemporary Feminism as Portrayed in Popular Media." *Summer Research* 413: 1–35.

Banet-Weiser, Sarah. 2018. *Empowered: Popular Feminism and Popular Misogyny*. Durham, NC: Duke University Press.

Banet-Weiser, Sarah, and Laura Portwood-Stacer. 2017. "The Traffic in Feminism: An Introduction to the Commentary and Criticism on Popular Feminism." *Feminist Media Studies* 17, no. 5: 884–8.

Bigman, Fran. 2019. "What's Wrong with Popular Feminism?" *Los Angeles Review of Books* (blog), April 19, 2019. https://lareviewofbooks.org/article/whats-wrong-with-popular-feminism/.

Conway, Janet M. and Nathalie Lebon. 2021. "Popular Feminism(s) Reconsidered: Popular, Racialized, and Decolonial Subjectivities in Contention." *Latin American Perspectives* 48, no. 4: 3–24.

Evans, Elizabeth and Prudence Bussey-Chamberlain. 2021. "The Problems with Feminist Nostalgia: Intersectionality and White Popular Feminism." *European Journal of Women's Studies* 28, no. 3: 353–68.

Flood, Michelle Laura. 2021. "Popular Feminism – Should Feminism Ever Be Chic and Trendy?" *Tell Magazine,* October 7, 2021. https://gwsstellmagazine.sites.uiowa.edu/news/2021/10/popular-feminism-should-feminism-ever-be-chic-and-trendy.

Gill, Rosalind. 2011. "Sexism Reloaded, or, It's Time to Get Angry Again!" *Feminist Media Studies* 11, no. 1: 61–71.

Harris, Anita. 2004. *Future Girl: Young Women in the Twenty-First Century*. New York: Routledge.

Kokerov, Maya. 2022. "What is 'Popular Feminism' and How Can We Escape It?" My Goddess Complex (blog), January 11, 2022. https://mygoddesscomplex.com/2022/01/11/what-is-popular-feminism-and-how-can-we-escape-it/.

Lauri, Johanna, and Marcus Lauri. 2023. "Selling Feminist Stories: Popular Feminism, Authenticity and Happiness." *European Journal of Cultural Studies* (April): https://doi.org/10.1177/13675494221137371.

McRobbie, Angela. 2004. "Post-feminism and Popular Culture." *Feminist Media Studies* 4, no. 3: 255–64.

McRobbie, Angela. 2009. *The Aftermath of Feminism: Gender, Culture and Social Change*. London: SAGE.

Rottenberg, Catherine. 2014. "The Rise of Neoliberal Feminism." *Cultural Studies* 28, no. 3: 418-437.

Verma, Jyni. 2021. "What Is Pop Feminism?: Unpacking The Layers of 'Girl Power' Feminism." *Feminism India*, December 10, 2021. https://feminisminindia.com/2021/12/10/what-is-pop-feminism-unpacking-the-layers-of-girl-power-feminism/.

Watson, Katarina. 2020. "Feminism's Popularity Reaches All Time Highs, Study Shows." *Ms. Magazine*, August 10, 2020. https://msmagazine.com/2020/08/10/feminism-popularity-reaches-all-time-highs-study-shows/.

POST-RACISM

"Post-racism" is a term for a collection of ideas that argue racism no longer has a significant impact on society. For some people, the successes of the Civil Rights Movement in the United States signaled that the fight against racism had been won, allowing many white people in particular to imagine that people of all races were now on an even playing field. In this narrative, racism is a thing of the past—society has progressed to an era of "post-racism" in which everyone is supposedly judged by "the content of their character" and a person's race has little determination on their lives (King 1963). Two of the primary discourses that express post-racism include *colorblind ideology* and the *post-racial myth*. Feminist scholars have long critiqued post-racism; far from being a thing of the past, racism is a systemic and persistent feature of society.

It is not difficult to see that racism continues to this day. Neighborhoods and schools remain highly segregated, the Black and white wealth gap is increasing, and Black and brown bodies are disproportionately imprisoned. Post-racism, then, should be understood as a fantasy. Claims of post-racism are alluring to many people, making these claims powerful, but they do not match our racial reality. The fantasies of post-racism appeal to many people because they place the harsh violence and outcomes of racism in the past, focus on progress rather than present problems, and because—with racism supposedly removed from the picture—unearned privileges can be attributed to merit. For many white people, acknowledging that racism persists would require admitting that their personal success and status was at some level achieved through a racist advantage. Instead, many would rather imagine a post-racist society, because a society that has moved past racism is good and one's privileged place need not be questioned. Post-racism is a fantasy that ignores the realities of racism, protects white privilege, and maintains the status quo.

Colorblind Ideology

One of the first and most successful post-racism discourses was colorblind ideology. In the 1960s, the Civil Rights Movement helped pass the Civil Rights Act and the Voting Rights Act. Some people interpreted these laws as the movement's only goals, ignoring civil rights leaders' calls for more systemic change. In the late 1960s and 1970s, this new interpretation of the Civil Rights Movement became widespread, claiming that Dr. Martin Luther King's "Dream" was only for formal equality before the law (Crenshaw 1988). In the second half of the twentieth century, colorblindness became the guiding principle of racial reform for both individuals and institutions.

For individuals, colorblindness is best summed up by the phrase, "I don't see color." Eduardo Bonilla-Silva's (2018) landmark book *Racism Without Racists* argues that colorblind ideology allows white individuals to express racist ideas while claiming they are not talking about race at all. Advocates for colorblindness claim that the only way to be fair is to ignore race completely. But this supposed fairness ignores the long-accumulating effects of "past and contemporary discrimination on the social, economic, and educational status of minorities" and allows individuals to hide racial prejudice behind phrases like "Some of my best friends are Black" or "I'm not racist, but" (Bonilla-Silva 2018, 59).

One strategy of colorblind racism is to move from talking about race to culture. Rather than talk about Black or Latinx inferiority, white people talk about other racial groups' cultures as inferior. In interviews, Bonilla-Silva notes how white participants would say things like "Mexicans do not put enough emphasis on education" or "Blacks have too many babies" to explain why these groups had higher rates of poverty (2018, 56). Colorblind ideology puts the blame for systemic racism on "cultural deficiencies," and culture becomes a way to talk about race without talking about race. Broadly, colorblind ideology asserts that talking about race is bad, and that those who do are the ones who are actually being racist. This assertion severely limits the ability of anti-racists to persuade others to address racial inequalities. Colorblind beliefs often leave white people baffled and angry when frank conversations of racism take place.

For institutions, colorblindness became a way of justifying exclusionary policies and racist outcomes without talking about race. Legal institutions, businesses, government agencies, and universities embraced the colorblind idea of "equal opportunity" as a remedy to the openly racist laws and policies of the Jim Crow era. In colorblind ideology, if everyone theoretically has the *chance* to succeed, society cannot be considered racist. The outcomes do not matter, as long as the opportunity is given to all. Kimberlé Crenshaw, preeminent thinker of both feminist and critical race theories, critiques colorblind ideology's reliance on "equal opportunity," saying, "Society has embraced the rhetoric of equal opportunity without fulfilling its promise; creating a break with the past has formed the basis for the neoconservative claim that present inequities cannot be the result of discriminatory practices because this society no longer discriminates against Blacks" (1988, 1347). Crenshaw points out that equal opportunity only makes sense if we ignore how historical racism has shaped the present. How can opportunities be equal if people of different races start from different places in a racist hierarchy?

For example, colorblindness greatly influenced fights over policies like affirmative action, including the civil rights policy of considering race in college admissions. In the 1970s, a vehement white backlash to these policies took place. Equipped with colorblind ideology, many white people claimed that they were losing admission spots to "unqualified" people of color. These white people argued that affirmative action ran counter to the principle of equal opportunity and the belief that institutions should not see color. This argument is often expressed as "reverse racism," the idea that people of color receiving race-specific remedies to historical wrongs is actually racism against white people (Crenshaw 1988). In this way, colorblind ideology not only attempts to block anti-racist solutions but also flips power dynamics on their head to claim that not only should society not see color but that when it does white people become victims.

The Post-Racial Myth

Another prominent expression of post-racism is the post-racial myth, which emerged around the election of the first Black president in the United States. This myth asserts that not only is society past racism but that it has progressed beyond the usefulness of race at all. The post-racial myth is an evolution of colorblind ideology for the twenty-first century. Brandi Thompson Summers writes that the post-racial myth "suggests that we are beyond conversations about race in the determination of the economic, political, and social lives of individuals" (2020, 247). Rather than pretending not to see color, the post-racial myth claims that race is just no longer significant.

One justification for this belief was the 2008 election of Barack Obama as president of the United States. Catherine Squires (2014) tracks how the term "post-racial" entered the public lexicon in earnest during Obama's campaign as reporters and pundits tried to make sense of the first US Black president. Even more so than colorblindness, the post-racial myth emphasizes progress. Barack Obama became the ultimate symbol of progress; a Black president showed how far the nation had come since the days of Black slavery. Although this progress is true and important to acknowledge, the post-racial myth takes this claim too far. Celebrating the first Black president by no means meant that race no longer mattered, but it did make for an appealing fantasy. Obama became evidence that racism had supposedly diminished and that race was now superficial.

The supposed superficiality of race is a key part of this myth. For example, Anjali Vats (2014) examines post-racial practices in 2009 in high fashion. Vats tracks how designers in several fashion shows, *Vogue Paris* and *America's Next Top Model*, began using makeup and costuming to visually change the race of their models. In these images, models would put on blackface, whiteface, or yellowface to "racechange." Or, more commonly, models would don cultural costumes to look "African," "Native American," "tribal," or "exotic." Vats argues that these practices in high fashion demonstrate how the industry believed the post-racial myth and tried to visualize race as an accessory. These designers displayed race as something superficial and disconnected from social or political contexts; race became something people could "put on" and "take off." The post-racial myth, in its belief we are beyond race, attempts to strip race of its significance, which creates a problem for those making anti-racist critiques.

The greatest challenge to the post-racial myth during the Obama era came from the feminist-founded Black Lives Matter (BLM) movement. While post-racial media narratives told a story of a nation that had progressed past race and racism, BLM offered a counternarrative that showed how racism still threatens Black lives. It should not come as a surprise that after decades of colorblind and post-racial rhetoric much of the United States responded to BLM with the phrase "All Lives Matter." Under a post-racism framework, many white people balked at BLM's explicit use of race in their critiques. People who had lived in the post-racism fantasy for too long could not believe that the United States was still a racist country or that Black lives were particularly threatened by police, because, after all, hadn't the country just elected a Black president? The post-racial myth helped convince these people that racism was a thing of the past.

Feminist Critiques of Post-Racism

Post-racism is a network of ideas such as equal opportunity, not seeing color, cultural hierarchy, reverse racism, progress, and the first Black president. This collection of ideas can be used by a white majority to shut down anti-racist critiques and maintain the status quo—as we saw in the "All Lives Matter" response to "Black Lives Matter." For this reason and others, feminists have long critiqued post-racism (hooks 1990; Hill Collins 2005). Not only are efforts to ignore racism and diminish race antithetical to feminist goals, but they also conflict with feminist theories like intersectionality. Race, like gender, is immensely important in a racist and sexist world. To ignore this part of identity would be folly and would severely limit the ability of theorists and activists to right wrongs and identify systemic oppression.

Feminist scholars such as Sarah Banet-Wieser (2007) have noted how post-racism and post-feminism often go hand in hand. Catherine Squires and her colleagues have also noted how these impulses to be "post-" are revealing about how the politics of identity work in our society today. Squires summarizes this impulse writing, "The joke is on those who continue to view history . . . as a continual progressive movement . . . Identities seem to get in the way, don't they? If we could only get past these identities! If we could only be color-blind, unisex, and all middle class, it would all be fine, wouldn't it?" (Squires et al. 2010, 212). As Squires notes, the post-identity impulse tries to eliminate difference, but as Crenshaw's theory of intersectionality reminds us, difference can be "the source of social empowerment and reconstruction" (1991, 1242). Rather than pretend identities should be overcome, feminists embrace the much harder task of negotiating our differences and working together to build a better world.

Rather than a never-ending story of progress, history is filled with backlashes. Post-racism and post-feminism, despite their sometimes optimistic focus on progress, should be understood as backlashes to the successes and critiques of the civil rights movement and feminist movements of the twentieth century. These backlashes can hide themselves in celebratory discourses like colorblind ideology and the post-racial myth, but they are ultimately fantasies that undermine anti-racist and anti-sexist efforts.

Daniel J. DeVinney

See Also: #BlackLivesMatter; Affirmative Action; Backlash; Civil Rights Act: Title VII; Civil Rights Movement; Crenshaw, Kimberlé; Intersectionality; Postfeminism; White Privilege

Further Reading

Banet-Weiser, Sarah. 2007. "What's Your Flava? Race and Postfeminism in Media Culture." In *Interrogating Postfeminism: Gender and the Politics of Popular Culture*, edited by Diane Negra and Yvonne Tasker, 200–26. Duke University Press.

Bonilla-Silva, Eduardo. 2018. *Racism Without Racists: Color-Blind Racism and the Persistence of Racial Inequality in America*, 5th ed. Lanham, MD: Rowan & Littlefield.

Crenshaw, Kimberlé Williams. 1988. "Race, Reform, and Retrenchment: Transformation and Legitimation in Antidiscrimination Law." *Harvard Law Review* 101, no. 7: 1331–87. https://doi.org/10.4324/9781315184555-4.

Crenshaw, Kimberlé Williams. 1991. "Mapping the Margins: Intersectionality, Identity Politics, and Violence against Women of Color." *Stanford Law Review* 43, no. 6: 1241–99.

Hill Collins, Patricia. 2005. *Black Sexual Politics: African Americans, Gender and the New Racism.* New York: Routledge.

hooks, bell. 1990. *Yearning: Race, Gender and Cultural Politics.* Boston: Southend Press.

King, Martin Luther, Jr. 1963. "I Have A Dream." Speech, Washington, D.C.

Squires, Catherine R. 2014. *The Post-Racial Mystique: Media & Race in the Twenty-First Century.* New York: New York University Press.

Squires, Catherine, Eric King Watts, Mary Douglas Vavrus, Kent A. Ono, Kathleen Feyh, Bernadette Marie Calafell, and Daniel C. Brouwer. 2010. "What Is This 'Post-' in Postracial, Postfeminist . . . (Fill in the Blank)?" *Journal of Communication Inquiry* 34, no. 3: 210–53. https://doi.org/10.1177/0196859910371375.

Thompson Summers, Brandi. 2020. "'Haute [Ghetto] Mess:' Postracial Aesthetics and the Seduction of Blackness in High Fashion." In *Racism Postrace*, edited by Roopali Mukherjee, Sarah Banet-Weiser, and Herman Gray, 245–63. Durham: Duke University Press.

Vats, Anjali. 2014. "Racechange Is the New Black: Racial Accessorizing and Racial Tourism in High Fashion as Constraints on Rhetorical Agency." *Communication, Culture & Critique* 7, no. 1: 112–35. https://doi.org/10.1111/cccr.12037.

POSTCOLONIAL FEMINISM

In the middle of the twentieth century, former colonial powers gave up direct control of their colonial holdings, which ushered in a so-called postcolonial era. What followed was a movement of historical change, literary exploration, and academic reflection in the wake of European colonialism. Within this movement, a group of women academics emerged in what is sometimes called postcolonial feminism. In this academic movement, scholars resisted the universalism of mainstream Western feminism. Instead, they studied the particular oppressions ordinary women face in their everyday lives and analyzed them against the backdrop of larger historical, political, and economic forces. Postcolonial feminist writers make a special contribution to feminist reflection, offering better ways scholars can attend to the real lives of women from across the world.

Postcolonialism: Historical, Literary, and Academic

In the middle of the twentieth century, many former European empires recognized the independence of their colonial holdings, moving from direct to indirect rule. While this indirect rule is often referred to as neocolonialism, the historical moment is described as a postcolonial situation. Postcolonialism (or postcoloniality), in this sense, describes the economic, material, historical, and political events that took place in "formerly colonized Asian, African and South American nations," after former empires surrendered direct control (Nayar 2010, 3).

In the wake of postcolonialism, writers from across the world reflected on the impact of colonialism, in what is sometimes called postcolonial literature. For example, Martinique psychologist Frantz Fanon (1952) writes about the psychological impact of colonialism on colonized peoples. Martinique politician and poet Aimé Césaire (1972) argues that colonialism harms both the colonizer and colonized and called for colonized people to recover their cultures, wisdom, and identity. Novelists also reflect on similar themes. Nigerian writer Chinua Achebe explores the wounds colonialism brought upon Igbo culture in *Things Fall Apart* (1958). Salman Rushdie, perhaps the most famous postcolonial novelist, traced the events surrounding India's independence from Britain in *Midnight's Children* (1981).

Academics, many from formerly colonized countries who were educated in the West, explore the ramifications of colonial legacy. Postcolonial scholarship exists in a wide variety of disciplines, including but not limited to anthropology, literature, philosophy, and communication and media studies. While no singular methodology or theory exists within academic postcolonialism, scholars often write to aid in the political, cultural, and psychological liberation of colonized peoples.

While there are many academics who contribute to postcolonial scholarship, two key authors include literary scholars Edward Said and Homi K. Bhabha. In Said's book *Orientalism*, he argues that when Western colonialists communicated about those peoples and cultures in the East, the West assumed its superiority to the East (1978, 15). As a result, colonialism was not only a process of physical violence, but it was also a process of *discursive* violence, or violent in the way the West communicated, wrote, talked, and represented colonized peoples (Shome 1996, 42). Bhabha argues in *The Location of Culture* that, in many places, colonizers failed to fully colonize people, languages, and cultures. What was produced, instead, was *hybridity*, or a mixed people, language, and culture. Within that hybridity, Bhabha sees a potential for subversion or resistance against colonization (1994, 59, 128). For example, imagine a Lakota tribal member who becomes a lawyer in the US legal system and uses their knowledge of the law to fight for Indigenous land sovereignty. Hybridity points to the reality that no return to a pure "pre-Western past" exists for any of us (Shome 1996, 44). Rather, liberation requires, in part, ways of resisting the strict binary thinking of colonizer/colonized and embracing the in-betweenness of hybrid existence.

Feminists Theorize Postcolonialism

Within academic postcolonialism, a group of women emerged in a postcolonial feminist movement. Both postcolonial academics and white feminists tended to gloss over the experiences of women of color in dealing with harmful conditions such as poverty, landlessness, sexism, or racism, be they in India, Egypt, or southern Texas. In contrast, postcolonial feminists insist "on local readings of 'ordinary women' . . . paying attention to the most minute detail of everyday lives" (Rajan and Park 2005, 63). These writers favor deep contextualization of the experiences of women, keeping the everyday oppression women face tied to larger historical, political, and economic realities. Three representative examples provide a sense of postcolonial feminism.

First, in her landmark essay, "Can the Subaltern Speak?", literary scholar Gayatri Chakravorty Spivak offers an example of how subaltern, or marginalized peoples do not have the option of speaking. Spivak offers an example of the suicide of a young Indian woman, Bhubaneswari Bhaduri. In puzzling through the details of the suicide, it seems that no reasonable account exists of why she ended her life, not even from Bhaduri's family. Spivak concludes that those in power and privileged positions cannot hear or make sense of marginalized people's rhetoric or protests. Spivak provocatively concluded this essay by saying that "the subaltern cannot speak" (1988, 308) and further explained that any attempt to speak for them is, in effect, a projection of the one speaking. Although Spivak later describes her conclusion as a "lament" and "inadvisable" (1999, 308), she clarifies that her point was to underscore the reality that when subaltern figures perform acts that vary from social norms (like Bhaduri's inexplicable death), institutions can render those people speechless when they fail to validate the experience of subaltern peoples (2010, 228). The task, she submits, is to unlearn one's privilege and attend in better ways to the concrete experience of peoples on the margins (1988, 295–6).

Second, anthropologist Saba Mahmood reflects on the lives of pious Muslim women in Egypt and suggests the way they wear hijab (or, the veil) challenges mainstream "feminist theory" (2005, 2). She argues that much of mainstream feminism centers on the notion that all women everywhere have a universal longing for liberation, or "an innate desire for freedom" (2005, 5). As a result, some feminists argue that social norms can function as site for suppression or subversion (2005, 22). Discussion of the wearing of veils by Muslim women tends to fall within this suppression/subversion binary, either as a site of oppression of Muslim women or as a site of resistance against encroaching Western values. The binary, however, misses much of the complexity by which Mahmood's subjects—pious Muslim women in Egypt—understand their own veiling. For them, the veil has to do with *habitus*, or the process in which people use outward bodily acts (like wearing the veil) in order to cultivate inward spiritual virtues (2001, 215). The veil is a practice that helps them change their natural desires into pious ones. The example of the veil suggests that there are a variety of ways women inhabit social practices (2005, 22), ways that supersede the assumed universal desire for liberation and binarism of suppression/subversion.

Finally, feminist studies scholar Chandra Talpade Mohanty argues in her essay "Under Western Eyes: Feminist Scholarship and Colonial Discourses" that Western feminists tend to imagine colonized women from across the world in a singular, demeaning, and violent way—as powerless victims of more powerful forces, be those forces men, traditional religions, colonial governments, and the like (Mohanty 1984, 338). Western feminists do this, she argues, because they imagine themselves as the universal norm for all women across the world (Weedon 2007, 289). Centering or universalizing themselves deprives colonized women from the complexity and agency of their actual lives. Mohanty says that Western feminists should, instead, learn how the injustices colonized women face in their everyday lives are linked to larger economic, historical, and political forces or how "the micropolitics of everyday life" are linked to "the macropolitics of global economic and political processes" (Mohanty 2003, 509).

For example, Mohanty cites a study of housewives in India who, because of the requirements of their caste, cannot leave their homes. In this situation, housewives make lace doylies to generate income, and multinational companies sell these doylies on the international market. Both local caste custom and the international market exploit the labor of these women. However, the lace makers "resist, challenge and subvert the process at various junctures," particularly through their relationship to caste (Mohanty 1984, 345). In one discussion, the housewives admit that they looked down on lower-caste women who could work in factories. If given the chance, however, the housewives would be willing to break with caste custom and leave the house to work with these lower-caste women. Their willingness to keep and break with caste shows that the housewives are more complex than mere powerless victims.

Based on these kinds of studies, Mohanty suggests that Western feminists can learn to see both similarities and differences between their own lives and the lives of women across the world. And perhaps more importantly, Western women can enter into solidarity with all women, noting "the interconnectedness of the histories, experiences, and struggles of US women of color, white women, and women from the Third World/South" (Mohanty 2003, 522).

Naaman Wood

See Also: Decolonialism; Patriarchy; Racist Stereotypes of Arab and Muslim People; Settler Colonialism; Strategic Essentialism; Structural Oppression; Third World Women's Alliance and Black Woman's Manifesto; White Supremacy

Further Reading

Achebe, Chinua. 1958, 2006. *Things Fall Apart*. London: Penguin Classics.

Bhabha, Homi. 1994. *The Location of Culture*. New York: Routledge.

Fanon, Frantz. 1952, 1986. *Black Skin, White Masks*. Translated by Charles Lam Markmann. London: Pluto Press.

Césaire, Aimé. 1972. *Discourse on Colonialism*. Translated by Joan Pinkham. New York: Monthly Peview Press.

Mahmood, Saba. 2001. "Feminist Theory, Embodiment, and the Docile Agent: Some Reflections on the Egyptian Islamic Revival." *Cultural Anthropology* 16, no. 2 (May): 202–36.

Mahmood, Saba. 2005. *Politics of Piety: The Islamic Revival and the Feminist Subject*. Princeton: Princeton University Press.

Mohanty, Chandra Talpade. 1984. "Under Western Eyes: Feminist Scholarship and Colonial Discourses." *Boundary 2*, 12, no. 3 (Spring - Autumn): 333–58.

Mohanty, Chandra Talpade. 2003. "'Under Western Eyes" Revisited: Feminist Solidarity through Anticapitalist Struggles." *Signs* 28, no. 2: 499–535.

Nayar, Pramod K. 2010. *Postcolonialism A Guide for the Perplexed*. New York: Continuum International Publishing Group.

Rajan, Rajeswari Sunder and You-me Park. 2005. "Postcolonial Feminism/Postcolonialism and Feminism." In *A Companion to Postcolonial Studies*. Edited by Henry Schwarz and Sangeeta Ray, 53–73. Malden, MA: Blackwell Publishing Ltd.

Rushdie, Salman. 1981, 2008. *Midnight's Children*. London: Penguin Classics.

Said, Edward. 1978. *Orientalism*. London: Routledge & Kegan Paul.

Shome, Raka. 1996. "Postcolonial Interventions in the Rhetorical Canon: An 'Other' View," *Communication Theory* 6, no. 1 (February): 40–59.

Spivak, Gayatri Chakravorty. 1988. "Can the Subaltern Speak?" In *Marxism and the Interpretation of Culture*, edited and with an Introduction by Cary Nelson and Lawrence Grossberg, 271–313. London: MacMillan Education.

Spivak, Gayatri Chakravorty. 1999. *A Critique of Postcolonial Reason: Toward a History of the Vanishing Present*. Cambridge: Harvard University Press.

Spivak, Gayatri Chakravorty. 2010. "In Response: Looking Back, Looking Forward." In *Reflections on the History of an Idea*, edited by Rosalind C. Morris, 227–36. New York: Columbia University Press.

Weedon, Chris. 2007. "Postcolonial Feminist Criticism." In *A History of Feminist Literary Criticism*, edited by Gill Plain and Susan Sellers, 282–300. Cambridge: Cambridge University Press.

POSTFEMINISM

The term "postfeminism" emerged in the 1980s and 1990s to describe the belief that feminism is no longer needed or desired as a political or social movement. The term "postfeminism" has been used to describe both the feminist achievement of gender equality and a backlash against the feminist movement. Instead of a unified movement or theoretical perspective, postfeminism is better understood as a "set of ideas, images and meanings" that circulate through popular culture and popular media representations (Banet-Weiser, Gill, and Rottenberg 2020). Although a clear-cut definition is hard to come by, postfeminist culture generally highlights individual choice, control over appearance, and consumerism as the key elements for female empowerment. In this way, any choice made by a woman regarding her life, body, or finances supposedly becomes an expression of female power. By shifting the focus of equality from questions of political and social power structures to questions of individual feminine empowerment, postfeminism works to impede feminist activism. Postfeminism operates as a smokescreen, obscuring the ongoing importance of the fight for gender equality with messages that portray feminism as irrelevant or outdated and that divert attention with illusions of feminine empowerment.

Take, for example, the online subculture that emerged around "tradwives," which gained popularity in the early 2020s. Tradwives, short for "traditional wives," believe in traditional gender roles and emphasize marriage and motherhood as key elements of feminine identity. Although primarily comprised of millennial or Gen Z women, online influencers within the tradwives community promote a feminine aesthetic reminiscent of the classic 1950s housewife, characterized by floral aprons and impeccably styled hair and makeup. Many within the tradwives community hail from conservative, religious backgrounds where traditional gender roles are deeply ingrained. Nevertheless, they vehemently defend their decision to embrace the roles of housewife and mother, viewing it as an empowering choice that allows women to escape the pressures of contemporary society. Many tradwives assert that assuming these roles is a matter of personal choice and emphasize that they don't perceive their duties as mothers or housewives as inferior to those of men. As one commentator put it, "But if a sister wants to bake up a storm, iron his shirts, believe her place is in the home and actively parent as a priority, knock yourself out. This is what we have been fighting for—choice. The last thing we need as women is for some of us to feel superior and judgmental of others" (Squires 2020). This response encapsulates the primary value of postfeminism: if women have the ability to choose the lifestyle that they find individually empowering, then any choice they make is (supposedly) inherently feminist. One of the main concerns of feminist scholars regarding postfeminism is that the emphasis on individual choice can undermine the urgency of addressing the broader cultural and societal structures that sustain gender inequality.

What Is Postfeminism?

While postfeminism emphasizes the belief that the feminist movement has become largely irrelevant, people disagree on why that is the case. Some argue that the feminist movement is no longer necessary because women have achieved equality. Others believe feminism is a failed endeavor and prefer to distance themselves from the feminist label while still endorsing many of its principles, including equal pay and reproductive choice. Still others embrace a form of anti-feminism, advocating for women to adopt traditional homemaking roles (Hall and Rodriquez 2003). Despite these differences, there are a few key themes that characterize postfeminist media. These themes include: an emphasis on personal choice and individual empowerment, an understanding of women as active participants in their sexuality (rather than as sexual objects), a belief that appearance is central to femininity (such as feeling more confident or empowered after a makeover or haircut), a return to the idea that there are clear biological differences between men and women, and an emphasis on buying things as a way to address feminine needs (Riley, Evans, and Robson 2022, 4–5; Gill 2007).

In postfeminist media, the political and cultural ideals of feminism are caricatured and dismissed as outdated or extremist. Instead, the emphasis shifts to more comforting narratives in which traditional femininity can coexist alongside the ideals of gender equality. In postfeminism, "girl power" becomes a main point of emphasis, promoting the idea that women can "have it all." In other words, women don't have to pick between being wives and mothers or pursuing a career. They can be strong and independent while also valuing their appearance and sexuality. This "have it all" message often points women toward the commercial products that seemingly help them achieve this success.

Consider, for instance, the success of beauty influencers on social media platforms such as TikTok and Instagram. Like the many makeover reality shows that came before them (Banet-Weiser and Portwood-Stacer 2006), these influencers frequently stress the ways that beauty regimes and cosmetic surgeries enhance confidence and serve as a form of self-care. However, they often promote particular products or services that promise to deliver these outcomes. In the process, they also reinforce traditional beauty standards that tie a woman's worth to her ability to be sexually appealing to heterosexual men. In this way, the ideals of empowerment, confidence, and self-care are redirected in ways that continue to stress the value of physical appearance and encourage viewers to become consumers to achieve these beauty standards. These influencers encourage viewers to believe that by purchasing just one more cosmetic product, they might finally attain the self-confidence needed to pursue their dreams. As this example demonstrates, "postfeminism fetishizes female power and desire," yet it sets limitations on how these can truly be attained (Negra 2008, 4). In this case, the confidence needed to succeed is directly linked to purchasing the products needed to improve your physical appearance, making a focus on physical appearance a requirement for female empowerment.

Additionally, postfeminist culture emphasizes the idea of individual choice and autonomy. In other words, if women are to have full control over their bodies, then they should have the freedom to make decisions about their bodies, even if those choices reinforce traditional gender roles or perpetuate objectification practices rooted in misogyny. This is the underlying justification for the existence of "tradwives" culture, as discussed above. The notion that women should have the freedom to make choices about their bodies appears beneficial. But feminists note that, because patriarchal systems of gender inequality still exist, this freedom can be turned against women. For example, Frazier (2021) demonstrates how "under the terms of postfeminism, a sexy body is viewed as the ultimate source of women's power" (405). Yet, even as women are encouraged to embrace their sexuality and sex appeal, those same behaviors are treated as evidence that "sexualized bodies are . . . 'asking for' victimization" and sexual assault (405). In this way, the supposedly "empowering" elements of postfeminism serve to justify sexual violence and rape culture.

Crucially, the ideals of postfeminism are inherently linked to white femininity. Images of white, heterosexual, middle-class women dominate postfeminist media because their relative social power means they can easily be portrayed as embracing postfeminism's consumerist and sex-positive messages of empowerment. Individuals with less social and economic power, such as women of color, LGBTQIA+ individuals, disabled women, and working-class women, lack the same privilege to readily conform to the consumerist demands of postfeminist culture. Additionally, postfeminism's emphasis on individual empowerment obscures the ways that individual freedom is often linked to the oppression of others. That is, the luxuries emphasized in postfeminist culture often rely on the exploitation of the workers whose labor enables them. In this way, postfeminism maintains the long tradition of centering affluent white women as the epitome of femininity and using the idea of individualism to mask larger systems of inequality.

Feminist Theorizations of Postfeminism

Most feminist scholarship follows Angela McRobbie and Rosalind Gill in theorizing postfeminism. Angela McRobbie (2009) understands postfeminism as "a process by which [the] feminist gains of the 1970s and 1980s are actively and relentlessly undermined" (11). This undermining process occurs predominantly through popular culture, in which postfeminist media "positively draws on and invokes feminism . . . to suggest that equality is achieved" and that feminism "is no longer needed," that feminism "is a spent force" (McRobbie 2009, 12). In this way, postfeminist culture retains some of the appealing elements of feminism—such as sexual freedom and economic independence—while dismissing the more political or radical elements of feminism as outdated or unnecessary. Postfeminism's emphasis on individual choice is utilized to silence feminist critiques on subjects such a pornography or marriage. Because women have the ability to individually choose their own path, postfeminist logic argues, those choices cannot be subject to feminist critique that draws attention to how those choices continue to uphold patriarchal and misogynistic power structures. Overarching questions of political and societal power are replaced with a focus on individual empowerment.

Following Gill (2007), many feminist scholars approach postfeminism as a "sensibility" rather than a specific theoretical perspective or philosophy. By calling postfeminism a sensibility, Gill (2007) means that postfeminism is a cultural phenomenon that relies on the circulation of specific ideas, representations, and themes about femininity via popular culture. These representations and ideas can "influence subject formation and everyday social relations," offering understandings of femininity that women can choose to replicate in their daily lives (Riley et al. 2017, 7). Therefore, feminist scholars understand postfeminism as a "critical object" rather than a coherent perspective or viewpoint (Banet-Weiser, Gill, and Rottenberg 2020). Essentially, this means that feminist scholars are more interested in studying how the term and its related set of ideas circulate and are employed in different circumstances than in treating it as a coherent theoretical framework that exists on the same level as, say, feminist theory (Banet-Weiser, Gill, and Rottenberg 2020).

Emerging Alternatives to Postfeminism

Even as postfeminist sensibilities continue to circulate in popular media, we are beginning to see the rise of new public forms of feminist activism. These efforts include social media campaigns such as #EverydaySexism and #MeToo. They also encompass protest movements such as the Women's Marches in the United States, protests for women's rights in Iran, and the significant mobilization efforts to advocate for and safeguard reproductive rights following the US Supreme Court's decision to overturn *Roe v. Wade* in June 2022. These movements, with varying degrees of success, have also worked to broaden the feminist movement to include marginalized populations that have traditionally been left out, including women of color and the LGBTQIA+ community. As a result, feminist activists have mobilized to support a broad range of issues, including reproductive healthcare, transgender healthcare and rights, and voting rights. While popular media continues to be the primary platform for disseminating postfeminist messages, it also serves as a significant source for feminist activism that pushes for the continued need to fight for gender equality. Via social media campaigns, feminist activists work to reach a wide audience. While the actual power of these "popular" feminist movements to bring about real change is heavily debated, these movements appear to be making at least some difference. In 2020, a Pew Research Center poll found that 61 percent of US women said the term "feminist" described them (Barroso 2020).

Courtlyn Pippert

See Also: Gender; Girl Power; Misogyny; Popular Feminism; Rape Culture

Further Reading

Banet-Weiser, Sarah, and Laura Portwood-Stacer. 2006. "'I Just Want to Be Me Again!': Beauty Pageants, Reality Television and Post-Feminism." *Feminist Theory* 7, no. 2: 255–72.

Banet-Weiser, Sarah, Rosalind Gill, and Catherine Rottenberg. 2020. "Postfeminism, Popular Feminism and Neoliberal Feminism? Sarah Banet-Weiser, Rosalind Gill and Catherine Rottenberg in Conversation." *Feminist Theory* 21, no. 1: 3–24.

Barroso, Amanda. 2020. "61% of US Women Say 'Feminist' Describes Them Well; Many See Feminism as Empowering, Polarizing." *Pew Research Center*, July 7, 202. https://www.pewresearch.org/short-reads/2020/07/07/61-of-u-s-women-say-feminist-describes-them-well-many-see-feminism-as-empowering-polarizing/.

Frazier, Kathryn E. 2021. "'Up for It' or 'Asking for It'? Violence against Women in the Age of Postfeminism." *Feminism & Psychology* 31, no. 3: 404–23.

Gill, Rosalind. 2007. "Postfeminist Media Culture: Elements of a Sensibility." *European Journal of Cultural Studies* 10, no. 2: 147–66.

Hall, Elaine J., and Marnie Salupo Rodriguez. 2003. "The Myth of Postfeminism." *Gender and Society* 17, no. 6: 878–902.

McRobbie, Angela. 2009. *The Aftermath of Feminism: Gender, Culture and Social Change*. London: SAGE.

Negra, Diane. 2008. *What a Girl Wants?: Fantasizing the Reclamation of Self in Postfeminism*. New York: Routledge.

Riley, Sarah, Adrienne Evans, Sinikka Elliott, Carla Rice, and Jeanne Marecek. 2017. "A Critical Review of Postfeminist Sensibility." *Social and Personality Psychology Compass* 11, no. 12. https://doi.org/10.1111/spc3.12367.

Riley, Sarah, Adrienne Evans, and Martine Robson. 2022. *Postfeminism and Body Image*. London, New York: Routledge.

Slaughter, Anne-Marie. 2012. "Why Women Still Can't Have It All." *The Atlantic*, July/August, 2012. https://www.theatlantic.com/magazine/archive/2012/07/why-women-still-cant-have-it-all/309020/.

Squires, Wendy. 2020. "Is It Any Wonder the 'Tradwife' Lifestyle Is So Alluring?" *The Sydney Morning Herald*, February 21, 2020. https://www.smh.com.au/lifestyle/life-and-relationships/is-it-any-wonder-the-tradwife-lifestyle-is-so-alluring-20200220-p542rf.html.

PREGNANCY DISCRIMINATION ACT (1978)

In 1978, the US Congress passed the Pregnancy Discrimination Act, amending Title VII of the Civil Rights Act of 1964. Title VII protects job applicants and employees from discrimination "based on race, color, religion, sex and national origin" (US Equal Employment Opportunity Commission). The Pregnancy Discrimination Act added to or clarified Title VII by prohibiting workplaces with fifteen employees or more from discriminating "on the basis of pregnancy, childbirth, or related medical conditions" (US Department of Labor).

In short, the Pregnancy Discrimination Act makes it illegal to treat an applicant or an employee "unfavorably in any aspect of employment, including hiring, firing, pay, job assignments, promotions, layoffs, training, fringe benefits (such as leave and health insurance), and any other terms or conditions of employment" (US Department of Labor). Moreover, it is "unlawful to retaliate against" a whistleblower—someone who believes a workplace is discriminating against an individual on the basis of pregnancy, childbirth, or related medical conditions and who files a discrimination charge or otherwise reports the incident under Title VII.

Feminist Activism: An Institutional Approach

The Pregnancy Discrimination Act was passed because of feminist activism. Feminists worked throughout the 1960s and 1970s to change US laws and policies, creating protections for women and expanding women's rights. Much of this activism is known as "institutional" activism or activism that uses "institutional" strategies. Institutional activism takes place within and through government institutions such as "the courts, legislatures, and governmental agencies" (McCammon and Brockman 2019, 5). Such institutional activism is contrasted with strategies that involve public protests.

In the late 1960s and early 1970s, feminists "began developing an extensive set of legal and policy advocacy organizations," such as the National Organization for Women, which originated in 1966. As McCammon and Brockman (2019) explain, by petitioning and advocating within the Equal Employment Opportunity Commission (EEOC), litigating cases through the court system—culminating in a partial win in the 1974 *Cleveland Board of Education v. LaFleur* Supreme Court ruling, and ultimately lobbying in Congress, feminist activists used the institutional processes and agencies that are open to all US citizens in order to protect pregnant people from being denied employment, fired, passed over, demoted, or required to take unpaid leave.

Leave Time, Accommodations, and Ongoing Discrimination

Currently, approximately 70 percent of women "work during their pregnancies" in the United States, and they typically continue to work right up to their due date (McCann and Tomaskovic-Devey 2021, 8). For instance, I worked until one week before my first child's due date and when I was pregnant with my second child, I worked continuously up to my due date—the only day I had off prior to delivery was the national holiday, Thanksgiving. Considering how much pregnant people work, it is important that pregnant people are protected from workplace discrimination and are able to obtain reasonable accommodations and leave time.

Most requested accommodations are minor, such as taking more frequent bathroom breaks or the time and a private place (not a bathroom) in which to pump breastmilk after childbirth. The Pregnancy Discrimination Act—in combination with the amendment for lactation accommodations within the Patient Protection and Affordable Care Act, the Fair Labor Standards Act, and the Americans with Disabilities Act—requires almost all employers to make these accommodations (US Department of Labor).

If a pregnant person becomes temporarily disabled and cannot perform their duties even with reasonable accommodations, then the situation becomes more complicated. The employer must treat the pregnant person who is temporarily disabled the same as they would treat any other employee who is temporarily disabled. For instance, imagine a restaurant where a waiter hurts their wrist and temporarily cannot perform their duties. If that restaurant would temporarily reassign the waiter to hosting duties, then the same type of reassignment must be made for an employee who is temporarily disabled due to pregnancy or a complication of pregnancy. Essentially, the employer must allow temporarily disabled pregnant people to do work that does not interfere with or exacerbate their temporary disability. However, some employers (e.g., construction companies) do not typically reassign a temporarily disabled person; they instead require that temporarily disabled person to take sick time or short-term disability leave. Employers with these policies can similarly require persons experiencing temporarily disability due to pregnancy or a complication from pregnancy to use sick time or take short-term disability leave.

Pregnant people can use short-term disability leave if they become temporarily disabled during pregnancy. Moreover, through the Family and Medical Leave Act of 1993 (FMLA) birthing people are entitled to up to twelve weeks of unpaid leave to care for a new child—if the employee has worked at their place of employment for at least twelve months prior to taking leave. For some employees, some portion of their up-to-twelve-weeks FMLA leave time might be paid or paid at a lower rate if they have earned or accrued paid leave time for sick days or short-term disability. This can vary widely based on state policies. This FMLA leave is colloquially known as "maternity" or "paternity" leave. The United States is the *only* developed nation that neither requires nor provides any paid leave for parents of new children.

Unfortunately, despite the Pregnancy Discrimination Act, discrimination against pregnant people runs rampant in US workplaces. Women who work in "low-wage" and "physically demanding occupations" and women who work in "high-wage occupations" are especially at risk for workplace pregnancy discrimination (McCann and Tomaskovic-Devey 2021, 2). Essentially, women in low-wage and physically demanding jobs are not given light work when they ask for accommodations and women in high-wage occupations are passed over for promotions or sidelined during (and after) their pregnancies (Silver-Greenberg and Kitroeff 2018; Kitroeff and Silver-Greenberg 2019).

Based on survey research, Carly McCann and Donald Tomaskovic-Devey (2021, 8–9) conservatively estimate that employers deny approximately 250,000 women pregnancy-related accommodations each year. McCann and Tomaskovic-Devey note, however, that this number is likely much higher, since around 36 percent of pregnant women report needing workplace accommodations and having that need go unmet rather than "ask their employer" and face even worse repercussions for having disclosed their condition to their employer. Ultimately then, workplace pregnancy discrimination remains a major problem in the United States.

Sarah Kornfield

See Also: Civil Rights Act: Title VII; Family and Medical Leave Act (FMLA, 1993); National Organization of Women (NOW); Reproductive Justice

Further Reading

Kitroeff, Natalie, and Jessica Silver-Greenberg. 2019. "Pregnancy Discrimination is Rampant Inside America's Biggest Companies." *NYTimes.com*, February 8, 2019. https://nyti.ms/2SXoxby.

McCammon, Holly J., and Amanda J. Brockman. 2019. "Feminist Institutional Activists: Venue Shifting, Strategic Adaptation, and Winning the Pregnancy Discrimination Act." *Sociological Forum* 34, no. 1: 5–26.

McCann, Carly, and Donald Tomaskovic-Devey. 2021. "Pregnancy Discrimination at Work: An Analysis of Pregnancy Discrimination Charges Filed with the US Equal Employment Opportunity Commission." *Center for Employment Equity*. https://www.umass.edu/employmentequity/sites/default/files/Pregnancy%20Discrimination%20at%20Work.pdf.

Silver-Greenberg, Jessica, and Natalie Kitroeff. 2018. "Miscarrying at Work: The Physical Toll of Pregnancy Discrimination." *NYTimes.com*, October 21, 2018. https://nyti.ms/2I8ZFrd.

US Equal Employment Opportunity Commission. n.d. *Title VII of the Civil Rights Act of 1964*. Accessed March 30, 2024. https://www.eeoc.gov/statutes/title-vii-civil-rights-act-1964.

US Department of Labor. n.d. *What to Expect When You're Expecting (and After the Birth of Your child) . . . at Work*. Accessed March 30, 2024. https://www.dol.gov/agencies/oasam/civil-rights-center/internal/policies/pregnancy-discrimination.

PRISON ABOLITION MOVEMENT

The prison abolition movement wants to end incarceration. It is a social campaign that began in the 1980s as a response to the increase in mass incarceration—which itself was a result of President Ronald Reagan's War on Drugs. The War on Drugs had massive ramifications, resulting in an increase in the US prison population from roughly 500,000 in 1980 to 1.3 million in 1990 and then 2 million in 2000 (Smith 2018). Since the 1980s, the ultimate goal of the prison abolition movement has remained the same: decrease the rates of incarceration through the utilization of alternative practices of justice for those who commit a crime. Feminism is about liberation, about creating a world without oppression—and for many feminists this means creating a world without incarceration.

Over the past five decades, the prison abolition movement has gained traction and now has countless grassroots movements and organizations, many of which focus on demographics who are at higher risk for incarceration due to interlocking oppressions, such as women of color and those who identify as LGBTQ+.

What the Prison Abolition Movement Does

The main focus of the prison abolition movement is reducing—even ending—incarceration, and while that sounds radical and revolutionary, much of the activism within the prison abolition movement is trying to reform the current system. Indeed, reform and abolition are intertwined, not mutually exclusive within the prison abolition movement because helping to prevent incarceration and helping formerly incarcerated people reenter society (thus preventing recidivism and their return to prison) reduce incarceration rates (Lawston and Meiners 2014). As such, the prison abolition movement often supports community centers that help prevent crime, supports public defenders—the lawyers who, usually without a fee, defend poor people accused of crimes—and helps provide resources for previously incarcerated individuals as they reenter society (Washington 2018).

Mass incarceration and the current prison system hurts everyone it touches. As such, prison abolition is for everyone! But it is especially focused on helping impoverished people, women, and people of color since these demographics are often profoundly affected by incarceration. Specifically poor women of color are disproportionately impacted by incarceration. Women are not only impacted by their own incarceration but are additionally impacted by the ramifications of the incarceration of their male partners, dependents, and relatives. Since the 1980s, incarceration has become so prevalent and has such a massive spillover effect, especially at a family level. For instance, a Harvard study published in 2015 found that 44 percent of Black women had a family member who was incarcerated (Hedwig et al. 2015).

Feminist Prison Abolition

Prison abolition feminism is a sector of feminism focused on eliminating the prison-industrial complex (Ragland 2023), which is often defined as the overlapping interests of government and industries that use surveillance, policing, and imprisonment as solutions to economic, social, and political problems (Tufts University 2024). Grassroots organizations such as Black and Pink, Critical Resistance, INCITE!, The Marshall Project and The National Council are examples of feminist prison abolition organizations. Each organization has a key focus. For instance, Black and Pink focuses on supporting incarcerated and formerly incarcerated women who identify as LBGTQ+ (Black and Pink 2024). Critical Resistance focuses on creating an international movement to end the prison-industrial complex for incarcerated individuals of all demographics (Critical Resistance 2024). INCITE!'s mission is centered on prison abolition for women of color and the dismantling of state violence (INCITE 2024). The Marshall Project seeks to spur criminal justice reform and maintain a sense of urgency for criminal justice reform with a focus on the US criminal justice system (The Marshall Project n.d.). The National Council focuses on prison abolition for incarcerated women and girls and their focus on the juvenile population sets them apart (The National Council 2024). Each organization is crucial to the overarching goal of prison abolition for all women and girls and prison abolition more broadly. Although prison abolition feminism focuses on women and girls who are or were incarcerated, the reform, rehabilitation, and general betterment of the criminal justice system positively impact all branches of the prison abolition movement.

Although each organization has distinguishing factors, feminist prison abolition activism is characterized by several common elements (Ragland 2023):

1. Feminist prison abolition requires solutions to gender-based violence that are not dependent upon the carceral state.
2. Abolition feminism seeks to find alternatives to the use of policing or prisons to protect victims of gender-based violence. It recognizes that intimate violence is a microcosm of macro systems of violence rooted in capitalism, imperialism, patriarchy, and other forms of oppression.
3. Abolition feminism works to reject reform as the only solution to systemic issues. Instead, it seeks solutions that focus on the macro level, creating systems, such as youth organization, equal access to K-12 education, and elimination of resource insecurity through community-wide support agencies that prevent incarceration before it happens.

One key factor of feminist prison abolition movement is criminal rehabilitation efforts that do not involve incarceration. Put simply, this means finding ways for justice to be served and for people who have committed crimes to be rehabilitated that do not involve going to prison or jail. This is important because, when incarcerated, women face a higher rate of sexual and interpersonal violence, increased challenges in accessing proper healthcare, and overarching ramifications related to pregnancy, childbirth, and motherhood. Essentially, incarceration is really bad for women—and their children. Feminist prison abolitionists want to end the hurt that incarceration often piles on top women who have already been hurt by poverty, a lack of education, gender violence, a lack of healthcare (including mental healthcare), and so on.

Alternatives to Incarceration

Feminist prison abolitionists often focus on what is known as Alternatives to Incarceration or ATI. ATI are sentencing options that do not entail time spent in prison or jail. The ultimate goal of ATI is to (1) repair the harm caused by a crime, (2) provide benefits for the community, and (3) better the outcomes for the individual who committed the crime. ATI vary depending on the nature of the crime committed and are very case dependent, making them challenging to institute at a governmental level. ATI can include community service, drug rehabilitation, mental health treatment, fines and restitution, home confinement, halfway houses, or some combination of the aforementioned programs. These programs are especially appropriate for women who are often victims of abuse or other systematic violence. ATI also reduce incarceration costs, lower recidivism rates, restore and strengthen family units, and support economic betterment at a small-scale level.

The prison abolition movement works to reform the criminal justice system with the ultimate goal of making the prison system obsolete. Through programs for community betterment, interpersonal violence prevention, criminal justice system reforms, and ATI, feminist prison abolition organizations work to make a better outcome for women and girls and everyone involved in the criminal justice system.

Josephine McClure

See Also: Capitalism; First Step Act (2018); Interlocking Oppression; Intersectionality; Prison-Industrial Complex

Further Reading

Black and Pink. 2024. "Our Story." Accessed August 5, 2024. https://www.blackandpink.org/about/#history.
Critical Resistance. 2024. "Mission & Vision." Accessed August 4, 2024. https://criticalresistance.org/.
INCITE!. 2024. "About." Accessed August 5, 2024. https://incite-national.org/history/.

Law, Victoria. 2014. "Against Carceral Feminism." *Jacobin*, October, 2014. Accessed August 13, 2024.https://jacobin.com/2014/10/against-carceral-feminism/.

Lawston, Jodie M., and Erica M. Meiners. 2014. "Ending Our Expertise: Feminist, Scholarship, and Prison Abolition." *Feminist Formations* 26, no. 2 (Summer): 1–25. https://doi.org/10.1353/ff.2014.0012.

Lee, Hedwig, et al. 2015. "Racial Inequalities in Connectedness to Imprisoned Individuals in the United States." *Du Bois Review* 12, no. 2: 269–82. https://doi.org/10.1017/S1742058X15000065.

Ragland, Alice. 2023. "Abolition. Feminism. Now." *International Viewpoint*, March 8, 2023. Accessed August 24, 2024. https://internationalviewpoint.org/spip.php?article8013.

Smith, Tana. 2018. "The Prison Abolition Movement (1985-)." *BlackPast*, March 12, 2018. Accessed August 24, 2024. https://www.blackpast.org/african-american-history/prison-abolition-movement-1985/.

The Marshall Project. n.d. "About Us." Accessed August 4, 2024. https://www.themarshallproject.org/.

The National Council. 2024. "Ending Incarceration of Women and Girls." Accessed August 3, 2024. https://www.nationalcouncil.us/#:~:text=The%20mission%20of%20The%20National,globally%20through%20its%20International%20Network

Tufts University. 2024. "What is the Prison Industrial Complex?" *Tufts University Prison Divestment*. Accessed August 13, 2024. https://sites.tufts.edu/prisondivestment/the-pic-and-mass-incarceration/.

Washington, John. 2018. "What is Prison Abolition?" *The Nation*, July 31, 2018. Accessed August 24, 2024. https://www.thenation.com/article/archive/what-is-prison-abolition/.

PRISON-INDUSTRIAL COMPLEX

Feminist philosopher and activist Angela Davis defined and explained the prison-industrial complex as the "business-government linkages" that make the penal system and mass incarceration profitable (Davis 1998, 2). Which is to say, the "prison-industrial complex" refers to the links between companies and government agencies (at the state and federal levels) that enable companies (and often the government) to financially profit from imprisoning people and other aspects of "justice" such as fees for everything from a court's "document storage" to "room and board" fees for imprisoned people within prisons (Semple and Kessel 2024).

The contemporary prison-industrial complex has its origins in 1971 when President Nixon described drugs as "public enemy number one" and announced a "war on drugs" (Diaz Pascual 2021). Founding the Drug Enforcement Agency (a special police force that targets "illegal drug use and smuggling") and instituting minimum sentences, Nixon's administration created mass incarceration across the United States (Diaz Pascual 2021). The imprisoned population ballooned from approximately 500,000 in 1980 to over two million in 2015; although the imprisoned population declined during the Covid-19 pandemic, it began to grow again in 2024 (Young 2020; "Mass Incarceration Trends" 2024). Notably, anti-drug policies and minimum sentencing requirements disproportionately affect "Black and Brown people," creating "a systemically unequal prison system" (Diaz Pascual 2021). Indeed, as Nixon's head of domestic policy John Ehrlichman explained, the so-called "war on drugs" was never intended to reform drug use; it was designed to imprison poor and Black people, many of whom lose their right to vote due to imprisonment (Diaz Pascual 2021).

Profiting from Prisoners

Many prisons are private prisons, meaning that they are owned by companies such as Corrections Corporation of America and Wackenhut Corrections Corporation, which are two of the largest private prison corporations in the United States. Privately owned prison companies have contracts with the government to build prisons and they are paid for every prisoner they house in their prison. Private prison companies have a financial incentive to maintain mass incarceration; as such, private prison corporations lobby for incarceration policies and to elect politicians who "will put more people in prison" (Young 2020). Since mass incarceration disproportionately affects communities of color, private prison companies are profiting from and perpetuating social and racial oppression.

Additionally, prisons and other corporations can profit from prisoners' labor. They do this by paying prisoners extremely low pay for the manufacturing of various products. Indeed, many of the "products we consume on a daily basis" are made—in part—by prisoners, including food products such as Frosted Flakes cereal, Gold Medal flour, and Coca-Cola products (Davis 1998, 3; Associated Press 2024). This exploitation was, again, designed during the 1970s. As Nixon's policies went into effect and mass incarceration ramped up, the US government made prisoners' labor easier to exploit in 1979 by passing a law titled the Justice System Improvement Act, which repealed "many restrictions against prison labor" (Haney 2010, 77). Since 1979, then, states set their own policies—often allowing companies to "set up shop in prisons," exploiting prisoners' labor in "traditionally feminine areas like textiles, data entry, and light industry" (Haney 2010, 77). Without regulations in prisons for pay, working hours, and safety, companies can exploitatively profit off inmates' labor. The prison-industrial complex dehumanizes incarcerated people, treating incarcerated people like cogs in a capitalist machine as companies profit from their imprisonment and their exploited labor.

Critical Resistance: A Feminist Response to the Prison-Industrial Complex

Critical Resistance is a charitable organization founded by feminists Angela Davis, Ruth Wilson Gilmore, and Rose Braz that works to end the prison-industrial complex. In 1998, Critical Resistance held a conference in Berkeley, California, bringing together approximately 3,500 activists from all sectors. This conference helped found Critical Resistance as an activist organization and helped many people recognize the importance of eliminating the prison-industrial complex. This movement has grown considerably, bringing together coalitions for prison reform and abolition. Critical Resistance works through local and regional chapters. For instance, there are currently chapters in cities such as New York, Portland, Los Angeles, and Oakland. As a result of their work, there is increased awareness of the prison-industrial complex and the injustice of the US justice system. Additionally, Critical Resistance works to develop community resources so that we can have safe and healthy communities without the prison-industrial complex.

Isabella M. Rodriguez

See Also: Civil Rights Movement; First Step Act (2018); Military-Industrial Complex; Prison Abolition Movements

Further Reading

Associated Press. 2024. "Prisoners in the US are Part of a Hidden Workforce Linked to Hundreds of Popular Food Brands." *US News & World Report*, January 29, 2024. https://www.usnews.com/news/best-states/louisiana/articles/2024-01-29/prisoners-in-the-us-are-part-of-a-hidden-workforce-linked-to-hundreds-of-popular-food-brands.

Critical Resistance. 2024. "History." Accessed October 22, 2024. https://criticalresistance.org/mission-vision/history/.

Davis, Angela. 1998. "Masked Racism: Reflections on the Prison Industrial Complex; What is the Prison Industrial Complex? Why does it Matter?" *Colorlines* 1, no. 2. https://www.proquest.com/docview/215541848?pq-origsite=primo&sourcetype=Magazines.

Diaz Pascual, Ignacio. 2021. "America's War on Drugs—50 Years Later." *The Leadership Conference on Civil and Human Rights*. https://civilrights.org/blog/americas-war-on-drugs-50-years-later/.

Haney, Lynne. 2010. "Working through Mass Incarceration: Gender and the Politics of Prison Labor from East to West." *Signs: Journal of Women in Culture & Society* 36, no. 1: 73–97. https://doi.org/doi:10.1086/652917.

"Mass Incarceration Trends: Report." 2024. *The Sentencing Project*, May 21, 2024. Accessed March 31, 2025. https://www.sentencingproject.org/reports/mass-incarceration-trends/.

Semple, Kirk and Jonah M. Kessel. 2024. "Grab Your Calculators. We're Going to Jail." *NYTimes.com*, October 16, 2024. https://www.nytimes.com/video/opinion/100000009730762/jail-fees-mass-incarceration.html?searchResultPosition=1.
Young, Sydney. 2020. "Capital and the Carceral State: Prison Privatization in the United States and United Kingdom." *Harvard International Review*. https://hir.harvard.edu/us-uk-prison-privatization/.

PUNK FEMINISM AND THE RIOT GRRRL MANIFESTO

During the late 1980s and early 1990s, the young women, or grrrls as they preferred to be called, who pushed back against the male-dominated punk music scene, founded punk feminism and what became known as the Riot Grrrl movement (Dunn and Farnsworth 2012). The punk feminist scene and accompanying music are famous for helping women push gender boundaries and express their power, anger, and aggression (O'Brien 2003).

This grassroots feminist movement combined punk music's DIY aesthetic—with its self-produced recordings—and genre elements such as fast beats, loud sound, and anti-establishment lyricism, which expressed their outrage at society (Downes 2012). Politically charged, popular punk songs addressed central Riot Grrrl issues, railing against rape and domestic abuse while supporting women's health, sexuality, and female empowerment (Dunn and Farnsworth 2012). While the male-dominated punk music scene relegated women to the roles of "groupie, girlfriend, or background singer," the punk feminist movement celebrated all-girl bands, such as Bikini Kill led by Kathleen Hanna (Gottlieb and Wald 1994, 256). Similarly, often relegated to the back of the venue, female fans could not safely participate in the mosh pits at male-dominated punk concerts; protesting this physical marginalization, Bikini Kill encouraged women to push to the front of the stage at their shows (Bikini Kill; see also Dunn and Farnsworth 2012). The "antithesis of polite and reasonable female speech," punk feminist lyrics further emphasized the movement's feminist agenda (Lusty 2017, 225). Often "misinterpreted as male bashing and reverse sexism" this practice led to women themselves—especially the Riot Grrrl punk performers—experiencing the brunt of harassment as men jeered at and assaulted them during shows (Kearney 1998, 155). In an interview, Kathleen Hanna stated that she has experienced verbal and sexual harassment including being "spit on, grabbed, and even punched" (Juno 1996, 90).

All-girl punk feminist band Bikini Kill encouraged female fans to push to the front of the stage at their shows (Raph_PH via Flickr, CC BY 2.0).

In their analysis of the punk feminist movement, Joanne Gottlieb and Gayle Wald (1994) describe the iconic punk feminist "scream" as a key example of how this movement pushed both gender and music boundaries. They describe the scream as a hallmark of all-female punk bands that conveyed many meanings and could simultaneously evoke "rage, terror, pleasure and/or primal self-assertion." Primarily, the scream expressed "feminist rage at the sexual uses and abuses of women"; it garnered attention and promoted the bands; and it also occasionally expressed pleasure—even orgasm. As a form of self-expression, screaming is not considered proper for women. Deemed unladylike, women often hold back their screams lest they become labeled "too emotional." As such, feminist punk bands expressed the central tenets of their movement in this wordless scream, protesting the marginalization of women in the music scene even as they protested the ladylike behavior and gender norms that constrain women's daily lives (Gottlieb and Wald 1994, 261–2).

Riot Grrrl Manifesto

The punk feminist movement launched Riot Grrrl and the Riot Grrrl Manifesto. Credited by mainstream media as Riot Grrrl's leader, Bikini Kill's lead singer Kathleen Hanna published the Riot Grrrl Manifesto in her band's zine, Bikini Kill #2. Published in 1991, the manifesto comprised a two-page list of maxims. "BECAUSE" began each sentence and a list of what the movement stood for and its social goals followed. The manifesto reads almost like Riot Grrrl lyrics, clearly fitting within the broader punk feminism movement (Lusty 2017).

The manifesto begins by referring to the author and audience as "girls" and spells out a reclamation of the term girls, stating, "BECAUSE we are angry at a society that tells us Girl = Dumb, Girl = Bad, Girl = Weak" (RIOT GRRRL MANIFESTO). Here, the manifesto reclaims the word "girl," rejecting its associated oppressive language. However, the "riot" and multiple "r's" symbolize an "enraged girl who empowers herself and others to speak out and fight against oppression" (Kearney 1998, 156). Additionally, the manifesto uses the word "riot" as a "call to action (Riot, grrrl!)" (Kearney 1998, 156). Mary Celeste Kearney wrote extensively about Riot Grrrl and the meaning behind the name. Kearney claims that the name "appropriates the traits of assertiveness and action" typically connected to male adolescence. In so doing, Riot Grrrl created a new identity for themselves that "better represents their revolutionary spirit" (Kearney 1998, 156). They changed the way society, and more specifically men and adults, saw adolescent girls by uniting as Riot Grrrls.

In the spring of 1991, several Riot Grrrl conventions and weekly meetings took place. Composed of "zine makers, activists, artists, musicians, and members of the punk community," these Riot Grrrl discussion groups offered resources for involvement in the movement (Dunn and Farnsworth 2012, 139). They talked about prevalent issues including sex and racism. Hanna said that the meetings became a "place for young feminists to support each other and exchange ideas" (Dunn and Farnsworth 2012, 139).

A new fashion aesthetic also arose out of Riot Grrrl. Scholars refer to it as an "anti-fashion style" comprised of an "uncategorizable amalgam of couture faux pas" (Kearney 1998, 158). This style featured a mishmash of many different things. Commonly, grrrls wore thrifted baby doll dresses, combat boots, tattoos, and piercings (Hopkins 1999). As such, in addition to appropriating the word "girl," their fashion also appropriated the symbols of girlhood and femininity. The result, an "ironic (dis)play and disruption of the signifying codes of gender and generation," combined the appropriated feminine styles and a typical punk aesthetic (Kearney 1998, 158).

Zine

The punk feminist movement also relied on DIY and self-published zines. Typically printed in the homes of Riot Grrrls, this underground publishing mode gave grrrls more agency over what they created. Due to a media blackout, the movement communicated and archived its history through zines (Dunn and Farnsworth, 2012). Young women expressed themselves freely regarding political issues through these zines. Natalya Lusty explains the making of zines and describing the use of old-fashioned materials including typewriters, magazine cutouts, felt-tipped pens, stickers, photos, and collages (2017). Zines also included spoken syntax and grammar, slang, profanity, misspelled words, and handwriting. In addition, the content was a startling combination of manifestos, sarcastic polemic, private and intimate letters, anecdotes, lists of favorite bands and zines, essays, editorials, and a variety of artworks, including straightforward line drawings, vandalized media, and commercial pictures (Lusty 2017). Additionally, the zines emphasized that "the personal is political" in many ways. They did this not only by bringing back the catchphrase ("the personal is political") but also by providing spaces for the sharing of intimate and deeply personal tales. This challenged conventional responses of guilt and blame often connected to sexual assault and other issues central to the Riot Grrrl cause (Lusty 2017). In this way, the zines reformulated feminism through the personal performances of everyday experience.

Joanna Thornburg

See Also: Anger; Cyborg Manifesto; Patriarchy; The Personal Is Political; Third World Woman's Alliance and Black Woman's Manifesto

Further Reading

Bikini Kill. 2018. "'Riot Grrrl Manifesto' Washington, D.C.; 1991." In *Feminist Manifestos: A Global Documentary Reader*, edited by Penny a. Weiss, 329–32. New York, NY: New York University Press.

Downes, Julia. 2012. "The Expansion of Punk Rock: Riot Grrrl Challenges to Gender Power Relations in British Indie Music Subcultures." *Women's Studies* 41, no. 2: 204–37. https://doi.org/10.1080/00497878.2012.636572.

Dunn, Kevin, and May Summer Farnsworth. 2012. "'We Are the Revolution': Riot Grrrl Press, Girl Empowerment, and DIY Self-Publishing." *Women's Studies* 41, no. 2: 136–57. https://doi.org/10.1080/00497878.2012.636334.

Gottlieb, Joanne, and Gayle Wald. 1994. "Smells Like Teen Spirit: Riot Grrrls, Revolution and Women in Independent Rock." In *Microphone Fiends: Youth Music, Youth Culture*, edited by Andrew Ross and Tricia Rose, 250–74. New York: Routledge.

Hopkins, Susan. 1999. "HOLE LOTTA ATTiTUDE COURTNEY LOVE AND GUiTAR FEMiNiSM." *Social Alternatives* 18, no. 2: 11–14.

Juno, Andrea, ed. *Angry Women in Rock, Vol. 1.* New York: Juno Books, 1996.

Kearney, Mary Celeste. 1998. "'Don't Need You': Rethinking Identity Politics and Separatism from a Grrrl Perspective." In *Youth Culture: Identity in a Postmodern World*, edited by Jonathan Epstein, 148–88. Blackwell Publishers.

Lusty, Natalya. 2017. "Riot Grrrl Manifestos and Radical Vernacular Feminism." *Australian Feminist Studies* 32, no. 93: 219–39. https://doi.org/10.1080/08164649.2017.1407638.

O'Brien, Lucy. 2003. *She Bop II (Gen): The Definitive History of Women in Rock, Pop and Soul.* London: Bloomsbury Publishing.

"RIOT GRRRL MANIFESTO." 1AD. *History Is a Weapon.* https://www.historyisaweapon.com/defcon1/riotgrrrlmanifesto.html.

PURITY CULTURE

Purity Culture is a "subculture" of religion, specifically evangelical Christianity, that believes people—especially women—should abstain from sexual acts before "heterosexual marriage" (Natarajan 2022, 316). Purity culture relies on gendered stereotypes, imagining men as being unable to control their sex drive and women as the "gatekeepers" of men's sexuality who must adhere to certain modesty guidelines. Because purity culture tends to think of men's sexual desire as uncontrollable, women and girls are unfairly tasked with the responsibility of staying pure. Ultimately, purity culture is based on sexist beliefs, and it defines womanhood—and individual women's and girls' value—in terms of virginity and abstaining from sexual acts. Without sexual "purity," women and girls are seen as decreasing in value.

Feminists have focused on the ways purity culture treats women's virginity as their most valuable asset and positions women and girls who have "lost their virginity" as being tainted or less worthy. For example, feminist author Jessica Valenti examines the various abstinence programs in the United States that target women and girls, summarizing their messages as, "Sex makes us less whole and a whole lot dirtier" (Valenti 2009, 41). She discusses how some abstinence programs describe women as candy. If women allow themselves to be "chewed" or "eaten" (aka have sex) and are unable to "fit back into" their "wrappers" they become unwanted (Valenti 2009, 33, 41). Women's and girl's "social and spiritual worth" is measured by their "sexual status" (Blyth 2021, 12).

Girls are encouraged to take abstinence pledges and although men and boys may also be encouraged to take a pledge, staying pure has primarily been the responsibility of women and girls as their virginity is equated with their worth and beauty (Valenti 2009, 30–2; Klement and Sagarin 2017, 207; Stanley 2020, 120). This belief "normalizes the oppression of women's bodies, restricts sexual agency" and "perpetuates rape culture" (Natarajan 2022, 316). Women and girls are told they must dress a certain way so as to not tempt men, who are "visually stimulated," often leading to victim blaming in cases of sexual abuse (Klement and Sagarin 2017, 215–16; Zimmerman 2023, 18). When women and girls are sexually abused, they are often asked, "how they might have contributed to their own victimization?" (Berra 2018, 30). For example, they may be asked, "what were you wearing?" implying that certain clothing may cause sexual assault. They are also often told to consider the "feelings and future of their attacker," who, assuming the attacker is a man, supposedly has uncontrollable sexual desire (2018, 30). Thus, it is up to women and girls to take responsibility for the abuse. By reinforcing rape culture myths, purity culture supports gender stereotypes such as men being unable to control their sexual desires and women having no desire at all. Purity culture treats premarital sex as something dirty and women's pleasure as immoral. It equates purity with "true" beauty, which is often associated with whiteness (Klement and Sagarin 2017, 212; Stanley 2020, 120; Mikkelsen and Kornfield 2021, 571).

For instance, feminist activists have emphasized how purity culture, specifically white women's "purity," has been "weaponized against Black people," because it treats white Christians' way of living as morally superior to those of a different race, class, or sexuality (Mikkelsen and Kornfield 2021, 564; Natarajan 2022, 316). Those who have historically embraced purity culture have been "white, middle-class, conservative Christians" (Stanley 2020, 119). For example, GirlDefined Ministries, an internet-based Christian organization run by two sisters, Bethany Beal and Kristen Clark, argues for biblical complementarianism and promotes what they consistently call "true femininity" or "God-defined femininity."

For GirlDefined, "true femininity" means highlighting "natural beauty," which is tightly if subtly linked to whiteness, as explained by Mikkelsen and Kornfield (2021, 571–2). Being naturally beautiful means partaking in purity culture by suppressing sexuality, saving oneself for marriage, and submitting to male leadership. Being sexually "pure" is what makes women beautiful in the eyes of GirlDefined and the broader Christian purity culture. Ignoring structural oppression, Beal and Clark (white women) use themselves as examples of naturally beautiful women who uphold purity, failing to acknowledge their standards of beauty (and thus purity) are unattainable for women of color and low-income women.

Brittany Cooper draws the same connection between purity culture and white supremacy, stating, "Purity culture demonizes Black women's bodies. It reinforces white supremacy . . . White supremacy said Black women were loud, unfeminine, out of control and ugly" (Cooper 2016). Black women have historically been depicted as hypersexual to a point where being pure is "altogether foreign" (Zimmerman 2023, 20). Purity culture perpetuates the same lie because it treats the white, nuclear family as the norm and demonizes those who don't (or are unable to) submit to this belief. White heterosexual women's beauty, which is deeply connected to their purity, is seen as natural and biblical, whereas women of color are seen as impure (Cooper 2016; Zimmerman 2023, 15). The standards of purity culture work to uphold a white supremacist, patriarchal society.

Ultimately, purity culture teaches women and girls that they are expected to remain chaste until they get married or else they lose value. Purity culture perpetuates rape culture by victim blaming and treats women's desires for sex as taboo. Feminists continue to push back against the harmful ideology of purity culture, arguing that women's value is not dependent on their sexual status.

Sage Mikkelsen

See Also: Biblical Complementarianism; Cult of True Womanhood; #MeToo; Rape Culture; Virginity

Further Reading

Berra, Robert. 2018. "Men's Ministries and Patriarchy: From Sites of Perpetuation to Sites of Resistance." In *Rape Culture, Gender Violence, and Religion*, edited by Caroline Blyth, Emily Colgan, and Katie B. Edwards, 27–51. Cham: Springer International Publishing.

Blyth, Caroline. 2021. *Rape Culture, Purity Culture, and Coercive Control in Teen Girl Bibles*. Abingdon, Oxon: Routledge.

Cooper, Brittney. 2016. "4 Reasons Why Black Women Should Reject Purity Culture." *crunkfeministcollective.com*, September 13, 2016. https://www.crunkfeministcollective.com/2016/09/12/4-reasons-why-black-women-should-reject-purity-culture/.

Klement, Kathryn R., and Brad J. Sagarin. 2017. "Nobody Wants to Date a Whore: Rape-Supportive Messages in Women-Directed Christian Dating Books." *Sexuality & Culture* 21, no. 1: 205–23.

Mikkelsen, Sage, and Sarah Kornfield. 2021. "Girls Gone Fundamentalist: Feminine Appeals of White Christian Nationalism." *Women's Studies in Communication* 44, no. 4: 563–85.

Natarajan, Madison, Kerrie G. Wilkins-Yel, Anushka Sista, Aashika Anantharaman, and Natalie Seils. 2022. "Decolonizing Purity Culture: Gendered Racism and White Idealization in Evangelical Christianity." *Psychology of Women Quarterly* 46, no. 3: 316–36.

Stanley, Olivia. 2020. "A Personal Encounter with Purity Culture: Evangelical Christian Schooling in Aotearoa/New Zealand." *Women's Studies Journal* 34, no. 1: 116–29.

Valenti, Jessica. 2009. *The Purity Myth: How America's Obsession with Virginity Is Hurting Young Women*. Berkeley, CA: Seal Press.

Zimmerman, Yvonne C. 2023. "Learning from Black Lives Matter: Resisting Purity Culture in US Antitrafficking." *Religions* 14, no. 4: 430.

Q

QUEER THEORY

Historically, the term "queer" has had a variety of meanings. It has been used to refer to something strange or unusual or to point out negative characteristics such as someone being "mad" or not fitting in with social norms (Littlejohn, Foss, and Oetzel 2021). More recently, the term has been reclaimed as a general word used to describe someone who is different due to their gender and/or sexual presentation or expression. In the LGBTQIA+ community "queer" is a multifaceted word that is used in various ways and means different things to different people. A queer person may have an attraction to people of many genders, or they may choose not to conform to cultural norms around gender and/or sexuality (Tuttlec 2011). Queer can also be used as a general term referring to all nonheterosexual people.

Queer theory is an interdisciplinary field that encourages people to embrace a view of the world that challenges traditional assumptions about gender and sexual identities, challenges traditional academic approaches, and challenges social inequality. In other words, queer theory is a critical theory that examines and critiques society's definitions of gender and sexuality, with the goal of revealing the social and power structures at play in our everyday lives. The term "queer theory" is attributed to Teresa de Lauretis who, in 1990, chose the phrase as a title for a conference she coordinated as a means to "disrupt the complacency of lesbian and gay studies" (Littlejohn, Foss, and Oetzel 2021, 79). De Lauretis proposes that queer theory could represent all the critiques of the social and power structures surrounding gender and sexual orientation and make it possible to rethink everything about sexuality. In the same year that de Lauretis coined the term "queer theory," an activist organization called Queer Nation adopted the term "queer" for chants such as, "We're here! We're queer! Get used to it!" ("Queer Nation NY" n.d.). As a result, queer theory has both academic (e.g., lesbian and gay studies and feminist theory) and activist origins.

Like all theories, queer theory is a way of seeing the world: the Greek word, θεωρία, from which English derives the word "theory" means "to see" or "perspective." While queer theory is broad in scope, it centers on a few core ideas or ways of seeing the world. First, queer theory and the queer analyses and research that stem from queer theory challenge the assumptions of heteronormativity. Heteronormativity is defined as the presumption and privileging of heterosexuality, gender conformity, and nuclear families over all other "deviant" forms of gender expression, sexuality, and families (Lloyd, Few, and Allen 2009). Queer theory challenges heteronormativity in that it actively fights against the institutions, practices, and structures that enforce heterosexuality. For example, queer theory challenges the historical and religious view that marriage can only be between a cisgender man and cisgender woman. Queer theorists would argue that any couple, regardless of sex, gender, and identity, should be allowed to marry and are entitled to the benefits and protections (e.g., insurance benefits, tax breaks, power of attorney, etc.) of being a married couple.

Second, queer theory understands that "privates are public and political" (Cloud 2007, 26). Here, queer theory recognizes that people's genitals and the most intimate or "private" parts of our lives are public and political—meaning that they are and always have been subject to legislation and to social and political governance. For instance, in 2003, the Supreme Court overturned a Texan law that outlawed homosexual sex, which was sometimes known as "sodomy." This decision, *Lawrence v. Texas*, made it legal for gay adults in the United States to have sex. Queer theorists point out that the existence of "anti-sodomy" laws are evidence that "privates" are "public and political." Governments have long been legislating and enforcing laws about who can have sex with each other and who can procreate with each other. These types of legislation are often part of population control and are theorized by Michel Foucault as biopower or biopolitics.

Third, queer theory rejects essentialized gender categories (e.g., woman or man; girl or boy) arguing that sexual orientations and identities are social, complex performances rather than stable aspects of one's identity (Littlejohn, Foss, and Oetzel 2021). Here, queer theorists such as Dana Cloud (2007, 29) argue that "establishing whether someone is queer is a social question." This means that although Western cultures generally assume that sexuality is an inherent, permanent, and foundational part of who someone is, the reality is more complicated. For instance, boys and men who are considered heterosexual (and who consider themselves heterosexual) often engage in male-male sex acts as part of "hazing" or team culture in sports teams and fraternities. Similarly, women who are attracted to other women might never act on these attractions and be unequivocally considered "heterosexual." Queer theorists remind us that gender categories and sexual orientations and identities are complex and social—not easily surmised or categorized.

Finally, queer theory recognizes intersexuality as part of reality rather than categorizing intersexuality as a "mistake" or trying to medically erase it through surgery. Intersex individuals have biological differences that do not fit with what is considered to be normal for a male or female individual. As such, both transgender and intersex people are queer and have identities that do not match the usual societal norm. Queer theory argues that sexuality cannot be disconnected from other parts of a person's identity, instead it shapes and is shaped by various social and cultural factors (Littlejohn, Foss, and Oetzel 2021).

Judith Butler was instrumental in expanding upon how the categories of sexuality, gender, and identity get normalized by society. Butler argued that we must continually question the existing traditional conversation around identity categories, thus allowing for different and more fluid meanings or understandings of identity to develop (Littlejohn, Foss, and Oetzel 2021). Furthermore, Butler contended that gender is performative, meaning that the performance of gender is what makes gender exist (Butler 1990).

Queer theory is demonstrated in contemporary pop culture through television shows such as *Queer Eye* and *"We're Here!" Queer Eye*, originally aired on Bravo and then rebooted by Netflix in 2018, is an American reality television show in which five openly queer male and nonbinary advisers spend a week using their expertise to help improve someone's life by refining their wardrobe, grooming, diet, cultural pursuits, and home décor ("Watch *Queer Eye*" n.d.). HBO's *"We're Here!"* follows renowned drag queens, Bob the Drag Queen, Eureka O'Hara, and Shangela, as they visit small towns across America ("We're Here" n.d.). During each visit, the queens recruit a diverse group of residents to share their stories, increase awareness, and promote acceptance in their communities by participating in one-night-only drag shows. The queens inspire their "drag daughters" to express their authentic selves in front of their families, friends, and communities, at times facing increased opposition and anti-LGBTQ+ legislation laws. Both shows are admired for challenging society's traditional understanding of gender and sexuality and celebrating the intersecting identities that make people unique. Through the continued work of queer and feminist theorists and the increasing normalization of gender and sexual fluidity, we can continue to challenge the oppressive social and power structures at play in our everyday lives.

Samantha F. Quinn

Also See: Biopower; Butler, Judith; Essentialism; Gender; Gender Performance; Intersex; *Lawrence v. Texas* (2003); Trans Theory

Further Reading

Butler, Judith. 1990. *Gender Trouble: Feminism and the Subversion of Identity*. New York: Routledge.

Cloud, Dana L. 2007. "The First Lady's Privates: Queering Eleanor Roosevelt for Public Address Studies." In *Queering Public Address: Sexualities in American Historical Discourse*, edited by Charles E. Morris III, 23–45. University of South Carolina Press.

Littlejohn, Stephen W., Karen A. Foss, and John G. Oetzel. 2021. *Theories of Human Communication:* 12th edn. Long Grove, IL: Waveland Press.

Lloyd, Sally A., April L. Few, and Katherine R. Allen, eds. 2009. *Handbook of Feminist Family Studies*. Thousand Oaks, CA: Sage Publications.

Tuttlec. 2011. "Definitions." Vanderbilt University, April 15, 2011. https://www.vanderbilt.edu/lgbtqi/resources/definitions.

"Queer Nation NY." n.d. Queer Nation New York. https://queernationny.org/history.

"Watch Queer Eye: Netflix Official Site." n.d. https://www.netflix.com/title/80160037.

"We're Here: Official Website for the HBO Series." n.d. HBO. https://www.hbo.com/were-here.

R

RACIST STEREOTYPES

A racist stereotype is a generalized and simplified belief about a particular racial group. The roots of such stereotypes can be traced back to ancient civilizations, where ethnocentric views and xenophobia were already present. In Greek and Roman civilizations, for example, there was prejudice against foreigners and people from other regions, who were often seen as inferior or barbaric (Williams 2012).

With the era of European colonialism these stereotypes took on a new dimension. To justify the exploitation and domination of other regions and peoples, European colonizers developed racial hierarchies, promoting the idea of racial superiority of European white people over Africans, Indigenous peoples, Asians, and so on. These ideas were reinforced by pseudoscience, such as social Darwinism, which used anthropology and biology to categorize human beings into racial types, supporting notions of racial hierarchy. In European literature and art, non-European peoples were often portrayed as "savage," "primitive," or "exotic" (Williams 2012; Mehta 1999; Pitts 2005; and Chiu and Taylor 2011).

The Europeans who colonized the land we now call the United States brought these stereotypes with them, embedding negative and dehumanizing ideas about Indigenous people, Jewish people, and people from Africa, Arabia, and Asia into daily life in colonial America. For instance, early Virginian colonists believed that heathenism was hereditary for Black people. This meant that according to early colonial laws in Virginia, Black people could never become Christians; they were considered permanently "primitive" in their spirituality and thus (unlike white indentured servants) could not claim their status as Christians to argue for the end of their exploitation (Goetz 2012).

In the United States, racist stereotypes continue to "other" people of color, marking them as different from the normal (i.e., white), as foreigners (i.e., as unamerican), and as inferior to white people. These racist stereotypes often have gendered and/or sexualized components that essentially disqualify men of color from white US idealizations of manhood and disqualify women of color from white US idealizations of womanhood.

This encyclopedia's entries on "Racist Stereotypes of Arab and Muslim People," "Racist Stereotypes of Asian People," "Racist Stereotypes of Black People," "Racist Stereotypes of Indigenous People," "Racist Stereotypes of Jewish People," and "Racist Stereotypes of Latinx People" provide synopses on some of the most common racist stereotypes in the United States. Their lists are not exhaustive, but they identify key racist stereotypes in US culture, media, and politics.

It is important to note that racist stereotypes often come in pairs where one stereotype is the inversion or flip side of another stereotype. Additionally, while some racist stereotypes are referred to by a general description (e.g., "Asian Geek" or "Indigenous Casino Owner"), many stereotypes are named after characters in US media who epitomized the racist stereotype (e.g., the Jezebel and Mr. Miyagi). Finally, many characters in contemporary US culture are an amalgam or mash-up of stereotypes. For example, a villain in an action movie might be a combination of the "Yellow-Peril" and the "Asian Geek" stereotype, featured as a nerdy computer whiz who is attempting to destroy the US economy so China can become an uncontested global superpower. Again, it is important to remember that racist stereotypes "other" people of color in the United States, marking them as different, as foreigners, and/or as inferior—and thus marking whiteness as normal, as American, and as superior.

Feminist Responses to Racist Stereotypes

Feminists resist racist stereotypes because they perpetuate harmful and inaccurate ideas about people based on their race—reinforcing systems of oppression and discrimination. Yet these stereotypes are intertwined with gender and sexuality, and they intersect to create unique forms of discrimination and marginalization. For example, stereotypes about Black women as "angry" and "aggressive" intersect with stereotypes about women being "emotional" or "irrational" even as they exclude Black women from (white) representations of femininity as gentle and demure—ultimately reinforcing negative perceptions of both Blackness and femininity. Similarly, stereotypes about Asian women as "submissive" and "exotic" intersect with stereotypes about women's sexuality, contributing to the fetishization and objectification of Asian women.

Intersectional feminism recognizes these complex intersections of identity and works to dismantle all forms of oppression, especially racism and sexism, recognizing that they are interconnected and cannot be addressed in isolation. Therefore, raising awareness about interlocking oppressions is crucial in combating racist and sexist stereotypes. By educating individuals about how these stereotypes intersect and reinforce each other, we can foster greater understanding and empathy, leading to more inclusive and equitable attitudes and behaviors.

Mariane Camargo

See Also: Colonialism; Essentialism; Interlocking Oppression; Intersectionality; Racist Stereotypes of Arab and Muslim People; Racist Stereotypes of Asian People; Racist Stereotypes of Black People; Racist Stereotypes of Indigenous People; Racist Stereotypes of Jewish People; Racist Stereotypes of Latinx People

Further Reading

Chiu, Yvonne, and Robert S. Taylor. 2011. "The Self-Extinguishing Despot: Millian Democratization." *The Journal of Politics* 73, no. 4 (October): 1239–50.

Goetz, Rebecca Anne. 2012. *The Baptism of Early Virginia: How Christianity Created Race*. Baltimore, MD: Johns Hopkins University Press.

Mehta, Uday Singh. 1999. *Liberalism and Empire: A Study in Nineteenth-Century British Liberal Thought*. Chicago: University of Chicago Press.

Pitts, Jennifer. 2005. *A Turn to Empire*. Princeton, NJ: Princeton University Press.

Williams, Robert A. Jr. 2012. *Savage Anxieties: The Invention of Western Civilization*. New York: St. Martin's Press.

RACIST STEREOTYPES OF ARAB AND MUSLIM PEOPLE

A racist stereotype is a generalized and simplified belief about a particular racial group—in this case, Arab and Muslim people. These stereotypes often have gendered and/or sexualized components that essentially disqualify Arab and Muslim men from white US idealizations of manhood and disqualify Arab and Muslim women from white US idealizations of womanhood—this ultimately creates and reinforces gendered and white supremacist hierarchies, privileges, and oppressions.

In the United States, it is fairly common to assume that anyone who appears Arab is part of the Muslim faith and vice versa. This is an ignorant assumption that equates region of birth or ancestry, culture, and/or skin color with religion—and it affects non-Arab people too. For instance, men of color wearing Sikh turbans are often mistaken as Arab and Muslim, even though Sikh is an entirely different religion than Islam, originating in northern India and Pakistan instead of the Arab region, and Sikh turban styles are very different from Muslim head coverings (Understanding Turbans n.d.). Because Americans often ignorantly conflate Arab people with Muslim people and vice versa, Arab and Muslim people experience both race-based and religion-based discrimination. For instance, 72 percent of white evangelical Christians believe that Islam and democracy are fundamentally incompatible (Gandhi 2021). Here, race and religion are clearly intertwined leading white evangelical Christians to be more likely to consider Muslim people of color as inherently anti-American.

Media in the United States has long portrayed Arab and Muslim people—especially men—as violent and passionate, and Anglo versions of stories such as *Arabian Nights* often present Arab and Muslim women as exotic victims who are also often deceitful and dangerous. After the 9/11 terrorist attacks, however, US media began depicting Arab and Muslim people much more negatively. For example, TV series such as *Homeland* and films such as *Argo* and *American Sniper* depict Arab and Muslim people "as dangerous, furious, duplicitous, violent, and extremist" (Gandhi 2021). Indeed, contemporary media almost exclusively portrays Arab and Muslim people in ways that connect them to war and terrorism.

These racist stereotypes have very real consequences. Hate crimes against Muslim people skyrocketed after 9/11 and remain high; they have never returned to their pre-9/11 levels ("Muslims in America After 9/11, Part II" 2023). Similarly, during his first term in office, President Donald Trump made a variety of anti-Muslim statements and implemented Executive Orders 13769 and 13780, both of which were titled, "Protecting the Nation from Foreign Terrorist Entry into the United States," and were more commonly and collectively known as the "Muslim Ban." These executive orders temporarily banned entry to the United States by nationals of Iran, Libya, Somalia, Sudan, Syria, and Yemen—all majority Muslim countries—in addition to vastly lowering the number of refugees admitted into the United States per year. Hate crimes against Arab and Muslim people are again on the rise in the United States, with a "337% uptick in incidents after Hamas' Oct. 7 attack on Israel" (Pinales 2023).

In the United States, racist stereotypes ultimately "other" people of color, marking them as different from the "normal" (i.e., white), as foreigners (i.e., as unamerican), and as inferior to white people. At the same time, then, racist stereotypes ultimately mark whiteness as normal, as American, and as superior.

Below are brief descriptions of some of the most common racist stereotypes of Arab and Muslim people. This is not an exhaustive list but rather illustrates some of the most common racist stereotypes in US culture, media, and politics.

- **The Orient:** This stereotype applies to Arab (and Asian) regions in general, and it clearly informs the gendered stereotypes for Arab and Muslim people. As theorized by Edward Said in his book *Orientalism* (1978), the West uses this racist stereotype to imagine Arab (and Asian) regions as backward, uncivilized, barbaric, and exotic lands. Think about the music that typically plays as a camera pans over a desert in films. This classic motif exoticizes Arab regions while framing it as desolate and backward. Generally, orientalism applies primarily to countries in Southwest Asia and North Africa—countries that are often known as the Arab region or the "Middle East," but orientalism can extend to South Asian and even East Asian countries as well. This stereotype conflates a "vast and diverse array of landscapes, peoples, and cultures into a single, unchanging unit," often presenting "countries as varied as Lebanon, Turkey and Iraq with little distinction" (Hibri 2023). For example, Disney's *Aladdin* (1992) is supposedly set in Arabia but incorporates a lot of Indian culture. The film features snake charmers, tigers, cobras, peacocks, and elephants, all of which are typically found in India, not Arabia (Anscombe et al. 2021). Ultimately, this stereotype frames Arab regions and cultures as hopelessly backward—with domineering men and exotic women. This stereotype sets the stage for Western military intervention and occupation and for neocolonial economic intervention into these regions. Indeed, as Said argued, by portraying Arab lands as mismanaged and Arab people as "inferior, subservient, and in need of saving," this stereotype justifies racist Western colonialism and imperialism (Hibri 2023).

- **The Terrorist:** Arab and Muslim men are often portrayed as terrorists in US films and TV series. They are portrayed as Islamist extremists and are typically presented as hyperviolent and controlling men who often brutalize and sexually assault women. Although these characters are typically portrayed as crafty with extremely well-planned terrorist attacks in films and TV series, these terrorists are usually thwarted by a single white man who outsmarts them and finally outmuscles or outguns them in a climatic fight scene at the end of the narrative. Amazon Prime's first season of *Jack Ryan* (2018) offers an extremely typical portrayal of this terrorist stereotype.
- **The Sheikh:** Sometimes known as the "Arab Oil Sheikh," this stereotype has a long history. It first presented Arab men as domineering and exotic leaders of desert kingdoms who kidnap and rape white women—who ultimately fall in love with the Sheikh. This was the plot of *The Sheikh*, a 1919 romance novel turned into a wildly popular silent film in 1921. In the contemporary era, this stereotype characterizes an Arab and/or Muslim man as an extremely rich, hypersexual playboy who overindulges in luxury items such as extremely expensive vehicles, sunglasses, and art. Although this stereotype presents these characters as occasionally charming, they often have unusual sexual appetites that objectify women, and they typically turn out to be brutally violent, controlling, and villainous characters in contemporary US media. This stereotype presents Arab and Muslim cultures as led by corrupt and (often grossly violent) lecherous men. This provides a convenient scapegoat, offering a built-in explanation for the poverty experienced in many Arab and Muslim countries—an explanation that overlooks how Western interventions (including war and neocolonial oil corporations) have affected the region (Harlock 2022).
- **Harem Girls:** This stereotype, also known as "Dancing Girls," refers to adult women as "girls." In so doing, this stereotype engages in the broader sexualization and eroticization of female children. The Arab and Muslim women depicted by this stereotype are hypersexualized. They are typically portrayed as scantily clad, exoticized belly dancers and/or as women in a harem. They are often nameless and speak few if any lines in US films and TV series. Instead, they exist as background—providing an exotic, sexualized spectacle that serves the male gaze. Again, Disney's *Aladdin* provides clear examples of this stereotype, featuring women in a harem during the song "One Jump Ahead" and as belly dancers during the song "Friend Like Me."
- **Women as Exotic Victims**: Arab and Muslim women are often stereotyped as exotic victims. They are portrayed as the wives, concubines, or daughters of men who are typically portrayed through the stereotypes of the terrorist or the Sheikh. Even Princess Jasmine from *Aladdin* fits this stereotype: she is forced into an arranged marriage (which is portrayed as backward) and

is hypersexualized throughout the film. Since 9/11, the women depicted through this stereotype are often seen being forced to wear clothing and head coverings such as burqas, niqabs, and hijabs. Here, a sign of Islamic religious devotion is often portrayed as patriarchal domination. This stereotype often presents Arab and Muslim women as demure and subservient (Jasmine was an exception to this rule in *Aladdin*). Ultimately, the exotic victim stereotype presents Arab and Muslim women as in need of saving and as worthy of being saved by Western intervention.

- **Women as Deceitful Villains:** Even as the stereotype of Arab and Muslim women as exotic victims circulates in US culture and Western cultures more broadly, so too does its mirror image—the stereotype of Arab and Muslim women as villains. Here, Arab and Muslim women are portrayed as duplicitous: acting as if they need saving when they are really dangerous. Western media often fixates on the "veil," demonstrating a "fascination with uncovering the veiled woman" and equating "feminine mystery" with both the exotic and the dangerous. In this stereotype, Arab and Muslim women are routinely depicted as carrying guns or explosives underneath their veils and coverings, and these women's "unveiling" becomes a climactic scene within many films and TV series (Eissa, Guta, and Hassan 2022, 3–4; Hancock and Mobillion 2019).

Racist stereotypes about Arab and Muslim people perpetuate harmful and inaccurate ideas. For instance, assuming that Arab and Muslim people are inherently violent and treacherous leads to hate crimes against Arab and Muslim people—as the post-9/11 data clearly demonstrates.

Ultimately, these racist stereotypes help create and reinforce systems of discrimination and oppression. For instance, not only do they contribute to hate crimes within the United States, but they were directly used to justify the US military invasion of Afghanistan. As communication scholar Tasha Dubriwny (2005) demonstrates, then First Lady Laura Bush advocated for US military intervention into and occupation of Afghanistan in 2001 and 2002 through the feminist-sounding appeal that such US intervention would rescue Afghani women and children from the Taliban's patriarchal rule. This advocacy invoked the classic stereotypes, portraying Afghanistan as a backward desert country (the orient) where men are terrorists who not only plot against the United States but also victimize women. These stereotypes neatly skipped over the history in which the United States and Soviets used proxy armies during the 1980s in a fight to control Afghanistan's oil—during which time the United States directly funded, trained, and gave weapons to the Taliban, helping them rise to power in Afghanistan (Stabile and Kumar 2005, 767).

Some of the first steps toward ending these racist stereotypes are being aware of them and calling them out when you see them in media or hear them in casual conversation. Bringing awareness to these stereotypes and naming them for what they are can help dispel their power in US culture.

Sarah Kornfield

See Also: Colonialism; Essentialism; Intersectionality; Male Gaze; Racist Stereotypes; Racist Stereotypes of Asian People; Racist Stereotypes of Black People; Racist Stereotypes of Indigenous People; Racist Stereotypes of Jewish People; Racist Stereotypes of Latinx People

Further Reading

Anscombe, Bridget, Promise Kim, Shourya Verma, and Kartika Tanguturi. 2021. *How to Spot Orientalism*, April 19, 2021. Accessed August 12, 2024. https://storymaps.arcgis.com/stories/7e57aa26b664437db87 53e916ef7c39c.

Dubriwny, Tasha N. 2005. "First Ladies and Feminism: Laura Bush as Advocate for Women's and Children's Rights." *Women's Studies in Communication* 28, no. 1: 84–114.

Eissa, Eiman A., Hala A. Guta, and Rana S. Hassan. 2022. "Representations of Arab Women in Hollywood Pre- and Post-9/11." *Journal of International Women's Studies* 24, no. 5: 1–20.

Gandhi, Insiya. 2021. "Reel to Real: Harmful Stereotypes of Arabs and Muslims in American Film and Television." *Rhētorikós: A Journal of Rhetoric & Composition.* Spring 2021. Accessed August 12, 2024. https://rhetorikos.blog.fordham.edu/?p=1738.

Hancock, Claire, and Virginie Mobillion. 2019. "'I Want to Tell Them, I'm Just Wearing a Veil, Not Carrying a Gun!' Muslim Women Negotiating Borders in Femonationalist Paris." *Political Geography* 69: 1–9.

Harlock, J. D. 2022. "The Troubling Persistence of the 'Arab Sheikh.'" *Blood Knife*, May 13, 2022. Accessed August 12, 2024. https://bloodknife.com/the-arab-sheikh/.

Hibri, Cyma. 2023. "Orientalism: Edward Said's Groundbreaking Book Explained." *The Conversation*, February 12, 2023. https://theconversation.com/orientalism-edward-saids-groundbreaking-book-explained-197429.

"Muslims in America After 9/11, Part II." 2023. *9/11 Memorial & Museum.* Accessed August 12, 2024. https://www.911memorial.org/learn/students-and-teachers/lesson-plans/muslims-america-after-911-part-ii.

Pinales, Tori Morales. 2023. "How Reports of Hate Crimes in the US Were Already at Record Highs, in 4 Charts." *CNN.com*, December 11, 2023. https://www.cnn.com/2023/10/29/us/hate-crimes-antisemitism-anti-muslim-dg/index.html.

Said, Edward. 1978. *Orientalism.* London: Penguin Books.

Stabile, Carol A., and Deepa Kumar. 2005. "Unveiling Imperialism: Media, Gender and the War on Afghanistan." *Media, Culture & Society* 27, no. 5: 765–82.

Understanding Turbans. n.d. *The Seattle Times.* Accessed August 12, 2024. https://special.seattletimes.com/o/news/nation-world/crisis/theregion/turbans.html.

RACIST STEREOTYPES OF ASIAN PEOPLE

A racist stereotype is a generalized and simplified belief about a particular racial group—in this case, Asian people. These stereotypes often have gendered and/or sexualized components that essentially disqualify Asian men from white US idealizations of manhood and disqualify Asian women from white US idealizations of womanhood—this ultimately creates and reinforces gendered and white supremacist hierarchies, privileges, and oppressions.

In the United States, Asian people have long been discriminated against. For instance, Chinese women were barred from entering the United States by the 1875 Page Act—which was in effect until 1943—and which banned Chinese women based on the assumption that they would become sex workers (Hwang and Parreñas 2021). During this time Asian men in the United States were prohibited from marrying white women due to anti-miscegenation laws. The Chinese Exclusion Act of 1882 barred all Chinese people from immigrating and was generally in effect through various updates or variations until (like the Page Act) it was dismantled in 1943. In the aftermath of the Second World War, the War Brides Act of 1945 allowed Asian women to immigrate to the United States, but it did so in explicitly sexualized terms: women were only admitted as wives.

Then, the 1986 Immigration Marriage Fraud Amendment went into effect. This law further sexualized Asian women, while seizing on the idea that Asian women are manipulative or duplicitous. During the 1980s, white men in the United States were using catalogues to "order" brides, primarily from the Philippines—again, demonstrating how Asian women are positioned as sex objects within US culture. The 1986 Immigration Marriage Fraud Amendment was enacted not to protect Asian women from such clearly predatory global patriarchy but to protect the supposed white male victims who were apparently at risk from these Asian women's sexual temptation and duplicitous natures (Hwang and Parreñas 2021). As these examples and immigration laws demonstrate, Asian people have long faced discrimination in the United States—and this discrimination has a decidedly sexualized component.

In the United States, racist stereotypes ultimately "other" people of color, marking them as different from the "normal" (i.e., white), as foreigners (i.e., as unamerican), and as inferior to white people. At the same time, then, racist stereotypes ultimately mark whiteness as normal, as American, and as superior.

Below are brief descriptions of some of the most common racist stereotypes of Asian people. This is not an exhaustive list but rather illustrates some of the most common racist stereotypes in US culture, media, and politics.

- **Yellow Peril:** This stereotype became especially prominent during the Second World War, when US war propaganda portrayed Asians and Asian Americans as a threat; during this time many Asian Americans were confined to internment camps. De Leon (2020) explains that the "yellow peril" stereotype portrays Asians, especially Chinese people, as an economic, cultural, and moral threat to the West. In contemporary times, this manifests itself in anti-Chinese sentiments, especially with China's economic rise and during crises such as the Covid-19 pandemic.
- **Model Minority:** This stereotype imagines Asian Americans as successful, highly educated, and hardworking immigrants. Although this stereotype seems positive, it is often wielded against other minority groups, particularly Black and Latinx communities. Additionally, it places significant pressure on Asian Americans to meet unrealistic expectations as Neil Ruiz (2023) describes.
- **Asian Geek:** This stereotype portrays Asian people as socially awkward, academically inclined, and technologically proficient, often at the expense of their social lives and personal charisma. While Asian Geek Girl characters are likely to be sexualized, Asian Geek Boy characters are likely to be portrayed as having abnormal sexual appetites and/or as being unable to attract women as sexual partners.
- **Geisha:** Asian women are often stereotyped as submissive, passive, and obedient. Specifically, the Geisha stereotype portrays Asian women—especially Japanese women—as sexually available to men while still demure and submissive. Celeste Nguyen (2016) shows how this stereotype results in exploitation in the workplace, abusive personal relationships, and the fetishization of Asian women. This stereotype objectifies Asian women as "exotic" and "mysterious."
- **Dragon Lady:** In contrast to the Geisha, the "Dragon Lady" stereotype portrays Asian women as power hungry and cunning. It also typically hypersexualizes Asian women, depicting them as seductive and manipulative femme fatales (Rieken 2022).
- **Tiger Mother:** This stereotype portrays Asian mothers—especially from East Asia—as domineering and focused on upward mobility. The so-called Tiger Mother forces her children into "grueling academic preparation activities" such as intense tutoring, in hopes of "securing their academic, and subsequently, life success" (Kobakhidze, Ma, and Tsaloukidis 2023). This stereotype has clear connections to other racist stereotypes for Asian people. Namely, the Tiger Mother is a sort of desexualized Dragon Lady who focuses her quest for power and domination at the family level. At the same time, the Tiger Mother and the Asian Geek stereotypes work in concert with one another, as Tiger Mothers are often credited for raising Asian Geeks.
- **Samurai:** Rooted in historical samurai imagery that has been popularized by Western media, the "Samurai" stereotype is a portrayal of Asian, particularly Japanese, men as stoic and honor-bound warriors. While it may seem to celebrate certain aspects of Japanese culture,

this stereotype also simplifies and distorts the complexities of both the samurai tradition and contemporary Japanese society.

- **Mr. Miyagi:** Named after the iconic character from the movie *The Karate Kid*, the Mr. Miyagi stereotype depicts Asian men as wise, humble, and self-sacrificing mentors who possess secret, almost mystical knowledge. The Mr. Miyagi stereotype is a version of the Samurai stereotype but typically for older men. This stereotype also marks Asian men as permanent outsiders in the United States, usually through a pronounced accent.
- **Desi Masculinity:** This stereotype focuses on South Asian men—especially men of Indian descent. It portrays these men as cute and funny but also pathetic. These men are depicted as largely unable to attract women and yet desperate for sex. Characters such as Raj Koothrappali from *The Big Bang Theory* (2007–19) and Asiz Ansari's character, Tom Haverford, on *Parks and Recreation* (2009–15) are clear examples of this stereotype (Na 2019).

Racist stereotypes about Asian people perpetuate harmful and inaccurate ideas. For instance, they put extreme pressure on people of Asian descent to excel in school (especially in math and science) and to conform to US culture. At the same time, Asian women are hypersexualized—either as passive Geishas or dangerous Dragon Ladies—and Asian men are often portrayed as desexualized and/or lascivious men of strange sexual appetites, who nonetheless cannot attract women.

Ultimately, these racist stereotypes help create and reinforce systems of discrimination and oppression. For instance, consider the response to Robert Aaron Long's targeted murder of women of Asian descent in 2021. Describing himself as a Christian and a "sex addict," Long purposefully murdered women of Asian descent, claiming he was eliminating "the temptation" rather than succumb to it (Hwang and Parreñas 2021). His reasoning relied on stereotypes such as the Geisha and the Dragon Lady, imagining women of Asian descent as inherently sexual and willing to satisfy his every whim and yet ultimately plotting or embodying his destruction. Even more troubling, the spokesperson for the Cherokee County Sheriff's Office, Captain Jay Baker, characterized Long as someone who was "pretty much fed up and had been at the end of his rope," continuing that "yesterday was a really bad day for him" (Hwang and Parreñas 2021). This statement positions a white man as the victim—as someone who had been pushed to "the end of his rope"—and builds sympathy for Long: Long (not his victims) is the one positioned as someone having a "really bad day." Such violence against Asian people and such sympathy for the white men who perpetuate such violence clearly demonstrate the horrifying outcomes of racist stereotypes.

Some of the first steps toward ending these racist stereotypes are being aware of them and calling them out when you see them in media or hear them in casual conversation. Bringing awareness to these stereotypes and naming them for what they are can help dispel their power in US culture.

Mariane Camargo

See Also: Essentialism; Intersectionality; Racist Stereotypes; Racist Stereotypes of Arab and Muslim People; Racist Stereotypes of Black People; Racist Stereotypes of Indigenous People; Racist Stereotypes of Jewish People; Racist Stereotypes of Latinx People

Further Reading

Bowman, Paul. 2024. "The Karate Kid at 40: Why the Film's Lasting Appeal Stems from a Simplistic Stereotyping of the 'Mysterious East.'" *The Conversation*, May 15, 2024. Accessed July 2, 2024. theconversation.com/the-karate-kid-at-40-why-the-films-lasting-appeal-stems-from-a-simplistic-stereotyping-of-the-mysterious-east-228433.

Chaiklin, Martha. n.d. "Bushidō and the Samurai." *Japan: Places, Images, Times and Transformations.* Accessed July 2, 2024. https://www.japanpitt.pitt.edu/essays-and-articles/history/bushid%C5%8D-and-samurai.

De Leon, Adrian. 2020. "The Long History of Racism against Asian Americans in the US." *PBS News Hour*, April 9, 2020. www.pbs.org/newshour/nation/the-long-history-of-racism-against-asian-americans-in-the-u-s.

Hwang, Maria Cecilia, and Rhacel Salazar Parreñas. 2021. "The Gendered Racialization of Asian Women as Villainous Temptresses." *Gender & Society* 35, no. 4: 567–76.

Kobakhidze, Magda Nutsa, Ying Ma, and Alexandros Tsaloukidis. 2023. "Tiger Parenting Beyond Cultural Essentialism: Discourses of Class, Culture, and Competition in Hong Kong." *ECNU Review of Education* 7, no. 3: 531-553.

Lee, Matthew. 2020. "Coronavirus Reveals How Quickly "Model Minority" Asians Become the 'Yellow Peril.'" *NBC News*, March 9, 2020. https://www.nbcnews.com/think/opinion/coronavirus-fears-show-how-model-minority-asian-americans-become-yellow-ncna1151671.

Na, Ali. 2019. "#AzizAnsariToo?: Desi Masculinity in America and Performing Funny Cute." *Women's Studies in Communication* 42, no. 3: 308–26.

Nguyen, Celeste. 2016. "Asian American Women Faculty: Stereotypes and Triumphs." University of San Francisco. Accessed August 13, 2024. https://Repository.usfca.edu/Cgi/Viewcontent.cgi?Referer=&Httpsredir=1&Article=1011&Context=Listening_to_the_voices#:~:Text=The%20lotus%20flower%2C%20or%20geisha,Females%20as%20feminine%20and%20passive.

Rieken, Sarah. 2022. "Representation of Asian Women in the Media." *The Women's Network*, March 24, 2022. Accessed August 13, 2024. https://www.thewomens.network/blog/representation-of-asian-women-in-the-media.

Ruiz, Neil G., et al. 2023. "Asian Americans and the 'Model Minority' Stereotype." *Pew Research Center*, November 30, 2023. Accessed August 14, 2023. www.pewresearch.org/2023/11/30/asian-americans-and-the-model-minority-stereotype/.

RACIST STEREOTYPES OF BLACK PEOPLE

A racist stereotype is a generalized and simplified belief about a particular racial group—in this case, Black people. These stereotypes often have gendered and/or sexualized components that essentially disqualify Black men from white US idealizations of manhood and disqualify Black women from white US idealizations of womanhood—this ultimately creates and reinforces gendered and white supremacist hierarchies, privileges, and oppressions.

In North America, the transatlantic slave trade and the US system of chattel slavery, which—combined—lasted several hundred years, relied on racist hierarchies, which in turn relied on essentialized understandings that imagined people of color as savages. After the American Civil War (1861–5) and the abolition of slavery, new forms of racial control and discrimination emerged in the United States, establishing legal segregation in public places, schools, transportation, and other areas of life. These laws and policies were known as Jim Crow laws. They were named after a minstrel character portrayed by Thomas Dartmouth Rice who—like most minstrel performers—was a white man who performed in blackface. The Jim Crow character and minstrel shows more broadly entertained audiences by making fun of Black people by portraying them through racist stereotypes that were commonplace across cartoons, advertisements, political speeches, and so on (Pilgrim 2023a).

In the United States, racist stereotypes continue to "other" people of color, marking them as different from the "normal" (i.e., white), as foreigners (i.e., as unamerican), and as inferior to white people. At the same time, then, racist stereotypes ultimately mark whiteness as normal, as American, and as superior.

Below are brief descriptions of some of the most common racist stereotypes of Black people. This is not an exhaustive list but rather illustrates some of the most common racist stereotypes in US culture, media, and politics.

- **The Coon:** This stereotype has its roots in the nineteenth-century minstrel shows, portraying Black men as avoiding work and responsibility, preferring leisure and idleness. As sociologist David Pilgrim (2024) explains, this stereotype depicts Black men as buffoons, incapable of taking care of themselves and typically needing and answering to white leaders, bosses, or overseers in popular entertainment. The Coon is almost always the butt of the joke.
- **The Tom:** The Tom stereotype (named after Tom in *Uncle Tom's Cabin*) depicts middle-aged and older Black men as nonconfrontational, gentle, and passive, reinforcing the idea that Black men happily accept subservient positions. A Tom character is unflaggingly kind and obedient to those in power.
- **The Mammy:** The Mammy is a stereotyped depiction of Black women that represents them as asexual caretakers—typically caring for white families. Mammy characters are often depicted with large bodies. As David Pilgrim (2012; 2023b) explains, both the Mammy stereotype and the Tom stereotype are characterized by unwavering loyalty and subservience to white employers: these stereotypes present Black people as happy and content with their subordinate roles.
- **The Buck:** This stereotype emerged during the era of slavery and continues to influence media representations and social attitudes. The Buck stereotype depicts Black men as being physically powerful, aggressive, and having insatiable sexual appetites—often fixated on white women. This portrayal fuels racist fears of Black masculine sexuality and the perceived threat it poses to white purity. As Ana Kocić (2017) details, the Buck stereotype is used to justify violence and discrimination against Black men, including lynching and other forms of extrajudicial punishment. It reinforces the notion that Black men are a threat to social order and must be controlled.
- **The Jezebel:** The Jezebel stereotype hypersexualizes Black women, portraying Black women as deceitful, lacking in moral values, and willing to engage in sexual activities deemed unacceptable by society. The Jezebel stereotype often represents Black women as villains—portraying Black women as manipulative, using their sexuality to seduce and control others (Pilgrim 2023a). This stereotype has been used to justify the sexual exploitation and abuse of Black women throughout history. It has also been used to pathologize Black female sexuality, portraying it as deviant and abnormal.
- **The Matriarch:** The stereotype of the Matriarch presents Black women as controlling and domineering family leaders—and thus as having usurped men's supposedly rightful place as head of the family. This stereotype and its evolutions have their roots in racist and sexist ideologies, portraying Black women as inherently volatile and difficult. These stereotypes are often used to dismiss the legitimate feelings and experiences of Black women, invalidating their emotions and delegitimizing their concerns and their families. This stereotype is often used to justify the mistreatment of Black women, suggesting that their anger makes them deserving of disrespect and violence.
- **The Welfare Queen:** The stereotype of the Welfare Queen is directly related to the Matriarch; however, the Welfare Queen is presented as a bad mother. Popularized by President Ronald Reagan in the 1980s, the Welfare Queen stereotypes Black women as lazy—especially stereotyping Black women as single mothers who have many children (by various fathers)

and who cannot financially provide for them, relying on "government handouts" and generally mistreating and neglecting their children.

- **The Sapphire or "Angry Black Woman":** This stereotype is again related to that of the Matriarch, and it portrays Black women as irrationally and constantly nagging and angry. Sometimes named after the character Sapphire Stevens from *Amos and Andy* (1928–60), and sometimes simply referred to as the "Angry Black Woman," this stereotype typically decontextualizes the Matriarch stereotype, taking it outside of the family setting as Daphna Motro, Jonathan B. Evans, Aleksander P. J. Ellis, and Lehman Benson III (2022) describe in their study of this stereotype within the workplace. The Angry Black Woman stereotype represents Black women as overly aggressive, hostile, and irrationally angry.

Racist stereotypes about Black people perpetuate harmful and inaccurate ideas. For instance, by delegitimating Black women's anger and imagining all young Black men as violent, stupid, and/or criminal, these racist stereotypes help create and reinforce systems of discrimination and oppression. Ultimately—as feminists, Civil Rights leaders, and anti-racist activists have long been pointing out—these racist stereotypes are often at play, negatively affecting Black people through systems such as the US justice system, de facto school and housing segregation, police practices, and so on.

Some of the first steps toward ending these racist stereotypes are being aware of them and calling them out when you see them in media or hear them in casual conversation. Bringing awareness to these stereotypes and naming them for what they are can help dispel their power in US culture.

Mariane Camargo

See Also: Essentialism; Intersectionality; Racist Stereotypes; Racist Stereotypes of Arab and Muslim People; Racist Stereotypes of Asian People; Racist Stereotypes of Indigenous People; Racist Stereotypes of Jewish People; Racist Stereotypes of Latinx People

Further Reading

Green, Laura. 2023. "Negative Racial Stereotypes and Their Effect on Attitudes toward African-Americans." *Jim Crow Museum*. Accessed August 13, 2024. jimcrowmuseum.ferris.edu/links/essays/vcu.htm.

Kocić, Ana. 2017. "From the Violent 'Black Buck' Stereotype to the 'Black Hero': Representations of African Americans and Black Masculinity in American Cinema." *Facta Universitatis: Linguistics and Literature* 15, no. 1: 85–96. https://doi:10.22190/FULL1702085K.

Motor, Daphna, Jonathan B. Evans, Aleksander P. J. Ellis, and Lehman Benson III. 2022. "The 'Angry Black Woman' Stereotype at Work." *Harvard Business Review*, January 31, 2022. Accessed June 17, 2024. https://hbr.org/2022/01/the-angry-black-woman-stereotype-at-work.

Pilgrim, David. 2012. "The Tom Caricature." *Jim Crow Museum*. Accessed June 17, 2024. https://jimcrowmuseum.ferris.edu/tom/homepage.htm.

Pilgrim, David. 2023a. "The Jezebel Stereotype." *Jim Crow Museum*. Accessed June 17, 2024. https://jimcrowmuseum.ferris.edu/jezebel/index.htm.

Pilgrim, David. 2023b. "The Mammy Caricature." *Jim Crow Museum*. Accessed June 17, 2024, https://jimcrowmuseum.ferris.edu/mammies/homepage.htm.

Pilgrim, David. 2024. "The Coon Caricature." *Jim Crow Museum*. Accessed June 17, 2024. https://jimcrowmuseum.ferris.edu/coon/homepage.htm.

Sonian, Smith. 2018. "Popular and Pervasive Stereotypes of African Americans." *National Museum of African American History and Culture*, October 23, 2018. Accessed August 13, 2024. nmaahc.si.edu/explore/stories/popular-and-pervasive-stereotypes-african-americans.

RACIST STEREOTYPES OF INDIGENOUS PEOPLE

A racist stereotype is a generalized and simplified belief about a particular racial group—in this case, Indigenous people. These stereotypes often have gendered and/or sexualized components that essentially disqualify Indigenous men from white US idealizations of manhood and disqualify Indigenous women from white US idealizations of womanhood—this ultimately creates and reinforces gendered and white supremacist hierarchies, privileges, and oppressions.

Since the colonial era, the Indigenous or Native people living in what we now call the United States have been exposed to viruses and diseases with genocidal effects, been stolen from, targeted in genocidal wars, had their children kidnapped and raised by white European people, and been violently relocated to undesirable land. At the same time, Indigenous or Native people living in what we now call the United States have been animalistically associated with nature.

In the territory now known as the United States, racist stereotypes "other" people of color, marking them as different from the "normal" (i.e., white), as foreigners (i.e., as unamerican), and as inferior to white people. At the same time, racist stereotypes ultimately mark whiteness as normal, as American, and as superior.

Below are brief descriptions of some of the most common racist stereotypes of Indigenous people in the United States. This is not an exhaustive list but rather illustrates some of the most common racist stereotypes in US culture, media, and politics.

- **The Spiritual Leader:** The "witchdoctor" or "spiritual indigenous leader" stereotype is a common depiction of Indigenous people—usually men—as having a special connection to spirituality, mysticism, and ancestral wisdom (Hirschfelder and Molin 2018). Although it may seem positive at first glance, this stereotype reduces individuals to a one-dimensional and exotic role, ignoring the diversity of beliefs, practices, and perspectives within Indigenous communities. Moreover, the connection to nature is often associated with animalism, which fundamentally dehumanizes Indigenous people.
- **The Indigenous Princess:** The Indigenous Princess stereotype can be understood as an idealized and romanticized representation of Indigenous women (Hirschfelder and Molin 2018). Perhaps there is no greater example of the Indigenous Princess stereotype than Disney's portrayal of Pocahontas, whose tribal name was Matoaka. This stereotype portrays Indigenous women as exotic guardians of nature, often associating them with mystical or spiritual narratives. This concept often combines elements of respect for the earth, spiritual connection with the natural environment, and a sense of harmony and balance with nature. These representations can be found in different forms of art, literature, cinema, and popular culture, where Indigenous women are symbolized as figures who have deep knowledge and a sacred relationship with the land, transmitting values of environmental conservation and sustainability. Also, like Disney's portrayal in *Pocahontas*, these women are typically hypersexualized.
- **The Casino Owner:** This stereotype oversimplifies the reality of tribal sovereignty, economic development, and the diverse experiences of Native communities. Originating from the Indian Gaming Regulatory Act of 1988 and fueled by media coverage and popular culture, this stereotype suggests that all tribes have casinos and equally benefit from them, ignoring the economic disparities among tribal nations. It can lead to the misrepresentation of economic realities, perpetuation of resentment and prejudice, and obfuscation of broader issues of tribal sovereignty and self-determination. It typically represents the Casino Owner character as a conniving leader.

Racist stereotypes about Indigenous people perpetuate harmful and inaccurate ideas. For instance, by continuously linking Indigenous people to nature (or radically separating them from nature through the associations of the Casino Owner), these stereotypes imply that Indigenous people are practically animals (or, in the case of the Casino Owner, have radically rejected their heritage and "nature"). As Indigenous rights leaders and feminists have long argued, these stereotypes subordinate Indigenous people so that—despite their lauded "knowledge" of nature—they are nonetheless subjected to outside governance and oppression.

Some of the first steps toward ending these racist stereotypes are being aware of them and calling them out when you see them in media or hear them in casual conversation. Bringing awareness to these stereotypes and naming them for what they are can help dispel their power in US culture.

Mariane Camargo

See Also: Essentialism; Intersectionality; Racist Stereotypes; Racist Stereotypes of Arab and Muslim People; Racist Stereotypes of Asian People; Racist Stereotypes of Black People; Racist Stereotypes of Jewish People; Racist Stereotypes of Latinx People

Further Reading

Hirschfelder, Arlene, and Paulette F. Molin. 2018. "I is for Ignoble: Stereotyping Native Americans." *Jim Crow Museum*. Accessed August 13, 2024. https://jimcrowmuseum.ferris.edu/native/homepage.htm.

RACIST STEREOTYPES OF JEWISH PEOPLE

A racist stereotype is a generalized and simplified belief about a particular group—in this case, Jews. These stereotypes often have gendered and/or sexualized components that portray Jewish men as greedy misers, power-hungry manipulators, or weak nerds and Jewish women as aggressive, shrill, and always *kvetching* (Yiddish for "complaining").

In Europe and elsewhere, anti-Jewish discrimination has included barring land ownership, expulsion, torture, forced conversions, pogroms, and the Holocaust (USHMM n.d.; Ryan n.d.). In the United States, anti-Jewish discrimination has included the sharing of false propaganda, exclusion from public places and social clubs, workplace discrimination, university quotas, immigration restrictions, lynchings, KKK and neo-Nazi violence, and attacks on synagogues and Jewish community centers (Horn 2022; Nadell 2022; Weisman 2018).

In the United States, racist stereotypes ultimately "other" people of color, marking them as different from the normal (i.e., white), as foreigners (i.e., unamerican), and as inferior to white people. At the same time, then, racist stereotypes ultimately mark whiteness as normal, as American, and as superior. In the United States, most Jews are of Ashkenazi (Eastern European) descent (see below). However, most non-Jewish Americans did not classify Jews as white until after the Second World War, and some Jews still do not identify as white, even if they are white-passing (Brodkin 1998; Kampeas 2020).

Below are brief descriptions of some of the most common racist stereotypes of Jews. This list is not exhaustive; instead, it identifies some of the most common racist stereotypes for Jewish people in US culture, media, and politics.

- **Christ Killers:** One stereotype about Jews is that because Jesus was put to death by Jewish people, and especially because Judas Iscariot betrayed Jesus, all Jews are forever guilty for Jesus's death. This stereotype has led to so much anti-Semitism that the Catholic Church actually issued an apology (*Nostra Aetate*) in the years after the Holocaust for perpetuating this stereotype (Kiewe 2011).

- **Blood Libel:** This is a false accusation that Jewish rituals, like making matzah for Passover, require the blood of non-Jewish (often Christian) children. The Torah actually forbids eating even the blood of animals (Lev. 17:10-14). Removing that blood with large grain salt (hence, kosher salt) is part of what makes certain meats kosher, so consuming human blood is considered especially *treif* (not kosher). Nevertheless, blood libels about children allegedly kidnapped by Jews for the sake of ritual sacrifice have led to many massacres of Jews as retaliation for "crimes" that they did not commit (ADL n.d.).
- **Power Hungry:** Another stereotype of Jews is that they are power hungry and seeking world domination. This stereotype largely comes from *The Protocols of the Learned Elders of Zion*, a Russian forgery "book" pretending to be a series of secret meeting notes among a Jewish cabal bent on taking over the world. Despite being completely fabricated, *The Protocols* has had so much influence that even US automaker Henry Ford recirculated their debunked claims (Maddow 2023; Shere et al. 2021).
- **Greedy (Shylock):** Another stereotype of Jews is that they are greedy. Ignoring the reality that—like any other population—some Jews are wealthy and some are not, this stereotype is that Jews are wealthy but only because they are cheap and manipulative. The slur "he *jewed* me down," meaning that someone cheated someone out of fair payment, is a good example. This stereotype of Jews as being wealthy and cautious with money comes from Jews being barred from professions other than moneylending in medieval Europe (Elvis 2024). Shakespeare's character Shylock from *The Merchant of Venice* is a good example of the greedy moneylender stereotype (Horn 2022).
- **Mort Goldman:** Another common Jewish stereotype is the caricature of Mort Goldman from *Family Guy* and others like him, who are portrayed as hopelessly nerdy, unattractive, awkward, and neurotic. This stereotype portrays Jews not only as bookish but also as bumbling fools: all book smarts and no street smarts. It's the antithesis of the power-hungry Jews, unless that power is to become the teacher's pet in the classroom.
- **Sheila Broflovski:** Jewish women are often portrayed as unattractive and neurotic as well, but unlike their male counterparts, they're more frequently presented as aggressive, overbearing, and prone to overreaction (Hidary 2010). For instance, on *South Park*, Kyle Broflovski's mother, Sheila, is regularly depicted as causing loud, angry riots over relatively trivial matters.
- **Homogenous:** This stereotype is that Jews are all the same. The reality is that Jews are divided across several lines, including but not limited to racial and religious traditions (Sephardic Jews from Spain, the Middle East, and North Africa and Ashkenazi Jews from Eastern Europe), religious observance (Orthodox, Reform, Conservative, Reconstructionist, and Renewal), and politics.
- **Dual Loyalty:** This stereotype suggests that Jews will be more loyal to their own kind than they are to the nation-states in which they live. Historically, this stereotype has manifested as claims that Jews are not capable of being fully American, British, French, Russian, German, and so on. Since the founding of the modern State of Israel in 1948, this stereotype sometimes manifests as insinuations that Jews are single-issue voters on Israel or that they are more loyal to that state than they are to their home countries. In reality, even on politics regarding Israel, it is important to note that Jews are not homogeneous. Rather, there is a wide spectrum from the American Israel Public Affairs Committee (AIPAC) and the Zionist Organization of America (ZOA) to J Street, IfNotNow, Jewish Voices for Peace (JVP), and Neturei Karta.

Racist stereotypes about Jews perpetuate harmful and inaccurate ideas. For instance, consider the Pittsburgh Tree of Life synagogue shooter's claims about Jews trying to "replace" white Christians with immigrants (an echo of the 2017 Charlottesville "Unite the Right" rally protesters shouting, "Jews will not replace us!" and a staple of so-called "Great Replacement Theory") or the 2022 Colleyville, Texas, synagogue hostage crisis.

One of the best ways to combat Jewish stereotypes is to speak to Jewish people directly about their faith and culture. Part of the Sheila Broflovski stereotype is that Jews are easily offended and that non-Jews need to walk on eggshells when asking questions. A good example of this is in the *Family Guy* episode "When You Wish Upon a Weinstein" (which is full of many of the Jewish stereotypes listed above). When Lois Griffin attends a synagogue service and tries to engage a Jewish woman in conversation, she repeatedly trips over her words, thinking that she has unintentionally offended the other woman: "Oh, we're not Jewish, but I hear you people have such lovely services. Oh my God, I didn't mean 'you people.' I didn't mean 'Oh *my* God' either. I know—I know he's your God, too." The Jewish woman's careful response, just a quiet "Shhh!" with the undertone of "you're more worked up about this than I am" implies that Lois, or anyone in her position, need not worry when genuinely trying to learn about Jews and their faith (MacFarlane, Zuckerman, and Blitt 2003, 14:00–14:18). One of the positive stereotypes that is pretty homogeneous about Jews is that they like teaching other people about their religion. Most would much prefer non-Jews to ask than to make bad assumptions, so please don't be afraid to ask.

Brad Serber

See Also: Essentialism; Intersectionality; Racist Stereotypes; Racist Stereotypes of Arab and Muslim People; Racist Stereotypes of Asian People; Racist Stereotypes of Black People; Stereotypes of Indigenous People; Racist Stereotypes of Latinx People

Further Reading

Anti-Defamation League (ADL). n.d. "Myth: Jews Use Christian Blood for Religious Rituals." Accessed October 25, 2024. https://antisemitism.adl.org/blood/.

Brodkin, Karen. 1998. *How Jews Became White Folks and What That Says About Race in America*. New Brunswick, NJ: Rutgers University Press.

Elvis, Toria. 2024. "Beyond the Stereotype: The Real Story of Jewish People and Money." *Medium*. Accessed October 25, 2024. https://medium.com/@toriaelvis/beyond-the-stereotype-the-real-story-of-jewish-people-and-money-6a00af15304b.

Hidary, Vanessa. 2010. "Hebrew Mamita." Slam poem, September 7, 3 min., 42 sec. https://www.youtube.com/watch?v=yAeWyGGTdEE.

Horn, Dara. 2022. *People Love Dead Jews: Reports from a Haunted Present*. New York: W.W. Norton & Co.

Kampeas, Ron. 2020. "US Census Poses a Dilemma for Jews: Are You White and What Are Your 'Origins?'" *The Times of Israel*. Accessed October 25, 2024. https://www.timesofisrael.com/us-census-poses-a-dilemma-for-jews-are-you-white-and-what-are-your-origins/.

Kiewe, Amos. 2011. *Confronting Anti-Semitism: Seeking an End to Hateful Rhetoric*. Leicester: Troubador Publishing.

MacFarlane, Seth, David Zuckerman, and Ricky Blitt, writers. 2003. *Family Guy*. Season 3, Episode 22. "When You Wish Upon a Weinstein." Aired November 9, Fox.

Maddow, Rachel. 2023. *Prequel: An American Fight Against Fascism*. New York: Crown.

Nadell, Pamela S. 2022. "Today in History: Antisemitism, an American Problem." *PBS*. Accessed October 25, 2024. https://www.pbs.org/wnet/exploring-hate/2022/03/14/today-in-history-antisemitism-an-american-problem/.

Nostra Aetate. October 28, 1965. Accessed October 30, 2024. https://www.vatican.va/archive/hist_councils/ii_vatican_council/documents/vat-ii_decl_19651028_nostra-aetate_en.html.

Ryan, Edward A. n.d. "Spanish Inquisition." *Encyclopedia Brittanica*. Accessed October 25, 2024. https://www.britannica.com/topic/Spanish-Inquisition.

Shere, Jeremy, Aaron Henne, Lisa Leff, and Pamela Nadell. 2021. *Adventures in Jewish Studies*. Episode 16, "The Protocols, Henry Ford, and The International Jew." *The Association for Jewish Studies*, March 11.

Podcast, 33 min., 35 sec. https://www.associationforjewishstudies.org/podcasts/the-protocols-henry-ford-and-the-international-jew-transcript.

United States Holocaust Memorial Museum (USHMM). n.d. "Why the Jews: History of Antisemitism." Accessed October 25, 2024. https://www.ushmm.org/antisemitism/what-is-antisemitism/why-the-jews-history-of-antisemitism.

Weisman, Jonathan. 2018. *(((Semitism))): Being Jewish in America in the Age of Trump*. New York: St. Martin's Press.

RACIST STEREOTYPES OF LATINX PEOPLE IN THE UNITED STATES

A racist stereotype is a generalized and simplified belief about a particular racial group—in this case, Latinx people. These stereotypes often have gendered and/or sexualized components that essentially disqualify Latinos from white US idealizations of manhood and disqualify Latinas from white US idealizations of womanhood—this ultimately creates and reinforces gendered and white supremacist hierarchies, privileges, and oppressions.

Racism and racist stereotypes about Latinx people in the United States are more focused on "culture" and less focused on "nationality" or "color" than other types of racism and racist stereotypes in the United States. This is largely because Central and South America are comprised by many countries and—due to European colonization of Central and South America—many Latinx people are white.

In the United States, racist stereotypes continue to "other" people of color and ethnic groups, marking them as different from the "normal" (i.e., European Americans), as foreigners (i.e., as unamerican), and as inferior to European Americans. At the same time, racist and ethnic stereotypes ultimately mark European-American whiteness as normal, as American, and as superior.

Below are brief descriptions of some of the most common racist stereotypes of Latinx people. This is not an exhaustive list but rather illustrates some of the most common racist stereotypes in US culture, media, and politics.

- **Machismo:** Latinos are often stereotyped as embodiments of machismo—a culture of sexism and male chauvinism exclusively associated with Latinos (Basham 1976). Stereotyping Latinos as machismos depicts Latino men as being excessively masculine, domineering, and having exaggerated beliefs in their own importance. This stereotype negatively depicts all Latinx cultures as backward, assuming that Latinos are more likely to be sexist than European American men, that Latinx communities treat women worse than US communities, and that Latinas are acculturated to such sexism and even consider sexist chauvinism normal and right (Brammer 2023).
- **Drug Lords:** During the 1980s, the US "War on Drugs" disproportionately focused on Black and Latinx communities. The media portrayed these communities as centers of criminal activity, especially associating Latino men with drug trafficking. This stereotype associates Latino men with crime—especially drug trafficking, gangs, and illegal immigration (Megía 2019).
- **Feisty Latina:** The "Feisty Latina" stereotype exotifies Latinas as sexy, hot-tempered women. It portrays Latinas as emotionally volatile, both in terms of love and anger (Barona 2018). This stereotype sexually objectifies Latinas, while dismissing them as overly emotional. Examples include characters like Gloria Delgado-Pritchett on *Modern Family* and Gabrielle Solis on *Desperate Housewives*.
- **Domestic/Manual Laborer:** These stereotypes imagine Latinx people as uneducated and capable only of physical labor. These stereotypes are gendered, associating Latinas with housekeeping jobs and Latinos with yardwork, agricultural work, and construction sites. Ignoring that these jobs are often the only types of jobs Latinx people can obtain in the United States, this stereotype imagines that Latinx people are specifically (and only) fit for hard labor.

- **Parasites:** This stereotype suggests that Latinx immigrants, specifically Mexicans, arrive in the United States just to take advantage of the social and economic benefits—and that they are stealing jobs and resources from US citizens. This stereotype became especially prominent during and after Trump's 2016 presidential campaign, in which he depicted Latinx immigrants as a threat to national well-being ("Mexican and Latino Stereotypes" 2024).

Racist stereotypes about Latinx people perpetuate harmful and inaccurate ideas. For instance, by sexualizing Latinas and imagining that Latinas accept, if not welcome, sexist behavior, these stereotypes perpetuate gendered violence against Latinas. Similarly, by imagining Latinos as violent, criminal, and dirty, these stereotypes pave the way for discrimination and oppression within the US justice system, de facto school and housing segregation, and so on.

Some of the first steps toward ending these racist stereotypes are being aware of them and calling them out when you see them in media or hear them in casual conversation. Bringing awareness to these stereotypes and naming them for what they are can help dispel their power in US culture.

Mariane Camargo

See Also: Colonization; Essentialism; Intersectionality; Racist Stereotypes; Racist Stereotypes of Arab and Muslim People; Racist Stereotypes of Asian People; Racist Stereotypes of Black People; Racist Stereotypes of Indigenous People; Racist Stereotypes of Jewish People

Further Reading

Barona, Juliana. 2018. "Stop Flinching! We Don't Bite: Why the 'Feisty' Latina Stereotype is Harmful." *Modern Brown Girl*, August 13, 2018. Accessed July 18, 2024. https://www.modernbrowngirl.com/blog/category/harmful-latina-stereotypes.

Basham, Richard. 1976. "Machismo." *Frontiers: A Journal of Women's Studies* 1, no. 2: 126–43.

Brammer, J. P. 2023. "Stereotype or Appropriate Diagnosis? Reluctantly Discussing Machismo." *De Los*, October 19, 2023. Accessed July 18, 2024. https://www.latimes.com/delos/story/2023-10-19/machismo-lgbtq-latino-community.

Hernandez, Rebecca. 2023. "The Misrepresentation of the Latine Community." *Nubian Message*, September 18, 2023. Accessed May 19, 2024. www.thenubianmessage.com/2023/09/18/13391/#:~:text=The%20most%20famous%20example%20being.

Megía, Carlos. 2019. "Latino Drug Dealers: The Clichéd Role that Spanish-Speaking Actors Willingly Accept." *El País*, October 8, 2019. Accessed July 18, 2024. https://english.elpais.com/elpais/2019/10/07/inenglish/1570461267_201013.html

Mesquita, Leah. 2023. "I Wish I Were a Spicy Latina." *The Arizona State Press*, October 17, 2023. Accessed August 14, 2024. www.statepress.com/article/2023/10/magazine-spicy-latina-culture.

"Mexican and Latino Stereotypes." 2024. *Jim Crow Museum*. Accessed July 18, 2024. https://jimcrowmuseum.ferris.edu/mexican.htm.

RADICAL FEMINISM

Radical feminism is a category of feminism that argues the root of women's oppression is due to the social domination women experience from men via patriarchal structures. These structures, such as social rights, laws, customs, and beliefs, privilege men and oppress women, according to radical feminists. In short, radical feminists assert women are oppressed by men through material means and the catalyst of this oppression is institutionalized patriarchy. Women's oppression is rooted in our psychology and social relations.

For example, in 1968 radical feminists protested the Miss America pageant to bring awareness to the sexism in beauty standards. During this protest material items such as dishcloths, girdles, and false eyelashes were tossed in a trash can, known as "freedom trash can," because of the material implications they carried for women. This event is often labeled as "bra-burning," though no bras were burned. Rather, items were placed in trash cans to symbolize that patriarchy cannot be reformed; rather, it must be dismantled to reach gender equality.

Marriage is also a complicated institution for radical feminists. Historically, marriage has made women the property of men (Barry 1984). Today marriage is still a vexing topic as often women do the majority of unpaid domestic labor in the home, known as the second shift.

History

The ideology and movement of radical feminism emerged in the late 1960s, and Kate Millett's work, *Sexual Politics*, is often cited as a key text to the movement's origins. Additionally, in 1970 Shulamith Firestone published *The Dialectic of Sex*, which asserts because women give birth, nurse, and often are the primary parent to raise children, they have been held in a class below men. Therefore, Firestone argues, women are not relegated to a class because they can give birth; rather, the world they give birth in creates material means that force them into a less-than-men position.

For example, still today women earn less than men, which is most commonly referred to as the gender wage gap. The logic of women staying home with children, as opposed to their male counterparts doing the same, is supported by paying women less to work and thereby encouraging women to stay home. But this condition is created by society to perpetuate gender inequality and could easily be remedied so anyone could stay home with children.

Many of the radical feminists who were writing and organizing during the 1960s and 1970s substantively changed US culture and significantly contributed to feminist and queer studies. For example, radical feminists such as Susan Brownmiller and Catherine MacKinnon worked to challenge intimate partner violence as naturalized in society. Andrea Dworkin wrote and spoke at length about the dangers of pornography for women. Monique Wittig and Gayle Rubin theorized feminist and queer studies. Mary Daly questioned the masculinization of God within Christian doctrines and retheorized a theology that does not rely on patriarchal values. Phyllis Chesler critiqued the assumptions that women are prone to madness, rethinking much of psychology's assumptions about women. Ti-Grace Atkinson advocated for women's sexual liberation and political lesbianism. And Carol Hanisch—who is known for the phrase, "the personal is political"—was famous for her activism, coleading the 1968 Miss America protest. These radical feminists and many more were foundational in organizations such as The Furies, Lavender Menace, New York Radical Women, Olivia Records, and the Redstockings. Their legacy of theory and activism continues to shape US feminisms.

Activism

Radical feminists are credited for introducing the use of consciousness-raising groups into the feminist movement. The purpose of consciousness raising was to create spaces where women could share their oppressive experiences with other women to understand how oppression is a collective experience and a result of repressive systems.

A tenant of radical feminist thought is that women should have complete bodily autonomy from men and structures that oppress them. Therefore, reproductive rights, violence against women, human trafficking, pornography, and rape are important topics that radical feminists address. The prevalence of women being objectified by society exemplifies that patriarchal ideas are embedded in culture.

Sarah Cooper

See Also: Bodily Autonomy; Consciousness Raising; Domestic Labor; Dworkin, Andrea; Feminization of Poverty; Patriarchy; Personal Is Political; The Redstockings and the Redstockings Manifesto; Reproductive Labor

Further Reading

Barry, Kathleen. 1984. *Female Sexual Slavery*. New York: New York University Press.
Bunch, Charlotte. 1972. "Lesbians in Revolt." *The Furies: Lesbian/Feminist Monthly*, January 1: 8–9.
Daly, Mary. 1978. *Gyn/Ecology: The Metaethics of Radical Feminism*. Boston: Beacon Press.
Dworkin, Andrea. 1974. *Intercourse*. New York: Free Press.
Gearheart, Sally Miller. 1982. "The Future – If There Is One – Is Female." *In Reweaving the Web of Life: Feminism and Nonviolence*, edited by Pam McAllister, 266–84. New Society Pub.
Hoagland, Sarah Lucia, and Julia Penelope, eds. 1992. *For Lesbians Only: A Separatist Anthology*. London: Onlywomen Press.
Lyon, Phyllis, and Del Martin. 1972. *Lesbian/Woman*. Volcano, CA: Volcano Press.
MacKay, Finn. 2015. *Radical Feminism: Feminist Activism in Movement*. London: Palgrave Macmillan.
Millet, Kate. 1970. *Sexual Politics*. New York: Columbia University Press.
Rubin, Gayle. 2011. "Blood Under the Bridge: Reflections on 'Thinking Sex.'" *GLQ: A Journal of Lesbian and Gay Studies*, 17, no. 1: 15–48.
Solanas, Valerie, 1968. *S.C.U.M. Manifesto*. New York: The Olympia Press Inc.
Wittig, Monique. 1992. *The Straight Mind and Other Essays*. Boston: Beacon Press.

RANKIN, JEANNETTE

Jeannette Rankin (1880–1972) was a suffragist, congresswoman, and a peace activist from Missoula, Montana. As a suffragist she helped make Montana one of the earliest states to grant women the right to vote. In 1916, she was elected as the first US congresswoman, before most women in the country could even vote. A controversial figure, her staunch pacifism led to controversy, particularly after she became the only member of Congress to vote against entering the Second World War.

Suffragist Jeannette Rankin was the first woman to be voted into the US House of Representatives in 1916 (Library of Congress).

As her biographer, Norma Smith (2002), notes, Rankin's feminism and pacifism were rooted in her deep concern for humanity, particularly children. As a former social worker, she saw children suffering but did not see the men in power doing much to help them. Based on this observation, Rankin persuaded many women who initially believed women should stay out of politics that women needed the right to vote so that they could vote to protect children. Throughout her life Rankin advocated for legislation and funding to help the many of the most vulnerable in society including reforms in foster and adoption programs, childcare, jail reform, food safety, and child labor laws. She stood against one of the most powerful mining companies in Montana because she believed miners deserved safe working conditions, despite knowing it would jeopardize her political career.

She was a firm pacifist, viewing war as simply answering violence with violence with limited long-term potential for peace. She was first elected to Congress shortly before they were asked to vote on whether the United States should enter the First World War, to which she voted "no." Despite the fact that forty-nine men in Congress also voted "no," newspapers focused on her "unmanly" vote (Smith 2002, 26 and 112). Critics of the suffrage movement used her vote as proof that women were too weak to be trusted with the vote. While Rankin was critiqued, there were many isolationists who supported her vote. She was elected to Congress again in 1940 where she again was forced to decide whether to vote for war after the attack on Pearl Harbor. In this case, she became the only person to vote against going to war. She argued her decision was based, in part, on the quickness of the decision to declare war before enough evidence was gathered to make an informed decision. Furthermore, she contended that, while she supported self-defense, she did not believe sending men to die in foreign lands would protect the American people. Rankin was reviled for her vote with critics calling her a "bitch," "old fossil," "Hitler aid," and a "disgrace and traitor" (Smith 2002, 184). She knew her vote would end her political career, yet she believed it was vital to her integrity to stand for what she believed was right rather than surrender under the pressure of the moment.

Feminist Perspectives of Jeannette Rankin

As a leader in the suffrage movement and the first woman in Congress in the United States, Rankin is an important figure in the feminist movement. The controversy around her war votes, however, has somewhat limited the attention given to her. Two Montanan-raised scholars, Shane Borrowman and Marcia Kmetz (2011), highlight the tension surrounding Rankin in Montana. By reflecting on their own educations, they demonstrate how Rankin's election is boasted as evidence of how Montana led the way in equality for women. They note, however, that Rankin's rhetoric and actions are largely ignored other than her war votes, which is framed as a source of shame for Montanans. Both Borrowman and Kmetz express concern about the silence, oversimplification, and hostility surrounding Rankin's rhetoric and decisions. They urge scholars and the public to learn more about Rankin's political career, which included not only peace advocacy but also universal suffrage, social change, and opposition to corporate greed.

In studying Rankin's suffrage rhetoric, feminist scholar Sara Hayden (1999) demonstrates how Rankin utilizes the conceptions of domestic ideology and the feminine style in her speeches. Hayden highlights how both men and women were anxious of how giving women the right to vote would disrupt traditional gender roles. Here, Rankin can be seen as using "strategic essentialism" by supporting a "domestic ideology" that defined women as being tied to domestic duties, while strategically using that tie as the reason women are needed to participate in politics. She argued that women could use their domestic knowledge to improve the lives of other women and children. Hayden notes that although this strategy reinforced strict gender roles that could limit women, it also offered a logical argument for expanding women's rights and power in a way that was not deemed threatening to men and women who were concerned gender roles would change if women got the right to vote.

Hayden (1999) also highlights how Rankin strategically shifted her rhetoric depending on her audience. When speaking to a mixed audience of men and women, she took on a more feminine style of speaking. Karlyn Kohrs Campbell (1983, 1989, 1995) suggests that although there were norms regarding proper feminine behavior that limited how women could speak during the suffrage movement, they were able to use a feminine style that allowed them to speak effectively without being perceived as a threat to social norms. For example, when speaking to a mixed gender audience, Rankin spoke to her audience as peers rather than taking on her own sense of authority; she also utilized personal experiences, applied a personal tone, and made requests and suggestions rather than demands, which are all classic hallmarks of the feminine rhetorical style. Moreover, she focused on how gaining the vote would help Montana women help those *outside* of Montana, making their voting appear more about helping others than changing Montana. As Hayden (1999) argues, such an approach allowed her to make logical and emotional appeals about the benefits of women voting in a way that was "less threatening to men" (94). Yet, in speeches to a women-only audience, Rankin largely abandoned this "feminine style" instead opting to use fewer personal anecdotes, making more bold claims such as the need for women to "force legislatures" to make changes to help children of Montana when they get the vote, and utilizing direct calls to action.

Rankin offers a potent example of the complexities women suffrage and political leaders faced in the 1900s. Women such as Rankin found their actions could be used against the whole suffrage movement when critics deemed them "proof" of women's failure to engage properly in politics. They had to reinforce some patriarchal ideologies in order to ease concerns that women's right to vote would not alter gender roles. They had to choose their language and tone carefully depending on who they were speaking to. While they needed to persuade women to join the movement, they had to be careful to not appear too threatening to the men who had the power to make suffrage happen. As an upper-class, educated, white woman raised in Montana where gender roles were often more blended due to ranch and farm life (Jameson 1984), Rankin had more access to speaking to the public than many women. She used careful rhetorical strategies to speak to different audiences in order to achieve suffrage in Montana. As a staunch pacifist, she was often encouraged by those close to her to vote for war to stave off critique but chose to stand by her conscious to maintain her integrity rather than buckle under social pressure. Feminist scholars have urged the need to explore her rhetoric and politics in more depth.

Kristina M. Lee

See Also: Chisholm, Shirley; Domestic Labor; Hegemonic Masculinity; Labor Activism; Nineteenth Amendment; Strategic Essentialism; Suffrage; Temperance

Further Readings

Borrowman, Shane, and Marcia Kmetz. 2011. "Divided We Stand: Beyond Burkean Identification." *Rhetoric Review* 30, no. 3: 275–92. https://www.jstor.org/stable/23064027.

Campbell, Karlyn Kohrs. 1983. "Femininity and Feminism: To Be or Not to be a Woman." *Communication Quarterly* 31, no. 2: 101–8. https://doi.org/10.1080/01463378309369493.

Campbell, Karlyn Kohrs. 1989. *Man Cannot Speak for Her: A Critical Study of Early Feminist Rhetoric*, vol. I. New York: Praeger.

Campbell, Karlyn Kohrs. 1995. "Gender and Genre: Loci of Invention and Contradiction in the Earliest Speeches by Women." *Quarterly Journal of Speech* 57, no. 4: 479–95. https://doi.org/10.1080/00335639509384130.

Hayden, Sara. 1999. "Negotiating Femininity and Power in the Early Twentieth Century West: Domestic Ideology and Feminine Style in Jeannette Rankin's Suffrage Rhetoric." *Communication Studies* 50, no. 2: 83–102. https://doi.org/10.1080/10510979909388476.
Jameson, Elizabeth. 1984. "Women as Workers, Women as Civilizers: True Womanhood in the American West." *Frontiers: A Journal of Women Studies* 7, no. 3: 1–8. https://doi.org/10.2307/3346233.
Lopach, James J., and Jean A. Luckowski. 2005. *Jeannette Rankin: A Political Woman.* Boulder: University Press of Colorado.
Smith, Norma. 2002. *Jeannette Rankin.* Helena, MT: Montana Historical Society Press.

RAPE CULTURE

Rape culture is the pervasive idea that violence—especially against women—is normal, even sexy. By referring to rape culture as a "culture," feminists highlight now society participates in sexual violence through jokes, music, films, television programs, and so on that make sexual violence seem funny, normal, and romantic.

For example, feminist media scholar Casey Ryan Kelly points out that the *Twilight* series epitomized love and teenage romance for a whole generation, yet the romance between Edward Cullen (a vampire) and Bella Swan is marked by domination and sexual violence. Edward watches Bella while she sleeps, disables her truck to prevent her from visiting her friend Jacob, lies to her, controls who she can see, and makes important decisions without her. When they have sex for the first time, it is violent. Edward's supernatural strength destroys the bed and Bella is left "covered in bruises and contusions." Yet the soundtrack during this violent sexual encounter is "soft" and "sentimental," eroticizing sexual violence as a depiction of love and pleasure. Afterward, Bella describes the encounter as the best sex possible. Together, the "romanticized portrait of Edward's manipulative behavior," the physical violence of their sex scene, and "Bella's enjoyment of pain during sex" combine to create a message that "women derive pleasure from physical and emotional abuse" (Kelly 2016, 36).

Twilight's romanticization of sexual violence is hardly an isolated example. Rather, *Twilight* is a product of its culture and whole swaths of romance novels, pornography, music videos, and films reinforce the same message, making violence seem normal, romantic, and sexy. Even advertisements routinely participate in rape culture. For instance, Budweiser's #UpForWhatever campaign promoted Bud Light as the "perfect" beer for "removing 'no' from your vocabulary for the night," and Domino's Pizza ran an artisan pizza campaign with the tagline, "No is the new yes" (Kutner 2015; Zerlina 2023). Both of these campaigns make light of consent, suggesting that an enthusiastic "yes" is unnecessary for pleasure. By drawing attention to rape culture, feminists connect the dots between this type of messaging, instances such as the men's march through Yale's campus where fraternity brothers chanted "No means yes, yes means anal," and statistics demonstrating that at least a quarter of women and almost 4 percent of men experience rape—and that the statistics for sexual harassment are much higher (Polk 2016; Centers for Disease Control 2022). Notably, these statistics only measure what people recognize as violence, leaving out all the instances of sexual violence where people considered the violence normal and therefore unremarkable and unreportable.

Feminist Responses to Rape Culture

By mobilizing against rape culture, feminists move from asking, "who would commit such a crime?" to "what type of society would produce people who commit such crimes?" (Johnson 2017, 24). This shifts the conversation from individuals to US culture—and this shift helps make patterns within sexual violence more visible. For instance, the originator of the #MeToo movement Tarana Burke (2018) consistently argues that sexual violence is not about individuals, it is about power. Here, Burke is pointing out that there is a pattern within US sexual violence: people with less power and privilege are targeted, and power and privilege often enable perpetrators to enact this violence. For example, as organizational scholars Tiffany Dykstra-Devette and Carlos Tarin (2019) explain, workplace sexual harassment does not occur merely because an individual chooses to harass; rather, it is the result of a "toxic workplace culture" where an individual experiences certain privileges and the workplace's policies, behaviors, and attitudes enable the situation. For instance, a workplace manager might sexually harass an intern or a temporary employee. Clearly, the harasser is at fault, yet by thinking of this scenario from a rape culture framework, feminists can recognize that power and privilege—and lack thereof—make this sexual harassment possible. The power difference between the manager and the intern or temporary employee and the difficulty that an intern or temporary employee would have reporting harassment are key components of this situation and they facilitate or sponsor an environment in which sexual violence can easily occur.

Feminist researchers such as V. Jo Hsu (2019) vertically map sexual violence, revealing the hierarchical connections among those causing harm, those experiencing harm, and the cultural norms, policies, and institutions that structure this violence. For example, as Aaron Jeckell, Elizabeth Copenhaver, and Alex Diamond (2018) explain, fraternities and men's athletic teams often haze new members in ways that include male-male sexual violence. Consider, for instance, a hazing attack in which five seniors on the Wheaton College football team abducted a first-year member of the team. The victim recounts that they threatened to rape him, attempted to sodomize him, and left him partially naked in a field for the night—in addition to severely injuring him and duct-taping his arms, legs, and chest (Stack and Hauser 2017). Made aware of the attack, Wheaton College originally found the attackers' statements of innocence credible and allowed them to remain enrolled and continue playing football—until they were arrested on criminal charges, to which they eventually pled guilty (ABC News 2017; CBS News 2019). Vertically mapping this violence demonstrates how power operates within teams and institutions and that sexual violence expresses power—the powerful prey upon the powerless within a social hierarchy.

Recognizing how rape culture enables the powerful to hurt those with less power further reveals patterns in sexual violence in the United States. Members of the LGBTQ+ community, people of color, and undocumented immigrants experience increased levels of sexual violence in the United States (Curry 2019; National Alliance to End Sexual Violence 2023; Human Rights Campaign 2023). These people are targeted because they have limited access to resources and because they are already stereotyped as untrustworthy in US culture making it less likely that they will be believed if they report the sexual violence committed against them. Legal scholar Kimberlé Crenshaw notes that Black women are vulnerable to sexual violence "not only because of racial bias against them, but also because of stereotypes"; for instance, that Black women "expect less nurturing," are "more willing to have sex," and that "no one will believe them." The combination of racist bias and these racist/gendered stereotypes marks Black women "as prey to men of all races" (Crenshaw 2019, 19).

Activist Responses to Rape Culture

Feminist activists resist rape culture, attempting to change culture itself so that sexual violence becomes less common. For instance, Laura Bates (2017) launched the Everyday Sexism Project to raise awareness of the way sexism affects people's lives. This digital activism space reveals the prevalence of sexual violence—revealing rape culture itself. Similarly, the feminist activism of #YesAllWomen and #MeToo revealed the widespread prevalence of sexual violence. Organizations such as Alteristic's Green Dot for Colleges directly applies feminist research on rape culture in order to reduce sexual violence on college campuses in the United States. Instead of treating men as "potential perpetrators" and women as "potential victims," Green Dot works to change college cultures, treating all "students, staff, administrators, and faculty as allies" in order to create a culture where everyone "does their small part" as bystanders to create a "safe campus culture that is intolerant of violence" (Alteristic 2023).

Ultimately, rape culture makes sexual violence seem normal, enabling those with more power and privilege to prey upon those with less. Feminists vertically map rape culture, revealing how power and privilege inform sexual violence, and work to change US culture so that people can recognize sexual violence as violence and resist it.

Sarah Kornfield

See Also: Burke, Tarana; Compulsory Heterosexuality; Crenshaw, Kimberlé; Rape Myths

Further Reading

Alteristic. 2023. "Green Dot for Colleges." Accessed October 9, 2023. https://alteristic.org/services/green-dot/green-dot-colleges/.

ABC News. 2017. "Wheaton College Doubted Football Player's Story of Alleged Hazing: Documents." *ABC News*, September 22, 2017, https://abcnews.go.com/US/documents-show-wheaton-college-doubted-story-alleged-hazing/story?id=50023705.

Bates, Laura. 2017. "What I have Learned from Five Years of Everyday Sexism." *The Guardian*, April 17, 2017. https://www.theguardian.com/lifeandstyle/2017/apr/17/what-i-have-learned-from-five-years-of-everyday-sexism.

Burke, Tarana. 2018. "MeToo is a Movement, Not a Moment." Filmed November, 2018, at TED Video. Video. https://www.ted.com/talks/tarana_burke_me_too_is_a_movement_not_a_moment.

CBS News. 2019. "Final Wheaton Football Player Pleads Guilty, Concluding the 2016 Hazing Case." *CBS News*, March 22, 2019. https://www.cbsnews.com/chicago/news/last-wheaton-football-player-pleads-guilty/.

Centers for Disease Control and Prevention. 2022. "Violence Prevention." Last modified June 22, 2022. https://www.cdc.gov/violenceprevention/sexualviolence/fastfact.html.

Crenshaw, Kimberlé. 2019. "We Still Have Not Learned from Anita Hill's Testimony." *UCLA Journal of Gender and Law* 26, no. 1: 17–20. https://doi.org/10.5070/L3261044346.

Curry, Tommy J. 2019. "Expendables for Whom: Terry Crews and the Erasure of Black Male Victims of Sexual Assault and Rape." *Women's Studies in Communication* 42, no. 3: 287–307. https://doi.org/10.1080/07491409.2019.1641874.

Dykstra-Devette, Tiffany and Carlos Tarin. 2019. "Isolating Structures of Sexual Harassment in Crowdsourced Data on Higher Education." *Women's Studies in Communication* 42, no. 3: 371–93. https://doi.org/10.1080/07491409.2019.1641873.

Hsu, V. Jo Hsu. 2019. "(Trans)forming #MeToo: Toward a Networked Response to Gender Violence." *Women's Studies in Communication* 42, no. 3: 269–86. https://doi.org/10.1080/07491409.2019.1630697.

Human Rights Campaign. 2023. "Sexual Assault and the LGBTQ Community." Accessed October 9, 2023. https://www.hrc.org/resources/sexual-assault-and-the-lgbt-community.

Jeckell, Aaron Slone, Elizabeth Anne Copenhaver, and Alex Benjamin Diamond. 2018. "The Spectrum of Hazing and Peer Sexual Abuse in Sports: A Current Perspective." *Sports Health* 10, no. 6: 558–64. https://doi: 10.1177/1941738118797322.

Johnson, Allan. 2017. "Patriarchy, The System: An It, Not a He, A Them, or an Us." In *Introduction to Women's Studies and Sexuality Studies Interdisciplinary and Intersectional Approaches*, edited by L. Ayu Saraswati, Barbara Shaw, and Heather Rellihan, 23–31. New York: Oxford University Press.

Kelly, Casey Ryan. 2016. *Abstinence Cinema: Virginity and the Rhetoric of Sexual Purity in Contemporary Film*. New Brunswick, NJ: Rutgers University Press.

Kutner, Jenny. 2015. "'The Perfect Beer for Removing 'No' From Your Vocabulary': Bud Light Apologizes for Avoidable Tone-Deaf Tagline." *Salon.com*, April 28, 2015. https://www.salon.com/2015/04/28/the_perfect_beer_for_removing_%E2%80%98no%E2%80%99_from_your_vocabulary_bud_light_apologizes_for_avoidable_tone_deaf_tagline/.

National Alliance to End Sexual Violence. 2023. "Racism and Rape." Accessed October 9, 2023, https://endsexualviolence.org/where_we_stand/racism-and-rape/.
Polk, Sam. 2016. "How Wall Street Bro Talk Keeps Women Down." *NYTimes.com*, July 7, 2016, https://www.nytimes.com/2016/07/10/opinion/sunday/how-wall-street-bro-talk-keeps-women-down.html.
Stack, Liam and Christine Hauser. 2017. "Wheaton College Football Players Charged with Violent Hazing Attack," *NYTimes.com*, September 19, 2017. https://www.nytimes.com/2017/09/19/us/wheaton-college-hazing.html.
Zerlina. 2012. "Domino's Pizza Thinks Rape is a Joke." *Feministing.com.* Accessed October 9, 2023. http://feministing.com/2012/07/10/dominos-pizza-thinks-rape-is-a-joke/.

RAPE MYTHS

Rape myths are widely held beliefs about rape that are quite simply false. Rape myths are harmful because they can make it hard for survivors to recognize their experiences as rape, to understand that they are not to blame for what happened, and to get help. Moreover, rape myths are harmful because they can prevent the rest of society—friends, family, school administrators, authority figures, police officers, lawyers, judges, and legislators—from helping survivors, enacting justice, and changing policies and cultural norms to address and prevent rape.

In the United States, some of the most common rape myths are (1) that the survivor was asking for it or led someone on; (2) that the perpetrator didn't mean to; (3) that rape is extremely rare; (4) that most reports of rape are false or malicious—spread by women who are just trying to hurt good men; (5) that a specific instance wasn't *really* rape; (6) that there are very few rapists but they are responsible for all the instances of rape; and (7) that men cannot be raped (Payne, Lonsway, and Fitzgerald 1999, 59). These rape myths "coalesce" into a general belief that most "reports of sexual violence" are false, "casting an aura of suspicion over all disclosures of sexual violence" (Kornfield and Jones 2022, 1660).

However, the reverse is actually true. The vast majority (between 90 and 98 percent) of rapes reported to the police are accurate (Kornfield and Jones 2022, 1660; Lisak et al. 2010). In reality, rape is widespread and 80 percent of the time, it is perpetrated by someone the survivor knows—such as a friend, family member, coworker, acquaintance, or romantic partner. Approximately one in five women and one in seventy-one men are raped during their lifetimes (National Sexual Violence Resource Center 2015).

Rape myths hurt survivors. They help create cultures—replete with laws, police policies, sentencing standards, and so on—that make it harder for survivors to obtain justice and more likely that rape and sexual violence will remain widespread. Feminists refer to this as "rape culture."

Rape myths particularly affect Black women and other women of color, making them more at risk and less likely to be believed and thus obtain justice when they report rape. Here, rape myths interact with racist stereotypes—such as the geisha for Asian/Asian American women, the "feisty/sexy" stereotype for Latinx women, and the Jezebel stereotype for Black women—that imply women of color are inherently sexy, always want sex, and are excited by violent sex. The combination of rape myths and these racist stereotypes "marks" Black women and other women of color "as prey to men of all races," making them more likely to be targeted for sexual violence and less likely to be believed when they report sexual violence (Crenshaw 2019, 19).

While men experience rape at a lower rate than women in the United States, it is important to understand how ideals for and assumptions about masculinity interact with rape myths. One of the prevalent rape myths is that men cannot be raped (Curry 2019). This rape myth speaks to a basic assumption about what it means to "be a man." Men are typically stereotyped as being strong and in control and *always* wanting sex from women. So if a woman initiates sex (even violently) the assumption is that the man is going to want it—or else, he isn't "really" a man.

Relatedly, since experiencing sexual violence is associated with women, men who experience sexual violence are perceived as being *like women* because they (1) didn't want sex and (2) experience the same crime/subordination that many women experience. Here, we can see that experiencing sexual violence is actually one of the defining features of being a woman in contemporary Western cultures. Moreover, treating a man like a woman is one of the clearest and most effective ways to discipline or subordinate him—making it obvious that he holds less power, is less important, and is less of a "man" than other men. This enacts a clear hierarchy in which men and masculinity are considered more powerful and better than women and femininity. Moreover, since storylines about male victims of sexual violence are often played for laughs in entertainment media, it becomes clear that laughing at men is a clear sign of denigrating them—of treating them as being unworthy of respect and unable to wield authority—in Western cultures.

As such, the rape myth that men cannot be raped and the rape jokes often seen in popular films and stand-up comedy that make light of sexual violence against men (especially same-sex violence within prisons) often reassert what it means to be a "real" man and in ways that continue to subordinate women and everyone considered to be "like" women. Essentially, by making light of sexual violence against men and by laughing at male victims of sexual violence, rape cultures perpetuate the assumptions that "real" men are tough, powerful, always want (heterosexual) sex, and always initiate sex—and that everyone else is "less than" by comparison, even to the point of deserving violence that "puts them in their place."

Sarah Kornfield

See Also: Crenshaw, Kimberlé; Hegemonic Masculinity; #MeToo; Rape Culture; Violence Against Women Act (1994)

Further Reading

Crenshaw, Kimberlé. 2019. "We Still Have Not Learned from Anita Hill's Testimony." *UCLA Journal of Gender and Law* 26, no. 1: 17–20. https://doi.org/10.5070/L3261044346.

Curry, Tommy J. 2019. "Expendables for Whom: Terry Crews and the Erasure of Black Male Victims of Sexual Assault and Rape." *Women's Studies in Communication* 42, no. 3: 287–307. https://doi.org/10.1080/07491409.2019.1641874.

Kornfield, Sarah, and Hannah Jones. 2022. "#MeToo on TV: Popular Feminism and Episodic Sexual Violence. *Feminist Media Studies* 22, no. 7: 1657–72. https://doi: 10.1080/14680777.2021.1900314.

Lisak, David, Lori Gardinier, Sarah Nicksa, and Ashley Cote. 2010. "False Allegations of Sexual Assault: An Analysis of Ten Years of Reported Cases." *Violence Against Women* 16, no. 2: 1318–34. https://doi:10.1177/1077801210387747.

National Sexual Violence Resource Center. 2015. "Statistics about Sexual Violence." Accessed March 29, 2024. https://www.google.com/url?sa=t&source=web&rct=j&opi=89978449&url=https://www.nsvrc.org/sites/default/files/publications_nsvrc_factsheet_media-packet_statistics-about-sexual-violence_0.pdf&ved=2ahUKEwi1ztHknZqFAxWRjYkEHdH4DTgQFnoECA8QAQ&usg=AOvVaw0EkhJkasp7g-_Nkj7yrhRm.

Payne, Diana, Kimberly A. Lonsway, and Louise F. Fitzgerald. 1999. "Rape Myth Acceptance: Exploration of Its Structure and Its Measurement Using the Illinois Rape Myth Acceptance Scale." *Journal of Research in Personality* 33, no. 1: 27–68. https://doi:10.1006/jrpe.1998.2238.

THE REDSTOCKINGS AND THE REDSTOCKINGS MANIFESTO

Redstockings is a radical feminist organization launched in January 1969 "To Defend and Advance the Women's Liberation Agenda." The group, sometimes known as Redstockings of the Women's Liberation Movement, was founded by Ellen Willis and Shulamith Firestone after the breakup of the short-lived New York Radical Women. The Redstockings survives online, as does its Redstockings Manifesto, probably its most famous and most reprinted document (Redstockings 1969).

The organization's name incorporates red, associated with leftist and revolutionary politics (although Redstockings accuse socialists, including socialist feminists, of privileging Marxist-type class struggle over women's liberation), and bluestocking, a nineteenth-century term used to ridicule feminist intellectuals. Consistent with the manifesto genre generally and the feminist version particularly, the Manifesto used strong, aggressive language in urging women to unite to reject male oppression, "the oldest, most basic form of domination." It explicitly declared its goal to expose the sexist foundation of social-political institutions, which it regarded as "tools of the oppressors," as a means to develop a consciousness across all women as an oppressed class. The concept of women's liberation therefore had, for radical feminists, a highly specific meaning—it was not a reference generally to the "women's movement" but a reference, indeed a demand, for women's liberation from patriarchy, capitalism, and oppression by men.

Early Actions

Within a month of its founding, Redstockings disrupted a hearing of a New York legislative committee that was considering abortion law reform; both mainstream and feminist media covered in detail the drama. Criticizing the committee for inviting fourteen men and one woman (a nun) to testify as experts, Redstockings members argued for repealing a law banning abortion, not simply liberalizing it by allowing abortion in cases of rape, incest, or when a woman's health was at risk (Asbury 1969, 42). Redstockings soon held its own open "hearing" on abortion, with its own "true experts": twelve women who had had illegal abortions. The Redstockings became famous for their abortion rights "speakouts" and "zaps," a public and often raucous form of political direct action, which was practiced beginning in the 1970s in the United States. *Ms.* magazine cofounder and coeditor Gloria Steinem, who had an abortion at age twenty-two, wrote that covering that first Redstockings abortion "hearing" was a milestone in her feminist activism, although her *New York* magazine article about the "rock-bottom, personal truth-telling" event was objective (1983, 17–18). The Redstockings participated in many dramatic protests, especially against Miss America beauty pageants and advertising that objectified and/or exploited women's bodies, as well as commemorating the twentieth anniversary of their first speakout with a major event.

The membership and organization changed often. The New York group's approximately twenty members split up in 1970 but reformed in 1973 with some of the original members, including Kathie Sarachild, who wrote or developed many crucial Redstockings documents and policies. Ellen Willis, working as a journalist and known for her criticism of the sexual puritanism of anti-pornography feminists, was barely involved with the new Redstockings. Firestone, who had designed Redstockings' logo, left to form—with other radical separatists—the group the New York Radical Feminists (which attributed the oppression of women to men's egos, rather than men's power) and then, after a falling out with that group's leadership and organization, left that group, too.

In 1975, consistent with its confrontational spirit and building on an investigation reported elsewhere, the Redstockings first presented and then published a lengthy press release accusing Gloria Steinem of working for the CIA many years before: Steinem had served as director of the Independent Research Service, an organization secretly funded by what turned out to be the CIA. In that role, Steinem also worked to send non-Communist American students to the 1959 World Youth Festival. Many feminist publications exchanged subscriptions, so the accusations gained a lot of traction. Redstockings also suggested that *Ms.* magazine, which Steinem cofounded and coedited, was both a government tool and a way for Steinem to decenter and deauthorize radical feminism and replace it with her more centrist mainstream version. In letters sent to five feminist newspapers that had covered the allegations, Steinem said she was hurt and angry at the McCarthyite style of the accusation, noting that "denying false and fantastic charges does absolutely nothing but spread false and fantastic charges" (1975, 6). Nevertheless, she denied being a CIA employee or providing the CIA with information; she did repeat an earlier acknowledgment that the foundations that backed the youth festival got funding from the CIA (22–3). Analyzing the story, the editorial collective that ran the long-running feminist publication *off our backs* (*OOB*) found no evidence that Steinem was a CIA agent and asserted that "a number of unsupported assumptions are offered as support for extremely shaky conclusions" (*OOB* 1975a, 8). On the other hand, *OOB* commended Redstockings for their courage and willingness to make themselves vulnerable by calling Steinem to account and concluded the unsavory association demanded a public explanation. *OOB* agreed *Ms.* was a capitalist, commercial enterprise (*OOB* 1975b, 8). *Big Mama Rag*, a feminist monthly newspaper also run by a collective, however, wondered if the lengthy attack on Steinem was in the spirit of feminist dialogue (Woodwoman 1975, 5). And Willis—one of the Redstockings' cofounders—resigned from her position as a *Ms.* contributing editor.

Consciousness Raising

Redstockings members practiced and advocated "consciousness raising" (CR). Already in 1967, members of New York Radical Women, including Firestone and Sarachild (who coined the phrase "Sisterhood Is Powerful"), began meeting to discuss and analyze issues in their own lives, including how they experienced oppression. By linking their individual feelings and experiences to broader structures, they aimed to raise their personal and thus collective consciousness. In 1968, at the First National Women's Liberation Conference, Sarachild (1978 [1975], 147) presented *A Program for Feminist Consciousness Raising*. Many women's liberation groups, including Redstockings, advocated CR, sometimes described as "bitch sessions," as a means through which women would come to understand that problems they assumed were "personal" and individual (rape, marital conflict, access to abortion) were widely shared and systematic. That is, the personal is political. The premise of CR, Sarachild wrote, was that feelings are meaningful and worth analyzing because they speak to a common situation. The goal was not sharing for the sake of individual problem-solving and therapy. The goal was to use pooled feelings and experiences to generate new ideas, which would lead to actions. Sarachild insisted that what counts in CR are results: radical truths lead to radical actions (1978 [1975], 147–8). The methods of CR involve going to the original sources, going to women themselves, and basing theory and strategy on what they say about their experiences. The Manifesto included this as crucial: questioning any ideologies or generalizations, as they are products of men's supremacist culture.

Redstockings positions were controversial in several respects. Redstockings opposed lesbian separatism because they regarded relationships with men as a crucial way to engage in feminist struggle, and they opposed cultural feminism, which they argued failed to engage in political struggle. Redstockings claimed to appreciate lesbianism, albeit as a political identity, but opposed homosexuality among men, which they regarded as rejecting women. Meanwhile, they dismissed liberal feminism and its equality/equal rights notions, which they claimed manifested in the thinking of the National Organization for Women (NOW) as reformist and ignoring male supremacy. The lesbian activist and novelist Rita Mae Brown, for example, joined the Redstockings but quit because of its lack of commitment to lesbians; she worked for NOW briefly and quit for the same reason (Faderman 2015, 232).

Meanwhile, the Redstockings were, as were many women's liberation groups of the time, largely white. In 2006 Carol Hanisch (2006) responded quite passionately to the accusation, which she took to be unfair, that Redstockings were racist. Hanisch's post angrily asked what these "Jenny-come-latelys" (not that the criticism had not been raised before) have done to combat racism:

> Have they risked their lives and careers, as so many of us did, and many instances still do, to fight racism? We did something about racism, we didn't just talk about it. . . . Somehow I never hear any convincing examples from our critics of just HOW we were racist, except that the WLM [Women's Liberation Movement] was mostly WHITE.

In 1981 the Redstockings announced a plan to become a grassroots women's liberation "think tank" in order to propose and test solutions as well as expose problems. More controversially, at the same meeting, it announced it was abandoning its commitment to a flat leaderless structure: henceforth, "voting and public spokesperson power would be based on experience, track record, and common political understanding, as well as demonstrated organizational and political commitment" (Giardina 2013, xvi).

Writing and Building an Archive

Essays by Redstockings members appeared in their journal *Feminist Revolution*, soon collected and republished in an anthology, *Feminist Revolution.* The journal carried the attack on Steinem and later the Redstockings' response to her response, but these particular articles were excised from the book, published in 1978. Random House gave in to Steinem after she threatened a libel suit, with the support of other powerful people, including Katharine Graham, publisher of the *Washington Post* and a friend of Steinem. As a result, the Redstockings published a booklet with the excised articles, some of the documentary evidence, and related materials and gave it to anyone who bought the book. The introduction to these materials, which remain available online, insists, "Gloria Steinem, media-corporate backed spokesperson of a 'women's movement' . . . weakened by the suppression of radical ideas and actions so vital to its beginnings (and beginning again), has been able to deny the public's right to know" (Redstockings 1979, 2). "The Redstockings Manifesto" and Patricia Mainardi's famous Redstockings essay, "The Politics of Housework," were included in the widely used and widely cited anthology *Sisterhood Is Powerful: An Anthology of Writings from the Women's Liberation Movement*, edited by Robin Morgan (1970). In the 1980s, the organization also launched the Redstockings Newspacket, a fast, informal way of sharing theoretical ideas, news of what Redstockings members were doing and information about Redstockings history, and participation at various events. The Newspacket also emphasized collaborative, "non-rip-off" consciousness; readers were asked to pledge to credit the Newspacket when they used its contents (Giardina 2013, xvi). In 2001, Redstockings self-published a spiral-bound report called *Confronting the Myth of America: Women's Liberation and National Health Care.*

In 1989 the group established a project, directed by Sarachild with substantial help from allies in Gainesville, Florida, to make widely available the Women's Liberation Archives for Action—radical feminist papers and original organizing materials, including pamphlets, broadsides, journals, and audiotapes. The Redstockings argued these materials corroborated the then virtually ignored impact of the Women's Liberation Movement organizers in galvanizing the renewed feminist upswell in the United States. In particular, the Redstockings asserted that radical feminism was the main engine of the Women's Liberation Movement's rapid spread, and that if its revolutionary practices were forgotten, its successes could be rolled back (Redstockings 2025). The project also circulates new theory on what to do about women's oppression. In 2009 the group worked with a commercial company to microfilm nearly all the public documents from radical women's liberation and feminist campaigners of the late 1960s and early 1970s. The microfilm included an "Introduction" by history professor and Redstockings member Carol Giardina (2013) that provided a history of Redstockings through 2013.

An independent group called Redstockings West started in San Francisco in 1969. Redstockings groups also formed elsewhere, including, starting in 1970, in Denmark and Iceland, with similar emphases on CR and analyses of and resistance to patriarchy. Their closest collaborators were radical feminists in Gainesville, Florida; in the 1980s, the Gainesville allies helped them distribute the Redstockings Women's Liberation Archives for Action (Brown 2015, 18).

More recently, the group launched a project to make available, through the Women's Liberation Archives for Action, additional papers and original source material about radical organizing. These build on the principle of "history for activist use" and the motto "Building on What's Been Won by Knowing What's Been Done" (Redstockings 2025). The project also puts out new theorizing on women's oppression and what to do about it. The group's website is still active and houses numerous documents and links to audio and video related to its activities; it appears to have been last updated in 2016 in reference to opposing sexist ads in New York City (Redstockings 2016). Sarachild is the only original Redstockings member still active. Following the election of Donald Trump as US president, Redstockings worked with the National Women's Liberation to organize the Women's Strike March in January 2017 (Fahs 2018).

Linda Steiner and Stine Eckert

See Also: Abortion; Consciousness Raising; Liberal Feminism; Marxist Feminism; National Organization for Women (NOW); The Personal Is Political; Radical Feminism; Socialism

Further Reading

Asbury, Edith Evans. 1969. "Women Break Up Abortion Hearing." *New York Times*, February 14, 1969. https://www.nytimes.com/1969/02/14/archives/women-break-up-abortion-hearing-shouts-for-repeal-of-law-force.html.

Brown, Jenny. 2015. "'This Oppresses Women' Stickers Go Viral." *Gainesville Iguana* 29, no. 7/8: 18. https://ufdc.ufl.edu/UF00073860/00072/pdf.

Faderman, Lillian. 2015. *The Gay Revolution: The Story of Struggle*. New York: Simon and Schuster.

Fahs, Breanne. 2018. *Firebrand Feminism: The Radical Lives of Ti-Grace Atkinson, Kathie Sarachild, Roxanne Dunbar-Ortiz, and Dana Densmore*. Seattle: University of Washington Press.

Giardina, Carol. 2013. "The Redstockings Women's Liberation Archives for Action." *The Redstockings Organizational Collection*. https://womenwhatistobedone.wordpress.com/wp-content/uploads/2013/09/redstockings-part-1-guide-carol-giardina-intro1.pdf.

Hanisch, Carol. 2006. "'The Personal is Political,' Attacking Women, Carnival of Feminists 17, and What the Heck." *Women's Space*. Originally posted June 1, 2006 (reposted June 22, 2006). https://redstockings.org/~rs/images/stories/redstockings/ClassOneReadings/10%20-%20reflections%20on%20the%201960s%20womens%20liberation%20movement%20as%20racist%20carol%20hanisch.pdf.

Morgan, Robin, ed. 1970. *Sisterhood Is Powerful: An Anthology of Writings from the Women's Liberation Movement*. New York: Random House.

OBB. 1975a. "Investigation." *off our backs* 5, no. 6 (July 8): 10–11.

OBB. 1975b. "Redstockings Statement." *off our backs* 5, no. 6 (July 8–9): 28–33.
Redstockings. 1969. "The Redstockings Manifesto." July 7. https://www.redstockings.org/index.php/rs-manifesto.
Redstockings. 1978 [1975]. *Feminist Revolution*. New York: Random House. https://www.redstockings.org/index.php/main/feminist-revolution.
Redstockings. 1979. "Major Articles Censored from the 1978 Random House Edition of Redstockings' Feminist Revolution." https://www.redstockings.org/images/stories/CatalogPDFs/FR/Feminist-Revolution-Complete-Censored-Section-Reduced2.pdf.
Redstockings. 2009. "A Collective Radical Feminist Declaration." https://www.redstockings.org/index.php/a-collective-radical-feminist-declaration.
Redstockings. 2013. "The Redstockings Organizational Collection: Redstockings Women's Liberation Archives for Action, 1940's–1991." https://womenwhatistobedone.wordpress.com/wp-content/uploads/2013/09/redstockings-part-1-guide-carol-giardina-intro1.pdf.
Redstockings. 2016. "Buttons and Stickers." https://www.redstockings.org/index.php/main/buttons.
Redstockings. 2025. "About Redstockings of the Women's Liberation Movement." https://www.redstockings.org/index.php/about-redstockings.
Sarachild, Kathie. 1978 [1975]. "Consciousness-Raising: A Radical Weapon." In *Feminist Revolution*, edited by Redstockings, 144–50. New York: Random House. https://womenwhatistobedone.wordpress.com/wp-content/uploads/2013/09/1973-consciousness-raising-radical-weapon-k-sarachild-redstockings.pdf.
Steinem, Gloria. 1975. "Statement from Steinem." *off our backs* 5, no. 8: 22–3. https://www.jstor.org/stable/25772314?seq=1.
Steinem, Gloria. 1983. *Outrageous Acts and Everyday Rebellions*. New York: Macmillan.
Woodwoman. 1975. "Gloria Steinem Accused." *Big Mama Rag*, July 5. https://www.jstor.org/stable/pdf/community.28033995.pdf.

RELIGIOUS RIGHT

The religious right is a political and cultural movement aimed at maintaining and reestablishing traditional cultural norms based on conservative religious values. Advanced by a network of religious and political leaders, the religious right grew in popularity in the 1970s in the United States, largely in response to the success of several social movements including the civil rights movement, feminist activism, and the secular movement. Although the movement appeals to conservatives from various religious backgrounds, its greatest support has come from white evangelicals.

Understanding the Movement

In the United States, the movement began to organize after the 1971 Supreme Court case of *Green v. Connally*, which ruled that if private religious schools refused to racially integrate, they would lose their tax-exempt status. Movement leaders rallied around Bob Jones University—a private college that maintained it would not admit African Americans because Jones argued that racial segregation was mandated by the Bible. Movement leaders argued that the issue was not about racial segregation but religious freedom. They contended this was a case of government overreach that threatened religious freedom (Balmer 2014). By the end of the 1970s and into the 1980s, the movement began to further rally around concerns regarding abortion access, reinstating teacher-led prayer and Bible readings in public school, opposing the feminist agenda (particularly the Equal Rights Amendment), and resisting LGBTQ+ rights.

The US religious right frames themselves as the "Moral Majority," arguing that there is a silent majority that opposes radical progressive social change as a threat to Christian moral society. They rely heavily on a persecution narrative in which they frame advances in gender and racial equality, LGBTQ+ rights, and religious pluralism as a threat to Christian religious freedom. The religious right frames themselves as victims of a culture war who are being forced to violate their religious beliefs to appease an immoral minority that threatens moral society (Conrad 1983; Dick 2021).

In the United States, the religious right draws heavily on a Christian nationalist ideology that presumes the nation was founded in conservative Christian values, the nation has gone away from those values, and that it needs to return to those values in order to survive. Within this narrative, conservative Christians are presented as true Americans who are the best citizens and leaders. As historian David Sehat (2011) argues, however, in making their arguments and expressing nostalgia for the "Christian foundation" of the United States, the movement relies heavily on the "Myth of American Religious Freedom," which ignores the long history of oppression toward religious and irreligious minorities in favor of Christian domination.

Patrick Buchanan's 1992 Republican National Convention speech is one of the strongest articulations of the ideologies and anxieties of the religious right. In the speech, which became known as the "culture war speech," Buchanan argued there was a "religious war" for the "soul of the country." He framed one side as wanting "radical feminism," "abortion on demand," "homosexual rights," "discrimination against religious schools" (a reference to Bill Clinton's opposition to state funding for private religious schools), and "women in combat." As Eric Miller (2012) notes, Buchanan's speech framed the threat to the United States as being a spiritual decline and he presented the Republican Party as the religious cure to this threat.

In the United States the religious right draws heavily on Christianity; however, it is important to recognize that the rise of the religious right is global phenomenon that manifests within dominant religions in different cultures. The Hindu nationalist movement in India, for example, draws on many similar narratives and ideologies as the religious right in the United States but from a Hindu perspective (See: Menon 2010; Thobani 2019).

Feminism and the Religious Right

In a special issue of *Signs: Journal of Women in Culture and Society*, feminist scholars note that anti-feminism and the resistance to gender equality are part of the core ideology within the global religious right and alt-right movements more broadly (Graff, Kapur, and Walters 2019). The movement frames feminism as a threat to the natural order, suggesting that it is "destroying humanity" (Graff, Kapur, and Walters 2019, 543). Their rhetoric includes calls to reinforce traditional gender roles, to resist what they perceive as sexual deviance regarding both women's sexual freedom and advancements in LGBTQ+ rights, and to limit reproductive care such as abortion and birth control. Such discourse is often presented as support for "family values" as demonstrated through organizations such as the American Family Association, Focus on the Family, the Family Research Council, and Family Watch International. The mission of such groups "underscores the nuclear (heterosexual, patriarchal) family in maintaining an orderly and healthy society" (Whitehead and Perry 2020, 125).

Although reinforcing patriarchal gender roles is a core tenet of the religious right, women are active members and leaders of the movement. One of the most prominent early leaders was Phyllis Schlafly. Schlafly championed the importance of "traditional" women, though she herself earned a master's degree, worked for the American Enterprise Institute, and ran for Congress in 1952 utilizing the slogan "A Woman's Place Is in the House." Schlafly is perhaps best known for her opposition to the Equal Rights Amendment (ERA), which would have confirmed in the US Constitution that "Equality of rights under the law shall not be denied or abridged by the United States or by any State on account of sex." Schlafly critiqued the proposed amendment based on her argument that women's oppression was not an issue in America, arguing instead that the American woman was one of the most privileged people in the world. She also opposed the notion of gender equality because, according to her, in a Judeo-Christian society differences between men and women needed to be upheld because it represented God's vision. She argued this vision involved men being the provider and women being homemakers. She argued that women liked being housewives and that the ERA was an attempt by radical feminists to force women out of homes. Schlafly framed opposition to the ERA as a religious issue and, in doing so, helped make opposition to gender equality a cornerstone of the religious right's agenda (Kobes Du Mez 2020, 66–73).

While the religious right often frames feminism as a threat, it is important to recognize that this trend does not suggest that religion or conservative politics is anti-women or anti-feminism. In an ethnographic study of contemporary evangelicals, the group most likely to support the religious right, feminist scholar Sarah Diefendorf (2019) found that there are three prominent responses to feminism: a creation of evangelical feminism that embraces the ideals of feminism as reflective of evangelical faith, an acceptance of some feminist ideals but self-distancing from the concept due to its perceived disconnect with traditional family values, and an active rejection of feminism as a contradiction of the Christian faith. These various responses reflect that, although the religious right often frames itself as speaking for Christianity, conceptions of religion, as well as feminism, are complex. Diefendorf (2019) urges feminist scholars to "pay attention to this messiness" (1023). Doing so will help feminist scholars and others engaging with the religious right recognize the complexity and avoid the hasty generalizations of beliefs relating to religion.

Kristina M. Lee

See Also: Abortion; Civil Rights Act: Title VII; Feminist Theology; Schlafly, Phyllis

Further Reading

Balmer, Randall, 2014. "The Real Origins of the Religious Right." *Politico Magazine*, May 27, 2014. https://www.politico.com/magazine/story/2014/05/religious-right-real-origins-107133/.
Conrad, Charles. 1983. "The Rhetoric of the Moral Majority: An Analysis of Romantic Form." *Quarterly Journal of Speech* 69: 159–70.
Dick, Hannah. 2021. "Advocating for the Right: Alliance Defending Freedom and the Rhetoric of Christian Persecution." *Feminist Legal Studies* 29: 375–97. https://doi.org/10.1007/s10691-021-09468-0.
Diefendorf, Sarah. 2019. "Contemporary Evangelical Responses to Feminism and the Imagined Secular." *Signs: Journal of Women in Culture and Society* 44, no. 4: 1003–26. https://doi.org/10.1086/702035.
Du Mez, Kristin Kobes. 2020. *Jesus and John Wane: How White Evangelicals Corrupted a Faith and Fractured a Nation.* New York: Liveright.
Graff, Agnieszka, Ratna Kapur, and Suzanna Danuta Walters. 2019. "Introduction: Gender and the Rise of the Global Right." *Signs* 44, no. 3: 541-560.
Menon, Kalyani Devaki. 2010. *Everyday Nationalism: Women of the Hindu Right in India*. Philadelphia: University of Pennsylvania Press.
Miller, Eric C. 2012. "Patrick Joseph Buchanan, 'Culture War Speech: Address to the Republican National Convention' (August 17, 1992)." *Voice of Democracy* 7: 47–59. https://voicesofdemocracy.umd.edu/wp-content/uploads/2013/08/Buchanan-Essay_Edited.pdf.
Sehat, David. 2011. *The Myth of American Religious Freedom*. Oxford: Oxford University Press.
Thobani, Sitara. 2019. "Alt-Right with the Hindu-right: Long-distance Nationalism and the Perfection of Hindutva." *Ethnic and Racial Studies* 42, no. 5: 745–62. https://doi.org/10.1080/01419870.2018.1468567.
Whitehead, Andrew L., and Samuel L. Perry. 2020. *Taking America Back for God: Christian Nationalism in the United States.* Oxford: Oxford University Press.

REPRODUCTIVE JUSTICE

Reproductive Justice (RJ) is a framework that extends beyond the pro-choice movement, emphasizing a comprehensive understanding of reproductive rights. Developed by women of color in the 1990s, RJ recognizes the intersectionality of race, gender, socioeconomic status, and other factors that impact individuals' reproductive lives. The four core principles of RJ are: (1) the right to own our bodies and control our future, (2) the right to have children, (3) the right to not have children, and (4) the right to parent the children we have in safe and sustainable environments.

Origins of Reproductive Justice

The term "Reproductive Justice" was coined in 1994 by an influential group of twelve Black women in Chicago. Frustrated that the mainstream feminist movement's focus on "choice" failed to address the systemic inequalities affecting marginalized communities, they created the Women of African Descent for Reproductive Justice (WADRJ) and jumped headfirst into fighting for healthcare reform (Leonard 2017, 41).

In 1997, SisterSong was founded by activists such as Luz Rodriguez and Loretta Ross to expand the RJ movement into a more diverse direction. As Ross wrote, by shifting the focus from the single issue of abortion to "reproductive oppression, including the control and exploitation of women, girls and individuals through our bodies," "sexuality," and "labor and reproduction," the reproductive justice movement develops a more inclusive vision of how to build a new movement (Ross 2006, 14).

Both SisterSong and RJ are deeply rooted in intersectionality, a concept coined by Kimberlé Crenshaw in 1989 that examines how various forms of oppression intersect. In the RJ context, identities such as race, gender, sexuality, disability, and socioeconomic status can cause individuals seeking reproductive healthcare to face additional accessibility challenges.

SisterSong saw "reproductive oppression" for what it truly was and continues to be: a perpetuation of violence against marginalized bodies tied directly to America's painful history of enslavement. As sociologist Dorothy Roberts writes, "the control of Black women's reproduction has shaped the meaning of reproductive liberty in America" (1997, 6). Today, the organization uses this history and grounded experience to inform their RJ activist efforts.

Core Principles of Reproductive Justice

The four core principles of RJ were created with intersectional and marginalized identities in mind and have been applied in various ways to center oppressed voices.

1. **The Right to Own Our Bodies and Control Our Future:** This includes access to comprehensive sex education, bodily autonomy, and freedom from violence and coercion.
2. **The Right to Have a Child**: This includes access to fertility treatments, prenatal and postnatal care, and the right to be free from coercive sterilizations—a practice that has historically targeted women of color and disabled women (Jarman 2021).
3. **The Right Not to Have a Child**: This principle encompasses access to contraception and safe, legal abortion. The landmark case *Roe v. Wade* (1973) is often cited for legalizing abortion nationwide. However, access remains inequitable as women of color—particularly Black, Indigenous, and Latina women—face higher barriers to reproductive healthcare due to factors such as restrictive laws, poverty, and geographic location (Roberts 1997). Moreover, the Supreme Court case *Dobbs v. Jackson Women's Health Organization* (2022) undid *Roe's* legacy, making abortion access more difficult across the United States.
4. **The Right to Parent Children in Safe and Supportive Environments:** This involves the right to raise children without fear of violence, environmental hazards, or state interference. For example, Dorothy Roberts's book *Shattered Bonds: The Color of Child Welfare* sheds light on how Black families are disproportionately impacted by child welfare policies that often remove children from their homes (2002).

Reproductive Justice in Practice

Organizations such as SisterSong, the National Latina Institute for Reproductive Justice, and Asian Communities for Reproductive Justice (ACRJ) work on the ground to implement RJ principles. These groups engage in advocacy, education, direct service provision, and policy initiatives. For instance, the Californian policy initiative SB 24, also known as the "College Student Right to Access Act," was signed into law in 2019. This legislation requires California public universities to provide medication abortion services at their student health centers, addressing the barriers students face in accessing abortion services ("Governor Gavin Newsom" 2019).

Despite this impactful progress, many challenges to the RJ movement remain. For example, the Hyde Amendment (1976)—which prohibits federal funding for abortion except in cases of rape, incest, or life endangerment—disproportionately affects low-income women who rely on Medicaid ("Hyde Amendment" n.d.). One of the most significant obstacles to RJ was the US Supreme Court's 2022 decision to overturn *Roe v. Wade*. This landmark decision, made in the case of *Dobbs v. Jackson Women's Health Organization*, ended nearly fifty years of federal protection for abortion rights. The Court's ruling handed the power to regulate abortion back to individual states, leading to a patchwork of laws across the country. States such as Alabama and Texas have enacted stringent bans and restrictions, while others have moved to protect and expand access to abortion services. These legislative changes exacerbate existing inequalities and disproportionately impact marginalized communities.

Through collectives like SisterSong, the transformative framework of RJ continues to advocate for a world where all individuals can make informed choices about their reproductive lives, free from discrimination and shaming.

Carole Yoke-kew Chee

See Also: Abortion; Bodily Autonomy; Intersectionality; *Roe v. Wade* (1973); SisterSong

Further Reading

"Governor Gavin Newsom Signs Reproductive Freedom Legislation, Including Bill to Expand Access to Care on College Campuses." 2019. *Governor of California*, October 11, 2019. Accessed July 13, 2024. https://www.gov.ca.gov/2019/10/11/governor-gavin-newsom-signs-reproductive-freedom-legislation-including-bill-to-expand-access-to-care-on-college-campuses/.

"Hyde Amendment." n.d. *Planned Parenthood Action Fund*. Accessed July 13, 2024. https://www.plannedparenthoodaction.org/issues/abortion/federal-and-state-bans-and-restrictions-abortion/hyde-amendment.

Jarman, Michelle. 2021. "Disability Rights through Reproductive Justice: Eugenic Legacies in the Abortion Wars." In *The Routledge Handbook of Disability and Sexuality*, 1st ed., vol. 1, edited by Russel Shuttleworth and Linda Mona, 132–43. New York: Routledge. https://doi.org/10.4324/9780429489570-12.

Leonard, Toni M. Bond. 2017. "Laying the Foundations for a Reproductive Justice Movement." In *Radical Reproductive Justice: Foundation, Theory, Practice, Critique*, edited by Loretta Ross, Lynn Roberts, Erika Derkas, and Whitney Peoples, 39–49. New York: Feminist Press at the City University of New York.

Roberts, Dorothy. 1997. *Killing the Black Body: Race, Reproduction, and the Meaning of Liberty*. New York: Vintage Books.

Roberts, Dorothy. 2002. *Shattered Bonds: The Color of Child Welfare*. New York: Basic Books.

Ross, Loretta J. 2006. "Understanding Reproductive Justice: Transforming the Pro-Choice Movement." *Off Our Backs* 36, no. 4: 14–19. http://www.jstor.org/stable/20838711.

Ross, Loretta J. 2017. "Conceptualizing Reproductive Justice Theory: A Manifesto for Activism." In *Radical Reproductive Justice: Foundation, Theory, Practice, Critique*, edited by Loretta Ross, Lynn Roberts, Erika Derkas, and Whitney Peoples, 170–232. New York: Feminist Press at the City University of New York.

REPRODUCTIVE LABOR

Reproductive labor refers to all the work—labor—that goes into birthing and sustaining life. Getting pregnant, bringing a pregnancy to term, child birth (which is known as *labor*), and breastfeeding are all parts of reproductive labor. So too are clothing and keeping an infant warm, feeding a toddler who cannot cut their own food, and even taking children to and from school—where they learn to be the next generation of laborers and citizens. As Barbara Laslette and Johanna Brenner wrote in 1989, reproductive labor includes "various kinds of work—mental, manual, and emotional—aimed at providing the historically and socially, as well as biologically, defined care necessary to maintain existing life and to produce the next generation" (383). Chief among the labor involved in reproductive labor are pregnancy, childbirth, childcare, meal preparation, procreation, sex, and emotional support (Brady 2023, 607). Feminists, especially Marxist feminists, theorize reproductive labor by putting it into conversation with larger economic and social structures—such as capitalism and domestic labor.

The contemporary exploitation involved in reproductive labor is directly related to the rise of capitalism. Capitalism created an "unequal 'wage relation' between men and women" (Brady 2023, 607). Essentially, as Miranda Brady explains, when Western cultures shifted toward industrialization, it became commonplace for women to perform unwaged labor in the home and in the fields surrounding the home while men performed waged labor in factories. At the same time, a hierarchy emerged wherein the "invisible unpaid forms of labor (and those who perform them) were devalued" while the "paid" forms of labor (and those who perform them) were valued (Brady 2023, 607). As such, within the newly emerging capitalist societies, waged labor (usually performed by men) became the coin of the realm while unwaged labor (usually performed by women and which used to be the standard form of labor) became devalued to the point of invisibility—but it did not disappear or stop being essential to life and society's well-being.

Importantly, waged labor occupies only a portion of a person's day. Meanwhile, "virtually all other activities are a preparation for work or a recuperation from it" (James [1983] 2012, 149). As such, women's unpaid domestic labor—supporting the preparation for and recuperation from waged labor—became the backbone for men's waged labor during early capitalist societies.

Today, approximately three-quarters or 75 percent of women aged twenty-five to fifty-four participate in waged labor in the United States, and 85 percent of these women work full-time (Almeida and Salas Betsch 2023). Yet women still provide the vast majority of the domestic labor—often known as the "second shift," enabling their own and their partners' waged labor. Additionally, women provide almost the entirety of reproductive labor in the United States.

For example, within a typical heterosexual family in the United States, both parents work full-time outside the home, yet it is the woman who manages their fertility (e.g., birth control), carries pregnancies to term and gives birth, arranges childcare, packs lunches, makes grocery lists and grocery shops, takes children to their medical appointments, rocks children to sleep when they are scared and unwell, and so on. This labor ensures the survival of well-adjusted people for the next generation of citizen laborers. As such, this reproductive labor is essential to society's future.

Capitalism is famous for producing a two-tier hierarchy where the "capitalists" are at the top, owning the means of production (e.g., the resources and factories), and the "proletariat" (the working class) are an oppressed class, laboring in factories and so on. However, feminist understandings of reproductive labor demonstrate that capitalism depends on a third class or tier that exists "underneath" the proletariat. That is, reproductive laborers (mostly women) are at the bottom or most exploited position in the hierarchy, and their labor supports the whole system through pregnancy, breastfeeding, childcare, cooking, cleaning, emotional support, and so on.

The oppression of women did not begin with capitalism, but it was intensified by capitalism. Indeed, capitalism specifically devalues reproductive labor since reproductive labor is unwaged, creating a more intense "exploitation of women as women" (Dalla Costa [1972] 2016, 274). Mariarosa Dalla Costa described capitalism's exploitation of the uterus as one that cuts off women's creative possibility, the possibility of women's "working activity," and the expression of women's "sexual, psychological, and emotional autonomy" ([1972] 2016, 280).

In contemporary Western societies, reproductive labor is often described as "love." That is, women are expected to perform the unwaged reproductive and domestic labor that enables men's waged labor and that births and sustains the life of the next generation of citizen laborers, because they "love" their partners and children. This labor is colloquially referred to as a "labor of love," as if women were uniquely (by sex and/or gender) programmed to perform this labor out of the goodness of their (biological or metaphorical) hearts rather than being socialized and forced into such labor by structural inequalities. Within this context—and highlighting the ways in which women's reproductive labor sustains both national and corporate populations over generations—Silvia Federici quipped that when they say such labor "is love," feminists say "it is unwaged work" ([1975] 2020, 11).

Sarah Kornfield

See Also: Capitalism; Domestic Labor; Emotional Labor; The Personal Is Political

Further Reading

Almeida, Beth and Isabela Salas-Betsch. 2023. "Fact Sheet: The State of Women in the Labor Market in 2023." *AmericanProgress.org*, February 6, 2023. Accessed September 15, 2024. https://www.americanprogress.org/article/fact-sheet-the-state-of-women-in-the-labor-market-in-2023/.

Brady, Miranda, J. 2023. "'I Think the Men are Behind It': Reproductive Justice and the Horror of Second Wave Feminism." *Feminist Media Studies* 23, no. 2: 606–20.

Dalla Costa, Mariacosta. [1972] 2016. "Women and the Subversion of the Community." In *Revolutionary Feminism: Communist Interventions*, edited by Communist Research Cluster, vol 3, 297–317. New York: Communist Research Cluster. Accessed September 15, 2024. https://www.google.com/url?sa=t&source=web&rct=j&opi=89978449&url=https://legalform.blog/wp-content/uploads/2020/05/dalla-costa-2015.pdf&ved=2ahUKEwim1u3v_sWIAxWBmokEHcuSCTkQFnoECBUQAQ&usg=AOvVaw0lt1DMRlthlQgXuw-FMN6p.

Federici, Silvia. [1975] 2020. *Revolution at Point Zero: Housework, Reproduction, and Feminist Struggle.* New York: PM Press.

James, Selma (ed). [1983] 2012. "Marx and Feminism." In *Sex, Race, and Class: The Perspective of Winning: A Selection of Writings 1952–2011*, 141–60. Oakland: PM Press.

Laslette, Barbara and Johanna Brenner, 1989. "Gender and Social Reproduction: Historical Perspectives." *Annual Review of Sociology* 15, no. 1: 381–404.

RIGHT TO PRIVACY

The right to privacy is a legal concept that has evolved through centuries of constitutional interpretation and judicial decision-making, though it only became a central focus of debate in the United States when the Supreme Court "discovered" such a right to be embedded in the Constitution in the 1960s, despite the lack of explicit or overt language in the founding document. At its core, the right to privacy assumes that individuals possess personal autonomy that cannot be subject to governmental intrusion by ordinary legislation. From a feminist perspective, privacy is especially significant due to its close association with bodily autonomy, reproductive rights, and gender equality.

Many feminist legal scholars argue that privacy rights are essential for empowering women and marginalized groups, allowing them to make decisions about their personal, sexual, and family lives free from government interference. The right to privacy, however, has been deeply contested in the judiciary. Key Supreme Court cases have shaped the contours of privacy, especially concerning reproductive justice, where privacy law intersects with feminist claims for bodily integrity and freedom from patriarchal control.

Historical Origins of the Right to Privacy

The origins of the right to privacy in the United States can be traced to the late nineteenth century, notably through the writings of Samuel Warren and Louis Brandeis, the latter of whom joined the Supreme Court as a justice in 1916. In their 1890 *Harvard Law Review* article, Warren and Brandeis (1890) argue that privacy—or the "right to be let alone"—is a legal right independent of property or contract law, specifically as a protection against intrusive (then-new) technologies like photography and mass media. In his famous dissent in *Olmstead v. United States* (1928), Brandeis expanded this argument, writing that the Fourth Amendment protected not just physical spaces but also the privacy of one's thoughts and communication. Brandeis's expansive view of privacy laid the groundwork for future constitutional interpretations that would emphasize personal autonomy and freedom from government interference.

However, early interpretations of privacy often centered on protecting property and domestic life, largely reinforcing traditional patriarchal structures that privileged men's control over households and excluded women from meaningful participation in these protections. Indeed, feminist critiques of this early understanding of the right to privacy emphasize how it overlooked or even reinforced the systemic subordination of women. Legal scholars like Catharine MacKinnon (1989) have pointed out that privacy was used to shield male dominance within the family, effectively excluding women's rights to control their bodies and reproduction. In this context, privacy was not an empowering tool for women but a concept that largely reinforced patriarchal power dynamics.

Supreme Court Jurisprudence: Expanding and Limiting Privacy Rights

The evolution of privacy as a constitutional right in the United States was propelled through several key Supreme Court rulings, particularly those related to contraception, abortion, and family autonomy. For feminists, these decisions are landmark moments that reflect both the successes and limitations of the right to privacy when applied to women's rights.

The first major Supreme Court case to explicitly recognize the right to privacy was *Griswold v. Connecticut* (1965). In this case, the Court struck down a Connecticut law that banned the use of contraceptives, even for married couples, finding that the law violated the "right to marital privacy." Justice William O. Douglas, writing for the majority, argued that various guarantees within the Bill of Rights create "penumbras" or "zones of privacy." The Court argued that, while not explicitly in the text, a careful reading of the First, Third, Fourth, Fifth, and Ninth Amendments provides justification for a fundamental right to privacy, including the right of married couples to make decisions about contraception without government interference. This decision was groundbreaking in recognizing privacy as a constitutional right, yet it was rooted in the context of marital relations, implicitly excluding unmarried women, and it failed to address gendered power dynamics within marriages (McClain 2006). Despite its problematic limitations, the decision laid the groundwork for expanding reproductive rights in future cases, where privacy would become a crucial legal tool in the fight for women's autonomy.

In 1972, the decision in *Eisenstadt v. Baird* expanded the right to privacy the Court first recognized in *Griswold* to unmarried individuals. The case concerned a Massachusetts law that prohibited the distribution of contraceptives to unmarried persons. In striking down the law, the

Court emphasized that the right to make decisions about contraception belonged to individuals, not just couples. "If the right of privacy means anything," wrote Justice William Brennan, "it is the right of the individual, married or single, to be free from unwarranted governmental intrusion into matters so fundamentally affecting a person as the decision whether to bear or beget a child." This shift from marital privacy to individual autonomy was a critical moment in feminist legal theory, as it more directly acknowledged women's rights to control their own reproductive choices outside the institution of marriage.

Perhaps the most significant case concerning the right to privacy and feminist legal concerns is *Roe v. Wade* (1973). In *Roe*, the Supreme Court held that a woman's decision to terminate a pregnancy fell under the constitutional right to privacy, rooted in the due process clause of the Fourteenth Amendment. The Court's opinion, authored by Justice Harry Blackmun, recognized that the right to privacy "is broad enough to encompass a woman's decision whether or not to terminate her pregnancy." Feminists hailed *Roe* as a landmark victory for women's autonomy and bodily integrity, providing legal protection for reproductive choices. However, the framing of abortion rights in terms of privacy, rather than equality, left the decision vulnerable to attack (Siegel 2008). By couching the right to abortion in privacy terms, the Court failed to fully engage with the gendered implications of reproductive control, leaving subsequent challenges to abortion rights room to argue that state interests could outweigh individual privacy. Moreover, the trimester framework set out in *Roe*, which allowed for increasing state regulation as pregnancy progressed, reflected a compromise that limited the scope of reproductive freedom.

In the decades following *Roe*, the Supreme Court continued to uphold and reaffirm its central holding in the case as it continued to grapple with its understanding of the right to privacy. In one of the most important of these progeny cases, *Planned Parenthood of Southeastern Pennsylvania v. Casey* (1992), the Supreme Court reaffirmed the core holding of *Roe* but replaced its trimester framework with the "undue burden" standard. This allowed states to impose restrictions on abortion so long as they did not place a "substantial obstacle in the path of a woman seeking an abortion before the fetus attains viability." The undue burden standard introduced ambiguity and gave states more power to regulate abortions, disproportionately affecting low-income women and women of color, who may face greater barriers to accessing care (Abrams 1999).

The Constitutional right to privacy has also been central to cases involving sexual autonomy for gay couples. In *Lawrence v. Texas* (2003), the Supreme Court struck down laws criminalizing consensual same-sex sexual activity, ruling that such laws violated the right to privacy. Justice Anthony Kennedy, writing for the majority, argued that the state could not demean the existence of individuals by making their private sexual conduct a crime. The decision in *Lawrence* not only expanded the right to privacy but also paved the way for the Court's later decision in *Obergefell v. Hodges* (2015), which recognized same-sex marriage as a constitutional right.

The most dramatic shift in the Supreme Court's privacy jurisprudence came with *Dobbs v. Jackson Women's Health Organization* (2022), which overturned *Roe v. Wade* (1973). In *Dobbs*, the Court ruled that the Constitution does not confer a right to abortion, effectively returning the issue to the states. Feminists argue that the *Dobbs* decision marks a profound regression in reproductive rights and privacy, stripping women of the protections established under *Roe* and *Casey*. Many feminist theorists see the ruling as a culmination of decades of conservative legal activism aimed at eroding reproductive freedoms under the guise of states' rights and moral concerns (Goodwin 2020). Furthermore, *Dobbs* has raised alarms about the future of other privacy-based rights, including access to contraception and same-sex marriage, which have been predicated on similar privacy arguments.

Intersectionality and Privacy

An intersectional feminist perspective on privacy underscores how the right to privacy has not been equally accessible to all women. Black feminist legal theorists, such as Kimberlé Crenshaw (1991), highlight that while privacy protections have expanded for some women, they often fail to account for the compounded vulnerabilities of women of color, LGBTQ+ individuals, and those from low-income backgrounds. Restrictions on abortion and contraception, for instance, disproportionately affect marginalized communities, for whom privacy rights do not always translate into practical access to healthcare or bodily autonomy.

Moreover, intersectional feminist critiques focus on the digital age, where privacy is increasingly threatened by surveillance, data collection, and online harassment. Feminists argue that privacy protections must evolve to address these new challenges, particularly as they disproportionately impact women, especially those from disenfranchised or vulnerable backgrounds, who are often the targets of cyberbullying, doxxing, and revenge porn (Citron 2014).

The Future of Privacy and Feminist Advocacy

The right to privacy remains a key battleground in feminist legal theory, particularly as it intersects with reproductive rights, bodily autonomy, and gender equality. The Supreme Court's jurisprudence on privacy has both expanded and limited these rights over time, reflecting broader social debates about the role of women and marginalized groups in US life. Feminist legal scholars continue to advocate for a more inclusive and intersectional understanding of privacy, one that fully recognizes the diverse experiences of women and the challenges they face. As the legal landscape shifts, particularly in the wake of *Dobbs*, the future of privacy rights will likely remain contentious, with feminists continuing to play a critical role in defending and expanding the scope of personal autonomy through a fundamental right to privacy.

Rachel A. Spooner

See Also: Bodily Autonomy; Crenshaw, Kimberlé; *Dobbs v. Jackson Women's Health Organization* (2022); *Eisenstadt v. Baird* (1972); *Griswold v. Connecticut* (1965); Intersectionality; *Lawrence v. Texas* (2003); *Obergefell v. Hodges* (2015); Reproductive Justice; *Roe v. Wade* (1973)

Further Reading

Abrams, Kathryn. 1999. "From Autonomy to Agency: Feminist Perspectives on Self-Direction." *William and Mary Law Review* 40, no. 3: 805–46.

Citron, Danielle Keats. 2014. *Hate Crimes in Cyberspace*. Cambridge, MA: Harvard University Press.

Crenshaw, Kimberlé. 1991. "Mapping the Margins: Intersectionality, Identity Politics, and Violence against Women of Color." *Stanford Law Review* 43, no. 6: 1241–99.

Dobbs v. Jackson Women's Health Organization, 597 US 19. 2022.

Eisenstadt v. Baird, 405 US 438. 1972.

Goodwin, Michele. 2020. *Policing the Womb: Invisible Women and the Criminalization of Motherhood*. New York: Cambridge University Press.

Griswold v. Connecticut, 381 US 479. 1965.

Lawrence v. Texas, 539 US 558. 2003.

MacKinnon, Catharine. 1989. *Toward a Feminist Theory of the State*. Cambridge, MA: Harvard University Press.

McClain, Linda C. 2006. *The Place of Families: Fostering Capacity, Equality, and Responsibility*. Cambridge, MA: Harvard University Press.

Obergefell v. Hodges, 576 US 644. 2015.

Olmstead v. United States, 277 US 438. 1928.

Planned Parenthood of Southeastern Pennsylvania v. Casey, 505 US 833. 1992.
Roe v. Wade, 410 US 113. 1973.
Siegel, Reva B. 2008. "The Right's Reasons: Constitutional Conflict and the Spread of Woman-Protective Antiabortion Argument." *Duke Law Journal* 57, no. 6: 1641–92.
Warren, Samuel D., and Louis D. Brandeis. 1890. "The Right to Privacy." *Harvard Law Review* 4, no. 4: 193–220.

ROE V. WADE (1973)

In 1970, a woman using the moniker "Jane Roe" sued the district attorney of Dallas County, Texas, challenging a law that made abortion illegal except to save the life of the mother. Roe claimed that the laws were unconstitutionally vague and abridged her right of personal privacy, protected by the Court's established interpretations of the First, Fourth, Fifth, Ninth, and Fourteenth Amendments.

Partially agreeing with Roe's claim, the Court concluded that the "Due Process Clause" of the Fourteenth Amendment includes a fundamental "right to privacy," which protects a pregnant woman's choice whether to have an abortion. However, this right is balanced against the government's interests in protecting women's health and protecting "the potentiality of human life."

Justice Blackmun explains in *Roe* that

> The principal thrust of appellant's attack on the Texas statutes is that they improperly invade a right, said to be possessed by the pregnant woman, to choose to terminate her pregnancy. Appellant would discover this right in the concept of personal "liberty" embodied in the Fourteenth Amendment's Due Process Clause; or in personal, marital, familial, and sexual privacy said to be protected by the Bill of Rights or its penumbras. (*Roe v. Wade* 1973)

Justice Blackmun's argument is that the decision turns on the right to privacy, not women's right to abortion itself. So, how does the Court justify that claim?

What many find surprising is that *Roe* is not actually a case about the right to have an abortion, but at its heart is about the right to privacy. Blackmun wrote that "the Constitution does not explicitly mention any right of privacy." However, for decades, the Court "has recognized that a right of personal privacy, or a guarantee of certain areas or zones of privacy, does exist under the Constitution." Indeed, the First, Fourth, Fifth, and Ninth Amendments have all been interpreted in ways that make clear that personal rights are "fundamental" or "implicit in the concept of ordered liberty" and that this is a "guarantee of personal privacy." These judicial interpretations make it clear that in relation to marriage, procreation, contraception, family relationships, and childbearing and education, the right to privacy is "broad enough to encompass a woman's decision whether or not to terminate her pregnancy" (*Roe v. Wade* 1973).

To put it more succinctly, the right to privacy isn't explicitly stated in the Constitution but the Constitution has been interpreted in such a way that the right to privacy is implied by a number of its amendments. And a woman's decision to terminate her pregnancy is a private matter. It is covered by her right to privacy. The government has no business being a part of that decision.

The Right to Privacy—and Its Overturning in *Dobbs v. Jackson* (2022)

Essentially, the 1973 ruling in *Roe v. Wade* is built on the 1965 ruling in *Griswold v. Connecticut*, which argued that the Fourteenth Amendment guarantees a right to privacy even though privacy is not enumerated—or listed—in the Constitution or its Amendments. That is, the right to privacy was inferred from other rights that are enumerated, such as the First Amendment's right to assembly, the Third Amendment's right "to be free from quartering soldiers during peacetime," and the Fourth

Amendment's right "to be free from unreasonable searches of the home" (Kornfield 2024). Put simply, the Court argued that these rights—the right to gather freely, the right to refuse to house soldiers during peace, the right to refuse to let law enforcement into one's home for unreasonable searches, and so on—imply that one has a right to *privacy*, a right to keep private who one associates with and what one does within one's own home.

First established in *Griswold* (1965), the right to privacy was used to further a wide range of rights and freedoms that civil rights, feminist, and queer activists have worked so hard to legally establish. These include the rights of interracial couples to marry (*Loving v. Virginia* 1967), of unmarried individuals to use contraception (*Eisenstadt v. Baird* 1972), access to abortion (*Roe v. Wade* 1973), same-sex sexual conduct (*Lawrence v. Texas* 2003), and the right of same-sex couples to marry (*Obergefell v. Hodges* 2015).

In 2022, the Supreme Court reversed course, deciding in *Dobbs v. Jackson Women's Health Organization* that US citizens do not have a right to privacy or abortion since neither "privacy" nor "abortion" is listed in the Constitution or its Amendments. This overturned decades of legal precedence and millions of people lost the right to access abortion care overnight as states implemented "trigger bans" or laws that were already passed but couldn't go into effect unless *Roe* was overturned.

The impact of the *Dobbs* decision, however, is much bigger than losing abortion access because *Dobbs* overturned the right to privacy itself—deciding that US citizens and residents do *not* have a right to privacy. This means that many of the freedoms established through civil rights, feminist, and queer activism within the court system since the 1960s—freedoms that depended on the right to privacy—are now up for grabs.

By denying the right to privacy and thus overturning *Roe*'s right to abortion, the *Dobbs* ruling is a threat to queer rights, women's rights, and possibly even the rights of people of color, if *Loving v. Virginia*—which also hinges on privacy—were to be taken to task.

M. Elizabeth Thorpe

See Also: Abortion; Choice; *Dobbs v. Jackson* (2022); *Eisenstadt v. Bard* (1972); *Griswold v. Connecticut* (1965); Right to Privacy

Further Reading

Kornfield, Sarah. 2024. *Invoking the Fathers: Dangerous Metaphors and Founding Myths in Congressional Politics*. Baltimore: Johns Hopkins University Press.

Roe v. Wade, 410 U.S. 113. 1973.

S

#SAYHERNAME

The #SayHerName campaign grew out of the intersectional #BlackLivesMatter (BLM) movement in response to the police and state violence against Black women and women of color. In order to fully understand the #SayHerName campaign, we have to start with BLM.

BLM was founded by three radical Black feminist organizers—Alicia Garza, Patrisse Cullors, and Opal Tometi. It serves as an important intervention into the way Black liberation movements are often dominated by Black men's leadership and center Black cisheterosexual men's experiences with racism. Prominently arguing that Black *lives* matter, the BLM movement centers Black women's leadership and the experiences of Black women, Black LGBTQ+ people, and Black disabled people.

Garza, Cullors, and Tometi shaped the BLM movement through social media with #BlackLivesMatter as a political platform and organizing tool that made anti-Black police and state violence more visible (Black Lives Matter 2017). The hashtag became prominent following the 2013 acquittal of George Zimmerman, a self-deputized neighborhood watch captain who killed Trayvon Martin, a seventeen-year-old Black boy (Thebault 2022). The hashtag also documented the backlash against and violent police repression of protesters following the August 9, 2014, police killing of Michael Brown, an eighteen-year-old Black man from Ferguson, Missouri (Lowery 2017). With the advent of social media and smartphone cameras, recordings of the protests and the aftermath of Brown's death, in particular, catapulted the BLM movement into mainstream media and political discourse.

However, as the BLM movement gained national attention, the police-sanctioned killings of Black men and boys, such as Trayvon Martin (2013), Tamir Rice (2014), and Michael Brown (2014), dominated mainstream news coverage of the BLM movement as well as policy discussions across legislative bodies in the United States. This coverage focused on Black men's experiences with anti-Black police and state violence. The ways in which Black women and girls experience police violence were largely ignored. This excluded Black women and girls from the media coverage and from the policymaking and reform efforts, meaning that anti-Black violence that affects Black women in gendered ways remained unaddressed—with little to no accountability for their deaths.

To rectify this injustice, in 2014 the African American Policy Forum launched the social media campaign #SayHerName to raise awareness of and organize around Black women's unique experiences with police and state violence (Crenshaw et al. 2015, 3). This was a direct counter to mainstream discourse and policymaking that had appropriated the BLM movement while focusing on Black cisheterosexual men's experiences, maintaining the historic exclusion of Black women from political deliberation and policy.

#SayHerName creates an important space to understand how Black women's interactions with police are often different from Black men's, yet still result in unjust violence and fatalities. For instance, when Black women seek police intervention, such as in cases of intimate partner violence, sexual abuse, or mental health crises, they risk facing further abuse, violence, or death from police instead of receiving the help or treatment they need to be safe. Consider, for example, what happened to Michelle Cusseaux, a fifty-year-old Black woman with psychiatric disabilities from Phoenix,

Arizona. She was killed by police in 2014 during a court-ordered mental health pickup. Officer Percy Dupra fatally shot Cusseaux, alleging he felt threatened when he saw her holding a hammer as she opened her apartment door (Cassidy 2015). Racist stereotypes frame Black women as inherently aggressive and unnaturally strong; when police and other state agents see Black women through this racist and sexist lens, it can increase the level of violence with which they respond to Black women—often with fatal outcomes for Black women.

By focusing on the ways in which anti-Black state violence shapes Black women's experiences and deaths, #SayHerName also highlights the destructive ripple effects Black communities experience through this violence. Black women hold important positions in family and community life. Their incapacitation, imprisonment, and deaths due to anti-Black police violence are tragic injustices not just at the personal level but also at the familial and community levels.

The #SayHerName campaign works to end Black women's experiences of police violence and death. #SayHerName is doing important political and activist work and has practical recommendations for feminist activism. For example, the African American Policy Forum released a scholarly report with recommendations for activists such as displaying and incorporating the faces and stories of Black women along with Black men at protests as well as developing social movements that create community spaces to materially and emotionally support the families of police violence victims (Crenshaw et al. 2015, 30–1).

Sergio Peña

See Also: #BlackLivesMatter; Intersectionality; Racist Stereotypes of Black People

Further Reading

Black Lives Matter. 2017. "Herstory." *Black Lives Matter*, July 7, 2017. Accessed August 24, 2024. https://blacklivesmatter.com/herstory/.

Cassidy, Megan. 2015. "Phoenix Police: 2014 Fatal Shooting of Michelle Cusseaux was 'Outside' Policy." *The Arizona Republic,* September 17, 2015. https://www.azcentral.com/story/news/local/phoenix/breaking/2015/09/17/phoenix-police-michelle-cusseaux-shooting-outside-policy/72370792/.

Crenshaw, Kimberlé W., Andrea J. Ritchie, Rachel Anspach, Rachel Gilmer, and Luke Harris. 2015. "Say Her Name: Resisting Police Brutality Against Black Women." *African American Policy Forum*, July 2015. Accessed August 21, 2024. https://scholarship.law.columbia.edu/faculty_scholarship/3226/.

Lowery, Wesley. 2017. "Black Lives Matter: Birth of a Movement." *The Guardian,* January 17, 2017. https://www.theguardian.com/us-news/2017/jan/17/black-lives-matter-birth-of-a-movement.

Thebault, Reis. 2022. "Trayvon Martin's Death Set Off a Movement that Shaped a Decade's Defining Moments." *The Washington Post*, February 25, 2022. https://www.washingtonpost.com/nation/2022/02/25/trayvon-martins-death-set-off-movement-that-shaped-decades-defining-moments/.

SCHLAFLY, PHYLLIS

Phyllis Stewart Schlafly (1924–2016) was a conservative activist and political leader best known for her successful campaign to prevent the ratification of the Equal Rights Amendment (ERA). She was born Phyllis Stewart into a two-parent working-class household on August 15, 1924, in St. Louis, Missouri, and grew up during the Great Depression (Cunningham 2024). Schlafly's parents were devout Roman Catholics, and she was raised in the church and attended a private Catholic school. Schlafly excelled at school, receiving top marks, which enabled her to obtain a scholarship to attend Maryville College of the Sacred Heart, now known as Maryville University of St. Louis ("Life Story" n.d.). In search of a more rigorous educational experience, Schlafly transferred to Washington University (an elite private college in St. Louis) where she had to work the night shift in a munitions factory to pay tuition for the degree in political science she completed in 1944. Schlafly went on to earn a master's degree from Radcliffe University, and, in the late 1970s, she returned to school to earn her law degree from Washington University Law School in St. Louis, Missouri (Cunningham 2024).

Throughout her political career, Schlafly presented herself as an idealistic model of what it means to be a (white) conservative, empowered Christian woman. Schlafly's political career began with a brief stint at the American Enterprise Institute, a conservative think tank before she returned to St. Louis. In 1949 she married John Fred Schlafly who was a wealthy lawyer. They raised their six children in Alton, Illinois, a suburb of St. Louis. John shared Phyllis's political views and encouraged her activism (Johnson 2024).

In 1967, Schlafly launched the Phyllis Schlafly Report, a conservative newsletter (Cunningham 2024). By 1970, she had amassed a subscriber base of 35,000 individuals across the United States. Schlafly's newsletter encouraged conservative women to be politically active but to do so through their supposed place of empowerment—the home (Hemmer 2016).

Schlafly's STOP ERA Campaign

The ERA was introduced on December 10, 1923, in an attempt to amend the US Constitution to explicitly affirm the equal rights of women before the law. Suffrage and women's rights advocates thought this proposed amendment would help women more fully exercise their natural rights (Martin 2016). For roughly fifty years, women's rights activists supported the ERA without gaining much traction, but in 1972, the ERA garnered enough momentum to get close to being enacted.

When Schlafly started opposing the ERA, it had already passed the two houses of Congress and been ratified by thirty of the thirty-eight states needed in order for it to become a constitutional amendment. The ratification of the ERA appeared inevitable when, in October of 1972, Schlafly initiated her STOP (Stop Taking Our Privileges) ERA campaign through her newsletter. Schlafly built the STOP ERA campaign upon conservative feminine rhetoric that denounced the capability of women and equal opportunity under the law in pursuit of a more conservative position. Essentially, Schlafly scared people, arguing that, if ratified, the ERA would have negative moral implications. Specifically, Schlafly's STOP ERA campaign scared people into thinking that women would be drafted into the armed services and forced to work outside the home if the ERA was passed, both of which were framed as moral problems. This framing of the ERA gained enough traction due to Schlafly's campaign that the ERA was indeed stopped.

It is imperative to note that while this political discourse took place almost fifty years ago during the 1970s, at the time of writing, this same type of rhetoric is being deployed by conservative women in the United States. Phyllis Schlafly laid the groundwork for future conservative white women to sound like they are championing women's empowerment while denouncing feminism; moreover, Schlafly role modeled a rhetorical strategy that made freedom look like imprisonment by framing the ERA as something that would hurt (white middle- and upper-class) women. Because of Schlafly's efforts in fighting the ERA, white middle- and upper-class women were able to find comfort in having fewer rights than men, reasoning that this protected them from being drafted into the armed services or being required to work a nine-to-five job (Cady 2020). Today, movements such as the #TradWife movement similarly celebrate women's submission and traditional gender roles as "freeing" for women. Schlafly pioneered a conservative political strategy that claimed to be feminist (or at least empowering for women) and appropriated feminist rhetoric. Her campaign against the ERA was a great example of this.

Feminist Analyses of Schlafly's Rhetoric

Schlafly engaged in fearmongering, arguing that ratifying the ERA would *require* women to work outside the home (Miller 2015). In reality, ratifying the ERA would have ensured that men and women have equal rights—including the right not to be discriminated against during hiring and promotion—but at no point could the ERA ever force anyone to work outside the home. However, twisting what the ERA meant, Schlafly made mostly white middle- and upper-class people afraid that the ERA would actually remove (white) women's "right" to stay-at-home. Moreover, Schlafly succeeded at making it feel like (white, middle- and upper-class) women who were stay-at-home mothers and full-time homemakers were more empowered than feminists such as Betty Friedan, who famously supported the ERA (Hemmer 2016).

The success of Schlafly's STOP ERA campaign has led numerous communication scholars to study her persuasive appeals (Miller 2015; Solomon 1979; Foss 1979). For example, Kathryn A. Cady (2020) analyzed how Schlafly's rhetoric capitalized on the divide between working-class and middle- and upper-class women: Schlafly mobilized middle- and upper-class women against the ERA—which was widely supported by working-class women.

Conservative activist Phyllis Schlafly meeting with President Ronald Reagan in the Oval Office, 1983 (National Archives).

Phyllis Schlafly was clearly inspired by Betty Friedan's *The Feminine Mystique*; she co-opted the success of the feminist movement during the 1970s using rhetorical and persuasive appeals that made her position sound like it was empowering for (white middle- and upper-class) women even as she galvanized the nation to torpedo the ERA. Throughout her career and especially in the STOP ERA campaign, Schlafly modeled a conservative white feminine rhetoric that continues to resonate throughout the United States. Yet Schlafly's educational, career, and political opportunities were all made possible through feminists' labor and activism—leading some to ironically refer to Schlafly as the woman who owes feminism the most.

A. J. Delgado

See Also: Cult of True Womanhood; Equal Rights Amendment (ERA); *The Feminine Mystique*; Friedan, Betty; Nineteenth Amendment

Further Reading

Cady, Kathryn A. 2020. "'Woman as Sign,' Class, and the 1972–1982 Equal Rights Amendment Controversy." *The Northwest Journal of Communication* 48, no. 1: 61–96.

Cunningham, John M. 2024. "Phyllis Schlafly." *Encyclopedia Britannica.* Accessed August 19, 2024. https://www.britannica.com/biography/Phyllis-Schlafly.

Foss, Sonja K. 1979. "Equal Rights Amendment Controversy: Two Worlds in Conflict." *Quarterly Journal of Speech* 65, no. 3: 275–88. https://doi:10.1080/00335637909383479.

Hemmer, Nicole. 2016. "What Phyllis Schlafly Owes Feminism." *Politico Magazine*, September 6, 2016. Accessed August 19, 2024. https://www.politico.com/magazine/story/2016/09/phyllis-schlafly-death-housewife-activ ism-feminism-214213/.

Johnson, Arbora. 2024. "Phyllis Schlafly." *National Women's History Museum.* Accessed August 19, 2024. https://www.womenshistory.org/education-resources/biographies/phyllis-schlafly.

"Life Story: Phyllis Schlafly." n.d. *Women & the American Story.* Accessed August 19, 2024. https://wams.nyhistory.org/growth-and-turmoil/feminism-and-the-backlash/phyllis-schlafly/.

Martin, Douglas. 2016. "Phyllis Schlafly, 'First Lady' of a Political March to the Right, Dies at 92." *The New York Times*, September 5, 2016. https://www.nytimes.com/2016/09/06/obituaries/phyllis-schlafly-conservative-leader-and-foe-of-era-dies-at-92.html.

Miller, Eric C. 2015. "Phyllis Schlafly's 'Positive' Freedom: Liberty, Liberation, and the Equal Rights Amendment." *Rhetoric & Public Affairs* 18, no. 2: 277–300. https://muse.jhu.edu/article/584317.

Solomon, Martha. 1979. "The 'Positive Woman's' Journey: A Mythic Analysis of the Rhetoric of Stop ERA." *Quarterly Journal of Speech* 65, no. 3: 262–74. https://doi:10.1080/00335637909383478.

SENECA FALLS CONVENTION (1848)

The Seneca Falls Convention of 1848 was the first recorded convention in the United States specifically focused on organizing for improving women's rights and lived experiences. The gathering of mainly aristocratic, Christian women and men developed the Declaration of Sentiments and Resolutions, a document essentially reproducing the tone of the Declaration of Independence in order to position the struggle for women's equality as a mission of self-determination. Today, many historians use the convention to mark the beginnings of the women's rights movement in the United States; it also provides a key example of the importance of applying intersectional frameworks to meaningful feminist practice.

Origins of the Seneca Falls Convention

During the early and mid-nineteenth century in the United States, socioeconomic changes were occurring for many nonenslaved white women. First, the Industrial Revolution, which shifted many labor practices outside of the home, altered family labor and home dynamics. Working-class white women participated in wage labor that contributed to family incomes, while upper-class white women were often found in domestic settings and typically supplemented by servants or enslaved laborers for domestic and childrearing tasks. Second, access to literature and schooling (outside of the higher education realm) offered opportunities for various levels of education for privileged women (Tong and Botts 2018). Reflections on women's intellectual, personal, and labor freedoms were not novel—many women had written about their freedoms prior to this point in time. The dovetailing changes from the Industrial Revolution and access to literature contributed further to women's consciousness of their lived experiences in comparison to nonenslaved men (Ritchie and Ronald 2001).

This period in women's history was also marked by limited participation for privileged white women in political organizing, such as the abolitionist movement that merged arguments against slavery with religious morality. Women participating in this movement included Susan B. Anthony, Angelina Grimké Weld, Lucretia Mott, Elizabeth Cady Stanton, Lucy Stone, and many others. Mott and Stanton met in 1840 while accompanying their spouses to the World Antislavery Convention hosted in London. Mott petitioned to speak at this convention but was denied. Women attendees were banned from participating in convention proceedings—relegated to only observe the convention. Mott and Stanton began discussing the idea of hosting a convention in the United States specifically focused on women's rights and access (Harris 1996; Tong and Botts 2018).

The Declaration of Sentiments and Resolutions

Several years later in 1848, Mott and Stanton, as well as Martha Coffin Wright, Jane Hunt, and Mary Ann McClintock, agreed to organize a convention on the "social, civil, and religious condition of woman" set for July 19 and 20 that year and published an announcement in the *Seneca Falls Courier* newspaper in New York (Report of the Woman's Rights Convention n.d.). Several days before the convention, Stanton served as the primary author and worked with Mary Ann McClintock and her two daughters, Elizabeth and Mary Ann Jr., to compose a document of grievances and resolutions concerning the inequities women experienced (Harris 1996). This draft became the origin of the Declaration of Sentiments.

The Seneca Falls Convention—named after the town in which it was held—gathered 300 women and men together for several sessions across two days (Harris 1996). The convening members were all white, save for Frederick Douglass, who was the lone person of color in attendance (Schneider 2023). The convention included the presentation, discussion, and ratification of the Declaration of Sentiments (Harris 1996). The document was modeled after the Declaration of Independence to tap into US patriotism, juxtapose women's struggles as comparable to the self-determination articulated in the original declaration, and to outline women's grievances under a tyranny of a patriarchal society (Kerber 1977; Ritchie and Ronald 2001).

The Declaration of Sentiments and Resolutions provides a litany of critiques that describe the hypocrisies, injustices, and inequities that women in the United States experienced during nineteenth-century patriarchy, as described by the writers. Across sixteen listed Sentiments, the document details women's inequity in terms of voting rights, representation, and participatory power in legislative bodies; just treatment before the law; property ownership and taxation; access to education; access to religious leadership; marriage and divorce rights; and an overall sentiment of a life that does not foster the full growth and capacity of a woman's capabilities (Declaration of Sentiments and Resolutions n.d.; Kerber 1977).

Eleven Resolutions followed the Sentiments, asserting that women should be seen and treated as equal to men, and that any legislation providing for the inferior treatment of women is "contrary to the great precept of nature" (Declaration of Sentiments and Resolutions n.d.). The document specifically states that women should have full access to education, improved access to labor and trades, and the franchise—among other rights. A third of the convention attendees added their signatures to the final ratified document (Declaration of Sentiments and Resolutions n.d.).

Reception, Conflicts with Abolitionism, and the Convention's Narrow Scope

After event organizers sent and published word of the Declaration of Sentiments and Resolutions, some newspapers responded positively while other publications, community members, and clergy gave negative or neutral reactions. The convention's production spurred subsequent conventions to be organized, such as the Rochester Women's Rights Convention of 1848 and the Ohio Women's Rights Convention of 1851 (McMillen 2009).

The women's rights movement in the United States grew out of the abolitionist movement, as not only did women's rights organizers agree with the moral concern of ending slavery, but they hoped attention might also be drawn to their own struggles in turn. Unfortunately, however, the simultaneous efforts for both abolition and women's rights for some organizers, such as Elizabeth Cady Stanton and Susan B. Anthony, were at odds with each other. Prior to and following the US Civil War, Stanton expressed some reservations about freed Black men being granted the franchise, a privilege that would follow with the ratification of the Fifteenth Amendment to the US Constitution. In Stanton's view, she felt white women were positionally equal, if not superior, to Black emancipated slaves and would be rendered inferior if Black men were granted voting rights like white men while women were not (Davis 1983).

Finally, the Seneca Falls Convention was primarily an event for middle- and upper-class, aristocratic, educated people—with all but one attendee being white. The convention's participants offered little to nothing for the perspectives of women of color and working-class women. The convention's outcome was the product of limited access to societal privileges, such as education, for most people and an unexpanded scope for women's rights organizers at the time (Tong and Botts 2018).

Legacy

The Seneca Falls Convention of 1848 marked a major moment in the history of women's rights and feminism in the United States due to its status as the first recorded convention and gathering for the specific discussion of women's rights in the United States. The Declaration of Sentiments and Resolutions, born out of the convention's process, elevated women's observations and grievances of their unequal treatment in a patriarchal society into public view. The convention's outcomes spurred subsequent motivation for future conversations and organizing aimed at securing equal rights and treatment for women, such as the eventual right to vote through the Nineteenth Amendment to the US Constitution. Although it would take many more decades to shed light on the lack of intersectional perspectives during the convention's proceedings, the outcomes provided the opportunities for women of color feminists and organizers to begin drawing attention through their available means at the interlocking oppressions that impacted their lives in comparison to white, privileged women.

Kale Wilk

See Also: Biblical Complementarianism; Liberal Feminism; Nineteenth Amendment; Suffrage

Further Reading

Davis, Angela. 1983. *Women, Race and Class*. New York: Random House.

Harris, Jennifer Chapin. 1996. "Celebrating Herstory: The History of Seneca Falls." *Off Our Backs* 28, no. 7: 9. https://www.jstor.org/stable/20836139.

Kerber, Linda. 1977. "From the Declaration of Independence to the Declaration of Sentiments: The Legal Status of Women in the Early Republic 1776–1848." *Human Rights* 6 (2): 115–24. http://www.jstor.org/stable/27879046.

McMillen, Sally. 2009. *Seneca Falls and the Origins of the Women's Rights Movement.* New York: Oxford University Press.

National Park Service. n.d. "Report of the Woman's Rights Convention." Accessed December 14, 2024. https://www.nps.gov/wori/learn/historyculture/report-of-the-womans-rights-convention.htm.

National Women's History Museum. n.d. "The Declaration of Sentiments and Resolutions." Accessed December 14, 2024. https://www.womenshistory.org/resources/primary-source/declaration-sentiments-and-resolution.

Ritchie, Joy, and Kate Ronald, eds. 2001. *Available Means: An Anthology of Women's Rhetoric(s).* Pittsburgh: University of Pittsburgh Press.

Schneider, Jennifer. 2023. "175th Anniversary of the Seneca Falls Convention." *Smithsonian American Women's History Museum,* July 13. Accessed December 14, 2024. https://womenshistory.si.edu/blog/175th-anniversary-seneca-falls-convention.

Tong, Rosemarie, and Tina Fernandes Botts. 2018. *Feminist Thought: A More Comprehensive Introduction.* New York: Routledge.

SETTLER COLONIALISM

Settler colonialism describes the ongoing, violent process by which one group of people displace and erase the Indigenous peoples (sometimes referred to as Native, American Indian, Native Alaskan, First Nations, and/or Aboriginal peoples) of a land. Gender plays a significant role in settler colonialism, impacting both settlers and Indigenous peoples. Because settlers cannot return to their countries of origin, reconciliation between settlers and Indigenous peoples describes a hoped-for future in which both settlers and Indigenous communities can live well together.

Defining Settler Colonialism

According to historian Patrick Wolfe, settler colonialism is comprised of two foundational acts of violence. First, settlers displace (or replace) Indigenous peoples from the land (1999, 1). Before settlers arrived, millions of Indigenous peoples populated the land currently called North America. One form of removal was biological. Settlers brought with them many diseases against which Indigenous peoples did not possess natural immunity. In some cases, settlers knowingly infected Native communities (Fenn 2000). Settlers also used so-called legal means. Through legislation such as the Indian Removal Act (1830), the US government forced relocation for many Native peoples. The Trail of Tears was one of the deadliest forced marches, killing thousands upon their removal from the American South to Oklahoma (Thornton 1984). Settlers also massacred Indigenous peoples, as in the case of the Wounded Knee Massacre, where soldiers murdered approximately 300 men, women, and children, all of whom were engaged in ceremony (Warren 2017). Some Indigenous peoples have been moved away from settler society into parcels of land called reservations (United States) or reserves (Canada, Australia) or places like the Gaza Strip (Israel).

Second, settlers attempt to erase or disavow Native peoples and cultures (Wolfe 1999, 2). The erasure of Native peoples and cultures takes a wide variety of forms. Settler laws and policies, political and educational institutions, and storytelling have attempted to disavow Native life and presence. In some places, like Australia, settlers might tell stories of an empty land void of Aboriginal peoples, referred to as the doctrine of *terra nullius*, which roughly translates as "nobody's land" (Veracini 2010, 81 and 93). In other places, such as the United States, settlers use the long-standing colonial trope of "savage/civilized," describing Indigenous peoples as primitive or violent peoples who did not attend to land in a so-called civilized way. The Declaration of Independence calls Indigenous people "merciless Indian savages," language that functions as one important and foundational example of disavowal in the national imagination (National Archives 2023).

Throughout American culture, disavowal stories abound. Settlers can read the *Little House of the Prairie* novels (or watch the television series), play the video game *Oregon Trail*, or watch many examples of Hollywood Westerns—like John Ford's *The Searchers* (1956) or *Stagecoach* (1939)—or their science-fiction incarnations, such as James Cameron's *Avatar* (2009) or Steven Spielberg's *War of the Worlds* (2005). Since erasure or disavowal often takes place in words and images (such as laws or stories), settler colonialism remains a powerful ideological force in settler societies (Wolfe 1999, 3).

The history of displacement and erasure has led to harmful outcomes for Indigenous peoples. Native people face high incarceration rates (Prison Policy n.d.). Indigenous women, girls, Two-Spirit, and queer people face profound vulnerability to sexual violence, murder, human trafficking, or disappearance (US Department of the Interior n.d., "Missing"). Native children are removed from their homes at higher rates than the general population (Association n.d., Washington 2021). Wealth and health disparities persist for Native communities (Grutman 2021). Stereotypes and caricatures of Indigenous people abound in the form of sports teams' mascots or popular images, like the Florida State Seminoles or the drunk Indian (FitzGerald 2013). As these outcomes illustrate, displacement and erasure are not events locked away in the past. Rather, settler colonialism is a "structure" or an ongoing way of life on stolen lands (Wolfe 1999, 1–3).

It is important to underscore that these attempts did not succeed. Indigenous peoples across the globe were not eradicated or assimilated into settler culture. Native communities have preserved their culture, languages, ways of life, and sovereignty as nations.

Settler Colonialism as a Gendered Process

Indigenous feminists point out how the process of settler colonialism is gendered, for both Natives and settlers. Settler governments often imposed heteropatriarchy upon Native communities. The "patriarchy" part of heteropatriarchy means that power and governance is attributed to men and masculinity; the "hetero" part of heteropatriarchy means that governance requires and assumes heterosexual marriages in which men lead and women submit. The settler government in Canada, for example, used the Indian Act (1876) to regulate "the marriage of Indigenous peoples to confer lines of descent, property, and landholding to men, even though most [Native] societies were matrilineal" (Arvin, Tuck, and Morrill 2013, 15). Furthermore, the government "elevated male leaders within bands as intermediaries with the state, which also specifically denied the traditional authority of women" (Aikau et al. 2015, 101).

Because many Indigenous peoples were matrilineal, community and status were often conferred through mothers. However, when settler governments imposed patriarchal inheritance and status, this meant, in part, that if Indigenous women married non-Indigenous folks both the mother and her children lost their governmentally recognized status. Without the governmental recognition, many people who would have been deemed Native by their communities lost access to resources, like reserve lands or healthcare, that the government promised to First Nations peoples. As a result, these families were often isolated from Native communities. The term "blood quantum" describes this process of erasing Natives from the governmental status, because they are "less Native" by blood than one of their parents. In these cases, imposed heteropatriarchy served as a means of erasure, both politically and culturally.

Within settler communities, heteropatriarchy advanced settlement across the emerging nation-state. In the United States, settlers valued the nuclear family, which created a need for and a focus on reproduction, birthing the next generation of settlers (Arvin, Tuck, and Morril 2013, 14–15; Morgensen 2011, 78). This is part of the ideological work of stories such as *The Little House on the Prairie*, naturalizing a heteropatriarchal nuclear family as one of the primary means of displacing Indigenous peoples.

Reconciliation

In settler societies, settlers cannot leave Native lands and return to their countries of origin, which means that a good future between settlers and Indigenous peoples must include some form of reconciliation. While settlers tend to think of reconciliation as putting the past to rest, it is better to think of reconciliation as the possibility that settlers and Indigenous peoples can live a life together on the land in a way that is beneficial to everyone.

While no nation-state can be said to have accomplished reconciliation, there have been attempts, as was the case with Canada's dealings with Residential Schools. Both American and Canadian settlers used Residential Schools as a means of erasure. These state-funded, Church-run schools attempted to convert Indigenous peoples to Christianity and assimilate them into settler culture. The government forcibly removed Indigenous children from their homes, placing them in schools sometimes thousands of miles away. Many experienced their education as a systematic assault on their bodies and culture. As Canadian prime minister Stephen Harper confessed in 2008, the purpose of the schools was "to kill the Indian within the child" (CBC 2008). To accomplish erasure, the Truth and Reconciliation Commission of Canada (TRC) recounts that educators cut students' hair, forbade traditional practices, and stripped Indigenous students of their names. Survivors report being strapped, humiliated, handcuffed, manacled, beat, neglected, locked away, and sexually assaulted. Furthermore, Indigenous children died at astronomical rates in these schools (TRC 2015, vi–xi), many of whom were placed in unmarked graves (Austen 2023; Associated Press 2022).

After the last Canadian Residential School closed in 1996, Residential School survivors filed lawsuits, and by 2005, there were over 18,000 cases. Eventually, one case proceeded to the Supreme Court, and the government settled the case out of court. As part of the settlement, the Canadian government provided funds for the TRC and officially apologized. From 2008 to 2015, the TRC heard testimony from survivors, held public hearings, and published a multivolume report, which included ninety-four Calls-to-Action, all of which the federal government committed to implementing.

The Calls-to-Action are, in effect, what the TRC believes Canada must do if settlers want reconciliation with Native communities. Some of these calls address systemic responses to the fallout of displacement and erasure in sectors like healthcare, the legal system, and education. Call-to-Action #1, for example, says, "We call upon the federal, provincial, territorial, and Aboriginal governments to commit to reducing the number of Aboriginal children in care" (TRC 2015, 319). Others address ideological concerns. Call-to-Action #49 says, "We call upon all religious denominations and faith groups who have not already done so to repudiate concepts used to justify European sovereignty over Indigenous lands and peoples, such as the Doctrine of Discovery" (TRC 2015, 327).

Other countries, like New Zealand and South Africa, have taken slightly different approaches. South Africa removed the Apartheid government, engaged in a Truth and Reconciliation Commission, and rewrote their constitution, although the success of such measures remains a matter of debate (Oyedemi 2021). New Zealand's reconciliation centered the founding treaty between settlers and Maori peoples, the Treaty of Waitangi. Reconciliation involved cash reparations, an apology from Queen Elizabeth II, and the return of land (Cineas 2023). No one would say that these countries have achieved reconciliation. They are merely evidence that Indigenous peoples are leading the way in imagining what a shared good future can be.

Naaman Wood

See Also: Colonialism; Decolonialism; Patriarchy; Structural Oppression; White Supremacy

Further Reading

Aikau, Hokulani K., Maile Arvin, Mishuana Goeman, and Scott Morgensen. 2015. "Indigenous Feminisms Roundtable." *Frontiers: A Journal of Women Studies* 36, no. 3: 84–106.

Arvin, Maile, Eve Tuck, and Angie Morrill. 2013. "Decolonizing Feminism: Challenging Connections between Settler Colonialism and Heteropatriarchy." *Feminist Formations* 25, no. 1 (Spring): 8–34.

Associated Press, The. 2022. "US Report Identifies Burial Sites Linked to Boarding Schools for Native Americans." *NPR*, May 11, 2022. https://www.npr.org/2022/05/11/1098276649/u-s-report-details-burial-sites-linked-to-boarding-schools-for-native-americans.

Association of American Indian Affairs. n.d. "Indian Child Welfare Act." Accessed February 1, 2023. https://www.indian-affairs.org/icwa.html.

Austen, Ian. 2023. "More Evidence of Children's Graves Is Found at Former Indigenous School." *The New York Times*, January 19, 2023. https://www.nytimes.com/2023/01/19/graves-indigenous-school-canada.html.

CBC. 2008. "Prime Minister Stephen Harper's Statement of Apology." June 11, 2008, https://www.cbc.ca/news/canada/prime-minister-stephen-harper-s-statement-of-apology-1.734250.

Cineas, Fabiola. 2023. "New Zealand's Māori Fought for Reparations — and Won." *Vox*, January 17, 2023. https://www.vox.com/the-highlight/23518642/new-zealand-reparations-maori-settlements.

Fenn, Elizabeth. 2000. "Biological Warfare in Eighteenth-Century North America: Beyond Jeffery Amherst." *The Journal of American History* 86, no. 4 (March): 1552–80.

FitzGerald, Michael Ray. 2013. *Native Americans on Network TV: Stereotypes, Myths, and the "Good Indian."* Lanham, MD: Rowman and Littlefield.

Grutman, Aurora J. 2021 "The Racial Wealth Gap Is a Racial Health Gap." *Kentucky Law Journal* 110, no. 1: 723–41.

Morgensen, Scott Lauria, 2011. *Spaces Between Us: Queer Settler Colonialism and Indigenous Decolonialization.* Minneapolis: University of Minnesota Press.

National Archives. 2023. "Declaration of Independence: A Transcription." Last modified October 11, 2023. https://www.archives.gov/founding-docs/declaration-transcript.

Oyedemi, Toks Dele. 2021. "Postcolonial Casualties: 'Born-Frees' and Decolonisation in South Africa." *Journal of Contemporary African Studies* 39, no. 2 (January): 214–29. https://doi.org/10.1080/02589001.2020.1864305.

Prison Policy Initiative. n.d. "Native Incarceration in the US." Accessed February 1, 2024. https://www.prisonpolicy.org/profiles/native.html#:~:text=Native%20people%20are%20incarcerated%20in,people%20(181%20per%20100%2C000).

Thornton, Russell. 1984. "Cherokee Population Losses during the Trail of Tears: A New Perspective and a New Estimate." *Ethnohistory* 31, no. 4 (Autumn): 289–300. https://www.jstor.org/stable/482714.

Truth and Reconciliation Commission of Canada (TRC). 2015. *Honouring the Truth, Reconciliation for the Future, Volume One: Summary, Final Report of the Truth and Reconciliation Commission of Canada.* Toronto: James Lorimer and Company.

US Department of the Interior: Indian Affairs. n.d. "Federal Indian Boarding School Initiative." Accessed February 1, 2024. https://www.bia.gov/service/federal-indian-boarding-school-initiative.

US Department of the Interior: Indian Affairs. n.d. "Missing and Murdered Indigenous People Crisis: Violence Against Native Americans and Alaska Natives Far Exceed National Averages." Accessed January 31, 2024. https://www.bia.gov/service/mmu/missing-and-murdered-indigenous-people-crisis.

Veracini, Lorenzo. 2010. *Settler Colonialism: A Theoretical Overview.* New York: Palgrave Macmillan.

Warren, Louis S. 2017. *God's Red Son: The Ghost Dance Religion and the Making of Modern America.* New York: Basic Books.

Washington, Jessica. 2021. "Minnesota's Foster Care System Perpetuates the Legacy of Racist Boarding Schools, Native Mothers and Experts Say." *The Fuller Project*, December 21, 2021. https://fullerproject.org/story/minnesotas-foster-care-system-perpetuates-the-legacy-of-racist-boarding-schools-native-mothers-and-experts-say/#:~:text=Native%20children%20in%20the%201970s,care%20than%20their%20white%20peers.

Wolfe, Patrick. 1999. *Settler Colonialism and the Transformation of Anthropology: The Politics and Poetics of an Ethnographic Event.* London: Cassell.

SEX EDUCATION

Sex education refers to the teaching and learning about sex and sexuality, primarily taught by institutions like schools. Sex education can include instruction on everything from puberty, consent, and healthy relationships to safe sex practices, birth control, and sexually transmitted infections (STIs). As of 2025, no federal laws dictate what sex education should look like or how it should be taught in schools, meaning sex education in many states does not have to be medically accurate or based in science. Decisions about sex education are made at the state and local level, which means that what type of information you get about sex, the body, and sexuality depends mostly on where you live.

Formal sexual education in schools as we know it only began in the 1900s as fears mounted about STIs and teen pregnancy (Filik 2021). In 1964, Dr. Mary S. Calderone, a physician who had served as medical director for Planned Parenthood, founded the Sex Information and Education Council of the US to "establish man's sexuality as a health entity . . . to the end that human beings may be aided toward responsible use of the sexual faculty toward assimilation of sex into their individual life patterns as a creative and recreative force" (Haffner 1989).

Despite this progressive focus, the culture wars of the 1960s and 1970s led to battles between Calderone's council and abstinence-focused groups. Everything changed in the 1980s with the AIDS epidemic. Fear led to an increase in sex education programs, changing from just three states to forty-seven states mandating sex education (Hall et al. 2016). The landscape has shifted again and currently fewer states support sex education programs, despite the growing need for more information about sexuality and gender.

Presently, there are two dominant approaches to sex education in the United States: abstinence-only and comprehensive sex education (CSE). Abstinence focuses on getting students to abstain from sex until marriage. Many proponents of abstinence-only education note that not having sex is the only 100 percent effective way to prevent teen pregnancy. Abstinence only programs are also federally funded, meaning that a grant program provides money to schools to present information about sex in abstinence-focused ways. For example, programs funded by the Title V Sexual Risk Avoidance Education note that "grantees to discuss contraception, but they are barred from providing demonstrations of how specific methods work" ("Federally Funded Abstinence-Only Programs" 2021). Abstinence-only curricula typically try and discourage students from having sex and describe sex within the context of heterosexual relationships. This means that queer youth often receive no formal education about what sex and sexuality looks like for them. Still, this is the primary form of sex education that most schools offer in the United States. Based on the most recent survey from the Guttmacher Institute, of the thirty-eight states and Washington, D.C. that mandate sex ed, twenty-nine states have rules that abstinence must be stressed ("Sex and HIV Education" 2023). In total, only eighteen states require that the information provided to students be "medically accurate" ("Abstinence-Only Education States" 2024). Most youth in the United States will receive some form of abstinence-only education, if they receive any education at all.

At the other end of the spectrum, CSE works to empower students with as much knowledge as possible so that they can make informed choices. According to the World Health Organization, CSE "gives young people accurate, age-appropriate information about sexuality and their sexual and reproductive health, which is critical for their health and survival" ("Comprehensive Sexuality Education" 2023). This type of education focuses on scientifically accurate information from a broad range of perspectives, including discussions of queer sex. CSE also has a strong emphasis on social and emotional health. For example, the Planned Parenthood CSE curriculum includes conversations about "sexual health, including sexually transmitted infections, birth control, pregnancy, and abortion" and "human development, including puberty, anatomy, sexual orientation, and gender identity," among many other topics ("What is Sex Education?" 2024). CSE aligns with a feminist view of sex education as they have similar goals. For instance, the National Organization for Women (NOW) describes a feminist approach to sex education as one that "shifts the lens from an abstinent-only view about sex education to empowering youth to make safe, informed, and thoughtful decisions regarding their sexual health" (Kim 2023).

Many feminist activists are pushing for a more comprehensive approach to sex education. For example, feminist organizations have begun to celebrate May as #SexEdForAll to raise "awareness of the critical need for national sex education" (Thimme 2021). CSE allows people to challenge society's view of sex and sexuality, leading to less shame and stigma around these important topics.

All in all, sex education looks remarkably different state to state and district to district. This means that students across the United States are receiving different information about their bodies, sex, and sexuality. Incorrect and incomplete education about sex leads to poor health outcomes, worsened mental health, and does not decrease the rate of sexual activity ("Comprehensive Sexuality Education" 2023). As with most issues concerned with bodily autonomy, sex, and choice, sex education will continue to be a battleground for discussions of morality, individual empowerment, and bodily control.

Hannah Taylor

See Also: Biopower; Bodily Autonomy; Choice; Menstruation; National Organization for Women (NOW)

Further Reading

"Abstinence-Only Education States 2024." 2024. *World Population Review*. Accessed July 19, 2024. https://worldpopulationreview.com/state-rankings/abstinence-only-education-states.

"Comprehensive Sexuality Education." 2016. *The American College of Obstetricians and Gynecologists*, November 2016. Accessed July 19, 2024. https://www.acog.org/clinical/clinical-guidance/committee-opinion/articles/2016/11/comprehensive-sexuality-education.

"Comprehensive Sexuality Education." 2023. *World Health Organization*, May 18, 2023. https://www.who.int/news-room/questions-and-answers/item/comprehensive-sexuality-education.

"Federally Funded Abstinence-Only Programs: Harmful and Ineffective." 2021. *Guttmacher Institute*, May 2021. Accessed July 19, 2024. https://www.guttmacher.org/fact-sheet/abstinence-only-programs.

Filik, Jessica. 2021. "The History of Sexuality Education in The United States." *Sexual Health Alliance*, June 8, 2021. Accessed July 19, 2024. https://sexualhealthalliance.com/nymphomedia-blog/the-history-of-sexuality-education-in-the-united-states.

Haffner, Debra W. 1989. "SIECUS: 25 Years of Commitment to Sexual Health and Education." *Sex Information Education Council of the US* 17, no. 4 (March/April): 1–24.

Hall, Kelli S., Jessica McDermott Sales, Kelli A. Kormro, and John Santelli. 2016. "The State of Sex Education in the United States." *Journal of Adolescent Health* 58, no. 6 (June): 595–97.

Kim. 2023. "A Call for a Feminist Approach to Sex Education." *National Organization for Women*, July 26, 2023. Accessed August 27, 2024. https://now.org/blog/a-call-for-a-feminist-approach-to-sex-education/.

"Sex and HIV Education." 2023. *Guttmacher Institute*, September 1, 2023. Accessed July 19, 2024. https://www.guttmacher.org/state-policy/explore/sex-and-hiv-education.

Thimme, Lucy. 2021. "Feminist Sex Ed: What It Is, Why We Need It, and How It Can End the Orgasm Gap." *Ms. Magazine*, June 25, 2021. https://msmagazine.com/2021/06/25/feminist-sex-ed-orgasm-gap-clitoris-women/.

"What is Sex Education?" 2024. *Planned Parenthood*. Accessed July 19, 2024. https://www.plannedparenthood.org/learn/for-educators/what-sex-education.

SEXUAL OBJECTIFICATION

Sexual objectification is the act of viewing another person as a tool or object to be used for one's own sexual goals (Kellie 2019). Sexual objectification occurs when a person's body or body parts are seen as separate from their person and consequently are viewed as a physical object of sexual desire (Szymanski 2011). Women and girls are more often the target of sexual objectification than boys and men (Calogero 2013). When a person's body or body parts are viewed as separate from their person, they are dehumanized or seen as less than human. When men dehumanize women, men become more willing to commit "sexually aggressive actions towards" women (Kellie 2019).

Sexual objectification has many negative effects like reduced cognitive flow, depression, eating disorders, and sexual dysfunction for victims, and it increases the likelihood of sexual violence from perpetrators. In addition, women who are sexually objectified are "perceived" by their perpetrators "to have less of a mind for thoughts or decisions" and thought to be "less deserving of moral treatment" (Kellie 2019). Sexual objectification is one of the main forms of sexual violence that women experience, and it infringes on women's liberation. This sexual discrimination and violence can come in many forms.

For example, sexual objectification is rampant in all forms of media including film, TV, ad campaigns, and social media. Women and girls are often subjected to catcalling on the street regardless of their physical appearance; in fact, 77 percent of women report experiencing verbal sexual harassment compared to 34 percent of men (Kearl 2018). Films and television shows are primary examples of women experiencing sexual objectification; women are often cast in roles or depicted in ways that prioritize their sexual appeal over their character's depth, skills, or intelligence. For example, Megan Fox's character, Mikaela Banes, in the *Transformers* film series is subjected to sexual objectification. The camera often does full-body pans that depict her as an array of body parts and her character receives multiple slow-motion scenes that emphasize her body parts (JCU 2022). Film theorist Laura Mulvey and queer comic artist Alison Bechdel have worked to raise awareness of sexual objectification in media by theorizing the "Male Gaze" and developing the Bechdel Test, respectively.

Feminists Theorize Sexual Objectification

Feminists theorize sexual objectification as a process that primarily targets women but which also targets LGBTQ+ people, reducing women and LGBTQ+ people to their physical appearance and sexual attributes, rather than being valued for their whole selves, including their intelligence, capabilities, and humanity. Sexual objectification often involves viewing women as instruments of male pleasure, stripping away their agency and subjectivity. Many feminists theorize that sexual objectification perpetuates gender inequality by reinforcing the idea that women's primary value lies in their sexual desirability to men. The sexual objectification of LGBTQ+ people also situates their primary value in their sexual desirability (or lack thereof) to straight cis men; here the sexual objectification of LGBTQ+ people can also ridicule or demonize them for their supposed failure to fully arouse or satisfy masculine desire.

Drawing on and further developing the psychological theory known as Objectification Theory, feminists demonstrate how sexual objectification damages women's mental health in ways that perpetuate sexism and gender inequality (Szymanski 2011). Objectification is understood to operate in two ways. First, direct experiences with sexual objectification—such as being catcalled on the street. And second, the internalization of sexual objectification where women come to see themselves and their own body through the so-called "Male Gaze" or through the eyes of sexual objectification (Vendemia 2024). The idea here is that women know they're going to be judged and sexually objectified, so they learn to self-objectify—to judge themselves—and filter their decisions (e.g., how to dress, how to position their bodies, how to comport themselves) in light of the reality that they will be sexually objectified. Self-objectification results in chronic self-surveillance of one's own physical appearance and the belief that one's physical appearance and attractiveness to others is more important than one's whole self. Self-objectification perpetuates the dehumanization of women and the reduction of a woman's value to her physical appearance. Sexual objectification as a whole perpetuates sexism and leads to internalized sexism (Calogero 2013).

Feminist Activism

Feminist activists have started many movements and organizations working to end the sexual objectification of women, girls, and LGBTQ+ people. For example, the #WomenNotObjects movement was started by Madonna Badger, a New York ad executive, in 2016 in order to end the sexual objectification of women in media ads. Badger released a two-minute-long YouTube video critiquing various advertisement campaigns that feature the sexual objectification of women, including ads for Skyy Vodka, Post-Its, Ford, DirecTV, and Tom Ford (O'Brien 2016). Another example of feminist activism to end sexual objectification is the Geena Davis Institute on Gender in Media. This organization has been on the forefront of groundbreaking research on the representation of women and other underrepresented minority groups in film and television.

Ultimately, sexual objectification dehumanizes people, reducing them to body parts for masculine pleasure rather than recognizing their humanity and respecting their bodily autonomy. Feminists reject sexual objectification believing that everyone deserves to be a sexual subject—not an object.

Ava Doty

See Also: The Bechdel Test; Bodily Autonomy; Internalized Sexism; Male Gaze; #MeToo; Misogyny; Rape Culture

Further Reading

Calogero, Rachel M. 2013. "Objects Don't Object: Evidence That Self-Objectification Disrupts Women's Social Activism." *Psychological Science* 24, no. 3: 312–18.

JCU, The Matthew. 2022. "Male Gaze and Female Objectification in Contemporary Cinema." March 15, 2022. https://thematthewrome.com/2022/03/15/male-gaze-and-female-objectification-in-contemporary-cinema/.

Kearl, Holly. 2018. "The Facts behind the #me Too Movement: A National Study on Sexual Harassment and Assault." *Stop Street Harassment.*

Kellie, Dax J., Khandis R. Blake, and Robert C. Brooks. 2019. "What Drives Female Objectification? An Investigation of Appearance-Based Interpersonal Perceptions and the Objectification of Women." *PLoS ONE* 14, no. 8: e0221388. https://doi.org/10.1371/journal.pone.0221388.

O'Brien, Sara Ashley. 2016. "#WomenNotObjects: 'Objectifying Women Is up There with Inequality.'" *CNNMoney*, January 26, 2016. https://money.cnn.com/2016/01/26/media/womennotobjects-ad-campaign/index.html.

Szymanski, Dawn M., Lauren B. Moffitt, and Erika R. Carr. 2011. "Sexual Objectification of Women: Advances to Theory and Research 1ψ7." *The Counseling Psychologist* 39, no. 1: 6–38. https://doi.org/10.1177/0011000010378402.

Vendemia, Megan A. 2024. "Sexual Objectification versus Empowerment: Examining the Effects of Sexualized Women's Facial Expression on Viewers' Evaluations of Social Cognition and Self-Objectification." *Body Image* 50 (September): 101721. https://doi.org/10.1016/j.bodyim.2024.101721.

SEXUAL PLEASURE

Sexual pleasure is "the physical and/or psychological satisfaction and enjoyment derived from solitary or shared erotic experiences, including thoughts, dreams and autoeroticism" (Global Advisory Board 2016). Feminist sexologists and sex-positive feminists are working to make sex safer and make sexual pleasure more accessible for everyone—especially women.

Patriarchal Sex Scripts

Cultural assumptions about sex are narrow and limiting for many people: in general, sex is thought to involve vaginal penetration by a penis in a heterosexual interaction. Sex advice columnist and gay rights activist Dan Savage (2013) refers to this as PIV, which stands for penis in vagina. PIV forms the basis for most cultural "sex scripts" or the assumptions about what constitutes sex, how people will behave in a sexual encounter, and how a sexual encounter will unfold. As Dan Savage points out, the PIV definition of sex and its typical sex script excludes many other forms of sex, such as sex in which two women orgasm without penetration or two men sexually penetrating each other without involving vaginas.

Most heteronormative sex scripts reinforce patriarchal roles. Men are assigned the dominant role: they must initiate, take charge, and satisfy their woman. Within heterosexual scripts, men are in control of the sexual encounter. Women are typically assigned submissive roles in heterosexual sex scripts: they must meet their man's expectations, help him achieve his goals, and ensure he feels manly throughout the sexual experience. These scripts play out across popular culture. Men are idealized in entertainment as romantic and sexual initiators who take control and provide women with unmatched pleasure by making them orgasm. Films and television series often feature plotlines where a man (romantically) chases a woman down, pursing her even after she says "no," and the woman seemingly experiences the greatest sexual pleasure when finally succumbing to his overwhelming desire. Moreover, entertainment such as Netflix's *Bridgerton* tends to idealize women as paradoxically virginal and yet sexually available to (heroic) men.

These cultural sex scripts affect people's real lives. Men's sense of self—their masculinity—is tied to their reputation for performing well in bed. Men are shamed if they cannot "get it up," cannot seduce women, or cannot bring women to orgasm. Patriarchal sex scripts insist that men have insatiable sex drives and valorize men who have many sexual partners. These scripts idealize the complete opposite in women. Women are typically idealized as not wanting or thinking about sex (unless aroused by the ideal man), and women are valorized for sexual abstinence.

The PIV sexual script is built around men's orgasms. This is a two-part script featuring a rising action/foreplay and then climax/orgasm. The orgasm is so essential to the heteronormative view of sex that its absence is jarring. In a study by Emily Opperman and her colleagues (2014, 507), adolescents named the orgasm as "the purpose and end of sex." Adolescents said that if their partner didn't orgasm, they felt bad about themselves that they couldn't make them come (Opperman et al. 2014). Women often fake orgasms rather than deal with a man's shame over failing to make her come (Thomas, Stelzl, and Lafrance 2016). As a result, heterosexual men can feel like they are doing a good job in bed even when they aren't (Thomas, Stelzl, and Lafrance 2016). Heterosexual men often delay (or attempt to delay) their own climax until they think the woman has climaxed; as such, faking an orgasm is a good way for women to end a sexual encounter that has grown boring or unpleasant—again, without having to deal with the fallout of a man's bruised ego (Thomas, Stelzl, and Lafrance 2016).

Theorizing Sexual Pleasure: More than Orgasm

Instead of using heteronormative scripts that center around PIV thrusting and orgasms, many feminist sexologists, gay rights activists, and sex activists encourage people to rewrite sexual scripts in ways that center reciprocity, comfort, and pleasure. Good sex typically occurs when partners feel comfortable with each other (Fahs and Plante 2016). Partners who are emotionally connected report higher rates of sexual pleasure (Fahs and Plante 2016). Feminist sexologists encourage everyone to abandon patriarchal sexual scripts in favor of developing scripts where everyone involved enthusiastically consents, experiences pleasure, and has control over the experience.

Many things contribute to bad sex, including poor body image. Women's bodies are under such tight scrutiny and so often shamed that many women feel uncomfortable being naked (Ralston 2021). Women need to feel good about their bodies to enjoy sex. Likewise, religion can factor into sexual pleasure. When people feel like they are sinning or disappointing religious leaders and family members, it can be harder for them to enjoy sex.

Feeling comfortable and happy with one's sexual partner can help counteract the negative messages that women internalize about their bodies, value, and morality. Feminists theorize sexual pleasure as more complex than just orgasming; pleasurable sex is emotionally and contextually informed, and people should always be in control of what happens to their bodies.

Sex-positive feminists remind us that people are unique and their sexual pleasures are also unique. From this perspective, sexual fetishes are normal. People like what they like. Sex positivity means respecting others' desires. In colloquial phrasing, sex-positive feminists don't "yuck other people's yum." This doesn't mean that feminists have to be game for anything, and it doesn't mean that people have to like or be enthusiastic about every sexual activity. Instead, the idea of not "yucking" someone's "yum" means that feminists respect others' consensual, healthy sexual desires, even when those desires lie outside their own interests (Buck 2021). For example, roughly 20 percent of college-age women in the Unites States report having consensually engaged in anal sex (Woodman-Maynard et al. 2009; Baldwin and Baldwin 2000). Sex-positive feminism doesn't encourage people who are uninterested in anal sex to engage in these behaviors, but it does require that we not shame or look down on others' pleasurable experiences.

Sex-positive feminists want people to experience healthy, enthusiastically consensual pleasure. There are so many types of sexual pleasure—both autoerotic and partnered—and sex-positive feminists are here for it all. Feminist sexologists often recommend that each person explore themselves through masturbation, fantasy, and erotica, to see what they enjoy. When engaging in sexual activity with other people, sexologists encourage us to communicate kindly and clearly about our desires. Our sexual partners are not mind readers; they are unlikely to know what we desire unless we tell them and show them.

Educating for Sexual Pleasure

Today, most sex education curricula focus on the potential dangers of sex. In public schools, sex education programs are limited by federal and state requirements; they typically focus on STI and pregnancy prevention. It is rare for high school sex education programs to mention pleasure. Similarly, current US legislation largely condemns sex work as illegal. This endangers sex workers (many of whom are women) and frames sex-for-pleasure as shameful. Moreover, in recent history, LGBTQ+ marriage, same-sex sexual activity, and contraception were illegal in the United States. These laws, privileges, inequalities, and histories result in a sexual landscape where lower-class women, younger women, less educated women, and women of color are more likely to report having bad sex (Fahs and Plante 2016). Meanwhile, disabled women have long experienced forced sterilization, removing their autonomy over their own sexuality.

Currently, sex education often denies women knowledge of their own bodies. Women often remain ignorant of where their clitoris is on the outside of their bodies and of the clitoris' large internal "leg" structure as it wraps around the vagina, creating what can be experienced as the "G spot." Similarly, women are often ignorant of the way their vestibular bulbs (internal erectile tissue that line the sides of the vagina) become engorged during arousal and thus squeeze the vagina creating an effect sometimes referred to as a "tight" vagina. A "tight" vagina has to do with arousal rather than the size or shape of the vagina itself. Likewise, women are often unaware of the range of shapes and sizes for the vulva's "inner" and "outer" labia (the so-called "lips" around the exterior of the vagina). The "inner" labia can be large, extruding beyond the "outer" labia. Moreover, women are often underinformed regarding the role the clitoris plays in sexual pleasure. The PIV script emphasizes penial thrusting into the vagina, but the clitoris is located toward the top of the vulva—above the urethra opening and toward the pubic bone. The clitoris is central to most women's physical sexual pleasure and orgasm, but it is located in a position that rarely receives stimulation through PIV sexual activity (Winston 2010). Denied the knowledge of their own bodies, women are often at a loss when it comes to sexual pleasure.

Within this context, sexologists such as Ruth Westheimer (known as Dr. Ruth, the author of many books on women's sexual pleasure), gay rights activists such as Dan Savage, and organizations such as OMGYes.com have been advocating for sexual pleasure in all its forms. The sex-positivity movement wants everyone to become comfortable with their bodies and to fulfill their sexual desires—whether this means abstinence, masturbation, or partnered sex in all its healthy and consensual forms. For instance, Dan Savage (2013) has long argued that rather than the adherence to patriarchal sex scripts that regard the rising action in sexual activity as "foreplay" (or not sex) and regard PIV activity as "intercourse" (or sex), we should instead consider all of this sexual activity as "coreplay." This perspective recognizes that so much of sexual touch and connection is pleasurable and thus is the "core" of sexual activity. By decentering the patriarchal focus on masculine orgasm, the "coreplay" perspective emphasizes sexual pleasure—including feminine orgasms—more broadly.

At the end of the day, feminist sexology and sex-positive feminism want everyone, especially women, to feel at ease in their bodies. More than that, sex-positive feminists hope that everyone will enjoy the type of consensual sex (or abstinence) they feel drawn toward. Not everyone has sexual urges and those who do not feel drawn to sex should not be pressured into it. Yet for those who have sexual desires, feminists hope they will abandon the constraining and pressuring patriarchal sex scripts, explore their own pleasures, and thoughtfully communicate with partners before, during, and after sexual experiences in ways that advocate for themselves and promote their own pleasure. Put succinctly, Dan Savage (2013) encourages everyone who engages in partnered sex to be "good, game, and giving," to set clear boundaries, and to expect and encourage the same from their partners.

Sex-positive feminists promote sexual pleasure—whether that pleasure is paradoxically found in sexual abstinence or found in masturbation or the various partnered activities Dan Savage calls "coreplay." At the same time, sex-positive feminists caution that a lot of the erotica marketed to women recreates patriarchal scripts in which men's overbearing, jealous, overprotective, and controlling behaviors are portrayed as sexy. Likewise, a lot of pornography portrays physical violence against women (e.g., choking, rape, gang rape) and the humiliation of women as sexy. In contrast, feminists invite everyone—and especially women—to experience and relish the many safe forms of sexuality that bring healthy, generous, and consensual pleasure.

Dulcinea Licavoli

See Also: Bodily Autonomy; Body Positivity; Enthusiastic Consent; Sex Education; Virginity

Further Reading

Baldwin, Janice I., and John D. Baldwin. 2000. "Heterosexual Anal Intercourse: An Understudied, High-Risk Sexual Behavior." *Archives of Sexual Behavior* 29, no. 4: 357–73.

Buck, Jesse. 2021. "'Don't Yuck Other People's Yum': Ericka Hart's Sex Positivity Talk Attended by over 70." *The Collegian*, October 22, 2021. https://www.willamettecollegian.com/post/don-t-yuck-other-people-s-yum-ericka-hart-s-sex-positivity-talk-attended-by-over-70.

Fahs, Breanne, and Rebecca Plante. 2016. "On 'Good Sex' and Other Dangerous Ideas: Women Narrate their Joyous and Happy Sexual Encounters." *Journal of Gender Studies* 26, no. 1: 33–44.

Fahs, Breanne, and Eric Swank. 2016. "Sex Positive Movement." In *The SAGE Encyclopedia of LGBTQ Studies*, vol. 3, edited by Abbie E. Goldberg, 1012–14. Thousand Oaks, CA: Sage Publications.

Global Advisory Board for Sexual Health and Wellbeing. 2016. "Working Definition of Sexual Pleasure." Accessed October 2, 2024. https://www.gab-shw.org/our-work/working-definition-of-sexual-pleasure/.

Gruskin, Sofia, Vithika Yadav, Antón Castellanos-Usigli, Gvantsa Khizanishvili, and Eszter Kismödi. 2019. "Sexual Health, Sexual Rights and Sexual Pleasure: Meaningfully Engaging the Perfect Triangle." *Sexual and Reproductive Health Matters* 27, no. 1: 29–40.

Opperman, Emily, Virginia Braun, Victoria Clarke, and Cassandra Rogers. 2014. "'It Feels So Good It Almost Hurts': Young Adults' Experiences of Orgasm and Sexual Pleasure." *The Journal of Sex Research* 51, no. 5: 503–15.

Ralston, Meredith L. 2021. *Slut-Shaming, Whorephobia, and the Unfinished Sexual Revolution*. Montreal: McGill-Queen's University Press. Accessed October 2, 2024. https://doi.org/10.1515/9780228007982.

Savage, Dan. 2013. *American Savage: Insights, Slights, and Fights on Faith, Sex, Love, and Politics*. New York: Penguin Group.

Thomas, Emily J. Monika Stelzl, and Michelle N. Lafrance. 2016. "Faking to Finish: Women's Accounts of Feigning Sexual Pleasure to End Unwanted Sex." *Sexualities* 20, no. 3: 281–301.

Tiefer, Leonore. 2017. "Unpacking the Popularity of a Paper on Feigning Sexual Pleasure: Consider Both Sexual Politics and 21st-Century Profits." *Sexualities* 21, no. 4: 706–9.

Winston, Sheri. 2010. *Women's Anatomy of Arousal: Secret Maps to Buried Pleasure*. Sebastopol, CA: Mango Garden Press.

Woodman-Maynard, Emily, Alex Carballo-Diéguez, Ana Ventuneac, Teresa M. Exner, and Kenneth H. Mayer. 2009. "Women's Experiences with Anal Sex: Motivations and Implications for STD Prevention." *Perspectives on Sexual and Reproductive Health* 31, no. 3: 142–9.

SEXUAL REVOLUTION

The Sexual Revolution, which took place during the 1950s–1970s, marked a significant shift in attitudes and behaviors regarding sex and sexuality. This movement arose largely in response to the strict social rules around sexuality that characterized the 1940s and 1950s. It was one of many social movements shaped by the political atmosphere of the time, alongside anti-Vietnam War protests, the Civil Rights Movement, the Women's Liberation Movement, and widespread critiques of the status quo. These movements reflected a period of significant social upheaval and demands for change. From feminist perspectives, the Sexual Revolution had positive and negative effects. In many ways, the Sexual Revolution expanded women's rights, promoted sexual freedom, and recognized women as sexual beings. Yet the Sexual Revolution also prioritized masculine pleasure and often further objectified women in ways that actually strengthened patriarchy (Jeffreys 2011, 92).

The Sexual Revolution responded in part to the "intense policing" of women's sexuality as women were encouraged to have many children to boost the post-Second World War population (Meyerowitz 2014). The revolution was influenced by several key factors, including the publication of Alfred Kinsey's *Sexual Behavior in the Human Male* (1948), which illuminated the sexual behavior of the average male in the United States at the time. This behavior included masturbatory practices, oral sex, and homosexual sex acts. This book, and the subsequent second volume, *The Sexual Behavior in the*

Human Female (1953), contributed to the public revelation that women and men engaged in sexual practices that were taboo.

A second key factor in the revolution was the invention and legal distribution of birth control pills. Before its legalization, women's sexual behavior was largely constrained by the fear of unintended pregnancy, limiting their ability to make autonomous choices about their sexual lives. The legal cases *Griswold v. Connecticut* (1965) and *Eisenstadt v. Baird* (1972), which expanded access to contraception for married and unmarried women, played critical roles in making oral contraception widely accessible. This reduced the risk and taboo surrounding premarital sex and allowed women more sexual autonomy without the fear of pregnancy. Additionally, as more women entered the workforce after the Second World War, women's greater economic independence further encouraged their sexual independence (Escoffier 2015).

Ultimately, during the Sexual Revolution, attitudes toward sex and sexuality changed dramatically, which led to shifts in behavior as well. Women and men began engaging in sexual activity younger and postponing marriage; this resulted in young people experiencing greater sexual freedom for a longer period of time than previous generations (Escoffier 2015).

Feminists Theorize the Sexual Revolution

Feminists have theorized the Sexual Revolution as a movement that profoundly shaped women's sexual identities and behaviors in the United States. Yet the Sexual Revolution is something of a paradox as it liberated women in so many ways and yet further oppressed them in others.

The Sexual Revolution made a significant step toward gender equality; it challenged the restrictive norms around female sexuality and expanded women's rights to sexual freedom, particularly through the availability of contraception and the destigmatization of premarital sex. The Sexual Revolution allowed women to reclaim control over their bodies and their sexuality, challenging the notion that sexual desire and autonomy are male-dominated spheres.

Paradoxically, however, the Sexual Revolution's sexual liberation largely came at the cost of women's liberation. For example, the focus for women's sexual liberation was often on reducing their "inhibitions" to please their male partner and resulted in the further objectification of women. Essentially, the Sexual Revolution urged women to have sex earlier in heterosexual relationships, have sex more often in heterosexual relationships, and be more sexually attractive and adventurous (read: submissive and objectified) in heterosexual relationships. As such, feminists note that the Sexual Revolution often prioritized masculine pleasure and maintained masculine dominance in heterosexual relationships.

Moreover, the Sexual Revolution focused on heterosexual relationships, reinforcing heteronormativity. Heteronormativity is the idea that "normal" sexuality is a heterosexual relationship; this means that any relationship that strays from heterosexuality (i.e., homosexuality, bisexuality, etc.) is viewed as abnormal. The various sexual advice books and articles that were popular during this time (*Sex and the Single Girl* (1962), *The Feminine Mystique* (1963), *Sexual Behavior in the Human Female* (1953)) were largely "unable to conceive of homosexuality in women or men as a reasonable alternative to heterosexuality" (Jeffreys 2011, 109). Ultimately then, feminists argue that the revolution failed to address deeper systemic inequalities, like the pressures of traditional heterosexual marriage, sexual violence, reproductive justice, or the complexities of women's economic and emotional autonomy, and argue that true sexual liberation for women requires challenging these structures more deeply.

Feminist Activism

Feminist activists were instrumental in advocating for the legalization of abortion, leading to the landmark *Roe v. Wade* Supreme Court decision in 1973, which recognized a woman's constitutional right to choose to have an abortion. Organizations like the National Organization for Women (NOW) and grassroots groups such as the Jane Collective, which provided underground abortion services in the pre-Roe era, were key in this fight. NOW was founded in 1966, in the heyday of the Sexual Revolution, by Betty Friedan (author of *The Feminine Mystique*) and a group of feminists to end sex discrimination. NOW was instrumental in the fight for legal abortion and for the Equal Rights Amendment (ERA). NOW members helped protest against the Miss America pageant. The myth of the bra burners was born at this event, but no bras were burned at this protest—though some were thrown in the trash ("History of Marches and Mass Actions" 2014). NOW is still a crucial feminist organization that continues to advocate and protest sex discrimination as well as access to reproductive healthcare. The Jane Collective was an "underground organization that provided illegal abortion services" in Chicago from the late 1960s until abortion became legal in 1973 (Horwitz 2017, 1). The Jane Collective worked with the Chicago Women's Liberation Union to provide women with safe and affordable abortions and reproductive healthcare to all women of the Chicago area. These activists framed reproductive rights as essential to women's bodily autonomy and gender equality. Feminist activism was essential to the Sexual Revolution and the shift in attitudes, behaviors, and even legislature that affected and still affects women's liberation.

Ava Doty

See Also: Bodily Autonomy; *Eisenstadt v. Baird* (1972); *The Feminine Mystique*; Friedan, Betty; Kinsey Institute; #MeToo; National Organization for Women (NOW); Reproductive Justice; *Roe v. Wade* (1973); Sex Education; Sexual Objectification; Women's Liberation Movement

Further Reading

Escoffier, Jeffrey. 2015. "The Sexual Revolution, 1960–1980." *GLBTQ*. http://glbtqarchive.com/ssh/sexual_revolution_S.pdf.

"History of Marches and Mass Actions." 2014. *National Organization for Women*, May 21, 2014. https://now.org/about/history/history-of-marches-and-mass-actions/.

Horwitz, Rainey. 2017. "The Jane Collective (1969–1973)." *Embryo Project Encyclopedia*, August 7, 2017. https://keep.lib.asu.edu/items/173375/view.

Jeffreys, Sheila. 2011. *Anticlimax: A Feminist Perspective on the Sexual Revolution*, 2nd ed. North Melbourne, VIC: Spinifex Press. https://research.ebsco.com/linkprocessor/plink?id=61f2e367-6fcd-3f31-bc65-7bbee2abf7e5.

Meyerowitz, Joanne. 2014. "The Liberal 1950s? Reinterpreting Postwar American Sexual Culture." In *Gender and the Long Postwar: Reconsiderations of the United States and the Two Germanys, 1945–1989*. Baltimore, MD: Johns Hopkins University Press and Washington, DC: Woodrow Wilson Center Press. https://history.yale.edu/sites/default/files/files/liberal%2050s.pdf.

SISTERSONG

The SisterSong Women of Color Reproductive Justice Collective, known as SisterSong, is an organization based in Atlanta, Georgia, devoted to advocating for the reproductive rights of marginalized communities, especially women of color. The coalition's mission is "to strengthen and amplify the collective voices of indigenous women and women of color to achieve reproductive justice by eradicating reproductive oppression and securing human rights" ("What We Do" n.d.).

SisterSong is grounded in the concept of reproductive justice (RJ), a framework that combines reproductive rights with social justice and human rights, advocating for the right to bodily autonomy, to have children, to not have children, and to parent in safe and healthy environments. Specifically by representing Indigenous, African American, Arab and Middle Eastern, Asian and Pacific Islander, and Latina women, and LGBTQ people within their membership, SisterSong is committed to "growing and supporting the RJ movement" ("About Us" n.d.).

Origins of SisterSong

Founded in 1997 by a passionate group of women who represented sixteen different organizations, SisterSong's name came from HIV/AIDS activist Juanita Williams's comment that together, they could learn "not to sing the same song, but our individual songs in harmony" (qtd. in Strickler and Simpson 2017, 51). This namesake sentiment highlights the heavily intersectional foundation upon which SisterSong rests. Their motto, "Doing collectively what we cannot do individually," represents the shared SisterSong and RJ goals of valuing human rights by "com[ing] together as one movement with the power to win freedom for all oppressed people" ("About Us" n.d.). Other key members of SisterSong's founding team include Luz Rodriguez, who served as executive director of the Latina Roundtable on Health and Reproductive Rights, and Reena Marcelo, who was a Program Officer at the Ford Foundation's Reproductive Health Program. Funding to begin SisterSong came from the Ford Foundation (Strickler and Simpson 2017, 50).

Core Principles and Activities

SisterSong engages in various activities to achieve its mission, including advocacy, education, and direct action. They provide training and resources to community organizations, conduct research to highlight disparities in reproductive health, and work to influence policy at local, state, and national levels. Additionally, SisterSong has successfully advocated for comprehensive sex education, improved access to contraception, and better healthcare for incarcerated women ("About Us" n.d.). Their efforts have contributed to a broader understanding of RJ within the feminist movement and beyond.

One of SisterSong's notable achievements is the Trust Black Women billboard campaign, launched in response to racially biased anti-abortion campaigns targeting Black communities with misinformation and stigmatization. The campaign works to counter these narratives by promoting the voices and experiences of Black women, advocating for their autonomy and decision-making power ("Our History" 2018). SisterSong has also played a pivotal role in organizing multiple national RJ conferences, including the first National Reproductive Justice Conference in 2003 and the first Let's Talk About Sex Conference in 2007 (Price 2010; "History of LTAS" n.d.).

Ongoing Work

Despite its successes, SisterSong continues to face challenges. The political landscape in the United States has seen increasing attacks on reproductive rights, particularly targeting marginalized communities. SisterSong's commitment to intersectionality means they must address not only reproductive rights but also issues such as immigration, LGBTQ+ rights, and economic justice, which intersect with and impact reproductive health. SisterSong remains resilient in the face of these challenges, continually adapting its strategies and expanding its alliances. They emphasize the importance of solidarity and coalition building, recognizing that the fight for RJ is deeply interconnected with other social justice movements.

In a message written for SisterSong's twentieth anniversary, SisterSong's executive director Monica Simpson wrote, "We are a portal that must remain open for the people drawn to this movement—just as I was seven years ago. SisterSong will continue to be radical and real." She continued, writing, "We will continue to amplify the voices of Indigenous women and women of color, and people of all gender identities and races. We will continue to push radical reproductive justice farther and wider. And we will always stay committed to collective action" (2017, 136).

Carole Yoke-kew Chee

See Also: Bodily Autonomy; Intersectionality; Reproductive Justice; Sex Education

Further Reading

"About Us." n.d. *SisterSong*. Accessed July 17, 2024. https://www.sistersong.net/about-x2.

"History of LTAS." n.d. *LTAS*. Accessed July 18, 2024. https://www.letstalkaboutsexconference.com/page/ltas-history.

"Our History." 2018. *Trust Black Women*. Accessed July 17, 2024. https://trustblackwomen.org/our-roots.

Price, Kimala. 2010. "What is Reproductive Justice? How Women of Color Activists Are Redefining the Pro-Choice Paradigm." *Meridians: Feminism, Race, Transnationalism* 10, no. 2: 42–65.

Simpson, Monica. 2017. "Moving SisterSong Forward." In *Radical Reproductive Justice: Foundation, Theory, Practice, Critique*, edited by Loretta Ross, Lynn Roberts, Erika Derkas, and Whitney Peoples, 134–5. New York: Feminist Press at the City University of New York.

Strickler, Rachael, and Monica Simpson. 2017. "A Brief Herstory of SisterSong." In *Radical Reproductive Justice: Foundation, Theory, Practice, Critique*, edited by Loretta Ross, Lynn Roberts, Erika Derkas, and Whitney Peoples, 50–7. New York: Feminist Press at the City University of New York.

"What We Do." n.d. *SisterSong*. Accessed July 18, 2024. https://www.sistersong.net/what-we-do.

SOCIALISM

Socialism, like democracy, is a political theory and system. Emerging in the early nineteenth century as a response to the inequalities and hardships caused by the Industrial Revolution, socialism is a way of organizing people, governance, and the economy. In 1848, Karl Marx and Friedrich Engels published *The Communist Manifesto*, which became one of the most influential socialist texts. They argued class struggles shape our societies and that capitalism ought to be replaced by a classless society. They theorized socialism as a temporary form of government for when a society transitioned from capitalism to communism. In the early twentieth century, socialism gained momentum with the Russian Revolution of 1917 led by Vladimir Lenin. This revolution resulted in the creation of the Soviet Union, which ceased to exist in 1991. Today, however, many countries such as India and Nicaragua have socialist constitutions, others such as Greenland and Iceland have socialist ruling parties in their governments, and many more, including Brazil, New Zealand, Norway, Spain, and Germany, are democratic socialist countries.

In the United States, socialism often has a bad reputation given its association with communism and the authoritarian regime of the Soviet Union. However, feminists have long been concerned with how people, governance, and the economy are organized, and feminist socialism has a long history with activists and reformers such as Florence Kelley in the 1800s, theorists such as Barbara Ehrenreich during the women's liberation movement of the 1960s and 1970s, and important political figures such as Representative Alexandria Ocasio-Cortez in the contemporary moment (Norwood 2017; Ehrenreich 1976; Whipps 2023; Socialist Feminist Working Group 2024).

Theorizing Socialism

In Marx's theories, the people whose labor produces goods and value are known as the proletariat. Marx imagined socialism as a governance in which the proletariat are the political leaders and collectively own the means of production—the factories, land, and natural resources—paving the way for a classless society. Again, socialism was imagined as a transition from capitalism to communism, and at this stage the state would coordinate the transition, ensuring an equitable distribution of resources. Marxist theories imagine that as society advances, the state would gradually become unnecessary and disappear, giving way to a fully developed communist society. However, socialism is now often theorized and actualized as a stand-alone means of governance (not a transitory state) and is often combined with democratic systems, creating democratic socialism.

Today, socialist theorists and activists advocate for the collective ownership of the means of production: the factories, land, and natural resources. Currently, in capitalist economies, the means of production are primarily owned and controlled by private individuals and corporations. Socialists argue that this deprives communities of necessary resources. Socialists typically argue that the means of production should instead be owned by the community or the state so that the benefits of work and resources are shared fairly among all members of society.

The pursuit of economic equality is one of the central goals of socialism. Socialists typically argue that wealth and resources should be distributed fairly to reduce inequalities and provide everyone with a decent standard of living. To this end, socialists advocate on behalf of strong social welfare systems that include health, education, and social assistance accessible to all. For example, the Nordic countries and Canada enact these more socialist welfare systems. The objective is to ensure that no one is left destitute in times of need, thereby promoting a social safety net that supports all citizens, regardless of their economic situation.

Moreover, socialism is fundamentally concerned with the equitable treatment of workers—ensuring workers are not exploited. This means that workers must receive fair compensation for their work and have greater control over their working conditions. Socialism seeks to end the dynamic where capitalists profit disproportionately from the labor of others, which is known as wage theft.

Additionally, socialist systems prefer economic planning over free market capitalism. That is, rather than letting the economy be guided by unpredictable market forces, socialists advocate for economic planning that meets the needs of the population and avoids economic crises. Planning aims to ensure sustainable and balanced development. Here, it becomes clear that values such as solidarity and cooperation are fundamental to socialism. Instead of encouraging unbridled competition, socialists promote cooperation and working together for the common good. This strengthens the sense of community and mutual support, creating a more united and supportive society.

Socialist Feminism

Socialist feminists argue that the oppression of women and other vulnerable populations is tangled up with capitalism (Holmstrom 2003). That is, gendered oppression has an economic aspect. For instance—as the US pay gap demonstrates—within a free market, women are often paid less because they are women. Within an ideal socialist system, the state would prevent such gendered inequities. Indeed, socialism has a central focus on equality. Socialist feminists argue that economic equality cannot be achieved without gender equality, as women face economic barriers including pay gaps, glass ceilings, the motherhood penalty, the feminization of poverty, and the double shift—where women perform paid labor outside the home *and* unpaid labor inside the home.

Put simply, socialist feminism is a part of feminism that looks at how both gender and class affect people's lives, arguing that women are oppressed not only by patriarchy but also by capitalist systems. Indeed, as socialist feminists such as Clara Zetkin and Alexandra Kollontai have famously theorized, in order to achieve equality, society must change both the way it treats women and the way it handles economics. Socialist feminists—including Zetkin and Kollontai—have long worked for women's economic independence through social reforms. While some feminisms focus solely or primarily on gender, socialist feminists believe that society cannot fix gendered inequality without also fixing economic inequality.

Such social reforms can only be accomplished through collective action and radical solidarity. Here, socialist feminists join the *Communist Manifesto*'s famous conclusion by calling out, "Workers of the world, unite!" and encouraging the international solidarity of the working class in the fight against capitalist oppression.

Mariane Camargo

See Also: Capitalism; Equal Pay; Feminization of Poverty

Further Reading

Armstrong, Elisabeth. 2020. *Marxist and Socialist Feminism*. Northampton, MA: Smith College. Accessed May 21, 2024. https://scholarworks.smith.edu/cgi/viewcontent.cgi?article=1014&context=swg_facpubs.

Arnold, Samuel. 2024. "Socialism." *Internet Encyclopedia of Philosophy*. Accessed May 21, 2024. https://iep.utm.edu/socialis/.

Ehrenreich, Barbara. 1976. "What is Socialist Feminism?" *WIN Magazine*. Accessed May 2024. https://www.marxists.org/subject/women/authors/ehrenreich-barbara/socialist-feminism.htm.

Holmstrom, Nancy. 2003. "The Socialist Feminist Project." *The Monthly Review: An Independent Socialist Magazine*. Accessed May 21, 2024. https://monthlyreview.org/2003/03/01/the-socialist-feminist-project/.

Leonard, Sarah. 2020. "Socialism Is the Answer to Corporate "Girl Boss" Feminism." *Teen Vogue*, May 5, 2020. www.teenvogue.com/story/what-is-socialist-feminism.

Norwood, Arlisha R. 2017. "Florence Kelly." *National Women's History Museum*. Accessed May 20, 2024. https://www.womenshistory.org/education-resources/biographies/florence-kelley.

Socialist Feminist Working Group. 2024. *Democratic Socialists of America*. Accessed May 2024. https://www.dsausa.org/working-groups/feminism/.

Whipps, Judy D. 2023. "American Feminist Socialism 1830–1930: A Century of Social Experimentation." In *The Oxford Handbook of American and British Women Philosophers in the Nineteenth Century*, edited by Lydia Moland and Alison Stone. Oxford: Oxford University Press. Accessed May 2024. https://doi.org/10.1093/oxfordhb/9780197558898.013.28.

Wong, Nellie. 1991. "Socialist Feminism: Our Bridge to Freedom." In *Third World Women and the Politics of Feminism*, edited by Chandra Talpade Mohanty, Ann Russo, and Lourdes Torres, 288–96. Bloomington: Indiana University Press. Accessed May 21, 2024. https://alejandroquinteros.wordpress.com/wp-content/uploads/2021/10/third-world-women-and-the-politics-of-feminism.-chandra-talpade-mohandy.pdf#page=301.

STANDPOINT THEORY

Standpoint theory is a feminist theoretical perspective that argues that an individual's knowledge and understanding are shaped by their social positions (i.e., how racism, sexism, heterosexism, and class position them in society) and lived experiences. As such, standpoint theory emphasizes the importance of marginalized perspectives in producing complete and accurate collective knowledge. That is, for a society to understand something, society needs to consider that thing from various "standpoints" or the perspectives from multiple social positions—including those of marginalized people. Theorized by philosopher Sandra Harding during the 1970s, standpoint theory was inspired by Marxist theories that focused on the perspectives of oppressed classes. Standpoint theory began by examining "how inequalities between men and women influence" the production of knowledge and has expanded to multiple aspects of identity (Borland 2020).

Standpoint theory works hand in hand with the concept of epistemology, the philosophical study of the nature, origin, and limits of human knowledge. Together, these concepts challenge traditional notions of "objectivity," which are often determined by dominant groups. In short, standpoint theory utilizes epistemology to uplift marginalized groups as the experts of their own lives.

Major Contributors

Feminist scholar Dorothy Smith wrote in the 1980s that by "excluding women from the ideological work of society," history has been created and taught from men's perspectives, therefore "othering" women in the way we think. Harding expanded on this theory in the 1990s to include the perspectives of other marginalized groups, advocating for beginning research from the bottom up to prevent bias in knowledge creation. She pushed for increased "focus on gender differences . . . between women's and men's situations which give a scientific advantage to those who can make use of the differences" (Harding 1991).

Also in the 1990s, sociologist Patricia Hill Collins demonstrated how the theory should be inclusive of Black feminist thought. She explained how considering multiple, intersecting areas of identity could "create a collective identity among African-American women about the dimensions of a Black woman's standpoint" (Collins 2009).

Applications and Influence

Through the work of these scholars and endless others, standpoint theory's impact has reached many fields. One area includes research methods, where researchers have been challenged to consider the social location of both the subjects and the researchers themselves. By doing so, they can become more aware of potential biases and blind spots in their work, placing more value on the perspectives of the communities being studied (Haraway 1988).

The theory is also used to analyze power dynamics and social inequalities, offering insight into how different groups experience and resist oppression. For example, it is influential in feminist, critical race, and intersectional studies, where scholars examine how overlapping social identities relate to systems of oppression and privilege (Crenshaw 1991). Standpoint theory encourages scholars in these fields to prioritize marginalized voices and experiences in their analyses.

Various social justice movements have also been significantly impacted by standpoint theory, which highlights the importance of amplifying marginalized voices in the struggle for equality and justice. For example, the Black Lives Matter movement emphasizes the lived experiences of Black individuals in addressing systemic racism (Taylor 2016). Similarly, environmental justice movements have adopted standpoint approaches to address how environmental issues disproportionately affect marginalized communities (Bullard 1990).

Criticisms

As the theory becomes more widespread, feminists and other critical scholars worry about its application. One concern is that a sloppy use of this theory could lead to relativism "where all perspectives are equally valid" and truth is difficult to find (Wylie 2012). Another concern is fragmentation, where focusing on different perspectives could make it hard to build a unified understanding. Additionally, some people fear that emphasizing different perspectives might introduce more bias, making it harder to achieve unbiased knowledge (Wylie 2012).

Standpoint theorists have responded to these concerns by explaining that standpoint theory doesn't mean all perspectives are equally valid or that everyone in a group thinks the same. They also focus on a "feminist [standpoint] rather than a women's standpoint" to avoid generalizing the experience of all women (Borland 2020).

Carole Yoke-kew Chee

See Also: Collins, Patricia Hill; Crenshaw, Kimberlé; Critical Race Theory; Feminist Methodologies

Further Reading

Borland, Elizabeth. 2020. "Standpoint Theory." *Encyclopædia Britannica Online*. Accessed August 29, 2024. https://www.britannica.com/topic/standpoint-theory.

Bullard, Robert D. 1990. *Dumping in Dixie: Race, Class, and Environmental Quality*. Boulder, CO: Westview Press

Collins, Patricia Hill. 2009. *Black Feminist Thought: Knowledge, Consciousness, and The Politics of Empowerment*. New York: Routledge.

Crenshaw, Kimberlé. 1991. "Mapping the Margins: Intersectionality, Identity Politics, and Violence against Women of Color." *Stanford Law Review* 43, no. 6: 1241–99. www.jstor.org/stable/1229039.

Haraway, Donna. 1988. "Situated Knowledges: The Science Question in Feminism and the Privilege of Partial Perspective." *Feminist Studies* 14, no. 3: 575–99. https://doi.org/10.2307/3178066.

Harding, Sandra. 1991. *Whose Science? Whose Knowledge?: Thinking from Women's Lives*. Ithaca, NY: Cornell University Press.

Smith, Dorothy E. 1987. *The Everyday World As Problematic: A Feminist Sociology*. Boston: Northeastern University Press.

Taylor, Keeanga-Yamahtta. 2016. *From #BlackLivesMatter to Black Liberation*. Chicago: Haymarket Books.

Wylie, Alison. 2012. "Feminist Philosophy of Science: Standpoint Matters." *Proceedings and Addresses of the American Philosophical Association* 86, no. 2: 47–76.

STONEWALL RIOTS (1969)

The Stonewall Riots—also known as Stonewall, the Stonewall Uprising, the Stonewall Revolution, the Stonewall Rebellion, and the Stonewall Protests—took place at the Stonewall Inn, a bar in the Greenwich Village area of New York City popular with LGBTQ+ people. The local police routinely raided the Stonewall Inn throughout the 1960s (D'Emilio 1983). At the time, it was illegal for adults to engage in same-sex sexual activity and police often rounded up the patrons at the Stonewall Inn. Same-sex sexual activity between consenting adults remained illegal in the state of New York until 1980.

Although police raids of the Stonewall Inn were common, in 1969 a mayoral campaign affected the local politics and "the clean-up of the bar took on a new impetus" (Hines 2009, 150). The Stonewall Inn was particularly vulnerable to police: it "operated without a liquor license" and had "ties to organized crime"; it additionally employed "scantily clad go-go-boys" to entertain patrons, and it served LGBTQ+ people who were unwelcome at the more upscale gay bars in the area—making it a "sanctuary for genderqueers," trans people, and working-class gay and lesbian people (D'emilio 1983, 231; Wilchins 2002). All of this combined to make the patrons at the Stonewall Inn particularly vulnerable to police.

On June 28, 1969, the police came to raid the Stonewall Inn and to their surprise the clientele fought back—resisting arrest. Specifically, trans woman Sylvia Rivera is credited for "initiating the Stonewall uprising by throwing a bottle at the police" (Hines 2009, 150). In his analysis of the Stonewall Riots, David Carter (2004) documents that over the subsequent five days of protesting, approximately 2,000 protesters joined the Stonewall uprising.

The Stonewall Inn on Christopher Street in New York City, site of the 1969 Stonewall Riots, where LGBTQ+ clientele fought back during a police raid, kicking off protests and galvanizing the gay rights movement (Lei Xu/Dreamstime.com).

Sociologist Sally Hines (2009, 149) notes that Stonewall is remembered as "the birth of the modern lesbian and gay movement in the West" but LGBTQ+ people had long been organizing and resisting. For instance, the Mattachine Society was founded in 1950 as a national gay rights organization; likewise, the Daughters of Bilitis—a lesbian rights organization—was founded in 1955. Moreover, in California during 1966, a similar riot had taken place. Compton Cafeteria was an all-night restaurant in San Francisco and a "popular queer gathering spot" (Levin 2019). The manager became annoyed with a noisy table and called the police. When the police officer attempted to arrest one of the drag queens who frequented the establishment, she threw her coffee at him, and mayhem erupted. Police reinforcements arrived but for the first time, the drag queens banded together and fought back, ultimately besting the cops (Hines 2009, 148).

The Stonewall and Compton Cafeteria Riots are key moments in the history of LGBTQ+ liberation because they are early examples of how the LGBTQ+ community can band together and resist oppression—and these protests "had results" (Hines 2009, 149). Following the Compton and Stonewall Riots, lesbians, gay men, trans people, drag queens, genderqueer people, and women's liberation activists formed alliances with each other and with other local minoritized people—such as sex workers (Hines 2009). Stonewall remains a call to solidarity and activism within the LGBTQ+ and feminist liberation movements.

Sarah Kornfield

See also: Drag; Queer Theory; Trans Theory

Further Reading

Carter, David. 2004. *Stonewall: The Riots that Sparked the Gay Revolution.* New York: St. Martin's Press.

D'Emilio, John. 1983. *Sexual Politics, Sexual Communities: The Making of a Homosexual Minority in the United States, 1940–1970.* Chicago: University of Chicago Press.

Hines, Sally. 2009. "Riding the Waves: Feminism, Lesbian and Gay Politics, and the Transgender Debates." In *1968 in Retrospect: History, Theory, Alterity*, edited by Gurminder K. Bhambra and Ipek Demir. New York: Palgrave Macmillan.

Levin, Sam. 2019. "Compton's Cafeteria Riot: A Historic Act of Trans Resistance, Three Years Before Stonewall." *TheGuardian.com*, June 21, 2019. https://www.theguardian.com/lifeandstyle/2019/jun/21/stonewall-san-francisco-riot-tenderloin-neighborhood-trans-women.

Stryker, Susan (director, writer). 2005. *Screaming Queens: The Riot at Compton's Cafeteria* (documentary). San Francisco: Frameline.

Wilchins, Riki A. 2002. "A Woman for Her Time: In Memory of Stonewall Warrior Sylvia Rivera." *Village Voice*, February 26, 2002. Accessed December 31, 2024. https://www.villagevoice.com/a-woman-for-her-time/.

STRATEGIC ESSENTIALISM

Strategic essentialism is when a group of people takes up one or more of the stereotypes society thinks are "essential to their nature" and uses it to their advantage. For instance, early suffragists used the stereotype that women are "virtuous" to argue that they should be given the vote—because who wouldn't want virtuous people voting? Those who believed that women had good moral character due to their "essential nature" as a woman could then rationalize supporting their suffrage efforts (Cohen 1996).

To understand strategic essentialism, we must first understand essentialism. Essentialism can be defined as a belief that a group or category of people share an intrinsic or biological essence—a shared nature—and thus they all share a few characteristics which are considered to be their "essence" (Riley 1988). For example, women are often thought to share an "essence," meaning that all women are—supposedly—fundamentally the same in certain ways. To have this "essence" is to be a woman, and vice versa, to be a woman is to have this essence. Usually, women's "essence" is described as attributes like being nurturing, being emotional, and so on.

In the case of essentialism, belief shapes interpretation, meaning what we believe or assume about a group of people shapes how we interpret their identity and behavior. Historically, essentialism leads to loops and cycles of stereotyping, categorization, ranking, and, thus, oppression (Riley 1988). Essentialism limits people to their labels. Society often punishes those who step outside of an essentialized identity to which they have been assigned, while rewarding those who—to put it simply—stay in their box. For example, women with stereotypically feminine presentations, such as wearing dresses and heels, often receive compliments that serve to reinforce their behavior. On the other hand, women who have more masculine presentations receive pointed looks, jokes at their expense, and are generally treated poorly. To be accepted and deemed "acceptable" in society, we have to behave the way society claims is "essential" to who we are. Strategic essentialism offers a route toward activism without risking the punishments of rejecting essentialism.

For example, consider how mothers are stereotyped as being extremely defensive of their children. This "essential" characteristic of all mothers can be used to qualify mothers as advocates for automatic weapon control. Using this widely accepted idea that "mothers know best" in caring for their children, mothers argue that they should be trusted as they advocate for their children's safety (Park, Banchefsky, and Reynolds 2015).

Theorizing Strategic Essentialism

In 1988, Denise Riley outlined the relationship between essentialism and strategic essentialism. She identified social categories as the first step in a line that leads to the oppression of different demographics. She uses the category of "woman" as an example. First, she notes that the category of "women" is historically constructed and always constructed in relation to other categories which also change. This means that, over time, different ideas about women have been stuck to that identity, which has resulted in an unstable category built upon centuries of stereotypes. We know this category is made up and not intrinsic, because it keeps changing. This ever-changing nature proves to be problematic for those who belong to this unstable category of "woman." Feminists like Riley point out that these categories aren't natural or inherent, and that nobody is responsible for upholding their essentialized identity (Riley 1988). The binary structure of social categories, like man and woman, Black and white, gay and straight, leaves no room for those who understand themselves outside these categories to feel accepted and gain the same rights as dominant groups.

Gayatri Spivak coined the term "strategic essentialism," developing the feminist theory around this form of activism. She traces the concept back to Foucault's theories of power, using the method of "deconstruction" to understand the various elements at play. She starts by identifying that the structuring of society is based on made-up categories and that the idea of a dominant or elite group creates inferior rankings below this group (Spivak 1988). Racism is a clear example of this. White people were once thought of as inherently better, which then oppressed Black people and other people of color. This structure is evident in systems of slavery, racial violence, segregation, and so on throughout US history. Spivak terms the inferior, nondominant class of people as the "subaltern."

In the context of postcolonial theory, the "subaltern" refers to groups of people—such as Indigenous people, peasants, or slaves—who are excluded from power within an empire or colonization. Spivak's first attempt at using the tool of strategic essentialism was with the Subaltern Studies Group. The goal of this group was to deconstruct the British colonization of India (Eide 2010, 76). Strategic essentialism was a "minority strategy for influencing mainstream society," or in other words, an attempt to change the narrative about minority groups' experiences with colonization. Spivak used Britain's colonization of India as the foundation for this concept, but feminists now apply her ideas to other social structures like patriarchy.

Risks of Using Strategic Essentialism

Despite Spivak's groundbreaking work theorizing strategic essentialism as an activist tool, she sometimes questions and doubts whether it can be used to achieve positive long-term effects. Indeed, strategic essentialism becomes especially problematic when it is not a deliberate and careful choice (Spivak 1988). Sometimes, as minoritized people respond to public events and media scrutiny, they might "strategically" essentialize themselves in order to fit a current narrative and thus highlight issues that matter in their community (Eide 2010). Here, the minoritized group essentializes themselves in response to outside pressure. This is a risky move. Typically, for strategic essentialism to result in progress rather than further oppression, it must overcome the pressures that caused the essentialism in the first place. Without proper support and execution, Spivak argues that this feat often fails.

Moreover, strategic essentialism ultimately reinforces essentialist ideas (Spivak 1988). This outcome is a by-product rather than the focus of this activism. If labels are used to marginalize and stereotype groups anyway, minoritized groups may be better off using these labels in ways that benefit them. And yet many feminists remain skeptical of using strategic essentialism as a form of activism because it reinforces a harmful categorization as it works toward progress (Colebrook 2001). For many feminists, this seems like one step forward and two steps backward.

Additionally, strategic essentialism typically has very narrow benefits. It typically only benefits the particular minoritized group who is using it and does not result in larger progress. For example, the early suffragists who used their "virtuous" status in society to argue for women's suffrage were typically leveraging their white femininity as virtuous and suffrage only benefited white women. Black women were not associated with virtue and did not receive suffrage since they were largely excluded from voting through Jim Crow laws and other racist machinations until the Voting Rights Act of 1965. As such, strategic essentialism often leaves people behind (Cohen 1996).

Kersten Dekker

See Also: Colonialism; Deconstruction; Essentialism; Gender Performance; Patriarchy; Suffrage

Further Reading

Cohen, Philip N. 1996. "Nationalism and Suffrage: Gender Struggle in Nation-Building America." *Signs* 21, no. 3: 707–27. http://www.jstor.org/stable/3175176.

Colebrook, Claire. 2001. "Certeau and Foucault: Tactics and Strategic Essentialism." *The South Atlantic Quarterly* 100, no. 2: 543–74.

Eide, Elizabeth. 2010. "Strategic Essentialism and Ethnification: Hand in Glove?" *Nordicom Review* 31, no. 2: 63–78.

Grosz, Elizabeth. 2012. "A Note on Essentialism and Difference." In *Feminist Knowledge: Critique and Construct*, edited by Sneja Gunew, 332–44. New York: Routledge Press.

Park, Bernadette, Sarah Banchefsky, and Elizabeth B. Reynolds. 2015. "Psychological Essentialism, Gender, and Parenthood: Physical Transformation Leads to Heightened Essentialist Conceptions." *Journal of Personality and Social Psychology* 109, no. 6: 949–67.

Riley, Denise. 1988. *Am I That Name? Feminism and the Category of "Women" in History*. Oxford: Oxford University Press. https://doi.org/10.1093/oso/9780192892706.003.0042.

Spivak, Gayatri. 1988. "Can the Subaltern Speak?" In *Marxism and the Interpretation of Culture*, edited by Cary Nelson and Lawrence Grossberg, 271–313. London: Routledge.

STRUCTURAL OPPRESSION

Structural oppression refers to oppression that is baked into the policies and procedures for an organization or society more broadly. Structural oppression does not set out to target a single individual—the way sexist bullying might—but it still involves people. Afterall, people make and enforce organizational policies and cultural norms, and it is people who experience the harm from structural oppression.

Consider an example of structural oppression. I am a professor at Hope College, a small, liberal arts college in Michigan. Hope College is a premier institution for undergraduate learning: students and faculty work closely together, resulting in a truly impressive record of undergraduate research. A lot of this research is funded through summer grants that pay undergraduate students a living wage during the summer months, so they do not have to work other summer jobs. At the time of writing, however, for tax purposes, these summer grants can—with few exceptions—only be given to students who are residing in Michigan during the summer. This makes a significant portion of Hope's students of color ineligible if they wish to return to their families and hometowns during the summer. That is, while many of Hope's white students are from Michigan, far fewer of Hope's students of color are from Michigan. As such, many students of color face a choice (to go home or not during the summer) and if they choose to stay in Michigan for summer research, they face economic pressures to pay for summer housing; meanwhile, Hope's white students are much less affected by this tax policy since so many of them are from Michigan. This is an example of structural oppression: an institutional policy affects people in uneven ways, with a disproportionately negative effect for students of color compared to white students. In this example, the structural oppression is not an evil racist scheme developed to prevent students of color from important learning, mentoring, and professionalization.

And this tax policy does not only affect students of color—it affects all students who live outside the state of Michigan. However, since Michigan is a predominantly white state, it disproportionately affects students of color.

In many other instances, however, structural oppression is intentionally malicious. For example, the Jim Crow laws that oppressed Black people and other people of color (e.g., preventing them from voting, from attending public schools, from buying houses) in the United States are a prime example of intentionally malicious structural oppression. Moreover, even when intentionally oppressive structural policies seem to have been overturned, they can cast a long shadow. For instance, while the Jim Crow laws regulating where people of color can buy houses (often known as "redlining") have been overturned, those laws set up what is now de facto school and housing segregation in the United States. This de facto segregation is inherited from one generation to the next, keeping people in generational cycles where impoverished schools lead to impoverished communities and back again.

Structural oppression often seems like an intractable problem. Returning to the earlier example, Hope College did not create the tax system that affects its summer grants, and thus it is easy to more or less accept structural oppression as "the way it is"—if one even notices it. That is, structural oppression is often invisible. For instance, in the case of Missing and Murdered Indigenous Women and Girls, while it is clear that Indigenous women and girls experience violence at much higher rates than white women and girls, the policies for how this data is reported are part of the problem—meaning that US and Canadian governments have been slow to recognize that a problem exists and, even now, the actual extent of missing, murdered, and trafficked Indigenous women is still unknown (US Department of Justice 2008).

Indeed, recognizing structural oppression often requires some sleuthing. For example, feminist sociologist Christine Williams (2021) spent years studying why women are leaving the oil and gas industry. Studying the numbers, Williams discovered that women who had spent years obtaining advanced degrees in science and had secured lucrative jobs within the oil and gas industry disappeared from the industry within a decade or so—leaving the oil and gas industry chronically male-dominated. Numerically, this should not have happened. Plenty of women are earning masters and doctorates in scientific fields such as geology and chemistry, and plenty of women are hired at entry levels into oil and gas corporations. Nonetheless, oil and gas corporations are male-dominated. As such, Williams set out to discover why women were "opting out" of such a lucrative field. What she discovered instead is structural oppression. Women are not individually "opting out": they are disproportionally laid off from oil and gas corporations during the "busts" of this industry's endless cycles of "boom-and-bust" (Williams 2021, 27).

Feminist Approaches to Structural Oppression

Feminists respond to structural oppression with a two-pronged approach (Wieskamp and Smith 2020, 73). First, activists and researchers need to expose structural oppression. This begins at home. Feminists have to notice when a problem is structurally caused. We have to notice how practices and policies disproportionally affect women and other vulnerable populations—regardless of whether the oppression is intentional or an unintentional side effect of a policy that was created by people with privilege who did not think of others. This means training ourselves to think about how policies, practices, historical precedents, cultural norms, and even physical barriers could be contributing to the trends and problems we see. This is an important part of feminist methodologies (Sprague 2016). Although this first step—exposure—begins at home, it cannot stay there. Feminist activists work to show administrators, policy advisers, legislators, law enforcement, and the broader community how structural oppression impacts vulnerable populations.

The second step is creative: feminist activists work to develop new, better structures that are more humane—that do not recreate systems in which some are unfairly advantaged and others unfairly disadvantaged. For instance, right now, I am part of a team at Hope College that is sifting through our records and data, looking for trends to better understand not only how tax policies but also how other structures affect students and their ability to engage in high-level undergraduate research. More than that, we're working to create new policies (while still paying our taxes) that will support all of Hope's students in undergraduate research.

It is essential to use intersectional analysis, both when working to understand and expose structural oppression and when working to develop better policies. If feminists and other activists fail to understand how policies overlappingly affect people through gender, race, sexuality, class, ability, and so on, we will fail to recognize how structural oppression affects the most vulnerable among us and we are likely to simply create new structural oppressions. Ultimately, it is important to remember that while structural oppression can feel insurmountable, every structure—every policy, every practice, and every cultural norm—was made by humans. And if humans made it, we can remake it in better ways.

Sarah Kornfield

See Also: Interlocking Oppression; Intersectionality; Feminist Methodologies; White Privilege

Further Reading

Otis, Hailey Nicole. 2019. "Intersectional Rhetoric: Where Intersectionality as Analytic Sensibility and Embodied Rhetorical Praxis Converge." *Quarterly Journal of Speech* 105, no. 4: 369–89.

Sprague, Joey. 2016. *Feminist Methodologies for Critical Researchers: Bridging Differences*, 2nd ed. Lanham, NJ: Rowman & Littlefield.

US Department of Justice. 2008. *Violence Against American Indian and Alaska Native Women and the Criminal Justice Response: What is Known*, August. https://www.ojp.gov/pdffiles1/nij/grants/223691.pdf.

Wieskamp, Valerie N., and Cortney Smith. 2020. "'What to Do When You're Raped': Indigenous Women Critiquing and Coping Through a Rhetoric of Survivance." *Quarterly Journal of Speech* 106, no. 1: 72–94.

Williams, Christine L. 2021. *Gaslighted: How the Oil and Gas Industry Shortchanges Women Scientists*. Oakland, CA: University of California Press.

SUFFRAGE

Suffrage, or the legal right to vote in political elections (also called enfranchisement), has long been seen as a sign of national belonging. The right to vote—to have a political voice in government by voting—is a marker of one's full US citizenship and today is open to citizens at the age of eighteen. In a democracy, the idea is that citizens should have a say in the laws that impact their bodies. This idea resonates with the contemporary feminist activist T-shirt slogan "My Body, My Vote," connecting ideas about political voice, bodily autonomy, and reproductive justice in feminists' response to the US Supreme Court's overturning of *Roe v. Wade* (the constitutional ruling protecting the right to abortion) in 2022.

The legal right to vote has not come easily for many people. In colonial America, women, Black men, and poor people did not have the right to vote; there were exclusive religious, racial, land ownership, and residency qualifications. As writer Elaine Weiss says, "our esteemed Founding Fathers had absolutely no intention of giving women a voice in public affairs. Throughout the 19th and early 20th centuries, women were condemned from the pulpit and in the press for thinking about suffrage; they were spit upon and pelted with rotten eggs for speaking out about it; and they were jailed for demanding it" (2018, 2). Feminists have, then, shown how the right to vote has historically been used to reinforce the political status quo yet can also be used to resist it. In the United States, marginalized people, such as women, Black people, and working-class people, have fought for suffrage to increase their voices in national affairs, while people with more political power and privilege have often controlled or suppressed others' right to vote to maintain power and privilege.

Historical Suffrage Activism

Feminist scholars have associated the movement for women's suffrage in the United States with women's rights activism from the mid-1800s to early 1900s. This period spans the "Declaration of Sentiments" in 1848 (which asserted women's equality and their right to vote), to the Anthony Amendment (a women's suffrage amendment introduced into Congress in 1878), to the Nineteenth Amendment in 1920 (which finally granted women suffrage at the national level). As Weiss puts it,

> The women who launched the [suffrage] movement were dead by the time it was completed; the women who secured its final success weren't born when it began. It took more than nine hundred local, state, and national campaigns, involving tens of thousands of grassroots volunteers, financed by millions of dollars of mostly small (and a few large) donations by women across the country. (2018, 3)

Over this period, "suffragists" (early activists for suffrage) used different strategies to campaign for the vote—lobbying members of Congress, giving speeches, marching in suffrage parades, and even performing suffragist plays (Hovet 1995, 862). Because the idea of women voting was either unfamiliar or unsavory to the public, women worked to produce images in newspapers and flyers supporting the idea that they could have a capable public, political role beyond their private, domestic work (National Women's History Museum). By the early twentieth century, suffrage activists split into "mainstream" tactics of the National American Woman Suffrage Association, which emphasized voting's compatibility with motherhood, and the "militant" National Woman's Party, which stressed equality and personal empowerment (National Women's History Museum). These more "radical" strategies included a march on the White House and a hunger strike by the suffragists who were arrested and jailed, as depicted in the star-studded 2004 drama *Iron-Jawed Angels.*

Progress in the suffrage campaign was uneven on the ground; change occurred state by state as well as at the national level, so some women were able to vote in individual states before the Nineteenth Amendment ensured women's right to vote nationally. Yet the Nineteenth Amendment did not make the vote "one and done" for all women. Even though suffrage was guaranteed by the Fifteenth and Nineteenth Amendments, the right of suffrage for many women of color was delayed: the Snyder Act did not grant Native Americans suffrage until 1924; and local and state barriers, such as racial violence and intimidation in the South, would keep Black voters from enacting their right to vote until the Voting Rights Act of 1965 (CAWP 2020; Williamson 2020).

Complexities of Women's Suffrage Activism and Roots in Political Petitioning

Feminist scholars explain how the path to suffrage was not straightforward, either historically or racially. While the fight for "woman suffrage" (as it was called then) is commonly dated from 1848 to 1920, the right of women and other disenfranchised people to have a voice in government arguably has roots in political petitioning that predate 1848. These roots reflect how white women's fight for the right to vote was interwoven in complicated ways with other important national and racial issues, such as Native American land dispossession, the abolition of slavery, the temperance movement (for moderation in alcohol use), labor reform, and anti-war efforts.

For example, some feminist scholars have suggested that women's concern with the right to vote began earlier than 1848, with petitions by women who wanted a voice both for moral and legal reasons in national issues such as Native American land dispossession and slavery. As Susan Zaeske (2003) and Alisse Portnoy (2005) define, petitions were letters submitted to government authorities detailing complaints about things that their writers wanted changed. Accessible to nonvoting citizens such as women, free and enslaved Black people, and Native Americans, letters of petition were signed humbly, recognizing authorities' power to improve existing conditions, and they were increasingly used not just individually but also in large groups over the 1800s (Carpenter 2021). For example, Tiya Miles (2009) has shown that Cherokee women used petitions to collectively protest removal of their own people from their rightful land in the 1810s; this collective protest very likely inspired white women to write petitions on behalf of Native Americans in the next decade. And, as Daniel Carpenter (2021) has shown, both free and enslaved Black women and white women also used petitions to protest slavery long before the "Declaration of Sentiments" (1848), which has often been pegged as the start of the suffrage movement.

In sending letters of petition to Congress, women advocated both for other people and for their own say in national affairs—reflecting a complicated process that intertwined suffrage with, among other issues, abolition. The cause of women's suffrage was, then, often in competition with racial emancipation and the right of the nation's Black citizens to vote, even though some activists like Sojourner Truth and Frederick Douglass advocated for both. Still, as Portnoy (2005) argues, it is from *within* the debates over Indian Removal and slavery that we can best understand the complexity of women's fight for suffrage. As Louse Michele Newman (1999) has shown, the origins of feminism in the United States were racially loaded.

After the Civil War, some activists advocated for Black men's suffrage and others prioritized white women's right to vote, causing splits in the movement and its organization. The women-only National Woman Suffrage Association, led by Elizabeth Cady Stanton and Susan B. Anthony, promoted the vote and economic and political equality for women, often using racist rhetoric to get political support; while the American Woman Suffrage Association, led by Lucy Stone and Henry Blackwell, focused on the single issue of suffrage and advocated promoting Black male suffrage while delaying women's suffrage until after Reconstruction (Borish 1995, 860–1). Even after Black male suffrage became national in 1870, many people in favor of women's suffrage argued problematically that the vote "of native white women would secure the social order, whereas undesirable black and immigrant male voters endangered it" (Kruman 1991, 1046). Clearly, this argument was flawed because of its racial bigotry; it also faultily reduced white women to a morally superior role because of their ability to have children and reproduce a (white) nation.

Additional political arguments, whether for or against women's right to vote, revolved around US business concerns. For instance, the liquor industry resisted women's suffrage because they feared women would vote for the prohibition of the sale of alcohol, and the textile industry worried that women voters would restrict child labor (Kruman 1991, 1046). Similarly, in the United States as in England, class tensions were always present in the suffrage movement—as we see in the famous *Mary Poppins* movie scene, when the affluent Mrs. Banks sings praises of the coming vote for women, while completely ignoring the working women "sisters" under her own roof (Bromley 2012, 135–6). These class tensions suggest a reality of intersectional feminism: just because women can raise their voices in political affairs (whether through their votes or their representation in government offices), this does not necessarily mean that intersectional feminist values are represented. Just because women vote or hold office, the interests of all women, including the rights of women of color, working women, or young women who choose bodily autonomy, are not necessarily being advanced.

Relevance and Necessity of Suffrage Activism Today

Still, the right to vote remains essential for women and marginalized citizens in our democracy today. The redrawing of voting districts (known as redistricting) can impact election outcomes for feminist candidates running for congressional office (CAWP 2024). Currently, politicians across the country have attempted to restrict access to the vote, particularly in communities of color, making it difficult to register to vote. Such restrictions undermine democratic elections at all levels (ACLU). In the early twenty-first century, voter turnout at elections is a persistent problem, as there is lower "continued voter engagement" among minority communities and young adults; voter identification laws, transportation, and taking time off work are challenges to suffrage today (Williamson 2020). This is why activist efforts like "Rock the Vote" and "Get Out the Vote" (or GOTV) campaigns by organizations like the League of Women Voters, efforts focused on registering voters and getting voters to cast their ballots, continue to be lynchpins in the feminist effort for suffrage.

It may be tempting to think that gender equality was achieved when suffrage was won. Yet as feminist scholars like Dorothy Sue Cobble, Linda Gordon, and Astrid Henry (2014) remind us, feminist movement is never finished and must continually reinvent itself. Ensuring the right to vote for *all* citizens, regardless of sex, race, or class, is one way to continue reinventing feminism alongside evolving a democratic society.

Amy Dunham Strand

See Also: Bodily Autonomy; Nineteenth Amendment; Patriarchy; Reproductive Justice; *Roe v. Wade* (1973); Seneca Falls Convention (1848); Temperance Movement

Further Reading

American Civil Liberties Union (ACLU). 2024. "Voting Rights." Accessed October 13, 2024. https://www.aclu.org/issues/voting-rights.

Borish, Linda J. 1995. "Suffrage Movement." In *The Oxford Companion to Women's Writing in the United States*, edited by Cathy N. Davidson and Linda Wagner-Martin, 860–2. New York: Oxford University Press.

Bromley, Victoria L. 2012. *Feminisms Matter: Debates, Theories, Activism.* North York, ON: University of Toronto Press.

Carpenter, Daniel. 2021. *Democracy by Petition: Popular Politics in Transformation, 1790–1870.* Cambridge, MA: Harvard University Press.

Center for American Women and Politics (CAWP). 2020. "100 Years of Women's Suffrage." New Brunswick, NJ: Center for American Women and Politics, Eagleton Institute of Politics, Rutgers University-New Brunswick. Accessed October 13, 2024. https://cawp.rutgers.edu/programs/100-years-womens-suffrage.

Center for American Women and Politics (CAWP). 2024. "Redistricting Effects on Women Congressional Incumbents." New Brunswick, NJ: Center for American Women and Politics, Eagleton Institute of Politics, Rutgers University-New Brunswick. Accessed October 13, 2024. https://cawp.rutgers.edu/redistricting-effects-women-congressional-incumbents.

Cobble, Dorothy Sue, Linda Gordon, and Astrid Henry. 2014. *Feminism Unfinished: A Short, Surprising History of American Women's Movements.* New York: Liveright/Norton.

Hovet, Ted, Jr. 1995. "Suffragist Plays." In *The Oxford Companion to Women's Writing in the United States*, edited by Cathy N. Davidson and Linda Wagner-Martin, 862. New York: Oxford University Press.

Kruman, Marc W. 1991. "Suffrage." In *The Reader's Companion to American History*, edited by Eric Foner and John A. Garraty, 1043–7. Boston: Houghton Mifflin.

League of Women Voters. 2022. "Empowering Voters. Defending Democracy." Accessed October 14, 2024, https://www.lwv.org.

Miles, Tiya. 2009. "'Circular Reasoning': Recentering Cherokee Women in the Antiremoval Campaigns," *American Quarterly* 61, no. 2: 221–43: https://dx.doi.org/10.1353/aq.0.0078.

National Women's History Museum. 2024. "Crusade for the Vote: Creating a Female Political Culture." Accessed October 13, 2024, https://www.crusadeforthevote.org/creating-a-female-political-culture.
Newman, Louise Michele. 1999. *White Women's Rights: The Racial Origins of Feminism in the United States.* New York and Oxford: Oxford University Press.
Portnoy, Alisse. 2005. *Their Right to Speak: Women's Activism in the Indian and Slave Debates.* Cambridge, MA: Harvard University Press.
"Rock the Vote." 2024. Accessed October 14, 2024, https://www.rockthevote.org.
Weiss, Elaine. 2018. *The Woman's Hour: The Great Fight to Win the Vote.* New York: Penguin.
Williamson, Nicole. 2020. "The 19th Amendment at 100: Modern Challenges." *Harvard Journal of Law & Gender.* Accessed October 14, 2024. https://journals.law.harvard.edu/jlg/2020/01/the-19th-amendment-at-100-modern-challenges/.
Zaeske, Susan. 2003. *Signatures of Citizenship: Petitioning, Antislavery, and Women's Political Identity.* Chapel Hill, NC: The University of North Carolina Press.

SURVIVORS' BILL OF RIGHTS ACT (2016)

The Survivors' Bill of Rights Act of 2016 established legal rights for sexual assault survivors under the US federal criminal code for the first time. Amanda Nguyen, founder of a sexual assault survivor advocacy group, Rise, spearheaded the bill to equalize the rights of sexual assault survivors in the United States. Before the bill was passed, state policy varied widely, and it was difficult for assault survivors in many states to seek justice. For instance, Ms. Nguyen was raped in Massachusetts, where untested rape kits were destroyed after six months even though the statute of limitations for rape was fifteen years. Other states, like California, Texas, and Colorado, preserved tests for a longer amount of time, and those states afforded survivors legal recourse if their tests were wrongfully destroyed (Nguyen 2016). The Survivors' Bill of Rights standardized how states handle these tests, preserving rape kits for twenty years or the maximum applicable statute of limitations, whichever is shorter. So, if a survivor has fifteen years to press charges after an assault, the survivor's rape kit would be preserved for fifteen years.

Additionally, the bill includes a survivor's right not to be prevented from or charged for receiving a forensic medical examination (also known as a rape kit or test), the right to be informed of test results, the right to receive written notification before their test is destroyed and to further preserve the test if requested, and the right to be informed of these rights and policies, as policies vary state by state (US Congress 2016).

Furthermore, the bill clarifies that "sexual assault" is any nonconsensual sexual act prohibited by law, which includes sexual acts that occur when one person does not have the capacity to consent. For instance, if someone is intoxicated or asleep, the person does not have the capacity to consent to a sexual act and acts performed on them or to them are thus sexual assault (US Congress 2016).

This bill gained unanimous support from both houses of Congress. President Barack Obama signed the bill into law on October 7, 2016.

Zoë Hess Carney

See Also: #MeToo; Violence Against Women Act (1994)

Further Reading

Nguyen, Amanda. 2016. "Obama Expected to Sign Sexual Assault Survivors' Bill of Rights into Law. Interview by Renee Montagne." *NPR*, September 9, 2016. Audio. https://www.npr.org/2016/09/09/493228724/obama-expected-to-sign-sexual-assault-survivors-bill-of-rights-into-law.
US Congress. "Text - H.R.5578 - 114th Congress (2015–2016): Survivors' Bill of Rights Act of 2016." October 7, 2016. https://www.congress.gov/bill/114th-congress/house-bill/5578/text.

T

TEMPERANCE

The Temperance Movement was a moral and social movement during the 1870s–1920s that aimed to end alcohol abuse and consumption. Often characterized as "wet blankets," temperance activists are now remembered as early feminists who actually opposed personal freedom and bodily autonomy when it came to alcohol (Appleby 1997). Put simply, temperance activists are now remembered as being "no fun." However, a historical understanding of the Temperance Movement demonstrates not just the complexity of feminist activism but also the ways in which gendered stereotypes and sexism profoundly shape how women experience oppression and how they resist.

History of Temperance

In the 1700s, alcohol was socially viewed as an essential component of life and the "average American over 15 years old consumed nearly seven gallons of pure alcohol a year," which is three times today's consumption ("Roots of Prohibition" 2025). For instance, alcohol was a routine part of farmers' lives, with neighbors routinely treating eachother to alcoholic drinks after helping one another with a harvest or other work (Rohrer 1990, 232). Then, starting around 1795, physicians and religious leaders began to oppose "intemperance" or the excessive consumption of alcohol (Appleby 1997; Krout 1923). Around the same time, drinking culture changed: instead of drinking in the home, men shifted to a "saloon culture" and began drinking in public gathering places. Concurrently, the United States experienced a renewed concern with "conservative Christian values" known as the Second Great Awakening (Thompson-Gillis 2007).

The simultaneous rise of saloon culture and the Second Great Awakening led to the Temperance Movement. Benjamin Rush and Dr. Billy J. Clark were some of the earliest voices to advocate against alcohol consumption or "intemperance" as medical doctors began to realize heavy alcohol consumption wreaks havoc on the body (Appleby 1997; Krout 1923). During this era, men—often Civil War survivors—were heavily consuming alcohol, and this negatively affected women and children. During this era, women who worked outside the home often had their wages taken by their husbands, as husbands typically controlled the household's money. As a result, men's heavy alcohol consumption in saloons spent the family's money—and men often returned home from saloons in violent and combative states. Put simply, women's rights advocates saw the Temperance Movement as a way to improve women's lives by ending the way alcohol consumption impoverished and contributed to the abuse of women and their children.

The Temperance Movement gained traction alongside the women's rights and suffrage movements during the late 1800s and early 1900s. As women advocated for rights, such as the right to vote and to retain their wages, they also advocated for the right to be free of the abuse and impoverishment caused by men's alcohol consumption. At the time, women's rights and "temperance" were clearly connected: both advocated on behalf of women's well-being. By 1875, women were responsible for three-quarters of temperance activism (Thompson-Gillis 2007).

During this time, gender roles largely barred women from speaking in public. It was considered wrong for women to address men as a leader, teacher, or preacher. Gender roles, however, are tricky and complex: although barred from teaching men, white middle-class women were assumed to be paragons of virtue and goodness—this was known as the Cult of True Womanhood. White women's reputations as paragons of virtue gave them credibility on the topic of drunkenness (Thompson-Gillis 2007). Temperance activism, then, became a feminist tool for suffrage. Women were able to lean into their moral reputations in order to gain a public stage. For instance, famous suffragist Susan B. Anthony began her public speaking career as one of the Daughters of Temperance (Novara 2023).

Frances Willard was a leading activist, spearheading women's involvement in politics. "Willard argued that as the nurturers of children and as moral guardians of the home, women should be more involved in public policy and politics" (Novara 2023). Willard led the Temperance Movement, becoming the president of the national Women's Christian Temperance Movement, which was the largest organization for temperance. Willard understood "intemperance" as a social problem sustained by masculine supremacy rather than an issue of personal morality. For Willard, temperance and suffrage were conjoined issues.

The Temperance Movement, however, achieved widespread support through religious and moral arguments that opposed the working-class, immigrants, and gay men (Chauncey 1994). Essentially, anti-saloon rhetoric portrayed the working-class, immigrant, and gay men who drank in saloons as dirty and bad. As the Temperance Movement gained momentum, it became increasingly expedient to blame US social problems on these minoritized populations.

Temperance and the Eighteenth Amendment

The Temperance Movement is broadly remembered as an anti-alcohol and anti-fun movement that tried to control people's choices and constrain bodily autonomy. This stereotype overlooks the social complexities and oppressions of the time and ignores how women's rights activists embraced what is now known as strategic essentialism by using sexist gender roles to their advantage.

The Temperance Movement seemingly accomplished its goal when the Eighteenth Amendment was ratified in 1919. This constitutional amendment banned the manufacture, sale, and transportation of "intoxicating liquors." In reality, this amendment inaugurated what is known as the Prohibition Era—a decade in which alcohol sales flourished in speakeasies and on the black market and in which organized crime became more prominent.

In 1933, the Eighteenth Amendment was repealed by the Twenty-First Amendment. This was an unprecedented decision, and the Twenty-First Amendment is still the only amendment that repeals a prior amendment in the US Constitution.

Current Impacts of Alcohol Use

It is no wonder that doctors and women were the leading activists for the Temperance Movement; today, women and healthcare workers remain the most affected by alcohol abuse and alcoholism. "Statistics show approximately 40% of American hospital beds are in use at any given moment due to alcohol-related causes, especially illnesses that have been caused by or worsened due to excessive consumption of alcohol" (Gonzales 2021). Currently, approximately 10 percent of US citizens struggle with alcohol use disorder (NIAA 2023).

The gendered differences noted during the Temperance Movement are still relevant. For example, today, sexual violence is often perpetrated in conjunction with alcohol consumption. A recent study of sexual assault found "that 70% of women and 80% of men had been drinking when a sexual assault occurred" (Alcohol and Sexual Assault n.d.). To be clear, alcohol is *not* the cause of sexual assault. In fact, being drunk makes it more difficult for perpetrators or would-be perpetrators to carry out acts of violence. However, the consumption of alcohol reduces inhibitions, impairs judgment, and heightens aggression—and these effects directly contribute to sexual assault. In other words, "drinking makes it easy for the perpetrator to ignore sexual boundaries, while the victim's intoxication makes it more difficult to guard against an attack" (Alcohol and Sexual Assault n.d.).

Many people recognize how alcohol contributes to violence against women, but it also contributes to negative outcomes for men. For instance, in 2019, men's alcohol-related deaths were almost twice that of women's; likewise, men have higher hospitalization rates caused by alcohol-related diseases and injuries. Moreover, men are approximately three times as likely to die by suicide than women and are more likely to have been drinking prior to attempting suicide (Centers for Disease Control and Prevention).

Alcohol is a drug that permeates US culture and its negative impacts should not be overlooked. In recent years, feminist scholars have been investigating the effects of alcohol on social roles and gender performances. By asking questions such as who drinks alcohol, on what occasions, and with what purpose, feminists begin answering the questions of how gendered differences and the social use of alcohol impact women.

Elizabeth Johnson

See Also: Cult of True Womanhood; Nineteenth Amendment; Strategic Essentialism; Suffrage

Further Reading

"Alcohol & Sexual Assault." n.d. *Butler University*. Accessed November 7, 2024. www.butler.edu/well-being/counseling-services/alcohol-sexual-assault/#:~:text=Quick%20Facts%20About%20Alcohol%20Use.

"Alcohol Use Disorder (AUD) in the United States: Age Groups and Demographic Characteristics." 2023. *National Institute on Alcohol Abuse and Alcoholism*. Accessed November 7, 2024. www.niaaa.nih.gov/alcohols-effects-health/alcohol-topics/alcohol-facts-and-statistics/alcohol-use-disorder-aud-united-states-age-groups-and-demographic-characteristics.

Appleby, Joyce. 1997. "The Personal Roots of the First American Temperance Movement." *Proceedings of the American Philosophical Society* 141, no. 2: 141–59.

Centers for Disease Control and Prevention. "Suicide Data and Statistics." *Suicide Prevention*, Centers for Disease Control and Prevention, May 13, 2024. www.cdc.gov/suicide/facts/data.html.

Chauncey, George. 1994. *Gay New York: Gender, Urban Culture, and the Making of the Gay Male World 1890-1940*. New York: Basic Books.

Duignan, Brian. 2018. "Temperance Movement." *Encyclopædia Britannica*, April 27, 2018. Accessed November 7, 2024. www.britannica.com/topic/temperance-movement.

"The Eighteenth and Twenty-First Amendments." 2024. *Jack Miller Center*, July 5, 2024. Accessed November 7, 2024. jackmillercenter.org/our-work/resources/the-eighteenth-and-twenty-first-amendments.

Gonzales, Andrea. 2021. "12 Scary Facts about Alcohol Abuse." *Sage Neuroscience Center*, April 30, 2021. Accessed November 7, 2024. sageclinic.org/blog/12-scary-facts-about-alcohol-abuse/.

Krout, John A. 1923. "The Genesis and Development of the Early Temperance Movement in the New York State." *The Quarterly Journal of the New York State Historical Association* 4, no. 2: 78–98.

Novara, Elizabeth. 2023. "Temperance and Suffrage Movement Collections Connections." *Library of Congress Blogs*, August 24, 2023. Accessed Spetember 18, 2025. https://blogs.loc.gov/manuscripts/2023/08/temperance-and-suffrage-movement-collections-connections/#:~:text=Willard%20argued%20that%20as%20the,in%20public%20policy%20and%20politics.

Rohrer, James R. 1990. "The Origins of the Temperance Movement: A Reinterpretation." *Journal of American Studies* 24, no. 2: 228-235.

"Roots of Prohibition." 2025. PBS: Prohibition a Film By Kenn Burns and Lynn Novick." Accessed September 18, 2025. https://www.pbs.org/kenburns/prohibition/roots-of-prohibition.

Thompson-Gillis, Heather. 2007. "'Maddened by Wine and by Passion': The Construction of Gender and Race in the Nineteenth Century American Temperance Literature." Thesis, Miami University of Ohio. https://www.google.com/url?sa=t&source=web&rct=j&opi=89978449&url=https://etd.ohiolink.edu/acprod/odb_etd/ws/send_file/send%3Faccession%3Dmiami1181073516%26disposition%3Dinline&ved=2ahUKEwjaz7v8hsuJAxW9kYkEHRduJd4QFnoECBkQAQ&usg=AOvVaw3_nrRotBuNL8oJ46S4HCMX.

Tillett, Paul. 1964. "Review of Symbolic Crusade: Status Politics and the American Temperance Movement by Joseph R. Gusfield." *American Political Science Review* 58, no. 2: 429–30. https://doi.org/10.1017/S0003055400289004.

Wagner, Ella. 2022. "'The Saloon Is Their Palace': Race, Immigration, and Politics in the Woman's Christian Temperance Union, 1874–1933." Dissertation, Loyola University, Chicago. https://www.google.com/url?sa=t&source=web&rct=j&opi=89978449&url=https://ecommons.luc.edu/cgi/viewcontent.cgi%3Farticle%3D4955%26context%3Dluc_diss&ved=2ahUKEwj8_sfrhcuJAxUPj4kEHWXDBIUQFnoECBYQAQ&usg=AOvVaw2eLIBKzTl6xyscyEgaHNnQ.

THIRD WORLD WOMEN'S ALLIANCE AND BLACK WOMAN'S MANIFESTO

The Third World Women's Alliance was a revolutionary socialist organization led by Black women and women of color in the United States from 1968 to 1980. The organization held active chapters in New York City, New York, and Oakland, California. The Alliance was formed during the Civil Rights Movement and women's liberation era in the 1960s and 1970s. The term "third world" was and still is used by people in the United States to refer to impoverished nation-states (usually in South America, Africa, or Asia); when used in this way it is a derogatory term. The Alliance, however, used "third world" to draw attention to the ways racism, sexism, and imperialism affect the lives of women whether in Mumbai, India, São Paulo, Brazil, or New York City.

The Alliance was organized in response to racism, sexism, and imperialism that impacted Black women and women of color domestically and globally. One of the main goals of the Third World Women's Alliance was to create a sisterhood among women of color devoted to unifying Third World communities and eliminating all forms of oppression. The Alliance ran on an ideological platform that advocated for "a socialist system that guarantee[d] full, creative, non-exploitive lives for all human beings, fully aware that we will never be free until all oppressed people are free" (Third World Women's Alliance 1971). That is, the Alliance reimagined and worked toward building a society that was free of racism, sexism, and economic exploitation.

The Alliance formally began as a Black women's caucus in 1968 within the Student Non-Violent Coordinating Committee (SNCC), a civil rights organization cofounded by Black woman activist Ella Baker, that consisted mostly of Black college students in the 1960s. Frances Beal, a member of SNCC and one of the cofounders of the Third World Women's Alliance, presented at a 1968 SNCC personnel meeting in New York. In her presentation, Beal advocated for a space within SNCC to uplift and center Black women's intersectional oppression. Although there was initially some pushback, a Black women's caucus was formed within SNCC and named the Black Women's Liberation Committee. A year later, in 1969, the Black Women's Liberation Committee split from SNCC while maintaining close ties to focus more on Black women's struggles related to sterilization abuse and welfare rights in the United States. At this point, the organization changed its name from the Black Women's Liberation Committee to the Black Women's Alliance.

Double Jeopardy

In 1969, while Beal was coleading the Black Women's Alliance, she coined the term "double jeopardy" in her article "Double Jeopardy: To Be Black and Female." Double jeopardy was an early conceptualization of the term "intersectionality" coined by Kimberlè Crenshaw in 1989. Beal offered an analysis of Black women's experiences related to racism and sexism in the Civil Rights

Movement, women's liberation movement, and society. Beal's essay contributed to the genealogy of Black feminist intellectual thought from Sojourner Truth, Anna Julia Cooper, Mary Church Terrell, Angela Davis, bell hooks, and Patricia Hill Collins.

Triple Jeopardy

In her article, "Double Jeopardy: To Be Black and Female," Beal often mentioned how Black women and Puerto Rican women experienced similar forms of intersectional oppression. That is, Black women and women of color both suffered from racism and sexism. Black feminist scholar Kimberly Springer noted how Puerto Rican women activists approached the Black Women's Alliance with interest in joining the organization but were met with some pushback from Black women members of the alliance who had concerns that Black women's issues may be diluted if non-Black women joined the organization (2005, 48). However, Beal supported a multicultural alliance and advocated for women of color to join them in the fight for liberation, and this stance was supported by the majority (2005, 49). Hence, the Black Women's Alliance once again renamed itself, becoming the Third World Women's Alliance and opening its doors and membership to Asian, Chicana, Middle Eastern, Native American, and Puerto Rican women. Therefore, the alliance shifted its objectives from solely focusing on racism and sexism impacting Black women (known as double jeopardy) to racism, sexism, and imperialism impacting Black women and women of color (known as triple jeopardy).

Third World Women's Alliance published and distributed a groundbreaking newspaper called *Triple Jeopardy* (1971–5), which expanded its mission and centered on the intersectional struggles of women of color domestically and globally. The *Triple Jeopardy* newspaper provided a space for the Alliance to recruit women of color, raise awareness of political issues, and engage in community action. For example, the newspaper featured a "Letter from Angela Davis" while she was in Marin County Jail in 1971. Davis, a Black woman political activist, was on trial and was charged with three felonies. Davis called for judicial fairness and support for her trial. She noted, "My life is at stake, but as I have repeatedly said, not simply the life of a lone individual, but a life which belongs to Black people and all who are tired of poverty and racism and the unjust imprisonment of tens of thousands" (Davis 1971). Like Davis, the Third World Women's Alliance understood that intersectional solidarity from women of color was needed to eliminate all forms of oppression.

Triple Jeopardy featured stories related to women during the revolution in China, the US intervention in Vietnam, and the struggles of Sudanese women. Other topics of interest included commentary on abortion rights, the history of welfare in the United States, healthcare, International Women's Day, citizenship, and imprisonment. Each issue ended with an editorial piece from the Third World Women's Alliance's editorial board that reinforced the Alliance's stance and action toward the interlocking oppression of racism, sexism, and imperialism.

Legacy

The Third World Women's Alliance was one of the first social movement organizations to engage in intersectional activism and adopt a transnational lens. The Alliance contributed to feminist theories and provided a template for intersectional unity. Their critiques of the interlocking oppression of racism, sexism, and imperialism continue to inform social justice frameworks. Today, when women's bodily autonomy is withdrawn and global injustices against nondominant individuals are rising, the strategies, liberation frameworks, and political consciousness of the Third World Women's Alliance continue to hold prominence.

Victoria T. Fields

See Also: Colonialism; Consciousness Raising; Davis, Angela; Intersectionality; Postcolonial Feminism; Socialism; Transnational Feminism

Further Reading

Alexander, M. Jacqui, and Chandra Talpade Mohanty. 2010. "Cartographies of Knowledge and Power: Transnational Feminism as Radical Praxis." In *Critical Transnational Feminist Praxis*, edited by Amanda Lock Swarr and Richa Nagar, 23–45. Albany, NY: SUNY Press.

Anzaldúa, Gloria. 1987. *Borderlands/La Frontera: The New Mestiza.* San Francisco: Aunt Lute Books.

Beal, Frances. 1970. "To Be Black and Female." In *The Black Woman: An Anthology*, edited by Toni Cade Bambara, 90–100. New York: New American Library.

Collins, Patricia Hill. 2000. *Black Feminist Thought: Knowledge, Consciousness, and the Politics of Empowerment*, 2nd ed. New York: Routledge.

Crenshaw, Kimberlé. 1989. "Demarginalizing the Intersection of Race and Sex: A Black Feminist Critique of Antidiscrimination Doctrine, Feminist Theory and Antiracist Politics." *University of Chicago Legal Forum* 1: 139–67.

Davis, Angela Y. 1971. *If They Come in the Morning.* New York: The Third Press.

Davis, Angela Y. 1981. *Women, Race, & Class.* New York: Random House.

Farmer, Ashley. 2017. *Remaking Black Power: How Black Women Transformed an Era.* Chapel Hill: University of North Carolina Press.

Jordan, June. 1981. *Civil Wars: Observations from the Front Lines of America.* New York: Simon & Schuster.

Licona, Adela C., and Karma R. Chávez. 2015. "Relational Literacies and their Coalitional Possibilities." *Peitho* 18 (1): 96–107

Mohanty, Chandra Talpade. 2003. *Feminism Without Borders: Decolonizing Theory, Practicing Solidarity.* Durham: Duke University Pres

Moraga, Cherríe, and Gloria Anzaldúa, eds. 1981. *This Bridge Called My Back: Writings by Radical Women of Color.* New York: Kitchen Table: Women of Color Press.

Roth, Benita. 2003. *Separate Roads to Feminism: Black, Chicana, and White Feminist Movements in America's Second Wave.* Cambridge: Cambridge University Press.

Sandoval, Chela. 2000. *Methodology of the Oppressed.* Minneapolis: University of Minnesota Press.

Springer, Kimberly. 2005. *Living for the Revolution: Black Feminist Organizations, 1968–1980.* Durham: Duke University Press.

Third World Women's Alliance. 1971. "Women in the Struggle." *Triple Jeopardy* 1, no. 1. Accessed September 18, 2025. https://www.marxists.org/history/erol/ncm-6/women-in-struggle.pdf.

TITLE IX (1972)

In 1972, president of the United States, Richard Nixon, signed into law the Higher Education Amendments of 1972. These amendments are most significantly remembered for one in particular: Title IX. Under Title IX, sex-based discrimination is prohibited in any school or educational program that receives funding from the federal government. The law developed out of a broader concentrated effort by women's rights groups for gender equality in education during the 1960s and 1970s. While the law passed in 1972, it took until 1975 for the Department of Health, Education, and Welfare (HEW) to publish the final regulations that would describe how Title IX could and would be enforced on campuses. To this day, Title IX works against sex-based discrimination in areas including oversight over educational recruitment, admissions, financial assistance, sex-based harassment, employment, and many more facets of school and campus life. On college and university campuses, Title IX is an important part of governing how reports of sexual harassment and assault are handled.

Even though Title IX encompasses so many elements of educational institutions, the law is overwhelmingly known for its effects on athletics and women's sports. Title IX steadily converted "parents, administrators, educators, and politicians to join the surge of advocacy for gender equity in sports" (Cahn 2015, 284). In 1972, fewer than 300,000 girls took part in high school athletics—by 2012, the number was over 3.2 million (Cahn 2015). Culturally, Title IX is considered a fundamentally successful legal, political, and social effort "at 'steering' the gender regimes of schools and universities toward gender equality" (Cooky and Messner 2018, 59). Even in the twenty-first century, Title IX is often invoked to explain the strength of American women's professional sports success in the twentieth and twenty-first centuries, particularly in the areas of soccer and basketball (Chuck 2015).

While Title IX has largely been deemed successful, in recent years, there has been pushback to its focus on the sex binary of male and female. Due to the fact that "Title IX does not directly address race, gender identity, disabilities or other characteristics besides sex," complicated questions have been raised about the law's ability to handle contemporary issues (Tumin 2023). In 2023, the US Department of Education, under President Joseph Biden, proposed a new rule that would permit schools to refuse the inclusion of transgender athletes "from competing on sports teams that align with their gender identity when questions of physicality and fairness arise" (Tumin 2023). While this rule would hinder schools' ability to issue absolute bans on transgender athletes, it also could create a framework for gender policing of female athletes and discrimination against transgender athletes.

Dafna Kaufman

Community members show their support for trans students at an Illinois school board meeting in April 2025 after the group Awake Illinois filed a Title IX complaint against the district over bathroom access (Paul Goyette via Flickr, CC BY 2.0).

See Also: Essentialism; Gender; Patriarchy; The Personal Is Political

Further Reading

Blinde, Elaine M. 1986. "Contrasting Orientation Toward Sport: Pre- and Post-Title IX Athletes." *Journal of Sport and Social Issues* 10, no. 1: 6–14. https://doi.org/10.1177/019372358601000102.

Cahn, Susan K. 2015. *Coming on Strong: Gender and Sexuality in Women's Sport*, 2nd ed. Urbana: University of Illinois Press.

Chuck, Elizabeth. 2015. "A Level Playing Field: Why the USA Is So Strong in Women's Soccer." *NBC News*, July 5 2015. https://www.nbcnews.com/storyline/world-cup/level-playing-field-why-usa-so-strong-womens-soccer-n385346.

Cooky, Cheryl, and Michael A. Messner. 2018. *No Slam Dunk: Gender, Sport and the Unevenness of Social Change*. New Brunswick, NJ: Rutgers University Press.

Edwards, Amanda Ross. 2010. "Why Sport? The Development of Sport as a Policy Issue in Title IX of the Education Amendments of 1972." *Journal of Policy History* 22, no. 3: 300–36. https://doi.org/10.1017/S0898030610000126.

Heinecken, Dawn. 2013. "'Fit for Everything': The Framing and Consumption of the Female Athlete in Title Nine." *Feminist Media Studies* 13, no. 1: 29–45. https://doi.org/10.1080/14680777.2011.647968.

Lane, Julie B. 2018. "Women Are a Problem: Title IX Narratives in the New York Times and the Washington Post, 1974–1975." *Communication & Sport* 6, no. 1: 25–40. https://doi.org/10.1177/2167479516685578.

Mertens, Maggie. 2022. "50 Years of Title IX: How One Law Changed Women's Sports Forever." *Sports Illustrated*, May 19 2022. https://www.si.com/college/2022/05/19/title-ix-50th-anniversary-womens-sports-impact-daily-cover.

Tumin, Remy. 2023. "Title IX and the New Rule on Transgender Athletes Explained." *The New York Times*, April 7 2023. https://www.nytimes.com/article/title-ix-transgender-athletes-school-sports.html.

Verbrugge, Martha H. 2012. *Active Bodies: A History of Women's Physical Education in Twentieth-Century America*. New York: Oxford University Press.

Wushanley, Ying. 2004. *Playing Nice and Losing: The Struggle for Control of Women's Intercollegiate Athletics, 1960–2000*. New York: Syracuse University Press.

TOKENISM

Tokenism refers to the promotion or celebration of one or a few people from minoritized backgrounds whose success is then typically used as proof that a company or society is *not* racist, sexist, heterosexist, and so on. Feminists and cultural theorists sometimes refer to tokenized people as "tokens." Tokens are often alone—for instance, the only woman in a board room—or almost alone, they are typically under intense scrutiny known as "hypervisibility," and while they are lauded, their ideas are also easily dismissed and their positions are quite precarious. Typically, tokens are fired and even publicly shamed if they attempt to make significant changes or attempt to reveal how sexism, heterosexism, or white supremacy operate within a company or community.

For example, in many ways Colin Kaepernick was tokenized. Kaepernick is a biracial Black man. A star player in the National Football League (NFL), Kaepernick quarterbacked for the San Francisco 49ers from 2011 to 2016. While the NFL employs many Black men as professional football players, it is still fairly rare for a Black man to hold a quarterback position. The quarterback position is typically considered a position of leadership and (white) quarterbacks are praised for their strategic thinking, discipline, strong work ethic, and other qualities that are rarely associated with Black men within white supremacist cultures (Cramer 2019). As such, Kaepernick was tokenized—one of the very few Black men promoted to this level of excellence and visibility within the NFL during this era. The NFL is a cultural touchstone within US society and occupies a media spotlight, more broadly tokenizing Kaepernick within US society. As a Black quarterback, Kaepernick was hypervisible and celebrated as a role model for young Black men and as proof that the NFL and the United States more broadly were not racist. Here, tokenism clearly provides cover for white supremacy. Having promoted Kaepernick, the NFL could essentially argue, "We can't be racist! Look! We have a Black man as quarterback." During this time, in many ways President Obama was similarly tokenized and many white Americans likewise argued that America could not be considered racist since it had a Black man as president.

However, in 2016, during the pregame pageantry, Kaepernick first quietly sat and then kneeled during the national anthem. Kaepernick's peaceful protest supported #BlackLivesMatter and called attention to racism in the United States. As Steve Martin and George McHendry Jr. (2016) recount, the backlash was swift and decisive. For instance, Donald Trump—who was campaigning for president at the time—suggested that Kaepernick was ungrateful and unpatriotic, stating, "I think it's a terrible thing, and you know, maybe he should find a country that works better for him, let him try, it's not going to happen" (qtd. in McDermott 2016). Kaepernick was quickly benched, shunned, and ultimately fired. This dismissal was possible because Kaepernick was a token. One cannot imagine the NFL or American public treating white quarterbacks in a similar manner.

Here, it becomes clear that tokens are always "outsiders" to the organizations that promote and celebrate them. They are always under scrutiny and the moment they "misbehave," they are replaced. This means that while tokens are celebrated as proof of progress (proof that the NFL or a Fortune 500 Company isn't sexist or racist), they are not allowed to progressively enact change. Indeed, they are usually fired or otherwise sidelined and demoted whenever they try to create real progress.

Moreover, people who are tokenized are often perceived negatively, even as an organization celebrates them. For example, consider a woman who is promoted from professor of psychology to dean of social sciences at a university, becoming the first woman to be a dean at that university. While the university provost and president and the university's marketing department announce her promotion with great fanfare (the first woman!) the other deans and her subordinates whisper that she only got the job *because* she was a woman. She is isolated and feels alone during Dean's Council meetings. The other deans stereotype her, joking that she might become too emotional during meetings and asking her to take notes when their administrative assistant cannot attend the meeting. She finds herself under a lot of pressure to perform perfectly since her work is singled out because she is "different" from the rest of the deans. Facing these rejections and pressures, she might even begin to doubt herself. As Mariateresa Torchia, Andrea Calabrò, and Morten Huse (2011, 301) describe, these are the conditions that most tokens find themselves in—whether they are tokenized as women, as a person of color, as both a woman and a person of color, or other minoritized identites.

As awful as tokenism is, there is a fairly straightforward solution. As feminist scholars such as Torchia, Calabrò, and Huse (2011) demonstrate when studying how tokenism affects women in company boards, the solution is to reach a "critical mass" of minoritized people at these high-level positions rather than promoting (and then isolating and scrutinizing) one or two tokens. And here, the math is fairly simple, for company boards comprised of six to twelve board members, at least three of the board members need to be women in order for their expertise and contributions to be taken seriously and for them to be respected leaders who can effectively implement structural change.

Sarah Kornfield

See Also: #BlackLivesMatter; Post-racism; Structural Oppression

Further Reading

Cramer, Linsay. 2019. "Cam Newton and Russell Westbrook's Symbolic Resistance to Whiteness in the NFL and NBA." *Howard Journal of Communications* 30, no. 1: 57–75.

Martin, Steve, and George F. McHendry Jr. 2016. "Kaepernick's Stand: Patriotism, Protest, and Professional Sports." *Journal of Contemporary Rhetoric* 6, no. 3/4: 88–98.

McDermott, Nathan. 2016. "Trump On Kaepernick." *Buzzfeed*, August 29, 2016. https://www.buzzfeed.com/natemcdermott/trump-on-49ers-kaepernick-maybe-heshould-find-a-country-tha?utm_term=.tfrGrEb0G6#.uuxk4epNkY.
Torchia, Mariateresa, Andrea Calabrò, and Morten Huse. 2011. "Women Directors on Corporate Boards: From Tokenism to Critical Mass." *Journal of Business Ethics* 102: 299–317.

TRANS THEORY

Trans theory is a body of knowledge and a way of thinking that focuses on understanding gender identity and the lived experiences of trans people, with particular emphasis given to the fluidity and malleability of gender presentations within this diverse community. Trans theory emerged as a response to the inadequacies of feminist and queer theories to fully address the breadth of gender-based experiences within the trans community (Stryker 2004). The need for trans theory became especially clear during 2014 as trans identities and gender fluidity suddenly became more visible in US popular culture—a year now known as the Trans Tipping Point (Steinmetz 2014). Trans theory has since become a staple in both feminist and queer scholarship and activist toolkits, helping address gaps and oppressions in public policy and legal statutes.

History of Trans Theory Scholarship

In its infancy, the scholarship on trans theory was quite varied, with different ideas about what this new theory would become. During this time, scholars from fields such as women's and gender studies as well as queer theorists and social scientists from disciplines such as psychology and social work all contributed to what we now call trans theory. Now considered a pioneer in the field of trans studies, Susan Stryker (2004) discussed the early stages of the field, noting how trans studies coalesced through a series of theoretical developments that merged into a critical orientation. These developments include Judith Butler's *Gender Trouble* (1990), Sandy Stone's essay "The 'Empire' Strikes Back: A Posttranssexual Manifesto" (1992), and Leslie Feinberg's *Transgender Liberation* (1992). Through these early works, these theorists cut their scholarly teeth on what is now known as *transgender studies*, leading to the eventual emergence of *trans theory* (Stryker 2004).

Around the same time, social science scholars such as Julie Nagoshi emphasized embodiment in relation to gender and sexual identity. Nagoshi also introduced what is now known as intersectional approaches to gender identity, particularly within the broader discipline of trans studies. This brings the embodied nuances of gender, race, class, and other aspects of social identity into focus as scholars work to understand the individual experiences of trans-identified folx in the United States (Nagoshi and Brzuzy 2010). Ultimately, early trans theorists took issue with feminist and queer theory's inability to address trans realities; their scholarship is united by the shared goal to develop a theoretical lens that can address the myriad of experiences of gender identity within the trans community.

Contemporary Trans Theory

Today, trans theory examines diverse gender identities within US culture and addresses what Stryker (2004) refers to as "all forms of gender trouble"—by which they mean the gender identities that exist beyond the essentialized binary of the male/female paradigm. This can be seen as part of queer theory's contribution to trans theory, especially as this aspect of "gender trouble" works to destabilize the power structures that reinforce binary ways of thinking about sex and gender. For instance, Sedgwick (1998, 208) wrote that *queer* "can refer to the open mesh of possibilities, gaps, overlaps, dissonances and resonances, lapses and excesses of meaning when the individual's gender or sexuality are not made to be signified monolithically." In this instance, *queer* works as a descriptive concept to accentuate the nonnormative aspects of trans identity, as well as celebrating the potentiality of transness to go beyond the binary and to express gender in a multitude of identities that are unique, personal, and worthy of analytical and cultural consideration.

In recent years, the United States has seen a marked increase in anti-trans/anti-gender ideology activism and violence. Not only is legislation being weaponized to regulate trans individuals' presence in public life, but the threat of physical violence against trans individuals is ever present—as evidenced by the continued documentation of anti-trans homicide rates throughout the United States. For instance, between 2017 and 2021, the number of trans individuals who were murdered in the United States nearly doubled (Mandler 2022). This violence is intersectional: approximately 13 percent of trans people are Black, but nearly 75 percent of the known victims of anti-trans violence are Black trans women (Mandler 2022; Herman, Flores, and O'Neill 2022). Age, as well as race and class, contributes to anti-trans violence. For instance, one in four or 25 percent of trans people who are murdered were between ages nineteen and twenty-five, and an additional 6 percent of those murdered were eighteen or younger. Trans sex workers are also a high-risk group for anti-trans violence; sex work is the highest targeted occupation among trans individuals (Wareham 2024).

By focusing on anti-trans violence, trans theory can create a space where scholars, academics, researchers, and allies alike can collectively work to end these dangers while remaining ever so mindful that the experiences of one trans individual do not mirror the experiences of an entire community. During 2024, US legislators set a record for proposing anti-trans legislative bills (Trans Legislation Tracker n.d.), heightening the necessity of trans theory as a way for feminist and queer scholars to become coalitional activists and as a way in which allyship can help generate a more gender-inclusive and liberated space for those who dare to trouble gender.

Jeffrey "JJ" Jones

See Also: Essentialism; Intersectionality; The May Test; Nonbinary; Queer Theory

Further Reading

Butler, Judith. 1990. *Gender Trouble*. New York: Routledge.

Feinberg, Leslie. 1992. *Transgender Liberation*. New York: World View Forum.

Herman, Jody L., Andrew R. Flores, and Kathryn K. O'Neill. 2022. "How Many Adults and Youth Identify as Transgender in the United States?" *UCLA School of Law Williams Institute*, June 2022. Accessed February 7, 2025. https://williamsinstitute.law.ucla.edu/publications/trans-adults-united-states/.

Mandler, C. 2022. "Murders of Trans People Nearly Doubled Over Past 4 Years, and Black Trans Women are Most At-Risk, Report Finds." *CBS News*, October 13, 2022. https://www.cbsnews.com/news/transgender-community-murder-rates-everytown-for-gun-safety-report/.

Nagoshi, Julie L., and Stephan/ie Brzuzy. 2010. "Transgender Theory: Embodying Research and Practice." *Affilia: Journal of Women and Social Work* 25 (4): 431–3.

Sedgwick, Eve K. 1998. "What's Queer?" In *Gender Inequality: Feminist Theories and Politics*, edited by Judith Lorber, Los Angeles, CA: Roxbury.

Steinmetz, Katy. 2014. "The Transgender Tipping Point." *Time*, May 29, 2014. https://time.com/135480/transgender-tipping-point/.

Stone, Sandy. 1992. "The 'Empire' Strikes Back: A Posttranssexual Manifesto." *Camera Obscura* 10, no. 2: 150–75.

Stryker, Susan. 2004. "Transgender Studies: Queer Theory's Evil Twin." *GLQ: A Journal of Gay and Lesbian Studies* 10, no. 2: 212–15.

Trans Legislation Tracker. n.d. "Anti-Trans Bills Tracker." Accessed February 7, 2025. https://translegislation.com/.

Wareham, Jamie. 2024. "350 Transgender People Murdered in 2024: 'Will the Violence Ever End?'" *Forbes*, November 16, 2024. https://www.forbes.com/sites/jamiewareham/2024/11/16/350-transgender-people-murdered-in-2024-will-the-violence-ever-end/.

TRANS-EXCLUSIONARY RADICAL FEMINISTS (TERFS)

The phrase "trans-exclusionary radical feminists" is a descriptive phrase, often abbreviated to "TERFs," and refers to people who call themselves radical feminists but exclude trans women, refusing to recognize trans women as women. TERFs often partner with conservative politicians who are enacting anti-trans legislation. Most TERFs do not like being called TERFs; feminists use the term TERFs to distinguish between feminists and the activists excluding trans people.

Feminist theorists and activists such as Judith Butler argue that there are no "right or wrong ways to be a woman" and that any versions of feminism that claim to represent the interests of "real" women cannot be feminism because they assert a "right" or "real" way to be a woman. Yet TERFs have actively championed cis women as "real" women since at least 1979, when Janice Raymond published an anti-trans book containing what many feminists consider to be hate speech (Hay 2019).

Feminist philosopher Carol Hay writes that when TERFs deny the status of "real" women to trans women, they typically consider cis women's experiences of marginalization and oppression as the defining factor—or essence—that makes cis women "real" women. At the same time, TERFs seem to rely on the false assumption "that all trans women have lived in the world unproblematically as men at some point" (2019).

For people who call themselves feminists, TERFs seem to spend inordinate amounts of energy (as well as time and money) protesting and organizing against trans women rather than against patriarchy.

Sarah Kornfield

See Also: Butler, Judith; Essentialism; Gender; Queer Theory; Trans Theory

Further Reading

Butler, Judith. 2024. *Who's Afraid of Gender?* New York: Farrar, Straus and Giroux.
Hay, Carol. 2019. "Who Counts as a Woman?" *The New York Times*, April 1, 2019. https://www.nytimes.com/2019/04/01/opinion/trans-women-feminism.html?smid=url-share.

TRANSNATIONAL FEMINISM

Like most feminists, transnational feminists aim to "end sexism, sexist exploitation, and oppression" (hooks 2000, xii), and they emphasize the ways in which social identities such as race, class, ability, religion, gender, and sexuality coconstruct to shape lived experiences. In addition, transnational feminists are particularly attentive to how borders of local and global significance such as nationality, state, and citizenship shape the lives of women and sexual minorities living in the so-called "Third World," which is more recently known as "Two-Thirds World" or "Global South." Transnational feminists ask questions such as: How does the language used to describe cultural Others shape our worldview? How is the everyday life of a rural woman farmer impacted by global development projects? How are women and sexual minorities denied human rights through global economic policies? Is transnational surrogacy ethical? What practices work toward solidifying the representation of women in the Global South as victims of their culture? Thus, rather than ignoring or transcending borders, transnational feminists explicitly engage with borders in their work.

Notably, such attention to borders is why terms such as "Third World," "Two-Thirds World," "Global North," "Global South," "Western," and so on are vigorously debated and contested by transnational feminists. The concern is that these language choices shape who and what counts as worthy of study for transnational feminist researchers and how that research is carried out. Additionally, these language choices are made conscientiously because transnational feminists are very aware of how language—especially naming—can reinforce oppressive binary thinking, such as us/them, Western/Eastern, Global North/Global South, First World/Third World, and developed countries/developing countries (Shohat 2002, 69–71).

Likewise, the term "transnational feminism" is a product of transnational feminists' attention to the power of labels and categories. Previous iterations of the phrase have included "global feminism" and "international feminism," which have been critiqued for reasons such as failing to account for the interconnectedness of the global and local, internal hierarchies within a community, and ongoing colonial formations (Mason 2017, 66–72). One takeaway from such theorizing is that language and other symbols, particularly when used to represent cultural Others, need to be used thoughtfully and intentionally. Transnational feminists realize that these phrases and labels can subtly and not so subtly center different goals and agendas. In other words, these labels are not value-neutral; they can reflect and create power hierarchies and can shape feminist theory, politics, and activism.

This entry primarily uses the terms Global North to refer to what was formerly known as "developed countries" and Global South to refer to what was formerly termed "developing countries." Although these terms are contested, I've used them because they tend to be most often used in current transnational feminist literature and because they are preferable to some other terms such as "Third World" that are deemed pejorative. However, when referencing the work of transnational feminists, I have tried to use the terms they themselves used.

Power Relations: Connecting Local and Global

Transnational feminist research often tries to show how power structures, policies, and economics connect the local and the global. There are three main approaches to this type of research. The first focuses on showing how capitalism and globalism interact, specifically noting how this interaction manifests through the polices of multinational corporations to affect impoverished women. The second focuses on studying transnational neoliberal policies, which typically privatize community resources (for instance, making healthcare a private, for-profit industry) and weaken government regulation and oversight of corporations in ways that negatively affect women and sexual minorities in the Global South. Third, transnational research often focuses on colonialism and neocolonialism by studying how conquest, occupation, political regimes, economic regimes, and so on affect people (Mason 2017).

Importantly, transnational feminists reject the idea that the local and global are in opposition to each other or separated from each other. Rather, they emphasize the intimate, complex interconnections between the local and global. For example, in "Love and Gold," Arlie Hochschild (2012) upends claims that celebrate transnational nannying for providing poor women with lucrative jobs by highlighting the deep emotional costs borne by the transnational nannies and their children. In a similar vein, Cynthia Enloe's (2014) analysis exposes the ways in which multinational corporations exploit poor women for the Global South by devaluing their labor, disregarding their safety, paying them lower wages, and so on. Both these authors expose how globalization and neoliberalism not only exacerbate but also create human suffering and, more specifically, feminize suffering. Their work aligns with Inderpal Grewal and Caren Kaplan's (1994) call to examine the different ways in which modern capitalist formations affect people globally, an approach which highlights that while people with different histories and in different locales are all impacted by these formations, the ways in which this impact is experienced are not the same.

Moreover, transnational feminist research has developed theoretical frameworks that demonstrate how the Global North's global agenda and local politics often further marginalize already vulnerable people. Border imperialism, a framework developed by Harsha Walia (2014), for example, exposes the heteropatriarchal, racist, and classist nature of contemporary immigration systems. Another example is Jasbir Puar's (2008) theorizing of homonationalism as a process whereby contemporary Western nation-states expand rights and opportunities for their queer citizens while using these terms of inclusion to justify imperialist aspirations and encourage the participation of queer people in these imperialist projects.

Politics of Representation

Transnational feminism initially arose as a critique of the ways in which feminists from the Global North were engaging in practices such homogenization and cultural imperialism. Chandra Talapde Mohanty (2003), for example, responded by deftly critiquing the ways in which Western feminism represents "Third World women." She argues that Western feminism generally imagines "Third World women" by using colonial frameworks such that "Third World women" are often seen as always poor, victimized, and primitive and therefore in need of saving, ostensibly by Western feminists.

Transnational feminists have also critiqued a form of cultural relativism practiced by Western feminists, wherein "Third World" cultures are characterized as inherently patriarchal and as a result, feminist goals get pitted against multicultural sensitivity. This strategy "obscures the influences that in fact shape cultural practices, hides the forces besides culture that affect women's lives, elides the way women exercise agency within patriarchy, and masks the level of violence within the United States" (Volpp 2001, 1181). In fact, when Western feminists embrace "cultural explanations" for violence experienced by "Third-World women" they are engaging in a form of decontextualization that prevents building productive feminist connections and activist agendas (Narayan 1997, 96–113).

Practicing Solidarity

Having a complex understanding of difference can allow transnational feminists to build solidarity that goes beyond a simplistic understanding of "global sisterhood," which naively (and dangerously) assumes shared feminist goals by advocating gender as the sole basis for solidarity. However, international feminist collectives have often struggled with acknowledging multiple goals. Tripp (2006) explains how feminists from the Third World have often had to advocate for causes that were not at the forefront of First-World feminists' agendas. For example, during the 1980 United Nation's World Conference on Women in Copenhagen, while Third World feminists advocated for development-related issues, First-World feminists did not see these issues as gender-specific or feminist concerns. The 1985 United Nation's Third World Conference on Women in Nairobi marked a turning point as Global South feminists succeeded in expanding definitions of gender violence from a narrow definition that encompassed only domestic abuse and rape to include violence caused by economic deprivation, war, and political repression. In short, transnational feminists are called to enact solidarity by realizing that not all women want the same thing and that not all women believe in doing things the same way.

Transnational feminists also build solidarity by incorporating "invisible" histories to reconfigure the scope, impact, and subjects of feminism. One example of this is including women-led anti-colonial struggles as feminist theorizing (Shohat 2002). Another way in which transnational feminists engage in solidarity is by being mindful of the dangers of applying a US perspective to non-US contexts. For example, the usual categories of intersectional analysis used in the United States might not be very useful or transferable in the context of South Asian countries, where issues of religion, caste, and ethnicity are in focus and more problematic than race. Similarly, transnational feminists realize that Indigenous understandings of sexuality might not directly correspond with Western categories of sexuality (Ballestín 2020).

Practicing transnational feminist solidarity always calls for deep and ongoing self-reflection so that feminists can name and grapple with power relations as they enter into alliances with each other. The book *Playing with Fire* (Sangtin Writers and Nagar 2006) offers an example of such solidarity in action. Although the project was initiated by Richa Nagar, a professor employed at a US university, she is not the sole or lead author. Instead, authorship is shared by the Sangtin Collective, a group of grassroots activists employed by a nonprofit organization in rural India. By choosing to share authorship, Nagar demonstrates how US feminists can amplify rather than speak over the voices and agendas of grassroots activists from the Global South. Additionally, the seven grassroots activists developed the book based on their diaries and conversations with each other and thus in the book they tell their stories on their own terms, positioning themselves as knowledge makers. This move is in contrast to the majority of transnational feminist theorizing by US feminists that uses knowledge from communities from the Global South but does not acknowledge their role as knowledge producers.

Finally, transnational feminists can build solidarity by amplifying feminist agency and activism from the Global South. Doing so can address an ongoing issue of feminists from the Global North silencing, dismissing, or ignoring activism and advocacy enacted by feminists from the Global South and thereby lapsing into "white saviorism."

Marissa Joanna Doshi

See Also: Capitalism; Colonialism; Neoliberalism; Third World Women's Alliance and Black Woman's Manifesto

Further Reading

Ballestín, Lucas. 2020. "Gender as Colonial Object." Accessed March 25, 2024. https://publicseminar.org/2018/07/gender-as-colonial-object/.

Enloe, Cynthia. 2014. *Bananas, Beaches and Bases: Making Feminist Sense of International Politics.* Berkeley: University of California Press.

Grewal, Inderpal, and Caren Kaplan, eds. 1994. *Scattered Hegemonies: Postmodernity and Transnational Feminist Practices*. Minneapolis: University of Minnesota Press.

Hochschild, Arlie Russell. 2012. "Love and Gold." In *Family, Ties and Care: Family Transformation in a Plural Modernity*, edited by Hans Bertram and Nancy Ehlert, 177–88. Farmington Hills: Verlag Barabara Budrich.

hooks, bell. 2000. *Feminism is for Everybody: Passionate Politics*. London: Pluto Press.

Mohanty, Chandra Talpade. 2003. "'Under Western Eyes' Revisited: Feminist Solidarity Through Anticapitalist Struggles." *Signs: Journal of Women in Culture and Society* 28 (2): 499–535.

Mason, Corinne. 2017. "Transnational Feminism." In *Feminist Issues: Race Class and Sexuality*, 6th ed., edited by Nancy Mandell and Jennifer Johnson, 62–89. Australia: Pearson Education.

Narayan, Uma. 1997. "Cross-cultural Connections, Border-crossings, and 'Death by Culture': Thinking about Dowry-Murders in India and Domestic-Violence Murders in the United States." In *Dislocating Cultures: Identities, Traditions, and Third World Feminism*, edited by Uma Narayan, 81–117. New York: Routledge.

Puar, Jasbir. 2008. "Feminists and Queers in the Service of Empire." In *Feminism and War: Confronting US Imperialism,* edited by Robin L. Riley and Chandra Talpade Mohanty, 47–55. London: Zed Books.

Sangtin Writers, and Richa Nagar. 2006. *Playing With Fire: Feminist Thought And Activism Through Seven Lives In India*. Minneapolis: University of Minnesota Press.

Shohat, Ella. 2002. "Area Studies, Gender Studies, and the Cartographies of Knowledge." *Social Text* 20, no. 3: 67–78.

Tripp, Aili Mari. 2006. "The Evolution of Transnational Feminisms." In *Global Feminism: Transnational Women's Activism, Organizing, and Human Rights*, edited by Myra Marx Ferree and Aili Mari Tripp, 51–75. New York: New York University Press.

Volpp, Leti. 2001. "Feminism Versus Multiculturalism." *Columbia Law Review* 101: 1181–218.

Walia, Harsha. 2014. *Undoing Border Imperialism*, vol. 6. Oakland: AK Press.

V

VAGINA MONOLOGUES

The Vagina Monologues is a production created by V (formerly Eve Ensler) in 1996. It is an episodic play in which the cast performs a series of monologues about vaginas. On Valentine's Day in 1998, V and a group of New York women founded the activist organization V-Day, which "demands that violence against all women, girls, and the Earth must end" (VDAY 2025). From 1998 until 2020, *The Vagina Monologues* was annually performed on Valentine's Day by "local volunteers and college students" as benefit performances to raise awareness and funds "for anti-violence groups" within the performers' own communities (VDAY 2025). Although *The Vagina Monologues* is not currently performed as part of V-Day's campaigns, it remains a licensed play and can be performed; V-Day encourages those who license and perform the play to still use it as a fundraising benefit to end violence.

The play typically opens with a monologue set in V's own voice, in which she explains that she interviewed over 200 women about their vaginas and that she developed the monologues from those interviews. V writes that "some of the monologues are close to verbatim interviews, some are composite interviews" and that others are more loosely based on the "the seed of an interview" (V 2001, 7). The monologues range from outrageously funny, to thought-provoking, to heartbreaking and rage-inducing.

Over the decades, there have been many drafts of *The Vagina Monologues*, with V adding a new monologue each year. Most notably, V added a monologue titled, "They Beat the Girl Out of My Boy . . . Or So They Tried," which was performed "for the first time by an all transgendered cast" in 2004 (Jamie 2014), and she added "I Was There in the Room," a monologue describing her granddaughter's birth as a graphic and emphatic celebration of vaginas.

V published the monologues as a book (2001), which has been translated into over forty-eight languages, and in 2002, HBO produced a TV version starring V. Both the book and TV screening are also titled *The Vagina Monologues*. This means that you can read and watch *The Vagina Monologues*—which I highly recommend—but they are still best experienced live.

Sarah Kornfield

See Also: Intimate Partner Violence; Violence Against Women Act (1994)

Further Reading

Jamie S. 2014. "They Beat the Girl Out of My Boy . . . Or So They Tried." *PFLAG Coeur D'Alene/Kootenai Country*. Accessed February 27, 2025. https://pflagcda.wordpress.com/2014/04/10/they-beat-the-girl-out-of-my-boy-or-so-they-tried/.

V (Eve Ensler). 2001. *The Vagina Monologues*. New York: Villard Books.

V (Eve Ensler). 2002. *The Vagina Monologues*. New York: HBO Film .

VDAY. 2025. "The Vagina Monologues." Accessed February 27, 2025. https://www.vday.org/art-activism/the-vagina-monologues/.

VIOLENCE AGAINST WOMEN ACT (1994)

Originally passed in 1994, the Violence Against Women Act (VAWA) was the first piece of federal legislation focused on addressing harms related to sexual violence and domestic abuse. Its central provisions include (1) providing funding for law enforcement agencies to address gender-based violent crimes and (2) creating enhanced sentencing for repeat offenders of such crimes (Hanson 2023). The law also created a domestic violence hotline and funded services for survivors of gender-based violence. Research suggests VAWA has been critical and effective in addressing and remedying such violence (Boba and Lilley 2009; Gover and Moore 2021; Modi, Palmer, and Armstrong 2014), although others emphasize its effect has been limited (Cho and Wilke 2005).

Since its passage, the legislation has undergone several changes. In 2000, the Supreme Court struck down one controversial provision in the VAMA that allowed victims of gender-based violence to sue their attackers (Schmidt 2015). This provision, a civil rights remedy, delayed the original passage of the legislation because of controversy that surrounded it. Debate about the provision centered on whether Congress had the authority to enact it, whether it was effective, and whether it would cause the federal court system to become overwhelmed.

VAWA must be reauthorized every five years, meaning the legislation expires unless Congress votes to renew it. During the effort to reauthorize VAWA from 2012 to 2013, controversy arose around provisions to augment protections for LGBTQ+, immigrant, and Indigenous women. After being excluded from the Republican-controlled House version of the bill, these provisions—including the first domestic violence services for LGBTQ+ people—were finally passed (LeTrent 2013).

When reauthorized in 2022, the law included additional provisions to address cybercrimes, services for LGBTQ+ individuals, and statutes to allow Indigenous authorities to prosecute non-Native people who allegedly committed gender-based crimes (Hoang 2024). Ahead of VAWA's reauthorization, Representatives Ayanna Pressley and Marie Newman highlighted the specific need to address violence against trans women of color (Yurcaba 2021).

Before the changes to VAWA in 2013, Indigenous woman faced unique and difficult barriers to address the gender-based violence and domestic abuse they survived. Indigenous tribes cannot prosecute non-Native people, even when those individuals commit a crime on tribal lands. Some abusers had even called tribal police to taunt them for their lack of ability to address the violence they committed. In 2013, however, Congress expanded tribal authority in persecuting gender-based violence (Crepelle 2020). Thus, VAWA has expanded to protect and assist more people.

VAWA's legacy is this: It was the first legislation to address the public health crisis of gender-based violence, and it has helped remedy that violence since its enactment.

Joshua H. Miller

See Also: Intimate Partner Violence; #MeToo; Missing and Murdered Indigenous Women and Girls; Rape Culture; Rape Myths

Further Reading

Boba, Rachel, and David Lilley. 2009. "Violence Against Women Act (VAWA) Funding: A Nationwide Assessment of Effects on Rape and Assault." *Violence Against Women* 15, no. 2: 168–85. https://doi.org/10.1177/1077801208329146.

Cho, Hyunkag, and Dine J. Wilke. 2005. "How Has the Violence Against Women Act Affected the Response of the Criminal Justice System to Domestic Violence." *Journal of Sociology and Social Welfare* 32, no, 4: 125–39. https://doi.org/10.15453/0191–5096.3118.

Crepelle, Adam. 2020. "Tribal Courts, The Violence Against Women Act, and Supplemental Jurisdiction: Expanding Tribal Court Jurisdiction to Improve Public Safety in Indian Country." *Montana Law Review* 81, no. 1: 59–95. https://scholarworks.umt.edu/cgi/viewcontent.cgi?article=2459&context=mlr.

Gover, Angela R.-, and Angela M. Moore. 2021. "The 1994 Violence Against Women Act: A Historic Response to Gender Violence." *Violence Against Women* 27, no. 1: 8–29. https://doi.org/10.1177/1077801220949705.

Hanson, Emily J. 2023. "The 2022 Violence Against Women Act (VAWA) Reauthorization." *Congressional Research Service*, May 22, 2023. https://crsreports.congress.gov/product/pdf/R/R47570/2.

Hoang, Vivian. 2024. "What to Know about the Violence Against Women Act as the Landmark Law Turns 30." *PBS News*, September 13, 2024. https://www.pbs.org/newshour/politics/what-to-know-about-the-violence-against-women-act-as-the-landmark-law-turns-30.

LeTrent, Sarah. 2013. "Violence Against Women Act Shines a Light on Same-Sex Abuse." *CNN*, March 14, 2013. https://www.cnn.com/2013/03/14/living/same-sex-domestic-violence-and-vawa/index.html.

Modi, Monica N., Sheallah Palmer, and Alicia Armstrong. 2014. "The Role of Violence Against Women Act in Addressing Intimate Partner Violence: A Public Health Issue." *Journal of Women's Health* 23, no. 2: 253–9. https://pmc.ncbi.nlm.nih.gov/articles/PMC3952594/.

Schmidt, Caroline S. 2015. "What Killed the Violence Against Women's Act's Civil Rights Remedy Before the Supreme Court Did?" *Virginia Law Review* 101: 501–57. https://www.virginialawreview.org/wp-content/uploads/2020/12/Schmidt_101-501.pdf.

Yurcaba, Jo. 2021. "Exclusive: Violence Against Women Act to Offer Support to LGBTQ Survivors." *NBC News*, March 17, 2021. https://www.nbcnews.com/feature/nbc-out/exclusive-violence-against-women-act-offer-support-lgbtq-survivors-n1261331.

VIRGINITY

Virginity is widely defined as the status of never having had sexual intercourse (Bersamin et al. 2007). At first glance, this definition seems straightforward—yet as feminists have been pointing out for decades, it crumbles almost immediately upon closer inspection (Hans and Kimberly 2011). For instance, what counts as sexual intercourse? Does oral sex count as sexual intercourse or only vaginal intercourse? If the answer is "only vaginal intercourse" then what about gay sex where there are no vaginas involved? What about lesbian couples who achieve orgasm without penetration? What about masturbation? Or, tragically, what about people who have never chosen to have sexual intercourse but have been raped?

Feminists argue that virginity is a social construct rather than a natural state of being. This means that society has made up—or constructed—the concept of "virginity" in order to use it. Consider, for example, the category of "blondes." "Blonde" is also a social construct: it refers almost exclusively to women with blonde hair but romanticizes them as gorgeous, carefree, and naïve or stupid. As an unspoken rule, this category only applies to white women (Cottom 2023). Almost immediately, it becomes clear that "blonde" is a social construct rather than a naturally occurring state of being: plenty of white blonde women are savvy rather than naïve; plenty of white blonde women are not gorgeous; many brunette women dye their hair blonde and are indistinguishable from people with naturally blonde hair; some women with blonde hair dye their hair darker colors; a lot of white men have blonde hair but aren't considered "blondes." Clearly, the category of "blondes" is not a meaningful natural category. Yet as a construct, the category of "blonde" remains useful to society. It creates hierarchies among women, reinforcing white women at the top of the hierarchy even as it stratifies white blonde women above brunettes, and so on. At the same time, the idea of "blondes" subordinates all women—even the most glamorous women—as naïve or simple-minded, insinuating that women need men's advice and exist to please men. The construct of "blonde" has economic uses for society as well: dying hair blonde is an expense that a lot of women consistently pay. Like the category "blonde," the category "virgin" is a social construct: rather than being a natural state of being, the category of "virginity" is socially defined.

Constructing Virginity

By conceptualizing virginity as a social construct, feminists turn our attention to examining how this concept was constructed and how it is used today. Virginity has a whole host of ideals tied to it, including femininity, purity, innocence, and overall value. Consider, for instance, how important "virginity" is in the context of religion and marriage. For example, Christianity often emphasizes virginity in the story of Jesus's birth—and Jesus's mother, Mary, is often known as the Virgin Mary (Mulya 2018). Depending on how this story is told, Mary's virginity is often framed as that which made her fit to carry the human form of God, emphasizing the importance of virginity and thus "purity" in connection to women's spiritual value.

Across time and in different places and cultures, people have believed different things about virginity. What someone thinks about virginity depends on their beliefs, exposure, group identity, experiences, and education (Bersamin et al. 2007). Most basically, people differ in their understandings of virginity based on their understanding of what counts as "sexual intercourse."

In the United States, virginity is largely understood within a heteronormative framework, meaning that one's ideas about virginity rely on the understanding of sex as a penis penetrating a vagina. But as feminists and LGBTQ+ activists have long argued, penetrative heterosexual sex is not the only or the defining version of sex. Yet because so many people in the United States think of sex in this heteronormative way, many believe that anal and oral intercourse preserves "virginity" if there is no vaginal penetration. These forms of penetration and other ways to achieve orgasm are widely used as a "loophole" that enables sexual pleasure while still preserving "virginity."

The Hymen

For a long time, people in the United States thought that an intact hymen was proof that a woman was still a virgin (Allan, Santos, and Spahr 2016). The hymen is a thin membrane that covers or partially surrounds the vaginal opening; it typically bleeds a small amount when it breaks or tears. In a lot of cultures, vaginally penetrative intercourse was thought to be the only way the hymen could break or tear. This inaccurate belief has long been used to police girls and women: that is, since women can supposedly "prove" their virginal status by bleeding during their first vaginally penetrative experience (and men cannot), the focus on women's virginity has become paramount in many cultures, including the United States. Indeed, this belief held so much importance that mothers would discourage or ban their daughters from using tampons, for fear that it would "take their virginity." And here, it becomes clear that virginity is linked to ideas of both loss and possession (Allan, Santos, and Spahr 2016). For example, two individuals having sexual intercourse with each other for the first time would simultaneously be "losing" one's own virginity and "taking" the other person's.

Medical advancements have demonstrated that the hymen is not an indicator of virginity. The hymen can tear as a result of any number of things, including horseback riding, rigorous exercise, injury, bike riding, etc. Therefore, the hymen is not a valid way to determine one's status as a virgin.

The long-standing focus on the hymen, however, points to patriarchal societies' strong association of virginity with femininity. Feminists have observed that historically, Western societies disproportionally focused on women's virginity and the idea that women could be proven as virgins (or not) on their wedding nights enabled husbands to possess and control their wife's sexuality—or discard the woman if it was suspected she wasn't "pure" (Allan, Santos, and Spahr 2016). Controlling women's sexuality is essential in patriarchal societies where inheritance and the family line is passed from father to son, since controlling women's sexuality is the only way to ensure that the son is the father's offspring. This is not the case in matrilineal societies where the family line follows the mother.

While the hymen has received the most attention when it comes to virginity, in medieval Europe, the uterus was considered the main indicator of having had intercourse. The bleeding that occurred during first intercourse was thought to be a product of a "reshaping of the uterine passage" rather than from the hymen stretching or breaking (Allan, Santos, and Spahr 2016). In medieval Europe, virginity was not just a physical state but a spiritual one as well.

Virginity Today

To this day, virginity is often associated with spirituality and morality—again, especially for girls and women (Allan, Santos, and Spahr 2016). When a culture considers virginity in more spiritual terms, then physical indicators are no longer fully able to determine "virginity." For instance, in some Christian circles, women might self-describe as "born-again virgins." Here, women who have previously had vaginally penetrative intercourse reclaim their virginity in a spiritual sense after religiously committing themselves to sexual abstinence (Conner 2009). On the other hand, when virginity is primarily considered a physical matter, then its arbitrary nature becomes more obvious. That is, since the hymen is not an indicator of virginity (and could only indicate for half the population anyway), we are left picking one thing (such as an orgasm, or penetrative vaginal intercourse, or any penetrative intercourse, etc.) as the marker of virginity. It becomes fairly clear that whatever we pick as an indicator of virginity, the choice is relatively arbitrary—since there are other options to choose among. Currently, many religions and ideologies assume that virginity is physical and yet involves a spiritual or moral state of purity.

Society has come a very long way in understanding misconceptions about virginity, and yet virginity as a social construct is still used to subjugate women. One example of this subjugation is the virgin/whore dichotomy. This phenomenon refers to the cultural stereotype that imagines women as either innocent virgins or hypersexual whores. This dichotomy perpetuates sexual violence against women who are labeled as "whores" (Mulya 2018). Within this ideology, once a girl or woman loses her "innocent virgin" status, she becomes a "whore" and thus "deserving" of sexual violence. And here, women are seen as "asking for it" even—or perhaps especially—when "it" is sexual violence, and the sexual violence committed against women is shrugged off as unimportant since women have already supposedly lost their value by being "deflowered." The stereotype that frames sexually active women as "whores" is often accompanied by the misconception that sexually active women are "used" or "stretched out," which then cheapens the supposed value of their sexuality. In contemporary US society, a woman's sexual status is often used to judge and label her moral character.

Virginity is still treated differently on the basis of gender. Due to men's supposedly extensive sexual needs, men are rarely held to the same standards as women when it comes to virginity. Besides, since there is no supposed physical proof or marker of men's virginity" (the way the hymen often still continues to operate in US society), it seems almost silly to think of policing men's virginal status. Women, on the other hand, are instructed to maintain their supposedly inherent purity, gentleness, and moral goodness—by keeping their legs closed (Mulya 2018).

Virginity is also treated differently on the basis of age. Adult men who haven't lost their virginity are often seen as less-than and teased for being a "loser" (Kelly 2016a). In fact, having a lot of sex during one's youth is typically considered admirable for men. For women, age plays a role depending on one's subculture. Within highly religious communities, virginity is typically of paramount importance regardless of a woman's age. But in secular cultures, women are often caught in a trap where having "lost" one's virginity too soon is seen as reckless and promiscuous (again, the "whore" stereotype comes into play), but still being a virgin in middle age is also penalized—middle-aged women who are sexually abstinent are often portrayed as prudes or spinsters.

Ultimately, our bodies are politicized. Sex is important to communities and governance because sex is the means to reproduction. Controlling when and in what circumstances people have sex allows institutions like governments and religions to create the reproductive structures they deem "ideal" (Kelly 2016b). Our bodies contribute to a larger social fabric, which is why they are so heavily policed (Kelly 2016b). Feminists resist these systems of control and surveillance, arguing for individual choice and bodily autonomy. Everyone should have the right to make choices about their bodies for the sake of their own pleasure and well-being.

Kersten Dekker

See Also: Biopower; Birth Control; Compulsory Heterosexuality; Hegemonic Masculinity; Matriliny; Purity Culture; Sex; Sex Education; *Vagina Monologues*

Further Reading

Allan, Jonathan A., Cristina Santos, and Adriana Spahr, eds. 2016. *Virgin Envy: The Cultural (in)Significance of the Hymen*. Regina: University of Regina Press.

Bersamin, Melina M., D. A. Fisher, S. Walker, D. L. Hil, and J. W. Grube. 2007. "Defining Virginity and Abstinence: Adolescents' Interpretations of Sexual Behaviors." *The Journal of Adolescent Health: Official Publication of the Society for Adolescent Medicine* 41, no. 2: 182–88. https://doi.org/10.1016/j.jadohealth.2007.03.011.

Conner, Vilma. 2009. *Born-Again Virgin: How to Transform Your Life from Promiscuity Back into Purity*. Beaumont, TX: Miracon Enterprises.

Cottom, Tressie Mcmillan. 2023. "The Enduring, Invisible Power of Blond." *The New York Times*, January 19, 2023. www.nytimes.com/2023/01/19/opinion/the-enduring-invisible-power-of-blond.html.

Hans, Jason D., and Claire Kimberly. 2011. "Abstinence, Sex, and Virginity: Do they Mean What We Think They Mean?" *American Journal of Sexuality Education* 6, no. 4: 329–42. https://doi.org/10.1080/15546128.2011.624475.

Kelly, Casey Ryan. 2016a. *Abstinence Cinema: Virginity and the Rhetoric of Sexual Purity in Contemporary Film*. New Brunswick, NJ: Rutgers University Press. https://doi.org/10.36019/9780813575131.

Kelly, Casey Ryan. 2016b. "Chastity for Democracy: Surplus Repression and the Rhetoric of Sex Education." *The Quarterly Journal of Speech* 102, no. 4: 353–75. https://doi.org/10.1080/00335630.2016.1209548.

Wijaya Mulya, T. 2018. "Queering the Virgin/Whore Binary: The Virgin Mary, the Whore of Babylon, and Sexual Violence." In *Rape Culture, Gender Violence, and Religion*, edited by Caroline Blyth, Emily Colgan, and Katie B. Edwards, 51–65. Palgrave Macmillan. https://doi.org/10.1007/978-3-319-70669-6_4.

W

WHITE PRIVILEGE

White privilege is the idea that white people in the United States are able to move through their daily life with the advantage of having social systems work for them and feeling as though they belong and that their skin color will not disadvantage them. Just as racism puts some at a disadvantage, white privilege works to advantage white folks in ways that often go unrecognized. Another way to understand white privilege is majority group advantage (McTaggart and O'Brien 2022). Feminist scholarship on white privilege has examined what white privilege is, how it impacts interracial solidarity, and how white privilege can be used to further feminist gains.

What White Privilege Is, and What It Is Not

Peggy McIntosh explains white privilege using the metaphor of an "invisible weightless knapsack of special provisions, maps, passports, codebooks, visas, clothes, tools, and blank checks" available to white people (1989, 10). As a white woman, McIntosh provides forty-six examples of ways she experiences white privilege, including being able to be in the company of people of her own race most of the time, being able to go shopping alone without fear of harassment, seeing people of her race represented widely and positively in news media, not being asked to speak for all people of her racial group, feeling relatively safe when being pulled over by a traffic cop, being able to find bandages in a "flesh" color that matches her skin, and easily being able to purchase posters, picture books, greeting cards, dolls, and toys featuring people of her race (1989). Each of these examples demonstrates how McIntosh's identity as a white person allows her to feel normal, accepted, and part of the social system.

While white privilege advantages white individuals in different ways, it does not mean that white individuals do not face challenges. For example, people of all races face the challenge of looking for a new job, but white privilege typically provides an advantage to white people even within this challenging situation as individuals with Black-sounding names are chosen for interviews far less than individuals with white-sounding names. Similarly, people of all races might face the challenge of trying to sell or purchase a home, but white privilege typically makes all neighborhoods available to white people and makes it easier for them to secure loans and mortgages within this challenging situation. Meanwhile, Black individuals are more likely to have their existing home devalued and are less likely to be shown properties in so-called "desirable" (white-majority) neighborhoods. Redlining is a historic practice in the United States that used color-coded maps to identify areas with large minority populations. These areas were then deemed "high risk" for lending and investment, making those properties less valuable and making it more difficult for people of color to obtain a loan to purchase a home in a Black neighborhood (they were often legally prohibited during the redlining era from purchasing homes outside Black neighborhoods).

White privilege manifests in the economy, education, criminal justice system, media, and pop culture (McTaggart and O'Brien 2022). For example, analyzing mainstream American literature (including the work of Poe, Melville, Whitman, Emerson, Thoreau, etc.), Toni Morrison (1992) explained how the idea and value of American individualism is made in the image of whiteness and has been built through the exclusion of Blackness. This creates a social and political space where whiteness is seen as normal and Blackness is seen as other.

White privilege became the topic of national conversation in 2020 following the police killings of Breonna Taylor and George Floyd. As the nation reckoned with police violence against Black people, activists and celebrities centered white privilege in calls for defunding the police. For example, Natalie Portman posted on Instagram, "When I first heard #defundthepolice, I have to admit my first reaction was fear." She explains that for her whole life, the police made her feel safe, and then writes, "that's exactly the center of my white privilege: the police make me as a white woman feel safe, while my Black friends, family, and neighbors feel the opposite: police make them feel terror." Continuing, Portman writes that Black people have good reason to fear the police, since the police "are the 6th leading cause of death for Black men in this country." Finally, Portman concludes by saying, "These are not isolated incidents. They are patterns and part of the system of over-policing of Black Americans" (Stone 2020).

Alongside coverage of police violence against Black people, examples of white women using police as their "personal protection agency" in disagreements with people of color emerged across social media sites. This made the differential treatment of white and Black folks by police even more apparent. One such video showed Amy Cooper, a white woman, calling the police on Christian Cooper, a Black man, because he asked her to leash her dog while in Manhattan's Central Park. The video showed Amy Cooper using a more distressed voice with the police, alleging that an "African American" was "threatening" her (Gruber 2020). This is a clear example of white privilege in action: Amy Cooper felt entitled to police intervention in a simple disagreement, while Christian Cooper felt compelled to record the interaction to prove his innocence when police arrived.

White Privilege as Roadblock and Resource

White privilege was discussed as a roadblock to feminist organizing even before the specific term "white privilege" was coined. For example, in 1977 the Combahee River Collective, a Black feminist group, identified a range of issues they faced, including a lack of racial privilege and racism by white women within the women's movement. Kimberlé Crenshaw extended the discussion in 1989 by coining the term "intersectionality," which states that our identities overlap to experience different intersections of relative privilege or oppression. In the 1960s and 1970s, most white feminists did not recognize how centering their whiteness excluded the experiences of Black feminists. This led to separations in the women's rights movement, as Black feminists and womanists sought to address issues that affected them.

Feminist scholars have taken white feminists' uncritical embrace of their white privilege to task: Marilyn Frye (1983) argues that white feminists must opt out of the "whiteliness" club and transform their consciousness to understand the experiences of others. Sarita Srivastava (2005) identifies white women's perceptions of their own morality as a roadblock to feminist organizing: when white feminists recognize their white privilege, they tend to center their guilt rather than the work necessary for moving an intersectional feminist project forward. Others have moved the conversation on white privilege to understanding how it can be used to resist the different forms of oppression women face. For example, Linda Alcoff (2015) imagines ways white feminists can use white privilege to further intersectional feminist goals. As an example, we can consider the "White Women for Kamala" groups that emerged during the 2024 presidential election. In these groups, white feminists came together to acknowledge their privilege, recognize the work of Black women, and organize together in support of Harris, a Black woman, for president.

Andrea J. Terry

See Also: #BlackLivesMatter; Combahee River Collective; Crenshaw, Kimberlé; Intersectionality; Morrison, Toni; Whiteness as Property

Further Reading

Alcoff, Linda Martín. 2015. *The Future of Whiteness*. Cambridge, UK: Polity Press.
Combahee River Collective. 1986. *The Combahee River Collective Statement: Black Feminist Organizing in the Seventies and Eighties*. 1st ed. Albany, NY: Kitchen Table.
Crenshaw, Kimberlé. 1991. "Mapping the Margins: Intersectionality, Identity Politics, and Violence against Women of Color." *Stanford Law Review* 43 (6): 1241–99. https://doi.org/10.2307/1229039.
Frye, Marilyn. 1983. *The Politics of Reality: Essays in Feminist Theory*. 1st ed. Trumansburg, New York: Crossing Press.
Gruber, Aya. 2020. "Why Amy Cooper Felt the Police Were Her Personal 'Protection Agency.'" *Slate Magazine*, May 27, 2020. https://slate.com/news-and-politics/2020/05/amy-cooper-white-women-policing.html.
McIntosh, Peggy. 1989. "White Privilege and Male Privilege," in Alison Bailey and Chris Cuomo (eds), *The Feminist Philosophy Reader*. New York: McGraw Hill.
McTaggart, Ninochka, and Eileen O'Brien. 2022. *White Privilege: The Persistence of Racial Hierarchy in a Culture of Denial*. Rev. 1st ed. San Diego, CA: Cognella.
Morrison, Toni. 1992. *Playing in the Dark: Whiteness and the Literary Imagination*. Cambridge, MA: Harvard University Press.
Srivastava, Sarita. 2005. "'You're Calling Me a Racist?' The Moral and Emotional Regulation of Antiracism and Feminism." *Signs: Journal of Women in Culture and Society* 31, no. 1: 29–62. https://doi.org/10.1086/432738.
Stone, Megan. 2020. "Natalie Portman Calls out her White Privilege in Post Supporting Defunding the Police." *ABC News*, June 9, 2020. https://abcnews.go.com/GMA/Culture/natalie-portman-calls-white-privilege-post-supporting-defunding/story?id=71149992.

WHITE SUPREMACY

White supremacy is an ideology based on the belief that white people, and white men specifically, are inherently superior to other racial groups and should exercise authority over them (Bonds and Inwood 2016, 719–20). It consists of personal beliefs about racial superiority but also includes larger cultural and political systems that "create unequal outcomes along racial lines" in terms of "wealth, freedom, health, and happiness" (Belew and Gutiérrez 2021). White supremacy often relies on circular reasoning, in which the dominance of white men in positions of power is used as evidence of their natural superiority. Simultaneously, this dominance helps perpetuate systems that hinder the success of others, including women and people of color. While white supremacy represents a belief system with pervasive influence across various facets of US society, there have been several organizations explicitly committed to upholding and safeguarding its principles. The most notorious of these is the Ku Klux Klan, which emerged in the aftermath of the Civil War and employed intimidation and violence to resist Reconstruction initiatives aimed at granting rights to Black southerners, such as the right to vote and own property (Daniels 2016). More recent examples include the National Association for the Advancement of White People, the White Aryan Resistance, and the National Socialist Movement.

Throughout history, white supremacist beliefs have been supported by various distinct justifications. During slavery and into the contemporary era—as represented by the Religious Right—Christianity and biblical scripture have been invoked to justify white supremacy (Jones 2020). Likewise, beginning in the late 1800s, white supremacists endeavored to employ science to argue for the biological existence of racial differences, thereby legitimizing social and political hierarchies based on race and gender. For example, the field of phrenology, which measured the skull sizes of different racial groups with the goal of finding physical evidence that Black people were intellectually inferior to white people, was hugely popular in the early nineteenth century (Jones 2020). Even after phrenology was discredited, some scientists continued to try to prove the intellectual and physical superiority of white men over other groups (Jones 2020). These include studies that attempted to prove that Black Americans had lower IQs and that they were predisposed toward criminal behavior (Harvard Library n.d.). These purported biological differences were used as evidence that Black Americans were unfit for positions of authority. While the consensus among contemporary scientists is that racial categories have no basis in biology, many of the ideas of scientific racism continue to persist into the present (Harvard Library n.d.).

Crucially, ideas of manhood and masculinity are central to white supremacy (Daniels 2016). As Daniels (2016) argues, in white supremacy, "race, class, gender, and sexuality are woven together in complex, and mutually reinforcing ways." Because of this, any threat to white male power—even if that threat comes from white women—is seen as a threat to white supremacy. White supremacist belief systems promote conventional gender roles, seeing women as homemakers and mothers and men as the financial providers and heads of households. In this way, white supremacy and patriarchy work to mutually reinforce one another (Anti-Defamation League 2018). White women are seen as valuable, if largely powerless, assets in furthering white supremacist goals.

Indeed, white supremacists express significant concern about the birth rate among white women, often opposing the use of contraceptives (Anti-Defamation League 2018). In contrast, Black women's reproductive capacities have historically been perceived as a challenge to white supremacy, leading to the forced sterilization of many Black women in the decades following the abolition of slavery (Stafford 2023).

The sanctity of white women has also been historically used to justify racial violence. The supposed protection of white women's virtue from Black men was used as justification for many lynchings across the South. White supremacy's fixation on white women's role in securing the future of the white race has resulted in the heightened surveillance of white women and their bodies. In fact, US white supremacist groups have long championed a mantra known as the "14-words," which states, "We must secure the existence of our people and a future for white children" and is often followed by the phrase, "because the beauty of the white Aryan woman must not perish from the earth" (Michael 2009).

As such, preserving white women's "virtue" is frequently emphasized as essential, with any sexual relations outside of marriage viewed as damaging to a white woman's reputation and respectability. Moreover, to uphold racial purity, white supremacists advocate that white women must only marry white men (see Daniels 2016; Anti-Defamation League 2018). For much of US history, these beliefs were enshrined in legislation known as anti-miscegenation laws. For example, until *Loving v. Virginia* (1967), it was illegal in many states for a white person to marry a person of color (Archie 2022).

White women who seek to defy the norms imposed upon them by white supremacy—whether by not marrying, not having children, or pursing relationships with nonwhite or nonmale partners—are often labeled as rebellious traitors to the white race. In this way, gender has been and remains a crucial aspect of white supremacy.

White Nationalism

Much has been said about white supremacy's role in shaping the United States as a nation (Jung 2015; Belew and Gutiérrez 2021; Jung et al. 2011). Many of the most cherished American rights, such the right to vote, were originally granted only to property-owning white men (Belew and Gutiérrez 2021). Moreover, the purported innate inferiority of Black people was employed to rationalize slavery. Similarly, supposed white superiority has been used to justify imperialism, epitomized by the concept of the "white man's burden," which asserted the moral obligation of white colonizers to govern and "civilize" Indigenous populations deemed incapable of taking care of themselves (Brantlinger 2007). Ultimately, white supremacists view the United States as a nation created by and for white men (Daniels 2016).

In contemporary culture, white supremacists oppose immigration, as well as the ideas of multiculturalism and globalism, because they promote the intermingling of people from different cultures and races (Southern Poverty Law Center 2022). This is seen as a threat to the United States' supposed status as a white nation, even though this has never truly been the case. White supremacists also oppose feminism and feminist movements, which they see as undermining the traditional gender hierarchies inherent in white supremacy (Anti-Defamation League 2018).

One example of white supremacist beliefs in contemporary society is the growing spread of the "great replacement theory." This theory argues that "Jews, racial minorities and immigrants are actively seeking to replace white native-born Americans through higher fertility rates and migration" (Altschuler and Blumin 2022). The theory has been promoted both online on message board sites like 4chan and by prominent conservative media figures, such as Tucker Carlson. It is a resurgence of a common fear that crops up among white Americans when the United States experiences periods of increased immigration (Altschuler and Blumin 2022). According to a 2022 poll, three in ten Americans believe in the "great replacement theory." The continued prevalence of the fear that nonwhite groups are "replacing" white Americans gestures to the ways that white supremacist beliefs remain deeply embedded in contemporary US society.

Scholars have theorized white supremacy as a series of "structures and logics" that underly racism and systems of privilege (Bonds and Inwood 2016). As Belew and Gutiérrez (2021, 6) have argued, "whiteness is a socially constructed category that has changed dramatically over the course of United States history." It was first understood as a social or political identity category and wasn't seen as a biological category until the nineteenth century. Which ethnic groups counted as "white" has changed dramatically over time. Until the twentieth century, Irish, Italian, and Polish immigrants were not considered "white" (Belew and Gutiérrez 2021, 6; see also Daniels 2016). This demonstrates the ways that white supremacy can adapt to maintain its power.

Jung has described white supremacy as "compris[ing] a web of crisscrossing discursive and practical ties" rather than a set hierarchical relationship between white and nonwhite racial groups (2015, 68). In this web, the fundamental principles of white supremacy persist, yet space is allowed for participation by nonwhite groups, creating an illusion of their inclusion as active members of society. This creates a vision of a unified society—such as the vision of the United States as a cultural melting pot—even when that society still contains inherent divisions that hierarchize racial groups (Jung 2015, 69–70). For example, even though the United States no longer has a segregated healthcare system, Black women are almost three times more likely to die during pregnancy or childbirth than women of other races (Stafford 2023). This is tied, in part, to racial biases within the medical profession that result in some healthcare providers continuing to falsely believe in biological differences between people of difference races (Stafford 2023). Thus, even as the US healthcare system appears to be available to all Americans regardless of race, the lived realities of that system demonstrate the racial disparities that continue to persist.

While various feminist and Civil Rights efforts have worked to undermine and draw attention to white supremacist systems and practices, white supremacy remains a powerful force in the United States. White supremacist ideology has been cited as the motive behind several mass shootings in recent years, including the 2022 mass shootings in Buffalo, New York, and Colorado Springs, Colorado. In 2022, white supremacists committed over 80 percent of extremist-related violence in the United States (Singh 2023). Additionally, structural inequalities, such as the fact that Black and Latinx Americans are more likely than white Americans to be sentenced to prison for the same crimes, continue to persist (Raymond 2023). In 2021, despite comprising only about 30 percent of the US population, white men occupied 62 percent of political offices (Villarreal 2021). In this way, the underlying power structures upheld by white supremacy continue to persist and thrive.

Courtlyn Pippert

See Also: Anti-Miscegenation Laws; Colonialism; Patriarchy; Religious Right; Structural Oppression; White Privilege

Further Reading

Altschuler, Glenn C., and Stuart M. Blumin. 2022. "The 'Great Replacement' Theory Rises Again, Ending in Tragedy." *The Washington Post*, June 2, 2022. https://www.washingtonpost.com/outlook/2022/06/02/great-replacement-theory-rises-again-ending-tragedy/.

Anti-Defamation League. 2018. "When Women Are the Enemy: The Intersection of Misogyny and White Supremacy." July 20, 2018. Accessed March 26, 2024. https://www.adl.org/resources/report/when-women-are-enemy-intersection-misogyny-and-white-supremacy.

Archie, Ayana. 2022. "Take a Look Back at the History of Interracial and Same-Sex Marriages." *NPR*, December 9, 2022. https://www.npr.org/2022/12/09/1141819649/interracial-same-sex-marriage.

Belew, Kathleen, and Ramón A. Gutiérrez. 2021. *A Field Guide to White Supremacy*. Oakland, CA: University of California Press.

Bonds, Anne, and Joshua Inwood. 2016. "Beyond White Privilege: Progress in Human Geography." *Progress in Human Geography* 40, no. 6: 715–33. https://doi.org/10.1177/0309132515613166.

Brantlinger, Patrick. 2007. "Kipling's 'The White Man's Burden' and Its Afterlives." *English Literature in Transition, 1880–1920* 50, no. 2: 172–91. https://doi.org/10.1353/elt.2007.0017.

Daniels, Jessie. 2016. *White Lies: Race, Class, Gender and Sexuality in White Supremacists Discourse*. New York: Routledge.

Harvard Library. n.d. "Scientific Racism." Accessed March 29, 2024. https://library.harvard.edu/confronting-anti-black-racism/scientific-racism.

Jones, Robert P. 2020. *White Too Long: The Legacy of White Supremacy in American Christianity*. New York: Simon and Shuster.

Jung, Moon-Kie. 2015. *Beneath the Surface of White Supremacy: Denaturalizing US Racisms Past and Present*. Stanford, CA: Stanford University Press.

Jung, Moon-Kie, João H. Costa Vargas, and Eduardo Bonilla-Silva, eds. 2011. *State of White Supremacy: Racism, Governance, and the United States*. Stanford, CA: Stanford University Press.

Michael, George. 2009. "David Lane and the Fourteen Words." *Totalitarian Movements and Political Religions* 10, no. 1: 43–61. https://doi.org/10.1080/14690760903067986.

Raymond, Nate. 2023. "Study Finds Racial Disparities in Whether US Judges Impose Prison." *Reuters*, November 14, 2023. https://www.reuters.com/legal/government/study-finds-racial-disparities-whether-us-judges-impose-prison-2023-11-14/.

Singh, Kanishka. 2023. "White Supremacists Behind over 80% of Extremism-Related US Murders in 2022." *Reuters*, February 23, 2023. https://www.reuters.com/world/us/white-supremacists-behind-over-80-extremism-related-us-murders-2022-2023-02-23/.

Southern Poverty Law Center. 2022. "White Nationalist." Accessed March 26, 2024. https://www.splcenter.org/fighting-hate/extremist-files/ideology/white-nationalist.

Stafford, Kat. 2023. "Why Do So Many Black Women Die in Pregnancy? One Reason: Doctors Don't Take Them Seriously." *Associated Press*, May 23, 2023. https://projects.apnews.com/features/2023/from-birth-to-death/black-women-maternal-mortality-rate.html.

Villarreal, Alexandra. 2021. "White Male Minority Rule Pervades Politics across the US, Research Shows." *The Guardian*, May 26, 2021. https://www.theguardian.com/us-news/2021/may/26/white-male-minority-rule-us-politics-research.

WHITENESS AS PROPERTY

The concept of "whiteness as property" was introduced by legal scholar Cheryl I. Harris in 1993. Broadly, this idea draws on critical race theory (CRT) to examine how race and racism are embedded in legal systems and social structures. Harris describes whiteness as property by stating that it involves "the legal legitimation of expectations grounded in white privilege and economic advantage" and that "whiteness has functioned as self-identity in a realm in which whiteness and property were conflated," thus becoming "a means of deriving value and maintaining status" (Harris 1993, 1713). Put more simply, Harris argues that whiteness, both historically and legally, has functioned like property in the United States. In other words, being white has given people social and material advantages, much like owning "property" does. For instance, consider an inventor who—through patent law—owns the "idea" of how to make something and profits from this patent; in a similar way, Harris demonstrates that US law has treated whiteness and white privilege as something that white people own and profit from. This perspective expands understandings about race and privilege by linking the social construct of race to the legal and economic structures of society.

Harris traces this concept back to slavery and segregation in the United States. During that time, the status of whiteness meant freedom, access to rights, and economic opportunities, while Black people were designated and treated as literal property—a dehumanizing status which served as grounds for their enslavement and the exploitation of their labor. The legal system in the United States ensured that only white people could own land, vote, pass goods and property to their children though inheritance laws, and possess full citizenship, reinforcing the idea that whiteness was not just a racial identity but something that provided immense privilege, profit, and control (Harris 1993, 1721–2). Even after slavery, segregation laws like Jim Crow continued to secure the social, political, and economic value of whiteness, evidenced as white populations consistently experienced superior access to education, housing, legal counsel, employment, healthcare, politics, and more.

Specifically, Harris (1993, 1731–45) outlined four ways in which whiteness operates as property in the United States. First, property laws involve the *right of disposition*, meaning that the owner has the right to decide whether to transfer ownership and to whom. Likewise, white people historically designed family laws to ensure that children with Black mothers and white fathers could not inherit the rights and status of white people regardless of the child's skin color. Second, owners have the *right to use and enjoy* their property. In a similar way, whiteness is something that can be used and enjoyed when—for example—applying for loans or encountering police officers. Third, the *right to reputation and status* means that ownership confers a reputation on the owner—like a form of inherent credibility. Similarly, whiteness confers status on white people in the United States. For example, white people are seen as "real" Americans, making it easier for them to vote. Finally, property ownership includes the *right to exclude*; this is seen most obviously in "no trespassing signs." Like property, whiteness has long maintained the right to exclude, as seen in the Naturalization Act of 1790, which limited citizenry to white people in the United States, and in contemporary immigration laws and de facto school and housing segregation.

Whiteness as Property Today

This idea of whiteness as property continues to be relevant today. Although the overt legal systems of segregation have largely been dismantled, the privileges of whiteness are still deeply ingrained in sociocultural norms and structures. For instance, homeownership has long been a factor in economic stability, but racist housing policies like redlining historically ensured that Black and nonwhite people were excluded from certain neighborhoods. As a result, white people were able to accumulate wealth through property ownership in ways that people of color could not. This kind of historical exclusion has contributed to the racial wealth gap that persists in the United States today (Lipsitz 2024).

Similarly, understanding whiteness as property has implications that extend far beyond race alone, particularly when viewed through the lens of intersectional feminism, which attends to the ways race, gender, class, and other identities interact to shape people's experiences with privilege and discrimination (Crenshaw 1991). Women of color have historically been marginalized within feminist and civil rights movements, where the concept of whiteness as property can be applied to explain why their needs and desires are often overlooked. White women in feminist movements, for instance, have often prioritized gender issues without fully accounting for the racial and economic barriers that women of color face (Davis 2011). Consequently, feminist movements have often reproduced patterns of white supremacy and privilege by centering issues like workplace equality and reproductive rights in ways that primarily benefit middle-class white women (Moraga and Anzaldúa 2015, xxv). This exclusion reinforces Harris's argument that whiteness operates as property that can be guarded or extended even within social justice spaces, as white women have access to feminist platforms and resources that many women of color do not.

This kind of intersectional analysis shows that whiteness as property is not just about individual acts of racism or privilege; rather, it is about a system that benefits certain populations over others. As a result, Harris emphasizes that whiteness operates as a form of "status property" that people defend and protect, even when it comes at the expense of justice and equality. This explains why efforts to promote racial equity—like affirmative action or reparations—are often met with strong opposition from those who fear losing the privileges that whiteness affords (Harris 1993). In other words, it is not so much that white people aim to hold onto whiteness as an identity marker but that they want to maintain the social status and opportunities whiteness provides in a white supremacist culture.

To summarize, Harris's notion of whiteness as property highlights how race has been used to maintain systems of power and privilege by furthering understandings of its cultural and material effects. Conceptualizing whiteness as property helps us grasp how historical injustices are connected to contemporary inequalities, offering a framework for addressing racial injustice in a way that acknowledges both individual and systemic issues. Keeping these ideas in mind, Harris invites us into critical reflection about the ways race and privilege operate together to shape social and structural inequities, as well as what opportunities might exist for creating a more just society.

Dakota J. Sandras

See Also: Affirmative Action; Crenshaw, Kimberlé; Critical Race Theory; White Privilege

Further Reading

Alexander, Michelle. 2010. *The New Jim Crow: Mass Incarceration in the Age of Colorblindness.* New York: New Press.

Crenshaw, Kimberlé. 1991. "Mapping the Margins: Intersectionality, Identity Politics, and Violence Against Women of Color." *Stanford Law Review* 43, no. 6 (July): 1241–99. https://doi:10.2307/1229039.

Davis, Angela Y. 2011. *Women, Race, and Class.* New York: Vintage.

Harris, Cheryl I. 1993. "Whiteness as Property." *Harvard Law Review* 106, no. 8: 1707–91. https://doi.org/10.2307/1341787.
Lipsitz, George. 2024. *The Danger Zone is Everywhere: How Housing Discrimination Harms Health and Steals Wealth.* Oakland, CA: University of California Press.
Moraga, Cherríe, and Gloria Anzaldúa, eds. (2015), *This Bridge Called My Back: Writings by Radical Women of Color*, 4th ed, Albany, NY: State University of New York Press.

WITCHES

The story of witches in US history is one of colonization, gender roles, and religion. It is a story of control and domination. By and large, the historical record we have of witches in the United States is actually a record of the accusations of witchcraft and the trials (and executions) that followed such accusations.

Witch trials targeted people—mostly women—who did not fit social expectations. For instance, in New England, only 20 percent of those accused of witchcraft were men (Godbeer 2017). Regardless of their gender, the accused typically transgressed patriarchally defined gender expectations. For the most part, women were accused of witchcraft when they deviated from the submissive role that was expected of them.

Witchcraft: A Colonial Construct

The settlers who colonized the land we now call the United States brought European beliefs about witchcraft with them. These beliefs have a long history and eventually took center stage during the witch trials in colonial America. Historian Elaine Breslaw (2000) notes that pre-Christian peoples used the idea of witchcraft to make the unfamiliar and inexplicable more understandable. European societies had no modern sense of coincidence and minimal scientific knowledge, so they turned to magical explanations to account for negative events. Witchcraft, in this framework, was understood as an intentional use of ritual or practice to cause harm. The harm could manifest in serious ways, causing death or disease, or less severe ways, causing stumbles and minor injuries. In the late Middle Ages, Christianity was spreading in Europe and the notion arose that witches had come by their power to cause harm through a pact with the devil. In 1486, Heinrich Kramer's *Malleus Maleficarum* (*The Witches' Hammer*) asserted the connection between witchcraft and devilry (Broedel 2003). Throughout the 1500–1600s in Europe, the ideas from the *Malleus Maleficarum* shaped peoples' understanding of witches and dictated methods of witch hunting, prosecution, and execution.

Ultimately, between the 1300s and the end of the 1600s, "tens of thousands of supposed witches—mostly women—were executed" in Europe (Blumberg 2022). It is important to remember that just because someone was accused of witchcraft does not mean that they were practicing witches. Many people who were accused of witchcraft were simply undesirables within their communities (Breslaw 2000). Witch hunts were well-established in British and Spanish cultures by the time the British and Spanish colonized the land now known as America, and anxiety about witchcraft followed settlers to the colonies.

Accusations of witchcraft erupted in a variety of places and times across colonial America. By focusing on Salem, Massachusetts, and Abiquiú, New Mexico, we can get a sense of the different roles colonization played in witchcraft accusations. Regardless of region, however, moments of witch hysteria in colonial America almost always reinforced social gender expectations, punishing both women and men who did not conform.

Salem Witch Trials

The Salem Witch Trials are famous—and Arthur Miller's 1953 play, *The Crucible*, has generally cemented this story into US popular culture. The Salem Witch Trials were, however, part of a larger drama of colonization, gender, and religion. These trials took place within a frenzy of religious rhetoric by Puritan preachers—most notably Reverend Increase Mather and his son, Reverend Cotton Mather—who preached and published against witchcraft.

During the colonial era in New England, the women accused of witchcraft typically threatened the religious community order (Baker 2014). The few men who were accused were often connected to these women (Karlsen 1998). Both the women and men accused of witchcraft were often known for having come into contact with Indigenous people (Norton 2002). Indeed, as Matthew Dennis and Elizabeth Reis (2015) write, the witch trials in New England combined a toxic brew of patriarchy and colonialism, primarily targeting women and leveraging racist, colonialist, and religious structures against them.

This is perhaps best exemplified in the story of Tituba, a central figure in the 1690s Salem Witch Trials. As Elaine Breslaw (1996) details, Tituba was an Indigenous woman who was enslaved on the Thompson plantation in Barbados. When the plantation owner died, she was inherited by Reverend Samuel Parris. He brought her to colonial Massachusetts where he was the minister in Salem Village. Because she was enslaved, many assume Tituba was African or of African descent, but records indicate she was an Indigenous woman from the Caribbean and/or Central America. The Salem community treated Tituba and her husband as Indigenous people—her husband was even called John Indian.

Reverend Samuel Parris accused Tituba of witchcraft, leveraging the racist, religious, and colonialist stereotype of "the Indian as Devil worshipper" against her. Parris enacted physical violence against Tituba to force her confession, and she agreed to name others who were involved in the supposed act of witchcraft, thereby setting in motion the events that would launch the Salem Witch Trials. During the Salem Witch Trials, over 200 people were accused of witchcraft and 20 were executed. Tituba, however, survived by cleverly confessing she had used magic to ward off evil while claiming others were making pacts with the devil and using witchcraft to cause harm.

Witch Hysteria in the Southwest

The Southwest region of what we now call the United States was colonized by the Spanish, not the British. This fundamentally changed the way witch accusations and witch hunts were handled in the Southwest. First, the Spanish colonists were primarily Catholic (unlike the New England colonists who were primarily Puritans). Second, the Spanish colonizers lived amid the Indigenous people they were colonizing, coexisting in the same communities. This was not the case in New England, where—with the primary exception of Indigenous people who were enslaved or bound in indentured servitude—colonists lived separately from and warred against Indigenous people.

In the Southwest, Spanish Catholic missionaries attempted to Christianize the Indigenous people along the Rio Grande River. These missionaries largely equated Indigenous religious practices—often healing practices—with witchcraft (Simmons 1974). Suppressing, policing, and punishing Indigenous religious practices as witchcraft, Spanish colonizers attempted to stamp out Indigenous beliefs. While the witch trials in Salem centered around colonists who had come into contact with Indigenous people, the witch hysteria in the Southwest focused on ending Indigenous religious practices. For example, between 1756 and 1766, the town of Abiquiú (located in what is now New Mexico) experienced a tumult of witch trials that foregrounded the intertwining of patriarchy, colonization, and religion. At the time, Governor Tomás Vélez Cachupín had granted the land of Abiquiú to the Indigenous people known at the time as the Genízaro Indians—a mix of Indigenous people who had been influenced by Spanish colonization. The people of Abiquiú resisted Christianization, refusing to give up their religious practices.

When the Franciscan priest, Juan José Toledo, began ministering in Abiquiú, his "religious and political authority" was severely challenged (Martinez 2021). Father Toledo accused an Indigenous man known as "El Cojo" of bewitching him. As Malcolm Ebright and Rick Hendricks (2006) explain, this conflict escalated, resulting in the destruction of Indigenous religious artifacts, exorcisms performed by Father Toledo on girls who claimed to have been demonically possessed, and the arrest and imprisonment or enforced servitude of many of the accused witches in Abiquiú—including Indigenous women who were community leaders. Eventually, Governor Cachupín—along with official word from the Inquisition in Mexico City—ended the tumult and the Catholic Church urged missionaries to learn local languages in order to "better Christianize" the Indigenous people and "wean them of their pagan religious practices" (Martinez 2021).

Witches Today

In contemporary popular culture, witches often represent feminine power and are associated with nature. Fantasy and romance fiction routinely feature witches as protagonists (e.g., *A Discovery of Witches*), embracing the idea of women's magic as sexy, empowering, and alluring. Moreover, within popular feminism, it is fairly routine practice to celebrate witches as proto feminists. For instance, the phrase "we are the granddaughters of the witches you couldn't burn" is a common slogan at feminist protests. The phrase itself is a paraphrase from Tish Thawer's 2015 novel, *The Witches of BlackBrook* (Toon 2021).

Today, some people identify as witches and hold beliefs and engage in rituals that they may call magic. Some witches practice a particularly feminist spirituality. Wendy Griffin (2006) notes that feminist witches often move between women's spiritual groups and exist both in and out of established religions. Because of this flexibility, as Helen Berger (2006) explains, feminist witches have impacted not only witchcraft communities but the larger women's spiritual movement as well. Some modern witches practice within established New Age religions, such as Wicca. Wiccan women find spiritual strength in their practice and often value nature. Rituals in Wicca often include the five elements: Spirit, Water, Fire, Earth, and Air. Studying Wiccan rituals, anthropologist Susan Greenwood argued that these rituals function as a "form of resistance to mainstream culture" and that they offer a "healing space" for women to "redefine and empower themselves" (1998, 101–2, 106). Michael York emphasizes that many New Age practices in the United States have been appropriated from Indigenous cultures and that this "appropriation represents simply the latest stage of Western imperialism" (2006, 19). Many modern witchcraft practitioners take great care to avoid rituals that may be appropriative.

Overall, in the US context it is important to remember the role colonialism played in the gendered, raced, and religious persecution of those accused of witchcraft. For contemporary witches, it is also important to not appropriate spiritual practices from colonially oppressed cultures.

Nancy A. Heise

See Also: Colonialism; Gender; Popular Feminism; Racist Stereotypes Against Indigenous People; Settler Colonialism

Further Reading

Baker, Emerson W. 2014. *A Storm of Witchcraft: The Salem Trials and the American Experience*. New York: Oxford University Press.

Berger, Helen A., ed. 2006. *Witchcraft and Magic: Contemporary North America*. Philadelphia: University of Pennsylvania Press.

Blumberg, Jess. 2022. "A Brief History of the Salem Witch Trials: One Town's Strange Journey from Paranoia to Pardon." *Smithsonian Magazine*, October 24, 2022. Originally published October 23, 2007. https://www.smithsonianmag.com/history/a-brief-history-of-the-salem-witch-trials-175162489/.

Breslaw, Elaine. 1996. *Tituba, Reluctant Witch of Salem: Devilish Indians and Puritan Fantasies*. New York: New York University Press.

Breslaw, Elaine. 2000. *Witches of the Atlantic World: A Historical Reader and Primary Sourcebook*. New York: New York University Press.

Broedel, Hans Peter. 2003. *The Malleus Maleficarum and the Construction of Witchcraft*. Manchester: Manchester University Press.

Dennis, Matthew, and Elizabeth Reis. 2015. "Women as Witches, Witches as Women: Witchcraft and Patriarchy in Colonial North America." In *Women in Early America*, edited by Thomas Foster. New York: New York University Press.

Ebright, Malcolm, and Rick Hendricks. 2006. *The Witches of Abiquiú: The Governor, the Priest, the Genízaro Indians, and the Devil*. Albuquerque: University of New Mexico Press.

Eller, Cynthia. 1998. *Living in the Lap of the Goddess: The Feminist Spirituality Movement in America*. Boston: Beacon Press.

Godbeer, Richard. 2017. "'Your Wife Will Be Your Biggest Accuser': Reinforcing Codes of Manhood at New England Witch Trials." *Early American Studies* 15, no. 3: 474–504. https://dx.doi.org/10.1353/eam.2017.0018.

Greenwood, Susan. 1998. "The Nature of the Goddess: Sexual Identities and Power in Contemporary Witchcraft." In *Nature Religion Today: Paganism in the Modern World*, edited by Joanne Pearson, Richard H. Roberts, and Geoffrey Samuel, 101–10. Edinburgh: Edinburgh University Press.

Griffin, Wendy. 2006. "Webs of Women: Feminist Spiritualities." In *Witchcraft and Magic: Contemporary North America*, edited by Helen Berger. Philadelphia: University of Pennsylvania Press.

Karlsen, Carol F. 1998. *The Devil in the Shape of a Woman: Witchcraft in Colonial New England*. New York: W. W. Norton.

Martinez, Rob. 2021. "In 1760s, Witchcraft Gripped Abiquiú." *Santa Fe New Mexican*, December 5, 2021. Originally Published October 30, 2020. https://www.santafenewmexican.com/news/local_news/in-1760s-witchcraft-gripped-abiqui/article_10f3c77e-1ac2-11eb-beab-630f9a188581.html.

Norton, Mary Beth. 2002. *In the Devil's Snare: The Salem Witchcraft Crisis of 1692*. New York: Alfred A. Knopf.

Simmons, Marc. 1974. *Witchcraft in the Southwest: Spanish and Indian Supernaturalism on the Rio Grande*. Lincoln: University of Nebraska Press.

Thomas, Keith. 1971. *Religion and the Decline of Magic*. London: Macmillan.

Toon, Francine. 2021. "'We are the Granddaughters of the Witches You Couldn't Burn.'" *Penguin Books*, March 24, 2021. Accessed August 29, 2024. https://www.penguin.co.uk/articles/2021/03/francine-toon-pine-inner-witch-violence-against-women.

York, Michael. 2006. "Webs of Women: Feminist Spiritualities." In *Witchcraft and Magic: Contemporary North America*, edited by Helen Berger. Philadelphia: University of Pennsylvania Press.

WOMAN-IDENTIFIED WOMAN MANIFESTO

The Woman-Identified Woman is a manifesto that was collectively written by the grassroots radical feminist group Radicalesbians in 1970. The manifesto was distributed as part of a protest during the Second Congress to Unite Women, which was hosted by the National Organization for Women (NOW) in New York City. The protest, largely referred to as the Lavender Menace protest, was in response to Betty Freidan's comment that lesbians were a "lavender menace." According to Freidan, the presence of lesbians in the women's movement would destroy the credibility of feminists and reduce them to a group of "man haters" in public opinion.

In protest to Freidan, a group of women entered the conference wearing T-shirts with "LAVENDER MENACE" on the front and distributed copies of "The Woman-Identified Woman." While the manifesto was written by Rita Mae Brown, Cynthia Funk, Lois Hart, Artemis March, Ellen Shumsky, and Barbara XX, others joined in distributing the manifesto such as Karla Jay (Jay 2000).

Lesbian: A Political Identity

The manifesto noted lesbian identity must be a focus for feminist politics as a resistance to patriarchy. For Radicalesbians, lesbianism was as much an erotic identity as a political one: "A lesbian is the rage of all women condensed to the point of explosion" (Radicalesbians 1970). The woman-identified woman must be defined without reference to men and male-dominated structures. Her sense of identity must come from herself and other women. For example, the manifesto states, "By virtue of having been brought up in a male society, we have internalized male's cultural definition of ourselves" (Radicalesbians 1970). The manifesto thus affirms that society keeps women from connecting with other women and instead requires women to bond to men for safety and security. We can see this play out in society when women are told they need protection and to be with a man is to ensure protection. However, we might better ask: protection from what or whom? If there wasn't any danger from a male-dominated society, then women would not have to align with "safe" men to ensure protection.

The manifesto acknowledges that heterosexuality is an institution because those who function within heterosexual relationships are privileged in society. For example, there are protections and benefits legally associated with marriage. The manifesto insists, "As long as woman's liberation tries to free women without facing the basic heterosexual structure that binds us in one-to-one relationship with our oppressors, tremendous energies will continue to flow into trying to straighten up each particular relationship with a man" (Radicalesbians 1970). For example, if women are focused on how to be a better wife, they will not be able to liberate themselves as women because their primary identity is that of wife.

For Radicalesbians, the only way to liberate oneself was to turn toward other women. The most radical act one could perform in a heterosexual world was to love another woman.

Sarah Cooper

See Also: Compulsory Heterosexuality; Friedan, Betty; Liberal Feminism; National Organization for Women (NOW); Patriarchy; Radical Feminism

Further Reading

Faderman, Lillian. 2015. *The Gay Revolution: The Story of the Struggle*. New York: Simon and Schuster.

Irigaray, Luce. 1980. "When Our Lips Speak Together." *Signs* 6, no. 1: 69–79.

Jay, Karla. 2000. *Tales of the Lavender Menace: A Memoir of Liberation*. New York: Basic Books.

Radicalesbians. 1970. *The Woman Identified Woman*. Pittsburgh, PA: Know, Inc.

Rich, Adrienne. 1978. "It Is the Lesbian in Us." In *On Secrets, Lies, and Silence: Selected Prose 1966–1978*, edited by Adrienne Rich, 199–202. New York: W. W. Norton & Company.

Rich, Adrienne. 1980. "Compulsory Heterosexuality and Lesbian Existence." *Signs* 5, no. 4: 631–60.

Wittig, Monique. 1980/1992. "The Straight Mind." In *The Straight Mind and Other Essays*, edited by Monique Wittig, 21–33. Boston: Beacon Press.

WOMANISM

Womanism is a school of thought extended from the creation of Black feminism and intersectionality. While Black feminism tends to address issues of racism, sexism, and classism simultaneously, womanism also included religiosity as a simultaneous element to consider within the lens of Black women and women of color's lives. The term "womanist" was first coined in 1983 by Black American woman author, Alice Walker, in her book, *In Search of Our Mothers' Gardens: Womanist Prose*. In this book, she offers a four-part definition illustrating what a womanist is.

First, she situates womanist as the opposite of "girlish" and the opposite of "frivolous, irresponsible" and "not serious." Describing "womanist" as a Black feminist or feminist of color, Walker continues, explaining that she has taken the term "womanist" from the Black folk expression said to female children, "You acting womanish," explaining that this phrase means one is acting "like a woman" and usually refers to "outrageous, audacious, courageous or *willful* behavior," including being interested in grown-up things. Walker concludes this first definition of womanist by writing that womanist means "Responsible. In charge. *Serious*" (1983, xi).

Second, Walker defines womanist as "a woman who loves other women, sexually and/or nonsexually" and who "appreciates and prefers women's culture, women's emotional flexibility . . . and women's strength." Although a womanist might sometimes love "individual men" a womanist is committed to the "survival and wholeness of entire people, male *and* female." Here, Walker adds that womanism is "traditionally universal," explaining this with an imagined exchange between a daughter and mother: "Mama, why are we brown, pink, and yellow, and our cousins are white, beige, and [B]lack?" to which the mother replies, "Well, you know the colored (*sic*) race is just like a flower garden, with every color flower represented." Walker concludes this second part of her definition of womanism by stating that a womanist is "capable" and again offering an exchange between mother and daughter to illustrate her point. The daughter states, "Mama, I'm walking to Canada and I'm taking you and a bunch of other slaves with me," to which the mother replies, "It wouldn't be the first time" (1983, xi–xii).

The third and fourth parts of Walker's definition are more concise. She writes that "womanist" means love in the sense of loving to dance, loving "food and roundness," and loving Black people and yourself. Walker emphatically closes this third definition by situating this joyous Black-affirming and self-affirming love as something womanists do "*Regardless*." Finally, the fourth part of Walker's definition states, "Womanist is to feminist as purple is to lavender" (1983, xi–xii). This analogy highlights the richness and strength of womanism as compared to mainstream feminism.

While much of the social sciences and humanities took up the lens and methodological frame of Black feminism and intersectionality, the religious studies and theological discipline took to using womanism as their lens and methodological frame to explore Black women's lives, naming it womanist theology. It should be noted that while womanism was initially taken up in Christian theology, it has been adapted to explore similar elements of systems of power and oppression within other faith traditions and practices, such as Islam. Prior to the adoption of womanism in theology, many Black theologians utilized a liberatory theology titled, Black Liberation Theology. Black Liberation Theology was created in the 1960s with the intent to counter the prominent narrative of Black inferiority by using the life of Jesus Christ and reframing biblical teachings to demonstrate that God was with Black people as the oppressed in US society. Yet, Black Liberation Theology was not inclusive of Black women's perspectives or needs. As such, womanist theology's primary goal was to reframe theological ideology and biblical texts, centering women as the subjects of their lives instead of passive objects.

Some of the earliest womanists/womanist theologians and womanist ethicists include Dr. Katie Geneva Canon, Dr. Dolores Williams, Dr. Jacqueline Grant, Dr. Emilie Townes, and Dr. Kelly Brown Douglas. Later "generations" of womanists include Dr. Judy Fentress-Williams, Dr. Stacey Floyd-Thomas, Dr. Kimberly Russaw, Dr. Nichole Renee Phillips, Dr. Monique Moultrie, Dr. Shively Smith, Dr. Gay Byron, and Dr. Vanessa Lovelace. Because womanism/womanist theology is a relatively young field, many of the foundational womanist scholars are still alive and contributing greatly to the further development of the field, in the form of scholarship and mentoring younger generations of womanists.

One of the most prominent social scientists who straddles both social scientific and womanist theological research is Cheryl Townsend Gilkes.

Critiques of Womanism

While many readily adopted Walker's foundational definition of womanism, it has also been met with much controversy. Many theological scholars, particularly some within the Christian faith, have taken serious issue with the normalization of homosexuality in Walker's womanist definition, as they believe homosexuality is "incompatible with the Christian theological and ethical principles" (Douglas 1994/2019, 100).

Prominent Black feminist scholar Patricia Hill Collins (1996) also critiqued Walker's definition of womanism, taking issue with its implied juxtaposition of Black and white women. Collins writes that while Walker claims womanism is universalist, Walker's definition constructs Black women's experiences "in opposition to those of white women," ultimately suggesting that Black women are "somehow superior to white women" because of their traditions (Collins 1996, 10–11).

Methodologies of Womanism

As with any theory, there must be methods to employ the theory. While Walker provided the definition to help us understand who a womanist is, the methodological approaches to employ womanism were incomplete. As such, womanist ethicist Dr. Stacey Floyd-Thomas (2006b) addressed this methodological gap in her book, *Mining the Motherlode: Methods in Womanist Ethics*. Floyd-Thomas explores and demonstrates methodological approaches across the disciplines of English/literature, sociology, and history. Floyd-Thomas maps Walker's definition onto the general principles of womanist ethics: radical subjectivity, traditional communalism, redemptive self-love, and critical engagement.

For instance, in field of English/literature,

- Audre Lorde's method known as "biomythography" corresponds to the womanist value of radical subjectivity and functions by bringing together "biological fact and mythically resonant fiction" in order to "locate the struggle for moral agency and self-identity in a context of social oppression" (Floyd-Thomas 2006b, 21).
- The method of virtue ethics corresponds to the womanist value of redemptive self-love and functions by charting or mapping Black women's perspectives of "the particularities of [B]lack women's moral character" (Floyd-Thomas 2006b, 33).
- The method of diasporic analysis corresponds to the womanist value of traditional communalism and functions to "explain circumstances and conditions under which [B]lack women strive to foster inclusivity and freedom" for the entire Black community (Floyd-Thomas 2006b, 51).

In the field of sociology,

- The method of case study analysis corresponds to the womanist value of traditional communalism and is intended to "convey the inextricable bond between the individual . . . to her larger community as a unique case's relevance to larger social phenomena" (Floyd-Thomas 2006b, 69).
- The method of the dance of redemption corresponds to the womanist value of redemptive self-love and was originally used by Katie G. Cannon, who borrowed from Beverly Harrison's work. This method is an "exploratory process to discern [what] mechanisms of exploitation and identity patterns that must be altered in order for justice to occur" (Floyd-Thomas 2006b, 82).
- The method of emancipatory metaethnography corresponds to the womanist value of radical subjectivity and functions to analyze "[B]lack women's religious formation" while also aiming to "debunk the inappropriate social scientific study of [B]lack women by treating them as subjects, not objects" (Floyd-Thomas 2006b, 91).

Finally, in the field of history,

- The method of slave narratives corresponds to the womanist value of radical subjectivity and functions by focusing on "the horrific truth concerning the social manufacturing and religious roots of racism, sexism, and classism as American core values." As such, these narratives "provide a profound insight into the radical subjectivity with [B]lack women's history" (Floyd-Thomas 2006b, 115–16).
- The method of moral biography and autobiography corresponds to the womanist value of traditional communalism. Through biography and autobiography, this method "can reveal much about the historical exigencies and ethical framework that gave rise to life in the contemporary [B]lack community . . .This entails an intentional method for Black historical recovery" (Floyd-Thomas 2006b, 131, 135).
- The method of emancipatory historiography corresponds to the womanist value of redemptive self-love and functions to explore "specific episodes or critical junctures in the life history of a person when ethical formation and racial identity politics are ultimately redefined" (Floyd-Thomas 2006b, 153).

Stephanie House–Niamke

See Also: Black Liberation Theology; Feminist Methodology; Feminist Theology; Intersectionality

Further Reading

Collins, Patricia Hill. 1996. "What's in a Name? Womanism, Black Feminism, and Beyond." *The Black Scholar* 26, no. 1: 9–17.

Douglas, Kelly Brown. 1994/2019. *The Black Christ.* Maryknoll, NY: Orbis Books.

Floyd-Thomas, Stacey M., ed. 2006a. *Deeper Shades of Purple: Womanism in Religion and Society.* New York: New York University Press.

Floyd-Thomas, Stacey M. 2006b. *Mining the Motherlode: Methods in Womanist Ethics.* Cleveland, OH: Pilgrim Press.

Gilkes, Cheryl Townsend. 2001. *If It Wasn't for the Women—: Black Women's Experience and Womanist Culture in Church and Community.* Maryknoll, NY: Orbis Books

Mitchem, Stephanie Y. 2002. *Introducing Womanist Theology.* Maryknoll, NY: Orbis Books.

Walker, Alice. 1983/2004. *In Search of Our Mothers' Gardens: Womanist Prose.* Orlando, FL: Harcourt.

WOMEN'S LIBERATION MOVEMENT

The Women's Liberation Movement arose in the mid-twentieth century as a response to social, cultural, and political inequality for women. During a time when a married woman needed her husband's permission to get a credit card, landlords could refuse to rent to a single woman or a woman with children, and there were not yet any domestic violence shelters, the Women's Liberation Movement rose up to address gender inequality. It challenged traditional gender roles and expectations that were at the root of gender discrimination and demanded equal job opportunities, equal pay for equal work, equal education, free contraception, abortion on demand, free childcare, legal and financial independence for women, an end to the discrimination against lesbians, the right to self-define sexuality, and an end to violence against women. The Women's Liberation Movement played a pivotal role in reshaping societal attitudes toward women and women's rights.

While the roots of the Women's Liberation Movement can be traced back to the women's rights convention in Seneca Falls during 1848 and activism around voting rights, and women's access to education and employment, the focus of the Women's Liberation Movement saw *liberation from* rather than *access to* a system they defined as fundamentally flawed as the solution to the oppression women faced. Rather than focusing on access to cultural and political institutions as liberal feminism did, the focus of the Women's Liberation Movement was to liberate women from the oppression of patriarchy.

Betty Friedan, in her book *The Feminine Mystique* (1963), challenged the idea that women found fulfillment solely in domesticity and motherhood by calling their plight "the problem that has no name" after interviewing women who were depressed despite the fact that they were living the ideal of femininity and motherhood. Though Friedan's work is often credited with sparking the Women's Liberation Movement in the United States, there was also a larger context that made her work well-timed.

In 1961 President John F. Kennedy formed the Presidential Commission on the Status of Women to advise him on women's inequality and policy changes and legislation necessary to address it. The commission was chaired by former First Lady Eleanor Roosevelt. The work of the commission produced some consequential results, including the 1963 *Presidential Report on American Women*, the Equal Pay Act of 1963, Title VII of the Civil Rights Act of 1964, and the formation of the Equal Employment Opportunity Commission to enforce it.

Following the third meeting of the Presidential Commission on the Status of Women in 1966, a group of attendees, including Betty Friedan, Flo Kennedy, and Pauli Murray, gathered to form the National Organization for Women (NOW), the grassroots arm of the feminist movement. NOW was instrumental in reintroducing the Equal Rights Amendment (ERA), a proposed amendment to the US Constitution that would bar sex-based discrimination. The Equal Rights Amendment was first introduced by feminists in 1923 and was repeatedly introduced thereafter. The newly formed National Organization for Women made it a goal to push for ratification of the amendment, particularly through Women's Strike for Equality in 1970; however, thus far, the amendment has yet to be implemented.

Women's Liberation Movement of the 1960s–1980s was not a singular movement. It had many branches and included three major strands of thinking: liberal feminism, socialist feminism, and radical feminism. The Women's Liberation Movement looked at women as a class of people oppressed under patriarchy and focused on undoing strict gender roles. The Women's Liberation Movement refers not just to the feminist movement but also to a way of thinking about women's experiences that emerged during the feminist movement from the 1960s through the 1980s.

Liberal feminists, like Betty Friedan and the National Organization for Women, focused on women gaining access to the system; radical feminist disagreed, in part, because this approach often excluded lesbians and women of color. Rather than seeking access to the system, radical feminists sought liberation from it. Rather than focusing on women's discontent as wives and mothers, radical feminists protested in order to raise consciousness about patriarchy as an oppressive system that defined women in terms of their relationship to men.

While the Women's Liberation Movement was responsible for a cultural revolution in thinking about gender, it faced criticism from within and outside the feminist community. Consciousness-raising groups, one of the key methods of growing the movement, often overlooked the particular experiences of women of color and lesbians in favor of the experiences of white women generalized to all women. Some women of color, working-class women, and LGBTQ activists felt that the movement was too centered on the concerns of white, middle-class women and did not sufficiently address the intersectional issues of race, class, and sexuality.

Critiques of liberal feminism by Radicalesbians and the Combahee River Collective led to the more intersectional approach to feminism through analysis of the ways in which race, class, and sexuality intersect in the experience of lesbians and women of color in patriarchal oppression. This led to the development of more intersectional feminist perspectives in the 1980s and beyond.

The Women's Liberation Movement paved the way for later feminist activism as well as Women's Studies, feminist analysis, and feminist cultural production and thus has had a lasting impact on women's rights, gender equality, and social progress.

Danielle M. DeMuth

See Also: Civil Rights Act: Title VII; Combahee River Collective; Consciousness Raising; Equal Pay; Equal Rights Amendment (ERA); Friedan, Betty; Liberal Feminism; Marxist Feminism; National Organization for Women (NOW); Patriarchy; Radical Feminism; Seneca Falls Convention (1848); Socialism

Further Reading

Berkeley, Kathleen C. 1999. *The Women's Movement in America.* Westport, CT: Greenwood Press.

Colbert, Laurie, and Dominique Cardona, dir. 1997. *My Feminism: Second Wave Feminism in the 1990s*. New York: Women Make Movies, 1997. 55 min.

Dicker, Rory C. 2016. *A History of US Feminisms*. Berkeley, CA: Seal Press.

Humm, Maggie. 1989. *The Dictionary of Feminist Theory*. Columbus: Ohio State University Press.

Kolmar, Wendy K., and Frances Bartkowski, eds. 2010. *Feminist Theory: A Reader*, 3rd ed. New York: McGraw-Hill.

WOMEN'S MARCH ON WASHINGTON (2017)

The Women's March on Washington was a demonstration in protest of President Donald Trump and in support of women's rights. The march, along with its sister demonstrations, took place one day after Trump's first inauguration, on January 21, 2017, and became the largest single-day protest in US history. Approximately 470,000 people demonstrated either on or near the mall in Washington and 4.1 million people participated across the United States (Felmlee et al. 2017; Wallace and Parlapiano 2017).

Approximately 470,000 people demonstrated on or near the National Mall in support of women's rights and in protest of President Donald Trump on January 17, 2017, the day after his first inauguration (3000ad/Dreamstime.com).

Teresa Shook, a retired attorney in Hawaii, conceived of the idea of a march on November 8, 2016. Shook posted "I think we should march" on a private Facebook group page as the results of the 2016 election were being processed. By the next morning, 10,000 group members wanted to join the march. In New York, activist Bob Bland had begun organizing a march in a separate Facebook group. Shook and Bland, along with other organizers, merged the two Facebook groups, igniting what became the Women's March (Women's March Organizers and Nast 2018).

Early in the organization process, activist Vanessa Wruble reached out to Bland, who had taken over organizing the march. Wruble critiqued the lack of representation of people of color in leadership and offered to help build a diverse coalition of leaders. Soon Carmen Perez, Tamika Mallory, and Linda Sarsour joined Bland as co-chairs and national organizers (Women's March Organizers and Nast 2018).

The organizers worked together to establish the goals of the march, known as the Unity Principles, which aimed to ensure Women's March issues were inclusive of a diversity of women. The Unity Principles included: ending violence, reproductive rights, LBGTQIA+ (lesbian, bisexual, gay, transsexual, queer, intersex, and asexual) rights, worker's rights, civil rights, disability rights, immigrant rights, and environmental justice (Women's March Organizers and Nast 2018).

Many Women's March demonstrators wore pink knit hats with cat ears, called "pussy hats," in reference to an offensive statement made by Trump in a 2005 recording, which had circulated during the 2016 presidential campaign.

Zoë Hess Carney

See Also: Hashtag Activism; #MeToo

Further Reading

Felmlee, Diane H., Justine I. Blanford, Stephen A. Matthews, and Alan M. MacEachren. 2020. "The Geography of Sentiment Towards the Women's March of 2017." *PLOS ONE* 15 (6): e0233994. https://doi.org/10.1371/journal.pone.0233994.

Wallace, Tim, and Alicia Parlapiano. 2017. "Crowd Scientists Say Women's March in Washington Had 3 Times as Many People as Trump's Inauguration." *New York Times,* January 22, 2017. https://www.nytimes.com/interactive/2017/01/22/us/politics/womens-march-trump-crowd-estimates.html

Women's March Organizers, and Condé Nast. 2018. *Together We Rise: Behind the Scenes at the Protest Heard Around the World.* New York: Dey Street Books.

Editor's Afterword

We need change. Only change will end violence, poverty, and oppression. In 1984, Audre Lorde wrote that each of us "must look clearly and closely at the genuine particulars" or conditions of our lives and "decide where action and energy is needed and where it can be effective." She continues, writing, "Change is the immediate responsibility of each of us, wherever and however we are standing, in whatever arena we choose" (Lorde 1984/2012, 136).

Change is our responsibility. Each of us, wherever we are, ought to make change right there. Perhaps Mary McLeod Bethune is the best example of this type of change. In 1904, she opened a school, and then a hospital, and then created affordable housing in the town where she lived (Daytona, Florida). She joined local and regional feminist organizations and through those networks joined and became a leader in national politics, ultimately founding the National Council of Negro Women (NCNW), which is still creating much-needed change today. Change begins where we are—because change begins with us.

I do not know the particulars of your life, and so the advice I can offer is partial and incomplete. But here are some places to start:

- You can join national feminist organizations such as the National Organization for Women (NOW), the National Council of Negro Women (NCNW), the National Indigenous Women's Resource Center (NIWRC), MANA: A National Latina Organization, the Asian American Feminist Collective, or ACT UP. You could intern for the Feminist Majority Foundation (FMF).
- You can educate yourself and learn about activism and opportunities by following feminists and activists on social media. In addition to following the national organizations listed above, consider following feminist sociologist Tressie McMillan Cottom (@Tressiemcphd), feminist activist and author Jessica Valenti (@JessicaValenti), and law professor and queer and trans liberation advocate Dean Spade (@spade.dean). I also recommend following feminist collectives such as @feminist on Instagram.
- If you enjoy reading, I recommend Sara Ahmed's *Living a Feminist Life* (2016), Tressie McMillan Cottom's *Thick* (2019), Dean Spade's *Love: How to Build Relationships in a F*cked-Up World* (2025), Jessica Valenti's *Abortion: Our Bodies, Their Lies, and the Truths We Use to Win* (2024), and Judith Butler's *Who's Afraid of Gender?* (2024). I recommend *everything* by bell hooks. If you're looking for a classic, Audre Lorde's *Sister Outsider* (1984/2012) is terrific. If you like fiction, I recommend Octavia E. Butler's *Fledgling* (2005).

To make change, however, my primary recommendation is that—like Mary McLeod Bethune—you start where you are: join a local chapter of Habitat for Humanity, volunteer at your local public library, join your town's Boys & Girls Clubs of America. Because creating affordable housing is a feminist project. Providing free access to knowledge is a feminist project. Caring for children is a feminist project. For instance, I volunteer my time teaching at a local men's prison, because education is proven to make life more livable behind bars and significantly increases people's ability to stay on the outside once on parole. And this, too, is a feminist project because feminism is about making life more livable and increasing people's freedom.

Change is our responsibility. My most sincere hope is that the information collected in *Feminism and Feminist Movements in America: An Encyclopedia of Ideals and Activism* might help you create feminist change in the wildly important places where you are.

Sarah Kornfield

Further Reading

Ahmed, Sara. 2016. *Living a Feminist Life*. Durham, NC: Duke University Press Books.
Butler, Judith. 2024. *Who's Afraid of Gender?* New York: Farrar, Straus and Giroux.
Butler, Octavia E. 2005/2011. *Fledgling*. New York: Seven Stories Press.
hooks, bell. 2018. *All About Love: New Visions*. New York: William Morrow Paperbacks.
Lorde, Audre. 1984/2012. *Sister Outsider*. Trumansburg, NY: Crossing Press.
McMillan Cottom, Tressie. 2019. *Thick*. New York: The New Press.
Spade, Dean. 2025. *Love: How to Build Relationships in a F*cked-Up World*. New York: Algonquin Books.
Valenti, Jessica. 2024. *Abortion: Our Bodies, Their Lies, and the Truths We Use to Win*. New York: Crown.

Index

About the Editor and Contributors

ABOUT THE EDITOR

Sarah Kornfield (PhD, Penn State) is a feminist communication scholar who studies the public persuasion of sexism. Dr. Kornfield is a professor of communication and women's and gender studies at Hope College, and she is the author of *Contemporary Rhetorical Criticism* (2021), *Invoking the Fathers: Dangerous Metaphors and Founding Myths in Congressional Politics* (2024), and *Watching Women: Femininity on TV* (2025).

ABOUT THE CONTRIBUTORS

Terrence Adams is a Madqueer trans and disabled poet-researcher who appreciates the ways people carve out spaces for themselves and communities with care. They like walking their dog and writing thank you notes.

Kelsey Taylor Alexander is completing her doctorate in English with a rhetoric concentration at Indiana University. Her current research focuses on rhetorical economies, specifically the ways in which the work ethic evolves in reaction to dominant ideologies in times of sociopolitical and economic crises.

Cherokee S. Bauer (BA, Hope College) is a theatre and feminist scholar who currently works as a costume designer in the midwestern United States.

Amanda N. Brand (PhD, University of Nebraska–Lincoln) adopts a critical feminist lens in her teaching and research. She teaches courses regarding lost and recovered feminist rhetoric(s), masculinities in the media, and writing. Her scholarship attends to the ways in which publics mediate accountability in cases of gendered and racial violence.

Carrie A. Bredow (she/her/hers) is an associate professor of psychology and the director of Women's and Gender Studies at Hope College (Holland, Michigan). She regularly teaches psychology of gender and researches the way that gender interacts with other social and cognitive factors to influence romantic relationship development.

Katie P. Bruner (PhD, Illinois) teaches in the Writing, Rhetoric, & Public Communication program at MIT. Her research examines the nature and legacy of visual media during the mid-twentieth century, and she is currently working on a book manuscript about the life of Harold Edgerton.

Mariane Camargo, from Brazil, is completing her bachelor's degree in communication and economics with a minor in women's and gender studies at Hope College. She aims to work around the world to create space for minority voices. Whether through activism, media, or public speaking, she seeks to foster an environment where marginalized groups can express themselves freely and challenge systemic inequalities.

Dominique Nicole Campbell is a PhD candidate in communication at the University of Illinois Urbana-Champaign. She studies political rhetoric, specifically the history of prisons and prison abolition in the United States.

Zoë Hess Carney, PhD, is a professor of practice of corporate communication and public affairs at Southern Methodist University. Her research focuses on political communication in a global era.

Carole Yoke-kew Chee (BA, Hope College) works in the University of Michigan Bentley Historical Library in Ann Arbor, Michigan, where she facilitates archival research.

Kristin Coletta (PhD, the Pennsylvania State University) is a communication scholar who studies rhetoric used in passing policies impacting the poor and working class. She focuses on the rhetoric of the US labor movement. Dr. Coletta is currently an associate teaching professor at Penn State.

Sarah Cooper (PhD, Clemson University) is an assistant professor in the English Department at Colorado State University. Dr. Cooper's interdisciplinary research resides at the intersection of archives, rhetoric, gender and queer theory, and sexuality studies.

Elsie Craig is completing her bachelor's degree at Hope College with majors in business and communication and a minor in peace and justice studies.

Brandy Daniels (PhD, Vanderbilt; MDiv, Duke) is an assistant professor of theology and codirector of gender, women, and sexuality studies at the University of Portland. She is the author of *How (Not) to Be Christian? Identity, Formation, and the Future in Feminist Theologies* (forthcoming).

Emma Darby earned her BA in English from Abilene Christian University and her MA in communication studies from the University of North Texas. Emma's research analyzes digital humor and culture through rhetorical perspectives in order to better understand the affective communication between internet memes and fandom communities.

Kersten Dekker (BA, Psychology and Women's and Gender Studies, Hope College) studies sexuality and feminism in the context of mental health. She intends to complete a PhD in clinical psychology with a focus on gender studies.

A. J. Delgado (BA, University of North Texas) is completing their MA in communication studies at the University of North Texas. They study rhetoric at the intersections of whiteness, femininity, conservatism, and civility.

Danielle M. DeMuth is an associate professor of women, gender, and sexuality studies at Grand Valley State University in Michigan, where she has taught since 2006. Her research is centered on the lesbian literary history, lesbian and queer literature, and feminist pedagogy.

Daniel J. DeVinney (PhD, University of Illinois at Urbana-Champaign) is an assistant professor of political rhetoric at Florida Atlantic University in the School of Communication and Multimedia Studies. He specializes in visual culture and race and is currently working on a book project on the visual logics of the post-racial myth.

Marissa Joanna Doshi is an associate professor of communication at Hope College. Her research draws on feminist perspectives to examine the creative and cultural dimensions of media and technology use. Her secondary research interests include intercultural communication and issues of representation in mass media. Her research has been published in journals such as *Communication Research, Journal of International & Intercultural Communication, International Journal of Communication,* and *Women's Studies in Communication.* She is currently editor of the journal *Women's Studies in Communication.* At Hope College, she teaches courses on transnational feminisms, cultural studies, media writing, and social media activism.

Max Dosser (PhD, University of Pittsburgh) is a senior lecturer of communication studies at Vanderbilt University and the cofounder and editor of the literary magazine *Flash Point Science Fiction.* His current book project, *Nostalgic Futures: The Reactionary Fantasies of Speculative Fiction Fandoms*, examines the relationship between the affective attachments fans have to speculative media and the logics of violence/exclusion that fuel broader reactionary groups.

Ava Doty (BA, Chemistry and Women's and Gender Studies, Hope College) studies sexuality and feminism in the context of reproductive health. She intends to complete her MD in the coming years.

Sage Drisker (BA, Texas A&M University) is completing their MA in communication studies at the University of North Texas. They study the intersection of Blackness and gender as it pertains to rhetoric within popular culture.

Rosa A. Eberly is an associate professor of rhetoric in the Departments of Communication Arts & Sciences and English at Penn State.

Stine Eckert, PhD, is an associate professor in the Department of Communication at Wayne State University, Detroit. She is coeditor (with Linda Steiner) of the book *We Can Do Better: Feminist Manifestos for Media and Communication.* She is coeditor of the bilingual journal *Journalistik/Journalism Studies.*

Cassidy D. Ellis (PhD, University of New Mexico) is an assistant educator professor at the University of Cincinnati where she teaches and conducts research on cultural narratives at the intersection of rhetoric and media. Her major research projects concern settler colonialism and contemporary anti-abortion narratives.

Victoria T. Fields is a former McNair Scholar, doctoral candidate, and instructor of record in the Department of Communication at the University of Illinois at Urbana-Champaign. Victoria's research centers on Black women's rhetoric, rhetorical history, archival rhetorics, social movements, and sports.

Samantha Gillespie-Hoffman (PhD, University of Nebraska–Lincoln) is a lecturer for the Department of Communication Studies at the University of Nebraska–Lincoln. Her research explores rhetorics of health and well-being in digital media spaces to expand feminist critique on popular culture and democratic freedoms.

Riley Gruppen is completing her bachelor's in political science and women's and gender studies at Hope College.

Ryan Hall is a graduate student in communication arts and sciences at Penn State University studying queer rhetoric.

Nancy A. Heise (MA, Texas State University) is earning their doctorate from Texas A&M University where their current research explores American religion and religious history from critical rhetoric and gender theory perspectives.

Theon E. Hill (PhD, Purdue University) serves as an associate professor of communication at Wheaton College where his research and teaching lie at the intersections of African American rhetoric, politics, and popular culture.

Stephanie House-Niamke is a sociologist who specializes in race, gender, and religion, particularly Black liberation theology and the sociology of womanism. House-Niamke was trained at West Virginia University and calls Roanoke, Virginia, home.

Elizabeth Johnson is earning a bachelor's degree in psychology and women's and gender studies at Hope College. She intends to attend a graduate program to earn a MA in social work.

Hannah Jones (MSLIS, University of Illinois Urbana-Champaign) is the Information Literacy Librarian at the University of Minnesota Duluth. Her teaching and research are centered around critical information literacy and feminist pedagogy, and she is the author of "When you wish upon a stall: Toilet facilities as a factor in library satisfaction among trans and gender nonconforming users," published in *User Experience in Libraries: Yearbook 2024.*

Jeffrey "JJ" Jones is a doctoral candidate in communication and information sciences at the University of Alabama, where they specialize in queer and trans rhetorics, political discourse of embodiment, and digital cultures of gender and sexual minorities. Their dissertation research utilizes rhetorical cartography to analyze the emergence of an internal displacement and mass migration movement of trans and gender-nonconforming bodies in response to the anti-gender/anti-trans movement in the United States.

Dafna Kaufman (MA, Georgia State University) studies communication at the University of North Carolina, Chapel Hill. Her research examines the relationship between spectatorship, visibility, and the construction of the gendered, raced body in American visual and athletic culture.

Talia E. Kibsey (MA, Florida Atlantic University) is completing their dual-title PhD in communication arts and sciences and women's, gender, and sexuality studies at Penn State University. Talia's research bridges critical feminist methodologies with rhetorical theory to study disability, madness, and neurodivergence—and the stigmas that accompany them—in Western popular culture.

Soyeon Kim (MA, Sogang University) is completing her doctorate in the English Department at Texas A&M University. She is the author of "Reclaiming a Space in American History with the

Collective Voices of the Japanese Picture Brides in Julie Otsuka's The Buddha in the Attic," published in *Feminist Encounters: A Journal of Critical Studies in Culture and Politics*.

Kristina M. Lee (she/her) is an assistant professor in the Department of Communication Studies at the University of South Dakota. Her research focuses on the intersection of religious and political rhetoric, Christian nationalism, theistnormativity and Christonormativity, and the marginalization of atheists.

Dulcinea Licavoli (BS, Biology, Hope College) studies sexuality and feminism in the context of Christianity. She intends to complete her MD in the coming years.

Alex Mahan is completing their bachelor's in political science and sociology with an emphasis on criminal justice at Hope College.

Jessie Marinho is a second-year PhD student at the University of Nebraska–Lincoln, studying rhetoric and public culture with an emphasis on feminist and queer media studies.

Josephine McClure is completing her bachelor's degree in political science, with a minor in women's and gender studies, at Hope College. She intends to obtain a Juris Doctorate and serve as general counsel for a nonprofit organization.

Sage Mikkelsen graduated from Texas Woman's University with a MA in multicultural women's and gender studies and currently works as an advocate at a domestic violence shelter. Her research examines gender, race, and sexuality in the context of Christian nationalism.

Leah Miller studies chemistry and women's and gender studies at Hope College, where her research currently focuses on social determinants of health.

Joshua H. Miller earned his PhD from the University of Wisconsin-Milwaukee in 2018. He is now an independent scholar, who teaches for the Hope Western Prison Education Program.

Pujarinee Mitra (PhD candidate, Texas A&M University) is a doctoral student who studies the intersections between South Asian literary and cultural studies, anti-fascism, affect theory and gender studies. Pujarinee has published articles in *Journal of Comparative Literature and Aesthetics* (2021), *Feminist Encounters* (2023), and *Humanities* (2023).

Tapaswinee Mitra is a PhD student at the Harriet Tubman Department of Women's Gender and Sexuality Studies at the University of Maryland-College Park. In her proposed PhD project, Tapaswinee hopes to explore the relationship between settler colonialism and the rise of religious fundamentalism in the sociopolitical context of contemporary South Asia.

Camryn O'Riley received her MA in communication from Texas A&M University where she studied the role of media in sexual violence advocacy. In addition to her academic research, Camryn spends time volunteering as a victim advocate for those experiencing sexual assault and domestic violence.

Kendra R. Parker (PhD, Howard University) is an associate professor at Georgia Southern University. She is the author of *She Bites Back: Black Female Vampires in African American Women's Novels, 1977–2011* (2018), coeditor of *The Bloomsbury Handbook to Octavia E. Butler* (2020), and author of *Understanding Octavia E. Butler* (2025).

Sergio Peña (MA, Penn State) is completing their dual-title doctorate in communication arts and sciences and women, gender, and sexuality studies at the Pennsylvania State University.

Courtlyn Pippert (PhD, University of North Carolina at Chapel Hill) is a critical media studies scholar who studies how popular media functions as a form of knowledge production that upholds white supremacist and patriarchal power structures. She is an assistant professor of communication at Coker University.

Samantha F. Quinn (PhD, University of Wisconsin-Milwaukee) is a communication scholar specializing in interpersonal communication and communication technologies and is an assistant professor in the Communication Studies Department at the State University of New York at Oswego. Her work can be found in the *Journal of Social and Personal Relationships*, the *Journal of Human Communication and Technology*, and the Annals of the International Communication Association.

Isabella Rodriguez is completing her bachelor's in women's and gender studies and sociology at Hope College. She intends to work in the field of diversity, equity, and inclusion to create sustainable change from within.

Dakota J. Sandras is an assistant professor of strategic communication in the Media and Entertainment Department at Colorado State University—Pueblo. Her research is rooted in critical rhetorical approaches and primarily investigates the ways power dynamics are negotiated at intersections of race and gender within popular culture and media.

Elaine Schnabel (she/her) is an assistant professor of organizational communication at Weber State University. Her research, which explores the dark side of Christian organizing, appears in *Management Communication Quarterly*, the *Journal of Communication and Religion*, and *Critical Studies in Media Communication*.

Brad Serber is an assistant teaching professor at Penn State University and an adjunct lecturer at SUNY New Paltz.

Amber Sodemann is completing her bachelor's in social work and women's and gender studies at Hope College. She intends to complete a MA in social work and later go into victim advocacy.

Rachel A. Spooner is an assistant professor of political science at Hope College, specializing in American politics with a focus on the Supreme Court and constitutional law. Her research and teaching examines judicial decision-making and its implications for governance in the United States.

Sutton Steensma (BA, Hope College) is pursuing her MSW at Boston University specializing in trauma and violence. She is passionate about the intersection of feminist theory and social justice as it informs her work with survivors of domestic and sexual violence.

Linda Steiner is a professor of journalism and the associate dean for Faculty Affairs and Inclusion in the University of Maryland's College of Journalism. Steiner is coauthor, editor, or coeditor of eleven books and is a UMD Distinguished Scholar-Teacher.

Arrington Stoll is an assistant professor at Valdosta State University. She teaches undergraduate and graduate courses in the areas of communication and public relations.

Amy Dunham Strand is an associate professor and the director of Women's and Gender Studies at Aquinas College in Grand Rapids, Michigan, where she also teaches in the English Department, General Education Program, and Women's and Gender Studies program. She is the author of *Political Prayer in Nineteenth-Century American Literature* (2024) and *Language, Gender, and Citizenship in American Literature, 1789–1919* (2009).

Hannah Taylor (PhD, Clemson University) is a scholar of feminist rhetoric and reproductive justice. Dr. Taylor is faculty at Duke University in the Thompson Writing Program and has published in *Peitho*, *Women's Studies in Communication*, and *College English*.

Lakelyn E. Taylor (PhD, University of Central Florida) is a postdoctoral associate working on a grant-funded project about flood warning communication at the University of Vermont. She is a lead coauthor of "Human or machine: How much difference in understanding and trust does a human element make in storm forecasts?" published in *Electronic News* (2023).

Andrea J. Terry is an associate professor in communication studies at Sacramento State, where she teaches courses on rhetoric, social movements, gender, and political communication. Her research is regularly put to work in her activism with the California Faculty Association, where she uses her expertise to advocate for rights, respect, and justice for her fellow workers.

Joanna Thornburg studies communication and studio art at Hope College, where her current research focuses on the intersection of feminism and popular media.

M. Elizabeth Thorpe is an associate professor at SUNY Brockport. Her scholarship focuses on legal rhetoric and the first amendment. She is an author of *The Rhetoric of Western Thought* (2020) and coeditor of *Communication Law Review*.

Kevin Timpe currently holds the William H. Jellema Chair in the Philosophy Department at Calvin University. His scholarship focuses on ethics, disability, and philosophy of religion.

Devon S. Torchiana (MA, Penn State) is a human resources professional specializing in talent strategy, leadership development, and change management.

Anna Whittle is a student at Hope College studying environmental studies and women's and gender studies. She plans to complete a MA of divinity with a concentration in religion, gender, and sexuality and be ordained within the Christian Church (Disciples of Christ).

Kale Wilk earned his master's degree in communication from Purdue University Northwest and has research interests in communication and feminist studies. He also serves as a communications specialist with Purdue University Northwest's office of marketing and communications.

Naaman Wood (PhD, Regent University) teaches courses in communication studies at Saint Paul College. Previously, he served as the founding faculty and chair in the Media and Communication Studies program at Redeemer University and as faculty at Tidewater Community College. He is the coauthor of the monograph *A Critical Companion to Sofia Coppola* and coeditor of the books *Humility and Hospitality: Changing the Christian Conversation on Civility* and *Words and Witnesses: Communication Studies in Christian Thought from Athanasius to Desmond Tutu.*

Jennie Young is a professor of English, rhetoric, and women/gender studies at the University of Wisconsin-Green Bay. She specializes and publishes in applied rhetoric, feminism, humor, and education.